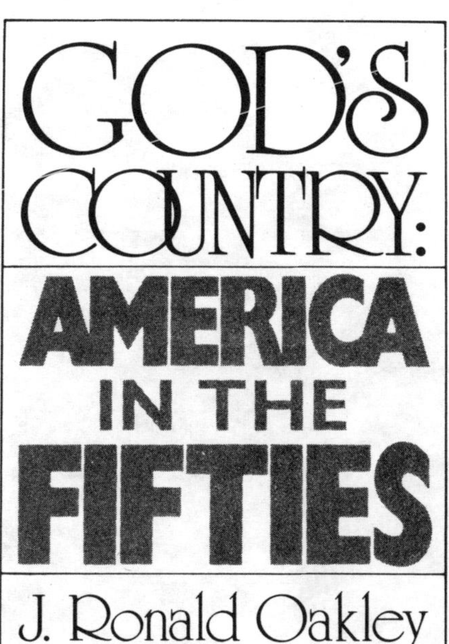
GOD'S COUNTRY:
AMERICA
IN THE
FIFTIES
J. Ronald Oakley

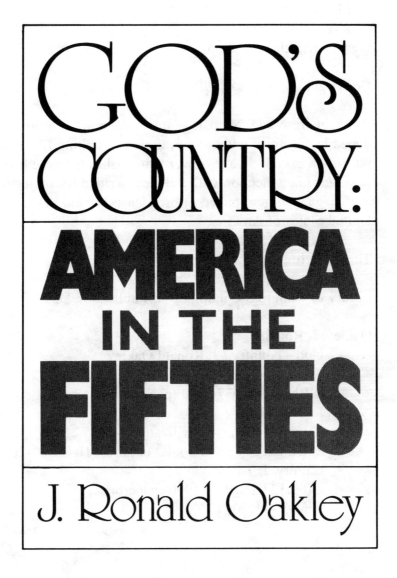

# GOD'S COUNTRY: AMERICA IN THE FIFTIES

J. Ronald Oakley

New York

Barricade Books
150 Fifth Ave.
New York, NY 10011
www.barricadebooks.com



Third Printing

Lbrary of Congress Cataloging-in-Publication Data

Oakley, J. Ronald
God's country / J. Ronald Oakley
p. cm.
ISBN: 0-942637-24-0 (paperback) : $14.95
Includes index.
1. United States—Civilization—1945-
2. United States—Popular culture—History—20th century. I. Title.
E169.12.02 1986, 1990 (paperback)
973.92—dc20

85-25316
CIP

**For my parents**

# CONTENTS

# PREFACE

In the fall of 1972, when the United States was being swept by one of its periodic waves of nostalgia for the 1950s, a nineteen-year-old drama student from the Juilliard School was chosen to portray a male character from the decade in a series of 7-Up commercials. Mandy Patinkin knew little about the fifties when he was first selected for the part, but as he told a *Newsweek* reporter, "That didn't matter. As soon as I put on the black leather jacket, the jeans and the boots, and combed my hair into a greasy ducktail, something happened to me. My shoulders dropped, my head cocked at an angle, and I felt tough and sexy. I felt on top of the world. And then I knew what the '50s were all about."[1]

For millions of Americans of the 1970s and 1980s, Patinkin's concept of "what the '50s were all about" has often been a part of what they have seen the decade as being all about, too. Like the 1920s, the decade has generally been looked at through nostalgic eyes that tended to focus on the good things while overlooking the bad. It has usually been viewed as "the fabulous fifties," "the nifty fifties," and, as a popular television show of the seventies saw it, as "happy days." It was the time before race riots, drugs, the assassination of two Kennedy brothers and Martin Luther King, Jr., the Vietnam War, violent student protests, the Kent State tragedy, Watergate, the energy crisis, and other problems of the 1960s and 1970s. It was a golden age of peace and prosperity, rock'n'roll, greasers, sock hops, big cars, suburban homes, cheap gasoline, Hula Hoops, Davy Crockett, 3-D movies, live television, Willie Mays, Mickey Mantle, James Dean, Elvis Presley, Marilyn Monroe, and Lucy. It was the time when everybody liked Ike, the grandfatherly president who always had a big grin on his face, continually assured the people that everything was going to turn out all right, and always seemed to have a golf club in his hand as he hurried off to the golf course to play a few rounds while Sherman Adams and other presidential aides ran the country. It was a happy, simple, placid time, only occasionally marred by such aberrations as the Korean War, McCarthy, Little Rock, Sputnik, and fear of thermonuclear bombs. Or so many people have thought.

*God's Country: America in the Fifties* provides a different view of the fifties, one made possible by the perspective offered by the passage of a quarter of a century and by the appearance of a wealth of books, articles, and other materials on the events and people of the time. The last few years, in particular, have brought the publication of an abundance of new information—private papers, diaries, letters, and other primary materials—on the presidencies of Harry Truman and Dwight Eisenhower, along with the memoirs, diaries, and letters of people close to them and to the events of their presidencies. New biographies and other studies of their administrations have also been appearing with increasing regularity, solidifying the high opinion historians have long held of Truman and dramatically elevating the historical reputation of Eisenhower, who held the office for eight years of the decade now commonly referred to as the Ike Age. Today, with the better perspective offered by time and these new historical materials, it is no longer possible to view the fifties as a happy, complacent, and sterile age presided over by a well-meaning but mediocre chief executive.

*God's Country* is a narrative history of the United States from the beginning of 1950 until the inauguration of John F. Kennedy in 1961. It depicts the 1950s as an exciting and seminal period when many of the features of today's society—such as the Cold War, ban-the-bomb movements, television, the youth culture, the drug culture, national educational debates, the civil rights movement, space travel, and rock'n'roll—were born or came into their own. This book also emphasizes that the fifties was a period of puzzling paradoxes. It was, for example, an age of great optimism along with the gnawing fear of doomsday bombs, of great poverty in the midst of unprecedented prosperity, and of flowery rhetoric about equality along with the practice of rampant racism and sexism. Finally, it portrays the man who presided over most of this complex age as a skillful, successful, and often underrated leader who deserves the high marks historians have recently begun to give to his presidency. Eisenhower, not his aides, ran the presidency, and he ran it very well. He kept the peace in a dangerous age and preserved the basic reforms of the New Deal–Fair Deal era, belying his contemporary critics' charges that his eight years in the White House were spent "golfing and goofing."

Although foreign affairs are not neglected, this fresh look at one of the most nostalgic decades in our past concentrates on major domestic events and on social and cultural history, particularly the television shows, movies, sports, books, music, fashions, customs, fads, and follies of the day. It also emphasizes people, devoting several chapters to Presidents Truman and Eisenhower and substantial sections to Joe McCarthy, Douglas MacArthur, Richard Nixon, John F. Kennedy, Julius and Ethel Rosenberg, Martin Luther King, Jr., James Dean, Elvis Presley, Marilyn Monroe, and other luminaries of the day. And finally, it devotes special attention to blacks, women, and the young, three groups whose impact on the nation's history steadily increased as the decade progressed. Although the narrative does have a wide focus, it cannot and does not claim to cover everything. It provides only the main threads of political history, not the minute details, and it emphasizes the mass or popular culture of the time rather than the high culture.

Many individuals have contributed to this book—knowingly and unknowingly. Hundreds of authors and editors made possible the written materials I have drawn upon in my research; my debt to them is further acknowledged in the chapter notes and bibliography. Several librarians at the University of North Carolina at Greensboro and at my own institution, Davidson County Community College, assisted me in locating materials. Brenda James, a member of the community college library staff, was particularly helpful in locating hard-to-find books through the interlibrary loan system. Three of my colleagues, Ashley Whitfield, Virginia Fick, and Sam Bright, read parts of the manuscript and offered valuable suggestions and encouragement. My editors, Anna Dembner and Ann Finlayson, ironed out the rough spots in my prose and provided candid and extremely helpful criticism of the contents. My typists, Lola Hoover and Sharon Koontz, somehow managed to decipher my rough drafts and numerous revisions and turn them into polished text. And above all, I am indebted to my wife Kathy, who during the five years I spent researching and writing this book gave me encouragement when I needed it most and cheerfully tolerated the long hours of work that of necessity took time away from domestic chores, vacations, and social engagements.

# PART ONE

# The Age of Fear and Suspicion, 1950–1952

# 1

# *Entering the Fifties*

The Second World War had ended over four years earlier, but reminders of that conflict were everywhere as Americans entered the 1950s. President Harry Truman was the same chief executive who had brought a dramatic end to the war by dropping atomic bombs on Hiroshima and Nagasaki. General Dwight D. Eisenhower of D-Day renown was the highly visible president of Columbia University and a popular choice for the presidency of the United States in 1952, while General Douglas MacArthur, the hero of the Pacific war against Japan, was completing his remarkable reform of Japanese society before making yet one more return, this time to the battlegrounds of Korea. Millions of war veterans, some still sporting GI haircuts from their military days, were taking advantage of generous veterans' benefits to crowd into college classrooms or buy homes in the new suburban developments springing up all across the country. Rogers and Hammerstein's *South Pacific* was delighting audiences on Broadway while picking up the Pulitzer Prize for drama. Winston Churchill's monumental history, *The Second World War*, was running in daily installments on the front pages of *The New York Times*, and war novels like John Hersey's *The Wall* were hovering near the top of the best-seller lists. In the movie theaters, millions were leaving their new television sets long enough to see the endless parade of grade B war movies being churned out by Hollywood, while critics were hailing a new star in Marlon Brando, making his movie debut as a paraplegic war veteran in *The Men*.

These reminders of the war were only surface indications of how much that cataclysmic conflict had molded the world in which Americans lived at the midcentury mark. "The greatest revolution the world has ever known,"[1] as Charles de Gaulle called it, brought far-reaching domestic and international changes. The United States quickly became the arsenal of democracy, using the safety of the oceans and the powers of its industry to turn out millions of tons of supplies for the fighting effort. Sixteen million men and women were put into uniform, while millions more left rural areas and small towns to find lucrative work in the burgeoning war industries. Unprecedented military spending, totaling close to $300 billion, brought a massive stimulus to industrial and agricultural production and inaugurated a new era of economic expansion and prosperity. The demands of the war effort accelerated by years—or even decades—revolutionary developments in atomic and conventional weapons, jet airplanes, rockets, electronic computers, and hundreds of other technological areas. The war also hastened the urbanization of the nation, promoted the centralization of the national government, and elevated the status and aspirations of women and blacks by giving them the opportunity to perform many jobs formerly reserved for white males. In these and in dozens of other ways, the war contributed to a vast social, economic, and technological revolution that was transforming the face of the nation.

The war also brought an international upheaval that changed the old world order, and America's place in it, almost beyond recognition. The original objective of the Allies—the defeat of fascism—was achieved, for the grand alliance of Great Britain, Russia, and the United States had dealt total defeat to Germany, Italy, and Japan. But it was obtained at a terrible price, fulfilling Hitler's prediction that "we may be destroyed, but if we are, we shall drag a world with us—in flames."[2] The war killed 40 million soldiers and civilians, wounded millions more, and brought crushing government debts and unprecedented physical destruction to nations across the world. Coming so soon after the First World War and the great depression, it was the final blow to Europe's world hegemony, for six years of modern warfare brought ruin to European victors and vanquished alike. It hastened the collapse of European colonialism and the birth of dozens of unstable nations in Asia, Africa, and the Middle East, shrinking Europe's boundaries to what they had been before the voyages of Columbus. Europe, the mighty continent, was devastated by its second civil war within a generation, leaving a worldwide power vacuum that could be filled only by two nations that had been second-rate powers in 1939, the United States and the Union of Soviet Socialist Republics.

At the end of the war these new superpowers divided the world between them. Protected by geography from the terrible destruction suffered by the other belligerents, the United States emerged from the war with the world's greatest economic machine, with military bases and occupying troops spread across the globe, and with a monopoly of the most destructive weapon in human history, the atomic bomb. As the world's greatest power, it had also acquired responsibilities it could not ignore as it had after the First World War. The Soviet Union was also a beneficiary of the war. In spite of staggering human and material losses, its swollen military establishment contained the largest land army in the history of the world, and its occupying troops were bringing Eastern Europe, North Korea, and other vital areas under Soviet control. Along with the British, these two giants celebrated in the summer of 1945 their joint victory over the Axis powers, and although strains of their unholy alliance had already appeared long before the end of the conflict, there was widespread hope in the West that with the help of the new United Nations, Russia and the Western democracies could construct a new world order based on international cooperation and permanent world peace.

But it was not to be. The ink had barely dried on the documents ending the conflict when Russia and America began quarreling over the peace treaties and the structure of the postwar world. Former ally and friend Joseph Stalin no longer talked about allied unity but instead warned of the inevitable battle between communism and capitalism. Even as he spoke, he was taking advantage of the collapse of the great European powers to establish a series of satellite states in Eastern Europe and Asia and to back colonial rebellions against the European powers. President Truman responded with equally tough rhetoric, with military and economic aid to rebuild Western Europe, with military assistance to Greece and other countries threatened by Russian-backed insurgents, and with an airlift of supplies to West Berliners cut off from the outside world by a Russian land blockade. He also led in the founding of an American-dominated military alliance, the North Atlantic Treaty Organization, to protect Western Europe from Soviet invasion.

But communism continued to advance, in spite of all America's efforts to contain it. In August of that terrible year of 1949 Russia successfully tested her atomic bomb, signaling the end of America's atomic monopoly and the inauguration of a new age of warfare that could bring Russian atomic bombs raining down on American cities. At the end of the year, the civil war in China between the forces of the American-backed Chiang Kai-shek and the communist leader Mao Zedung ended with Chiang's defeat and the evacuation of his army and government to the little island of Taiwan. Eight hundred million Chinese, constituting nearly one fourth of the world's population, had fallen under the grip of communism.

To many Americans at the beginning of 1950 the world appeared to have been turned upside down in just a few short years. World War II had not brought the permanent peace that so many had sacrificed so much for but had instead merged into another life-and-death conflict. Russia and America, so recently allied in the war against the fascists, were now locked in a Cold War that threatened to erupt into a hot one, while the three fascist nations were now America's allies and friends. Fascism was no longer a threat to world order, but it seemed now that large areas of the globe might share Eastern Europe and China's fate by falling to fascism's totalitarian twin, communism. The atomic bomb, which America had developed and which was supposed to guarantee American security for decades to come, now also belonged to the other side and could be used against the American people. And on top of all these worries was the fear that the communist victories had been partly won with the help of traitors inside the United States and Great Britain. Spies had been arrested for passing atomic secrets to the Russians, and congressional committees, ambitious politicians, and sensational journalists were charging that communists and their sympathizers in the State Department had worked to hand over Eastern Europe and China to communism. The United States, many were saying, was in danger of falling to communism, not from external conquest, but from internal subversion.

Americans entered 1950, then, under the shadow of the Cold War and the atomic bomb. Never had the nation been more powerful, but not since the early dark days of World War II had the American people felt so puzzled and so threatened by world events. Everywhere there was talk of Joseph Stalin and the Russians, of the "loss of China," of a communist plot to rule the world, of the Cold War and World War III, of subversives in the State Department, colleges and universities, entertainment industry, and no telling where else. Instead of celebrating the onset of a new year and a new decade, many of the nation's newspapers and popular magazines began the year with pessimistic assessments of the state of the nation and the world and with calls for a new crusade of right against wrong. In its special New Year's edition, for example, *Life* magazine declared that "the mid-century American is called upon . . . to resist the communist threat to the world" and "to rally his world to battle for the life and freedom of all men."[3] No wonder that when George Gallup sent his army of questioners out to find what the American people were thinking, they found that 70 percent of the public felt that Russia was trying to rule the world, 41 percent expected the United States to fight a war in the next five years, and 75 percent feared that American cities would be bombed if the country got into another war. A small but growing number, 19 percent, predicted that another world war would bring an end to the human race.[4]

Nineteen hundred and fifty turned out to be a dreadful year in the history of the republic. It was the year when accused communist and former State Department official Alger Hiss was convicted of perjury, when President Truman inaugurated a terrible new phase in the arms race by ordering a crash program to build a superbomb (H-bomb) that would dwarf the bombs used against Japan, and when Russia and China seemed to draw together in the struggle against the West by signing a Treaty of Friendship and Mutual Assistance. It was the year when Julius and Ethel Rosenberg and several other Americans were arrested for conspiring to pass America's atomic secrets to the Russians, when Joe McCarthy began his rise to national fame with his reckless charges that the State Department was riddled with communists, and when two Puerto Rican nationalists tried to assassinate President Truman. But worst of all, it was the year when North Korean forces invaded South Korea, plunging the United States into a frustrating and divisive war less than five years after the end of the Second World War. The year ended with Chinese troops routing the United Nations forces in Korea and with President Truman proclaiming a state of national emergency. When the editors of *The Nation* reviewed the year's events in January of 1951, they were moved to write that "the late 1950 was the kind of year in the affairs of this country that few of us can look back on with pleasure" and to declare that it had been the darkest time since the early days of the Second World War.[5]

It would be wrong, in looking back upon 1950, to think that all Americans were obsessed with the great political issues of the period and that they were living in great fear and anxiety. Some were, of course, but the great majority, even those who kept up with the news and had informed opinions about what was going on, learned to put these problems in the backs of their minds while they went about their daily business. If it often seemed to be the worst of times, it seemed to be the best of times, too, for even in the midst of great danger most Americans realized that they lived in the richest and most powerful nation on earth. The Second World War had failed to bring world peace, but it had brought something else: an end, perhaps a permanent end, to the great depression that had scarred so many lives in the terrible thirties. Worried as they were about the communists and the atomic bomb, most Americans were more concerned with enjoying the fruits of a great economic boom that was transforming American life and ideals. The fat, consumer-oriented decade of the fifties was about to begin.

During the boom years of the war millions of citizens enjoying the benefits of a superheated war economy kept looking back over their shoulders at the recent depression. Would these good times disappear once the war was over, plunging the nation back into the days of 25 percent unemployment, Hoovervilles, railroad bums, and public works projects? Many economists predicted that when the guns fell silent and the government war orders stopped, the factories would close their doors or return to short time, throwing millions out of work. The ripple effect, it was said, would devastate the rest of the economy, and the millions of men streaming back from the battlefields would return not to a hero's welcome but to long unemployment and relief lines.

But it did not happen. There had indeed been problems since the end of the war—labor unrest, inflation, shortages of some agricultural and industrial products, unemployment, lags in converting back to peacetime industry and absorbing job-seeking veterans, and a recession in 1948–1949—but the basic trend had been upward as the economic boom of the war years continued. Spurred by easy credit terms, government defense spending, and the rush by consumers to spend $150 billion in wartime savings, the Gross National Product jumped from $212.3 billion in 1945 to $286.2 in 1950. By the middle of 1950 the federal minimum wage had risen to seventy-five cents an hour and the average weekly pay for industrial workers had reached a record $60.53. The outbreak of the Korean War would bring high inflation and a partial return to price controls and other governmental restrictions on the economy, but it would also stimulate the economy, reduce unemployment to 1.9 million, and contribute to the prosperity that would become so notable in the 1950s.[6] Americans had plenty of money to spend, not just for necessities but for a wide range of luxury items and leisure activities.

One obvious beneficiary of the prosperity of the period was the garment industry, for Americans at midcentury were buying more clothing than ever before. The end of wartime shortages and the repeal of Government Regulation L-85, which restricted the amount of fabric that could be used in clothing, helped to free the imaginations and fill the coffers of designers and manufacturers. In 1947, Christian Dior's New Look, and the many inexpensive imitations of it, had swept the female fashion world in large cities and small towns alike, forcing women to replace entire wardrobes and causing men to complain that the full-flowing fashions, with skirts barely twelve inches above the floor, did not show enough leg. Other kinds of formal wear flourished too, but the long-term postwar trend was toward informal fashions. By 1950, the demand for suits and hats for men and women alike leveled off or declined, while the sales of casual dresses, slacks, sport shirts, blouses, sport coats, and other types of informal clothing continued to boom. Nylon shirts became a craze in 1950, while the bikini, which had caused such a stir when it was imported from France in 1948, was seen less on American beaches in 1950 as young women turned to more modest swimsuits, pedal pushers, and strapless suntops. Young people of high school and college age were buying more sweaters, dungarees, sneakers, loafers, and ballet-type shoes.[7] Fashions for both men and women were becoming not only more casual but also more faddish than at any time in the forties, providing more than a hint of the sack dresses, pink shirts, Bermuda shorts, tube dresses, and rogue trousers to come later in the decade.

Automotive sales and housing starts had been one of the major barometers of America's economic health ever since the 1920s, and in 1950 both were booming. During World War II a huge pent-up demand developed when practically no new automobiles were produced for over three years, and both gas and tires were rationed, forcing the American people to pool rides, drive old clunkers, walk, or take other forms of transportation. Meanwhile they saved their money and waited for the day when their love affair with the automobile could be resumed. When the war ended, Americans went on an automobile buying spree, snapping up cars at full list price as fast as Detroit could make them. New car sales jumped from 69,500 in 1945 to 2.1 million in 1946 and to 5.1 million in 1949, surpassing for the first time the 1929 record of 4.5 million. In 1950, sales rose to 6.7 million, well on the way toward the decade's peak of 7.9 million, reached in 1955.[8]

Since postwar buyers would pay full list price for every automobile Detroit could turn out, manufacturers made few changes in the styles or mechanical operations of the models produced between 1945 and 1950. Americans wanted big, roomy boxes like those they had bought in the past, and the automakers gladly obliged. In 1950 the typical automobile in the popular price range had an 8-cylinder, 100-horsepower engine, sealed-beamed headlights, a manual transmission, and a list price of around $1,800. Radios and heaters were popular options, but most new buyers passed up the 6-cylinder engines, automatic transmissions, and other options offered by Detroit. Depending on the model and options, a new Chevrolet could be bought for as little as $1,329 or as much as $1,994, while Fords ranged from $1,329 to $2,262, Chryslers from $2,134 to $5,384, and Cadillacs from $2,761 to $4,959.[9]

Most of the new cars were produced by the big three—General Motors, Ford, and Chrysler—who in 1950 were already threatening to drive the other six domestic automakers out of the market. Only 16,336 foreign-made cars—one quarter of 1 percent of all automobiles—were sold in the United States that year, and the nation's single Volkswagen dealer sold only 300 of the odd-looking German cars born in Hitler's Germany.[10] Like other foreign makes, the Volkswagen would become very popular later in the decade, but in 1950 few buyers were impressed with its low initial cost (around $1,300), mechanical reliability, and high gas mileage, regarding it and other small cars as quaint affectations of college professors, students, old misers, and other eccentrics.

The housing industry was having a very good year in 1950. After the severe housing shortages of the depression and war years, which had forced millions of families to live in cramped apartments or to share homes with parents or in-laws, postwar Americans had rushed out to buy up new homes as soon as they became available. Taking advantage of low prices, low interest rates, and GI loans, these eager homeowners bought almost 1.4 million new homes in 1950. Many of them were in the rapidly growing suburbs, where William J. Levitt and his many imitators all across the country were offering small, standardized houses for as little as $6,000. For the more affluent buyers, realtors in cities like Greenwich, Connecticut, were offering eight-bedroom houses on two-acre lots for around $62,000. Ever atune to the temper of the times, some builders in this first year of the H-bomb scare offered to add bomb shelters for a few hundred more dollars, while realtors around the nation's capital were advertising suburban homes located "a safe 58 miles from Washington," or "out of the radiation zone," or "out beyond atom bombs."[11]

Unlike the majority of existing homes, most of the new ones being built in 1950 had central heat, usually an oil or natural gas furnace. These two convenient and inexpensive fuels were rapidly replacing coal as the major heating sources for American homes and industries. More and more new homes—as well as older ones—were also being equipped with modern appliances as American homemakers continued a trend that had begun back in the 1920s when labor-saving appliances were first produced for the mass market. By 1950, over 86 percent of the homes wired for electricity had refrigerators, 70 percent had modern cooking stoves, 57 percent had vacuum cleaners, and 72 percent had washing machines. However, some of the newer appliances—first available after the war—were as yet in few homes. Only 1.4 percent of the wired homes had electric or gas clothes dryers, only 7 percent had home freezers, and less than 1 percent had electric dishwashers. Few homes—or banks, retail stores, offices, or schools, for that matter—had air-conditioning.[12] Often the first buildings in town to get air-conditioning were the movie theaters and restaurants, whose owners tried to lure people away from their television sets and other summertime amusements with icicle-framed signs promising "It's Cool Inside!" Air-conditioning had been around since the early part of the century and would make the transition from luxury to necessity in the 1960s, but at the midcentury mark people survived, as they had for thousands of years, without it.

By far the most successful of all the appliances that appeared on the mass market after the war was television. In 1946, when television sets cost over $500 and only a few television stations were in operation, only 7,000 sets were sold. Sales jumped to 975,000 in 1948 and zoomed to 4.4 million in 1950, when over 5 million[13] homes were enjoying Captain Video, the Aldrich Family, Perry Como, the Lone Ranger, Hopalong Cassidy, Milton Berle, Frank Sinatra, the Goldbergs, and dozens of other personalities, game shows, talk shows, dramas, comedies, and news programs. Television was already transforming America as no invention had done since the automobile. It was already being hailed as a boon and as a threat to family life, a promising tool for the education of America's children and the cause of their ignorance and delinquency, a destroyer of radio, books, magazines, and newspapers, and the precipitator of hundreds of other real or imagined changes occurring in American life. At the end of 1949 the influential editor of the *Saturday Review*, Norman Cousins, was already labeling television the "billion dollar blunder" and lamenting that "the most magnificent of all forms of communication" was pandering to the lowest levels of taste and intelligence. "Television," he declared, "is being murdered in the cradle."[14] But television would survive, despite Cousins and all the other critics. In the decade ahead it would change the face of America.

Television had not yet soured the love affair with the radio that had bloomed when that wonderful invention went on the market in the early 1920s. The 80 million radio sets in use in 1950 were being served by over 2,800 stations at a time when only 97 television stations existed in the entire country.[15] At the beginning of the year radio could boast of 108 shows that had been on for at least twenty years. Radio profits were up over the previous year, and Jack Benny, Bing Crosby, and other favorites seemed as popular as ever. But by the end of the year radio's popularity was slipping, with many of its performers and much of its audience defecting to television. Radio would survive and even prosper in the decade ahead, but it would be forced to change its format drastically.[16]

Radio was still the major source of the popular music the nation was so fond of at midcentury. There was as yet no distinct teenage music—teenagers listened to the same music as their older siblings and parents, and in 1950 that music continued to be dominated by the sounds of the big band and swing music of the 1940s. Most popular songs were idealistic, sentimental portrayals of a dream world of love and romance, untainted by serious social and personal problems. With few exceptions, the singers were dignified, restrained crooners like Frank Sinatra, Bing Crosby, Perry Como, and Rosemary Clooney, or amiable groups like the Ames Brothers and the Andrews Sisters. These and other pop artists turned out dozens of hits for their grateful fans, who purchased 189 million records in 1950, 80 million more than just five years earlier at the end of the war. The best-selling pop record of 1950 was "Goodnight Irene," a remake by the Weavers of an old song, but record buyers also bought millions of copies of "It Isn't Fair" (Sammy Kaye), "Mule Train" (Frankie Laine), "Mona Lisa" (Nat King Cole), and "Music, Music, Music" (Teresa Brewer). Then at the end of the year came one of the best-selling records of all time, "Rudolph the Red-Nosed Reindeer," which earned a small fortune for the singing cowboy, Gene Autry.[17]

The radio and recording industries' attempt to satisfy the appetite for popular music was now joined by the new medium of television. The most popular singer of the decade, Perry Como ("Mr. C"), entertained large audiences three nights a week at 7:30 on CBS. Millions also tuned in to *Your*

*Hit Parade, The Voice of Firestone, The Fred Waring Show, The Frank Sinatra Show, Arthur Godfrey and His Friends*, and other musical and variety shows featuring the top performers of the day. Those who liked amateur talent and wanted to see the stars of tomorrow discovered right before their eyes could turn to *The Original Amateur Hour*, where Ted Mack provided an array of hopeful piano players, one man bands, kazoo players, singers, dancers, an occasional talented performer, and the dancing Old Gold cigarette pack and matchbook. They could also watch "the old redhead" promote new talent on *Arthur Godfrey's Talent Scouts* or the King of Jazz search for young performers on *Paul Whiteman's TV Teen Club*. Viewers who wanted to become performers themselves could receive dance lessons on *The Arthur Murray Show* from Arthur and Katherine Murray, or enjoy fifteen minutes of ukulele lessons from the master himself on *Arthur Godfrey and His Ukulele*. Those who were better at recognizing music than playing it or dancing to it could test their skills with Jan Murray on *Sing It Again* or with Bert Parks on *Stop the Music*. What viewers could not do, if they turned on their television or radio in 1950, was to avoid Arthur Godfrey, the most popular television personality of 1950 and of the decade to come.

At a time of widespread racism and segregation, popular music was broad enough to include some forms of black music and some types of black musicians. Jazz, blues, spirituals, crooners like Nat King Cole, and black "big band" music were widely appreciated by the white audiences that bought recordings and frequented clubs, theaters, and hotel ballrooms across the country. However, outside the mainstream of popular music there was a separate current of black music that had been around for decades but had been little noticed by white audiences. Called race music by people in the music trade, it was played on black music stations in the rural South and ghettoes of the North and recorded and sold by Atlantic and other small black record companies. Race music had a hard-driving, rhythmical beat, sexually suggestive lyrics and titles, and references to "rocking and rolling," a phrase used in the black community to denote both dancing and sexual relations.

In 1949, recognizing that race music was reaching a wider audience, including many white teenagers, *Billboard* began to refer to it as "rhythm and blues" and to carry charts of its top sellers. In 1950, a New Orleans singer and pianist named Antoine Domino saw his first record, "Fat Man," make the rhythm-and-blues charts, along with Ivory Joe Hunter's "I Almost Lost My Mind," Johnny Otis's "Double Crossing Blues," and Ruth Brown's "Teardrops from My Eyes." As the fifties proceeded, Fats Domino and his fellow makers of race music would move into the mainstream of white popular music and help produce the rock'n'roll musical revolution of the second half of the decade.[18]

Although the nation was rapidly moving away from its rural past as people migrated to cities and suburbs, country music was still very popular in 1950. Every Saturday night, thousands of people from all over the nation came to Nashville, Tennessee, and stood in line for hours to get into the mecca of country music, the Grand Old Opry. Along with the millions of Americans tuned in to WSM radio between 7:30 and midnight, they wanted to hear Hank Williams, Eddy Arnold, Ernest Tubb, Webb Pierce, Roy Acuff, and the rest of the Opry's cast of over 120 musicians and comedians, the cream of the country-music crop. Country music was in the midst of a golden age that had begun during the prosperity following the Second World War. It was becoming more popular, more national, more commercial, and less country as it experienced a boom in record sales and live performances that made millionaires of many of its top stars. It was now called "country and western" rather than "hillbilly," but through all its changes in nomenclature and style, it continued to focus on unrequited love, death, infidelity, alcoholism, unemployment, and other tragic themes that popular music chose to avoid in its portrayal of a white dream world. Occasionally, however, pop singers would capitalize on country songs, as when Patti Page recorded "The Tennessee Waltz," written as a country song in 1948, and turned it into a 5-million-copy hit that went to the top of the pop charts in 1950 and 1951.[19]

The most popular country music star of 1950 and one of the chief contributors to its rise to national prominence was Hank Williams. Drawing much of his material from his own troubled life, he wrote and recorded a long series of hits, including "Your Cheating Heart," "Half as Much," "Cold, Cold Heart," and "So Lonesome I Could Cry." Williams often said that to write and sing country music you had "to know a lot about hard work" and "to have smelt a lot of mule manure." His special interpretation of life's pleasures and tragedies endeared him to millions of fans who listened to his music in truck stops, pool rooms, taverns, and simple homes all across the country. At the height of his popularity, from 1949 to 1953, he made eleven records that sold at least a million copies each. On New Year's Day in 1953, with his life ruined by alcohol and drugs and with his career on the skids, he died at the age of twenty-nine in the back seat of an automobile as he was being driven to a concert in Canton, Ohio. Over 20,000 people jammed the city auditorium in Montgomery, Alabama, for his funeral service. Within three years of his death many country singers would begin to change their style in order to join the rock'n'roll bandwagon that was pushing country music and the older styles of popular music out of the national limelight.[20]

If 1950 was part of the golden age of television, as some believed, it was becoming increasingly clear that the golden age of Hollywood was in the past. The star system, the magnificent downtown theaters, the large audiences, the fat profits, the annual production of hundreds of new feature length and short films, the tremendous unifying and homogenizing force of motion pictures—all these familiar elements of the movie industry since the twenties were rapidly disappearing at midcentury. The industry was suffering from a host of legal and labor troubles and a debilitating conflict over communist subversion and blacklisting, but its major problem came from the competition of the rapidly expanding television industry. Sales of television sets doubled between 1949 and 1950, and with the linking that year of seventy-two television stations in forty-two major markets by the Long Lines Department of the American Telephone and Telegraph Company, almost 70 million people—almost half the population—were brought within the range of television broadcasts.[21]

All these problems were having a devastating effect on the movie industry. In its heyday, in the late 1930s, Hollywood was producing over 500 feature films and 700 short subjects a year and average weekly theater attendance was around 85 million. But in 1950 Hollywood produced just 383 feature-length films, and average weekly attendance, which had still stood as high as 90 million in 1947, had dropped to 36 million.[22] All across the country theaters were curtailing their operating hours, closing their doors, or being converted to bowling alleys, furniture stores, and restaurants. Between the summer of 1950 and 1951, over 3,000 theaters closed across the United States, including 21 in Cleveland, 134 in Southern California, and 100 in Philadephia. Some officials in the movie industry claimed that the effect of television was temporary because, in the words of one top industry executive, "people soon get tired of staring out at a plywood box every night."[23] But most officials knew better and were backing an industrywide promotional campaign headed by the slogan "Movies Are Better Than Ever."

Hollywood did provide some fine movies in 1950 with outstanding performances by established stars like Bette Davis (*All About Eve*), Gloria Swanson (*Sunset Boulevard*), and Spencer Tracy (*Father of the Bride*). Marilyn Monroe (*The Asphalt Jungle*), Marlon Brando (*The Men*), and other newcomers seemed to promise in their debuts that perhaps the best was yet to come. But the decline in attendance, profits, and productions would continue, even though for the rest of the decade Hollywood would try gimmick after gimmick to lure the movie faithful back to the theaters.

Hollywood recouped some in its theater losses by leasing movies to the drive-in theaters. First appearing in Camden, New Jersey, in 1933, their number had grown to over 1,100 by 1949 and to over 3,000 by the end of 1950.[24] Some were little more than cleared cornfields containing a screen, concession stands, rest rooms, and steel posts equipped with amplifiers, but others were more ornate. In Rome, Georgia, a drive-in was built on a thirty-five-acre plot with an elaborate Southern plantation theme, and in Miami one was constructed around an exotic garden theme complete with palm trees, tropical flowers, and hanging gardens. A Washington, Pennsylvania, drive-in boasted that it was "the only drive-in theater in the world that offers lake fishing."[25]

The drive-ins attracted young married couples with children, the elderly, the handicapped, and others who found it too inconvenient or expensive to go to indoor movies. Already dubbed "passion pits with pix," they especially attracted young dating couples, who found the privacy of the automobile much better than indoor movie balconies for heavy necking and, their parents suspected, for even worse transgressions. The problem was so serious, *The New York Times* reported in October of 1950, that some owners were hiring watchmen to patrol the lot with instructions, according to one manager's manual, to look "casually into every car without disturbing the occupants" in order "to prevent any sort of misconduct." Noting the increasing popularity of outdoor theaters, the *Times* concluded that "the drive-ins seem here to stay—and to grow."[26] The *Times* was correct: The number of drive-in theaters would increase to over 4,000 by the end of the decade.

The attractions of television had not yet challenged America's long-standing reputation as a nation of newspaper, magazine, and comic book readers. In 1950 the country had 1,772 daily newspapers with an average circulation per issue of 53.8 million, and nearly 7,000 magazines with total annual sales of nearly 147 million.[27] At only five cents per issue (up from three cents in 1949), the daily newspaper was one of the best bargains around, as were the popular magazines, which ranged from fifteen cents for *Time* and other mass weeklies to twenty cents for the *Saturday Review*, twenty-five cents for *Reader's Digest*, and fifty cents for *Harper's* and *The New Yorker*. *Reader's Digest* was the leading magazine with 9 million sales per issue, but there were 7 other magazines with circulations over 3 million and 8 with circulations over 2 million.[28] The decade ahead would bring stiff competition from television for consumers and for advertising revenue, and the demise of some daily newspapers and mass magazines, but both the newspaper and magazine industries would continue to prosper and to exercise great influence over American taste and opinion.

Much to the dismay of many teachers and parents, millions of young Americans shunned newspapers and magazines for comic books. During the Second World War, studies of periodical sales at American military posts around the world showed that comic books outsold *Reader's Digest*, *Life*, and *The Saturday Evening Post* by a ten-to-one margin, and as the fifties began, young Americans were buying between 60 and 90 million comic books a month.[29] Millions of Americans, young and old, also followed the adventures of dozens of comic-strip characters in the daily newspapers. In addition to reading older strips like "Dick Tracy" and "Blondie," readers were becoming fans of "Pogo," started in 1949 by Walt Kelly, a former artist with Walt Disney, and of several other new strips. In October of 1950 Charles Schulz, who had been drawing a strip called "L'il Folks" for a St. Paul newspaper, renamed the strip "Peanuts" and saw it picked up by the United Features

Syndicate. His galaxy of lovable child characters with all kinds of emotional problems caught on quickly at a time of increased public interest in popular psychology. In that same year Mort Walker started his highly successful "Beetle Bailey," with Beetle as "Joe College." When the Korean War broke out, Beetle was made into a reluctant draftee, and the strip changed from a satire on college life to one on military life. It became so popular among soldiers that when the Tokyo edition of *Stars and Stripes* dropped the strip in 1954 because of its irreverent attitude toward the army, a chorus of GI complaints forced the editors to put it back in.[30] Americans, it seemed, took their comic strips seriously.

It spite of all the dire warnings that television would destroy the book industry and create a nation of illiterates, book sales were healthy in 1950 and, aided by population growth and the paperback revolution, would double by the end of the decade. The best-seller list in fiction in 1950 was headed by Henry Morton Robinson's *The Cardinal*, a story of a Catholic priest's rise to power, which sold 435,516 copies in paperback and 152,879 in cloth and heralded the changes to come in book publishing by becoming the first major book to be issued in both hardcover and paperback editions. Led by *Betty Crocker's Picture Cook Book*, the nonfiction list reflected the contemporary interest in homemaking, children, self-improvement, and religion.[31] The bookstores were also crowded with how-to books, as millions tried to follow supposedly simple instructions on how to make home or car repairs, make love, become pregnant, raise children, play bridge, write and spell better, paint, stay young, enjoy growing old, cook, marry, get divorced, work, retire, and even how to write how-to-do-it books. For those who were too lazy or too busy that year to read much of anything, the *Reader's Digest* corporation launched a condensed-book club. It would be highly successful: By 1952, each quarterly volume would be selling over a million copies.[32]

Spectator sports were enjoying a boom in 1950, with baseball still leading the way as the national pastime. This uniquely American game had been part of the nation's culture since the middle of the nineteenth century and was still played much the same as it had been then. Year after year, through two world wars, the great depression, and thousands of other momentous events of American history, baseball had commanded national attention and acquired a history of its own that was familiar to millions. Legions of loyal fans possessed remarkable knowledge of current or past star players, pennant races, World Series, batting averages, pitching records, great catches, and other team and individual performances. In the first week of every October other events were pushed into the background as the nation focused its attention on the World Series. Many workers and students traditionally called in sick so that they could be home near their radio or television sets, while many schools and offices across the country gave in to popular demand and played radio broadcasts of the games over intercom systems. No summer would have seemed the same without the summer game, for baseball was as essential to American culture and Americanism as the flag, apple pie, and motherhood.

In 1950 millions of fans turned out to the ballparks or tuned in to their radio and television sets to follow their favorite teams and star players like Ted Williams, Joe DiMaggio, Stan Musial, Jackie Robinson, and Bob Feller. Baseball in many ways was still the "the New York game," for media attention and the dominance of the Brooklyn Dodgers, New York Giants, and New York Yankees kept the city in the national eye. The Yankees were in their heyday, both loved and hated all across the country for their consistently winning ways. Most people expected it to be another Yankee–Dodger subway World Series, but Richie Ashburn, Robin Roberts, and the rest of the Philadelphia Whiz Kids made it a Yankee–Phillie fall classic by beating the Dodgers on the last day of the season for the first Phillie pennant in thirty-five years. But the pennant celebration had scarcely ended and Dodger fans had barely stopped moaning "Wait'll next year" before the Yankees swept the Whiz Kids in four straight games to take their second consecutive World Series title en route to a record-setting five straight under "the old perfessor," Casey Stengel.

After a decade of problems stemming from the Second World War and the competition of rival leagues, professional football in 1950 was set to offer a serious challenge to baseball as the land's most popular spectator sport. Mergers of the two rival leagues at the end of the 1949 season allowed the National Football League to begin the decade with Bert Bell as the commissioner of the only pro football league around. Under Bell the league in 1950 adopted the free substitution rule, which, by legalizing the two-platoon system, freed players from having to play both offense and defense and allowed them to develop specialized skills at one position. Football now became a more exciting game, and this, along with the decision to black out the televising of home games, brought millions of fans into the stadium. Attendance at NFL games reached an all-time high of 1,977,556 in 1950, when the Cleveland Browns won the league championship by beating the Los Angeles Rams 30–28 on Lou Groza's field goal with twenty-eight seconds left in the game. Professional football was ready to enter a new age of popularity and prosperity.

Sports fans found 1950 to be a good year all around. College basketball had not yet attained the popularity it would enjoy in later decades, but college football had a banner year that was kicked off on January 1 when over 100,000 fans jammed the stadium in Pasadena to watch Ohio State win the Rose Bowl by defeating California 17–14. In professional sports, George Mikan led Minneapolis over Syracuse for the National Basketball Association championship, Detroit beat Toronto to take the Stanley Cup and end the Leafs' three-year reign in professional hockey, and Middleground won the

Belmont Stakes and the Kentucky Derby. In tennis and golf, two sports that had not yet attained mass appeal, Arthur Larsen won the men's singles title in the United States Lawn Tennis Association championship, while golfer Ben Hogan won the United States Open but was surpassed in total earnings by Sam Snead, who won $35,758 for his year's efforts on the links. In boxing, a very popular sport in arenas and on television, 1950 provided the spectacle of an aging and portly Joe Louis attempting to come out of retirement to take the heavyweight crown from reigning champion Ezzard Charles, who won an easy fifteen-round decision over the Brown Bomber, who had aroused so much black pride and thrilled so many fans of all races in the thirties and forties. In women's sports, thirty-one-year-old Florence Chadwick swam the English Channel in thirteen hours and twenty-eight minutes, a new record for women. Margaret Osborn du Pont won the women's singles title in the United States Lawn Tennis Association championship for the third consecutive time, and Babe Didrikson Zaharias regained her golf title in the United States Women's Open.

The prosperity enjoyed by midcentury Americans was bringing more than a boom in consumer goods and leisure activities. It was also helping to make Americans healthier, for they were the beneficiaries of an ongoing revolution in the diagnosis, treatment, and prevention of some of man's oldest maladies. Beginning with penicillin, discovered back in the 1920s but not put into widespread use until the Second World War, the 1940s had witnessed the development of streptomycin and dozens of other antibiotics, cortisone, ACTH, antihistamines, and many other wonder drugs. In research centers and operating rooms, doctors in the late 1940s learned how to perform open-heart surgery, repair heart valves, correct congenital heart defects (the "blue baby" condition), and to do other complicated repairs of the heart and other organs. Life expectancy, which in 1900 had stood at a little over forty-nine years for whites and thirty-three for nonwhites, had jumped to sixty-five for whites and over fifty-three for nonwhites in 1940, and then rose to almost sixty-nine for whites and sixty for nonwhites by 1950.[33] Medical authorities expected the coming decade to bring even greater medical wonders.

The treatment and prevention of some disorders, however, continued to elude medical researchers in 1950. One was cancer. Another was poliomyelitis, a crippling and sometimes fatal disease that was the cause of more fear and despair than any other single malady. In 1950 the National Foundation for Infantile Paralysis reported 31,989 cases on top of the previous year's record 41,442 cases.[34] To retard the spread of the disease, which primarily affected the young, many schools closed early in the spring and opened later in the fall, while in affected areas movie theaters, swimming pools, playgrounds, and other gathering places for young people either closed or barred children under sixteen years of age. Anxious parents refused to let their children play with other children or even to touch their books or toys, and they canceled or postponed summer vacations that would take the family into crowded areas. Everyone seemed to know or to have heard of a child who had died, been placed in the dreaded iron lung, or been left with a withered "polio leg." Each year millions of people contributed to the March of Dimes to fight the disease, but few even dared to dream that medical researchers were closing in on a preventive vaccine that would bring miraculous results by the end of the decade.

Revolutionary medical advances were not able to overcome the effects of poverty and poor health knowledge and practices among large segments of the population. Too many Americans ate the wrong foods, smoked and drank too much, failed to seek proper medical care, and doctored themselves with home remedies or patent medicines of questionable value. One of the fastest-selling over-the-counter drugs in 1950 was Hadacol, a cure-all invented and marketed back in 1947 by Dudley J. LeBlanc, a Louisiana state senator. A mixture of vitamins, minerals, water, honey, and ethyl alcohol, Hadacol was promoted as a remedy for heart trouble, high blood pressure, rheumatism, cancer, strokes, hay fever, arthritis, ulcers, fatigue, and virtually any other ailment—all for only $1.25 for a half-pint bottle or $3.50 for the twenty-four-ounce family size. To make sure that everyone got the message about his wonderful product, LeBlanc blanketed newspapers, magazines, billboards, barns, and television and radio shows with Hadacol health claims and with testimonials from Mickey Rooney, Bob Hope, Burns and Allen, Jimmy Durante, Jack Dempsey, and other notables. He also dreamed up the idea of a barnstorming Hadacol Good Will Caravan made up of Hadacol buses, trucks, automobiles, and five airplanes trailing advertising banners. Like the old-time medicine shows, the Hadacol Good Will Caravan put on shows in ball parks and fair grounds, charging only the Hadacol box top as the price of admission.

It worked. Sales went from $75,000 in 1947 to almost $2 million in 1949 to $24 million in 1950, when sales were so brisk that LeBlanc was unable to fill all the orders that came in. The bubble burst later in the year when the Federal Trade Commission began to investigate Hadacol's fraudulent health claims and the Internal Revenue Service became interested in the taxes LeBlanc had neglected to pay. LeBlanc would sell the company in 1951, but legal and financial problems would plague the new owners throughout the decade and force them into bankruptcy in 1960, compelling millions of apparently satisfied customers to look elsewhere for miracle cures and twenty-five-proof drinks.[35]

The United States in 1950 was a powerful and prosperous nation in the throes of revolutionary changes that promised to transform the country and its people in the decade ahead. In a few short years it had become a global power with worldwide responsibilities and with nationwide fears of the Russians, Chinese, and atomic bombs. The economy was expanding and moving toward greater emphasis on luxury goods and services, plastics and electronics, credit purchases, advertising, automation, and research and development. Television sales and stations, marriage rates, birth rates, and urban and suburban populations were all booming. More and more women were having their horizons broadened and their expectations raised as they went off to college or entered the work world. Large numbers of black citizens, crowding into the slums of northern cities or languishing in impoverished small towns and farms in the South, were becoming more resentful than ever before of their second-class citizenship. Teenagers (the term was still relatively new in 1950) were increasing in number and showing signs of developing a distinct subculture with values and consumer products of its own. In these and in many other ways, America was a nation in rapid transition.

Yet in many respects the country seemed at midcentury to belong to an earlier, more placid age. It was still a man's world—and a white man's world at that—for white males controlled the seats of power and used law and custom to keep women, blacks, and other minorities in their "proper place." The nation's leaders, songs, clothing, movies, and sexual attitudes and practices still bore the distinct stamp of the forties. In small towns across the country milkmen delivered their products directly to the front door according to the directions scrawled on a note inside an empty bottle. Neighbors frequently visited one another and on hot spring and summer nights sat talking on front porches, at least until it was time to retreat inside to watch the antics of Milton Berle or Sid Caesar and Imogene Coca. A first-class letter cost three cents to mail, and soft drinks and candy bars sold for a nickel. People wrote with fountain pens, filled from a bottle with real ink, not with ballpoint pens. Most kids went swimming in lakes and ponds and other swimming holes, not in swimming pools, and the flotation devices used were real inner tubes from derelict automobile tires rather than artificial substitutes. Most people still regarded airplane travel as a novel and dangerous experience. The railroads, while declining, still carried 488 million passengers, and travelers could choose from among a dozen daily trains making the sixteen- to eighteen-hour trip between New York and Chicago. Even the Korean War, which lasted well into the decade, was a forties-type war; the jet fighter planes and helicopters were new, but the commanders, uniforms, battlefield strategies and tactics, and much of the equipment were of World War II vintage.

In the America of 1950 almost 90 percent of all families did not have a television set and 38 percent of the population had never seen a television program. No one could buy a TV dinner; that dubious improvement in the American diet did not appear until 1954. There was no color television or coast-to-coast television transmission, though both were being developed and would shortly be implemented. There was no nudity in movies or magazines, except in what most people called "dirty movies" shown in run-down theaters in the worst part of town, in nudist magazines kept behind the counters of newsstands, or in *National Geographic*, where it was considered permissible to display bare-breasted females if they were dark-skinned women from exotic foreign cultures. *Playboy*, with its famous first centerfold of Marilyn Monroe, would not hit the newsstands until 1953. There were few national fast-food chains—McDonald's was still a local chain owned by two brothers, and it would remain that way until Ray Kroc bought them out in 1954 and proceeded to revolutionize the hamburger business and the nation's eating habits. There were no thirty-minute newscasts, federal interstate highways, legal abortions, birth control pills, direct distance dialing, or Sunday afternoon doubleheader football games on television. There were few shopping centers, supermarkets, homes with air-conditioners, or cars with automatic transmission, tubeless tires, power brakes, or power steering. In many ways, the United States in 1950 still bore a resemblance—albeit a rapidly fading one—to the small-town America idealized in the Norman Rockwell paintings that graced the covers of *The Saturday Evening Post*.

But ahead lay great changes. The coming decade would bring more economic and technological growth, more social upheaval, more domestic strife, more involvement in world affairs, a hot war in Korea, and the spread of the Cold War across the globe. By 1961, when the reins of political power passed from Dwight D. Eisenhower to young John F. Kennedy, the United States would be a far different nation from the one presided over by Harry S. Truman at the midcentury mark.

# 2

# The Man from Independence

The man who occupied the White House in 1950 was living proof of the old adage that in America almost anyone can be president. The third child of John and Martha Truman, Harry S. Truman was born on a western Missouri farm in 1884 but grew up in nearby Independence, where the Trumans moved in 1890. Afflicted with poor eyesight and forced to wear glasses from the age of six, young Harry was a voracious reader who spent most of his days with books rather than with his young friends on the playground. His formal education ended with his graduation from high school in 1901, for his poor eyesight blocked any hopes of a West Point appointment, and strapped family finances prevented him from going anywhere else. He tried a variety of jobs—with a railroad, newspaper, and bank—before entering a ten-year farming partnership with his father. He joined the army in 1917, rose to the level of captain, and saw military action in France in the last battles of the war as the commander of Battery D of the 129th Field Artillery. At the end of the war he witnessed Paris's tumultuous reception of President Woodrow Wilson, who was joining other statesmen from around the world to sit down at the Paris Peace Conference to remake a world torn apart by the Great War. The young captain could not have known that a quarter-century later he would be called upon to end another great war and to make another attempt at world peace.

Discharged at the end of the war as a major, Truman returned to civilian life and to his midwestern roots. In June of 1919, when he was thirty-five and she was thirty-four, he married his childhood sweetheart, Elizabeth Virginia Wallace, whom he had courted for five years before he went off to war. He and a friend soon formed a partnership in a haberdashery in Kansas City, Missouri, but it went bankrupt in 1922, leaving the Trumans in debt for years to come. At the age of thirty-seven, when most successful men have settled into their careers, Truman was an apparent failure with a dim future.

Truman's life took a new turn in 1923, when he entered politics with the Pendergast machine in Jackson County. He served several terms as county judge before being elected to the Senate at the age of fifty in 1934. His ties to the corrupt Pendergast machine led reporters and fellow politicians to refer to him as the Senator from Pendergast, but his hard work, party loyalty, and support of the New Deal made him a popular senator. During the Second World War he served as the chairman of the Special Senate Committee to Investigate the National Defense Program, commonly called the Truman Committee, and his diligent efforts as the watchdog over war contracts soon won him admiration in the Senate and across the nation. He even made the cover of *Time* magazine and was the subject of a *Reader's Digest* article.[1] His Senate record, along with the party regulars' dislike of Henry Wallace and other controversial candidates, led the party to turn to Truman as a compromise choice as Roosevelt's running mate in the election of 1944. Roosevelt won an easy victory for an unprecedented fourth term, and on January 20, 1945, Truman settled into the vice-presidency, resigned, as he often said, to playing the role of the "political eunuch."

Truman's life changed dramatically on April 12, 1945, when—less than a month before final victory in Europe and four months before the defeat of Japan—the popular president who had guided the nation through the dark days of the depression and the Second World War died of a cerebral hemorrhage. When summoned to the White House and told of Roosevelt's death by his widow, Eleanor, a stunned Truman asked, "Is there anything I can do for you?" Eleanor shook her head and responded, "Is there anything we can do for you? For you are the one in trouble now."[2] And indeed he was, for the man who had entered national politics at the age of fifty, served ten years in the Senate, and only eighty-two days in the vice-presidency, was now the head of the most powerful nation in the world near the end of the worst war the world had yet seen. When he took the oath of office the next day, he told reporters: "Boys, if you ever pray, pray for me now. I don't know whether you fellows ever had a load of hay fall on you, but when they told me yesterday what had happened, I felt like the moon, the stars, and all the planets had fallen on me."[3]

The first president from the state of Missouri and only the fifth Democratic president since the Civil War, Truman would occupy the White House during eight of the most turbulent, controversial, and formative years in American history. He also had the unenviable task of succeeding the nation's most popular and powerful president. Roosevelt had been president for so long—over twelve years—that it was difficult for many people in Washington and throughout the country to think of anyone else occupying that office. Truman would long labor in Roosevelt's shadow, damned by those who thought he was not enough like Roosevelt and by still others who thought he was too much like him. But he would not be another Roosevelt, for he brought to the most powerful job in the world his own unique blend of experience, personality, ideas, leadership style, strengths, and weaknesses, that would enable him to leave his distinct mark on the presidency and the nation.

Truman was a bespectacled, scholarly looking man who was fond of saying that he looked just like fifty other people you might pass on the street. Plain and unpretentious, he preferred simple foods (ham, roast beef, potatoes, chili, fruit) to gourmet dishes, enjoyed coarse humor (especially political yarns), did not smoke but drank a little bourbon now and then, loved to play poker (a "study in probabilities," he called it), and chose the company of plain people and hometown buddies over that of intellectuals and artists. He was a Baptist who began each day with a prayer for humility, but he was not a regular churchgoer, especially when he moved into the presidency and saw that his presence attracted too much attention from the rest of the congregation. He liked almost all kinds of music except opera, which he detested, but his favorite pieces were works by Bach, Mozart, Beethoven, Chopin, and Johann Strauss. He loved to play the piano, and when he played before friends he rarely passed up the opportunity to tell them that "if I hadn't become President, I sure would have made a helluva good piano player in a whorehouse."[4] He was a combative and outspoken man—his contemporaries in politics and the press described him as cocky, spunky, brash, pugnacious, irascible, gritty, and blunt—who rarely hesitated to use colorful or profane language to express how he really felt about a personality, issue, or event. He was also independent, stubborn, and slow to forget a slight against himself, the presidency, or his beloved family. Harry Vaughan, a close Truman aide and friend, told author John Hersey in 1950 that Truman was "one tough son of a bitch of a man."[5] Truman would have beamed at this characterization.

The thirty-third president had some rather glaring weaknesses when he stepped into the office vacated by his powerful predecessor. Although he had been a popular and effective senator who knew his way around Washington, he had little training and experience in foreign affairs. In fact, he knew little about the fast-breaking developments in the war beyond what he read in the newspapers, for Roosevelt was gone from Washington much of the time in 1945, and even when he was in town, he had not included the vice-president in high-level policy conferences. Truman was not even informed of the progress of the atomic bomb project. He also lacked many of Roosevelt's skills, particularly the latter's ability to manipulate his party, Congress, and public opinion, and he fell far short of his oratorical abilities. Roosevelt had been one of the most charismatic, spellbinding, and quotable speakers of all time, and in this area, as in so many others, he was a hard act to follow.

In private conversations or in extemporaneous speeches delivered before enthusiastic campaign crowds, Truman could be very dynamic, particularly in his patented "give 'em hell" lambastings of Republican opponents. However, his prepared speeches sounded, as one critic said, "like a musical comedy which doesn't have tunes you can whistle."[6] Truman used speechwriters, but he did a great deal of editing to make sure that his speeches were short and to the point and contained no "two dollar words." But he sometimes read his speeches too fast, using as many as 150 words a minute (compared to 125 for Roosevelt and many other accomplished speakers), and his speed and poor eyesight combined to cause him to mispronounce words or to stumble and lose his place. He also spoke with a nasal twang in a seemingly uninspired monotone. He was a straightforward, serious speaker, not an eloquent and inspiring one, and his most quotable words—and there were many—came not from his prepared texts but from his private conversations or public outbursts at his political opponents or the press.[7]

Truman had other faults, too. His loyalty to old friends and cronies led him to appoint too many of them to federal jobs and to stand stubbornly by them even when they were obviously guilty of incompetence or dishonesty. In his approach to some of the basic issues of the day, he was sometimes simplistic and inconsistent, and in political quarrels his fierce partisanship often caused him to attack his opponents' motives or character rather than to deal with the issues. Along with his stubbornness and penchant for sticking to a decision even when it turned out to be wrong, his partisanship led him to defend lost causes and to go down to defeat when compromise could have saved part of the program or policy he was trying to promote. And he could be maddeningly petty, rarely forgetting a real or imagined wrong done to him or his family.

Although Truman came to the presidency poorly prepared, he did bring to the job some important qualities. He had a keen mind, a retentive memory, and a great deal of common sense, a trait sadly lacking, he often noted, in the nation's capital. He was a Jacksonian Democrat, an unpolished "man of the people" whose common touch was appreciated by millions of his fellow citizens. He was a genuinely modest man, who often claimed that a million other Americans were more qualified than he to be president, and he never forgot that all of his power and fame resulted from the office he held and not from his importance as Harry S. Truman. He possessed a strong sense of duty and great personal integrity, and he was scrupulously honest, having shunned all opportunities his long political career had given him to enrich himself at the public till. Corruption was a way of life in the Pendergast machine and even touched some members of the Truman administration, but through over thirty years of political life Harry Truman maintained a spotless record in his personal finances.

One of Truman's greatest attributes was his ability to make quick, usually sound decisions. Dean Acheson, his close friend and controversial secretary of state, probably described this talent best: "When a problem was brought before him, he always asked how long he had to make the decision. He always made it on time, and he never looked back and second-guessed."[8] Truman took full responsibility for his decisions, never backed away from a problem or a decision, and refused to be intimidated by his critics. "If you can't stand the heat," he was fond of saying, "get out of the kitchen."

The first president without a college education since Grover Cleveland, Truman was defensive about his educational background and often chided the "ivory tower professors" who presumed to criticize the way he ran the country. He was certainly not an intellectual, but he was intelligent and well-read. In spite of his backbreaking workday, he managed to continue his lifelong habit of reading a surprising number of books on a variety of subjects. He occasionally read mysteries, like his predecessor, and he always looked forward to receiving an autographed copy of the latest Perry Mason thriller from mystery writer Erle Stanley Gardner.[9]

But his favorite reading matter was history and biography. Truman had a great love of history, and his knowledge of it ranged from ancient times to his own day. He read critically, often making notations in the margins like "bunk" or "True, true, true!" or "Where did he ever get a damn fool notion like that?"[10] His diary and letters are full of historical allusions, and he loved to discuss history with anyone who would listen. Sometimes reporters or other visitors who had debated with Truman some of the finer points of history would be surprised a few days later by a presidential letter or phone call following up on their previous conversation. His own sense of history and the importance of his office led him to be one of the few presidents in history—along with John Quincy Adams, James K. Polk, Dwight Eisenhower, Richard Nixon, and Jimmy Carter—to keep a diary. Written on White House stationery, appointment sheets, and leather-bound diary books, his diary reveals a fascination with history and a firm conviction that the lessons of the past can be applied to the problems of the present.[11]

Truman's knowledge of history undoubtedly contributed to one of his greatest strengths—his keen sense of the importance and sanctity of the presidency of the United States and a firm determination to defend it against all attackers, from Senator McCarthy and General MacArthur to the partisans in Congress trying to restrict the office's constitutional powers. Well-versed in the histories of his thirty-two predecessors in the office, Truman was fondest of what he considered the strong presidents—George

Washington, Thomas Jefferson, Andrew Jackson, Abraham Lincoln, both Roosevelts, and Woodrow Wilson.[12] He was resolved to be a strong president in the mold of his favorite, Andrew Jackson, and to pass the powers of his office—completely intact—to his successor, even if it happened to be someone he did not particularly care for, like Dwight D. Eisenhower. An appreciation of this trait in Harry Truman is absolutely essential to an understanding of why he acted as he did in the eight years he spent in the White House.

Like many of the great figures of history, Truman was an energetic man with an enormous capacity for hard work. Although he turned sixty-six years of age in May of 1950, he was a vigorous and healthy man who exercised daily, kept the weight on his 5-foot 9-inch frame at between 165 and 175 pounds, and followed a daily schedule that many younger men would have had trouble maintaining. He had never lost the habit, acquired a half century before on the Missouri farm with his father, of getting up early and putting in a hard, full day's work. He rarely seemed to tire. His old friend and press secretary, Charles Ross, claimed that Truman "put in a sixteen- to eighteen-hour day and was fresher at the end than I was at the beginning."[13]

In 1950 a typical workday in the life of President Truman began not at 1600 Pennsylvania Avenue but across the street at Blair House, where the Trumans resided during most of his second term while the living quarters of the White House were undergoing badly needed repairs. His long day usually began at around 5:30 A.M., when he awoke, shaved, dressed, wrote letters, and read several newspapers. Around seven he began his legendary morning walk around the streets of Washington, covering close to two miles at a 120-steps-a-minute military pace that left the Secret Service and trailing reporters panting to keep up. At the end of his walk he usually went by the White House for an additional workout on the rowing machine in the gym or for a quarter-mile swim (with his glasses on) in the pool built by Roosevelt. At eight he returned to Blair House for breakfast with his family or, if they were visiting back in Missouri, to eat alone. After a breakfast consisting of an egg, strip of bacon, fresh fruit, and half a glass of skimmed milk, he rode in a bullet-proof limousine across the street to work in his White House office.[14]

At 8:30 or so he would be in the Oval Office at his seven-foot-long mahogany desk, usually cluttered with a telephone, his engagement list, four clocks, six desk calendars, books, folders, papers, and the famous sign bearing the slogan "The Buck Stops Here." On a frame hung on the wall was another one of his favorite slogans, this one from Mark Twain: "Always do right. This will gratify some people and astonish the rest." Behind his desk was a table with family portraits and several books that the busy president might be reading in his spare moments. Over the door of the office was a lucky horseshoe Truman had found during the Senate campaign of 1940. The office also contained dozens of other mementoes, including a portrait of Franklin Roosevelt, a small statue of Andrew Jackson, and globe given to Truman by General Dwight D. Eisenhower.[15]

The early morning hours were usually taken up with dictation to Rose Conway, his private secretary, of official government correspondence or of fiery letters to his congressional and media critics. The rest of the morning was occupied with the laborious task of signing documents, meeting with his staff members or congressional leaders, calling or writing members of Congress, answering a select few of the 12,000 to 15,000 letters he received every week, and keeping appointments with heads of state, other dignitaries, and a countless parade of groups like the Gold Star Mothers (mothers of men killed in the war), the Elks, and the Boy Scouts. At one o'clock he went back to Blair House for lunch, usually consisting of a small serving of fish or meat, a light vegetable, and fruit dessert. He then napped until around three, when he went back to his office to work until around six, when he left again for Blair House with a briefcase full of papers he referred to as his homework. After having dinner with his family, and occasionally with friends, he would go to his study and work for several more hours before retiring at midnight. He rarely had trouble sleeping, even after the most problem-ridden day, a gift he attributed to his avoidance of coffee and his conviction that he had done his best and could not affect the outcome of the day's decisions by carrying the problems to bed.[16]

This routine was altered, of course, to accommodate special meetings, unexpected problems, or periodic press conferences. Truman had 324 press conferences during his eight years in office, an average of 3.5 per month as compared to Franklin Roosevelt's 6.9 and Eisenhower's 2.0. Held on Thursdays in the Indian Treaty Room in the Old State-War-Navy Building across the street from the west wing of the White House, these conferences were attended by as many as 200 newsmen. Truman gave direct answers to direct questions, responded to all questions—even to some that should have gone unanswered—and was frequently drawn into fiery exchanges with reporters. He often made candid or heated remarks about foreign or domestic issues that would have to be "clarified" later. One observer said that at some of these sessions Truman resembled "the backwoods Baptist laying down a personal testament of God and Mammon to the congregated reporters."[17]

Truman generally had good relations with the press, but like many other presidents, he often complained that he had been misquoted or misinterpreted and that some newspapers were out to get him. In his conversations and diary he referred to various newspapers as "the snotty little Howard paper," "the sabotage sheet," and "lie outlets."[18] He also had no use for pollsters. He rarely passed up an opportunity to ridicule the 1948 pollsters who had predicted Dewey's victory, and he often remarked that no one would ever have heard of Moses or Martin Luther if they had taken a poll every time they were faced with a decision.[19]

Throughout his long workday President Truman was always punctual, orderly, decisive, and cheerful. He was also easy to work with. He was warm and friendly to his cabinet and staff members, conducted his meetings in a dignified yet relaxed manner, and listened carefully and politely to reports, proposals, and opinions. He engaged in good-natured ribbing and enjoyed a good joke on himself as well as on others. Secretary of State Dean Acheson, the suave intellectual who was so different from the president yet became one of his closest advisers, wrote that Truman was always "the patient, modest, considerate, and appreciative boss, helpful and understanding in all official matters, affectionate and sympathetic in any private worry or sorrow."[20] Truman's considerate treatment of fellow workers extended down to the butlers, maids, and other staff members who worked behind the scenes in the White House. He always treated them as important people, not as mere auxiliaries to the presidency. Often stuffy foreign dignitaries, including kings, presidents, and premiers, were surprised when the Trumans introduced them to the doorman or to the butler who was serving the tea or coffee. This was not done in foreign capitals, and it was not done under the Roosevelts, but it was a common practice with the plain, unpretentious couple who now occupied the White House.[21]

Harry and Bess Truman were certainly one of the most loving and ordinary couples ever to serve as president and First Lady of the United States. They were deeply devoted to one another and to their only child, Margaret, who was born in 1924 and lived with them in the White House while she attended George Washington University and tried to launch a singing career. To Truman, the First Lady was "Bess" or "the boss." She had served as his paid secretary and unofficial adviser while he was in the Senate, and when he shouldered the burdens of the presidency, he continued to seek her advice on everything from military and political matters to the wording of a speech. "She is my chief adviser," he once said. "I never write a speech without going over it with her."[22] The independent, fiery president with a "give 'em hell" public image was in private a romantic and sentimental man who loved his family deeply, was miserable when separated from it, and wrote love letters to his wife and affectionate, fatherly letters to his grown daughter.

Truman tried to shield his wife and daughter from the public eye and to lead a private family life even in the fishbowl of the presidency. The three had breakfast and other meals together whenever they could, and at night, when he could steal time from his thick briefcase of official papers, they talked, read, or played the piano together. Sometimes Bess listened to a baseball game on the radio while her husband worked in a nearby chair. Bess and Margaret often went down to the basement for a game of Ping-Pong or watched television, but except for an occasional prize fight or quiz show, the president rarely watched the new invention that was sweeping the country. The Trumans also entertained relatives from Missouri or had old friends in for dinner, a card game, or a movie.[23] When Truman had to travel from Washington on official business or when Bess and Margaret went back to Missouri for long visits, a lonely president called or wrote them every day. "Your pop had missed you and your mother very much," he would write in letters that reached their Independence home almost before the Truman women could unpack.[24] They were a typical middle-class, midwestern family that just happened to be the first family in the land.

From the very beginning of her husband's presidency Bess had shown that she would not try to emulate her popular predecessor, Eleanor, an outgoing First Lady who had acquired an international reputation in her own right as an advocate of numerous causes. Bess always maintained that, since she had not been elected to anything, her opinions were not important, so she refused to give interviews or hold press conferences. She rarely spoke in public, and when she did, she did not discuss politics. She cheerfully carried out her social chores—the endless round of teas and receptions—and gained a reputation as a gracious hostess with an uncanny knack for remembering names. But she never liked these responsibilities, preferring to stay out of the limelight and to play the role of the dignified and reserved First Lady and dutiful wife and mother. She often called long-distance to chat with friends in Missouri, and she once had her old bridge club fly to Washington so she could catch up on her card playing and conversation. In the summer she would ride the train back to Missouri to stay for weeks at a time. Wherever she was, she was devoted to her husband and dependent upon him. When asked by a friend to describe the most important thing in her life, she answered without hesitation, "Harry and I have been sweethearts and married for more than forty years, and no matter where I was, when I put out my hand, Harry's was there to grasp it."[25]

Through more than a half-century of marriage Bess was bothered by her husband's language, for he had an apparently uncontrollable habit of punctuating his speech with profanities from his farming days in Missouri and his days with the boys in Battery D. His repertoire included the whole range of barnyard expressions, four-letter words, and compound phrases, like "son of a bitch," one of his favorites. Other presidents—notably Eisenhower, Kennedy, Johnson, and Nixon—swore more in private than Truman, but what was so shocking in the late forties and early fifties was that Truman sometimes used profanity in public, such as at press conferences or on the campaign trail.[26] He also used it in his letters, diary, and other written materials. Bess spent much of their married life trying to induce her husband to modify his verbal indiscretions, but to little avail. According to one story making the rounds in Washington, Bess was once visited by a prominent party woman who complained about Truman's characterization of another politician's comments as "a bunch of horse manure," only to be told by Bess that "you don't know how many years it took me to tone it down to that!"[27] That story may be a delightful fabrication, but several of the servants at the White House testified that one of the most frequent expressions in the Truman household was the First Lady's "you didn't have to say that."[28]

Truman's fondness for coarse humor and language was usually kept under control in mixed company, for like many men of his age and background he had Victorian ideas about womanhood and chivalry, believing that women should be placed on pedestals and treated like ladies while men ran the world. In an age that did not know the meaning of sexism, he called women's rights "a lot of hooey," and answered questions about the possibility of a woman president with a stock reply: "I've said for a long time that women have everything else, they might as well have the presidency."[29] At times he could be shy around women and prudish about sex. He called the Folies Bergère "disgusting" when he saw it in Paris at the end of World War I, and years later, at the age of fifty, he proudly wrote that he had "come to the place where all men strive to be at my age" by acquiring control over his carnal desires.[30]

Truman believed that, although he himself, as a public figure, was fair game for criticism from the public and the press, his family was private and should be off-limits. He always bristled at any criticism of his family and indignantly rose to their defense. Two members of the House of Representatives, Clare Boothe Luce and Adam Clayton Powell, were barred from all White House social functions when they dared to criticize Bess, but perhaps the most notable of the Truman wars in defense of his family came in an incident in 1950 involving his daughter and Paul Hume, a music critic for the *Washington Post*. In a December 6 review of a recital Margaret had given the night before at Constitution Hall, Hume had several unkind remarks to make about Margaret's performance, including the observation that "she cannot sing with anything approaching professional finish" and "she communicates almost nothing of the music she presents."[31]

When Truman read the review, he was so outraged that he sat down and wrote in longhand a blistering letter, put his own stamp on it since it was private business, and carried it to the mailbox himself. The letter called Hume "a frustrated old man who wishes he could have been successful," characterized his review as "lousy" and "poppycock," and promised that if the two ever met Hume would "need a new nose, a lot of beefsteak for black eyes, and perhaps a supporter below." It was signed "H.S.T."[32]

The letter to the thirty-four-year-old music critic was soon on the front page of all newspapers. When Margaret heard the news while in Nashville on a concert tour, she said, "I am absolutely positive my father wouldn't use language like that."[33] But Truman confirmed that he had, and though an embarrassed Margaret then took a "no comment" stance, the rest of the country did not, particularly the press, which wrote article after article deploring the president's rough language and misplaced paternal pride. The letter was certainly ill-considered and abusive, even by the standards of the hot-tempered Truman, who wrote it in haste while dealing with several international crises, including the Chinese intervention in the Korean War, and while coping with the loss of his press secretary and friend from his high school days, Charles Ross, who died of a heart attack while working at his White House desk just hours before Margaret's ill-fated concert. But the president never apologized for the attack on the young critic and never doubted that he had done the right thing. Hume "put my baby as low as he could and he made the young accompanist look like a dub," he wrote in his diary. "It upset me, and I wrote him what I thought of him."[34]

Hume was not alone in the category of those who received angry letters from the president, for Truman often fired off literary broadsides at his critics in Washington and across the country. Many of his letters never reached the intended recipient. Mrs. Conway wisely filed some of her boss's most intemperate epistles before they reached the mailbox, and the president himself prudently stashed others away in his desk drawers, apparently feeling so much better after letting off steam that he saw no need to mail them. Unpublished until 1982, these letters reveal a candid president unveiling his innermost thoughts about journalist Westbrook Pegler ("the greatest character assassin in the United States"), Senator Estes Kefauver ("Cowfever"), Senator Richard Nixon ("Squirrel-Head Nixon"), and other personalities of the day.[35]

Truman's family loyalties extended beyond his wife and daughter to other members of his and Bess's family back in Missouri. He was especially kind to Bess's mother, Madge Gates Wallace, whom he helped to support from the time he and Bess were married in 1919 until Mrs. Wallace's death in 1952. He and Bess lived in her home on 219 North Delaware Street when they were in Independence, and while he was president Mrs. Wallace had her own room at the White House, even though the arrangement inconvenienced the Trumans. Bess would have it no other way: "It's a daughter's duty to look after her mother," she said.[36] Truman agreed, and always treated his mother-in-law with utmost respect even though she often belittled her son-in-law's appearance, decisions, speeches, or anything else that came to mind. When Truman fired General MacArthur, an unhappy Mrs. Wallace asked Bess, "Why did Harry fire that nice man?"[37] As always, Bess defended her husband, and as always, Harry continued to act as he pleased.

Truman was almost as loyal to his friends as to his family. He had many friends from his early years in Missouri, his army days, and his memberships in the Elks, Lions, American Legion, and some two hundred other organizations he had joined over the years. Even in the busy years of his presidency he found time to send letters and cards to his old friends, to attend funerals or send condolences to the survivors, and to travel back to Independence for special dinners or parades. Early in 1945, when he was still vice president, Truman had insisted on flying back to Missouri to attend the funeral of Tom Pendergast, his old mentor who had helped launch his political career, even though his closest aides feared the renewed association with the unsavory Missouri political boss would hurt Truman's political career. At heart Truman was a small-town midwesterner who valued family and friends and never forgot them or his humble roots.

Truman was a hard worker who seemed to enjoy being president. However, he sometimes tired of the burdens of the office and longed to get away from what he called "the Great White Prison" on Pennsylvania Avenue. Whenever he could, he sought relief from his duties through his morning walks and swims, afternoon naps, evenings with his family, and a few hours of recreation carved out of busy weekends. His favorite weekend activity was sailing down the Potomac in the presidential yacht, the *Williamsburg*, with his family, staff members, and close friends like Chief Justice Fred Vinson, Clinton Anderson, Averell Harriman, Clark Clifford, and Lyndon Johnson. Although he still had to attend to the business of the presidency, signing documents or doing other paperwork, Truman used these river trips for reading, playing poker, sunbathing, swimming, drinking a little bourbon, and talking politics. He also spent an occasional weekend at the presidential retreat at Shangri-la in the Catoctin Mountains in Maryland, and he took two vacations a year at Key West, Florida, soaking up the sun at the naval reservation with his family, staff, old friends, and reporters. At all of his vacation retreats Truman greatly enjoyed the exercise and relaxation, the political gossip, the drinking and poker playing, the talk of politics and history and other current events. He was constantly making little wagers with friends over correct dates of important historical events, names of rulers, the exact wording of Biblical and literary quotations, and the correct answers to a wide range of important and trivial questions. Because of his wide reading and good memory, he usually won.[38]

Truman also enjoyed parties and other social gatherings with close friends, but the demands of his office and his reluctance to disrupt weddings and other festive occasions with his retinue of Secret Service agents led him to decline many social invitations he otherwise would have accepted. Security arrangements became even more elaborate and annoying after an attempt on his life in late 1950. Around two o'clock on the afternoon of November 1, two Puerto Rican nationalists, Oscar Collazo and Griselio Torresola, stormed the front door of Blair House carrying guns and thirty-nine rounds of ammunition. The guards opened fire, and in about three minutes thirty-one shots were exchanged. Torresola and guard Leslie Coffelt were killed, two other guards were wounded, and Collazo was wounded, captured, and later sentenced to life imprisonment. Awakened from his afternoon nap by the gunfire, Truman ran to the upstairs window in his underwear and looked out, but ducked back inside when a guard saw him and shouted, "Damn it! Get back! Get back!" After the incident an unshaken Truman dressed and left for a speaking engagement. "A President has to expect these things" was his reaction.[39]

After this scare the Secret Service roped off the sidewalk and steps in front of Blair House, forced the president to use the bullet-proof limousine even for the short trip across the street between the White House and Blair House, and transported the president to a different part of Washington each day for his morning walk. Truman was annoyed by the new restrictions on his movements, but he complied in order to avoid worrying his wife and daughter or endangering the lives of his guards. But he complained in his diary that "it's hell to be President of the Greatest Most Powerful Nation on Earth—I'd rather be 'first' in the Iberian Village."[40]

Harry S. Truman was an extraordinarily common man thrust by fate into the presidency of the strongest nation in the world during one of the most crucial of all periods of history. He would make many mistakes, especially in his early years, and he would be vilified by the press, public, and Congress as few presidents had been before him. But he would do many things that were right, especially in foreign policy, and he would preserve the powers of the presidency at a time when it came under its greatest attack since the days of Reconstruction, when a power-hungry Congress had stripped Andrew Johnson of many of his constitutional powers and had come within one vote of impeaching him over political differences. Truman's efforts would be little appreciated at the time; in fact, he would leave office in 1953 with one of the lowest popularity ratings ever recorded for a modern president. But with the passage of time, knowledgeable observers would place him where he belonged—in the company of the great presidents he had often praised in his diary late at night in the lonely confines of the White House.

# 3

# "A Hell of a Job"

Harry S. Truman became president in the last months of World War II and went out of office eight years later with American troops fighting a bloody, no-win war in the hills and rice paddies of Korea. The time in between would constitute eight of the most turbulent years in the history of the republic. Hardly a day went by, it seemed, without a domestic or foreign crisis to engage the attention of the press and the public and to plague the harassed president and his advisers. In foreign affairs it was the time of the final defeat of the Axis powers, the outbreak of the Cold War, the communist takeover of China, the Korean conflict, and the growing threat of atomic war. On the domestic front it was the time of demobilization from one war and remobilization for another, of shortages, inflation, a rash of strikes in the major industries, political stalemate and intense partisanship in Congress, charges of corruption in the Truman administration, and a new Red Scare that made rational political debate virtually impossible. Harry Truman would have few carefree days in the White House.

In the first few months of his presidency, Truman seemed overwhelmed by the magnitude of the job and by the crises that seemed to crop up every day. "This is a hell of a job," he wrote his mother a few weeks after he took the presidential oath.[1] He often vacillated, and he made many mistakes, leading his delighted Republican opponents to quip that "to err is Truman" and members of his own party to despair over the future of the Democratic party and of the nation. The despair worsened as the country was buffeted by one crisis after another and as the popularity of the president and his party plummeted. In the election of 1946 the Republicans won control of both houses of Congress for the first time since 1930, signaling the end, political pundits said, of the formidable New Deal coalition that had kept the Democrats in power for over thirteen years.

Both the political pundits and the Republicans underestimated the skills of the president and the staying power of the Democratic coalition. Truman was a fast learner and a scrappy fighter, and after a few months in office he emerged as a strong and confident leader who wielded the powers of his office effectively and more than stood his ground in disputes with Congress, the press, and the Russians. In the election of 1948 he scored one of the biggest upsets in the annals of American politics. Much of the left wing of his party, disillusioned with Truman's sparse domestic reform record and his hard line against the Russians, defected to Henry A. Wallace and his new Progressive party, while the conservative wing, alienated by Truman's support of civil rights, formed a States' Rights party (the Dixiecrats) under Senator J. Strom Thurmond of South Carolina. Thus divided, the Democrats, led by Truman and vice-presidential candidate Alben W. Barkley of Kentucky, ran against popular Governor Thomas E. Dewey of New York and Governor Earl Warren of California. Officials of both parties, all the public opinion polls, and most of the press predicted a massive defeat for the Democrats. A week before the election *Life* magazine ran a picture of Dewey over the caption, "The Next President Travels by Ferry Boat over the Broad Waters of San Francisco Bay," and as late as the day before the election, newspapers and magazines hit the newsstands with articles speculating on the actions of the new Dewey presidency.[2]

But Truman won, receiving 24.1 million votes to Dewey's 22 million, 49.5 percent of the popular vote to Dewey's 45 percent, and 303 electoral votes to the governor's 189. The Democrats carried both houses of Congress, winning a majority of twelve seats in the Senate and ninety-three in the House. With all the wisdom of hindsight, political analysts decided that Truman had won because of the popularity of his foreign policy, the Democratic party's record on prosperity and reform, the voters' rejection of the extremism of both Wallace and Thurmond, and Truman's personal campaigning. Taking his cause to the people, Truman had barnstormed across the nation, traveling over 30,000 miles and delivering over 356 speeches giving his opponents hell, attacking the "do nothing" Eightieth Congress, and reminding the voters of the Democrats' long record on prosperity and of his own record in standing up to the Russians. "Truman won," the *New York Sun* editorialized, "because this is still a land which loves a scrapper, in which intestinal fortitude is still respected."[3]

Whatever the cause of his victory, Truman was jubilant; few people in the country escaped seeing the famous picture of a smiling Truman holding up an early edition of the *Chicago Tribune* with its front-page headline, "DEWEY DEFEATS TRUMAN." A stunned Dewey likened his reaction to that of a man "who had been buried in a coffin with a lily in his hand, and said to himself, 'What am I doing here? And if I am dead, why do I have to go to the bathroom?'"[4] George Gallup and other chastened pollsters rushed to investigate their polling techniques, and unhappy Republicans lamented with Senator Robert A. Taft that Truman's victory "defies all common sense."[5] But Truman had won, and the Democratic coalition had held together, preserving the New Deal for yet a little while longer and guaranteeing the Democratic party twenty consecutive years in the White House.

Truman's dramatic victory did little to advance his domestic programs, however. By 1950 it had become obvious to most careful observers of his administration that any claims he might have to presidential greatness would rest on his foreign-policy record, not on his domestic accomplishments. A moderate, pragmatic liberal who often called himself "left of center," Truman was not a social experimenter or radical reformer, but he had strongly supported Roosevelt's New Deal programs during his Senate years and as president he fought to preserve and expand them. From 1945 on he sent proposal after proposal to Congress, even going beyond Roosevelt to advocate federal aid to education, a national health care plan, sweeping civil rights legislation, and other social and economic reforms. After his victory in 1948 he began to push even harder for passage of his social welfare measures, proclaiming to Congress and the public that "every segment of our population and every individual has a right to expect from our government a fair deal."[6]

But he had little success in advancing Roosevelt's New Deal or his own Fair Deal. After years of sacrifice and rapid change during the depression and war years, the postwar nation was in a conservative mood and wanted prosperity and stability rather than social and economic reform. Congress was controlled by a conservative coalition of Southern Democrats and midwestern Republicans determined to vote against any extension of what they regarded as "socialistic" New Deal programs, and big business and powerful pressure groups like the American Medical Association lobbied against further reforms. It was also a time of intense partisanship and bitter conflict between the White House and Congress—during his two administrations Truman used the veto 250 times, more than any other president except Franklin Roosevelt (631 times) and Grover Cleveland (374 times). He also had twelve vetoes overridden, the most of any president since Andrew Johnson of Reconstruction days almost a century before.[7] And sometimes Truman was his own worst enemy, bombarding Congress with sweeping reforms that had little chance of passing, concentrating too much on lambasting his political opponents and "do nothing" Congresses rather than working behind the scenes to smooth the way for passage of his legislation, and devoting more time to foreign affairs than to domestic legislation—an understandable emphasis, given the world tensions of the time, but one that hurt his domestic programs.

When he left office in 1953, Truman could point to only a few successes on the domestic front. At his behest Congress had voted additional funds for slum clearance and public housing, increased Social Security benefits and extended them to an additional 10 million persons, and raised the federal minimum wage from forty to seventy-five cents an hour. And although Congress had overridden his veto of the Taft-Hartley Law, which eroded some of labor's gains during the New Deal years by outlawing the closed shop and placing new restrictions on union political activities and strikes, he had managed to preserve the other reforms of the New Deal in the face of a hostile conservative coalition in Congress attempting to roll them back. In areas outside social welfare, Congress had adopted his legislation providing for the consolidation and streamlining of the departments and agencies of the executive office, creating a Council of Economic Advisers to advise the president on economic matters, establishing a National Security Council to advise the president on matters of national security, creating the Central Intelligence Agency to aid in the collection of information essential to the national security (and which by 1950 was already operating an elaborate espionage operation behind the Iron Curtain and other strategic areas in the Cold War), and centralizing the branches of the military under a new cabinet level position—the Department of Defense—headed by a civilian. Ironically, in passing these measures Congress had inadvertently increased the powers of the president along the lines charted earlier by Franklin Roosevelt.

Although he knew that his actions would alienate the large southern wing of his party, Truman did more than Roosevelt or any other previous twentieth-century president to advance the civil rights of the nation's black minority. He used his executive powers to initiate the desegregation of the military and other federal agencies. He appointed a commission on civil rights and strongly endorsed its report, *To Secure These Rights* (1947), which called for national antilynching and antipoll tax laws and for sweeping federal action to end discrimination and segregation in American life. He was the first president to invite blacks to all the functions surrounding his inauguration, to appoint a black to the federal judiciary, to address a meeting of the National Association for the Advancement of Colored People, and to campaign in Harlem. And although the odds were stacked against him, he courageously tried to push Congress for passage of antilynching laws, antipoll tax laws, and other civil rights measures.

Most of Truman's civil rights legislation, like his proposals for federal aid to education and national health insurance, were rejected by Congress. But

Truman's support of these progressive ideas injected them into the national political debate and into the national consciousness. Partly because of his efforts, future presidents, operating in a more favorable political climate, would be able to turn these ideas into legislative realities.

It was clear by 1950 that the greatest achievements of Truman's presidency had been in the area of foreign policy, where his executive powers were not as fettered by Congress as his domestic powers were and where he had wide support from Congress and the country in his dealings with the Russians. Ironically, before he assumed the presidency Truman had been abroad only once, when he traveled to France as a soldier in 1918, and during all his years as a senator he had concentrated on domestic issues and had developed little expertise in foreign affairs. Yet as president he would spend far more time on foreign problems than on domestic ones and would lead the country into a revolutionary era in international affairs.

Truman had led the military effort of the United States in the final months of World War II and ordered the use of atomic bombs on Hiroshima and Nagasaki to bring that conflict to a close. He had made the United States the leader in the new United Nations, often going before the General Assembly himself to advocate specific resolutions and policies. He had persuaded Congress to endorse the Truman Doctrine (1947), which proclaimed that "it must be the policy of the United States to support free peoples who are resisting attempted subjugation by armed minorities or by outside pressures,"[8] and to vote $400 million in military aid to support the right-wing governments of Greece and Turkey in their battle against communist-backed insurgents. He had secured congressional support of the Marshall Plan (1948), which provided financial aid to Western European nations to help them rebuild their shattered economies and thus blunt the major economic appeals of the fast-growing European communist parties. He had responded to Stalin's blockade of Berlin (1948–1949)—a reckless attempt to test the resolve of the West and drive it out of the city—by joining with the British in a massive airlift of food and supplies that relieved the pressures on the city, forced Stalin to end the blockade, and dealt Russia a major psychological defeat in the Cold War. He had taken the lead in the formation of the North Atlantic Treaty Organization (1949), a mutual defense pact aimed at protecting the Western nations against communist aggression. He had made long-range bombers with their deadly atomic payload the first line of American defense against Russia and was surrounding the Soviet Union with military, naval, and air bases. And finally, he was in the process of forming alliances with America's former enemies—Germany, Italy, Japan, and Spain—and extending American military and economic aid to democratic and dictatorial regimes threatened by internal and external communist aggression.

In just five short but crisis-ridden, dramatic years, Truman had led the nation through a revolution in foreign policy. After a century and a half of isolationism, the United States had become a global power actively involved in the United Nations, the reconstruction of wartorn Europe, the defense of countries thousands of miles beyond its borders, and the containment of communism. The United States was attempting, in essence, to impose a Pax Americana upon the rest of the world, a peace based upon American economic dominance, assumed moral superiority, and a military preponderance resting on the monopoly of atomic weapons. And this revolution had been carried through with the approval of most Americans, who seemed somewhat bewildered that World War II had not brought peace but the inauguration of a dangerous Cold War. It was also done with the support of Congress, which in spite of all its bickering with Truman over domestic matters had generally given him bipartisan support in the area of foreign policy. There had been many congressional dissenters, of course, but those who felt that the nation should return to its traditional isolationist policy or who claimed that Truman had provoked Russian aggression by his own bellicose attitudes and actions were usually outvoted by the majority who felt that the president's actions were the only possible reaction to Russian belligerence.

After following a policy of isolationism for so long, after refusing to lift a hand to help the Western democracies against the spread of fascism in the 1930s, after failing to come to Europe's aid as Germany defeated France and took over the continent in 1940, and after entering the war only after the attack on Pearl Harbor made it impossible to stay out, why did the United States in the second half of the forties assume the leadership in the battle against the spread of Russian communism? Few Americans of the immediate postworld war period fully understood the nature and causes of the foreign policy revolution they were living through, and even today historians are divided on the nature and purity of America's motives in leading the West in the battle against communist expansion.

If the man on the street had been asked in 1950 why the United States had assumed the mantle of world leadership, he probably would have said that Joe Stalin was leading a communist conspiracy to take over the world and that if Americans did not fight the communists in Europe or Asia, they would eventually be fighting them in New York and California and all the places in between. In his own simplistic way, he would have summarized some of the basic assumptions about the containment policy worked out by Truman, George F. Kennan, Dean Acheson, Charles Bohlen, and other state department officials in response to Russian aggression in the postwar period.

This policy was really based on the lessons that had been learned from fascist appeasement in the 1930s. Instead of preventing the Second World War, appeasement had only made its occurrence more certain by encouraging the fascist dictators to make more and more "territorial demands" until the British and French had no choice but to stand up and fight. Similarly, the containment policy was based on the idea that Russia was an insecure and insatiably ambitious nation following a policy of aggressive expansion designed to increase her power and security, that Stalin and his colleagues would not respond to ordinary rules and principles of diplomacy and intercourse among civilized nations, and that the only thing that they understood was force or the threat of force. Appeasement would only lead to more appeasement, to humiliations like the Munich agreement, to more aggression and acquisition and war. The word in the White House and State Department in the late 1940s was "no more appeasement, no more Munichs," and that since Europe was too weak to stand up to Russia, the United States would have to undertake the burden. As George F. Kennan had written, the United States would have to resist every direct or indirect Russian challenge by "long term, patient but firm and vigilant containment," concentrating on "the adroit and vigilant application of counterforce at a series of constantly shifting geographical points, corresponding to the shifts and maneuvers of Soviet policy."[9]

But the origins of America's new foreign policy activism and anticommunism go far deeper than the lessons of the appeasement of the 1930s. America's rabid anticommunism stretches back to the founding of that ideology in the middle of the nineteenth century, for ever since then communism had been regarded as an alien and atheistic ideology threatening democracy, Christianity, private enterprise, and all the other ideals Americans thought Americanism stood for. The United States joined an allied expeditionary force sent to Russia in 1918 in an unsuccessful attempt to defeat the new communist regime and bring Russia back into the war against Germany, suffered through an hysterical Red Scare at the close of that war, withheld diplomatic recognition of the communist regime until 1933, and allied with Stalin in the common war against Hitler only out of military necessity. America's fears and suspicions of the Soviet Union existed, then, long before 1945, and were only heightened in the postwar period by Russian secrecy about what was happening in the countries under her occupation, by the bickerings over the agreements made in the wartime conferences at Yalta and Potsdam, by disputes over the peace treaties, and by Russia's expansion at the expense of little innocent countries. It had also became clear by then that in an age of high speed bombers and atomic bombs, even America was no longer safe from the aggressions of totalitarian countries.

Like the American public, Truman and the other architects of containment never seemed to consider that their policies might be wrong, that their tough rhetoric and economic and military containment programs might be provocative to a paranoid Joe Stalin with his long memory of Western hostility toward Russia in the past. After all, Russia had been attacked by Napoleonic France in 1812, by Imperial Germany in 1914, by an allied expeditionary force in 1918, and by Nazi Germany in 1941, and the communist regime had been treated as an outcast by the West ever since it came to power in 1917. There were critics like Henry Wallace, who argued that Truman had not done enough to defuse the Cold War and was in fact contributing to it by his own aggressive behavior, and even George F. Kennan, the main architect of containment, who left the State Department in 1950, complained that the containment policy had hardened into a dangerous emphasis on military responses to Soviet expansion. A later generation of revisionist historians would also argue that Truman's bellicosity and America's capitalistic designs had provoked Stalin's militancy and contributed as much to the Cold War as Stalin had. But Truman and his advisers saw it differently: Russian communist aggression was threatening the world, the United States had to take the lead in stopping it if World War III were to be prevented, and the only way to stop Russia was to stand up to her, not to appease her.

Thus was born the containment policy. Although it would be modified by future presidents, it would remain the cornerstone of American foreign policy down to the present day. Whatever its causes and merits, it would provide the rationale for a staggering American military buildup, the formation of military alliances with democratic and dictatorial nations across the globe, American intervention in the internal affairs of dozens of countries, and protracted conflicts in Korea and Vietnam. Fear of Russia and of communism had revolutionized America's role in the world.

As America entered the fifties, the containment policy had produced mixed results. It had brought an end to communist threats to Greece and Turkey, a dramatic economic recovery to the European democratic states, an equally dramatic decline in the strength and danger of Western European communist parties, an end to the Berlin blockade, and the formation of NATO. But in the meantime, Czechoslovakia had fallen to a communist coup in 1948, Soviet control over the rest of its Eastern European satellites had been consolidated, Germany had moved closer to a permanent division with the establishment of a democratic West German state (the Federal Republic of Germany) and a communist East German state (the German Democratic Republic), Berlin remained a divided city deep in the heart of East Germany, Korea remained divided into a Russian puppet state in the north and a American-backed military dictatorship in the south, China had fallen to Mao Zedung's communist forces, and Russia had acquired the atomic bomb. And Truman and the American people did not know it yet, but the toughest test of containment still lay ahead, with the outbreak of the Korean War in June of 1950.

* * *

The inauguration of a radically new international posture was not the only revolutionary aspect of Truman's presidency, for he also had the dubious distinction of being the first atomic age president. He was the first president—and so far the only one—to use the atomic bomb against another nation, and he initiated the policy of stockpiling atomic weapons and making their use—or the threat of their use—the mainstay of American military policy. Truman never seemed to doubt the wisdom or morality of these actions. He did understand, as Secretary of War Henry L. Stimson had said two months before the bombs were dropped on Japan, that these new weapons had brought "a revolutionary change in the relations of man and the universe."[10] But Truman also believed that the bomb had brought a quick end to the war and had saved millions of lives on both sides, and that it was the best deterrent against Soviet aggression and the outbreak of a third world war. In the first four years after the war, as America basked in the knowledge that the monopoly of atomic weapons had made it the world's number one power and rendered it immune from Russian attack, the Truman administration and most of the public regarded the bomb as a cheap way of exercising military superiority. Even though Russian ground forces and conventional weapons greatly outnumbered those of the West, the United States and its allies could shun a big buildup in troops and conventional weapons and deter Russian aggression by the mere threat of atomic destruction.

Actually, the atomic bomb was a vastly overrated weapon in the American arsenal in these early years of the atomic age. Atomic weapons were neither powerful enough, nor numerous enough, to destroy Russia if war broke out, and if Russia had invaded Europe, the United States would have been faced with the uncomfortable prospect of dropping atomic bombs inside the borders of its allies. But America's leaders, her allies, and the world press treated the bomb as the ultimate weapon that gave the United States an unprecedented world power and influence. Americans had a false sense of power and security, and they were therefore terribly shocked and frightened when Russia learned the secrets of this horrible weapon.

America's atomic advantage was short-lived, for in the late summer of 1949 instruments aboard an air force B-29 bomber engaged in routine scientific research detected unmistakable evidence of an atomic blast. It could only have been set off by the Soviet Union, which had somehow learned the secrets of this mysterious weapon some three to five years ahead of the predictions of most American scientists. The stunned Truman administration waited three weeks before releasing this information to the public on September 23, and the public was as shocked as government officials had been. It was obvious that a new era in American history had arrived. The most powerful nation in the world had lost its atomic monopoly and the security that went with it. Russia now had the bomb, and in an age of rapid revolutionary development in weaponry, it would be only a matter of time before she could drop it not just on America's allies in Europe and Asia but also on New York and Washington and other American cities. Americans were now gripped by a fear of atomic war and destruction as they read newspaper and magazine accounts of the probabilities and dangers of atomic war and saw military experts' predictions of 10 to 20 million Americans, or more, being killed if an atomic war broke out. Thus, just a few months before the fifties began, the atomic nightmare that would dominate so much of the actions and thinking of the decade had arrived.

The last quarter of 1949 was spent in high-ranking, frantic discussions within the Truman administration on how to deal with the new threat posed by Russia's development of the atomic bomb. It was finally decided that the only possible response was to build an even greater bomb, a superbomb many times more powerful than the two that had been dropped on Japan less than five years before. On January 31, 1950, Truman announced that "it is part of my responsibilities as Commander-in-Chief of the armed forces to see to it that our country is able to defend itself against any aggressor. Accordingly I have directed the Atomic Energy Commission to continue its work on all forms of atomic weapons, including the so-called hydrogen or super-bomb."[11]

The decision to build a hydrogen bomb instigated a widespread debate among American scientists, many of whom had never been comfortable with their role in producing the original atomic bomb. Many opposed the thermonuclear bomb on the grounds that it would not work or could not be delivered to its target, but most opposed it on moral grounds, contending that the destructive powers unleashed by such a bomb could not be confined to military targets and would bring the slaughter of millions of innocent civilians and perhaps the death of the entire human race. Dr. J. Robert Oppenheimer, who had been the director of the Los Alamos project that produced the original atomic bomb in 1945, argued vigorously against producing the new weapon, as did Dr. Enrico Fermi and many other physicists. Albert Einstein, whose revolutionary findings in physics decades earlier had paved the way for the harnessing of atomic energy, went on television to warn that "if these efforts prove successful, radioactive poisoning of the atmosphere, and hence, annihilation of all life on earth, will have been brought within the range of what is technically possible."[12] But others, like the Hungarian-born physicist Edward Teller, swept aside these moral and practical objections, claiming that they were exaggerated, that the Russians would build the bomb whether America did or not, and that the United States could not allow them to gain an atomic advantage.

The Truman administration appointed Teller to direct the American superbomb project, and on March 10, 1950, the president approved a crash program to build "the super," as it was now called. Teller had no objections to becoming the father of the hydrogen bomb, and under his direction American scientists worked frantically to beat the Russians in the race to build it. By the fall of 1952 Teller was ready, and testing equipment was moved to the Eniwetok atoll in the Marshall Islands. All ships in the area were ordered to stay at least fifty miles away, and from the safe distance of fifty miles the American scientific team watched the bomb explode at dawn on November 1, 1952.

The test exceeded all expectations. The bomb blast created a fire ball 5 miles high and 4 miles wide and a mushroom cloud 25 miles high and 100 miles wide, completely destroyed the mile-wide island, left a hole in the Pacific floor a mile long and 175 feet deep, and created a temperature at the center of the blast five times greater than the center of the sun. If detonated above ground on land, it would have vaporized cities the size of Washington, D.C., could have destroyed most of St. Louis or Pittsburgh, and leveled all of New York City from Central Park to Washington Square.[13]

But the Russians were not far behind. It had taken them four years to catch up with the atomic bomb, but now it took only nine months to match the technology of the hydrogen bomb. On August 12, 1953, only six months after Truman left office, Russia successfully tested its first hydrogen bomb in Siberia, prompting Premier Georgi Malenkov to boast that "the United States no longer has a monopoly on the hydrogen bomb."[14] Other powers were getting into the race, too. Britain had tested its first atomic bomb in the Monte Bello Islands, off the western coast of Australia, on October 3, 1952, shortly before the American H-bomb test at Eniwetok, and by the end of the decade France would join the atomic club with a test in the Sahara desert on February 13, 1960. The secrets of atomic fission and fusion, though hidden in nature and labeled "classified information" by governments, were impossible to keep.

Clearly a new era of death and destruction had dawned. In less than ten years the modern weapons of destruction had gone from the large conventional bombs of World War II, with an explosive force equal to a single ton of TNT, to the Hiroshima bomb (a fission bomb whose explosive force came from the splitting of uranium atoms) with a force of 20,000 tons of TNT, to the hydrogen bomb (whose force came from the fusion of hydrogen atoms under extreme temperatures) with its force of 5 megatons or 5 million tons of TNT. As the decade progressed the 10-megaton bomb would become the standard size nuclear weapon, but scientists would also be building 20-megaton bombs, and Nikita Khrushchev would be boasting of building a 100-megaton bomb.[15] For the first time in man's history, it was becoming possible to fulfill ancient religious prophecies of the destruction of mankind, only now it seemed that it would be wrought not by an angry God but by a foolish human race.

The fifties opened then, under a nuclear cloud that grew larger and larger with each new test and weapons breakthrough. In 1950 there was little danger from Russian attack, for bombs of any type still had to be dropped from airplanes and there was little possibility that Russian planes could reach targets in the United States. Still, it was felt that no chances could be taken, for research into atomic bombs, jet airplanes, and rockets was proceeding so rapidly that breakthroughs in weapons and delivery systems could come in just a few short years. (Indeed, ICBM's would be operational by the end of the decade.) "I cannot tell you when or where the attack will come or that it will come at all," Truman told the American people. "I can only remind you that we must be ready when it does come."[16]

The Truman administration proceeded on several fronts to try to meet the atomic threat from the Russians. The first line of defense, of course, was the Strategic Air Command, which kept some of its planes in the air at all times, poised to carry their deadly atomic payloads to targets in the Soviet Union should the Russians be so foolish as to attack the United States or its European allies. While Truman was not an atomic-bomb rattler, and indeed refused to use it in Korea, he was careful in his public statements never to rule out its use in Korea or anywhere else. Truman also approved in April of 1950 a National Security Council document, commonly called NSC-68, calling for a massive buildup in American military manpower and atomic and conventional weaponry in order to guarantee American worldwide military superiority over the Soviets. And finally, the Truman administration started a civil defense program designed to help the nation survive an atomic attack and win the war against the Russians.

The civil defense program of the Truman administration was poorly planned, poorly executed, and based on a great deal of ignorance and misunderstanding about the effects of atomic war and the possibilities of surviving it. The Civil Defense Act of 1950, passed by a frightened Congress, left most of the responsibility for civil defense up to the states and limited the federal government's role, under the Federal Civil Defense Administration, to that of providing policy suggestions and disseminating information to the public. Consequently, very little money was spent by the federal government or the states, both of whom acted as little more than public information agencies. Although some funds were provided for fire and rescue trucks, communications equipment, and the training of civil defense personnel, the nation's civil defense system under Truman was concerned primarily with convincing people that they could survive an atomic war if they planned for it.[17]

Through such manuals as *You Can Survive* and *Atomic Attack*, the government downplayed the dangers of fire storms, radiation sickness, radiation contamination, and other problems and concentrated on instructing the public on the precautions necessary for survival. The American people were told to build bomb shelters in their backyards, to stockpile food, water, and other essential supplies, to buy Geiger counters, and to practice attack drills at home, at school, and at work. Following the directions of civil defense manuals, teachers and administrators held drills teaching schoolchildren to curl up in a fetal position under a desk or heavy table and to file out of the building in an orderly fashion after the attack so that they could be picked up by their parents. Some businesses and industries held similar exercises, and hospitals held seminars and drills on how to treat victims of an atomic attack. The general public was told to seek shelter in schools, subways, basements, and other well-fortified areas, and was given maps of evacuation routes to be followed in case of general evacuation. People were also told that they might get radiation sickness and experience vomiting and loss of hair, but that with proper treatment they would recover and their hair would grow back. Coming through all the literature was the simple message: Atomic war might come, we must prepare for it, you can survive it, we can win, and we must win.[18]

The "you can survive" theme was reiterated in the newspapers and popular magazines of the day, which is not surprising since most reporters and feature writers had little training in the complexities of atomic physics and thermonuclear war and had to rely on information supplied them by the civil defense officials or by scientists who were engaged in weapons research or supported such research. Standard reference books, such as almanacs, also repeated the same theme and offered helpful suggestions on how to survive an atomic war. In "What to Do in Case of an Atomic Bomb Attack," on the contents page of the 1951 *World Almanac*, readers were told: "Always shut windows and doors, pull down shades, turn off pilot lights, close stove and furnace doors," and "Seek shelter below ground, in subway, basement or cellar. Duck under table or bed. Flatten against base of wall or dive into ditch or doorway." They were also promised that "a thick wall or overhead covering will protect you from the prompt radioactivity of the bomb, even if you are close to it."[19]

Many of the popular magazines of the day went far beyond the support of civil defense programs and supported the building of more and more atomic weapons as deterrence against Russian aggression. In the October 10, 1951, issue of *Look*, in "Atomic Weapons Will Save Money," author Richard Wilson claimed that it is a fiction that "atomic bombs are very costly," for in fact "they are one of the cheapest forms of destruction known to man." These weapons would get even cheaper, he predicted, for "we will soon be able to make atomic projectiles which can be fired from heavy artillery pieces or as guided missiles." And if America followed a big building program, "we could produce such an overpowering force—held in reserve and never becoming obsolete—that no aggressor would accept the risk of destruction we could inflict upon him." The use or threatened use of atomic bombs might "prevent World War III and make general war a military impracticability."[20]

Government officials could not have expressed the Truman administration's position on atomic weapons any better.

In these early years of the atomic age most people reacted to the threat of atomic war by denying its probability, convincing themselves that it could not happen because it was too terrible to happen or because God or the American government would not let it happen. But there were others who took the threat seriously, worrying about it enough to read civil defense manuals, hold drills at home with the children, and stockpile essential supplies in a basement or backyard bomb shelter. Some built their own shelters in the basement or backyard out of earth, concrete, and steel from plans provided in civil defense manuals. But commercial manufacturers quickly saw the possibilities of this new market and rushed into it with shelters ranging from glorified foxholes and prefabricated spartan quarters to elaborate underground living quarters complete with carpet, phones, and other luxuries at a cost of several thousand dollars. The shelter program was in its infancy during the Truman administration, but already it was becoming something of a fad or mark of status for those who could afford one. In January of 1951, after a construction company had built Mrs. Ruth Calhoun of Los Angeles a $2,000 underground shelter near her patio, she held a groundbreaking ceremony that was attended by some Hollywood stars, television cameramen, reporters, and officials of the construction company. She told the reporters that it was a reasonable thing to do, and besides, "It would make a wonderful place for the children to play in." It would also "be a good storehouse, too. I do a lot of canning and bottling in the summer, you know."[21]

There were few protestors against the government's decision in the early fifties to prevent atomic war by building bigger and better atomic weapons and teaching civilians how to survive a Russian atomic attack. In the Cold War atmosphere of the early fifties, pacifists and other critics of the government's military and civilian defense policies were roundly condemned by the public, the press, and government as misguided zealots, traitors, or communists. Serious criticism of atomic weapons and atomic defense would have to wait until later in the decade.

At the beginning of the 1950s war correspondent William L. Shirer returned to the United States after spending most of the previous twenty-five years in Germany and other European countries, where he had observed Nazism and other ideologies of the right and left at first hand. As he traveled around his homeland, he witnessed many things that reminded him of the totalitarian countries he had lived in, especially Germany. People were afraid to speak out on controversial issues, the FBI was investigating applicants for jobs in even the lowest levels of government, Senator Joe McCarthy was using Hitler's "big lie" technique to smear well-known public figures, liberals and intellectuals were being branded as communists or socialists or "pinkos," and the Democratic party was being accused by the Republican opposition of taking the country down the road toward socialism and communism. "There was an atmosphere throughout the land that year of suspicion, intolerance, and fear that puzzled me," he wrote in *Midcentury Journey*. "I had seen these poisons grow into ugly witch hunting and worse in the totalitarian lands abroad, but I was not prepared to find them taking root in our own splendid democracy."[22]

What Shirer was describing was an ugly time in American history when large numbers of Americans were caught up in an irrational fear of a great communist conspiracy, orchestrated from the Kremlin, that was supposedly subverting the country from within, causing the setbacks the nation was suffering in foreign affairs, and contributing to the onward march of world communism. Similar periods of hysteria had appeared before in American history, most notably during the Salem witchcraft trials in 1692, in the paranoid South in the decade before the outbreak of the Civil War, and under the Wilson administration at the end of the First World War. But none of these earlier periods of irrational behavior got as much national attention or affected America's domestic and foreign policy as much as the Great Fear or Red Scare of 1949–1954. As if he did not already have enough problems to contend with, Harry Truman was now plagued during his second administration with a growing congressional and public fear that communism was about to take over the country and that the government was doing nothing to stop it and, in fact, was itself riddled with communists and communist sympathizers who were aiding the Kremlin's cause.

The causes of the Great Fear are complex, involving a large number of political, economic, social, and psychological factors. It was partly the result of a long-standing American suspicion of anyone or anything that threatened—or seemed to threaten—American capitalism, democracy, and Christianity. It was partly the result of widespread ignorance of the nature of the basic ideologies of the twentieth century—many Americans knew very little about the capitalism and democracy they held so dear, wrongly viewed communism and socialism as synonymous isms, saw liberalism as an alien ideology that was little different from socialism and communism, and were willing to suspend basic civil rights and liberties in the battle against a highly overrated communist threat. It was partly the result, too, of a naive but widespread belief that Russia was such a backward nation that it could not have developed the atomic bomb—and certainly not so quickly—without being given its secrets by Western spies. But most importantly, it was the result of the long conflict with Russia and fear of communist expansion which stemmed back to the Communist Revolution of 1917.

The Communist Revolution had shocked the Western world and raised the fear that communism was an epidemic threatening to spread everywhere. At the end of the First World War, the United States was swept by a great Red Scare that brought the arrest of thousands of real and imagined communists and other radicals, the deportation of over 500 alien radicals, and the ruin of the reputations and careers of thousands of innocent victims. Fear of communism became permanently entrenched in America after this hysterical period, and the fear grew in the 1930s as many intellectuals in the country joined other Western intellectuals in turning to communism or socialism as the answer to the terrible economic depression and the rise of fascism. Many Americans in the thirties also began to equate Roosevelt's New Deal with communism and to believe that communists and socialists had infiltrated the government and were working to destroy capitalism at home and advance the cause of communism throughout the world. The fear became so great that in 1938 Congress had established the House Un-American Activities Committee (HUAC) to investigate these alleged subversives. The Roosevelt alliance with Russia only deepened the suspicions of these rabid anticommunists, who saw the alliance as part of a wide conspiracy and felt that Roosevelt and Truman had sold out to Russia at the wartime conferences called to plan military strategy and postwar political and territorial settlements. As these diehard anticommunists saw it, a communist conspiracy, led by dedicated American communists and abetted by naive sympathizers or "fellow travelers," had led American domestic and foreign policy down the communist road ever since Roosevelt and the Democrats took over in 1933.

Several developments since 1945 had contributed to the steady growth of the atmosphere that led to the Great Fear. Communism continued to spread behind the Iron Curtain, moved into North Korea, China, and Indochina, endangered innocent countries in the Middle East, and threatened to turn the Cold War into a hot war over the Berlin Blockade. Russia got the bomb, ending the American monopoly, and spy rings were uncovered in Canada, Britain, and finally in the United States itself. These events prompted federal and state governments and patriotic organizations all across the country to mount a campaign to ferret out the communists or other radicals in the government, universities, public schools, newspaper staffs, and churches. In 1947 HUAC fanned the flames of the witchhunt by initiating its investigations of subversives in the movie industry, the government, labor unions, and education, amidst widespread publicity and wild rumors and charges. And in Washington, many members of the Republican party, anxious to end the long reign of the Democratic party in Washington, found the loyalty question a good issue to put before an electorate already scared to death of the Russians.

The Truman administration inadvertently fed the Great Fear that was threatening to tear the government and the country apart. Truman's tough talk and actions toward the Russians helped to magnify the communist threat in the eyes of the public, as did his attempts to defend his administration against the charges that he had sold out to the Russians and was covering up subversives in his own government. To prove his own purity as an anticommunist ideologue, Truman in 1947 launched his own loyalty program with an executive order initiating a loyalty check of all federal employees. In October of 1949, at the end of the controversial ten-month trial, the Truman administration obtained the conviction and imprisonment of eleven communists charged with violating the Smith Act of 1940, which made it illegal to advocate the violent overthrow of the United States government. This conviction would be upheld by the Supreme Court in *Dennis* v. *U.S.* in 1951, encouraging the Justice Department to speed up its anticommunist campaign and obtain the conviction of some forty communist party leaders across the country.

Meanwhile, at the orders of the president, Attorney General Tom C. Clark had released the names of ninety-one groups considered to be subversive and dangerous to the country and to initiate a program to find and deport subversive aliens. Clark's successor, J. Howard McGrath, continued these programs and went around the country making speeches to patriotic groups about the communist danger in American schools, libraries, and other institutions. "Communists are everywhere—in factories, offices, butcher stores, on street corners, in private business," he told them. "And each carries in himself the death of our society."[23] And always there to fan the anticommunist hysteria was Director J. Edgar Hoover of the FBI, who in countless speeches, reports, interviews, and pamphlets warned the nation of a widespread communist conspiracy aimed at undermining American institutions, capturing the minds of gullible Americans of all ages, and destroying the American way of life.

The Truman administration was also damaged by its association with accused communist Alger Hiss. A graduate of Harvard law school and a former secretary to Justice Holmes, Hiss had served in the State Department for some fourteen years in the 1930s and 1940s, had been a member of Roosevelt's wartime staff, and had participated in the Yalta conference and several other key postwar conferences. He was also a strong backer of the United Nations, president of the Carnegie Endowment for International Peace, and a friend of Dean Acheson, Adlai Stevenson, John Foster Dulles, and several key members of the liberal community. Hiss's name was injected into the subversive hunt in 1948 by Whittaker Chambers, a senior editor of *Time* magazine who had once been a member of the Communist party (1924–1937) and a Russian agent. In sensational testimony before HUAC in the summer and fall of 1948, Chambers testified that in the 1930s Hiss had given him copies of important State Department documents to pass on to Russian agents. To prove his charges, Chambers carried members of HUAC to his Maryland farm and showed them microfilmed documents, allegedly given to him by Hiss, hidden in a hollow pumpkin. These sensational charges led to dramatic confrontations between Hiss and Chambers before HUAC, an appearance by Chambers on *Meet the Press*, where he repeated the charges, a highly publicized campaign by Congressman Richard Nixon to prove the charges, a slander suit filed against Chambers by Hiss, and fierce denials of all charges by Hiss, who claimed he was being pursued as a scapegoat by opponents of the New Deal and the United Nations. Although the statute of limitations prevented Hiss from being tried for treason, he was tried for perjury by a federal court in the spring of 1949. A hung jury resulted in a second trial in November of 1949, which ended on January 21, 1950, with his conviction and a five-year sentence for perjury.[24]

Hiss was convicted of perjury, not of treason, but his lies concerned passing secret government documents to a communist agent, and many Americans believed that he was a traitor and that there were many others like him working in the government and other vital institutions across the country. The Hiss case split the liberal community, strengthened the hand of the anticommunist witchhunters, and brought further discredit to New Dealers, the United Nations, the State Department, American liberals, and the Truman administration. When the charges against Hiss had first been brought up, Truman had dismissed them as "a red herring," and four days after Hiss's conviction Secretary of State Dean Acheson had said at his weekly news conference that "I should like to make it clear to you that, whatever the outcome of any appeal which Mr. Hiss or his lawyer may take in this case, I do not intend to turn my back on Alger Hiss."[25] Hiss appealed his case all the way to the Supreme Court, but failed to secure a reversal of his conviction, and on March 21, 1951, he began serving his sentence. He would be paroled in November of 1954 for good behavior.

Acheson's defense of Hiss and his refusal to turn his back on him confirmed many people's belief that this striped-pants secretary of state was soft on communism. To many people, he was the epitome of what was wrong with America. Born into wealth, educated at Groton, Yale, and Harvard law school, he had served as undersecretary of the treasury and assistant secretary of state under Roosevelt and as the undersecretary of state under Truman before being appointed secretary of state when George Marshall retired early in 1949. He had been at the center of important foreign policy decisions for almost a decade and secretary of state when Russia exploded the atomic bomb and China fell to communism. He was also an intellectual, a suave, dapper dresser, and a bona fide member of the liberal, New Deal community. Many people of the time found him a convenient scapegoat for all of America's problems and would have agreed with Senator Hugh Butler of Nebraska, who once said: "I watch his smart-alec manner and his British clothes and that New Dealism, everlasting New Dealism in everything he says and does, and I want to shout, Get out, Get out. You stand for everything that has been wrong with the United States for years."[26]

Hiss's trial and conviction occurred at a time when the nation was still reeling from the news of the communist takeover of China. Ever since the 1930s the Chinese Nationalist army of Chiang Kai-shek had been engaged in a civil war with Mao Zedung's communist forces for control of that ancient country. During the Second World War, as both factions kept a wary eye on the other while they fought the Japanese invaders, the United States supported Chiang with advisers and military and economic aid. While Mao pursued an aggressive and effective military campaign against the Japanese, Chiang often exasperated President Roosevelt and American military advisers in China by avoiding major engagements with the Japanese army and concentrating on saving his troops and stockpiling his weapons for the resumption of civil war with the communists once World War II was over. American aid to Chiang continued during the full-scale civil war that broke out in that country between Chiang and Mao after World War II, as the United States saw the Christian and Western-oriented Nationalist leader as the best hope in the battle to unify all of China and prevent communism from taking over still another country. However, Chiang failed to make the reforms needed to gain the hearts of the peasantry, mismanaged the American aid, and was generally outsmarted and outmaneuvered by the more wily Mao. In 1948 and 1949, Mao's forces won one victory after another, capturing Peking in January of 1949 and finally forcing Chiang and his forces to flee at the end of the year to the little island of Taiwan under the protection of the American fleet. In spite of Chiang's 3 million troops and $82 billion in American aid, China had been taken over by communism.

This had come as a great shock to most Americans, who knew very little of the actual history of China or of the civil war but had a dreamy, romantic picture of that Asian country as the land of the Open Door, Christian missionaries, Pearl Buck, the Great Wall, and magnificent palaces and mountains and rivers. Americans had somehow come to think of China as "theirs"—as a land America was building into a Christian, democratic civilization. This belief that China was "theirs"—which it never really was—now led to the belief that they had "lost" it. Military experts and State Department officials knew that a million American troops and billions of American dollars could not have saved the hopelessly demoralized, inefficient, and corrupt Nationalist regime and would only have been resented by the masses of Chinese people. But most Americans could not believe this, for to many it was inconceivable that the country that had never lost a war and had liberated Europe twice could not protect Chiang's regime and keep it in the Western camp. In the halls of Congress and all across the country the myth spread that China had been lost not by Chiang's incompetence and corruption but by the insufficient support, bungling, and perhaps even treason, of the Truman administration. The loss of China was quickly turning into an issue that would bring about the fall of bipartisan foreign policy and contribute to the rapidly spreading anticommunist hysteria.

In the first half of 1950 the bad news kept coming. In February Dr. Klaus Fuchs, a British scientist who had worked on the atomic bomb project at Los Alamos, was arrested on charges of supplying atomic bomb secrets to the Russians. In his trial he admitted to passing atomic secrets to the Russians between 1942 and 1947 and was convicted and sentenced to fourteen years in prison. The breakthrough in the Fuchs case soon led to the arrest of several of Fuchs's American accomplices: Harry Gold, a Philadelphia chemist; David Greenglass, a New York machinist who had worked at Los Alamos during the war; Greenglass's wife, Ruth, and his sister and brother-in-law, Ethel and Julius Rosenberg, a young New York couple with backgrounds in various socialist and communist causes and organizations; Morton Sobell, an old City College classmate of Julius Rosenberg; and several acquaintances of the Rosenbergs. All of the defendents were Jewish, fueling the belief among American right-wing groups that an international Jewish conspiracy was behind the postwar expansion of communism and many of the other problems plaguing the United States and the rest of the World. The unfolding of this spy ring in the spring and summer of 1950 caused a sensation, coming as it did at a time when the newspapers were full of news about Alger Hiss, China, the new superbomb project, the outrageous allegations of Senator Joe McCarthy, and the outbreak of the Korean War.

Communist expansion. Cold Wars. Atomic and hydrogen bombs. Traitors. Spies. Were not these ominous developments clear signs that the country was in danger from within and without? Since the United States was the strongest nation in the world, was it not obvious that these terrible events resulted from the bungling, communist sympathies, and downright treason of people in the government and other high places? Were not most of the people who had been in power for the last two decades members of the Democratic party and perhaps even clandestine socialists and communists? And were not Truman and Acheson and the rest of the administration trying to cover up these subversive activities and their own blunders? Unable to believe that America's problems were largely the result of honest human mistakes and complicated world developments beyond the control of American policymakers, many people in 1950 had come to believe that America's basic problems lay within the country, not outside in Russia, China, or other hot spots in the world.

It was time, many believed, for all Americans to close ranks against the common danger and to purge the nation of the critics, nonconformists, and subversives who were threatening the greatest republic God had ever put on this earth. Proof of the internal and external danger seemed to be everywhere, but if any more evidence was needed, it came in June of 1950, when the outbreak of the Korean War sent thousands of American boys to fight and die in a no-win war against the communists in Asia, far from the shores of America.

It was this climate that produced the Great Fear and the rise of the most gifted demagogue in American history, Joseph R. McCarthy.

# 4

# *The Great Fear*

The atmosphere of fear and suspicion settling over the land in 1950 was skillfully exploited by many men, but none was more adept at the politics of fear than Senator Joseph R. McCarthy of Wisconsin, who in the first few months of the year would rise from obscurity to become one of the most admired, hated, and powerful men in America.

When the year began, few people in America knew much about the senator. Born in 1908 in Wisconsin to poor Irish-American parents, he was a graduate of Marquette University, a former circuit judge, and a former marine who was elected to the Senate in 1946 after using smear tactics to defeat veteran Senator Robert M. La Follette, Jr., in the primary election and Democrat Howard McMurray in the general election. His first three years in the Senate were undistinguished. Although a junior senator, he refused to follow Senate rules and customs, specialized in malicious attacks on his colleagues, and frequently thwarted committee work by trying to inject trivial and extraneous matters into committee discussions. A lazy and ineffectual senator, he was an easy captive for any lobbyist willing to put a few extra bucks into his personal or political bank accounts. He fought so vigorously and effectively for the sugar and soft drink industries that he became known around Washington as the Pepsi Cola Kid, and his shameless efforts for the real estate industry earned him the nickname Water Boy of the Real Estate Lobby. But none of these activities had brought him the fame and power he so desperately sought, and early in 1950 he was anxiously looking for some issue to enhance his reputation and guarantee his reelection in 1952.

Then, at a dinner meeting at the Colony Restaurant in Washington on January 7, an acquaintance suggested that the communists-in-government issue would attract national publicity and enhance his chances for reelection. Like other conservative Republican senators, McCarthy had occasionally raised this issue before in his speeches, but he now saw that in the charged political atmosphere of the new year, it could become the salvation of his fading political career. "That's it," he told his companions. "The government is full of Communists. We can hammer away at them."[1] McCarthy left the dinner party excited about his new issue, and his ruthless exploitation of it would catapult him to national fame and, eventually, to disgrace.

Having "discovered" the communists-in-government issue, McCarthy asked the Senate Republican Campaign Committee to schedule several speaking engagements for him around the time of Lincoln's birthday. The committee obliged, and on February 9, McCarthy found himself speaking before the Ohio County Women's Republican Club in Wheeling, West Virginia. This was not quite the forum McCarthy had wanted, but he made the best of it. In a rambling, largely extemporaneous speech, he told the good Republican ladies gathered there that the United States had been the strongest nation in the world at the end of World War II but had since fallen from that pinnacle of power through the incompetence and treason of men high in the government, particularly in the State Department. Then, waving a sheaf of paper, he said that "I have here in my hand a list of 205—a list of names that were made known to the Secretary of State as being members of the Communist Party and who nevertheless are still working and shaping policy in the State Department."[2] The audience was stunned, and so was the rest of the nation when it read of these accusations on the front pages of the newspapers. McCarthy had found the issue he had been looking for.

McCarthy's Wheeling speech came at just the right time for maximum exposure and impact. Just a few months before, Russia had acquired the atomic bomb. Just a few weeks before, China had been "lost." Just three weeks before Hiss had been convicted of perjury. Just ten days before Truman had decided to build the H-bomb. And just six days before, Fuchs had confessed. McCarthy was as surprised as anyone at the national reaction to the Wheeling speech, but he quickly and skillfully capitalized on the issue. He could not remember what figure he had quoted at Wheeling—whether it was 205 or 209 or 57 or whatever—and his staff tried in vain to find someone who had recorded the speech so as to pinpoint the exact figure. But it did not matter to McCarthy. In Denver on February 10 he spoke of 205 "security risks," but in Salt Lake City the next day he transformed them into "57 card-carrying Communists," and in subsequent speeches the number of people involved and the nature of their crime continued to vary widely. By February 20, when he kept the Senate in session from late afternoon to around midnight with a rambling six-hour performance that embarrassed and outraged some senators, caused others to doze, and sent still others heading for the nearest exit, McCarthy was repudiating all his previous figures, talking about "81 cases," and bragging that he had penetrated "Truman's iron curtain of secrecy."[3]

Hoping to restore confidence in the Truman administration by disproving McCarthy's allegations, the Senate Foreign Relations Committee established a subcommittee headed by Democratic Senator Millard E. Tydings of Maryland to investigate McCarthy's charges. The Tydings Committee began its hearings on March 8, and finally on July 14, after bitter partisan infighting aggravated by the trauma surrounding the outbreak of the Korean War, it issued a majority report dismissing all of McCarthy's allegations and condemning them as "a fraud and a hoax perpetrated on the Senate of the United States and the American people."[4] However, Republican members of the subcommittee and of the Senate Foreign Relations Committee condemned the majority report and the Democrats who had signed it. Senator William E. Jenner accused Tydings of chairing "the most scandalous and brazen whitewash of treasonable conspiracy in our history."[5] As for McCarthy, he showed his ability to turn defeat into victory through the great publicity he received and through his charges that the report was "a green light to the Red fifth column in the United States" as well as "a signal to the traitors, Communists, and fellow travelers in our Government that they need have no fear of exposure."[6] In contrast to the Truman administration, which found itself in a no-win situation with the communists-in-government issue, McCarthy was, at least for the time being, in a no-lose situation. Many people were willing to believe his charges without any evidence or in the face of contrary evidence, and he profited from every bit of publicity—good or bad—that came his way.

Joe McCarthy was now one of the most famous men in America. He had made the front covers of *Time* and *Newsweek* and many other magazines, and pictures of him and accounts of his Red-hunting activities appeared almost daily on the front pages of the newspapers. He was one of the most sought-after public speakers in the land, he was constantly pursued by reporters and photographers and autograph-seekers, he was widely touted as one of the most eligible bachelors in Washington, and his office was inundated with mail, mostly favorable, and often containing donations that totaled close to $1,000 a day.[7] A Gallup poll on May 21 showed that 84 percent of the American people had heard of his charges against the State Department and that 39 percent of those who had heard of them felt that they were a good thing for the country.[8] The outbreak of the Korean War on June 25 would force the senator to share the headlines with events from that far-off land, but it also added fuel to his charges and gave him a new issue to use against the Truman administration, which he could blame for encouraging the North Korean attack and for mishandling the conduct of the war that was killing so many American boys. World events seemed to be playing into McCarthy's hands.

McCarthy would be in the spotlight for the next four years, gaining a power and influence usually beyond the reach of most senators and demagogues. He was a tireless campaigner for right-wing Republican candidates and was credited—probably erroneously—with securing the election of anywhere from six to twelve congressmen. He constantly harassed the Truman administration with his wild charges of incompetence and treason, with his brutal attacks on the State Department for losing China and giving Eastern Europe and the bomb to the Russians, with his attempts to block the president's nominees to State Department posts, and with his allegations of government bungling and treason in the conduct of the Korean war.

As McCarthy's fame grew, he became more vituperative and reckless, and instead of hinting at nameless "lists" and changing numbers of "communists in government," he began to name names—speaking always from the Senate floor, of course, so he could not be sued for libel. He branched out to attack and intimidate not just government officials but journalists, professors, and many other private citizens. He successfully resisted all attempts by the Senate and his own party to restrain him, cleverly manipulated the media, and gained even more power when the Republican victories of 1952 enabled him to assume the chairmanship of the Senate Committee on Government Operations and of that committee's Permanent Subcommittee on Investigations. In these positions he would overreach himself and bring about his own dramatic fall from power, but until then he basked in the publicity showered upon him by his supporters and critics, relished the myths of his political invincibility, and enjoyed the turmoil he was creating.

Joe McCarthy was certainly one of the most incredible men ever to hold a Senate office. Physically, he was thickset with broad shoulders, muscular hairy arms, a large head, a long pointed nose, a receding hairline, and a constant five-o'clock shadow. He had shifty eyes and a snickering laugh, especially when he was taunting witnesses. He dressed and acted like a slob—his shoes often needed shining, and his clothes were usually rumpled and bulging with notes sticking out of his pockets. He was a heavy drinker, always carrying a bottle of whiskey in the scruffy briefcase that supposedly contained his "documents," and he liked to brag about drinking a glass of whiskey for breakfast and belting down a fifth every day. In public he had no qualms about belching, using obscenities, or employing rough language that seemed straight out of a Mickey Spillane novel, for he frequently talked of hitting people in the groin, kicking them in the rear, kicking their brains out, or working them over with a club. When attractive women appeared as witnesses before his Senate committee, he leered at them and jokingly told his aides to get their phone numbers.[9] He spent more time at the poker table or placing bets with his bookies than on legitimate Senate business, and he prided himself on his tough-guy appearance and his violation of Senate protocol and civilized manners. He called strangers he had just met, no matter how important, by their first name and told them to call him Joe, and he appeared to be a friendly, ingratiating, good fellow to everyone he met—making small talk, shaking hands, and putting his hairy arms around their shoulders. He was a big fake and a Senate maverick, and he enjoyed playing the role.

McCarthy was ruthless, brutal, reckless, and unscrupulous. He was also a pathological liar. He lied about his early life, his college career, his military service, his opponents in his judicial and senatorial races in Wisconsin, and the facts he had about all the subversives he claimed to be uncovering. Incredibly, he lied when he did not have to lie, and he told lies that could easily be checked up on or that patently contradicted what he had said the day before or even just a few minutes before. He even lied in print, as when he fabricated footnotes to "document" the reams of lies and innuendoes in his book, *McCarthyism: The Fight for America* (1952).

McCarthy's accounts of his military career provide just one example from among many of his blatant disregard for the truth. In his speeches and press releases, he proudly touted his war record, claiming that his exploits had led his colleagues to name him Tail-Gunner Joe for his brave actions in the midst of heated air battles. The truth is that he had an uneventful war experience, seeing little combat action, and that his time in the tail-gunnery section was limited to occasional rides during peaceful flights. He did set a record for the largest number (4,700) of ammunition rounds fired from the tail-gunner's section in a single day, but these rounds were fired at coconut trees on an American island base while the plane was sitting on the ground. His campaign brochures always carried pictures of "Tail-Gunner Joe" and "Wisconsin's Fighting Marine," and with each retelling the number of combat missions he flew during World War II grew from the original fourteen to seventeen, to twenty-five, and finally to thirty, though military records indicate that he never went on any. After the war he walked with a slight limp, mostly an affected one, and he proudly but falsely claimed that his injury had been caused by "ten pounds of shrapnel" and that it had earned him a Purple Heart. He did hurt his foot during the war, but the mishap occurred when he fell down a stairwell during a party aboard the seaplane tender *Chandeleur*, far from the menace of Japanese guns. After he entered the Senate, he used his political influence to obtain an Air Medal and the Distinguished Flying Cross.[10]

McCarthy carried his lies to the floor and committee rooms of the Senate and to news conference and public events that were reported to audiences running into the millions. Most men would shrink from telling obvious lies under such public scrutiny, but not McCarthy. He lied about the backgrounds of his opponents, distorted their statements, and assassinated their characters with wild allegations. One of his favorite techniques was to pull a stack of papers from his old briefcase and, claiming that he held the evidence in his hand, taken from his files, to read from imaginary documents about imaginary people and imaginary events, making up names and numbers and events as he went along. Sometimes the "documents" were worthless sheets of paper, old government reports, or copies of legislation being deliberated by the Senate. It did not matter to McCarthy, who skillfully paraphrased and lied as he went along and warmed to his topic and audience. He denied requests to see the documents by claiming that they were secret documents given to him by his network of informants, parried requests for clarification by claiming that it was not his fault that the inquiring senator was too stupid to understand what he was saying, and evaded attempts to pin him down on his inconsistencies in the number of communists he had found by claiming that he was tired of this silly numbers game and wanted to get on to the heart of the matter. When backed into a corner and confronted with an obvious lie, he responded by attacking his adversary or dropping that line of investigation and going on to another. He would attack any person or organization as long as he got good publicity from it or until he ran into strong opposition; then he would drop that cause and pick up another.

McCarthy was a master at using inflammatory rhetoric that obscured his lack of facts, stuck in the minds of his listeners, and made newspaper headlines. For four years Americans were accustomed to hearing McCarthy lambast "left-wing bleeding hearts," "egg-sucking phony liberals," "Communists and queers who sold China into atheistic slavery," and "Parlor Pinks and Parlor Punks."[11] He frequently talked of the "Yalta betrayal," the "sellout of China," and a State Department that was full of homosexuals and traitors "more loyal to the ideals and designs of Communism than to those of the free, God-fearing half of the world." He called Owen Lattimore (a Far Eastern expert and former part-time State Department consultant) "the top Russian espionage agent" in the United States, and the "principal architect of our far-eastern policy" that had led to the communist takeover of China.[12] He habitually referred to Truman and Acheson as the "pied pipers of the Politburo," called Truman a "son of a bitch" after he fired General MacArthur, called Acheson the Red Dean and the Red Dean of Fashion, and characterized General George C. Marshall, the highly revered army chief of staff during World War II and the secretary of state and then secretary of defense under Truman, as "a man steeped in falsehood" who was part "of a great conspiracy, a conspiracy on a scale so immense as to dwarf any previous such venture in the history of man."[13] He said that Senator Ralph Flanders of Vermont was "senile" and that "they should get a man with a net and take him to a quiet place," and he described Senator Robert C. Hendrickson of New Jersey as "a living miracle in that he is without question the only man in the world who has lived so long with neither brains nor guts."[14]

These malicious attacks went on and on for four years, as did his pledge to continue his battle against communism "regardless of how high-pitched becomes the squealing and screaming of those left-wing, bleeding heart, phony liberals."[15] He was a ruthless, clever wordsmith. No wonder he became known as Low-Blow Joe, or that Joseph and Steward Alsop could write that "McCarthy is the only major politician in the country who can be labeled 'liar' without fear of libel,"[16] or that President Truman, when accused by Senator Robert A. Taft of libeling McCarthy, would ask a reporter, "Do you think that is possible?"[17]

McCarthy was as dishonest in his financial affairs as he was in his rhetoric and his "investigations" and "exposés" of communists and other traitors. As Senate investigations later revealed, he received thousands of dollars in cash or unsecured loans from lobbyists in return for his vote on crucial issues. A large amount of the donations he received for his "fight for America" crusade went not into the fight against communism but into his personal checking account, where it was used to pay off gambling debts, to play the stock market, and buy soybean futures. He also violated several federal and state laws and regulations in the area of bribery, taxes, banking, and commodity trading.[18]

What were the motives of this incredibly unscrupulous man? Many of his contemporary opponents compared him to Hitler and saw him as the leader of a right-wing totalitarian movement that was using the communist issue to establish a totalitarian state. McCarthy was like Hitler in his ruthlessness, his complete disregard for the truth, and his shrewd manipulation of the fears of the people. But here the comparison stops. Hitler was the leader of a ideological movement designed to take over the state and run it along totalitarian principles. McCarthy, however, had no social or economic program and did not seek control of the military or the government. He was not a fanatic or a fascist, and he never tried to organize or lead any movement. As historian Richard Hofstadter later wrote in his *The Paranoid Style in American Politics*, the slovenly senator "could barely organize his own files, much less a movement."[19]

What McCarthy sought was publicity, fame, and reelection to the Senate. He loved to manipulate people, to create turmoil and confusion, to be able to swagger into a room and command the attention of everyone there, to see his name and picture in the paper. There is little evidence that he ever believed his own lies, that he ever really thought that communism was boring from within to destroy the American republic. Everything he did and said was calculated to bring maximum publicity and the fame he thirsted for. His wild charges, his tantrums, his staged walkouts from committee hearings, his badgerings of witnesses, his taunts, his sneers, his roughhouse language—all were shrewdly calculated to put him at the center of attention and gather headlines and votes.[20] Communism in government was a convenient tool for him to use to further his own glory-seeking. Had the circumstances been different, he could just as easily have ridden the fears of a fascist, Jewish, or black "menace" to the top of the glory pole. He was a man without principles, scruples, beliefs, or proof of his sensational allegations. He never uncovered a single communist in the government, yet he had the support of millions.

McCarthy was not the first demagogue to appear in American history, but he was the first to have a national following, thanks to the power of modern communications, particularly television. He was a master at using the media. He knew when to release information in order to get maximum publicity and effect. He used the press to spring his wild charges and accusations, knowing that they would draw fire from his opponents, which would also be printed, and that he could then answer their countercharges and keep the publicity mill running. The newspapers and magazines strong enough or brave enough to oppose him he quickly branded as "communist" or "Red" publications—thereby generating even more publicity. When columnists Joseph and Stewart Alsop attacked him, he claimed that their articles were "almost 100 percent in line with the official instructions issued to all Communists and fellow travelers."[21] He tried to smear the names or ruin the reputations of his most troublesome editors and reporters, like James A. Wechsler, the editor of the *New York Post*. And sometimes he tried the physical approach, as when in December of 1950 he met his old nemesis, columnist Drew Pearson, in the cloakroom of the Sulgrave Club in Washington and, without provocation, punched Pearson in the head and kneed him in the groin. According to newly elected Senator Richard M. Nixon, the attack ended when he stepped between the two men and said, "Let a good Quaker stop this fight." Nixon then spent close to thirty minutes helping the intoxicated McCarthy find his car in the club parking lot.[22]

Who supported this demagogue, this ruthless "poolroom politician," as some contemporaries called him? In the beginning, in February of 1950, he seemed to have little support in Washington or across the country, but as he continued to press his charges and attract publicity, the public's approval of him grew, and more and more Republican congressmen began to back him. Throughout the McCarthy era, the single most important distinction between his supporters and his detractors was party affiliation. Many conservative Republicans believed that there was an internal Red menace and that while McCarthy's methods were extreme, he was doing the right thing. Many others saw him as a convenient tool for attacking the Democrats and ending that party's twenty-year reign in Washington. Many agreed with Senator Robert A. Taft, who said that McCarthy should "keep talking, and if one case doesn't work out, he should try another,"[23] and with Senator John Bricker, who told McCarthy that "you're a dirty son of a bitch, but there are times when you've got to have a son of a bitch around, and this is one of them." McCarthy took this as a compliment.[24] His strongest Senate supporters were conservative Republicans Barry Goldwater, William E. Jenner, Richard Nixon, Karl Mundt, Charles Potter, Robert Taft, and Everett Dirksen. But he was also supported by many congressional Democrats, who believed that there was some substance to his charges and were trying to show that they were working just as hard as McCarthy and the Republicans to root the communists out of government. Other Democrats gave him passive support or at least refrained from attacking him, fearing that he would retaliate by smearing them and campaigning against them in the next elections.[25]

McCarthy also received support from other quarters of the government. Many minor officials in various agencies of the executive department fed him vital—and sometimes classified—information that he could use in his broadsides against the Truman administration. He also won the endorsement of J. Edgar Hoover, who rivaled McCarthy in his ability to inflate the communist threat and who frequently praised McCarthy for his efforts in the battle against godless communism. In 1952, in one of his many favorable public statements on the senator, Hoover noted that McCarthy's Irish, marine corps, and amateur boxing background made him "a vigorous individual, who is not going to be pushed around . . . I view him as a friend and believe he so views me."[26]

McCarthy was also backed by many people outside the government. Much of the press was generally pro-McCarthy, either through agreement with his ideas or out of fear of opposing him. The Hearst and Scripps-Howard newspaper chains were among his strongest supporters, as were right-wing magazines like the *American Mercury* and conservative mass publications like *Reader's Digest*, *U.S. News and World Report*, *The Saturday Evening Post*, and *Time* and *Life*, though the two Luce publications eventually turned against him. He was supported by conservative radio commentators Paul Harvey, Walter Winchell, and Fulton Lewis, Jr.; the American Legion, the Veterans of Foreign Wars, the Daughters of the American Revolution, and other superpatriotic organizations; Billy James Hargis, Carl McIntyre, and other right-wing ministers and their fundamentalist followers; Joseph Kennedy, Archbishop Francis Cardinal Spellman of New York, and millions of other conservative Roman Catholics with strong anticommunist sentiments; the "China Lobby," which agreed with his attacks on the State Department's China policy and unrealistically hoped that he could lead the fight to reverse the communist revolution in China and restore Chiang Kai-shek to power on the mainland; long-term opponents of the intellectual, liberal eastern establishment; and by rabid haters of Roosevelt, Truman, and the New Deal. McCarthy played on the hopes and fears of millions of people from many walks of life, and one of his major appeals was that in a complex age he gave simple answers to difficult questions and simple solutions to difficult problems.[27]

McCarthy also had many courageous and vigorous opponents. Most of organized labor, the educational establishment, and organized religion resisted the appeals and attacks of McCarthy and his followers. *The New York Times* and the other top ten dailies in the country regularly condemned the senator, as did *The New Republic*, *The Nation*, and other liberal magazines. Political cartoonists lampooned him almost daily, and about a month after the Wheeling speech, Herbert Block (Herblock) drew his famous cartoon showing four Republican senators pushing an elephant toward buckets of tar, one of which was labeled "McCarthyism," instantly coining the word that came to be used to describe the methods not just of the Wisconsin senator but of his imitators all across the nation. More timid in its approach to McCarthy was the radio and television industry, where pressure from advertisers was much greater than in the printed media and where blacklisting was causing broadcasters to lose their jobs and watch their words. But even here Martin Agronsky, Elmer Davis, Edward R. Murrow, and a few others had the courage to reveal the senator for what he was.[28]

In political circles McCarthy was naturally opposed by more Democrats than Republicans. Democratic Senators Millard Tydings (Maryland), William Benton (Connecticut), and Scott Lucas (Illinois) fought against him in the Senate, but all three men were later defeated in their reelection bids, lending credence to the myth that opposition to McCarthy was political suicide. From the Republican side the strongest attack on McCarthy came from Senator Margaret Chase Smith of Maine, who in June of 1950 stood up in the Senate to denounce McCarthy and to plead with her fellow Republicans to refrain from joining the McCarthy bandwagon just for the purpose of wresting power from the Democrats. "The nation sorely needs a Republican victory," she told them, "but I don't want to see the Republican Party ride to victory on the Four Horses of Calumny—Fear, Ignorance, Bigotry, and Smear."[29]

President Truman and the top members of his administration regularly spoke out against the senator. From the Wheeling speech on, Truman had regarded him as a demagogue who was part of a Republican right-wing crusade to discredit the Democrats and win control of Congress and the presidency. As early as March 31, Truman was writing his cousin, Nellie

Noland, that McCarthy was a "pathological liar" who, along with Senator Kenneth S. Wherry, "a blockheaded undertaker," was "going along with the Kremlin to break up our bipartisan foreign policy."[30]

Truman consistently denounced McCarthy and his methods, denied that there were any communists in the government, and claimed that his own loyalty program was ferreting out all bureaucrats with suspicious political loyalties. But the more he denied the existence of communists in the government, the more McCarthy and his growing body of Republican followers attacked him for "covering up" subversives in high places. Ironically, Truman, Acheson, and the other top members of the administration were ardent anticommunists themselves and were known in the Kremlin, Peking, and European capitals as hard-liners in the Cold War, yet they had to endure McCarthy's daily taunts and allegations and spend valuable time trying to refute his wild charges. From the summer of 1950 onward, while he dealt with the Korean War and other troubles, Truman always had to consider the "McCarthy problem" when he gave a speech or made a major decision.

As much as Truman detested McCarthy, he refused to use the senator's dirty tactics in the battle against him—his own moral principles and reverence for his office would not allow it. This was dramatically demonstrated in February of 1951 in a presidential staff meeting called to discuss possible ways of dealing with the senator. One official at the gathering told the president that a thick file had been gathered on McCarthy's sexual escapades over the years, complete with names of motels and cities and sexual partners. If released to the press, the senator would be ruined, and the administration would be rid of one of the biggest thorns in its side. But Truman would have none of it. After listening to this proposal, he angrily slammed his fist on the table and proceeded to lecture his embarrassed circle on the sanctity of the presidential office and the dangers of lowering it into the gutter to fight a skunk and guttersnipe like McCarthy. Novelist John Hersey, who had been covering Truman's daily activities for months in preparation for writing a profile of him for *The New Yorker*, wrote that he carried away from this meeting a "burning memory . . . of his indignation, both at the vicious methods of McCarthy and at the idea that some of his trusted friends would wish to splatter mud on the man who lived in him, the President of the United States."[31]

McCarthy was the most famous of the witchhunters, but he was certainly not the only one, for throughout the country many individuals, organizations, and government agencies were working for the same hysterical cause. It began at the top, with the federal government. From 1947 until 1954, when the hysteria began to decline, federal employees under both the Truman and Eisenhower administrations were subjected to a series of executive orders, laws of Congress, and Supreme Court rulings on loyalty and security regulations. During this period federal employees were investigated, prosecuted, and dismissed for a wide range of activities, including subversion, espionage, sabotage, belonging to the Communist party or some other totalitarian organization, "furthering" the interests of a foreign power, having "questionable" loyalty to the United States, taking the Fifth Amendment during loyalty hearings or trials, being a "security risk" in a "sensitive" job, having "dangerous" associations, and for a variety of activities that were believed (whether true or not) to lay federal employees open to blackmail, such as homosexuality, sexual promiscuity, and immoral conduct of various kinds.

The loyalty issue put the whole federal service under a cloud of suspicion and subjected thousands of employees to investigations by the loyalty boards within their departments, by the Justice Department, by the FBI, HUAC, and other government agencies. "An ugly, sinister, and completely stupid process of intimidation is undermining the morale of completely loyal government workers," wrote A. Powell Davies in *The New Republic* in early 1952.[32] Federal employees were afraid to speak out on controversial topics, join organizations that might be tainted with the slightest suspicion of radicalism, subscribe to unusual periodicals, or associate with "suspicious" people. Employees under investigation quickly learned that they would be subjected to a whole range of questions and checks on their private beliefs and habits, such as what books do you read? Do you believe in God? Do you ever entertain black people in your home? Do you have any of Paul Robeson's records in your home? Do you believe that blood from white and black donors should be segregated in blood banks? In one silly incident, a Negro bootblack in the Pentagon was interviewed seventy times by the FBI before it finally decided that he was not a security risk and should be allowed to continue shining shoes there. The cause of this expensive and time-consuming investigation was the bootblack's $10 donation years before to a defense fund for the Scottsboro boys.[33]

The results of the loyalty and security programs and investigations certainly never justified the cost in dollars, man hours, or damages to the reputations and careers of innocent people. Thousands of people were investigated, but under Truman only 1,210 were dismissed and another 6,000 resigned rather than submit to the indignities and publicity of a hearing or trial. During Eisenhower's first administration, around 1,500 were dismissed, while another 6,000 resigned. The Truman and Eisenhower administrations also deported 163 alien "subversives," far fewer than the 900 deported during the Red Scare of 1919–1920. In neither administration did the investigations turn up a genuine spy or saboteur—the dismissals were for being a "security risk" or for engaging in some form of "misconduct," such as alcoholism, adultery, or homosexuality.[34] Many of those who resigned were valuable federal employees. The State Department was especially hard hit by the resignations, losing many of its foreign policy experts, especially those in the area of Far Eastern Affairs, who fell under the most suspicion because of the "loss" of China.

It was not just government employees who suffered. HUAC reached out to investigate and ruin the reputations of private citizens from all walks of life, and in December of 1950 the Senate, fearful of being left out in the crusade against communism, established its own version of HUAC, the Internal Security Subcommittee of the Committee of the Judiciary. And just a few months before, in September, the Senate and the House had joined to pass over Truman's veto the most restrictive of all the internal security measures, the McCarran Internal Security Act. Named for its major sponsor, Democratic Senator Pat McCarran of Nevada, this act required all communist organizations and communist-front organizations to register with the attorney general's office, banned communists from working in defense plants, prohibited government employees from contributing money to any communist organization or from being a member of any organization conspiring to set up a totalitarian state in the United States, and gave the government the power to halt the immigration of subversive aliens and to deport those already in this country. The bill also gave the president the power to declare a national security emergency, during which the government could arrest and detain in special concentration camps anyone suspected of conspiracy, espionage, or sabotage until they had been given a hearing before a Detention Review Board.[35] No one was ever put in these camps, but many critics found it astonishing that they were established in a country claiming to be the freest nation in the world and to be the free world's leader in the battle against international communism.

During the Great Fear the states followed the example of the federal government and joined in the anticommunist crusade. By the time Eisenhower took office in 1953, thirty-nine states had passed laws making it a criminal offense to advocate the violent overthrow of the government or join any organization advocating the violent overthrow of the government, twenty-six had passed laws prohibiting communists from running for public office, twenty-eight had closed civil service ranks to communists, thirty-two had enacted loyalty oaths for teachers, and most states had outlawed the Communist party. A Connecticut sedition law made it illegal to criticize the United States government, the army, or the American flag, while Texas made membership in the Communist party a felony punishable by twenty years' imprisonment. In many states laws were passed making the taking of the Fifth Amendment automatic proof of Communist party membership and automatic grounds for summary dismissal from government service. And at the local level, in municipal and county governments, authorities often tried to rival the state and federal government in the zeal with which they enacted antisubversive laws and regulations. Many towns passed their own loyalty oaths for public employees and ordered communists to register with the police, or simply ordered them to get out of town.[36]

It was virtually impossible in this atmosphere for accused communists to get a fair trial. The most publicized example of this was the fate of Julius and Ethel Rosenberg, arrested in 1950 for allegedly passing atomic secrets to the Russians. The trial of the Rosenbergs and several of their codefendents for violation of the Espionage Act of 1917 began on March 6, 1951, at the federal courthouse at Foley Square in New York, during some of the darkest days of the Korean War. During the two-week trial Ethel's brother and sister-in-law, David and Ruth Greenglass, testified that the Rosenbergs had recruited them as accomplices in a vast conspiracy to transmit secrets of the atomic bomb to Russia during the Second World War, when Julius had worked as a civilian engineer in the Brooklyn supply office of the Army Signal Corps before being dismissed by the army in March of 1945 on the grounds that he was a communist. According to the Greenglasses, the Rosenbergs were motivated by the belief that, if both Russia and America had the bomb, it would never be used, and world peace would be assured. The Rosenbergs denied all allegations, claimed that they had been framed by the government, and took the Fifth Amendment when asked if they were or had ever been communists. They steadfastly argued that they were the victims of American fascism, anti-Semitism, and the anticommunist hysteria of the time.[37]

But the jury believed otherwise, and on March 29 it pronounced the Rosenbergs guilty of a conspiracy to commit espionage. On April 15, Judge Irving Kaufman sentenced the Rosenbergs to die in the electric chair. Their crime, he told the court, was "worse than murder," because it had helped the Russians acquire the atomic bomb much earlier than they would have otherwise, had encouraged communist aggression in Korea, and furthered the goal of world communism. "It is not in my power, Julius and Ethel Rosenberg, to forgive you," he said. "Only the Lord can find mercy for what you have done."[38] The Rosenbergs' coconspirators were convicted of lesser degrees of conspiracy and given lighter sentences, ranging from fifteen to thirty years.

All across the country people kept up with the Rosenberg trial, read their published letters, followed the newspaper stories of their two little sons' visits with their parents at Sing Sing prison, and debated their guilt and their death sentence. Many felt that the Rosenbergs were guilty and deserved their fate, others accepted their guilt but believed that the punishment was too harsh, others believed that they were probably guilty but had not received a fair trial in Judge Irving Kaufman's court, and some felt that they were innocent victims of the anticommunist hysteria of the time and of a long-standing willingness by some to believe in an international Jewish conspiracy. Many were disturbed by the fact that the Rosenbergs were tried and convicted by the press long before they entered the courtroom, that most of the testimony against them came from confessed spies trying to reduce their sentence by turning witnesses for the prosecution, and that they were convicted of conspiring to pass secrets to Russia at a time when Russia was an ally of the United States, not an enemy. At home and abroad, the case was frequently compared to the Sacco and Vanzetti case of the twenties in America and to the Dreyfus case in France in the latter part of the nineteenth century. It would be a big headline-getter until the couple's execution in the early months of the Eisenhower administration.[39]

One of the major victims of the Great Fear was the movie industry, a natural target since it dealt with the dissemination of ideas to a mass audience. From the mid-1930s to the mid-1950s perhaps as many as 300 Hollywood writers, directors, actors, set designers, and others connected with the movie industry had joined the Communist party, which always drew a large percentage of its membership from the intellectual and artistic class in America. But few if any communist ideas ever got into Hollywood's movies, for the conservative business interests that financed the making of movies shied away from supporting films with controversial themes, much less communist ones. No film was ever proved to be communist in origin or content in spite of all the publicity surrounding the "communists in Hollywood" controversy.[40] But this didn't stop HUAC and other superpatriotic organizations from wreaking havoc on the industry.

The Great Fear began in Hollywood in 1947 when HUAC began a series of investigations and hearings on communist infiltration of the movie industry. Many people in Hollywood quickly caved in to HUAC and the Great Fear. Some appeared before HUAC and named names of colleagues who were communists or suspected communists or who had tried to recruit them for the cause. Blacklists were quickly circulated of communists or suspected communists or anyone else who did anything to arouse the kind of suspicion that might cause unwanted publicity and controversy for forthcoming pictures. According to some estimates, perhaps as many as 500 people—writers, directors, actors and actresses, and others associated with the making of films—found their name on the blacklists.[41] Among the prominent names on the list could be found those of actors Will Geer and Jeff Corey, pantomime Zero Mostel, and writers Lillian Hellman, Ring Lardner, Jr., and Arthur Miller. Some were never able to work again, while others, like Will Geer, could find little or no work for over a decade—and often it was too late by then to resume an aborted career.

In addition to the infamous blacklists, Hollywood also reacted to the Great Fear by severely reducing the number of films dealing with serious social issues and controversial subjects and replacing them with escapist entertainment—westerns, cops and robbers, comedies, and musicals. And to show just how patriotic it was, Hollywood turned out more and more war films and anticommunist films. About forty anticommunist films were made, with titles like *I Was a Communist for the FBI*, *The Steel Fist*, and *The Red Menace*.[42] Perhaps the best example of this genre was *My Son John* (1952), a morality tale about a nice, small-town boy who went off to college and was duped into becoming a pacifist, an atheist, and perhaps even a homosexual and communist by his intellectual professors and liberal friends, and was then assassinated gangland style on the steps of the Lincoln Memorial after his corrupters discovered that he had repented of his errors and was going to the FBI with his confession.[43] The effect that the suspicion was having on Hollywood can be also seen in the decision by Monogram Pictures in 1950 to cancel plans for a movie on Hiawatha because, according to studio executives, Hiawatha's attempts to arrange peace with the Indians "might be regarded as a message of peace and therefore helpful to Russian designs."[44]

Like the movies, the radio and television industry was a natural target of the anticommunist hysteria, because it dealt with a wide variety of ideas and broadcast to a mass audience. The industry was under attack from 1947 onward, but the major blow came in 1950 with the publication of *Red Channels: The Report of Communist Influence in Radio and Television*, written by former FBI agents Kenneth M. Bierly, John G. Keenan, and Theodore C. Kirkpatrick. Fear of lawsuits prevented the authors from claiming that any of the people listed inside the book were communists, but it contained an alphabetical list of 151 prominent people in the radio and television industry along with a "citation" of each individual's activities on behalf of various causes. These "citations" gave the unmistakable impression that these individuals had belonged to organizations and participated in activities that aided the communist cause. And what were they accused of, or "cited" for, in this literary smear? They were cited for fighting race discrimination, combatting censorship, criticizing HUAC, opposing Hitler and other fascists in the thirties and forties, advocating better Russian–American relations, favoring New Deal legislation, signing petitions for "liberal" or "pacifist" causes, supporting the United Nations, and campaigning for Henry Wallace. Among those cited for these so-called subversive activities were Lee J. Cobb, Leonard Bernstein, Aaron Copland, Jose Ferrer, Will Geer, Gypsy Rose Lee, Burgess Meredith, Edward G. Robinson, and Orson Welles.[45]

Published on June 22, just three days before the outbreak of the Korean War, copies of *Red Channels* soon found their way to the desks of radio and television executives and sponsors, who in the hysterical climate of 1950 wanted no connection with controversial ideas or controversial individuals. Without being given the opportunity to defend themselves against the charges in the book, many actors, directors, writers, and others connected with the industry suddenly discovered that their services were no longer needed. Among those who lost their jobs were Philip Loeb, who played Jake on the *The Goldbergs*, accused by *Red Channels* of communist sympathies for sponsoring an "End to Jim Crow in Baseball Committee." Banished from television and radio, he later died of a sleeping pill overdose.[46] The blacklisting also led to many ridiculous, humorous incidents, such as the New York Yankees' refusal to allow catcher Yogi Berra to appear on a television show with blacklisted actor John Gilford, even though a Yankee spokesman asserted that Berra did not know "the difference between communism and communion."[47]

Another major victim of the Great Fear was higher education. Communism in the United States had always drawn a large proportion of its followers and sympathizers from intellectuals, so it was not surprising that HUAC, state legislators, and other witchhunters would go after college professors. Many were deprived of their tenure, placed on probation, or fired for refusing to take state-imposed loyalty oaths, for taking the Fifth Amendment during investigations or trials, for holding unconventional opinions, for refusing to testify against their colleagues, or for signing petitions protesting violations of civil liberties by governments and vigilante groups. At the University of Minnesota, a black professor of philosophy who admitted to being a socialist and vice chairman of the Minnesota Progressive party was harassed by the administration and the FBI, subjected to unsubstantiated rumors that he was a homosexual and had engaged in sexual affairs with white female students, and finally dismissed by the administration for "lack of scholarly promise." At Kansas State Teachers College an economics professor lost his job for simply signing a petition urging the pardon of communists who had been arrested and imprisoned under the Smith Act.[48]

By the time the Great Fear had run its course, six hundred college professors had been dismissed. No wonder many professors were afraid to discuss controversial subject matter, to subscribe to leftist publications, or even to be associated with liberal—much less socialist or communist—ideas, causes, or organizations. Understandably, most signed the loyalty oaths. Joseph Heller, an English professor at Penn State who was working on his novel *Catch-22*, probably spoke for many when he said that he regarded the oath "as an infringement of liberty, but it was only a tiny inconvenience compared with having no job."[49]

The public schools, like the colleges and universities, also suffered from the Great Fear. All across the country public school educators were subjected to loyalty oaths, dismissals with or without a hearing due to real or alleged affiliation with radical groups, bans on the teaching of radical ideas, and scrutiny of teaching materials by local censors. This national crusade against communism in the schools was promoted by McCarthy and other politicians in Washington, by state legislatures, by state and local politicians, by superpatriotic organizations like the DAR and the American Legion, and by books and mass magazines. In the October 1951 edition of *Reader's Digest*, for example, author John T. Flynn warned in "Who Owns Your Child's Mind?" that social science teachers were spreading socialist propaganda in the public schools and urged parents to get actively involved in the surveillance of the teachers and books that were molding the minds of their children.[50] Hundreds of similar articles appeared in other magazines and newspapers, combining with right-wing books and pamphlets with titles like "How Red Is the Little Red Schoolhouse?" to spread the idea that subversives would capture the minds of the nation's young children unless parents and other concerned groups joined hands to fight the conspiracy.

Libraries were also favorate targets of overzealous patriots. In many cities, librarians were forced to purge from their shelves not just copies of the *Daily Worker* or the *National Guardian* but also of *The New Republic*, *The Nation*, *The Negro Digest*, *The Saturday Review of Literature*, *National Geographic*, *Look*, *Life*, and *Time*. Books by communist, socialist, liberal, or black authors were often pulled from the shelves, as were books and other materials critical of American capitalism, government, religion, or other American values and institutions or favorable toward the United Nations, disarmament, world peace, integration, interracial marriage, and even the fluoridation of city water supplies. Books on sex education or birth control were usually taboo, along with novels with obscene or suggestive passages. Sometimes it seemed that the censors were trying to outdo one another in the lengths they went to in trying to protect the public from "dangerous materials." In 1952, the Los Angeles Board of Education banned all UNESCO publications from the libraries and classes of the public schools, while in the winter of 1953 and 1954 one member of the Indiana State Textbook Commission tried to get books on Robin Hood expunged from the school curricula and libraries. His reason? The communists, he said, were trying "to stress the story of Robin Hood. They wanted to stress it because he robbed the rich and gave it to the poor. That's the Communist line. It's just a smearing of law and order."[51]

The Great Fear often reached even more ridiculous dimensions. Indiana required professional wrestlers to take a loyalty oath, while the District of Columbia refused to issue a retailers license to a secondhand furniture dealer who had taken the Fifth Amendment when questioned about communism. In New York one town required a loyalty oath for a license to fish from city reservoirs, and in another a court granted a woman an annulment of her marriage on the grounds that her husband was a communist.[52] In Cincinnati, the Cincinnati Reds' baseball club tried to demonstrate its Americanism by changing the club's name to the Cincinnati

Redlegs; however, the fans rejected this change in the name of the nation's oldest professional baseball team, stubbornly maintaining, as sportswriter Tom Swope put it, that "we were Reds before they were."[53] In Wisconsin, when the *Madison Capital-Times* sent a reporter out on the city streets on July 4, 1951, to ask passersby to sign a petition made up of quotes from the Declaration of Independence and the Bill of Rights, only one out of over a hundred people who examined the petition agreed to sign it. The others declined on the grounds that the ideas in the petition were communist, un-American, or in some other way subversive.[54] Newspapers in New Orleans and several other cities tried the same experiment that year and obtained basically the same results. No wonder that a few months later, in January of 1952, Claude M. Fuess wrote in a *Saturday Review* article on the temper of the times that "we are dominated by a fear so pervasive that it approaches hysteria."[55]

Just how strong was the communist menace in America? Not very. Founded in 1919 after the Bolshevik Revolution, the American Communist party had always recruited most of its followers from a handful of urban intellectuals, idealists, and malcontents who joined the party because they were alienated from American society or saw communism as the best solution to the problems of American capitalism. The party had always suffered because of its close ties to Moscow, which made it seem like an agent of a foreign country, from its stigma as an alien ideology in a nation that was inherently suspicious of un-American isms, and from its own internal quarrels and power struggles. Furthermore, the weak class consciousness in the country robbed the party of its appeal to the working classes, labor unions, and blacks. Consequently, the party had always been only a minor irritant in American politics and communism a vastly overrated danger to the country's security. The communist presidential candidate William Z. Foster received fewer than 103,000 votes in 1932, when party leaders had expected the depression to bring them millions of followers, and his successor, Earl Browder, was able to garner only 80,000 votes in 1936 and some 46,000 in 1940. After this third loss to Roosevelt, the party did not even put forth its own candidates, supporting instead Roosevelt in 1944 and Progressives Henry Wallace in 1948 and Vincent Hallinan in 1952. Furthermore, not a single communist candidate for Congress ever got elected.[56]

In terms of party membership, the party reached its peak during the days of Russo-American collaboration during the Second World War, when it numbered perhaps as many as 60,000 to 80,000 official members. But in the postwar period Russian aggression, the rise of the Cold War and arms race, government repression, and rapid growth of domestic prosperity combined to cause a dramatic decline in the party's fortunes. Party membership fell to 43,000 in 1950, to 10,000 in 1957, and to around 5,000 (including FBI agents and informers) in 1960, while the circulation of the party's organ, *The Daily Worker*, dropped drastically as well, falling from 23,000 in 1945 to 10,433 in 1953 alone.[57] In 1959 David Shannon was able to write in his history of the party, *The Decline of American Communism*, that "at this moment, the Communist Party seems destined to join a collection of other sects as an exhibit in the museum of American Left Wing Politics."[58]

Ironically, the greatest threat to American freedom in the fifties was not the communism that was feared by so many, but the spread of irrational anticommunism and the rise of right wingers and fascists who were willing to suspend civil liberties and other constitutional rights and freedoms in order to fight an overblown communist threat. As Truman and other critics tried to point out in the fifties, McCarthy and his type were the best friends the Soviet Union had in America, for they did much more to disrupt American foreign policy and domestic tranquillity than American communists could ever hope to do. Truman was not just engaging in political rhetoric in his often-repeated assertion that "the greatest asset the Kremlin has is Senator McCarthy."[59]

# 5

# Mr. Truman's War

On Sunday, June 25 (Korean time), 1950, North Korea launched a surprise, unprovoked invasion of South Korea, at the beginning of the summer monsoons. The predawn attack began with a two-hour barrage of mortar and artillery fire, followed by an invasion of 90,000 North Korean troops across the 38th parallel in a well-planned drive along a 150-mile front. Led by approximately 150 Russian-built tanks, the assault was accompanied by amphibious attacks along South Korea's eastern coast and aerial bombings of gasoline storage tanks, railroads, railway stations, airfields, army bases, and other strategic areas around Seoul, the capital of South Korea. Later in the day, some seven hours after the attack had begun, North Korean radio announced that North Korea was responding to attacks on the north by "the bandit traitor Syngman Rhee" and that he would soon be captured and executed.[1] Americans did not know it yet, but this was the beginning of the Korean War, a war that would plunge the country into another protracted conflict just five years after the end of World War II, resulting in bitter internal divisions, a heightening of the Great Fear, another revolution in American foreign policy, and the election of the first Republican president since Herbert Hoover.

The war that would have such a profound effect upon the United States would be fought in a faraway land whose people, culture, history, and even geographical location were largely unknown to most Americans. Korea was a little peninsula projecting from the Asian mainland between the Yellow Sea and the Sea of Japan. Only 600 miles long and 150 miles wide, it was a land of valleys, rice paddies, rolling hills, mountains that reached as high as 9,000 feet, and temperature extremes ranging from 105 degrees during the summer to 40 below in the winter. Its northern boundaries border on the Manchurian region of China, along the Yalu and Tumen rivers, while it also shares an eleven-mile boundary with Russia, the Russian city of Vladivostok lying only forty miles away from the eastern tip of Korea. The terrain and climate made this remote nation an unsuitable arena for a modern mechanized war, yet several thousand Americans would come to fight and die in a country that was itself a casualty of the unfinished business of World War II and the Cold War between East and West.

The "hermit kingdom" of Korea had for centuries served as the cultural bridge between China and Japan and had often been the battleground among China, Japan, and Russia. Japan acquired Korea as a protectorate in 1905 after defeating Russia in the Russo-Japanese War, annexed the little country (as the province of Chosen) in 1910, and ruled and exploited it until it was liberated in World War II. At the end of the war, Korea was temporarily divided, as provided by the Potsdam Conference, into a northern country occupied by Russia and a southern one occupied by the United States. However, this temporary partition, like the one in Germany and other areas, would become permanent due to the quarreling of the two superpowers. By 1948 it had become permanently divided into the Republic of Korea (South Korea) with its capital at Seoul and strongman Syngman Rhee, an ardent nationalist, as its president, and a People's Democratic Republic of Korea in the North, with Pyongyang as the capital and veteran communist Kim Il-sung as the premier. The Russians ended their military occupation in the summer of 1949, leaving behind a well-trained army backed by tanks, planes, and heavy artillery. The United States also withdrew its occupying troops in 1949, but it refused to equip the South Korean army with offensive weapons, fearing that Syngman Rhee, a petty dictator and unpredictable ally, would use them to launch an attack on the North in an attempt to unify all of Korea under his control. As the Americans withdrew, they left behind a weak country that must have been very tempting to the rulers in the North and their Russian and Chinese allies.

From the very beginning of the North Korean invasion, the Truman administration assumed that North Korea was not acting independently but at the behest of its sponsor, Russia. As the assistant secretary of state for political affairs put it, "the relationship between Russia and North Korea [was] the same as [that] between Walt Disney and Donald Duck."[2] Korea's other communist neighbor, China, was discounted as the primary force behind the invasion because North Korea was a puppet of Russia, not China, and China itself was thought to be controlled from the Kremlin. Besides, Mao Zedung, fresh from his victory over Chiang Kai-shek just a few months before, was deeply involved in consolidating his power within China and was thought to be too weak at this point to engage in international adventures. American officials did not entirely dismiss the possibility of China's culpability in the invasion, but most felt that the most likely candidate was Russia.[3]

The Truman administration did not debate for very long the cause of the North Korean invasion or the proper response to it. Truman would later write that as he flew from Independence back to Washington the day after the invasion he remembered the hard lessons of the 1930s and decided that "Communism was acting in Korea just as Hitler, Mussolini, and the Japanese had acted ten, fifteen, and twenty years earlier." If communist aggression was not stopped in South Korea, it would lead to further communist aggression and ultimately to World War III, just as appeasement had led to World War II.[4] Truman and his advisers believed that America was being tested by the communists and that if the nation did not meet the challenge, the whole containment policy would unravel, America would lose its allies in Europe and other parts of the world, NATO would probably come apart, and the communists would be encouraged to make aggressive moves in other areas. Truman decided to come to the defense of South Korea, although it would mean fighting a difficult war in a faraway land under very adverse circumstances with the risk of provoking war with Russia or China—or both. It was not an easy decision. Truman told Acheson that "everything I have done in the last five years has been to try to avoid making a decision such as I had to make" in Korea,[5] and in his memoirs he would write that it was the "toughest decision I had to make as President."[6]

Truman acted very quickly and decisively in Korea, using his executive powers to make extensive military, diplomatic, and economic commitments to the South Koreans. And he did it without congressional approval or even consultation, setting an important precedent that would later become so controversial during the Vietnam War. In the first week after the attack, he condemned the North Korean aggression, instructed General MacArthur to airlift supplies to the South Korean army, ordered air and naval support for South Korea, dispatched two divisions of ground troops to Korea, ordered a naval blockade of North Korea, and sent the Seventh Fleet into the Formosa Strait to protect Taiwan against possible Chinese invasion, an act which for the first time committed the United States to the defense of Nationalist China. He also increased American aid to the French forces fighting against a communist insurgency in Indochina led by Ho Chi Minh, and promised more aid to the Philippine government, which was also struggling against rebel forces.[7]

Regarding the attack on South Korea as an attack on the United Nations, which had supervised the elections that had created that country in 1948, Truman sought—and received—the support of the United Nations almost every step of the way. On Sunday afternoon, June 25, the Security Council endorsed an American-sponsored resolution condemning the North Korean attack, and on Tuesday, July 27, the Council passed another American-backed resolution branding North Korea as an aggressor and calling on all member states to come to the aid of South Korea. Both resolutions passed only because the Russian delegate, Jacob Malik, absent since January in a protest over the United Nations' refusal to give the new Chinese communist regime Taiwan's place on the Security Council, was not present to cast a veto. And a little over a week later, on July 7, the next obvious step was taken when the Security Council passed a resolution acknowledging the American leadership of the United Nations forces, and Truman named General Douglas MacArthur as the commander of the American and United Nations armies in Korea.

General MacArthur seemed to be the ideal choice. He was one of America's most popular and revered army officers, leading *The New York Times* to assert that "fate could not have chosen a man better qualified to command the unreserved confidence of his country."[8] A graduate of West Point at the turn of the century, he had served in the Philippines and Mexico before going to France during World War I, where he was wounded twice and decorated thirteen times. Between the two world wars he had served in several capacities—as commandant of West Point, as army chief of staff, and, after his retirement from the army in 1937, as field marshal of the Philippine forces. During the Second World War he was called out of retirement by President Roosevelt to serve as supreme allied commander in the South Pacific, where he helped plan the island-hopping campaigns, made good on his promise to return and recapture the Philippines, and accepted the Japanese surrender on the U.S.S. *Missouri* in Tokyo Bay. From 1945 until he assumed command of the United Nations and United States forces in Korea, he was the commander of the American occupying forces in Japan, where he earned the reverence of the Japanese people for his firm but compassionate approach to the eradication of militarism and fascism and the Westernization of America's former Pacific foe.

Arrogant, aloof, and domineering, MacArthur had a reputation as a flamboyant general capable of bold and sometimes brilliant military planning and execution. He also had an insatiable thirst for publicity and fame and a penchant for claiming credit when it was someone else's due and for shifting blame to others when it should have been his. Seventy years old at the time of the beginning of the Korean War, he was still a vigorous man who stood and walked with military erectness. He had to use glasses for close-up work like reading, though his vanity caused him to take them off when photographers were present. Now, in the twilight of his career, the Korean War was to give him one more chance to play the hero's role he loved so much.

* * *

From the very beginning Truman portrayed the Korean War as a conflict between North Korea and the United Nations and as a "police action" of that international body rather than a war between the United States and North Korea. Sixteen nations contributed troops to the United Nations forces, thirty others sent supplies or other forms of nonmilitary aid, and the troops fought under the blue flag of the United Nations. But General MacArthur, the commander of the United Nations forces, took his orders directly from the president of the United States, not from the United Nations. The United States contributed over 50 percent of the ground forces, 86 percent of the naval forces, and 93 percent of the air forces.[9] In spite of all the rhetoric to the contrary, it was an American war, and as it dragged on without an end in sight, it was inevitable that it would become "Truman's war" and "the Democrats' war."

But in the beginning Truman's actions were widely applauded at home and abroad. His cabinet, the National Security Council, and the military were almost unanimous in their approval of his actions. Members of both houses of Congress stood and cheered when his decision to aid South Korea was announced, even though he had acted without asking for congressional advice or backing; only Senator Taft and a handful of other congressmen attacked Truman for committing the nation to war without congressional approval. Most of the press, including *The New Republic, The Nation,* and other liberal publications praised him for making a very courageous decision and for taking a firm stand against communism. Truman's presidential opponent in 1948, Thomas Dewey, sent a telegram saying that "I wholeheartedly agree with and support the difficult decision you have made today,"[10] and even Truman's old antagonist, Henry Wallace, backed Truman's actions and condemned the Soviet Union.[11] Public opinion polls indicated that the great majority of the American public—73 percent, according to a Roper poll—approved of the president's actions, and for once a tally of the telegrams pouring into the White House showed a huge margin—ten to one—in favor of a presidential decision.[12] Ironically, most of the criticism of Truman at the beginning and throughout the Korean War came not from the left but from the right—from conservatives who opposed his limited war policies and believed that the United States should either withdraw from Korea or go all-out to defeat North Korea, unite the Korean peninsula, and liberate the rest of Asia as well.

The first six weeks of the war went badly for the South Koreans and their United Nations allies. The South Korean troops were no match for the larger, better-trained, and better-equipped North Korean forces, who were being supplied with Russian equipment and advisers. The United States was also ill-prepared to fight the war it had committed itself to. American army strength in June of 1950 stood at only 592,000, not even half the number in uniform at the time of the Pearl Harbor attack, and most of the 80,000 troops MacArthur had at his disposal in Japan were green draftees. Therefore, the surprise North Korean attack quickly turned into a South Korean retreat and then into a rout as the demoralized South Korean army fled southward. By the end of July, the North Korean army had pushed the South Korean and American forces to the easternmost tip of the peninsula before the advance was finally halted some fifty miles north of the port of Pusan. This was good news on the American domestic front, where six weeks of steady North Korean advances had shocked and demoralized the American people and seriously eroded the early bipartisan support for Truman's actions.

With the North Korean advance stalled, MacArthur now proceeded to amass troops and supplies in preparation for a counterattack. With the approval of Truman and the Joint Chiefs of Staff in Washington, he now launched a brilliant offensive on September 15 with an amphibious assault on Inchon, the port of Seoul near the western end of the 38th parallel, and a land strike through the Pusan encirclement. MacArthur's surprise landing of troops behind enemy lines trapped and killed thousands of North Korean troops and drove the others across the 38th parallel. By the end of September, Rhee had reestablished his government in Seoul, and MacArthur's troops were poised at the 38th parallel, awaiting further orders. The general had won a great victory at Inchon, and his surprise amphibious attack was widely hailed as a stroke of military genius and a turning point in the war, fortifying his belief in his own greatness. It would also be his last victory.

The victories of September had brought the Korean War to a turning point. The original reason for American and United Nations entrance into the war was containment—to protect South Korea from communist aggression by repelling the North Korean invaders. This objective had now been achieved, so the war could have ended here with the reinstatement of a divided Korea. But Truman, MacArthur, the Joint Chiefs of Staff, and the United Nations were now tempted to go beyond containment to the total destruction of the North Korean forces, the elimination of communism from the Korean peninsula, and the unification of the country under an anticommunist government. Truman decided to take the gamble. On September 27, the Joint Chiefs of Staff authorized MacArthur to cross the 38th parallel and to destroy the North Korean armed forces. He was specifically ordered, however, not to bomb China or cross the Chinese or Russian borders. For the first time since the onset of the Cold War, the United States had committed itself to the destruction of an established communist regime.

In the first two weeks of October MacArthur's troops drove across the 38th parallel and moved rapidly through North Korea, inflicting heavy casualties upon the enemy troops and forcing them to retreat northward toward their boundaries with China. Through public statements and diplomatic channels the Communist Chinese condemned the United Nations invasion and announced that they would not stand idly by and allow North Korea to be crushed and a unified Korea governed by Syngman Rhee to be established on their border. Most administration officials dismissed these statements as typical bombast by a nation too weak to risk war with the United States. But as the United Nations troops advanced Truman began to worry more and more about the intervention of Korea's huge neighbor, with its almost endless supply of manpower, so he arranged a rendezvous with the general at Wake Island on October 15 to discuss the situation.

Truman made the 18,000-mile round-trip flight to Wake Island, a square-mile patch of land between Tokyo and Honolulu, in order to review the military situation and make sure that the headstrong general understood the limited nature of the war he was conducting. The two men had never met (this would, in fact, be their only meeting), and MacArthur had not been to the States since 1937. Relations were already strained between the two strong leaders, with MacArthur chafing over the restraints Truman imposed on his warmaking and Truman incensed over the commander's public criticism of his Far Eastern policy. Before he left the States, Truman wrote his cousin that he had "to talk to God's righthand man."[13] At Wake Island, the two men got off to an uncomfortable beginning, as MacArthur kept the president's plane waiting before he came to meet him, did not salute his commander-in-chief, and was dressed, as Truman observed, rather sloppily, "with his shirt unbuttoned, wearing a greasy ham and eggs cap that evidently had been in use for twenty years."[14]

But most of their conversations were cordial. Although a great deal of controversy would later erupt over exactly what was said at Wake Island, Truman left after a five-hour visit with the definite impression that the war in Korea was all but won, that effective resistance would be over by Thanksgiving, that final victory would come in time to bring the boys home by Christmas, and that neither China nor Russia would intervene. According to Averell Harriman, MacArthur told Truman that "I know the Chinese will not intervene. If they do, it will be one of the greatest slaughters in history. Corpses will be piled six deep."[15] Truman also left with the impression that he and MacArthur saw eye-to-eye on who was running the war, that MacArthur understood the nature of limited war and the dangers of expanding it, and that there would be no more public criticism of the president's policy.[16] As Truman prepared to depart, Anthony Leviero of *The New York Times* asked him how things had gone, and the president replied, "Perfectly . . . I've never had a more satisfactory conference since I've been President." Leviero would later write that Truman "left Wake highly pleased with the results, like an insurance salesman who had at last signed up an important prospect while the latter appeared dubious over the extent of the coverage."[17]

Truman flew back to Washington in a pleasant and reassured mood, unaware that even as he and MacArthur conferred the Chinese were sending troops across the Yalu into North Korea. American military and civilian authorities—in spite of all the threats from China itself, signs of a buildup along the Manchurian border, and warnings from a few lonely voices in the State Department—had greatly misinterpreted the capabilities and intentions of the Communist Chinese. American policy makers refused to recognize that China would not tolerate an American-backed unified Korea on its doorstep and was almost paranoid in its fear of an American invasion of Communist China once Korea was conquered. After all, as the Chinese leaders saw it, America had supported Chiang Kai-shek in the civil war and was now protecting his regime on Taiwan, was aiding the French in their struggle against the communist insurgents in the war in Indochina, had rebuilt Japan, and seemed now to be rearming Japan as part of America's plan to replace its former World War II enemy as the major imperial power in that part of the world.

How wrong the policymakers were became very clear in the last week of October. As the United Nations troops advanced northward and approached the Yalu river, Chinese "volunteers" began to appear among the military captives and casualties, and soon entire divisions of Chinese troops began to inflict heavy losses upon the United Nations forces. But MacArthur still maintained that only 50,000 to 60,000 Chinese troops were involved, and on November 24, he ordered an "end the war" offensive that he claimed would finish the conflict by the end of the year. United Nations troops now drove almost eight miles toward the Yalu with no opposition. But on November 26, as Lt. Gen. G. E. Stratemeyer would later testify, "the whole mountainside turned out to be Chinese."[18] Thirty-three Chinese divisions, comprising around 200,000 troops, hit the middle of the unsuspecting United Nations line and ripped it to pieces. Overwhelmed, the troops were forced into a retreat that quickly became a rout. After so many confident assertions that the Chinese would not intervene, a surprised MacArthur had to send a message to the president with the news that his troops could not stop the Chinese attack and that "we face an entirely new war."[19] The lightly regarded Chinese army had outsmarted and outmaneuvered one of the world's most famous generals.

The war now became a nightmare for the United Nations forces. The Chinese seemed to be everywhere, attacking at night as well as in the day, knifing American soldiers as they tried to sleep in their sleeping bags on the frozen ground, engaging them in terrifying hand-to-hand combat, and fighting as if they were oblivious to the subzero temperatures, blinding blizzards, snow drifts, and impassable mountains that bothered the Americans so much. American soldiers were being slaughtered in such large numbers that it became difficult to give them a decent burial—after one battle 117 bodies were hurriedly buried in a mass grave by their fleeing comrades. The rapidly deteriorating military situation forced a grim Truman to appear on television on December 15 to announce that he was declaring a national emergency and that he was calling for all-out military and economic mobilization to meet the communist threat, necessitating an army buildup to 3.5 million men and the imposition of economic controls. "Our homes, our nation, all the things we believe in are in great danger," he told the American people. "This danger has been created by the rulers of the Soviet Union."[20] The roads southward were now filled with retreating United Nations forces and refugees from the war. By Christmas most of the United Nations forces had retreated below the 38th parallel, and during the first week of the new year of 1951 Seoul had to be evacuated for the second time in the war and more soldiers and civilian refugees had joined the trek southward.

The Korean war became even more unpopular now over the long winter of 1950–1951. More and more it was called "Truman's war," "the no-win war," "the Democrats' war," and a war that the United Nations would fight "to the last American." Truman's earlier decision not to seek advance congressional approval for his intervention in South Korea now came back to haunt him, for since Congress had not authorized the war many congressmen now withdrew their support and began to attack the president's management of the conflict. Americans were scared, and frustrated. House and Senate Republicans passed a resolution demanding that Truman fire Acheson because the secretary of state "had lost the confidence of the country." Truman ignored it.[21] A draft board in a small Montana town announced in December of 1950 that it would draft no more men until MacArthur had been given permission to use the atomic bomb in Korea. Americans felt humiliated because their troops had been beaten and forced to retreat by China. For the first time, a Western army had been defeated by communist forces, and now even MacArthur came under heavy criticism from the press for failing to anticipate and repel the Chinese invasion.[22]

In January of 1951 the Chinese advance was finally halted, and once again the regrouped United Nations forces launched a counterattack that drove the enemy forces back toward the north. Seoul was recaptured again in the middle of March, and once again the 38th parallel was reached and the temptations of victory loomed in front of the United Nations forces. But now Truman, his advisers, and America's allies felt that it was far too risky to invade North Korea again, and that it was time to pursue a negotiated settlement leading to a truce recognizing the existence of two Koreas—in short, settling for containment, the original goal in the war.

* * *

The military events of the winter of 1950–1951 brought to the fore the long simmering feud between President Truman and his popular general. Neither liked the other. MacArthur regarded his civilian boss as a little captain who had not seen war close-up since 1918 and was incompetent to conduct the Korean War even though he was the commander-in-chief. Truman viewed his egocentric general with equal disdain, often referring to him as "Prima Donna, Brass Hat, Five-Star MacArthur"[23] and as a showman and stuffed shirt who "went around dressed up like a nineteen-year-old Second Lieutenant."[24] Truman had long felt that MacArthur was an overrated military hero, and he had been incensed by the patronizing treatment he felt he had received from him at Wake Island and angered by the general's criticism of his military policies.

But the dispute between the two men went beyond personal differences to deep philosophical and political ones. In spite of all his rhetoric about the need for a worldwide battle against communism, Truman was a pragmatic president and commander-in-chief who had no intention of launching a third world war in order to destroy the communist menace he talked so much about. Except for the brief period when he had gambled on complete victory and the unification of Korea, he had tried to avoid taking great risks that might widen the conflict into a global war. Besides, he felt that Korea was the wrong place to take the ultimate stand against communism, and he was more concerned about the communist threat to America's allies in Western Europe than he was about the communist danger in Asia. From the very beginning of the Korean conflict, Truman had feared that Russia would take advantage of America's involvement in Asia to mount a surprise attack on Western Europe, so he did not want the United States to be drawn into a war with China that could only benefit the Soviet Union. Neither did he want to risk war with Russia. The United States was not prepared to fight a conventional war with the superior Russian ground forces, and such a conflict would inevitably result in the use of atomic weapons by both sides. Truman was also worried about retaining the support of America's allies, who were already alarmed over MacArthur's reckless actions and rhetoric and over Truman's statement at a November 30 press conference that the United States had considered using atomic weapons in Korea and would not rule out their use there or anywhere else America's interests were threatened.[25]

General MacArthur, however, was an Asia-firster, who ever since the early days of World War II had maintained that Europe was a dying civilization destined to fall under Russian hegemony, while "the lands touching the Pacific with their billions of inhabitants will determine the course of history for the next ten thousand years."[26] He had long believed that it had been shortsighted of the Roosevelt and Truman administrations to concentrate on Europe in the battles against totalitarian fascism and communism. The worldwide battle between communism and the free world was now centered in Asia, and with Europe lost anyway, the United States should go all-out to stem the communist tide on the Asian mainland. He had always opposed the fighting of a limited land war in Korea, and he often asserted publicly that the United States should bomb crucial targets in China, blockade Chinese ports, and use Nationalist Chinese troops—or withdraw from the peninsula. He believed that there was "no substitute for victory," that the concept of limited war was nothing but a policy of appeasement, and that the civilian leaders in Washington—along with the Joint Chiefs of Staff—were putting unreasonable and even stupid restrictions on his powers to conduct the Korean War. As his successor as commander of the United Nations forces, General Matthew B. Ridgway, would later write, "Like some other great figures on the world stage, past and present, MacArthur seemed at times to have decided that his innate brilliance, so frequently illustrated by military successes, rendered his judgment supreme, above that of all his peers and even of his duly constituted superiors."[27]

The Korean debacle of the 1950–1951 winter caused a great deal of criticism to be leveled at MacArthur by the press and by his superiors in the military. He was accused of misreading the strength and intentions of the Communist Chinese and of precipitating their entrance into the war, causing a great loss of life on both sides and perhaps prolonging the conflict by as much as eighteen months. MacArthur was not accustomed to such criticism, for throughout his career he and his aides had tried to sell to the public the image of the infallible, courageous conqueror. He had come to believe not only his own press clippings but his own press releases, and his belief in his own infallibility had led to a military catastrophe. Unable to accept the blame, he tried to redirect it to his superiors in Washington. In press releases, public statements, and interviews in *U.S. News and World Report* and other publications, he defended his actions, claiming that they had been misinterpreted. The United Nations setbacks were caused, he said, by the superior manpower of the Chinese army and by the restrictions placed upon his freedom to wage the war as he saw fit. He also insisted that his armies were not retreating in defeat but were engaging in a "tactical withdrawal" carried out in "a superior manner."[28]

In early December Truman instructed MacArthur to make no public statements on military or foreign policy without first clearing them with his superiors in Washington. MacArthur complied for a while, but he could not stay quiet for very long. Soon after the first of the year he resumed his condemnations of the president's limited-war policies and renewed his plea to be given the authority to go all-out for victory or else evacuate American forces from Korea. Many critics now believed that MacArthur was seeking either to cap his military career with one last great victory or to bail out of the war in such a way as to avoid tainting his record with the stigma of defeat.

When he was informed by the Truman administration on March 20 that it was planning to seek a negotiated settlement of the conflict, he sabotaged the plan by releasing on March 24 a statement of his "military appraisal" of the Korean War, in which he asserted that China had shown "its complete inability to accomplish by force of arms the conquest of Korea," and offered to meet with the commander-in-chief of the enemy forces to work out an end to the conflict. He also threatened that, if China would not agree to this proposal, then his forces might invade China.[29]

MacArthur's unauthorized offer to negotiate an end to the Korean conflict infuriated President Truman, who told Democratic Senator Harley Kilgore of West Virginia, "I'll show that son of a bitch who's boss. Who does he think he is—God?"[30] Truman and his military and civilian advisers now concluded that MacArthur had to go, but they decided to wait until the popular general made a mistake that would make it possible to fire him with the minimum of public outcry. They did not have to wait for very long, for on March 19 the general had written a letter to Joe Martin, the Republican minority leader in the House and one of the leaders of the conservative Republican critics of Truman's Asian policies, attacking the restrictions Truman had placed on his conduct of the war and claiming, with MacArthur's usual flair, that "there is no substitute for victory." As MacArthur had undoubtedly intended, Martin made the letter public, reading it on the floor of the House on April 5.[31]

The letter to Martin was, as Truman wrote in his diary, "the last straw."[32] He discussed this latest episode with his top civilian and military advisers, and all agreed that MacArthur must be dismissed, regardless of the public's reaction, because he had disobeyed orders and openly challenged the president's constitutional position as the chief foreign-policy maker and supreme commander-in-chief of the armed forces, an important constitutional principle that had helped to preserve the American republic in a world filled with military dictators unhampered by such democratic principles. At the heart of the Truman–MacArthur controversy was, as Truman would later write in his memoirs, "the principle of civilian control of the military."[33] It was a decision he did not want to make—in fact, had postponed for several weeks—but he had no other choice. "I was sorry to have to reach a parting of the way with the big man in Asia," he wrote Eisenhower on April 12, "but he asked for it, and I had to give it to him."[34] Truman did not like MacArthur, but that was not the reason for the firing. As he told one historian years later, "I fired him because he wouldn't respect the authority of the President. That's the answer to that. I didn't fire him because he was a dumb son of a bitch, although he was, but that's not against the law for generals. If it was, half to three quarters of them would be in jail."[35] The firing took courage, but Truman later told a reporter that "courage had nothing to do with it. He was insubordinate, and I fired him."[36]

In the early morning hours of April 11, Truman's press secretary released a statement announcing that MacArthur had been relieved of his duties in Korea and replaced by General Matthew B. Ridgway because MacArthur was "unable to give his wholehearted support to the policies of the United States government and of the United Nations in matters pertaining to his official duties."[37] That evening Truman gave a nationally broadcast address describing the firing as a regrettable but necessary action taken to preserve the principle of civilian control of the military and to remove "any doubt or confusion as to the real purpose and aim of our policy." He also defended his limited war policy, asserting that "we are trying to prevent a world war—not to start one," and told his millions of listeners that "it is with the deepest personal regret that I found myself compelled to take this action. General MacArthur is one of our greatest military commanders. But the cause of world peace is more important than any individual."[38]

The nation was stunned at the firing of one of its greatest heroes, but even Truman, who knew he had made a very unpopular decision, was surprised at the abuse that was heaped on him from across the country. In the first twelve days after the firing, the White House received over 27,000 letters and telegrams, and they ran 20 to 1 against the president. The total eventually ran to 78,000 before exhausted secretaries stopped counting. Some 1,700 of the letters and cards sent to the White House were so abusive and threatening that they were turned over to the Secret Service. Congressmen also received thousands of letters and telegrams, many of which were inserted into the *Congressional Record*. Many called for Truman's impeachment: "IMPEACH THE IMBECILE." "IMPEACH THE RED HERRING FROM THE PRESIDENTIAL CHAIR." "IMPEACH THE JUDAS IN THE WHITE HOUSE WHO SOLD US DOWN THE RIVER TO LEFT WINGERS AND THE UN." "SUGGEST YOU LOOK FOR ANOTHER HISS IN BLAIR HOUSE." "IMPEACH THE B WHO CALLS HIMSELF PRESIDENT." One particularly vitriolic communication said that the American eagle had been killed "BY PARASITES KNOWN AS FIVE-PERCENTERS, MUSCLE-INNERS, TRAITORS, HOMOSEXUALS, PINKOS, SEX PERVERTS . . . AND THOUSANDS MORE PARASITES OF LIKE SPECIES."[39]

Congress reacted quickly, too. Although most Democrats defended the firing on constitutional grounds, Joe Martin and other conservative Republicans suggested that the president and his advisers, particularly Acheson and Marshall, should be impeached. Senator William Jenner said on the Senate floor that the United States was "in the hands of a secret inner coterie which is directed by agents of the Soviet Union." The gallery applauded, and Jenner went on to declare that "our only course is to impeach President Truman and find out who is the secret invisible government which has so cleverly led our country down the road to destruction." Orland K. Armstrong, Republican representative from Minnesota, described MacArthur's firing as "the greatest victory for the Communists since the fall of

China."[40] Senator Joe McCarthy, of course, held nothing back, saying that "the son of a bitch ought to be impeached" and that when he made his decision to fire MacArthur he must have been drunk on "bourbon and benedictine."[41] And Senator Richard Nixon was quick to claim that "the happiest group in this country will be the Communists and their stooges. . . . The President has given them what they have always wanted—MacArthur's scalp."[42]

Outside Congress, other leaders spoke up on the controversy. Socialist Norman Thomas said that "if MacArthur had his way, not one Asian would have believed that the U.S. has a civilian government," and Mrs. Eleanor Roosevelt stated that "I do not think that a general should make policies." General Eisenhower agreed, telling reporters that "when you put on a uniform there are certain restrictions you accept." But Thomas E. Dewey felt that the firing was "the culmination of disastrous failure of leadership in Washington," and Herbert Hoover lamented that "a strong pillar in our Asian defense has been removed."[43] At the United Nations and in European capitals, most leaders were relieved at the firing of the impetuous general, for many had long feared that his reckless actions would spread the war to engulf the rest of Asia and perhaps Europe as well. The *London Evening Standard*'s headline was an irreverent "Mac Is Sacked."[44]

The press was divided on the firing, but even many normally anti-Truman papers supported him on this one because of the constitutional principles involved. As for the public, Gallup polls showed that only 29 percent of the people agreed with Truman's decision. In many towns across the country flags flew at half-mast, Truman and Acheson were hanged or burned in effigy, patriotic organizations met and drafted resolutions condemning the president and calling for his dismissal, fundamentalist preachers assailed the president from the pulpit, and endless arguments ensued over the merits of the decision. In Seattle, Washington, a heated altercation over the firing ended with one man pushing another's head into a bucket of beer after he had criticized MacArthur, and in Los Angeles a domestic strife over the firing ended when the husband hit his wife over the head with a radio. In Florida, California, Michigan, and Illinois, state legislators passed official resolutions condemning Truman's actions and praising MacArthur. And when Truman threw out the first ball of the new season at Griffith Stadium in Washington, he was roundly booed, the first president to suffer such an indignity at a sporting event since Herbert Hoover made the mistake of showing up at the 1931 World Series.[45]

Meanwhile, General MacArthur was preparing to bring a dramatic end to a distinguished military career and perhaps open the door to the presidency of the United States. Before he left Japan, he was visited by Emperor Hirohito, who broke down in tears in the presence of the man who had helped defeat his country in World War II and had ruled it ever since. As

MacArthur's car traveled the twenty miles from the embassy to the airport, an estimated 1 million Japanese lined the road and bowed as his car passed by, and at Haneda airport the departing general was given a nineteen-gun salute. When his plane landed at San Francisco on Tuesday, April 17, he was greeted by a large crowd estimated at 100,000 people. He flew on to Washington the next day, and was met at the National Airport shortly after midnight by the Joint Chiefs of Staff, who had unanimously recommended his firing, and a crowd of around 12,000. He had been invited by Congress to address a joint session the next day, and he already had his speech ready.

The speech was scheduled for shortly after noon. Around 12:30, after his wife, Jean, and the senators had marched in and taken their seats, and excitement had built to a fever pitch, the general strode down the aisle to a standing ovation to deliver a thirty-four-minute speech that was interrupted thirty times by applause. In a dramatic but controlled address, he reiterated his standard views on the Korean War, emphasizing his belief that "war's very object is victory—not prolonged indecision" and that "in war, indeed, there is no substitute for victory." At the end of the speech he called on an old army ballad containing the refrain "old soldiers never die, they just fade away," to tell his mesmerized audience that "like the soldier of that ballad, I now close my military career and just fade away—an old soldier who tried to do his duty as God gave him the light to see that duty. Good-bye."[46]

When the speech was over, many congressmen, including some who had agreed with his firing, were weeping uncontrollably. Republican Representative Dewey Short of Missouri exclaimed that "we heard God speak here today, God in the flesh, the voice of God."[47] In New York Herbert Hoover said that MacArthur was "a reincarnation of St. Paul into a great General of the Army who came out of the East."[48] Similar reactions occurred all across the country, where all other activities seemed to have stopped as Americans gathered around televisions and radios at home, in the office, or wherever they happened to be to listen to the general's speech. Attendance at baseball games that afternoon was sparse, as people stayed home to hear or watch the speech, and those who did come out to the ballpark carried portable radios so they could catch the hero's words. The Boston Marathon, held at the same time as the speech, drew less than half of the 250,000 spectators usually present at the event, and many of those had radios. In the White House Truman, Acheson, and other top advisers watched the address on television, and while some thought that it meant more trouble for the beleaguered administration, Truman dismissed it as "a hundred percent bullshit" and expressed disdain for the "damn fool Congressmen crying like a bunch of women."[49]

After the speech MacArthur made a triumphal journey down Pennsylvania Avenue, which was lined with some 300,000 adoring spectators, while jet bombers and fighters flew in formation overhead. From Washington, the general moved on to a tour of New York, Chicago, Boston, and dozens of other American cities, always drawing large, adoring crowds. In New York, he was welcomed by an estimated 7 million people along a nineteen-mile parade route, eclipsing by far the receptions given any previous dignitaries, including returning aviator Charles A. Lindbergh and war hero Dwight Eisenhower. And all across the country, enterprising vendors cashed in on the general's notoriety with sales of souvenir pipes, buttons, pennants, statues, and busts, while recording companies put out a dozen versions of "Old Soldiers Never Die," including one by Bing Crosby.

The nation had never seen anything like it before. It was quite a homecoming for a man who had just been fired by his commander-in-chief for insubordination, who was regarded by the Joint Chiefs of Staff as a pompous egotist, who in the previous winter had made several serious miscalculations leading to a military disaster, and who could have plunged the world into a third world war if he had been allowed to widen the Korean War in order to achieve the victory he had so often claimed was within his grasp. Ironically, while Truman's popularity had reached a new ebb and MacArthur was being hailed as a risen god, the nation's top military leaders agreed with Truman, not MacArthur, and public opinion polls showed that most of the public also wanted to confine the war to Korea and not to widen it in the manner advocated by MacArthur. The emotional outburst surrounding MacArthur's firing and homecoming was primarily directed at a genuine American war hero revered for his contributions to victory in World War II. The MacArthur remembered by the public in April of 1951 was the MacArthur of "I shall return" fame, not the aging general who had become a legend in his own mind and could not accept the complexities of fighting a limited war in which, for larger political considerations, a military giant like the United States was forced to fight with handcuffs on against a small country like North Korea. The American people did not understand this either, and much of their sympathy for MacArthur was born out of frustrations over the problems of the Cold War and Korea and out of indignation that a great war hero could be so shabbily treated by a little man in the White House dressed in a business suit and two-toned shoes.

The furor over MacArthur's firing gradually abated, with the last chapter being written during the Joint Senate Foreign Relations and Armed Services Committee hearings held in May and June of 1951. Called to investigate the general's dismissal, these hearings brought an extraordinary debate over the entire range of American foreign policy during the previous decade. The first three days were devoted to testimony by the general himself, who repeated his arguments for widening the war and the frustrations he was forced to endure by a president who was fighting a "half war." There was also voluminous testimony on the other side from Truman's civilian and military advisers. Major support for Truman's position came from General Marshall, a rival of MacArthur for almost forty years, and from the members of the Joint Chiefs of Staff, particularly the chairman, Omar Bradley, who argued that MacArthur's war plans would have brought the risk of war with Red China and allowed Russia to stand by and pick up the pieces: "Frankly, in the opinion of the Joint Chiefs of Staff, this strategy would involve us in the wrong war, at the wrong place, at the wrong time and with the wrong enemy."[50] The hearings came to an end without a formal report and without proving anything except, perhaps, that the issues were extremely complex and that only in a democracy could such a debate occur.

By the end of the hearings the national outburst over MacArthur's dismissal had run its course. Partly because of the hearings, more Americans had become aware of the dangers involved in MacArthur's ideas and of the merits of the limited-war policies that the Truman administration was pursuing. Most people did not like it, they found it very frustrating, and deep down inside they wanted to win the war, but they resigned themselves to the continuation of the limited conflict until an honorable exit could be found. As for MacArthur, he spent the next year crisscrossing the country giving speeches defending his policies and warning the nation of the dangers of Truman's "half-win" and "appeasement" policies, but after he failed to wrest the Republican nomination from Eisenhower, he faded away to the board of directors of the Sperry-Rand Corporation. He died on April 3, 1964.

In the spring of 1951 the Korean War entered its last phase. The Truman administration, the United Nations, and General Ridgway were all committed to the continuation of a limited war aimed at restoring the status quo of a divided Korea. It was obvious that there would not be another drive northward to the Yalu, and after the United Nations forces repulsed two major communist offenses in April and May, it became equally obvious that there would be no further communist gains in the south. The war settled into a stalemate along the 38th parallel, with neither side able or willing to mount a breakthrough offensive.

On June 23, 1951, the Russian ambassador to the United Nations, Jacob Malik, proposed an armistice providing for a cease-fire and a mutual withdrawal of both forces to their respective sides of the 38th parallel. The United States, with MacArthur gone from the scene, was ready. Armistice talks began on July 10 at Kaesong but were moved five miles east to Panmunjom in October. Here they would continue for another two years while opposing negotiators argued over exact boundary lines and the repatriation of prisoners of war. While the negotiators talked, thousands of men continued to die on both sides as heavy fighting continued on the battlefields. The American people seemed resigned to the continuation of this limited war, to an acceptable number of weekly casualties, even to the streams of reports about the torture and brainwashing of American prisoners of war in the hands of the North Koreans and Chinese Communists. But the people's hearts were no longer in the war. Neither the soldiers nor the public could see much point in risking lives to take hills, little towns, or rice paddies of no apparent value, or of killing thousands of Chinese or North Koreans when there were millions of others up in China waiting to take their places as the killers of American boys. As the war-weariness continued it became increasingly apparent that the frustrations of "Truman's war" would probably bring a Republican victory in 1952. The war would not end until the defeat of Truman and the death of Stalin paved the way for Eisenhower and the new Russian regime to bring the "police action" to a conclusion in the summer of 1953.

The Korean War had a great impact on the United States. By the time of the armistice, 33,629 young Americans had died in battle and another 103,000 had been wounded. Politically, it brought more discord to a country and government already bitterly divided, ended any faint prospects of the passage of additional Fair Deal legislation, fed McCarthyism by providing to the McCarthyites more evidence of administrative "incompetence" and "treasonable activities," and played a major role in the Republican gains of twenty-eight seats in the House and five in the Senate in the elections of 1950 and in the Republican capture of both houses and of the presidency itself in 1952. Economically, it brought mixed results. It gave rise to an economic boom that caused employment to rise to a new high of 62 million, but it also promoted inflation, shortages of strategic military and industrial materials, wage and price controls, and an increase in income, excess profits, and excise taxes. It also brought profitable defense contracts to manufacturers all across the country, greatly contributing to the rapid growth of the military-industrial complex that would become so powerful during the decade.

The war also produced great military changes. It provided the rationale for the rapid implementation of an April 1950 National Security Council Report (NSC 68) calling for a massive military buildup to meet the Soviet challenge to world peace. Military spending rose from $14 billion in 1949 to $44 billion in 1953, when it made up 60 percent of the federal budget. The nation's military arsenal was greatly expanded, and military personnel rose from 590,000 in June of 1950 to 3.6 million by the time of the armistice. Close to 5.7 million men were put into uniform during the conflict, about one third of the total of World War II. Thus the Korean hostilities contributed to the militarization of American society, a trend that would continue throughout the decade.

At the same time, the American alliance system, limited to the NATO signatories and a few other nations at the beginning of 1950, was greatly expanded as the nation signed military and economic pacts with anticommunist countries across the globe. The United States became the official protector of the reactionary governments of South Korea, Nationalist China, and the Philippines, and the main financier of the French counterrevolutionary effort against Ho Chi Minh's communist insurgents in Indochina. The United States also signed mutual defense pacts with Australia and New Zealand and concluded a separate (excluding Russia) peace treaty with Japan permitting the Japanese to rearm and giving the United States the right to maintain military bases in that country. In 1952 the United States for the first time gave more military aid to Asia than to Europe, clear evidence that the Korean War and conflict with Communist China was causing the Cold War to shift from Europe to Asia and to take on global dimensions. Europe was not forgotten, of course. The administration sought to strengthen NATO, backed the rearmament of Germany, and reversed its anti-Franco stance so dramatically that by 1953 American military bases were established in Spain in return for American economic aid.

Influential as it was, the Korean War would have had an even greater impact on the nation had it not been fought before television had become a pervasive national force. The Korean conflict was reported primarily by newspapers, magazines, radios, and movie newsreels, much as the Second World War had been. Americans of the early fifties could not sit night after night eating dinner in front of their television sets while they watched American boys fighting and dying in a faraway Asian land and domestic war supporters and opponents battling one another in the streets. Unlike the Vietnam conflict in another distant Asian country in another time, the Korean War was not a living-room war but a more remote conflict that generated few pacifists or protestors but few ardent supporters either. Most Americans just wanted to get it over with.

But it would be almost two more years before it would be over with. Meanwhile, most people resigned themselves to the senseless stalemate while they took advantage of the jobs and consumer goods the war economy was helping to generate. They also sought diversions from the daily news about battlefield deaths, traitors in the State Department, and other nagging problems. And one of the greatest diversions they turned to was television, the new communications marvel that was sweeping the nation.

# 6

# *The Magic Box*

In 1939, when television was still in its infancy, a Harvard professor of electrical engineering, Chester L. Dawes, predicted that the new gadget would never catch on in the United States. There were too many technical problems involved in producing both indoor and outdoor programs, he wrote, and television had other built-in limitations that would prevent it from ever becoming as popular as radio. People could listen to radio while doing other things, but "television viewing is limited to a few persons, it must take place in a semi-darkened room, and it demands continuous attention." Because of these and other problems, he concluded, "the growth and future of television is highly uncertain at this time."[1]

But the passage of time soon embarrassed Professor Dawes and other television skeptics. In just a few short years television would emerge as a fully developed commercial medium, transforming the institutions and living habits of postwar America in very dramatic ways. No other invention, not even the motion pictures, automobiles, or radio, brought so much change to so many people in so short a time.

The invention of a magic box that could bring the world into the living room was an age-old dream that first became possible in the twentieth century. The early years of the new century brought the invention of the wireless and the first true motion pictures, and in 1907 *Scientific American*, sensing that pictures as well as sound could be transmitted through the air, became one of the first publications to use the word, "television." The twenties saw the development of the radio, sound motion pictures, the iconoscope, and other devices necessary for taking, transmitting, and receiving pictures. Experimental television broadcasts, including one in color, were made in the late twenties, and in the thirties NBC, CBS, and other radio leaders established experimental television stations that transmitted fuzzy pictures to the few people who had sets. By 1940 there were twenty-three experimental stations and about 10,000 television sets in the country, NBC and CBS were ready to obtain licenses for commercial public telecasting, and industry officials were expecting a bright future. But then the Second World War intervened, creating serious material and manpower shortages that caused many stations to close their doors, almost completely halted the manufacture of new sets, and practically froze television technology for the duration of the world conflict.[2]

At the end of the war conditions were ripe for the rapid expansion of television. Postwar Americans had more leisure time and purchasing power than ever before, and they continued to move into urban and surburban areas where they could be served by television stations. The growth of the American economy and the resulting increase in business profits freed billions of dollars for advertising, a necessary prerequisite for commercial programming. And finally, the rise of the suburbs and the marriage and population explosions created a large population of young couples with children who would be immediately attracted by television's possibilities as home entertainment and as babysitter. This link between television and children was quickly recognized by the television and advertising industries. In 1950, the American Television Dealers and Manufacturers' Association ran an advertisement in newspapers across the country reminding parents that "there are some things a son or daughter won't tell you. . . . Do you expect him to blurt out the truth—that he's really ashamed to be with the gang—because he doesn't see the same shows they see?" Having aroused the appropriate guilt feelings, the advertisement continues with "how can a little girl describe the bruise deep inside? . . . Can you deny television to your children any longer? Youngsters today need television for their morale as much as they need fresh air and sunshine for their health."[3] How, indeed, could you deny your youngsters a set, especially when it could become, in the words of Buckminster Fuller, "a third parent,"[4] entertaining the children while mother and father did other things, including watching television?

Television expanded rapidly between the end of the Second World War and the end of the Korean War, in spite of the freeze on the licensing of new stations imposed by the FCC between 1948 and 1952 in an attempt to solve interference problems and to provide for a rational planning and reallocation of channels. Sports events were popular in the immediate postwar years; in 1946 fans lucky enough to have television sets saw the Joe Louis–Billy Conn world championship fight, while in the summer of 1947 they were enthralled by the telecast of a Brooklyn Dodgers–Cincinnati Reds baseball game. Then in the fall of 1947 an estimated 3.9 million people—many of them gathered around small screens in bars—saw the World Series. The popularity of this event helped to sell thousands of new sets, while the appearance in 1948 of Milton Berle's *Texaco Star Theater* and other regular programs promoted the purchase of hundreds of thousands more. An average of 250,000 sets per month were bought between 1949 and 1952, and millions of other Americans were saving their money and eagerly awaiting the day when television stations would serve their region.[5]

The real expansion of television could not come, however, until the Federal Communications Commission lifted the freeze on new station licenses. When the freeze was lifted in 1952, there were only 108 stations in sixty-four cities beaming out signals to the 15 million households with television sets, but by 1956 the number of stations had grown to almost 500 and the number of households with sets to nearly 35 million, and by the end of the decade the number of stations had risen still further to 562 and the number of households with sets had jumped to almost 46 million. Whereas sales of new sets had gradually grown from around 7,000 in 1946 to 975,000 in 1948 and 3 million in 1949, they averaged over 5 million per year in the 1950s and in some years reached the 7.5-million mark. By the early 1960s, 90 percent of all American homes had at least one television set.[6] Never had a new product expanded so rapidly or so quickly become an essential part of American life. In just a decade and a half, television had become one of the most democratic of all inventions, owned by rich and poor, black and white, urbanite and rural dweller, illiterate and intellectual.

In the 1950s mass production and technological advances brought major improvements to television. The size of the screen was expanded from the 12-inch screens of the early days to 19 and 21 inches, portable sets were perfected, the cost of sets was reduced from the $500 to $750 range of the late 1940s to as little as $200 by the midfifties, and color television was introduced in 1953. Another important improvement came in 1951, when the completion of the coaxial cable provided for coast-to-coast transmission. On his first *See It Now* show on November 18, 1951, which telecast simultaneous pictures of the Brooklyn Bridge and the Golden Gate Bridge, opening up a new era in television broadcasting, Edward R. Murrow commented that "we are impressed by a medium through which a man sitting in his living room has been able for the first time to look at two oceans at once."[7] Murrow was not the only one impressed, for this dramatic telecast persuaded thousands of holdouts to go out and buy a television set. And finally, another major breakthrough came in 1956 with the development of videotape by RCA, Ampex, and Bing Crosby Enterprises, making it possible to tape shows in advance, to correct mistakes, to rerun shows, and finally to give them eternal life in syndication.

The rapid spread of television into millions of homes reveals that it had enormous appeal to people from all walks of life. Television brought inexpensive, convenient entertainment for the entire family. It was also passive entertainment, requiring little effort or thought, and for many people it provided a pleasurable way of relieving boredom, relaxing after work, passing time while waiting for the spouse to come home from work, or putting off doing scholastic homework, housework, or other unpleasant tasks. But most of all, it brought the world into the living room—news, sporting events, drama, comedies, circuses, political conventions, musicians, dancers—almost anything one wanted to see. It provided instant gratification, and it was not necessary to dress up, pay a babysitter, fight traffic, look for a parking space, go out into the rain or snow, or spend money. No wonder that by the mid-1950s the A. C. Nielson Company was able to report that family members in television homes were watching the set almost five hours every day.[8]

What did Americans watch on television in the 1950s? As would be expected in a sports-minded nation, spectator sports were popular from the very beginning. Two of the earliest televised programs were a Columbia–Princeton baseball game in 1939 and a Brooklyn Dodgers–Cincinnati Reds game later that same year (using only two cameras), and when commercial programming began after the war, baseball and other team sports were standard fare on the little screens being installed in living rooms across the country. But in the late forties and early fifties, team sports took a back seat to wrestling, boxing, and roller derby, all of which took place in small arenas ideally suited to the cameras and other technological limitations of television in those early years. Boxing was so popular in the first decade of commercial programming that the networks aired five or six boxing matches every week, and pugilists like Archie Moore, Sugar Ray Robinson, Rocky Marciano, Kid Gavilan, and Ezzard Charles became household names. So did Gorgeous George, a wrestler who possessed eighty-eight different satin costumes, numerous ermine jockstraps, and a valet who preceded him into the ring carrying his mimeographed towels, prayer rugs, and atomizered perfumes. And long before football and ice hockey had acquired their reputation as the premier examples of televised organized violence, male and female skaters were committing legal mayhem on the roller derby.

But the favorite shows from the late 1940s on were the comedy shows, many of which were simply television productions of old popular radio shows, featuring stars like Bob Hope, essentially a stand-up comic, and Jack Benny, who never failed to delight with his stock jokes about his violin playing, old Maxwell, and parsimoniousness. Then there was Milton Berle, whose slapstick comedy enthralled viewers every Tuesday night from 1948 through 1956 and who was so popular that in the early days of television he was known as Mr. Television and credited with causing thousands of people to go out and buy a television set. Sid Caesar, Imogene Coca, Carl Reiner, and Howard Morris, backed by such writers as Neil Simon, Larry Gelbart, and Mel Brooks, provided some of the best satire of the decade on *Your Show of Shows*, a favorite of even the harshest critics in its four-year run (1950–1954) of live entertainment from 9:00 to 10:30 on Saturday evening. These early days of live television were filled with dozens of other comedians, including Jackie Gleason, Red Skelton, Jimmy Durante, Dean Martin and Jerry Lewis, Phil Silvers, Burns and Allen, Red Buttons, Ernie Kovacs, George Gobel, Amos and Andy, and Garry Moore.

Of all the comedies of the day the most popular was *I Love Lucy*, which debuted on CBS in 1951 and continued as a weekly program on that network for the next twenty-three years. Featuring Lucille Ball as the scatterbrained wife of Cuban bandleader Desi Arnaz, and William Frawley and Vivian Vance as their neighbors Fred and Ethel Mertz, *I Love Lucy* took only six months to zoom past Milton Berle and Arthur Godfrey to become the top show on television. Restaurant owners, theater managers, civic clubs, and PTAs quickly learned to expect small crowds on Monday nights, when everybody was home watching Lucy. On January 19, 1953, when the real-life Lucy gave birth to a son, Desi Arnaz IV, almost 70 percent of all sets were tuned in to the pre-filmed Lucy show about the blessed event. The next morning General Eisenhower was inaugurated president on television before a smaller audience than had seen Lucy the night before. The success of the *I Love Lucy* show persuaded other Hollywood stars to end their boycott of what they considered an inferior medium and to turn their talents to television, and Hollywood producers, cameramen, and others quickly followed.[9]

In addition to comedy, television viewers also liked action shows, especially those with violence. Network programmers gave it to them in dozens of crime shows such as *Man Against Crime*, in which Ralph Bellamy played hard-boiled detective Mike Barnett, and *Dragnet*, which drew millions of viewers through its dynamic musical theme and the deadpan manner in which detectives Joe Friday and Frank Smith went about seeking "just the facts" as they slowly got their man. Westerns such as *The Lone Ranger* and *Hopalong Cassidy* were popular with children and many adults, too, from the late 1940s on, but beginning in 1955 these children's heroes were pushed aside by *Gunsmoke*, *The Life and Legend of Wyatt Earp*, *Cheyenne*, and dozens of other "adult" westerns and violent urban crime shows. Many concerned individuals and groups complained about the violence, feeling that it was especially harmful to impressionable children, but the network programmers seemed to sense what most viewers wanted and gave it to them—and the sponsors' money kept rolling in.

One of the most popular types of television shows in the late 1940s and

1950s was the variety show. Milton Berle's *Texaco Star Theater, Arthur Godfrey and His Friends*, Ed Sullivan's *Toast of the Town*, and several other similar shows provided a seemingly endless stream of comedy acts, singers, dancers, acrobats, puppets, jugglers, and dancing animals. Many of these shows went off the air by the midfifties, but some, like the *Toast of the Town* (retitled *The Ed Sullivan Show* in 1955) survived into the early seventies, fulfilling Fred Allen's prophetic quip that "Ed Sullivan will be around as long as someone else has talent."[10] A columnist for the *New York Daily News*, Sullivan featured middle-brow and high-brow talent, often sandwiching operatic arias or classical ballet between animal acts or appearances of All-American football teams or the West Point Glee Club. He deliberately introduced and promoted black talents such as Pearl Bailey and Louis Armstrong at a time when their appearances invariably provoked hate mail from the South, and he launched or promoted the careers of many new performers, including the comedy duo of Dean Martin and Jerry Lewis and singer Elvis Presley.

Music was also a popular staple throughout the fifties, with the nation's favorite singers appearing on their own shows or on the many variety and special shows of the decade. Perry Como was the most popular television singer of the decade, but Bing Crosby, Dinah Shore, Rosemary Clooney, Frank Sinatra, and many others trailed not too far behind. The orchestras and vocal groups of Fred Waring, Kay Kyser, and Lawrence Welk attracted large audiences, as did *Your Hit Parade*, which, from 1950 until rock 'n' roll brought its demise in 1959, featured Dorothy Collins, Snooky Lanson, Gisele MacKenzie, and other cast members singing the top ten songs of the week every Saturday night. And in a class all by himself was pianist Liberace, whose effeminate ways, candelabrum on the piano, and elaborate costumes brought large audiences, vicious ridicule, and the performer's lighthearted response that his critics hurt him so much that he "cried all the way to the bank."[11]

Talk shows were a favorite of many viewers in the 1950s. The best-liked and most imitated of these shows was *The Tonight Show*, which began on NBC's flagship station, WNBT-TV, as a local New York show in 1953. In 1954 the show and its host, Steve Allen, moved to the network, which gambled that television was changing the habits of millions of Americans and that they would stay up from 11:30 P.M. to 1:00 A.M. to watch Allen play the piano, interview guest stars, ad-lib jokes, involve the audience in conversation and skits, and do his famous man-in-the street interviews. Millions did stay up to watch, thus beginning one of the longest-running shows on television. A young comic named Jack Paar succeeded Allen in July 1957, and from then until 1962 he entertained late-night watchers with his witty conversation, interviews, comedy sketches, and running bouts with the network over what he could and could not say on television. In 1962 he was succeeded by the less controversial Johnny Carson, the most durable of all late-night hosts.

Daytime television in the 1950s took on a form that it would keep on into the 1980s: game shows and soap operas. Both were inexpensive to produce, both were very profitable, and both were aimed at the busy housewife who often could not take time to sit down throughout the entire show. Game shows featured attractive male hosts, flashing lights, and lots of noise—all designed to catch the attention of the housewife. Successfully transplanted to television from radio, soap operas moved slowly, with the plot unfolding over months and even years, so that busy homemakers could miss several episodes and still catch up. Daytime television also featured talk shows, children's shows, cooking shows, variety and audience-participation shows like Art Linkletter's *House Party*, and "most enjoyable tragedy" programs like *Queen for a Day* and *Strike It Rich*. On *Queen for a Day*, ordinary people suffering from sickness, accidents, poverty, or some other desperate problem, competed with one another in relating their sad stories to host Jack Bailey and to the studio audience, which then voted (by applause) for its choice to be Queen for a Day and to take home all the prizes. On *Strike It Rich*, hosted by Warren Hull, similar victims of life's misfortunes recited adversities in hopes that viewers would call the Heartline phone number with offers to help pay for an operation, rebuild a burned-out home, or provide a job for a widow or widower with six or seven poor children. Although such shows were widely ridiculed by critics and comedians, the studio and home audiences were often moved to tears by the plight of these unfortunates. But they tuned in again the following day.

Television tried to show that it could inform as well as entertain, and almost from the very beginning of postwar programming the networks tried to provide news and other instructive programs. In 1946 NBC introduced the first regularly scheduled newscast with a ten- to fifteen-minute newscast running three times a week, and in 1948 NBC and CBS both introduced nightly news programs. Veteran newsman Douglas Edwards anchored the CBS program for almost fourteen years, until replaced by Walter Cronkite in 1962, while on NBC John Cameron Swayze's *Camel News Caravan* ran until its replacement in 1956 by Chet Huntley and David Brinkley, whose Huntley–Brinkley report ran for almost fourteen years. The third network, ABC, tried several unsuccessful news formats before it settled on a copy of the two other networks in 1953 with John Daly as the anchor—the same John Daly, incidentally, who was moderator on CBS's immensely popular *What's My Line?* In the early days of television the nightly news was little more than a telecast of a radio news show, for the newscasters sat at a desk and read from a script that was occasionally illustrated by still photographs, maps, and charts. The absence of videotape until the late fifties made it difficult for the networks to show films of current happenings, since film had to be flown in to New York from wherever it had been taken. Throughout the decade the nightly news programs were only fifteen minutes long—they would not expand to thirty minutes until 1963.

In January of 1952 the nightly news programs were joined by a morning news and talk show with the debut of *Dave Garroway's Today Show*. Featuring Garroway as host, Frank Blair as newsman, and eventually a colorful group of weather girls, sportscasters, and other regulars, including a chimpanzee named J. Fred Muggs, the show was broadcast live from New York from seven to nine each weekday morning. *The Today Show* would be a morning favorite for many viewers for over thirty years and earn the record for the longest-running morning show.

In addition to nightly newscasts, the networks also telecast political conventions, presidential press conferences and speeches, informative documentaries like NBC's *Victory at Sea* and CBS's *You Are There*, and interview shows like Ed Murrow's CBS production *Person to Person*, which with Murrow as host took the American people into the homes of Liberace, the Duchess of Windsor, Marilyn Monroe, John Steinbeck, Margaret Mead, and other famous personalities. On Murrow's other show, *See It Now*, Murrow raised television journalism to a new height through his discussions and investigations of the major concerns of the day. Murrow often took on controversial issues, such as McCarthyism and the security case of J. Robert Oppenheimer, and he captivated millions of viewers with a show featuring his visit to front-lines GIs in Korea. Ironically, he also did a famous and controversial show on the link between cigarette smoking and lung cancer, from which Murrow, a chain-smoker on- and off-camera, would die in 1965. His cigarette was one of his trademarks, as was the way he ended each broadcast with the words, "Good night . . . and good luck."

Live drama flourished on television in the fifties, leading even the severest of television critics to concede that these shows alone justified the purchase of a television set and the labeling of the period as a Golden Age of Television. Live drama began in 1947 with *Kraft Television Theatre*, and by the early 1950s no fewer than eleven live drama series were on every week under such titles as *Playhouse 90*, *Robert Montgomery Presents*, *The United States Steel Hour*, the *Philco–Goodyear Playhouse*, and *Studio One*. Those who tuned in were treated to live presentations of such plays as Paddy Chayefsky's *The Bachelor Party*, Rod Sterling's *Requiem for a Heavyweight*, J. P. Miller's *The Days of Wine and Roses*, George Orwell's *1984*, and Reginald Rose's *Twelve Angry Men*. Most live drama originated from New York, the location of most television networks and studios and a great pool of talent from Broadway and other areas of entertainment. Each week, television viewers could see some of the best acting talent in the land in some of the best dramas of the time. In 1953, when millions tuned in to a *Hallmark Hall of Fame* production of *Hamlet*, the bard's famous play was probably seen by more people than had witnessed all of its other performances over the three and a half centuries since its birth.[12]

Unfortunately live drama thrived for only a relatively short time, for by the midfifties Hollywood had abandoned its early opposition to television and had begun to exploit the tremendous commercial potentialities of the new medium. Hollywood began to sell old movies to television, to produce shows designed especially for it, and to lure television dramatists and actors to do films for Hollywood. Eva Marie Saint, James Dean, Grace Kelly, Paul Newman, Rod Steiger, and many others who began their careers as television actors now turned to Hollywood, where they could make more money. Television lost some of its best talent, but in return it received a huge backlog of old films and new specially-made-for-television features that allowed them to fill up the time formerly taken by live drama. These films were cheaper to produce than live drama, allowed the editing of mistakes or occasional slips of obscenity, and brought big profits—they could be rerun an endless number of times before being put into syndication where they could run, presumably, forever. Furthermore, Hollywood could be counted on to turn out formula programs emphasizing action and exciting special effects and providing regular characters and situations designed to build audience and sponsor loyalty. From the midfifties on, talent, scripts, and money migrated from New York to Hollywood. Live drama and most other live shows died, and the quality of television, which in its early live years had shown so much creativity and variety, declined into formula programming aimed at reaching mass audiences and wealthy sponsors. Television, which began the decade with almost a dozen live drama series, ended it with over thirty westerns.[13]

From the beginning television was a commercial medium, and from the beginning it was attacked for being so by critics who seemed to forget that television was only following the commercial practices of radio, newspapers, and magazines, and that like them, it depended on advertising revenues for its very existence. A public already accustomed to radio commercials offered no resistance to television ones; after all, seeing supersalesman Arthur Godfrey hawk a product on television was little different from hearing him advertise it on radio—in fact, the visual effects made it more interesting, especially in the beginning, before the novelty wore off. By 1956, American companies were spending over $488 million a year on network advertising, and the three networks were amassing riches that would have been unimaginable in the golden days of radio. CBS's profits jumped from $8.9 million in 1953 to $22.2 million in 1957 and continued to climb afterward, while the television industry as a whole saw its profits rise from $41.6 million in 1951 to $244.1 million in 1960.[14] These were truly golden days for the networks and television stations.

The expenditure of such large sums of money on television helps explain why the new medium was so commercially oriented from the outset. These were prosperous times, there was a huge consumer market to be tapped, and advertisers had plenty of money to spend. Viewers were looked upon as a mindless herd that could be persuaded to buy almost anything by thirty-second or one-minute commercials appealing to their greed, egos, guilt feelings, or other conscious and subconscious desires. Since sponsors wanted as many people as possible watching their shows, the ratings system sprang up to measure the size of the audience and let the sponsors know where best to spend their advertising dollars. It was only a short step then to letting the ratings determine the content of the show and even whether it lived or died. The accuracy of the ratings compiled by A. C. Nielson and other ratings companies was sometimes questioned by media critics and executives; in 1953 RCA's David Sarnoff complained that "our industry from the outset has been plagued by ratings systems which do not say what they mean and do not mean what they say."[15] But his views were shared by few people in the industry, and totally ignored by the sponsors.

In these early days of television, sponsors were afraid of offending anyone who might buy their products. Therefore they insisted that the programs they sponsored contain no material that could conceivably offend any individual or group. There was to be no direct criticism of American capitalism and no mention of a class struggle within the country or the existence of racism or large numbers of poor people. Criticism of the American government and the American way of life—whatever that might mean—was to be avoided, lest the House Committee on Un-American Activities or some private superpatriotic organization rise up in arms. Discussion or portrayal of interracial dating or marriage or segregation was to be avoided, and the Civil War handled carefully, so as not to offend southerners. The clergy, lawyers, doctors, and other professionals were to be portrayed in a positive light, to prevent them or their professional organizations from causing trouble for the network and sponsors. Sex, too, was to be handled gingerly: Husbands and wives were to be shown sleeping in separate beds, sexual relations were to be referred to only in euphemisms, and the ultimate goal of most lovers was apparently to be a passionate kiss. Rape and homosexuality were absolutely taboo, of course. So puritan was the television code that Lucy's famous pregnancy was always referred to as an "expectancy" or some other euphemism.[16]

Throughout the fifties, sponsors' fears of controversial topics led to ludicrous attempts to interfere with programming. On John Cameron Swayze's *Camel News Caravan*, cameras were forbidden to show No Smoking signs, and the only individual who could ever be shown smoking a cigar was Winston Churchill—perhaps because it was so difficult to get a picture of the British hero without his famous stogie. On *Man Against*

*Crime*, sponsored by this same tobacco company, the writers were given mimeographed sheets detailing exactly how smoking was to be handled on the show: Criminals and other disreputable or undesirable types were not to smoke cigarettes; no one was to be given a cigarette to calm his nerves, since this would imply that nicotine was a narcotic; fires or arson were not to be shown, for this might remind people that cigarettes caused fires; and never, ever, was anyone to cough on a show. Another cigarette company advertising its new filter-tip brand insisted that the villain in the show smoke unfiltered cigarettes, and when a guest on *Do You Trust Your Wife*? replied that his wife's astrological sign was Cancer, the tobacco company sponsoring the show ordered it to be refilmed and the wife's sign changed to "Aries." And in one of the most contemptible of all such sponsor-ordered changes, the American Gas Association, backer of *Judgment at Nuremberg* on CBS's *Playhouse 90* show, objected to a comment in the script on Nazi victims being sent to their deaths in "gas ovens." Fearing that the public would confuse the Nazis' cyanide gas with the natural gas used in America for cooking and heating, the skittish sponsor forced the deletion of the words "gas ovens" from the script.[17] "The association of a product . . . with a villain, a murderer, or whatever," the association excused itself primly, "is certainly something to be avoided."

The impact of television was the subject of much concern and debate in the 1950s. Hundreds of books and articles appeared on the subject, commentators and panelists analyzed it on radio and television programs, principals and teachers agonized over it in faculty meetings, and parents discussed it between themselves and with other parents. Perhaps never have the effects of a new invention been debated so widely and so quickly after its introduction, probably because few other inventions had such immediate consequences. It was obvious from the very beginning that television was profoundly affecting American life, and many were troubled by it.

A good example of contemporary views on the influence of television in the first decade of its existence was contained in the September 2, 1955, issue of *U.S. News and World Report*, the conservative newsweekly. In a special article entitled "What TV Is Doing to America,"[18] the magazine summarized the results of its polls and its interviews with teachers, parents, doctors, sociologists, and other people across the nation. It found that television sets were on almost five hours per day in the average household, that housewives watched it the most, followed by adult males and then by children, and that over 75 percent of the programs watched were entertainment shows. Most of the viewers who were surveyed admitted that if necessary they would pay to have the television repaired before they would pay the rent and that they read fewer books and magazines than they did before they purchased the set. The magazine also reported that television had promoted interest in most sports but had caused a serious decline in attendance at indoor movies and minor-league baseball games, and that some experts believed that television was causing children to make poorer grades in school and to commit violent, even criminal acts. Finally, the special report concluded that television had some beneficial effects. It provided—if only people would watch—a great deal of information and educational programs, it enabled people to see and hear the politicians they were voting for, and it was contributing to the breakdown of regionalism in thought and language. It was also found to be a great comfort for travelers, who now had a way to pass lonely nights in their motel rooms, and for the aged, handicapped, sick, and other shut-ins.

As this and similar studies showed, television's effect on America was indeed immediate and dramatic. In the late 1940s and early 1950s, a family's purchase of its first television was a major event, akin to the arrival of the first child. After talking about it for weeks, discussing it with their neighbors, and shopping around for the one with the best picture and the best price, the family would finally make the big decision. Since the first set was usually a heavy console model, it was delivered by the retailer, and often the entire family, and perhaps even the neighbors (if they did not already have their own set) would gather around to watch the set being unloaded and installed, complete with the telltale antenna, which not only received television signals from the studio but also sent out a signal of its own: This family has a television. The arrival of the first set was an exciting event and a mark of status.

As soon as the set came into the house, television began to change the family's living habits. The set was usually placed in the living room, the traditional center of family life, where members had met to entertain guests or to listen to radio, play family games, work puzzles, read, or talk. The living room remained the center of family life, but the nature of family life changed. Traditional evening activities seemed forgotten as family members sat shoulder to shoulder, rarely speaking except to comment on the programs or to suggest turning to another channel. Visitors were often ushered in quietly, almost as intruders, taking their places in the silent vigil. People seemed to visit less, either because they did not want to miss their favorite programs or because they did not want to interrupt the viewing of others. They also tended to go out less, reducing the opportunities for formal and informal social gatherings and causing declining revenues for movie theaters, restaurants, some sporting events, and other amusements. So in spite of the television advertisements in newspapers and magazines showing family and friends gathered in a warm, cozy atmosphere watching television, the introduction of television into the home often caused a deterioration of family life and friendships. Television reached an audience of millions and provided the greatest shared experience in the history of mankind, but as

T. S. Eliot perceived in the early days of the new marvel, it was "a medium of entertainment which permits millions of people to listen to the same joke at the same time, and yet remain lonesome."[19]

Television also changed some other personal habits. In 1954, apparently in response to a great national need, the TV dinner appeared, making it unnecessary to interrupt favorite programs for the preparation and consumption of food. This dietary loss was also a social one, for family conversation, already relegated to commercial breaks during the evening hours, was reduced even more now that the need to gather in the dining room was eliminated. Even the most fundamental body habits were now regulated by television scheduling, according to the city engineers of Toledo, Ohio, who triggered anxiety in advertising circles in 1953 by releasing a study showing that the periods of heaviest water consumption came at the beginning and midpoint of every hour, when viewers apparently took advantage of the commercials and station breaks to visit the bathroom.[20] Studies of the time also showed that the average fanily stayed up later at night when it got a television set, and other studies claimed that for many couples lovemaking became less spontaneous and instead was scheduled for times when favorite programs were not on or when the set had been turned off for the evening. In 1954, critic Louis Kronenberger, who often complained that television was filling up people's lives with passive entertainment and driving out many worthwhile activities, suggested only half tongue-in-cheek that "I don't know that it can lick the problem of sex, though with time it may simply extinguish the desire for any."[21] Other critics at mid-decade suggested that television was well on its way to becoming the opiate of the masses, fulfilling a prediction made in Aldous Huxley's 1932 novel, *Brave New World.*

From the very beginning most of the concern about the effects of television centered around what it was doing to the nation's children, who were watching not just *Captain Midnight*, *The Howdy Doody Show*, and *Kukla, Fran and Ollie*, but adult programs as well. All across the country parents, psychologists, and other experts on child behavior complained that television was causing children to neglect their schoolwork, to become passive and uncritical receivers of information, to read less, to acquire short attention spans, to stay up too late, to neglect healthy play activities, and to procrastinate in doing their homework or daily chores or even eating their meals. Some feared that television was robbing children of their childhood by exposing them so early and so frequently to the adult world shown day after day on the magic tube, and a growing number of adults—74 percent according to a 1954 Gallup Poll—believed that the constant parade of violence on the home screen was a major constributor to the growth of violent behavior, juvenile delinquency, and outright criminal behavior among the nation's young people. Many experts agreed with child psychologist Arthur R. Timme, who said that television violence was causing children to "grow up with a completely distorted sense of what is right and wrong in human behavior."[22]

The validity of all these assertions was not at all clear in the fifties and still is not today. And there were many observers of television and child behavior who pointed out the positive benefits of television. In a 1955 article, *Better Homes and Gardens*[23] claimed that television helped children to relax, kept them off the streets, increased their vocabularies, widened their interests, and made them better informed about the world at an earlier age than any generation in history. The evidence to back these statements was not clearly documented either. But what was clear by the late fifties was that the generation of children growing up with television would be greatly different from previous generations, and that television, along with rock 'n' roll, rising prosperity, and the population boom, would be one of the major contributors to these differences and to the much-heralded "generation gap" of the 1960s.

Some other effects of television were easier to determine, like its impact on the movie and radio industries. Hollywood lost half of its customers between 1947 and 1957, forcing the closing of many indoor theaters in cities all across the nation. A similar fate was predicted for radio, but radio endured and even prospered—in fact, the number of stations grew dramatically, from 1,522 AM and 158 FM stations in 1948 to 3,079 AM and 530 FM stations in 1957. Radio survived television by changing. Since television had captured most of the evening audiences, and since radio could not compete with television in drama, comedy, and variety shows, radio began to concentrate on music, news, talk shows, weather, public-service announcements, and specialized shows for specialized audiences. Radio played up its role as something to listen to while doing other things, such as driving, working, or playing. Its biggest audiences came during the morning and afternoon hours; in the evenings people turned to television.[24]

By the mid-1950s it was becoming increasingly clear that television was having a major impact on politics. For the first time in history, millions of Americans were able to watch their leaders and candidates in action—on the news, at the political conventions, in press conferences, on interview shows like *Meet the Press*, on paid political advertisements, and on special congressional investigating committees like Senator Estes Kefauver's Special Committee to Investigate Organized Crime. They could watch General MacArthur addressing the Congress after he had been fired by the president, Senator McCarthy badgering witnesses and in turn being humiliated by army counsel Robert Welch, vice-presidential candidate Richard Nixon saving his political career through his emotional Checkers Speech, Eisenhower announcing the end of the Korean War, and Mike Wallace grilling Governor Orval Faubus of Arkansas and the Imperial Wizard of the Ku Klux Klan. Television bred a familiarity with politicians and issues and transformed obscure figures into national heroes or villains. Unfortunately, it also made appearance more important than substance, as candidates were valued now as much for their television style as for their political and governmental skills.

In many of the debates over the influence of television, many argued that the new medium was not doing enough to educate the general population. But television did teach people, though not in a way that educators and other hopeful critics had wanted. Through its programming, television taught many subtle lessons: that blacks existed only as manual laborers, domestic servants like Jack Benny's Rochester, or buffoons like Andy Brown and Kingfish on *Amos 'n' Andy*; that men held the real jobs while women were scheming and scatterbrained housewives like Lucy, sexy but wacky secretaries like Irma Peterson, or old-maid schoolteachers like Miss Brooks; that guns and other weapons settled disputes between adults; and that Americans were screaming, greedy idiots like the contestants on daytime game shows. Through its commercials, television taught that Americans could and should buy all kinds of products for their health, looks, and happiness, and that they should aspire to own many products that they could not afford and often really did not need.[25] And through its programs and commercials, television taught the nation's impoverished black minority that there was a wonderful world of white, middle-class consumer comforts and conveniences largely denied to the black community, a realization that would contribute to the rising aspirations of blacks and to the civil rights revolution of the second half of the decade. Television taught all of these things, and at the time encouraged a homogeneity of interests, tastes, opinions, and consumption all across the country.

In the latter half of the decade television declined from what it had been in the golden age of the late forties and early fifties, when it had demonstrated a great variety in its programming and most shows were done live. As the decade progressed, the networks' fear of controversy, the entrenchment of the ratings systems, and the ability of Hollywood to provide inexpensive action shows caused television to resort to formula programming that would guarantee the highest ratings and attract the most money from sponsors. More and more, television relied on quiz shows, sporting events, situation comedies, and, very importantly, action series produced by Hollywood—the westerns and cops-and-robbers shows featuring spectacular chase scenes, fistfights, shootings, and other violence. By 1960, television had degenerated to the violent level of *The Untouchables*, a very successful show appearing on ABC, which was trying to improve its ratings with this and other action series, such as *77 Sunset Strip*, *The Rebel*, *Cheyenne*, *The Rifleman*, and *Hawaiian Eye*. Quinn Martin, producer of *The Untouchables* and several other such shows, went along with the violence, though he complained to his writers that there was too much repetition in the mayhem. He told one writer that killing people by running them down with cars had been overdone and that other methods should be employed. "I like the idea of sadism," he wrote, "but I hope we can come up with another approach." The popularity of *The Untouchables* was not lost on the other two networks, which tried to compete with violent shows of their own.[26]

By the time John F. Kennedy took office, many people inside and outside the industry were complaining about the decline of television in the second half of the fifties, but probably no one expressed what had happened to television better than Newton N. Minow, chairman of the FCC, in a speech to the thirty-ninth annual convention of the National Association of Broadcasters on May 9, 1961. Calling the modern period the Television Age, he told his audience that "when television is good, nothing—not the theater, not the magazines or newspapers—nothing is better. But when television is bad, nothing is worse." If they would sit down before their sets and watch one complete day of programming, he told them, they would "observe a vast wasteland." He went on to say that "you will see a procession of game shows, violence, audience participation shows, formula comedies about totally unbelievable families, blood and thunder, mayhem, violence, sadism, murder, western badmen, western good men, private eyes, gangsters, more violence, and cartoons. And, endlessly, commercials—many screaming, cajoling, and offending. And most of all, boredom."[27]

The Golden Age of Television, if indeed the fifties had ever been that, had come to an end.

# 7

# Home, Sweet Home

A revolution in foreign policy, a war in a far-off Asian country, a Great Fear sweeping the land, a revolution in telecommunications—the United States in the Truman years was obviously a nation in upheaval. But these were not the only forces transforming the country in the postwar period, for the nation was also undergoing dramatic social and economic changes. Perhaps nowhere was this better illustrated than in the shifts occurring in the distribution, composition, and size of its population. Americans were moving from farms and small towns into cities and suburbs, migrating to the South and West, getting married in larger numbers and at earlier ages than they had for decades, and having children at a record rate that defied all the predictions of the experts. In short, the United States was experiencing a demographic revolution that would profoundly affect its history for decades to come.

An examination of the demographic statistics for the 1950s helps to reveal the amazing transformations occurring in America's population. The total population jumped by almost 30 million, from 150.7 million in 1950 to 180 million in 1960—the largest numerical increase for any decade in the nation's history. The exodus from the farms, which had begun in earnest during the depression years, accelerated in the postwar period, with the total farm population dropping in the fifties from 23 million (15 percent of the total population) to 15.6 million (8.7 percent of the population). This fed the decades-old trend toward urbanization, as the percentage of urban dwellers rose from 63.7 in 1950 to 70.1 by the end of the decade. But what is perhaps most significant about the population gains of the decade is that 83 percent of the total population growth occurred in the suburbs. In New York City 1.5 million people moved to the suburbs in the 1950s, while outside Los Angeles, Orange County more than tripled in population, rising from 216,224 to 703,925. Similar growth occurred around many other cities across the country, until by 1960 almost 60 million people, making up about one third of the total population, resided in suburban areas.[1] All across the nation, people were moving from rural areas or central cities into the outskirts of town, turning pastures or forests into housing developments, shopping centers, and industrial parks.

People seemed to be on the move everywhere, not just from rural and urban areas into suburbia. Continuing a trend begun in the 1940s, industry and people continued to migrate from the Northeast to the South, particularly the Southwest, and to the Pacific Coast. Florida's population boomed, fed by the tourist industry, the influx of retirees, and the rapid expansion of the fruit industry, while in Texas the rapid growth of the petrochemical industry caused a rise in the population, wealth, and power of the Lone Star State. But the fastest growth occurred in California, as millions poured into that state seeking sunshine and jobs in agriculture, aircraft manufacturing, electronics, and other industries engaged in defense work. California was the fastest-growing state in the union in the fifties, enabling her to bypass New York to become the most populous and wealthy state by 1963. Throughout the fifties Americans rhapsodized about the "California phenomenon" and moved there in such large numbers that the state entered the sixties suffering from overcrowding, pollution, freeway congestion, overlapping and paralysis of governmental authorities, and other problems associated with too much growth too fast.[2]

Wherever they moved, Americans tried to avoid the problems of the city and the isolation of rural areas by moving to the outskirts of towns and cities. Suburbs had existed long before the 1950s, of course. Even in ancient times, people who could fled the large cities for the more peaceful life of the urban perimeter, but this kind of life-style was possible for few people until the early twentieth century, when transportation advances made the commuting life possible. But even then, suburban life was available chiefly to the upper middle class, who built comfortable suburban homes on roomy lots or, if they were truly wealthy, grand estates in exclusive wooded areas. It was not until the late 1940s and early 1950s that millions of working-class Americans obtained the wherewithal and the mobility that allowed them to flood into the suburbs.

The dramatic rise of the suburbs was made possible by several factors. It was partly caused by the rapid population growth—young couples with children needed two- or three-bedroom homes to house their growing families, and they wanted them in areas outside the central city so they could have lawns and playgrounds. It was encouraged by the federal government, which facilitated home buying with VA and FHA loans allowing for low down payments, low-interest-rate mortgages, and other easy terms. It was fostered by private lending institutions, such as the nationwide network of savings and loan associations, which also offered easy credit. It was furthered by federal and state governments, which constructed freeways, highways, and suburban streets and roads to facilitate travel between home and work, the shopping centers, and other destinations. It was promoted by the automobile industry, which turned out millions of automobiles at affordable prices, for without widespread ownership of automobiles, suburban life on a large scale would not have been possible. Finally, suburban growth was encouraged by the housing industry, which developed new techniques in construction and sales that brought low-cost housing within the reach of millions of young home buyers and of older ones who had been forced to postpone buying a home during the hard times of the depression or the material shortages of the war years.

A severe housing shortage existed at the end of the Second World War, but in the postwar period ingenious home developers rose all across the country to develop new ways of meeting the crisis in home construction—fast. Chief of these was William J. Levitt, who had originated the techniques of building standardized, low-cost housing while constructing some 2,000 units for the navy during the war. After the conflict ended, he and his sons revolutionized the housing industry by constructing entire new towns on land that had once been pototo fields, pastures, or forests. Like Henry Ford, the Levitts discovered that most Americans would trade variety and style for affordability and function, so they brought the assembly-line method to housing. The land was bulldozed flat, then covered with standardized houses on standardized lots connected by standardized streets. Trees and shrubbery were systematically added after the houses had been completed. By using a uniform floor plan, seven different color choices, the same basic exterior, as many precut or prefabricated materials as possible, standard appliances, and other cost-cutting techniques, the Levitts could offer a house with 721 square feet of floor space and a fully equipped kitchen for a little less than $8,000. Levittowns sprang up quickly on Long Island (with a population of 70,000 by 1953), then in New Jersey, Pennsylvania, and other parts of the country. Thousands of people who had formerly been unable to buy a house now became homeowners. Levitt and Sons made millions of dollars, and William J. Levitt, who liked to call his firm "the General Motors of the housing industry," became a national figure. On July 3, 1950, he appeared on the cover of *Time* magazine, which hailed him as the seller of "a new way of life."[3]

Other developers knew a good thing when they saw it, and imitators of the Levitts multiplied all across the country. Thousands of new communities sprang up, complete with their own churches and schools and neighborhood recreational facilities such as swimming pools, tennis courts, and playgrounds. Almost 2 million new homes were started in 1950, and for the rest of the decade the number of new housing starts averaged around 1.5 million a year before dropping off to 1.3 million in 1960 as the housing shortage ended. Almost 25 percent of all existing homes in 1950 had been built in the previous ten years, and the number of homeowners had jumped during that decade from 23.6 million to 32.8 million. The great majority of new homes built in this time were located in the suburbs—in fact, 11 million of the 13 million new homes built between 1948 and 1958 were located in the suburbs.[4]

The Levitts were reputable builders, but many of their imitators were not, causing the dreams of many new homeowners to turn into nightmares. Illegal or certainly unethical and shoddy building practices produced homes with faulty wiring and plumbing, cracked walls and ceilings, flooded basements, uneven floors, peeling paint, sinking floors, leaking roofs, cracked driveways, and malfunctioning septic tanks. Often cheap linoleum was substituted for expensive tile in bathrooms and kitchens, plywood was used in place of more expensive and durable hardwoods, and refrigerators and other appliances were placed in such tight spaces that the doors could not be opened. Insulation and other materials that could not easily be seen were skimped on or eliminated altogether, built-in appliances were not connected to their electrical or water supplies, bathtubs were not joined to the sewer line, and flowers sprouted in the living room in the cracks between the floor and the walls. Other evidences of skimping were harder to detect, like that of the Baltimore builder who was able to erect ninety-four houses on a development originally zoned for only ninety. How? By simply cutting one foot off the planned width of sixty of the houses.[5]

Most of the suburban development homes were copies or modifications of three basic styles: ranch, Cape Cod, or split-level. Architects accustomed to designing more stylish homes for wealthier clients called the new suburban homes ugly little boxes, and most of them would have agreed with author John Keats, who wrote (with considerable exaggeration) that "for literally nothing down—other than a simple two percent and a promise to pay, and pay, and pay until the end of your life—you too . . . can find a box of your own in one of the fresh-air slums we're building around the edge of America's cities." Sociologists and other critics of American life claimed that the people in these boxes were just as uniform, unimaginative, and boring as the houses themselves. Keats promised that if you bought one of these homes "you can be certain all other houses will be precisely like yours, inhabited by people whose age, income, number of children, problems, habits, conversation, dress, possessions and perhaps even blood type are also precisely like yours."[6]

Many of the suburban houses were no larger than apartments, since costs could be held down by eliminating a porch, dining room, usable attic or basement, or a third bedroom. Some young couples of middle-class origin realized that their homes were not as spacious or as well-constructed as those of their parents or grandparents; they constantly complained about the things that went wrong with the home, they found the neighbors' children and dogs tiresome, and they longed to move into a larger house in a better neighborhood. In time, most did.

To others, with nothing but a railroad tenement to compare it to, a Levittown house was the realization of a dream. It gave them the pride of owning their own home, and it was a good place to rear the children. To make their carbon-copy house even more "theirs," they could paint the front door or shutters a different color from their neighbors' or put up a little fence or plant different shrubs or buy a distinctive doorbell chime. In time, they might add a wing to their little house or a full second story, or re-side it with new material.

The population characteristics of these new suburbs differed markedly from that of the general population. They usually contained few poor or wealthy people, few if any blacks, and very few single adults, elderly people, or childless couples. Most development communities were inhabited by couples between the ages of twenty-five and thirty-five with one or two small children. Many of the men were veterans, which is not surprising since VA loans were one of the principle sources of home financing, most held middle-class jobs (as managers, salesmen, professionals, small business men) or were skilled craftsmen, and in the beginning a high percentage were college-educated, thanks to the GI bill. The average income of most of the men fell between $4,000 and $7,000, higher than that of the general population, but many of them still held second jobs in order to pay their mortgages and support their growing families. And finally, many suburbanites were transients, who moved frequently from one city or development to another as they rose up the economic or corporate ladder. In many communities, For Sale signs were almost as common as dogs and children, and all across the country men were joking that "this is only the first wife, first car, first house, first kids—wait till we get going."[7]

The absence of the extended family and the transient nature of suburban life turned many suburbanites into rabid organizers and joiners. Lacking close, long-term ties, suburbanites sought identity and companionship in PTAs, churches, swimming pool clubs, bridge clubs, political organizations, civic clubs, writing clubs, ceramic clubs, photography clubs, and dozens of other excuses for getting together with a group. "Get together a half-dozen like-minded Americans," Frederick Lewis Allen wrote in 1952, "and pretty soon you'll have an association, an executive secretary, a national program, and a fund-raising campaign."[8] In one community a minister calling on a new couple was unperturbed when they informed him that they were atheists: "Well, you should have a club," he said. "I'll see if I can't find some others and get you all together."[9] In addition to formal club meetings, neighbors frequently got together for dinner, cards, or some other games, and often larger groups met for backyard barbecues or block parties, where the beverage of choice was usually beer rather than wine or liquor. Group activities also extended to dozens of mutual sharings of tasks that in older communities and earlier times were done by family. Residents formed car pools and babysitting pools, helped each other with home repairs, and quickly came to one another's aid in time of emergency or sorrow.

There was another side to this friendliness and cooperation, of course, for the developers' building codes, the common background of suburban residents, and the close living arrangements tended to encourage conformity and keeping up with the Joneses. People tended to buy similar automobiles, clothing, mailboxes, and toys for their children. There was strong pressure to keep the grass mowed and to maintain the external appearance of one's home, and those who failed in these elementary housekeeping functions were sometimes criticized and even paid visits by neighbors who suggested that they might try to keep up the place a little better. People were also expected to think alike and to be part of the group rather than act as individuals. In some developments, those who read too many books, expressed unusual opinions, thought too much, or refused to go along with silly games at parties were often regarded as "too brainy" or "stuck up" or "too good for the rest of us." Once branded as not being part of the group, such individuals were often ostracized and relegated to living in a state of uncomfortable tolerance with their neighbors.[10]

The center of suburban life, especially during the day when the men (and many working wives) were at work, was the housewife. Many of the books and magazines of the day, particularly the women's magazines, tended to glorify the suburban housewife, portraying her as a happy babymaker and homemaker, who cheerfully bore children and took care of them, the house, and an untidy husband while he worked to support them all. *Time* magazine idealized her as "the key figure in all suburbia, the thread that weaves between family and community—the keeper of the suburban dream." The suburban housewife, *Time* continued, "with children on her mind and under her foot, . . . is breakfast getter, . . . laundress, housekeeper, dishwasher, shopper, gardener, encyclopedia, arbitrator of children's disputes." She was also the community chauffeur, sharing with other wives the tasks of funneling children to school, boy and girl scout meetings, ball games, dance lessons, and parties, and driving herself and her friends to PTA meetings, bridge parties, and other community activities. "If the theory of evolution is still working," *Time* jested, "it may well one day transform the suburban housewife's right foot into a flared paddle, grooved for easy traction on the gas pedal and brake."[11]

It all seemed so idyllic—the husband was the breadwinner, the wife kept the house and took care of the kids, and she was the beneficiary of his labors—the more he made, the more conveniences and luxuries she would have. And in the spirit of "togetherness," the husband did his part around the house, too. While many women were happy with the role society had conditioned them to play, many others were not. Although few women publicly complained, and magazines and books continued to carry stories of the happy, ideal housewife, many women lived lives of quiet desperation, bored with their children, with their housework, with the television programs they watched to while the day away, with their neighbors' incessant chatter about children and the newest floor wax, with their husbands who spent too much time on their work or with male friends. In an age that put such a high premium on what kind of job a person held and how much money he made, many women felt that, as mere satellites of their husbands, they were wasting their lives. This was especially true for college-educated women, who had had glimpses of a different world, but it was not confined to them. No wonder many housewives buried themselves in mindless television game shows and soap operas, sought volunteer work ouside the home, turned into closet alcoholics, became the biggest buyers of the new tranquilizers, or sank into a deep depression for which their husbands or male physicians could find no explanation or cure.

The suburbs were in the forefront of the nationwide emphasis on marriage, children, and family life. The fifties was a time of unprecedented sentimentalization of marriage and family life, and young men and women were going to the altar in unusually large numbers at unusually tender ages. In 1900, the median age of Americans at the time of their first marriage was 25.9 for males and 21.9 for females. The median showed a slow decline as the century progressed, and by 1940 it stood at 24.3 for males and 21.5 for females. At the end of the war, the marriage rate boomed, and the median age at first marriage began to drop, and in the 1950s the median age steadily declined to 22.8 for males and 20.3 for females. By 1953, almost one third of American females had married by the time they reached the age of 19, and by 1960, almost 75 percent of all women between the ages of 20 and 24 were married. And in an age that still looked upon divorce as a personal and even moral failure, both older married couples and young marrieds tended to stay married—the divorce rate, which had been rising ever since the 1920s and had peaked in 1947, leveled off in the early fifties to around one divorce for every ten marriages and remained at that level until it began a slow rise at the end of the decade.[12] Perhaps as a portent of what was to come, America's favorite television couple, Lucy and Desi Arnaz, got a real-life divorce in 1960.

What was causing Americans to rush into marriage in such large numbers and at such young ages in the fifties? A major factor, of course, was the great cultural emphasis on romantic love—the churches, schools, movies, television, novels, magazines (especially slick-paper magazines for women), comic books and other elements of American society constantly glorified romantic love, glamorized marriage and the happy home, and held up marriage and parenthood as the norm for every happy, well-adjusted American to strive for. The prosperity of the period also made it easier for young people to take on the economic responsibilities of marriage, the GI loans and flexible credit policies of lending institutions made it possible for young couples to buy a house, and the GI bill made it unnecessary for veterans to postpone marriage during their college years by providing them with allowances for their wives and children along with the payment of college expenses. The larger number of women entering college also contributed to the marriage rise by putting young men and women in close proximity to desirable mates—after all, many women of the time were conditioned to regard college as simply a happy hunting ground where they could find a husband who was likely to be wealthier and more successful than the boy back home who never went to college.[13] Many women apparently rushed into marriage because they feared that since women outnumbered men, and since so many young men were in military service, they had better find a husband before they were all gone. In 1955 a *New York Times* article on early marriages maintained that "a girl who hasn't a man in sight by the time she is 20 is not altogether wrong in fearing she may never get married."[14] And finally, the tensions and complexities of the new atomic age undoubtedly contributed to many young people's decision to seek the companionship and security of marriage.

The image of marriage that most young Americans seemed to have in the fifties was the one portrayed on the popular television show *The Adventures of Ozzie and Harriet*. Originally a radio show, this program, featuring the real-life family of Ozzie and Harriet Nelson, moved to television in 1952, where it reigned for almost fifteen years and 435 programs. The Nelsons were an ideal family—a mother who was always home (usually cooking meals or baking cookies in the kitchen), a father who apparently worked outside the house but was usually home and always had time to spend with the family, and two clean-cut teenage boys, David and Ricky. It was a family characterized by love, warmth, togetherness, honesty, respect, and stability, with all the members playing proper family roles. It was, in short, the ideal patriarchal family of the thirties and forties, not the family of the fifties in which the mother often worked and the cohesiveness of the family unit was being undermined by the demands and problems of a complex, tense, atomic age.[15] The popularity of this program, along with that of similar family shows like *Father Knows Best*, suggests that the fifties, the period which would later be the object of so much nostalgia, was itself an age in which the complexities of modern life were already leading people into nostalgic yearnings for an earlier age.

As Americans idealized family life in the fifties, they began to emphasize something called "togetherness"—a concept apparently coined by *McCall's* magazine in its 1954 Easter edition.[16] In theory and practice, "togetherness" meant that young couples now spent more time together than married people had in the past and that family roles were becoming less differentiated as couples shared the duties and burdens of maintaining a household and rearing children. The husband was now more home-oriented, assuming more of the burdens of childrearing and housekeeping than ever before, and wives were performing more traditional masculine tasks, like mowing the lawn or painting the living room. But it was the husband who was supposed to have changed the most. Magazines ran article after article on the new husband, who was shown working and helping around the house, attending classes with his wife on childbirth and child care, and being present in the delivery room when the blessed event occurred. In 1956 *Parents Magazine* wrote that "today, Dad finds families function best on a partnership basis. He shares in the daily care and companionship of small-fry—all sizes. As for discipline, he's replaced the 'woodshed' with a do-it-yourself workshop where everyone has fun."[17] And in the interest of family life, *The New York Times* reported in 1954, many young couples were forgoing movies, nightclubs, and other outside forms of entertainment for home activities, such as barbecuing in the backyard, playing family games, fixing up the marriage nest, and of course watching television.[18] In 1953 one student of suburbia found that many of the young couples he interviewed were almost ecstatic over television's beneficial effect on family life. Many claimed that television was "something we can share" and that it even "saved our marriage." One happy housewife told him that "until we got that TV set, I thought my husband had forgotten how to neck."[19]

Important as it was, "togetherness" was not the only purpose and function of marriage—married people were supposed to have children. After all, had not God in the very beginning exhorted mankind to "be fruitful, and multiply, and replenish the earth"? American women in the 1950s, in fact in the twenty years following World War II, took this command seriously. The birth rate, which had declined in the depression years of the 1930s to 19 per 1,000 women, began to rise during World War II until it reached its peak in the midfifties at 27 per 1,000 before it began to decline. The number of births per year, which stood at only 2.6 million in 1940, began to rise during the war, but the real boom began after the conflict ended: From 1946 to 1950 an average of over 3.6 million children were born each year, and from 1950 on there was a steady rise to the 4-million mark in 1954 and to an all-time high of 4.3 million in 1957—an average that year of one baby every 7 seconds, proud census officials pointed out. The birth rate stayed above 4 million until 1965, when it dropped to 3.8 million and began a steady decline as Americans entered a new demographic age, the time of the "baby bust."[20] The high birth rate, coupled with great progress in medical care, added almost 30 million to the total United States population.

The baby boom of 1946–1964 was not supposed to happen, or at the least was not supposed to last so long or produce so many children. In the United States, as in most other Western countries, the birth rate had steadily declined in the twentieth century, and many people, including government officials and professional demographers, had worried that the nation would experience a disastrous decline after World War II and would not have enough manpower to maintain the country's prosperity and world power. When women began to have children in large numbers after the war, population experts attributed the high birth rate to the pent-up demand of the war years and other temporary demographic aberrations, and confidently predicted that it would be short-lived. The birth rate did level off and decline in most Western countries in the late 1940s and early 1950s, but in the United States births continued to boom right down to the mid-1960s, confounding most of the experts. Among Western nations, only Canada, Australia, and New Zealand shared this aberration with the United States, which in some years had a birth rate higher than that of most of the underdeveloped countries, where the much-heralded population explosion was taking place.[21]

What was causing this big baby boom that was reversing long-term trends and shattering the predictions and reputations of demographers everywhere? As they examined the indisputable evidence, saw it mounting each year, and reexamined some of their cherished conceptions about birth rates in modern Western societies, the population experts began to come up with the explanations. Part of the answer was, of course, the satisfaction of pent-up demand, as after World War II and the Korean War young couples who had delayed marriage or having children now entered into homemaking and babymaking. The marriage boom inevitably fed the baby boom, and now not only were more people marrying and marrying earlier, but they were also having children at a younger age and having more of them. The ideal number of children was two, but in these days before "the pill" and other reliable contraceptives, many young couples wound up with three or four children. The prosperity of the times contributed to the baby boom, since young couples could afford to move into marriage and parenthood much easier than young marrieds could in the depression and war years, and the government promoted the baby boom by providing the GI benefits in education and home purchasing that helped eliminate the need to delay marriage or parenthood until education was finished or a large down payment was saved for a house large enough for a family. Finally, and very importantly, young people in the fifties were under the great influence of the Procreation Ethic, which held that marriage is infinitely preferable to being single, that single people are abnormal, that married couples should have children unless medical or financial problems prevented it, and that a couple should never have just one child. All of these factors, demographers finally agreed, were leading the United States to defy all the canons of population science by experiencing a population explosion that was supposed to happen to peasants in India, China, and Latin America, not to prosperous couples in the world's most industrialized and modern nation.[22]

Pregnant women seemed to be everywhere, especially in the suburbs, where housing developments were often nicknamed Fertile Acres and pregnancy was referred to as the Levittown Look and "our greatest industry." New attitudes about pregnancy seemed to be growing rapidly. In contrast to their mothers and grandmothers, who talked of sex and pregnancy in hushed tones and in euphemisms like "a wife's duty" or "in a family way," and avoided going out in public during pregnancy, suburban women of the fifties talked openly about sex and pregnancy, shared information and fears, proudly went to supermarkets and other public places in stylish maternity clothing especially designed to display the pregnant condition rather than hide it, and attended prenatal classes for advice and exercise, often accompanied by their husbands. Pregnancy was often the main topic of conversation when women got together, and it was celebrated as the greatest period in one's life, a time to be shared and openly discussed.

One of the biggest television events of the decade was the series of shows surrounding Lucy's pregnancy on the *I Love Lucy* show, and the joys of pregnancy and motherhood were frequently celebrated on other television shows and in the popular press. In its 1956 Christmas edition, for example, a *Life* magazine article on "The First Baby" pointed proudly to the fact that 4.2 million children had been born that year and that 1 million of these were the first babies for their parents. In the article, pictures and text lovingly depicted the pregnancy of Mrs. Georgette Mapes, of Mount Kisco, New York, as she tries on maternity clothes lent by a friend, shops for baby clothes with her husband, redecorates the baby's room and bassinet, struggles to rise from the sofa because of the extra twenty pounds she has gained during her pregnancy, gets settled in the hospital, holds her new child, and uses the telephone to tell all her friends about the new arrival.[23] Is there any wonder that young married couples who had no children were frequently asked when they planned to have them, or subjected to rude questions about the nature of their "problem"? Is there any wonder that childless couples or unmarried adults sometimes felt a little abnormal?

The baby boom had an immediate and profound impact on American society. Probably the most immediate effect was that it created a whole new consumer market: The fifties was a prosperous decade for manufacturers of maternity clothing, baby furniture, diapers, toys, baby food, bikes, clothing, washing machines, clothes dryers, and televisions, the new electronic babysitter. In 1958 alone, total toy sales reached $1.25 billion, and proud parents spent $5 million just for bronze-plating baby shoes and another $50 million for diaper services. In that same year *Life* magazine estimated that the average parents of a new baby would spend in the first year of his life about $800 for diapers, clothes, toys, medicine, soaps, formulas, milk, clothing, and other items. Looking at 4.3 million children born that year, *Life* predicted that they "represent a backlog of business orders that will take decades to fill."[24] America was bullish on babies, and businessmen rubbed their hands in anticipation of the profits each year's new crop of babies would bring.

Almost as quick to feel the effects of the baby boom were the nation's schools. The first wave of the baby boom generation began to enter the elementary grades in the early fifties, creating a shortage of classrooms and teachers that would follow them each year as they went from grade to grade, through high school, and finally into college in the early 1960s. Each year the entering class at every grade level was larger than the one the year before: Between 1946 and 1958, the number of students in grades 1 to 8 alone increased from 20 million to 30 million.[25] In the 1950s, the state of California, which accounted for an astounding 20 percent of the nation's population growth in the fifties, was opening up a new school on the average of once a week, but it still was not enough, and the problems of the largest state were being repeated, though usually not quite so acutely, in the other states of the union. By the early 1950s the nationwide teacher shortage reached 72,000, and it continued to soar with each passing year. The nation spent an astonishing $2.5 billion on its schools in 1958, and by 1964, when the babies born at the peak of the boom had reached school age, almost 25 percent of the nation's population was enrolled in the public schools.[26] In addition to creating classroom and teacher shortages, this tremendous influx of students would be partly responsible for the great problems the schools began to face in the second half of the fifties and throughout the sixties, when they tried to offer too many services to too many people, and were forced to become the vanguard of the desegregation movement and to assume other complex social responsibilities.

The baby boom was also causing problems in other areas. There was a shortage of doctors and nurses to treat the illnesses of this generation; female physicians, who often went into specialties connected with children, were in particularly short supply—not many were being trained, and many who had completed their training were taking time out, like thousands of nurses, to have their own children. Municipal recreation departments had trouble providing enough playgrounds and equipment, and other public and private organizations dealing with large numbers of children had trouble taking care of them all. From 1950 to 1960, for example, the number of girl and brownie scouts jumped from 1.8 million to 4 million, cub scouts from 766,635 to nearly 2.5 million, and Little League baseball teams from 766 to 5,700.[27] The nation was struggling with the nearly impossible task of assimilating a huge army of children.

Never in American history had a generation of children been so much the center of attention and so catered to as this generation born in the prosperous, child-centered years of the fifties. "Nothing is too good for the children" was a strong rule in most households, and it was used to justify all kinds of decisions—to buy a bigger house so the children could have a room of their own, to move close to a good school, to buy a television, to maintain a lifeless marriage, and to buy the millions of dollars' worth of goods and services that Americans needed for their children or were told by Madison Avenue that they needed. There was more than a little truth in the assertion, often made at the time, that America had become a "filiarchy" in which grandparents, parents, professionals, businesses, and service industries concentrated on satisfying—some said indulging—the wants and needs of the children.[28]

The patron saint of the filiarchy was Dr. Benjamin Spock, whose *Common Sense Book of Baby and Child Care* was a best-seller when it first appeared in 1947, sold almost a million copies every year in the fifties, and was eventually translated into twenty languages. In the mobile society of the fifties, millions of women were no longer near their mothers or grandmothers and could not turn to them for advice as the many generations before them had, so they turned to friends or to Dr. Spock. In his books Dr. Spock took an informal, relaxed, common-sense approach to childrearing that emphasized loving and other positive approaches rather than punishment in order to control and mold behavior. This approach would later be labeled "permissiveness" by people who blamed the good doctor for the way some of these children turned out.[29] His guilt in this matter was certainly questionable, but less debatable was his role in reinforcing the sexism of the times, through his teaching that women with children should be full-time mothers and should not be distracted by hobbies or jobs or careers, especially during the first three years of the child's life. Devoted maternal care, he argued, gave children the security and comfort they needed and produced good, well-adjusted children, while the lack of it produced problem children. Some experts of the time debated the validity of his teaching, but many women were induced by his books to forgo outside interests for motherhood or else developed guilt feelings about leaving the children with a sitter or at a nursery while they pursued careers or plunged into volunteer work.[30]

Whatever happened to the baby-boom generation, to the 76.4 million children born between 1946 and 1964? They grew up, of course, and in the process of growing up and entering young adulthood they profoundly affected the country's history, not just in the fifties but in the decades since then and in the decades still to come. Because of its huge numbers, this would be the single largest generation in the country's history, constituting almost one third of the nation's population in the early 1980s. Called War Babies, Spock Babies, the Sputnik Generation, the Vietnam Generation, and the Me Generation, this is the generation that fed American prosperity by its consumer needs, created the youth culture of the fifties and sixties, rode the first wave of rock 'n' roll, crowded the schools and colleges, participated in the first desegregation experiments in the public schools, marched and demonstrated in the name of civil rights and dozens of other causes, and fought and protested the Vietnam War. It was taught that it was an important generation, it acted like it was an important generation, and it was an important generation, important enough to lead *Time* magazine to choose the Under-25 Generation, male and female, as the Man of the Year for 1966.[31]

But by 1966 this generation was already running into trouble because of its sheer numbers. The baby boomers were facing overcrowded conditions not only in the schools but everywhere they turned, forcing them into fierce competition for places in graduate and professional schools, for jobs, for promotions, for housing, and for mortgages. Growing up in a time of prosperity in a world that seemed to be made for them, they entered the adult world in the 1970s to experience energy shortages, inflation, high interest rates, high unemployment, and other problems that would lead many of them to have to settle for a lower level of living than they had expected. And because there were so many of them, and because they themselves turned the baby boom into the baby bust by drastically reducing the birth rate, they face an uncertain future, when there may not be enough workers able or willing to pay their Social Security retirement benefits, for just as they grew up together, they will also grow old together.[32] As one of the best analysts of this generation has pointed out about the baby-boom generation, "What had once seemed its greatest strength—its overwhelming size—has turned out to be its tragedy."[33]

Although much of the attention given to suburbs in the fifties centered around its effects on housing, marriage, and children, the rise of suburbia was also transforming other areas of life as well. This could especially be seen in the effects it was having on America's large cities. As people moved to the suburbs, many cities, such as Washington, St. Louis, Detroit, and San Francisco, actually lost population in the central city. Very importantly, most of those who left were middle- and upper-class whites, leaving the core city composed primarily of the poorer, less-skilled, and less-educated blacks,

Puerto Ricans, and other minority groups. By 1960, for example, 40 percent of Newark and almost 50 percent of Washington were black.[34] Those who were left behind by the rush to the suburbs would not be a part of the prosperity and optimism of the fifties; instead, they sank into the poverty, despair, and alienation that would contribute to the rising crime rate, riots, and other great urban problems of later decades.

The flight of middle-class whites cost the cities billions of dollars in desperately needed tax revenues, which the influx of poor blacks and other minorities could not make up. Public transport, too, was hurt, since suburbanites tended to drive their cars in to work rather than to rely on commuter trains and buses, which often did not service far-out areas and in any case were not as convenient as one's own car. With declining ridership and revenues, public transportation could not maintain its facilities and services and declined in comfort, reliability, and number of routes. In New York City, for example, railroad commuters rode an estimated 277 million miles in 1950 but only 203 million miles in 1960, and the number of commuter railroads in the nation dropped from forty-six to thirty during the decade.[35] The prosperity of the cities suffered still further declines as industries began to locate near expressways in outlying areas, often in "industrial parks," seeking to be near the labor supply and to escape the high land prices and taxes of the inner city.

The growth of the suburbs also gave rise to the suburban shopping center, which brought major changes in the nation's shopping habits and created still more economic problems for the inner cities. Although shopping centers had appeared in a few large cities in the 1920s, it was not until the postwar period that they grew up outside the cities to serve the suburban customer. Usually built near the expressway and centered around one or two large department or discount stores, shopping centers provided retail stores (often branches of national chains), specialty shops, supermarkets, restaurants, barber and beauty shops, banks, and other services traditionally found in the inner center—plus a convenient large parking lot. By the mid-1950s there were over 1,800 shopping centers in the United States and hundreds more in the planning and construction stages.[36] Since the city had come to the suburbanite, he no longer saw any need to go to the city, which in addition to losing population and taxes was now losing retail customers as well. More and more the inner city was becoming a place to work but not to live or shop, as commuters swelled the cities in the daytime but rode back to the suburbs at night, leaving behind cities that took on the appearance of ghost towns between the evening and morning rush hours.

As the editors of *Fortune* pointed out in a series of articles collected and published in 1955 as *The Changing American Market*, the rise of suburbia was also creating a "lush new suburban market." With average family incomes of $6,500, almost 70 percent higher than that of the rest of the population, suburbanites had money to spend on both necessities and luxuries. Suburbanites constituted the best market for new homes, furniture, lawn furniture, backyard barbecue equipment, appliances, do-it-yourself books and materials, televisions, automobiles, and other necessities of suburban life. They were having millions of babies, opening up an almost insatiable market for baby food, clothing, toys, and other goods and services aimed at children. They also led the rest of the country in what economists were calling the trend toward "casualization" in clothing, spending millions of dollars each year on slacks, dungarees, casual shoes, sport shirts, skirts and sweaters, stadium coats, trench coats with zip-in linings, sports jackets, summer suits and shirts, ski outfits, lounging pajamas, summer pajamas, loafers, golf shoes, and dozens of other items that did not exist a bare ten years before or if they did exist could not have been afforded by the middle class. Fortune correctly predicted a huge increase in sales of casual wear and of clothes made of rayon, acetate, and the synthetic fibers like nylon, Orlon, and Dacron.[37]

Suburbanites also led the country in another revolution in eating habits: the shift away from diary products, grains, vegetables, and fruits to more meat and more canned and frozen vegetables. Prosperous Americans were eating more meat, especially beef—per capita consumption of beef rose from around 60 pounds in 1950 to almost 100 pounds by decade's end.[38] During that same period the per capita consumption of dairy products dropped from 29.4 to 25.6 pounds per year, fresh fruits from 107.4 to 101.5 pounds per year, and fresh vegetables from 139.5 pounds to 125.2 pounds per year.[39] Prosperity and an understandable desire to spend less time in the kitchen led more and more families, especially the young mothers in the suburbs, to use more convenience foods. Canned foods had been around for a long time, of course, but now young cooks had another boon: frozen foods, which first appeared in large quantities and varieties in the early fifties. Frozen-food production quadrupled between 1947 and 1953, and the most popular of all frozen products in the early fifties, orange juice, jumped in production from 560,000 gallons in 1947 to 70 million gallons in 1953—and still Minute Maid and other suppliers could not meet the demand. In 1954, just in time to meet the needs of the busy mother and television watcher, came the TV dinner, which prompted the editors of *Fortune* to marvel at how "in many supermarkets you can now buy a complete turkey dinner, frozen, apportioned, packaged. Just heat and serve."[40]

The shift to convenience foods also affected the children, as more and more young women began to feed them preprocessed canned baby food, which sold poorly when it first appeared in the depression, when times were hard and the birth rate low, but then picked up in sales in the Second World War and boomed along with the population explosion. As late as 1942 American babies were eating only 20 pounds of canned baby food per capita each year, but by 1953 annual per capita consumption had risen to 55 pounds.[41] Older children were eating more and more presweetened cereals (first introduced in 1949), and both children and adults were consuming more snacks—candy, cookies, potato chips, soft drinks, and other sweets—than ever before.[42]

Changes in eating habits combined with other changes in the American life-style to revolutionize the grocery business. Women wanted to shop less frequently, buy more on each shopping trip, and choose from a greater variety of products, and American grocers responded to these wishes by providing the large supermarket, where in air-conditioned comfort women could choose at leisure from a wide and growing variety of food and nonfood items. Supermarkets greatly expanded in size as they provided a large parking lot, rest rooms, lunch counters, and delicatessens, automatic doors, larger grocery carts, and other services. By 1953 there were over 17,000 supermarkets (stores with annual sales figures in excess of $375,000 per year) constituting only 4 percent of all grocery stores but accounting for 44 percent of all food sales. The day of the small, friendly grocer was passing, though as late as 1953, 44 percent of all grocery stores, primarily the small ones, still provided delivery service.[43]

The rise of suburbia was obviously bringing great changes to the American scene, and naturally suburbanites were the targets of much analysis by academics and the popular press. The flood of literature reveals just how new suburban life was, and how much it was influencing the country. Much of the literature was critical, especially that written by academic sociologists, who saw suburbia as an architectural wasteland inhabited by conformists, materialists, drab organization men, hordes of children, bored housewives, and harried husbands pushed to the brink of exhaustion by the daily commuting and corporate grind and worries over paying the bills incurred with keeping up with the Joneses. To others, however, suburbia was almost a new frontier—a refuge from the crime and other evils of the city; a place to lead an idyllic family life centered around backyard barbecues, block parties, the sounds of happy children, and volleyball and touch football; and a haven where the problems of fighting world communism took a back seat to that of neighbors who would not cut their grass or control their children or dogs. As *Time* magazine wrote in 1960, "the fact surrounding all the criticism and self-searching is that most suburbanites are having too good a time to realize that they ought to be unhappy with their condition."[44]

Whatever the truth about the merits of suburban life, there was one indisputable fact about suburbia: It was here to stay, and it was radically changing the face of America.

# 8

# *Time for a Change?*

The United States was a prosperous and progressive nation in 1952, but many of its people were weary. They were weary of the Cold War, of the Korean conflict, of high taxes, of inflation, of battles between labor and management, of communism and corruption in high places. They were weary, too, of President Truman, whom they blamed for most of these nagging, persistent problems. By the spring of 1952 his popularity had dropped to a low of 26 percent, and if he had chosen to run for reelection in the fall, he would surely have been defeated. To many voters, it seemed that it was time for a change, time to get Truman out of the White House and the Democratic party out of Washington after a reign of twenty years.

Partisan that he was, Truman would never have entertained the notion that the Democrats should be swept out of Washington, but he had decided as early as 1949 that he would not seek reelection in 1952. But not wanting to become a lame duck so early or to start a donnybrook among his possible Democratic successors, he did not publicly reveal his decision until the Jefferson–Jackson Day dinner at the National Guard Armory in Washington on March 29, 1952, when he told the assembled Democratic faithful that "I do not feel that it is my duty to spend another four years in the White House."[1] The reason he usually gave for this decision was that in a republic two terms were long enough for any man to hold the powerful office of the presidency. "There is a lure in power," he wrote in his diary. "It can get into a man's blood just as gambling and lust for money have been known to."[2] But his decision to reestablish a tradition broken by Franklin D. Roosevelt was certainly influenced by other considerations as well. Bess did not want him to run again, his popularity had fallen to a new ebb, and the job had been a tremendous burden. He often referred to the office as a "mankiller," and on one occasion he said that he was not going to run again because he "didn't want to be carried out of the White House in a casket."[3] The sixty-eight-year-old president was ready to go back home to Missouri.

Most liberals, including many of Truman's close friends and advisers, were relieved at his decision to forgo a bid for a second full term, which they felt would be disastrous and humiliating for him and for the party. The party now had the opportunity to choose a fresh candidate for the 1952 race. When the Democrats met in convention at Chicago's International Amphitheatre in late July, ten days after the Republicans had met in the same arena to choose General Eisenhower, a battle broke out among Governor Adlai Stevenson of Illinois, Senator Estes Kefauver of Tennessee, and several other contenders. On the third ballot the party nominated Stevenson, Truman's personal choice, and later tried to balance the ticket by selecting a segregationist senator, John Sparkman of Alabama, as his running mate. There was no southern walkout as in 1948, but many southern Democrats formed "Democrats for Eisenhower" organizations, and some southern senators and governors supported Eisenhower over their own party's nominee.

Sensing victory, the Republicans had met in the second week of July in the Chicago International Amphitheatre in the first presidential nominating convention ever nationally televised. As expected, a battle erupted between the conservative southern and midwestern wing of the party, supporting Senator Robert A. Taft of Ohio ("Mr. Republican"), and the liberal eastern wing, backing what it felt was a sure winner in the nonpolitical but enormously popular Dwight D. Eisenhower, the hero of the D-Day invasion in World War II and the supreme commander of the NATO forces in Europe. But once again in 1952 the top prize eluded Taft, as Eisenhower won an easy first-ballot victory. To give the party geographical and philosophical balance, he chose as his running mate Senator Richard M. Nixon, who had won a reputation as a fighter against subversion, a supporter of containment, and an effective critic of the Democrats, whom he had been lambasting for months for being too soft on communism and for mishandling the Korean War. According to one journalist, the young senator was a "Republican meld of Paul Revere and Billy Sunday."[4]

Eisenhower was a virtually unbeatable candidate. A very popular war hero, he had turned down offers of the nomination by both parties in 1948 and had been approached by both parties again in 1951 before announcing in January of 1952 that he was a Republican. Eisenhower disliked politics, but he entered the presidential sweepstakes in 1952 out of a strong sense of duty and out of the fear that the foreign policy of the Taft Republicans would bring disaster to the nation. Eisenhower had been a strong supporter of containment, agreeing with most of the foreign policy conducted by Truman and the Democrats since 1945, while in domestic affairs he was a moderate conservative who wanted to maintain most of the New Deal measures but to slow down their expansion and their rising costs. But he was a neophyte in politics, especially in domestic matters, and at the beginning of the campaign he shied away from debates on domestic issues with his better informed and more articulate opponent. His avoidance of issues and affection for generalities and patriotic homilies led reporters to remark that Eisenhower was "crossing the 38th platitude again."[5] But he was enormously popular, and became even more so as the campaign proceeded and a friendly press gave him a steady stream of favorable publicity, causing Stevenson to complain about "the extent to which we are developing a one-party press in a two-party country."[6] Eisenhower tried to pose as an independent candidate above partisan politics and issues, as the leader of a "great crusade" to restore America's freedoms, decency, and greatness. But he supported all Republican candidates, including Senators Joe McCarthy and William E. Jenner, even though he disapproved of their low tactics in the battle against domestic subversion and had been infuriated by their attacks on his old friend and mentor, General George C. Marshall. He even appeared on the same platform with Jenner in Indiana, and in McCarthy's home state he was persuaded by his advisers to omit from a Milwaukee speech a reference to Marshall's patriotism and greatness.

As the campaign proceeded, Eisenhower began to forsake his nonpartisan posture and to direct more attacks at the Democrats along the lines of the formula suggested by Senator Karl E. Mundt—$K_1 C_2$ (Korea, Communism, Corruption)—but he left most of the dirty work of attacking the opposition party to Nixon, John Foster Dulles, and other combatants who supplemented the Mundt formula with attacks on inflation and high taxes. But Eisenhower, too, began to talk about getting rid of the "crooks and cronies" in Washington and replacing the Fair Deal with "an Honest Deal."[7] Abandoning his earlier support of containment, he began to endorse Dulles's call for the "liberation" of the "captive peoples" of Eastern Europe and other communist-dominated areas and to attack Truman's conduct of the Korean War, which had emerged as the major issue in the campaign. He had no specific solution for the war and had, in fact, supported Truman's intervention in the conflict and the firing of MacArthur, but he assailed the Democrats for bungling the war and pursuing a "no win" policy. And like the other members of his party, he kept reminding the voters that twenty years of Democratic rule had carried the country to the brink of disaster and that it was time for a change. To refute the Democratic charge that the Republicans would dismantle the popular New Deal measures, he pledged again and again that he would not "turn back the clock" on social reform.

Eisenhower's campaign was carefully managed by his advisers and by the large advertising firm of Batten, Barton, Durstine, and Osborne. From the very beginning, the focus of the campaign was on the image of the candidate rather than on the content of his speeches. His arrivals, departures, speeches, press conferences, and other campaign activities were carefully orchestrated down to the smallest detail to present the image of a smiling, God-fearing, knowledgeable, and folksy man, an experienced man of action (rather than an ivory-tower intellectual like his opponent), a man who could be trusted to restore things as they ought to be in an America that had somehow gotten off the track. A major feature of his campaign was the making of fifty 20-second television commercials, filmed in one day at the Transfilm Studios in Manhattan, with Eisenhower reading from large, hand-lettered cue cards so he would not have to wear glasses. Most of these television spots began with a supposedly ordinary citizen asking Eisenhower a question, such as, "Mr. Eisenhower, what about the high cost of living?" And he would reply from the cue cards: "My wife, Mamie, worries about the same thing. I tell her it's our job to change that on November fourth." Eisenhower did not like the way his image was being sold in these ads. Between takes, as he sat talking to his brother Milton, he was seen several times shaking his head and saying, "To think that an old soldier should come to this."[8] But he reluctantly acknowledged that these spot commercials, costing $1.5 million to put on the air, got maximum exposure for the money. They concentrated on one issue that viewers could remember, oversimplified the issues, and made the popular general an even more familiar personality in homes all across the country. They also demonstrated television's power to sell the right "image," helping to revolutionize campaigning in subsequent years.

Eisenhower's opponent was a reluctant candidate who really preferred, as he said right up to the time of the nomination, to serve another term as governor of Illinois, but he finally succumbed to party pressures and his own sense of duty. The grandson of the first Adlai E. Stevenson, who was vice president under Grover Cleveland, the Chicago lawyer was educated at Choate, Princeton, Harvard, and Northwestern. He had held several posts under Franklin Roosevelt, serving as the assistant secretary of the navy and as a State Department official participating in the conferences leading to the founding of the United Nations. He served under Truman as a delegate to the United Nations in 1946 and 1947 before winning the governorship of Illinois in 1948, his only electoral victory but one which allowed him to earn a reputation as a liberal, effective governor. Fifty-two years old in 1952, he was urbane, scholarly, witty, articulate, and charming—a patrician in politics, it was often said. Old and new liberals alike regarded him as one of their own and spoke of him in glowing terms. Max Lerner thought that Stevenson was "the first figure of major stature to have emerged since

Roosevelt," while journalist Richard Rovere went even further and claimed that "his gifts are more imposing than those of any President or any major party aspirant for office in this century."[9]

Although, in these days of the Korean War and Red Scare, Stevenson seemed like a shining liberal, and is often fondly remembered as such, he was essentially a moderate who was actually more conservative than Truman on many domestic matters. He campaigned for the extension of the New Deal–Fair Deal programs, called for the revision but not the repeal of the Taft-Hartley Act, and took a moderate position on civil rights aimed at winning the support of southern blacks and whites. He was a staunch defender of civil liberties, opposing the McCarran Internal Security Act and the methods of McCarthy and his followers. "We must take care not to burn down the barn to kill the rats,"[10] he often said, and he frequently attacked those "who use 'patriotism' as a club for attacking other Americans" and who "hunt Communists in the Bureau of Wild Life and Fisheries while hesitating to aid the gallant men and women who are resisting the real thing in the front lines of Europe and Asia."[11] But he also supported Truman's loyalty programs, enforcement of the Smith Act, and the firing of communist teachers.[12] In foreign affairs, he was a Cold Warrior, differing little from Truman. He viewed Russia as the main threat to world peace and the United States as the bulwark of freedom throughout the world, and he supported Truman's containment policies and a negotiated "peace with honor" in Korea.

Although he defended the Truman administration against the Republican charges of communism and corruption, Stevenson also tried to disassociate himself from the discredited administration and to run as an independent candidate, emphasizing issues and running above politics, much like his opponent. He set up his campaign headquarters in Springfield, Illinois, chose his own party chairman, and had little contact with the president during the campaign. This angered Truman, as did Stevenson's inadvertent and unfortunate reference to "the mess in Washington," which was immediately exploited by the opposition.[13]

The "mess in Washington" was difficult to refute, for throughout most of his second term Truman's administration had been plagued by charges of corruption. Congressional investigating committees had revealed that several individuals high in the federal bureaucracy were involved in collecting fees to put businessmen seeking government contracts in touch with the right people in the right government department, that officials in the Bureau of Internal Revenue were accepting bribes from individuals seeking to avoid prosecution for delinquent or fraudulent tax returns, and that officials in the Reconstruction Finance Corporation were involved in influence peddling or questionable loan making. Although Truman's honesty was beyond reproach, the charges of corruption had reached into the White

House itself: Truman's close friend and military aide, Harry Vaughan, was accused of accepting a deep freeze, White House aide Donald Dawson was accused of intervening to secure Reconstruction Finance Corporation loans to businessmen engaged in questionable business practices, a former White House stenographer who was now the wife of an official of the Reconstruction Finance Corporation was also accused of receiving a mink coat worth almost $10,000 from suspicious sources, and White House appointments secretary Matthew Connelly was charged with accepting bribes in tax-fixing schemes.

For over three years the press and Truman's political opponents had a field day with the corruption charges. The press often compared the "Truman scandals" to those of the days of Harding and Grant, while few campaign speeches were given without mention of deep freezes, mink coats, five percenters, tax fixers, influence peddlers, and the rest of the "mess in Washington." Actually, the scandals were minor and in no way comparable to the Republican scandals of the Grant and Harding eras, but Truman had erred in moving too slowly, attacking the partisan motives of the investigators, and loyally sticking by his friends and appointed officials, maintaining for months that "my people are honorable—all of them are."[14] Eventually the executive office and various congressional committees moved to root out the scandals. The Reconstruction Finance Corporation and Bureau of Internal Revenue were thoroughly reorganized, and sixty-six employees of the Bureau of Internal Revenue and the Justice Department were fired or allowed to resign. Matthew Connelly was convicted of accepting bribes, and eventually nine employees of the Bureau of Internal Revenue and Justice Department, including an assistant attorney general, T. Lamar Caudle, went to jail. But the damage done to the Truman administration, and to the Democrats' 1952 presidential fortunes, was irreparable.[15]

In his nomination speech Stevenson had said: "Let's talk sense to the American people. Let's tell them the truth." The American people should be told that the future involved no "easy decisions" but "a long, costly, patient struggle against the great enemies of men—war and poverty and tyranny."[16] And Stevenson did try to talk sense to the American people. He and his advisers, not an advertising agency, ran his campaign, and he employed Arthur Schlesinger, Jr., John Kenneth Galbraith, and other liberal wordsmiths to help him with his speeches, which he read instead of using a Teleprompter. He did very few spot television commercials, declining to be sold "like a breakfast food."[17] Many of Stevenson's addresses sounded like college classroom lectures rather than campaign speeches, and he was often accused of talking over the heads of the people. But many liberals and intellectuals were attracted to his approach, especially to his subtle wit. In Bakersfield, California, he coined a phrase he would often repeat: "I have been tempted to make a proposal to our Republican friends: that if they stop telling lies about us, we would stop telling the truth about them."[18] In Fort Dodge, Iowa, he quipped that "Senator Taft is the greatest living authority on what General Eisenhower thinks."[19] And after hearing that a wooden platform from which Eisenhower had been speaking had collapsed, Stevenson said: "I'm glad the General wasn't hurt. But I wasn't surprised that it happened—I've been telling him for two months that nobody could stand on that platform."[20]

Stevenson's sense of humor appealed to many, but it was disliked by many others. It was not the folksy humor that so many Americans liked, but the sophisticated, subtle, often biting humor of an educated man. Eisenhower and his party often attacked Stevenson for making light of serious issues (a form of censure he called the Republican Law of Gravity), and the press also criticized him and many of his followers for being too intellectual, often associating intellectualism with liberalism (now a dirty word) and even socialism and communism. Columnist Stewart Alsop used the word "egghead" to describe Stevenson, and the word quickly caught on with the press and the public as a description not just of Stevenson but of intellectuals in general, making America one of the few countries in the world to use the word "intellectual" and its new synonym, "egghead," as terms of opprobrium. Stevenson tried to defuse the egghead issue with quips like "Eggheads of the world, unite—you have nothing to lose but your yolks," but the charge undoubtedly hurt him in the campaign, as did his lack of an athletic or military background (he had been a civilian in both world wars). To many people, he just didn't seem "manly" enough to be a tough politician and tough leader. He was widely viewed as an effeminate, bookish intellectual who did not know much about the real world and would not know how to use the reins of power if he were given them.[21]

The introduction of television into the 1952 presidential race could not eliminate the more grueling aspects of campaigning. This was the last real whistlestop campaign, and both candidates were subjected to tiresome rides by train, long workdays, and tight schedules. Both candidates were exhausted from trying to remember what town they were in, from pretending to know the local candidates they shared platforms with in cities and little towns all across the nation, from shaking hands when their fingers were already swollen from shaking too many hands, from hiding how tired and bored they were, from constantly smiling, from trying to recall what they had said or were going to say when they knew that television cameras and reporters from the printed media were capturing and circulating every word all across the nation. In one thirteen-hour period in Indiana and Illinois, Eisenhower traveled 139 miles by car and 232 by train (on the Look Ahead, Neighbor, Special) to make 13 speeches in twelve different cities.[22] He seemed to be the more energetic candidate and campaigned harder than his younger opponent, but he complained about the schedules drawn up by "those fools on the National Committee" and once angrily asked, "Are they trying to perform the feat of electing a dead man?"[23] By the time it was all over, Eisenhower had traveled almost 33,000 miles and given 228 speeches in forty-four states, while Stevenson had traveled 32,500 miles and given 203 speeches in thirty-two states. Together, the two parties spent almost $80 million, a figure inflated for the first time by the heavy use of television campaign commercials.[24]

It was a vigorous campaign, with both sides using all the tools of politics and communications to get their message to the voter. Inevitably, the campaign came to revolve around the images of the candidates, with basic issues being pushed into the background and reduced to slogans on political buttons, placards, hats, neckties, and almost anything else they could be written on. While Stevenson tried to talk sense to the American people, the public was inundated with buttons and other paraphernalia saying, "Adlai for Me," "All the Way with Adlai," "We're Madly for Adlai," "We Need Adlai Badly," "Vote Gladly for Adlai," "I Like Stevenson," "My Favorite *Son* Is Steven*son*," and "I Like Ike But I Am Going to Vote for Stevenson," and "Nix on Ike." And while Eisenhower was promising to lead a "great crusade," prospective voters were bombarded with such slogans as "I Like Ike," "We Like Ike," "Ike and Dick Sure to Click," "For the Love of Ike Vote Republican," "Make the White House the Dwight House," "Vote Right with Ike," "Peace and Prosperity," "Peace and Power with Eisenhower," and "Had Enough?" Meanwhile Richard Nixon was labeling Stevenson "Adlai the appeaser" and calling him "a graduate of Acheson's 'Cowardly College of Communist Containment,'" while McCarthy was describing Democratic rule as "twenty years of treason," referring to "Alger—I mean Adlai," and saying that "if somebody would only smuggle me aboard the Democratic campaign special with a baseball bat in my hand, I'd teach patriotism to little Ad-lie." And everywhere, Republican candidates were talking of "the no-win war," the "Mink Dynasty," "the mess in Washington," and "time for a change."[25]

The Eisenhower–Nixon bandwagon rolled along with increasing momentum until the middle of September, when the danger of derailment appeared with the issue of the Nixon fund. On September 18, the *New York Post*, a pro-Stevenson newspaper, printed allegations that Nixon had often paid some of his personal and campaign expenses (stationery, postage, hotel bills, travel, and the like) as senator from a secret slush fund of over $18,000 provided by a California "millionaire's club" made up of wealthy businessmen. This was not unusual or illegal, for other congressmen had done similar things before. The fund was not secret, and it was used not for personal financial gain but for his 1950 political campaign. Nixon claimed that he was a victim of a "smear" carried out by the "Communists and crooks in the Government,"[26] and Senator McCarthy came to his defense with the claim that "the left wing crowd hates Nixon because of his conviction of Alger Hiss."[27]

But the Republican party was deeply stung, for it had been promising to clean up the "mess in Washington." As Eisenhower said to reporters on his campaign train, "Of what avail is it for us to carry on this crusade against this business of what has been going on in Washington if we ourselves aren't as clean as a hound's tooth?"[28] He ordered an independent audit of the fund and of Nixon's financial affairs, and although the audit revealed that Nixon had stayed within the legal limits in his use of the fund, many of Eisenhower's top advisers felt that Nixon had become too great a liability for the party and urged Eisenhower to drop him from the ticket. But the general demurred, and told Nixon that he ought to take his defense before the public on radio and television to demonstrate his innocence and reestablish his moral and political credibility. Nixon would later write that Eisenhower's treatment of him during one of his deepest crises "made me feel like the little boy caught with jam on his face."[29]

On September 23, five days after the story of the fund first broke, Nixon appeared on television in a fight to save his political career. With his wife Pat in a nearby armchair and a portrait of Lincoln on the wall behind him, the thirty-nine-year-old vice-presidential candidate sat at a desk and read from five handwritten pages a melodramatic speech destined to become one of the most famous political speeches in history. He discussed the fund, denied any wrongdoing, described the audit that had cleared him, listed his assets (a 1950 Oldsmobile, equity in two houses, $4,000 in life insurance), his debts ($30,000 remaining on the two houses, a $4,500 loan from a Washington bank, a $3,500 loan from his parents, and a $500 loan on his life insurance), and said: "Well, that's about it. That's what we have. And that's what we owe. It isn't very much. But Pat and I have the satisfaction that every dime that we have got is honestly ours." And in a dig at the Democrats, he said: "I should say this, that Pat doesn't have a mink coat. But she does have a respectable Republican cloth coat, and I always tell her that she would look good in anything." He also managed to paint himself as a man of "modest means" while mentioning that Stevenson had "inherited a fortune from his father."

In the part of the speech that gave it its name, he related that someone in Texas had sent his family a cocker spaniel, which his six-year-old daughter Tricia named Checkers. "And you know, the kids, like all kids, loved the dog, and I just want to say this, right now, that regardless of what they say about it, we are going to keep it." He could not resist attacking Truman, Acheson, and Stevenson, or praising Eisenhower as the "only man who can save America at this time." He concluded by saying that "I don't believe that I ought to quit, because I am not a quitter," but he shrewdly told the 55 million people watching that the decision was not his to make but that of the

Republican National Committee, and he urged his viewers to write the committee and tell it whether he should stay on the ticket or not. He pledged to accept its decision, but he promised that "regardless of what happens, I am going to continue this fight. I am going to campaign up and down America until we drive the crooks and the Communists and those that defend them out of Washington."[30]

This maudlin but politically shrewd speech, watched by the largest television audience in history up until that time, caused a remarkable reaction. Over 200,000 letters and telegrams poured into the headquarters of the Republican National Committee, to local Republican headquarters, to Eisenhower, and to Nixon, and they ran overwhelmingly in the senator's favor. Almost $60,000 in contributions came in, too, almost enough to cover the $75,000 cost of the broadcast. From all across the country, people wrote that they had been moved to tears by the speech, and many of them sent handwoven dog blankets, dog collars, a dog kennel, a year's supply of dog food, and dozens of other canine gifts. Eisenhower had been infuriated by parts of the speech, particularly by the call for all candidates to reveal their financial status, which would have forced him to reveal the $635,000 in royalties he had received from his book, *Crusade in Europe*. He had been angered, too, by Nixon's plea for the people to express their feelings to the Republican National Committee, a move that shrewdly put pressure on the committee and on Eisenhower to keep Nixon on the ticket. But Eisenhower was also impressed by the political astuteness of the speech, and the next day, when he met Nixon at the airport in Wheeling, West Virginia, he put his arm around him and said, "You're my boy."[31] The speech not only saved Nixon's career, it also made him more popular than ever before. Furthermore, in this early age of television, it demonstrated the new medium's enormous power to make or break political candidates.

The Checkers speech eliminated the last major obstacle to a Republican victory, and the Eisenhower bandwagon rolled on as the Republicans continued to hammer away at the domestic and foreign policies of the Truman administration, particularly its handling of the Korean War. Eisenhower had no specific plan for ending the war, but in Detroit on October 24, eleven days before the election, he made a dramatic announcement on the Korean conflict. Eisenhower promised that after his electoral victory he would "forgo the diversions of politics and concentrate on the job of ending the Korean War. . . . That job requires a personal trip to Korea. Only in that way could I learn how best to serve the American people. I shall go to Korea."[32] By this time the Republicans undoubtedly had the election sewn up, but this dramatic gesture practically guaranteed a Republican victory at the polls.

Truman was chafing at the bit all through the campaign, and in the last two weeks of October he entered the fray in spite of reservations held by some of Stevenson's entourage who felt that their candidate should keep his distance from the discredited lame duck. Truman wanted a Democratic victory in the campaign, and he also wanted to defend his administration against the attacks by the Republicans. In a cross-country whistlestop tour punctuated with over a hundred speeches aimed at recapturing the "give 'em hell" style and effect of 1948, Truman lit into the Republican candidates with charges that their party would destroy the New Deal and Fair Deal programs and return the country to a depression and isolationism. He claimed that the Republicans were using Hitler's "big lie" techniques to fool the electorate,[33] attacked Eisenhower for endorsing "moral pygmies" like Jenner and McCarthy, and charged that in refusing to defend General Marshall against their attacks Eisenhower had "compromised every principle of personal loyalty."[34] He also called Eisenhower "a stooge for Wall Street," and said that he "has spent all his life in the army and doesn't know much."[35] For one last time, but this time in a losing cause, Truman was "giving 'em hell."

When the votes were counted on election day, Eisenhower had won by a landslide. In the largest voter turnout ever, he gathered 33.9 million popular votes to Stevenson's 27.3 million, and his 55.4 percent victory margin was the largest of any candidate's up to that time. In the electoral vote he won by 442 to 89, carrying thirty-nine states to Stevenson's nine (eight in the South plus West Virginia). He even wrested four states from the Democratic South, capturing Florida, Virginia, Tennessee, and Texas and running well in the others, and he won all six New England states, the first time a Republican had pulled off that feat since Coolidge's election in 1924. He won overwhelmingly in traditional Republican strongholds like the Midwest and suburban areas, but he even made heavy inroads into typically Democratic areas like the South, low income groups, ethnic groups, Catholics, and farmers (who gave Eisenhower 63 percent of their vote after giving Truman two thirds of it in 1948). The majority of new voters, young or old, also voted for him, as did most women.[36] In short, Eisenhower ran well in all sections of the country and among almost all classes and groups.

Many Republican leaders in 1952 talked of a new Republican majority, believing that their party had broken up Roosevelt's New Deal coalition and returned after an absence of twenty years to claim its rightful place as the nation's majority party. However, the victories of 1952 were victories for Eisenhower, not for the party, and the coattail effects of his victory were small. The Republicans managed a net gain of only twenty-one seats in the House and three in the Senate, giving them a majority of nine in the House and a forty-eight–forty-eight tie in the Senate. In gubernatorial races across the country, the Republicans won twenty of thirty contested races to wind up with a majority of twelve.[37] The decline of Republican strength in the elections for the rest of the decade, and the return of the Democrats to the executive office in 1960, would offer additional proof that the voters did indeed like Ike but were unable to transfer their traditional allegiances to his party. It was significant, too, that Stevenson garnered 27 million votes, more than any loser had ever received, and more than Truman had attracted in his winning effort in 1948.

Stevenson conceded defeat around one in the morning, Central Standard Time, and sent a telegram to Eisenhower at the latter's suite in the Commodore Hotel in New York, telling him that "the people have made their choice and I congratulate you. That you may be the servant and the guardian of peace and make the vale of trouble a door of hope is my earnest prayer."[38] It was a bitter blow to the reluctant candidate, who, borrowing a story from Lincoln, told his disappointed supporters that he felt like the little boy who had stubbed his toe in the dark, for "he was too old to cry but it hurt too much to laugh."[39]

Many of Stevenson's followers felt that his defeat was a defeat for American intellectuals and intellectualism and that the age of talent and brains in government that had been inaugurated by Franklin Roosevelt in 1933 had come to an end. On the other hand, many of Eisenhower's supporters believed that finally, after twenty years of drifting down the road toward socialism and communist appeasement, America was back on the right track. But Eisenhower's victory and Stevenson's defeat meant neither of these things. As was said by many pundits of the time, the two men could have exchanged speeches and party platforms and the results of the election would have been pretty much the same. Eisenhower's victory was the result of his great personal popularity and the widespread belief that he was the best hope for troubled times. Disillusioned with Truman's leadership and with the war in Korea, and deeply troubled by inflation, high taxes, and charges of corruption and communism in Washington, the voters looked to the man who had masterminded the conquest of Hitler as the only man who could provide the leadership for ending the Korean War and solving the nation's other vexing domestic and foreign problems. Eisenhower, it was hoped, would get the country out of the mess it was in, and if he seemed to offer simple solutions to complex problems, that was what the electorate wanted. And some were just voting for a change, feeling that twenty years in power was too long for any party.

Remembering how unprepared he had been to take over the presidency in 1945, Truman was anxious to brief his successor and provide for an orderly transition of power, always a difficult task when the opposing party defeats the incumbent one but a task made even more difficult in this case because of the hard feelings existing between the president and the president-elect. The two men had been on good terms in the late 1940s. Truman was then a great admirer of Eisenhower, writing him warm letters, praising him publicly and privately, and appointing him commander of NATO. Apparently there was also some substance to the rumors circulating in Washington that Truman had wanted Eisenhower to be his successor in 1948 before he decided to run again himself.

But during the 1952 campaign, relations between the two men badly deteriorated. Truman felt betrayed when Eisenhower decided to run as a Republican, and he was incensed by the general's attack on his administration, especially by his promises to "clean up the mess" in Washington and his charges that Truman had bungled the handling of the Korean War. He was also angry over Eisenhower's refusal to defend their mutual friend, George C. Marshall, from attacks by McCarthy, Nixon, and other right-wingers. Truman also felt insulted in August of 1952 when, during the height of the campaign, Eisenhower declined his invitation to come to the White House for briefings on domestic and foreign policy matters because his advisers thought it would hurt his candidacy to meet with the president. This caused Truman to fire off a letter to the general expressing regret "that you have allowed a bunch of screwballs to come between us."[40] For his part, Eisenhower was offended by Truman's own harsh comments during the campaign, especially his description of the decision to go to Korea as "a piece of demagoguery," his remark that "Ike has a brass halo," and his postelection telegram congratulating Eisenhower and sarcastically informing him that THE INDEPENDENCE WILL BE AT YOUR DISPOSAL IF YOU STILL DESIRE TO GO TO KOREA."[41]

However, Eisenhower did send several members of his staff to the White House for briefings by Truman's staff, and on the afternoon of November 18, Eisenhower and several of his advisers came to the White House for a briefing by Truman and key members of the cabinet. It was an awkward meeting for both men, only partially alleviated by Truman when he returned the world globe Eisenhower had used during World War II and then given to Truman when he came to Germany in 1945 for the Potsdam Conference. According to Truman, Eisenhower came into the office with "a chip on his shoulder," went through the entire briefing with a detached look on his face, and let everything that was told him go "into one ear and out the other." Truman also claimed that when the magnitude of the job began to sink in, "General Eisenhower was overwhelmed when he found what he faced."[42] The meeting reinforced Truman's belief that Eisenhower did not fully understand the burdens and complexities of the job. On one of his last days in office Truman told his aides that the general would sit in the Oval Office and give orders right and left, but "nothing will happen. Poor Ike—it won't be a bit like the Army. He'll find it very frustrating."[43]

The feud was very much in evidence on inauguration day. Truman had been angered over the Republican inauguration officials' request that traditional top hats be replaced by homburgs, but he reluctantly gave in, saying that "I refuse to have my last quarrel over a hat."[44] However, he balked at the suggestion that he ride in a parade car to the Statler Hotel to pick up Eisenhower instead of waiting, as was customary, for the president-elect to come to the White House to pick up the outgoing president. Truman's refusal irked Eisenhower, who nonetheless agreed to come by the White House for the Trumans. But Eisenhower declined to attend a customary preinaugural luncheon with the Trumans, and instead of going in to the Blue Room to greet the president, Eisenhower stayed in his limousine until a fuming Truman came out and got into the car. The two rode in silence down the parade route until an obviously irritated Eisenhower turned to Truman and asked who had embarrassed him by ordering his son John back from Korea to attend the inauguration, making it appear that he was receiving special treatment. An equally irritated Truman icily replied that "the President of the United States ordered your son to attend your inauguration. . . . If you think somebody was trying to embarrass you by this order, then the President assumes full responsibility." Joe Martin and Styles Bridges, riding in the car with them, were shocked at this exchange and tried to change the subject.[45]

After the inauguration, the Trumans went to Dean Acheson's home for a luncheon with close friends and administration officials. At five-thirty that afternoon, the Trumans left by train for Independence, taking with them Margaret's piano, 300 crates of Truman's books, several boxes of gifts, 400 steel files crammed with Truman's papers, 75 steel files containing Bess's correspondence, and dozens of boxes of clothing and mementoes.[46] Riding in a private car (his old campaign car, the Ferdinand Magellan) assigned to them by the new president, the Trumans journeyed back to Independence, to the old fourteen-room house on Delaware Street where they had lived before he went to Washington. Here he lived off his small government pension and savings from his White House years, took his usual fast-paced prebreakfast walk, talked with old friends and neighbors, went to the local barbershop, oversaw the construction of the Harry S. Truman Library to house his papers, wrote his *Memoirs*, corresponded with friends, and occasionally let the Republicans and even some Democrats know what he thought of them and their policies.

As expected, Truman continued to be critical of Eisenhower. Almost a decade after he left the White House he would tell Merle Miller that "the system we have under the Constitution that was set up by those fellows in Philadelphia has survived worse things than Eisenhower. Not much worse but some worse."[47] The two presidents met briefly at General Marshall's funeral in 1959, but their greetings went little beyond a perfunctory handshake. In November of 1961 the two men came together again, when Eisenhower visited the Truman library and when the two attended Sam

Rayburn's funeral in Bonham, Texas. They would meet again at John F. Kennedy's funeral in November of 1963, and after this meeting they ended their quarrel and resumed their friendship. Before he died in 1972, Truman had patched up relations with almost all of his old antagonists except General MacArthur and Senator McCarthy.[48]

On the afternoon of January 20, 1953, President Truman became citizen Truman and went back home to Missouri after eight troubled years in the presidency. He had seen the American electorate turn against him and his party by voting in the opposition party, and he left office as one of the most unpopular presidents in American history. A Gallup poll taken in January of 1953 revealed that only 30 percent of the American people approved of the way he was handling his job.[49]

While millions of Truman's contemporaries held him in low esteem, many others did not. While lamenting that Truman was no Roosevelt and that the Fair Deal made little progress, most historians of the time gave Truman high marks, especially in foreign policy. So did many of the politicians and statesmen who worked with him. Dean Acheson considered Truman to be one of the nation's best presidents—a decisive and courageous man who "was always doing his level best" in a very difficult job.[50] Another friend and admirer, Sam Rayburn, claimed that Truman was "right on all the big things, wrong on most of the little ones."[51] One of the greatest tributes to Truman came from Winston Churchill, who told him in a 1952 meeting that he had held him "in very low regard" when he first succeeded Roosevelt but was now convinced that "since that time, you, more than any other man, have saved Western civilization."[52]

Truman held no such lofty evaluations of his presidency. Several years after he left office, he said that "I wasn't one of the great Presidents, but I had a good time trying to be one, I can tell you that."[53] But perhaps he best summed up his own feelings about his administration in a story he told reporters in April of 1952 about a monument in a cemetery in Tombstone, Arizona, which read, "Here lies Jack Williams. He done his damnedest." Truman said that "I think that is the greatest epitaph a man can have—when he gives everything that is in him to the job he has before him. That is all that you can ask of him and that is what I have tried to do."[54]

As the years have passed, many have come to feel that Truman did, indeed, do his damnedest, and that his damnedest was good enough most of time. In 1962, just a decade after he left office but long enough to provide some perspective on his presidency, a poll of historians ranked him as the ninth best president in the nation's history, a "near great" trailing behind Lincoln, Washington, Franklin Roosevelt, Wilson, Jefferson, Jackson, Teddy Roosevelt, and Polk.[55] Other polls of historians and political scientists conducted since that time have consistently placed him in the top ten. A 1982 poll taken by the *Chicago Tribune*, for example, ranked him eighth.[56] Clearly, the perspective provided by the passage of time has only served to consolidate his historical reputation. Serving in what he often called "a hell of a job," this gutsy common man was a hell of a president.

# PART TWO

# The Good Years, 1953–1956

# 9

# *Ike*

Tuesday, January 20, 1953, was an important day for Republicans and for many disenchanted Democrats across the country, for on this bright but cold day in Washington the Republican party was returning to power after an absence of twenty years. The capital was crowded with Republican faithful who had come from all across the land to watch Dwight David Eisenhower take the oath of office and to participate in activities surrounding the most elaborate and expensive inauguration up to that time. In the late morning hours the streets along the parade route were jammed with spectators, while all across the nation people gathered in front of television sets to witness the day's events. There were many disappointed Democrats, of course, but for millions of others the inauguration of the man everybody called Ike symbolized the return of political sanity to Washington and the end of twenty years of Democratic giveaway programs, corruption, and communist appeasement. The mess in Washington was about to be cleaned up, and America was to be restored to its former greatness.

The new president did not disappoint his admirers on this special day. After being sworn in by Chief Justice Fred Vinson at 12:32 in a ceremony using one of George Washington's Bibles and one that Eisenhower had used at West Point, the thirty-fourth president of the United States shook hands with Vinson and ex-president Truman, strode across the platform and kissed Mamie, and began his address. He began by asking his audience to bow as he read a prayer he had written especially for the occasion, then launched into a speech that was heavily moral and internationalist in tone. Using the familiar Cold War rhetoric of the time, he pledged that the United States would continue to lead the worldwide fight against communism and other forms of tyranny, declared that the "forces of good and evil are massed and armed and opposed as rarely before in history," and warned that "freedom is pitted against slavery; lightness against dark." He promised that the United States would work for world peace but would not engage in "the futility of appeasement," and called upon the American people "to accept whatever sacrifices may be required of us."[1] The speech was followed by a luncheon, attendance at two inaugural balls, and a review of a ten-mile parade that reminded Eisenhower of an earlier time in his life when as a West Point cadet he had marched in Woodrow Wilson's inaugural parade.[2] The day's festivities went on until well after midnight. The Eisenhowers did not get to their new home until around one-thirty the next morning, when most Americans were already asleep, spending their first night under a Republican president since 1933.

The man who inherited the awesome responsibilities of governing the nation in a dangerous atomic age was born in a far different time in America's history. The last president born in the nineteenth century and the third of seven sons (one died in infancy) born to David Jacob and Ida Stover Eisenhower, hardworking parents of modest means, Dwight David Eisenhower entered the world on October 14, 1890, in Denison, Texas. At that time the United States was completing the conquest of the Indians with the Battle of Wounded Knee, Benjamin Harrison was in the White House, wealthy men like John D. Rockefeller and Andrew Carnegie and J. P. Morgan wielded more power than presidents, and millions of immigrants were pouring into the country to work in the factories and crowd the big cities. Soon after his birth, the future president's parents moved to Abilene, Kansas, where he was reared and educated in the public schools. After graduating from high school in 1909, he got a job at the local creamery and began saving his money for his and his brother Edgar's college educations. In 1910, at the age of twenty, he received an appointment to West Point, a stroke of fortune that would dramatically change the direction of his life.

At West Point Eisenhower was an average student who excelled in sports, especially football, until a knee injury suffered while tackling the legendary Jim Thorpe ended a promising athletic career. In 1915, after graduating sixty-first in a class of 164, he was commissioned a second lieutenant in the infantry and sent off to Fort Sam Houston in Texas, where he met and married Mamie Geneva Doud, a young lady from a comfortable middle-class family. He did not see combat in World War I, spending his army time in training camps in Texas and Gettysburg, Pennsylvania. From 1918 until the outbreak of World War II, he attended several special training schools and served in many peacetime posts in the United States and abroad, including almost eight years as General MacArthur's aide and speech writer. At the time of Pearl Harbor, he was a recently promoted brigadier general and the assistant chief of staff of the Operations Division of the War Department. His superior was General George C. Marshall, who took him under his wing and promoted his rapid rise during the Second World War.

The Second World War transformed Eisenhower from an obscure army officer who had never seen combat to a world-famous leader and potential candidate for the presidency of the United States. He helped plan and lead the invasions of North Africa, Sicily, and Italy, and then as the supreme commander of the Allied Forces in Europe he directed the invasion of Normandy, the liberation of France, and the conquest of Germany. At the end of the war he was a five-star general and the most famous American military leader in the world. He returned home to a hero's welcome in New York in 1945 and remained in the public eye as chief of staff of the army (1945–1948), president of Columbia University (1948–1950), and commanding general of NATO (1950–1952).

After turning down nomination feelers from both parties in 1948 and being courted by both again in 1951, he resigned his NATO post and successfully sought the nomination and the presidency as a Republican. Although he disliked many aspects of politics, he was only sixty-one years old, he was in good health, and he was not quite ready to be put out to pasture. He believed that the country could not stand another eight years under a liberal Democrat and that if the Taft wing of the Republican party captured the presidency, it might dismantle the NATO alliance and all the other foundations of the Western alliance that he so strongly believed in. He felt prepared for the job, he believed that he was the best man for the job, and he thought that it was his duty to serve his country once again, this time in a civilian capacity.[3]

Eisenhower shared some similarities with his predecessor, Harry Truman. Both men came from small towns in the Midwest—in fact, Abilene, Kansas, and Independence, Missouri, are less than two hundred miles apart. Both men came from honest, hardworking religious parents of modest circumstances and were reared in the traditional values of the Midwest—hard work, honesty, thrift, perseverance, loyalty, integrity, and patriotism—which they kept all their lives. Ironically, Truman had unsuccessfully sought an appointment to West Point, and as a young man working in a Kansas City bank, he had lived in the same rooming house as one of the six Eisenhower brothers, Arthur.[4] Both were pragmatic rather than ideological in their approach to problems, and both felt more comfortable in the company of businessmen or other men of affairs than in the presence of intellectuals. And in many ways, both came ill-prepared to the presidency, Truman after being kept in the dark by Roosevelt, and Eisenhower after having spent his life in administrative posts in the army where he became proficient at army politics but did not have to deal with a fickle electorate or quarrelsome Congress.

But here the similarities end, for the two men had led very different lives and developed very different personalities. Truman was an average man, average senator, and undistinguished vice president who was thrust into the president's chair by the death of Roosevelt. However, Eisenhower came to the presidency after achieving great fame and conquering virtually all the worlds a military man could conquer. The presidency seemed to be his next logical position, almost a reward or honorary degree for a long distinguished career. And unlike Truman, who had been dazzled by his new position and almost bewildered at first by the problems and awesome responsibilities of the job, Eisenhower felt right at home. On January 21, 1953, his first full day in office, he wrote in his diary: "My first day at the president's desk. Plenty of worries and difficult problems. But such had been my portion for a long time—the result is that this just seems . . . like a continuation of all I've been doing since July 1941—even before that."[5]

Eisenhower was a genuine American hero and a popular president. Taking office at the age of sixty-two, he was 5 feet 10½ inches tall and weighed 178 pounds, just 6 pounds over his weight as a West Point cadet some forty years before. He was a genuinely friendly and likable man with a good sense of humor and a broad, almost boyish smile that became his trademark and probably brought him more votes than any speech he ever gave. He came across as responsible, dependable, honest, and dignified—all of which he was. He came across as a regular guy, an outdoors type, a poker and bridge player, a golfer and a fisherman, a man's man, and an extrovert—all of which he was. He was a strong moralist who embodied and often spoke of old-fashioned virtues like honor, duty, patriotism, hard work, and perseverance. Although he was capable of bursting into blue language, especially when he lost his famous temper, he thought it distasteful to use four-letter words in public or tell off-color stories in mixed company. This sense of propriety even extended to his diary, where he occasionally would write out explicatives like "damn" and "hell" in full but more often would write the first letter of the word followed by dashes. Unlike MacArthur, Patton, and other military prima donnas, he was not a jealous or egotistical man, showing throughout his career a willingness to share credit with others and to give credit entirely to them when it was their due.

Eisenhower was a disciplined, forceful, and energetic man who looked forward to getting up every day and who approached his daily presidential tasks with a zest that belied his age. He had a dignified demeanor, rarely losing his temper in public or getting down into the gutter, as he often said, to deal with politicians like Joe McCarthy. He was also a calm and patient man who was not easily ruffled and could not be pushed into hasty, ill-considered decisions—"make no mistakes in a hurry"[6] was one of his favorite aphorisms. He was also enormously self-confident, coming to the presidency after holding big jobs in the military and dealing with strong individuals like Churchill, de Gaulle, MacArthur, Patton, and Montgomery. Although he was new at Washington politics and did not have a close friendship with many of the old professional politicians, they did know and respect him. And in a dangerous atomic age, it gave him considerable confidence to know that when he picked up the phone to talk to the chairman of the Joint Chiefs of Staff, he was talking to Omar Bradley, a man he had known for most of his adult life and considered one of his closest friends.

Eisenhower did not spend as much time on the job as his predecessor or some of his successors, but he worked long and hard at the never-ending task of being president. Perhaps unable to shake an old army habit, he was an early riser, usually having breakfast over a couple of newspapers around six-thirty. He normally arrived at the office by seven-thirty or eight, and from then until late in the afternoon his day was spent on his presidential tasks. His formal workday in the Oval Office usually ended around five or six in the afternoon, but he often spent another hour in an informal session with members of his staff, cabinet, or important congressmen like Lyndon B. Johnson, Sam Rayburn, Everett Dirksen, or William Knowland. During this hour, according to assistant to the president Sherman Adams, "over a drink and a canapé . . . Eisenhower smoothed the road for many of his goals and legislative purposes."[7] When he left his office around six he sometimes took a load of papers to his living quarters to work on that night, and often the evening would be taken up with an important appointment that could not be held in the day or with a state dinner of some kind.[8]

Eisenhower felt that in order to function effectively in the rigorous job of the presidency he needed regularly scheduled rests and vacations, so he tried to leave Wednesday and Saturday afternoons, and all of Sunday, open for leisure activities. He often vacationed at the Augusta National Golf Club, on his Gettysburg farm, in New England, and at his mother-in-law's home in Denver, Colorado. But to set the right tone for the austere economic program he hoped to implement, he sold the presidential retreat at Key West and put the presidential yacht, the *Williamsburg*, in dry dock. He also changed the name of the presidential retreat in the Catoctin Mountains from Shangri-la to Camp David, named after his father and grandson. Eisenhower looked forward to these vacation retreats, but even they did not provide him with the rest he wanted and needed. As has been the case with all modern presidents, he was never really off the job. There were still phone calls to take, reports to read, problems to mull over, and documents to sign. According to Eisenhower's appointments secretary, Robert Keith Gray, when the president vacationed at Augusta courier planes arrived from Washington daily to bring new paperwork for the president and to take back to Washington work he had finished the day or evening before. When his critics read in the newspapers that he had played nine or eighteen holes of golf at Augusta, they did not know that he had also spent several hours working on government business in his office there.[9]

Eisenhower's favorite leisure activity was golf, which he pursued with a passion. He loved golf so much that he had a driving range and putting green installed at the White House so that he could get in a little practice on days he was too busy to get to the links. On many occasions his secretary and staff noticed him looking wistfully out the window, wishing he could be hitting a few balls instead of reading and signing papers and attending to the many other onerous duties of the presidency. Soon pictures of the golfing Eisenhower began to appear regularly in the newspapers and popular magazines, and many golfing experts claimed that Eisenhower was partly responsible for the golfing boom of the early 1950s among middle-aged men who had never played the game before. Fred Corcoran, a prominent member of the Professional Golfing Association, said that the president's golfing was "the greatest thing that ever happened to the game."[10] He shot in the mideighties, not bad for a man his age, but he never had the luxury of playing in relaxing circumstances. Crowds inevitably gathered unless they were kept back by the Secret Servicemen, who always had to tag along with shortwave radios and carbine rifles hidden in golf bags or under their coats and to search the woods surrounding the fairways for assassins.[11] His golfing attracted a great deal of criticism from the press and his political opponents, who accused him of "golfing and goofing" when he should have been in the White House attending to important matters of state. Jokes about Eisenhower's golfing spread across the country throughout his presidency. One automobile sticker of the time read: "Ben Hogan for President. If We're Going to Have a Golfer for President, Let's Have a Good One."[12]

Eisenhower also relaxed in other ways. He occasionally swam in the White House pool when the weather was too bad for golf, but he never really liked swimming and made himself do it just for the exercise.[13] He dabbled in oil paintings of portraits and landscapes, and he was a good poker and bridge player, often playing the latter at nights and on weekends with numerous partners, including Democrats like Fred M. Vinson, who had played poker with Truman, and with bridge experts like Oswald Jacoby, who found him to be an excellent player. Eisenhower also liked to cook, specializing in pancakes, cakes, steaks, potato salad, fresh-caught fish, and, according to one reporter, "chili that sends you to the nearest fire-alarm box."[14] He enjoyed holding stag dinners at the White House in the evenings, having from fifteen to twenty men in for dinner and male conversation. He invited people from all fields to these dinners—old army buddies, his brother Milton, cabinet members, book and newspaper publishers, bankers, executives from General Motors and other large corporations, an occasional intellectual like Robert Frost, and old friends from the entertainment field like Freeman Gosden (Amos in the *Amos 'n' Andy* radio comedy).[15]

Eisenhower also read for relaxation, often at night while Mamie watched television. His favorite leisure reading was western magazines or paperback western novels, particularly those by Bliss Lomax and Luke Short. His love of westerns was often the butt of jokes by his detractors, who viewed this as simply another indication of his intellectual shortcomings, though they had not concluded this from Truman's occasional readings of whodunits and would not deduce it from President Kennedy's fondness for Ian Fleming's James Bond novels. Although he was not the history scholar that Truman was, Eisenhower from a very early age had been a devotee of histories, particularly Civil War histories, and of biographies of Lincoln, Lee, and the president he admired the most, Washington.[16] He read weekly news magazines and daily newspapers, but he strongly distrusted the press, particularly the big-city dailies like *The New York Times* and *Washington Post*. He thought that most radio, television, and newspaper reporters had an exaggerated sense of their importance, that their criticism was generally negative rather than constructive, and that government officials spent too much time trying to court them in an effort to gain a good press.[17]

Eisenhower embodied the simple religious faith so popular at the time. Although reared in a religious atmosphere in Abilene, he had been a sporadic churchgoer through most of his adult life and had not been an official member of any church until he joined the Presbyterian Church after his 1952 election. He understood and cared little for the complexities of theology, and his own beliefs seemed to be a fuzzy mixture of ill-defined feelings about God, Jesus, salvation, prayer, goodness, and Americanism.[18] He had no doubt that God was on the side of the Americans in the war against the godless Russians, could define democracy as "a political expression of a deep and abiding religion,"[19] proclaimed that "recognition of the Supreme Being is the first, the most basic expression of Americanism,"[20] and held that the twin cornerstones of American democracy were free enterprise and "a deep and abiding religious faith."[21]

Eisenhower often used religious phrases and talked about the need for religious faith and spiritual values. He frequently called on divine aid for himself and his country in his speeches, held prayer breakfasts, received church delegations in his office, and had Billy Graham and Norman Vincent Peale as overnight guests at the White House. He also began cabinet meetings with a prayer, usually asking Secretary of Agriculture Ezra Taft Benson, a Mormon, to lead or provide the prayer. Eisenhower once broke up a cabinet meeting with laughter when, after reading a note slipped to him by a secretary reminding him that the prayer had been forgotten, the president said, "Oh, goddammit, we forgot the silent prayer."[22] He and Mamie frequently attended Sunday morning worship services, but he sometimes chose instead to play a round of golf on a beautiful day. When he attended, he enjoyed singing hymns, usually put $5 or $10 in the collection plate, and almost always stopped to chat with the pastor and to tell him how much he enjoyed the sermon.[23]

Eisenhower's simple and unpretentious personality led many of his critics to brand him as anti-intellectual and unintelligent. A standard criticism of the time was that he was a good and well-intentioned man who was unfortunately too dumb for the complex job he had to do. All kinds of jokes were made about his intellectual shortcomings, such as the one that attributed his preference for one-page summaries of reports to the fact that his lips got tired if he had to read longer ones. It is true that he was not an intellectual, which he described as "a man who takes more words than is necessary to say more than he knows."[24] He was not a profound or original thinker, he was not broadly educated, he did not care for great literature or classical music, and he felt a little uncomfortable in the company of artists and intellectuals.[25] But he *was* intelligent, and those who denied this on the grounds that he was not an intellectual were as unfair as those who thought that Stevenson must be impractical and irreverent because he was intellectual and witty.[26] Eisenhower was not brilliant, but he had impressive analytical powers, great common sense, shrewdness, and a real affinity for organization, administration, and compromise. He was a practical, down-to-earth man who was interested in facts, action, and results—not in theories.

Eisenhower was not a good speaker, especially in spontaneous circumstances, and his clumsy syntax and unfortunate habit of stumbling over words also contributed to the impression that he simply was not very bright or well-informed. He was much better at written communication—he had a good vocabulary, almost perfect grammar, and a preference for concise, unadorned, uncontrived prose. He labored long over speeches that had been written for him, trying to assure a natural delivery unencumbered by overblown rhetoric. Most of his speechwriters attested that he had a good ear for the written and spoken word even though he did not perform as well in spontaneous situations as in formal, prepared ones.[27] As an aide to General MacArthur in the 1930s, he had written many of the dramatic speeches the publicity-seeking MacArthur was praised for delivering, and in 1945 he had written and given a speech in London that the London *Times* likened to the best efforts of Abraham Lincoln and Winston Churchill.[28]

Entering the presidency during the first age of television, Eisenhower realized the political value of the new media, so soon after his victory in 1952 he brought actor Robert Montgomery into the White House as a staff member to help with his television image. Montgomery coached him so that he could be more relaxed and folksy on the home screen, and gradually Eisenhower became a skillful user of the new medium that brought national politics and national political figures into the homes of so many citizens. He never became an eloquent speaker on television, but he had an infectious, winning smile and manner and came across as an honest, good, kind, and sincere man.

Eisenhower was a devoted family man. There was considerable gossip to the contrary, for during the Second World War rumors had circulated in army circles and even back in Washington that he was having an affair with Kay Summersby, a former English model and army lieutenant who served as his automobile driver during the Second World War and later wrote *Past Forgetting: My Love Affair with Dwight D. Eisenhower.*[29] But most Eisenhower scholars, along with his friends and family, believe that the two were close friends but not lovers, and that Mrs. Summersby fantasized the affair; the ghostwriters who finished the book after her death from cancer may have worked under the cynical expectation that stories of real or fictitious sex scandals involving the rich and famous attract lucrative book contracts. All evidence seems to point to the conclusion that Eisenhower was a faithful husband and that he and Mamie were compatible and devoted in spite of some very real marital strains caused by their frequent and lengthy wartime separations.[30]

Mamie was a popular First Lady who enjoyed all the activities and duties that befell her as a presidential wife. After moving some twenty-five times during her husband's army career, she relished the permanence that eight years in the White House afforded her and never seemed to tire of the endless rounds of teas, receptions, and other activities she had to host. But as she had throughout her famous husband's career, she stayed in the background, content to be a satellite of the man who was, she often said, "the star in the heavens."[31] She made no speeches and held no press conferences of her own, and he rarely consulted her on important matters of state. According to her, "Ike took care of the office, I ran the house."[32] Unlike the president, she did not like to fly, so she often did not accompany him on long plane trips. She would have taken these trips with him and been more active in general had she not suffered from rheumatic heart, asthma, headaches, and Ménière's disease, an inner ear condition that made her dizzy, affected her balance, and undoubtedly contributed to the widespread but apparently unfounded allegations that she was an alcoholic.[33]

Like the Trumans, the Eisenhowers were homebodies. Although they had to attend many evening social functions, they tried to stay at home as much as they could and to lead private lives. When the president came home, he changed into comfortable, casual clothing for dinner and, unless he had work to do, a relaxing evening with Mamie. Both were big television fans, and when color television appeared, they became the first presidential family—and one of the first American families—to get a color set. Their favorite shows were *I Love Lucy*, *You Bet Your Life*, and *Arthur Godfrey's Talent Scouts*. Mamie was also a big soap-opera fan. This all-American couple also watched movies in the White House movie theater on the ground floor, with the president preferring westerns like *High Noon* and *The Big Country* and Mamie enjoying romantic stories and musicals like *The King and I*. They occasionally invited friends in for dinner and cards, and they frequently entertained their three young grandchildren, who had their own upstairs bedrooms.[34] Pictures of the president playing with his young grandchildren appeared often in the newspapers, reinforcing the public's image of Eisenhower as a regular guy.

The eight years in the White House constituted the longest period of time the Eisenhowers had spent in one place since their marriage in 1916. For years Mamie had longed for a place of her own, and in 1950 a step in this direction was taken when they purchased a farm near Gettysburg containing a farmhouse nearly two hundred years old. The house was remodeled during Eisenhower's first term, allowing the couple to use it as a weekend retreat from the Washington fishbowl. When it was finished, Mamie's Dream House had fifteen rooms, eight baths, a putting green, a herd of Angus cattle, a guardhouse, fences with electronic surveillance systems, and a host of other security devices deemed necessary by the Secret Service. The Eisenhowers often entertained family and friends here, along with guests as famous as Nikita Khrushchev, Winston Churchill, Charles de Gaulle, and British Field Marshal Sir Bernard Montgomery, who signed the guestbook by his title: "Montgomery of Alamein."[35]

Eisenhower brought to the presidency political and administrative views learned and practiced over a long military career. Although his midwestern background had molded him along the lines of moderate Republicanism, he had never been a strong political partisan and in fact had not even voted until he was fifty-eight years old. Unlike Truman, who enjoyed the political trenches, he did not like the game of politics—the partisanship, the personal attacks, the competition, the infighting, the backstabbing, the horse trading, the patronage, and the moral and political compromising politicians engaged in. Neither did he relish the speechmaking, the motorcades, the television appearances, the press of large crowds, the handshaking, the chicken dinners, and all the other aspects of campaigning and running the presidency. As president, he was only as political as he felt he had to be in order to get the job done.[36]

The new president seemed to have trouble placing himself on the political spectrum. Throughout his two administrations he seemed to be searching for a label for his ideas, often identifying himself as "middle of the road" and his political philosophy as "the new Republicanism" or "modern Republicanism" or "dynamic conservatism" or "moderate progressivism" or "progressive, dynamic conservatism." All political labels aside, it is clear from Eisenhower's speeches and actions as president that he was a moderate

Republican who did not want to repudiate the past but did not want to rush too quickly into the future, either. Although he often spoke of the danger of "big government," "creeping socialism," and "giveaway programs," he accepted most of the basic tenets of the New Deal while opposing any dramatic extension of it. He hoped to return some governmental powers and functions to the states, balance the budget, cut taxes, and reduce government spending, but he knew that he could not turn back the clock. He once told his brother Edgar that if any party tried to abolish the New Deal, "You would not hear of that party again in our political history," and that while people like H. L. Hunt and "a few other Texas oil millionaires and an occasional politician and businessmen from other areas" might feel that you could reverse the New Deal programs, "their number is negligible and they are stupid."[37]

In spite of all the rhetoric about "Democratic appeasement" and "the liberation of captive peoples" from their communist overlords, Eisenhower's foreign policy views and practices would differ little from those of his predecessors. He would inaugurate a New Look in defense that emphasized atomic weapons over conventional ones, but in essence he would follow the broad outlines of the containment policy laid down by Truman. And much to the surprise of many within the administration and across the country, the old army veteran would resist strong pressures from within his own party for a huge and expensive military buildup—"you can't provide security just with a checkbook,"[38] he often said—and would launch peace initiatives that would have been impossible for Harry Truman or any other Democrat, and perhaps even any Republican with less stature than the general, to make. In many ways, the new president would be full of surprises.

Many of Eisenhower's critics, and even some of his supporters, thought that he would be a weak, caretaker president. Coming to the office at the relatively advanced age of sixty-two after a long and successful military career, he would be content, many felt, to delegate most of his authority and play the ceremonial role of head of state, much like a constitutional monarch. This would give him the time to do what he really liked best—golfing and playing bridge with his rich friends from the business world, fishing with his grandchildren, reading paperback westerns, and just generally enjoying the role of honorary president or White House hero-in-residence. He would reign, but he would not rule.

Eight years of the Eisenhower presidency would do little to change the minds of his critics, a broad group that included dyed-in-the-wool Democrats, right-wing Republicans, members of both parties who favored strong and active presidents in the Roosevelt-Truman mold, liberal intellectuals who always felt that the president's chair really belonged to Adlai Stevenson, and the liberal journalists and historians who wrote the first interpretations of the Eisenhower years. To his critics, the Eisenhower years were summed up in the popular joke depicting a golfing Eisenhower asking the party in front of him, "Do you mind if we play through? New York has just been bombed."[39] This unflattering portrait of Eisenhower persisted throughout the fifties and for many years after he left office.

It was a false image, however. It was an image fashioned in the heat of the politics of the age, before the passage of time could provide the perspective necessary for an objective appraisal of the man and his era. It was an image partly based on the longstanding popular belief that generals can wage and win wars but lack the political wisdom necessary for running the political arm of the government. It was an image partly fed by Eisenhower himself, for in public he appeared to be a smiling, friendly, ordinary guy who did not take himself or his job too seriously. And finally, it was an image based upon a woefully inadequate historical record, for the full publication of his presidential and private papers (including an invaluable diary), and of the memoirs, diaries, and other writings of his speechwriters and close aides, would not come until the 1970s and early 1980s, when many of these materials were declassified for the first time.

These new materials reveal a man and president far more complex and able than most of his contemporaries realized. The writings of some of Eisenhower's aides have claimed that Eisenhower was a political genius who compiled such an impressive record of domestic and international accomplishments that he deserves to rank among the nation's greatest presidents. Similar assertions have been made in some of the revisionist histories, biographies, and articles written by historians and journalists taking advantage of the new Eisenhower materials. These attempts to rehabilitate Eisenhower's reputation were long overdue, but in some cases they seemed overzealous as well, their authors claiming more than is warranted by the evidence.

What the evidence does suggest is that Eisenhower was no simple-minded man, no caretaker president, no puppet of his cabinet or "captive hero" of his millionaire business friends, no innocent babe in the political woods. He was an intelligent, confident, and hardworking president with a keen perception of the politics, politicians, issues, and problems of the day. He understood power and enjoyed using it. He loved his job. He ran the presidency himself, delegating power but never relinquishing it. He, not his aides, made the major decisions, and he, not his aides, must bear the blame and credit for them. And while he was no political genius, he was a talented politician who attempted—often successfully—to lead his party and the nation down the path he felt they should take. Historian Robert H. Ferrell was probably not too far off the mark when he wrote in his introduction to Eisenhower's diary that Eisenhower was "a marvelous politician" and that he "was a success, in the largest possible way, in American politics; no other politician of his time did nearly as well."[40]

One of the reasons for the contemporary misjudgment of Eisenhower lay in his view of the proper style of leadership and of the constitutional duties of the president. A man of strong will who was used to having his way, Eisenhower also believed in compromise and conciliation and tried to lead others in a low-keyed manner without their being aware that they were being led. The motto on his desk—*Suaviter in modo, fortiter in re* ("Gentle in manner, strong in deed")—was indicative of a leadership style that was poles apart from that of his blustery predecessor.[41] As he once told an associate, he did not believe that leadership required "hitting people over the head. Any damn fool can do that. . . . It's persuasion—and conciliation—and education—and patience. That's the only kind of leadership I know—or believe in—or will practice."[42] His leadership skills had served him well in the army, and now he would effectively use them in the presidency. His style and his skills did not surprise those close to him, nor those who had worked with him in Europe, when as the coordinator of the armies of several nations he had to persuade strong, egotistical men to reconcile their national, personal, and policy differences and work as a team in the invasion and conquest of Hitler's Europe.

Eisenhower held conservative views on the nature of the presidential office, regarding himself as a nonpolitical chief of state who would run the executive office and the nation in a bipartisan manner. His primary duty, he felt, was not to serve as the strong head of his party, leader of Congress, or agent of dramatic social and economic change, but to function as a promoter of harmonious relations among the three branches of government so that all could work together for the common national good. He had long felt that Roosevelt and Truman had lowered the dignity of the presidential office by engaging in too many personal and political quarrels, and he planned to avoid these disputes and refrain from public criticism of his opponents, even of men like McCarthy. If the president got too political, he felt, he would lower the prestige of the office, lose esteem among the people in the country, and endanger his effectiveness as the chief executive. It was far better to work behind the scenes to get things done while maintaining the public nonpolitical stance important to governing the nation and serving as a healer during very divisive times.[43]

Throughout his eight years in office, Eisenhower operated behind the scenes to try to win public support for his policies, to influence legislation being considered in Congress, and to manage the nation's domestic and foreign affairs. Out of the public eye, he instructed the party faithful to support legislation he favored and to oppose bills he did not want. Rather than publicly lambasting Congress or individual congressmen as Truman had, Eisenhower quietly twisted congressional arms by sending personal memos, making personal telephone calls, holding prayer breakfasts, and holding face-to-face meetings in the Oval Office with influential leaders from both parties. At other times he sent personal emissaries to congressmen or other public figures with a personal message from the president attempting to persuade them to do what he wanted them to do. He also exerted influence by employing the tremendous patronage powers of his office, and by using his press conferences to send messages to Congress on pending legislation. Through it all, he rarely used threats, but rather appealed to people's patriotism, party loyalty, or sense of what was morally right.

Always conscious of how Truman had lost popular support for the Korean War and other presidential actions, Eisenhower tried to use the new medium of television to gain public support for his policies. In addition to giving inaugural, state-of-the-union, and other formal addresses on television, Eisenhower decided in 1955 to allow television coverage of his press conferences. In these meetings with the press he tried to inspire trust in the president and his policies, to tell the public why he had made a particular decision, to send messages to Congress, and to delay questions on problems on which he had not yet made up his mind. In his first press conferences in 1953, he had often appeared to be ill-read, uninformed, and ignorant of many basic things that even ordinary newspaper readers knew. Gradually, with better coaching and briefing, he began to perform better, though he never got over his habit of straying from the subject or speaking in ungrammatical, convoluted sentences. Sometimes he really was ill-informed, especially on some domestic matters, and reporters became accustomed to press secretary Jim Hagerty's "clarifications" on what Eisenhower had said or meant to say a day or two earlier.

But often the obfuscation was deliberate—he was in greater control of his press conferences than appearances indicated, for he decided in advance what he would and would not say and steadfastly refused to depart from it. He was skillful in dodging questions, changing the subject, and confounding his listeners when he wanted them to be confounded. On one occasion, when Hagerty was worried about what Eisenhower should tell the press about a dangerous crisis that was developing over Taiwan, Eisenhower said, "Don't worry, Jim. If that question comes up, I'll just confuse them."[44] He did, too, on this occasion and many others. Throughout his eight years in office and 193 press conferences—more than any president before him—he rarely, if ever, divulged any information or any decision on any policy until he was ready to reveal it.[45] And his frequent appearances on television made him the most familiar president in American history up to that time.

In spite of his dislike of many newspapers and his belief that politicians spent too much time cultivating the press, Eisenhower sometimes used the newspapers to help build public support for his policies. Unlike Truman, he did not engage in name calling with the press, nor did he fire off heated letters to an offending reporter or columnist. He did not publicly condemn newspapermen when he disagreed with them or when they attacked him, but if he liked an article or column he would send a warm note to the writer or publisher. He felt that this was a much more effective way of encouraging a favorable press than by engaging in fiery public attacks. He also courted the press in other ways. On his vacations he often played golf with accompanying reporters or treated them to fish he had just caught and cooked, and on really important matters he sometimes met privately with members of the press to turn on the Eisenhower charm. In 1956, for example, after being told by Arthur Sulzburger, publisher of *The New York Times*, that the paper had not endorsed the Republican ticket because of reservations about Nixon, Eisenhower invited Sulzberger for lunch. Not long afterward, a *Times* editorial appeared with an endorsement of the Eisenhower-Nixon ticket.[46]

Eisenhower also tried to drum up public support for his policies by making telephone calls or writing letters to prominent publishers, industrialists, educators, businessmen, and other powerful opinion makers, asking them to support his policies and use their influence to get others to. And he used his famous stag dinners not just for relaxation, but to gather information and advice from these influential men and persuade them to help sell his programs. More often than not, guests at these affairs left pledging to "go out and help Ike on this one."[47] Eisenhower's critics often ridiculed these presidential efforts as naive, and he probably overestimated how much help this personal network was able to give him, but he regarded these personal appeals as an essential tool of his presidency.

Eisenhower's political skills would be demonstrated in the way he organized and ran his White House staff and cabinet. In keeping with his military background, he organized the White House staff along military lines of authority and operation. This helped to isolate him from partisan politics and Republican infighting and to free him to concentrate on broad policies while leaving the tactics to his subordinates. This staff was headed by the ex-governor of New Hampshire, Sherman Adams, who had so impressed Eisenhower as his campaign manager that he appointed him the assistant to the president. This position gave Adams considerable power, for he and his staff served as a clearinghouse of information and people, handling as many problems and people as they could and carefully screening which documents and people—aside from those who had direct access—got to the president's office.[48]

Adams was a taciturn New England Yankee who worked long days, generally from seven-thirty in the morning to six-thirty in the evening, Monday through Saturday, and occasionally came in on Sunday afternoon as well—and he expected his subordinates to share this same capacity for backbreaking work. He brought his lunch to work every day in a brown cardboard box, wore suits that, his colleagues joked, must have dated from his student days at Dartmouth, and rarely ever wasted time, words, or effort. In a normal working day, he talked on the telephone from 200 to 250 times, often annoying those on the other end of the line by omitting helloes and good-byes from the conversation and abruptly hanging up when he had conveyed what he had to say, even when he was talking to the president himself. He acquired a reputation for gruffness and coldness because he was a brief, direct, businesslike man with no time or inclination for small talk, courtesy, joking, or other lubricants of human contact.[49] His personality and power aroused resentment and jealousy among many other members of the administration and with Congress. Around the White House he was known as Sherm the Firm and the Abominable No-Man, and his power, which was perhaps as resented as much as it was exaggerated, led many of his opponents to call him the assistant president and to circulate jokes like "If Sherman Adams dies, who will become president?" or the one that asked, "What if Ike died and we got Nixon as president?" with a punch line that answered, "But what if Adams died, and we got stuck with Ike?"[50]

Eisenhower relied heavily on Adams, for like all modern presidents he was simply too busy to see all the people who needed—or thought they needed—to see the president. Eisenhower used him to streamline the administrative process and to say no to people or problems he did not want to deal with. But Adams never had as much power as his opponents thought. He was not a palace guard, and the widespread belief that he made major governmental decisions just by writing "OK, SA" on documents intended for Eisenhower's desk simply was not true. He made decisions on minor matters, such as the appointment of people far down in the administrative bureaucracy. But he did not make major policy decisions. Furthermore, White House organizational charts and the writings of many of Eisenhower's aides clearly indicate that many people had direct access to Eisenhower. Presidential press secretary Jim Hagerty, Milton Eisenhower, the cabinet heads, and many other top officials could go straight to Eisenhower without going through Adams or anyone else. Eisenhower received advice from many aides and friends inside and outside the White House, and he, not Adams or anyone else, made the major decisions of his presidency.[51]

Eisenhower filled most of his cabinet and other top-level administrative positions with wealthy businessmen rather than professional Republican politicians. This irritated party regulars like Senator Taft, and it caused liberal opponents like TRB of *The New Republic* to scoff that the new cabinet was composed of "eight millionaires and a plumber" (the plumber was the secretary of labor, Martin Durkin, who resigned after only eight months in office). Three of the new appointments had close ties with General Motors, prompting Adlai Stevenson to quip that "the New Dealers have all left Washington to make way for the car dealers."[52] Although Eisenhower had planned to grant all cabinet members equal importance and access, Secretary of the Treasury George M. Humphrey and Secretary of State John Foster Dulles soon emerged as his closest and most influential advisers. He also relied heavily on his more liberal younger brother, Milton, who had a long and distinguished career as a government official and college president. The president depended on him not just for advice but for companionship, as a sounding board, as a speech proofreader, and as a special envoy to other countries. He held his brother in such high regard that he often stated that he was the most qualified man in the country to be president, not excluding himself.[53]

Under the formal bureaucracy and formal chain of command that Eisenhower brought to the White House, the cabinet, which had declined under Roosevelt but had been resurrected by Truman, was restored to its former position as the president's highest consultative body. He also had the directors of the Central Intelligence Agency, the United States Information Agency, the National Security Council, the Budget, and the ambassador to the United Nations to meet regularly with the cabinet, and he met separately once each week with the National Security Council, which he relied on much more heavily than Truman had. Eisenhower delegated broad powers and responsibilities to his cabinet members, who soon learned that he expected them to deal with the day-to-day details of government while he concentrated on the most important areas of policy-making.

Eisenhower had promised that he would use the cabinet as a policy-making body, and he seemed to carry out that pledge by having ten cabinet meetings in his first eighty days as president and averaging thirty-four meetings a year over his eight-year presidency. But actually he used it for advice, not policy-making. He presided over most cabinet meetings, where he skillfully asked the right questions to get the information he needed to make a decision. Cabinet members were encouraged to contribute facts and opinions on what should be done and to argue with one another and even with the president. But no votes were ever taken, and he made the final decision himself.[54] He also sought advice from congressional leaders, the members of his stag dinner parties, his brother Milton, and, if it involved foreign policy, the heads of the governments of America's allies. There were times, of course, when he could not seek wide counsel, as when decisions had to be made quickly or when they involved delicate matters or secret ones involving national security. And there were issues on which he could have, but did not, solicit opposing views. He never really gave a fair hearing to those who advocated a more vigorous action against McCarthy, a more active stance on civil rights, more spending for the cities and Social Security and other domestic social programs, or a cessation of nuclear testing.[55] Once he had made the decision, he expected the staff to support it and to remain loyal to him and to his team, looked to the appropriate cabinet member to work out the details of its implementation, and held him strictly accountable for it. Attorney General Herbert Brownell would later recall that "it was almost scary how much power he delegated to you."[56]

To maintain his public stance as a nonpolitical president, Eisenhower used his subordinates as lightning rods to draw the criticism and blame that might otherwise be directed at him. Sherman Adams and John Foster Dulles were often used in this manner, but so were other top officials of his administration. Press secretary Jim Hagerty once recalled that, when he complained to the president that if he had to tell reporters what he had just been ordered him tell them, "I would get hell," Eisenhower gave him a friendly pat on the back and said, "My boy, better you than me."[57]

Eisenhower disliked being bothered with the details of policies or problems that he felt should be ironed out by the men he had assigned to deal with them. Men like Charles E. Wilson, who ran to him with details of policy-making, irritated the president, who once told his secretary of defense: "Look here, Charlie, I want *you* to run Defense. We *both* can't run it, and I *won't* run it. I was elected to worry about a lot of things other than the day-to-day operations of a department."[58] Eisenhower also preferred that memos to him be models of conciseness, providing him in only one page, if possible, the essential details of the problem and the possible options open to him in decision-making. He also disliked sending memos to others or talking over the telephone. He preferred to see cabinet and staff members in his office, face to face, where they could talk over problems in a direct manner and he could immediately ask for clarification or more information before he made a decision. One of the few major exceptions to his preference for direct meetings was in his dealing with Dulles, who often called him on the phone to discuss foreign-policy matters.[59]

Like some of the other modern presidents, Eisenhower could not resist the temptation to record private conversations with other governmental figures. He had a tape recorder installed in the Oval Office, with the equipment hidden in a piece of furniture in the office of his secretary, Ann Whitman, and the activating switch located under his desk. The recorder was used infrequently, for Eisenhower frequently forgot to turn it on. But the recordings were made without the knowledge or permission of those being recorded, and were later transcribed by his secretary, who also monitored phone calls to the Oval Office and took notes on them, again without the knowledge of the other party.[60] He was not the first president to engage in clandestine recordings of private conversations—Franklin Roosevelt holds that distinction—and of course his own vice president would later become the most famous secret recorder of candid Oval Office conversations. The reasons for Eisenhower's invasions of the right of privacy are not entirely clear, but he did once tell members of his cabinet that they should record or monitor their telephone calls because "it's a good thing when you're talking to someone you don't trust to get a record made of it. There are some guys I just don't trust in Washington, and I want to have myself protected so that they can't later report that I said something else."

Eisenhower usually had the recording machine on when he was talking to the vice president.[61] Regardless of reason for the tapings, the practice seems to have been out of character for Eisenhower and constitutes a stain on his admirable presidency.

Eisenhower's leadership style, combining a low public political profile with behind-the-scenes maneuverings, did not always work, partly because of weaknesses inherent in the style itself, partly because of Eisenhower's own political limitations and mistakes, and partly because many men, events, and problems of the time could not have been manipulated, much less controlled, by Eisenhower or anyone else sitting in the president's chair. His refusal to condemn McCarthy, southern diehard segregationists, and demagogues and troublemakers of all kinds undoubtedly encouraged them and their followers. By concentrating on compromise and conciliation, he failed to awaken the nation to some of the real problems of the day or to give it a vision to strive for. And sometimes, especially in domestic matters, he put himself so far above the battle that he really was not as much on top of things as he should have been.

But it was Eisenhower's style and it was his considered belief that it was the only possible approach for the times. He wanted to end the political divisions that had wracked the nation under Truman, he realized that he had a fragile congressional constituency, and he felt that the nation wanted a period of compromise, conciliation, and consolidation, not a continuation of party strife, executive–legislative battles, or strident calls for reforms. His style enabled him to accomplish far more than most of his detractors had predicted when he took office. His successes, and there were many, necessitate a modern upgrading of his presidential reputation to the near-great level; his failures prevent him from being labeled a truly great one. Clearly, he was a complex man whose presidency cannot simply be dismissed as a boring and stale interlude between the administrations of Harry Truman and John F. Kennedy.

The voters certainly approved of the way Eisenhower ran things. He seemed to be the right man for the times, a healer and a conciliator after so many years of conflict, a man who inspired trust and confidence and encouraged about as much change as the people were ready to accept. They liked Ike, and they would continue to like him regardless of the mistakes he made in one of the toughest jobs in the world. They would reelect him by a large margin in 1956, allowing him to become only the fifth president since Andrew Jackson (Grant, Cleveland, Wilson, and Franklin Roosevelt were the others) to serve two full terms in office, the first Republican since William McKinley to win two consecutive elections, and the first Republican since Grant to serve two full terms. During his eight years in office, monthly Gallup Poll surveys of the public's view of the way he was handling his job averaged an incredible 64 percent approval rate,[62] and in 1960 he could easily have won a third term if he had wanted it and not been denied it by the Twenty-second Amendment (ratified in 1951) limiting the president's tenure to two terms. Had it not been for that amendment, Walter Lippmann once said, "Ike could be reelected even if dead. All you need do would be to prop him up in the rear seat of an open car and parade down Broadway."[63] One of the least political of presidents, Dwight D. Eisenhower was, quite simply, a political phenomenon.

# 10

# *Charting a New Course*

On January 24, 1953, I. F. Stone wrote in his newsletter, the *I. F. Stone Weekly*, that "Ike is no fire-eater, but seems to be a rather simple man who enjoys his bridge and his golf and doesn't like to be too much bothered. He promises to be a kind of president *in absentia*, a sort of political vacuum in the White House which other men will struggle among themselves to fill."[1]

Stone's view of the new president was shared by many people inside the administration and across the country. But it was not the view of Eisenhower himself, and his actions in office over the next eight years would reveal that it was an inaccurate assessment of the old general turned president. After twenty years of Democratic rule, he hoped to chart a new course into the future, turning the nation away from creeping socialism, foreign-policy blunders, and political bickering that only served to paralyze the government and divide the country. Far from abdicating his presidential powers, Eisenhower would work hard at his job and would leave behind a considerable list of accomplishments in both domestic and foreign affairs. This record would be obtained in spite of opposition from the right wing of his own party, Democratic control of Congress for six of the eight years he spent in office, the problems inherited from his predecessor, and complex domestic and foreign events that were often beyond the influence—much less control—of the president of the strongest nation in the world.

In pursuing his domestic and foreign policies, Eisenhower was plagued by a split within his own party between the moderate eastern wing and the conservative to reactionary midwestern wing. Led by such men as Thomas E. Dewey and Harold Stassen, the eastern wing had backed Eisenhower in 1952, accepted the New Deal reforms, and generally supported Truman's international policies. By contrast, the midwestern wing had supported Taft in the 1952 election and generally opposed the New Deal and the European-centered containment policy of Truman. While some were isolationists in foreign policy, still holding to the old idea of Fortress America, others accepted a broader role for the United States in world affairs but were Asia-firsters who felt that Truman had emphasized Europe too much and that the real global battle against communism was to be fought in Asia. It was this wing of the party, led by Senator Taft and, after his death in 1953, by William Knowland, that supported Senator McCarthy and opposed Truman's China policies, the limited warfare in Korea, and the firing of General MacArthur. And it was this wing that gave Eisenhower the most trouble.

Conscious of the split in his party and the dangers it presented to his administration, Eisenhower went out of his way to gain the loyalty of the conservative wing of the party. He cultivated the friendship and backing of Taft and other leading conservatives, avoided a direct confrontation with McCarthy, and vigorously campaigned for conservative Republicans in congressional elections. In all of these efforts to placate the conservative wing of his party, he was only partly successful, and its opposition dogged him all the way through both administrations. He was never able to modernize the Republican party, but he did succeed in persuading most of it to support his international policies and to accept the New Deal legislation as a fait accompli.

In most of his domestic and foreign policies, the president often got more backing from the opposition party than from his own Republicans. In this he was extremely fortunate, for of the four Congresses elected during his two terms, the Republicans had a majority only in the Eighty-third Congress elected along with him in 1952. The Democrats regained control of Congress in 1954, enabling Sam Rayburn to return to his post as speaker of the House and Lyndon B. Johnson to become Senate majority leader. Eisenhower maintained good relations with these powerful Texans most of the time, and his ability to work with them and the rest of the Democrats was facilitated by the conservative nature of the Democratic party, which had a strong southern wing. Both parties, and most of the electorate, were in a conservative mood, enabling him to pursue policies aimed at bringing stability and tranquillity to the country after the political turmoil of the Truman years. Under Eisenhower, the political rancor that so characterized most of Truman's terms, diminished, particularly after the end of the Korean War in 1953 and the fall of Senator McCarthy in 1954.

The first Eisenhower administration neither repudiated nor significantly expanded the basic domestic programs of the Roosevelt–Truman era. True to his campaign promises and political philosophy, he worked to reduce the powers and expenditures of the federal government, ease governmental regulations of business, and return some governmental functions to the states. The Reconstruction Finance Corporation was abolished, government manufacturing firms competing with private industry were closed or sold to private owners, the economic controls imposed by Truman during the Korean War were terminated, and the rich oil and gas fields off the Gulf Coast were returned to the states for easier leasing to private investors and developers. The federal bureaucracy was reorganized and streamlined (eliminating some 200,000 civilian jobs), tax cuts were granted to affluent individuals and corporations, and the federal monopoly of atomic energy provided by the Atomic Energy Act of 1946 was ended by a new Atomic Energy Act of 1954, which authorized the AEC to license private firms to develop and sell atomic power. Further, Eisenhower gave only lukewarm support to, and sometimes actively opposed, legislation designed to aid the elderly and minorities or to promote education, public housing, public works, fair employment practices, urban renewal, mass transit, or a viable national health-insurance program.

But in some other areas Eisenhower showed in his first term that in modern times even the Republican party could not return to the policies of the Hoover era and pretend that the New Deal and depression had never occurred. He supported the extensions of some New Deal measures, signing into law bills continuing farm supports, extending Social Security benefits to an additional 10 million people (including federal employees, farmers, and domestics), appropriating more money for public housing, hiking the federal minimum wage from seventy-five cents to $1 an hour, and increasing unemployment benefits. He added a new department—the Department of Health, Education, and Welfare—to the federal bureaucracy he had promised to trim, and filled the new position with Oveta Culp Hobby, wife of a wealthy Texas publisher, who became only the second female cabinet member in history (Frances Perkins, Franklin Roosevelt's secretary of labor, was the first). He supported the passage in 1956 of the National Defense Highway Act, which by providing $26 billion for the construction by 1972 of nationwide interstate highway system of 42,000 miles became the largest public-works project in history. He also backed federal planning and financing of the St. Lawrence Seaway project, which provided for cooperation between the United States and Canada in constructing a deep-water link between the Great Lakes and the Atlantic.

One of the most difficult and frustrating problems Eisenhower had throughout both his administrations was his futile attempt to keep his campaign promises to balance the budget, an obsession the Democrats characterized as "better dead than in the red." Achieving a balanced budget was extremely difficult because of the existence of so many fixed costs (such as pensions, Social Security, and interest on the national debt), because decreases in the defense and foreign-aid budgets would endanger national security and harm a national economy that had become so dependent upon defense spending, and because cuts in agricultural supports would be political suicide in the farm belt. Although Eisenhower resisted pressures for a budget-busting arms race and in fact was able to trim Truman's defense budget from $50 billion annually to around $40 billion for the next eight years, he refused to make further cuts because he felt that they would endanger the national security. Consequently, he was able to achieve only two balanced budgets in his eight years in office. After dropping slightly from the $80 billion level of the last year of the Korean War, federal expenditures rose to peacetime records of $81.8 billion in 1957 and $98 billion in 1960. By the late 1950s the annual federal deficit had also reached record proportions and the federal debt had jumped from $266 billion in 1953 to nearly $291 billion.[2] Like so many other modern presidents, Eisenhower found the problems of balanced budgets and a steadily increasing national debt to be virtually insolvable.

In the first months of his presidency, Eisenhower had to deal with several problems inherited from Truman's administration. One of the most troublesome ones was the sensitive case of Julius and Ethel Rosenberg, who in April of 1951 had been convicted of conspiracy to commit espionage and sentenced to death under the Espionage Act of 1917. The Rosenbergs had remained in the spotlight for the next two years as they engaged in a round of appeals through the federal court system and petitioned the White House for clemency. Incarcerated in separate cells in the men's and women's sections of Sing Sing Prison in Ossining, New York, they wrote tender letters to one another affirming their innocence, revealing their sympathies for left-wing causes but never admitting that they were communists, and agonizing over the fate of their two young sons, who were being taken care of by friends and by their lawyer, Emanuel Bloch. They were also allowed to visit one another for one brief period each week or when they consulted with their attorneys. Meanwhile, the nationwide debate over their case had continued, kept alive by the Red Scare and by the press's continuing fascination with the case. Most newspapers had accepted their guilt from the very beginning, and after their conviction article after article appeared urging them to confess and implicate others so they could receive clemency, save their lives, and provide for the care of their two innocent sons.

The Rosenbergs' case had slowly crawled through the courts, where the conviction was upheld by the United States Court of Appeals on February 25, 1952. When the Supreme Court refused to hear the case in the fall of 1952, Judge Kauffman set the execution date for January 12, 1953. The first of 1953 brought Truman's rejection of a Rosenburg clemency petition, another postponement of the execution, marches and rallies in Washington, New York, and several other cities, vigils outside Sing Sing and the White House, and letters and telegrams to the White House from some 200,000 people—including Albert Einstein, Pope Pius XII, and the family of Captain Alfred Dreyfus—asking for clemency. But Truman refused to act on the clemency petitions, believing that the Rosenbergs had received a fair trial. Through it all, the ACLU and most other liberal organizations refused to take up the Rosenbergs' case, for like most of the general public they believed that the couple was guilty and had received a fair trial.

Eisenhower felt that the couple had been fairly convicted of a heinous crime, and he was prepared to offer clemency only if they confessed and implicated others. In the spring there were further stays of execution from the Circuit Court of Appeals and more refusals by the Supreme Court to hear the case, including one on the afternoon of Friday, June 19, the date set for the execution. Thirty minutes after the Supreme Court refused for the last time to review the case, President Eisenhower released a statement announcing that he would not intervene with an act of clemency because the couple had "received the benefit of every safeguard which American justice can provide." The statement also claimed that "by immeasurably increasing the chances of atomic war, the Rosenbergs may have condemned to death tens of millions of innocent people all over the world. The execution of two human beings is a grave matter. But even graver is the thought of the millions of dead whose deaths may be directly attributable to what these spies have done."[3]

Attorney General Brownell ordered the executions to take place shortly before sundown on Friday, June 19, so that they would not be put to death on the Jewish Sabbath, which begins at sundown on Friday. The Rosenbergs were given a few hours together that afternoon as they awaited their deaths, and they used this time to talk and to write a joint letter to their young sons, affirming their love for them and asking them to "always remember that we were innocent and could not wrong our conscience."[4] Meanwhile, their lawyers made frantic last-minute efforts to get a new stay of execution. In Paris, London, and other European cities thousands demonstrated in support of the Rosenbergs, while demonstrations and vigils were held in New York and other American cities, including one outside Sing Sing and outside the White House, where an estimated four hundred sympathizers gathered to picket. A telephone line was kept open between Sing Sing and the Justice Department in Washington, just in case the Rosenbergs made a last-minute decision to repent and confess.

But at 8:06 P.M. Julius Rosenberg went calmly and silently to his death in the electric chair at the age of thirty-five. A few minutes later, Ethel Rosenberg, who was two years older than her husband, was brought into the execution chamber, where she turned to the female guard, hugged her and kissed her tenderly on the cheek, and sat down in the chair. She died at 8:16. The next morning *The New York Times* reported that "stoic and tight-lipped to the end, Julius and Ethel Rosenberg paid the death penalty tonight . . . for their war-time atomic espionage for Soviet Russia." Both Rosenbergs, said the *Times*, "went to their deaths with a composure that astonished the witnesses."[5] Their deaths did not end the debate over their guilt, trial, and punishment—that controversy continues even today—but their case gradually dropped from the front pages of the newspapers and would no longer serve as a divisive force within the nation.

The summer of 1953 also brought the end of another critical problem inherited from the Truman era: the Korean War. When Eisenhower took office the war had been going on for over two and one-half years. It had killed thousands of Americans, Koreans, and Chinese, deeply divided the United States, and greatly endangered world peace. But it had been in a stalemate ever since the peace talks began in the summer of 1951, when it settled into a war of attrition along the 38th parallel with neither side able to mount a final, victorious offensive. The communists regarded the peace talks as another front in the war, using them as a propaganda vehicle and as a way of wearing down the American will to fight. Day after day, the United Nations negotiators were subjected to endless harangues, arguments over the size of the tables used for the talks, delays, cancellations of earlier agreements, and the introduction of new issues to the agenda. The talks at Panmunjom dragged on and on, with the communists obviously awaiting the outcome of the American presidential election and the first moves of Truman's successor.[6]

Early in December of 1952, Eisenhower kept his famous campaign promise by making a three-day trip to Korea, where he met with General Mark Clark, the United Nations commander, talked with South Korea's president, Syngman Rhee, and visited the front line and ate with the soldiers. Eisenhower returned without a plan for ending the war, but the visit did convince him that "we could not stand forever on a static front and continue to accept casualties without any visible results" and that "small attacks on small hills would not end wars."[7]

In the first few months of Eisenhower's presidency world events slowly moved the two sides toward the signing of an armistice. Truman's departure from office and Stalin's death on March 5 removed two of the original protagonists, while the power struggle in Russia was bringing the emergence of rulers who took a softer line toward the West while they fought their own internal battles. The death of Stalin affected the Chinese leadership, too, for the war-weary Chinese, with about a million troops in Korea early in 1953, had their own internal problems and were unsure, in the absence of Stalin, of future Soviet foreign policy toward Korea and China. In April and May Eisenhower stepped up the bombing of North Korea, while hinting through the Indian ambassador and other diplomatic channels that if meaningful progress was not made soon the United States might be forced to use atomic weapons in North Korea and maybe even on Manchuria.[8] The negotiations now made a few halting steps forward, while at the same time the Chinese mounted one last major offensive, inflicting heavy casualties, with the apparent hope of increasing their bargaining powers. Syngman Rhee, who opposed any settlement leaving his country divided, tried to torpedo the armistice by allowing some 27,000 prisoners who had opposed repatriation to "escape" into the countryside. But finally, on July 26 (Washington time), an armistice was signed. Thirty-seven months after it began and with the opposing troops facing each other only a few miles from where it had all begun, the Korean War had come to an end.

The armistice agreements called for a cease-fire, a division of Korea along the battle line just slightly north of the 38th parallel, the establishment of a demilitarized zone jointly policed by United Nations and communist forces, the establishment of a military commission to supervise the execution of the agreements, and the orderly but voluntary exchange of prisoners of war. Over 3,700 happy Americans were among the nearly 13,000 United Nations troops released from communist POW camps, but the communists gleefully publicized the fact that twenty-one Americans and 326 other United Nations POWs chose to stay in North Korea or Communist China. (The twenty-one soon returned home, disillusioned with the People's Republic.) Those who were released brought back horrifying stories of mistreatment—poor food, inadequate clothing and medical care, unbearably cold living quarters, forced marches through subzero weather, and systematic torture and brainwashing. Almost 38 percent of American POWs in Korea died in captivity, as compared with only 11 percent of those in the Axis camps in World War II.[9]

Eisenhower went on radio and television at nine o'clock on the evening of July 26 to announce the armistice and to warn his countrymen that "we have won an armistice on a single battleground—not peace in the world. We may not now relax our guard nor cease our quest."[10] Americans were glad that it was over, but they saw little else to celebrate. The war had cost the country some 33,000 lives, over 100,000 wounded, and $22 billion, but Korea was still divided, just as she had been at the beginning of the war. Some conservatives, including many in Eisenhower's party, called it "peace without honor" and reminded anyone who would listen that Eisenhower was the first president to preside over the end of an American war that did not end in victory for the United States. But most Americans were just glad it was over and looked forward to the return home of the 350,000 troops stationed there. They also gave the president credit for ending the war, even if he had settled for the same basic terms Truman had unsuccessfully sought. As many newspapers pointed out, Truman would have been roundly condemned if he had accepted such a settlement.

The end of the Korean War, however unsatisfactory its terms, was a great advantage for Eisenhower. True, he had settled for containment, not rollback, and he institutionalized Truman's containment policies in Korea by signing a mutual defense treaty with South Korea committing the United States to sending billions of dollars of military and economic aid to Rhee, even though he ran one of the most reactionary regimes in Asia. But the armistice freed him from the great problem that had paralyzed Truman during his last two years in office, ended a great drain on the budget, helped to heal the divisions and wounds within the United States, and allowed him to forge his own foreign policy without being tied to a ground war in Asia. It also contributed to the end of the Great Fear, for the end of the fighting in this far-off Asian land inevitably led to the gradual subsiding of the communist paranoia at home. With the end of the Korean War, Joseph McCarthy's days in the limelight were numbered.

The end of the Korean War would eventually help to break the power of Senator McCarthy by depriving him of that international issue in his battle against communism. But the demagogic senator's downfall was still more than a year away, and in the meantime he reached his height as a divisive force in the Republician party, which Stevenson and other Democrats were labeling "half McCarthy and half Eisenhower." Many Republicans who had gone along with McCarthy's attacks on the Truman administration for political reasons had hoped that his reckless actions would stop now that the Republicans were in the seats of power. The congressional victories of 1952 had put the Republicans in control of the committee system in Congress, but rather than award McCarthy a major committee, Taft and other party regulars assigned him what they considered the less harmful posts of chairman of the Senate Committee on Government Operations and chairman of that committee's Permanent Subcommittee on Investigations. Senator Jenner, who played more by the party rules, was entrusted with the chairmanship of the Internal Security Subcommittee.

But they underestimated McCarthy's political skills and his insatiable thirst for fame. He turned his position into a power and publicity base by hiring his own staff, headed by Roy Cohn, holding his own highly publicized committee hearings on subversion in government, and building a large network of workers in all areas of government—from the CIA to the army—who served as "informers" and "agents" and funneled documents and information to McCarthy instead of their own superiors, directly violating bureaucratic regulations and federal laws. His power was augmented even further when Secretary of State Dulles, hoping to prevent further splits in the party and avoid the fate of his precedessor, Dean Acheson, tried to appease the witchhunters by appointing McCarthy's close friend, Scott McLeod, as the director of the State Department's personnel program. McCarthy now had a direct link to the State Department, where McLeod set up his own loyalty standards and cleared hirings with the senator. The demagogue from Wisconsin was now more powerful than ever before.

McCarthy used his new committee as a forum for making sensational charges, launching "investigations," announcing new "exposés" and "findings" of subversion, and bullying and embarrassing innocent witnesses. His favorite target was the State Department, and it made little difference to him that it was now run by Republicans instead of Democrats. He attacked its Voice of America program as an agency infiltrated by communists, left-wingers, and other fellow-travelers. He unsuccessfully sought to block the appointment of Charles E. Bohlen, a valuable career officer with experience dealing with the Soviet Union going all the way back to the recognition of the communist government in 1933, on the grounds that he had served as Roosevelt's interpreter at Yalta and that his loyalty was "questionable." McCarthy also sent Roy Cohn and Cohn's wealthy young friend and "volunteer consultant," David Schine, on an investigation of books in the libraries of the State Department's International Information Agency (later renamed the United States Information Agency). In early April they made a whirlwind trip across Europe, staying a few hours in Paris, Bonn, Frankfurt, Munich, Vienna, Belgrade, Athens, Rome, and London while they carried out their "investigations." A typical investigation took about thirty minutes and involved a superficial and often boisterous rummaging through card catalogs or library shelves and loud demands that the librarians purge the offensive volumes from their collections. In Paris and other cities they also had lively evenings on the town, charging their expenses—which included such items as perfume and silk stockings—to the government and engaging in rowdy horseplay in the lobbies of their hotels. Everywhere they went they were followed by European reporters, who ridiculed the ridiculous actions of two ridiculous men who represented the United States of America and were making laughingstocks of themselves and of their country.[11]

When they returned and made their report to McCarthy, the senator claimed that the International Information Agency had over 30,000 books on its shelves by communist authors. The list included works by known communists and Marxists, but also by Edna Ferber, John Dewey, Robert M. Hutchins, Arthur Schlesinger, Jr., and even Foster Rhea Dulles, the brother of the secretary of state.[12] The State Department panicked, and ordered the directors of its 189 libraries to purge their shelves of books written by communists or containing "communist propaganda." Such nebulous guidelines led some library directors to rather ridiculous decisions, such as the order that all books critical of Nationalist China be taken from the shelves. There were even reports of book burnings by some librarians.[13]

But these were not the only embarrassments McCarthy caused the new administration. In March of 1953 he proudly announced that he had secured an agreement from Greek shipowners that they would not trade with Red China—a clear violation, if indeed such an agreement had been reached—of the president's treaty-making powers. Further embarrassments came in July when J. B. Matthews, a former staff member of HUAC now serving on McCarthy's subcommittee staff, charged in an article in the right-wing *American Mercury* magazine that some 7,000 Protestant clergymen were part of the Kremlin conspiracy and constituted "the largest single group supporting the Communist apparatus" in the United States.[14] This created an uproar from churchmen all across the country and provoked Eisenhower into making a rare and angry attack on Matthews, who was then fired by McCarthy. And in the middle of the summer, McCarthy spent an entire day holding hearings on an alleged assassination plot against him hatched by opponents of his work in rooting out the communists. And so it went, on and on, one circus and unfounded allegation after another from a man whose duplicity and search for publicity knew no boundaries.

McCarthy's charades presented a difficult problem for Eisenhower, who viewed him as the very epitome of the dirty, self-seeking politician the president felt was so harmful to the country. But he avoided a direct attack on the slovenly senator. Eisenhower believed that a public confrontation between the president and the senator would only harm the presidential office, the Republican party, and the nation without damaging the demagogue who was pursuing headlines, not communists. As Eisenhower wrote in his diary on April 1, 1953, he believed that "Senator McCarthy is . . . so anxious for headlines that he is prepared to go to any extremes in order to secure some mention of his name in the public press. . . . I really believe that nothing will be so effective in combating his particular kind of troublemaking as to ignore him. This he cannot stand."[15] Eisenhower said on several occasions that "I just will not—I refuse—to get into the gutter with that guy," and that "I just won't get into a pissing contest with that skunk."[16] He also thought that the disciplining of the senator should come from the legislative branch of government, not from the White House, and that if McCarthy were given enough rope, he would eventually hang himself.[17]

Although Eisenhower tried to avoid public clashes with McCarthy, he worked behind the scenes to try to curb the senator's influence and persuade him to restrain his words and actions. When Eisenhower appointed Dr. James B. Conant, president of Harvard, to become the United States high commissioner to Germany, McCarthy let it be known that he intended to fight the appointment on the Senate floor, on the grounds that Conant must be a communist sympathizer for denying that the Harvard faculty contained any communists in its ranks. Eisenhower dispatched Vice President Nixon to talk with McCarthy and also telephoned the senator himself, asking him to drop his opposition. As a result, McCarthy sent Eisenhower a note promising that he would not provoke a floor fight over Conant. He kept his word—a rare thing for McCarthy—and Conant was confirmed.[18]

While Eisenhower's behind-the-scenes actions worked in the Conant case, they were less successful in the case of Chip Bohlen, a talented and experienced career diplomat whom Eisenhower had appointed ambassador to the Soviet Union. McCarthy denounced the nomination, claiming that Bohlen, who had been an interpreter at the Yalta conference, was a security risk, one of the "architects of disaster" who had sold out to the Soviets at Yalta and had been appeasing them and aiding communist expansion ever since then. Although Eisenhower was infuriated at this ridiculous charge and at this challenge of his presidential authority, he did not attack McCarthy publicly, but he did not sit passively by either. He refused to give in to Dulles and other administrative advisers who wanted to cave in to McCarthy and drop the Bohlen nomination. Eisenhower also praised Bohlen publicly, sent Nixon to try to reason with McCarthy, persuaded a reluctant Taft to rally other Republican senators behind the nomination, and refused the request of McCarthy and other senators that FBI files containing possibly damaging information on Bohlen's family life be made available to the Senate during the hearings. Eisenhower was not able to persuade McCarthy to drop his opposition to the nomination, but he did win the battle. Bohlen's nomination was approved by a vote of 74 to 13 on March 27.[19]

Occasionally Eisenhower publicly touched on McCarthy's excesses, as when in a speech at Dartmouth College (June 14, 1953) after Cohn and Schine's European trip he told his young listeners, "Don't join the book burners," urged them to read anything they wanted to, and encouraged them to study communism so that they would know how to fight it.[20] But he did not mention McCarthy by name. At a news conference three days later he again denounced book burners, but when asked by reporters if he was talking about McCarthy, Eisenhower replied that "I think that we will get along faster in most of these conferences if we remember that I do not talk personalities; I refuse to do so."[21]

Eisenhower also fought McCarthy by trying to prove that in the ferreting out of security risks, he was more diligent than Truman had been. Soon after taking office, he inaugurated his own loyalty program, broadening the grounds for dismissal of federal employees to go far beyond loyalty to include "Fifth Amendment communists" and threats to "national security," which could be interpreted to mean almost anything. Under his loyalty program, some 10,000 federal employees resigned or were dismissed, and disability pensions and Social Security payments for communists, such as the aging William Z. Foster, were ended even though many had paid into the Social Security fund for almost twenty years.[22] Eisenhower also supported the suspension of the security clearance of Dr. J. Robert Oppenheimer, the father of the atomic bomb, because he had admitted to being a fellow-traveler from 1937 to 1942, had close friends and relatives who were communists, and had opposed the decision to build the hydrogen bomb. Oppenheimer's security clearance was suspended in 1954 by the AEC. (It would be reinstated in 1963, under a very different political climate.) Eisenhower authorized the FBI to continue investigations of subversive activities of American citizens and to employ wiretapping in national security investigations, and he allowed the vice-president to go around bragging that the Republicans were kicking the communists out of high places in government. The Eisenhower administration also passed the Communist Control Act of 1954, which declared communism to be a great danger to the nation and prohibited communists from running for public office. It is clear that although the president detested the personality and methods of McCarthy, he shared his anticommunist fears and goals.

Their shared feelings, and their shared party affiliation, undoubtedly helped to shape Eisenhower's approach to his trials with McCarthy. There was considerable merit in his attempts to work behind the scenes, but there were serious weaknesses as well. Eisenhower's unwillingness to condemn McCarthy in public undoubtedly emboldened the unscrupulous senator, encouraged his followers, and prolonged the Red Scare that was so harmful to the country. Even if a public battle with McCarthy had hastened his downfall by only a few months, the reputations of many of his victims would have been spared, some semblance of rational political debate would have returned to Washington sooner, and the president and his advisers would have been granted additional time and freedom of action that could have been used to deal with other problems facing the country. And if the president had faced the McCarthy problem head on from the very beginning, he would not have been placed in the uncomfortable—and untenable—position of remaining publicly silent while McCarthy attacked General Marshall and General Zwicker—both old friends of the president—and other good, decent, and honorable men. Eisenhower's refusal to take bold action against this dangerous demagogue constitutes one of the greatest political and moral failings of his presidency.

McCarthy's popularity began to slip in the second half of 1953. The end of the Korean War eliminated one of the major contributors to the Great Fear, and his tactics were beginning to trouble even some of his strongest supporters. As was typical of him, he tried to arrest his declining popularity with a diversion, announcing that he was launching an investigation of the CIA and its director, Allen Dulles, brother of the secretary of state, but this idea was quickly abandoned. On July 10, the Democrats on his committee protested his actions by walking out en masse and launching a boycott of committee meetings. In the fall, as more people seemed to tire of his self-promotional efforts, he sought a new area of investigation, this time looking into the army and Department of Defense. He took time out in late September to marry his long-time research assistant and girl friend, Jean Kerr, but cut his honeymoon short so as to return to his investigations. As he moved from the investigation of the Army Signal Corps' Engineering Laboratories at Fort Monmouth, New Jersey, to an investigation of several defense plants, he was steadily moving toward a direct confrontation with the Eisenhower administration. Early in 1954 he overreached himself by beginning an investigation of the army, a reckless act that would lead to his own downfall.

McCarthy's feud with the army is complex, but basically it began with the army's foot-dragging in its handling of the case of Irving Peress, a dentist who had been automatically promoted by the army before it learned of his membership in the left-wing American Labor party. Peress, who took the Fifth Amendment when the army and McCarthy's committee questioned him about his political beliefs, requested and obtained an honorable discharge. McCarthy then launched an investigation, claiming that he had proof that "certain individuals in the Army have been promoting, covering up, and honorably discharging known Communists."[23] When Peress's commanding officer, Brigadier General Ralph W. Zwicker, a highly decorated veteran of World War II, came before McCarthy's committee, McCarthy received his refusal to provide information on the case with the assertion that Zwicker was "not fit to wear that uniform" and did not have "the brains of a five-year-old."[24] Eisenhower still declined to move against the senator, in spite of all the urging to do so by others in his administration, and he even ordered Secretary of the Army Robert Stevens, who had been intimidated and humiliated by McCarthy, to agree to cooperate with McCarthy's investigation. But as McCarthy continued to intimidate top army brass, Eisenhower began to urge other members of the administration to attack McCarthy openly, and finally allowed the army to retaliate.

On March 11, 1954, the army finally did, releasing very damaging information involving David Schine, Cohn's close friend and companion on the trip to overseas libraries in the spring of 1953. It seemed that when Schine had been drafted into the army, McCarthy and Cohn had intervened to seek preferential treatment for the young man, unsuccessfully trying to blackmail the army into giving him a commission but succeeding in securing lighter duties and more passes and other privileges than were normally given to other men of the same rank in the same outfit. McCarthy claimed that these charges were fabrications and that the army was trying to blackmail him. But his own subcommittee decided to investigate the whole affair, with Senator Karl Mundt taking over as chairman while the hearings went on. McCarthy was forced to relinquish his positions on the committee temporarily while retaining the right to testify as a witness and to cross-examine.[25]

At the same time that the Army–McCarthy battle was shaping up, television was also contributing to the destruction of the senator. Troubled by its own blacklists, fears, purges, and cowardice, network television had been afraid to tackle the powerful grand inquisitor until Edward R. Murrow took him on in several broadcasts of his *See It Now* program in the spring of 1954. The first program, on March 9, was composed mainly of a series of clips showing McCarthy in action, and though the telecast contained occasional comments from Murrow, it was McCarthy's own words that proved him to be a fraud. Murrow ended the broadcast with the assertion that McCarthy "didn't create this situation of fear; he merely exploited it, and rather successfully. Cassius was right: 'The fault, dear Brutus, is not in our stars but in ourselves.'"[26] Another *See It Now* show aired the following week, showing McCarthy and his tactics during one of his hearings, again with little comment from Murrow. McCarthy finally appeared on the show in April, spending most of the time—in his typical fashion—evading the issues and attacking Murrow, calling him "a symbol, the leader and the cleverest of the jackal pack which is always found at the throat of anyone who dares to expose individual Communists and traitors."[27] More and more, the public was seeing what McCarthy was really like. Murrow later did another show on McCarthy, contributing still further to the unveiling of a demagogue. But it was the sensational Army–McCarthy hearings, held from April 22 through June 17, 1954, that were the beginning of the end for the reckless senator.

During the hearings Eisenhower was still unwilling to attack the senator directly. But he continued to encourage other administration officials to do so, and he severely damaged McCarthy's case by refusing to turn over to McCarthy and other members of the Army–McCarthy committee executive personnel records or to allow executive personnel to testify before the committee. This unprecedented use of executive privilege to deny Congress the right to subpoena executive documents and personnel denied McCarthy access to important information and people, shutting off a potential source for more of his distortions, "exposés", and grandstanding before the committee. It also set an important precedent that would later be used—and abused—by Eisenhower's successors in the Oval Office.[28]

Most of the hearings—some 187 hours—were televised, and at times as many as 20 million viewers tuned in to watch the complicated but fascinating proceedings. The subcommittee's lawyer was Ray H. Jenkins, a Taft Republican and trial lawyer from Tennessee, while the army chose sixty-three-year-old Joseph Welch, a Harvard graduate, wealthy lawyer, proper Bostonian, and proper Republican. McCarthy dominated the proceedings, and for the first time millions of Americans saw him for what he really was. What they saw was an uncouth, unscrupulous, dishonorable, and sneering bully who intimidated and threatened witnesses; attacked the personality and looks rather than the arguments of his opponents; changed or evaded the subject when things were not going his way; assigned guilt by association; constantly interrupted testimony and proceedings by crying out "point of order" so he could level a countercharge or diversion; and showed disdain and sarcasm for decent men trying to follow accepted rules of civilized behavior. And finally, they saw him overreach himself on the thirtieth day of the hearings, when he interrupted with a point of order to reveal to the committee and to the huge television audience that a member of Welch's law firm named Fred Fisher had once been a member of the National Lawyer's Guild, which had been accused of communist sympathies. This attack by a grinning McCarthy on a young lawyer who had nothing to do with the hearings was an obvious attempt to divert attention from McCarthy's rapidly deteriorating case by impugning the background and motives of the army's counsel.

Welch had heard enough, and he now proceeded to make mincemeat of McCarthy. "Until this moment, Senator, I think I never really gauged your cruelty or recklessness," he told him and the rest of the nation. "Little did I dream you could be so reckless and so cruel as to do an injury to that lad. . . . If it were in my power to forgive you for your reckless cruelty, I would do so. I like to think that I am a gentle man, but your forgiveness will have to come from someone other than me." McCarthy tried to interrupt and return to an attack on Fisher, but Welch broke in and said: "Let us not assassinate this lad further, Senator. You have done enough. Have you no sense of decency, sir? At long last? Have you left no sense of decency?" The whole room applauded, and Welch got up and walked out, passing right by McCarthy. As the room emptied, a sheepish-looking McCarthy threw up his hands and asked, "What did I do?"[29]

The trial lasted several more days, but McCarthy was through. The committee hearings were inconclusive, for when the committee reports were released on September 1 the Republican majority's report favored McCarthy and condemned the actions of the army while the report of the Democratic minority condemned McCarthy. But the particulars in the Army–McCarthy case were now forgotten, for the Senate was now moving to discipline its famous maverick member. Republican Ralph Flanders of Vermont had introduced a censure motion on the Senate floor on July 30, but this was followed by a long partisan debate until December 2, when the Senate voted by a 67 to 22 vote to "condemn" McCarthy for contempt and abuse of the Senate. All forty-four Democrats present voted for the resolution, as did independent Wayne Morse and twenty-two Republicans.[30] McCarthy thus became only the third senator in history to be censured by the Senate. Goldwater, Jenner, and other conservative backers of McCarthy defended him to the end, claiming that partisan Democrats and communist sympathizers were out to get him because he had been so effective, and of course the senator had no trouble blaming the communists and communist dupes for the resolution. Technically, he was "condemned" rather than censored, but the word "condemned" had been used in the other two censure cases and McCarthy's colleagues thought that this was what they were voting for. When reporters asked McCarthy about the intent of the resolution, he admitted that "it wasn't exactly a vote of confidence." But he then said, with a flash of his old theatrical skills, that "I'm happy to have this circus ended so I can get back to the real work of digging out communism, crime and corruption."[31]

But McCarthy's work was over, though he still had four years of his term to go. His favorable ratings in the Gallup Poll dropped from over 50 percent in January 1954 to 34 percent in July, and continued to drop thereafter. He had lost his public support. In the elections held the month before his censure he was also shorn of his political support, for the Democrats gained control of the Senate, and McCarthy was stripped of the chairmanship of the committee he had so cleverly used before. He now had few friends in the Senate, was dropped from social lists all over Washington, and was no longer followed by reporters seeking information about his latest "exposés" or "investigations." The Senate and the nation paid little attention to him now, even when he called Earl Warren "a good friend of the communists," apologized to the American people for telling them to vote for Eisenhower in 1952, and advocated that General MacArthur be put in charge of foreign policy.[32] In October of 1955, I. F. Stone wrote in his newsletter that McCarthy looked as if he "stood on the threshold of old age. He looks with his too eager smile like a man who feels that he has become disreputable, secretly agrees with the verdict passed upon him, but wishes people would like him anyway. He who made so many people infamous and drove them out of respectable society now stoops slightly, as if under the weight of a similar fate."[33]

McCarthy began to drink even more heavily and to appear in public obviously intoxicated, and he was frequently hospitalized for ailments ranging all the way from exhaustion and bursitis to liver and back trouble. He began to miss committee meetings and roll calls, and finally stopped going into the office altogether, staying home to drink, brood, and watch soap operas. In 1956 he did not even attend the Republican convention or campaign for any candidates. His health continued to decline, and on May 2, 1957, he died in the Naval Medical Center at Bethesda, Maryland, from hepatitis and other conditions complicated by alcoholism. After a formal service at St. Matthews Cathedral and another memorial service, at the request of his wife, in the Senate chamber, his body was flown to Appleton, Wisconsin, where he was laid to rest beside his parents in St. Mary's cemetery.[34]

While many Americans felt little or no remorse at the passing of McCarthy, and openly said so, most of his public opponents, including Truman, Acheson, and Joseph Welch, politely expressed their condolences to his widow and refused to speak ill of the dead, at least in public. But McCarthy's die-hard supporters were not so charitable toward the senator's opponents. Right-wing publications and patriotic organizations like the American Legion and DAR asserted that the senator was a martyr to the anticommunist cause and that he had been driven to his death by the homosexuals, pinkos, communists, liberals, fellow travelers, and dupes he had fought so long and hard against. A writer in the Fort Worth *Southern Conservative* claimed that "Joe McCarthy was slowly tortured to death by the pimps of the Kremlin,"[35] while New England publisher William Loeb wrote that McCarthy had been driven to death by a mob led by "the stinking hypocrite in the White House."[36] David Lawrence, editor of the conservative *U.S. News and World Report*, was moved to write a six-page editorial on "Justice to the Memory of Senator McCarthy," claiming that the senator's death "was due in part to a physical condition brought on by the months of agonizing tension growing out of the persecution he suffered at the hands of the Senate." He urged the Senate to repent of its earlier sins (the censure) and adopt "a simple resolution expunging from the record the vote of December 2, 1954."[37]

With McCarthy effectively silenced as the leader of the right, it had to look for new leaders. One of them was Barry Goldwater, an outspoken conservative from Arizona, a rising star in the Senate, and a future presidential candidate. Another was young William F. Buckley, Jr., who had caught the eye of the nation's conservatives in 1951 with the publication of *God and Man at Yale*. The son of an Irish Catholic from Texas who made his fortune in oil, Buckley had been relieved of the need to earn a living and was able to devote himself to politics and writing. In 1954, he and his brother-in-law, L. Brent Bozell, one of McCarthy's speech writers and aides, wrote a defense of McCarthy entitled *McCarthy and His Enemies*, which concluded that "as long as McCarthyism fixes its goal with its present precision, it is a movement around which men of good will and stern morality can close ranks."[38]

In 1955, with $450,000 raised from his father and seventy-nine other contributors, Buckley founded the *National Review* to serve as a vehicle of his ideas and those of other conservatives. Buckley's magazine campaigned against government regulation while touting the merits of free competition, generally opposed the policies of the Eisenhower administration as too liberal and too soft on communism, published a review of one of Dean Acheson's books by none other than Joe McCarthy, and attacked the Supreme Court's Brown decision on desegregation as "one of the most brazen acts of judicial usurpation in our history."[39] Buckley did not normally espouse the more extreme causes of the radical right, such as the John Birch Society, which he often condemned. Beginning with an initial press run of around 2,700, the *National Review*'s circulation rose from 10,000 at the end of its first year to 30,000 by 1960 and to 60,000 by the time of its support of Goldwater's candidacy in 1964.[40] The magazine provided American conservatives with a respectable literary voice at a time when most right-wing publications were vulgar screeds.

Farther to the right of Buckley was the radical right, which tended to cluster around new groups like the John Birch Society, established in 1958 by wealthy candy manufacturer Robert Welch, who had been a staunch supporter of Robert Taft and Joseph McCarthy and a vehement critic of Eisenhower. Founded at a meeting of right-wingers in Indianapolis in 1958, the society was named after a U.S. Army intelligence officer who had been killed by the communists in China ten days after the end of World War II. The John Birch Society claimed that anyone who was not part of the extreme right wing of the Republican party was procommunist—which would have included the great majority of the American people. It strongly supported the work of the late senator from Wisconsin and the views of Barry Goldwater. Firmly opposed to the United Nations, which it regarded as an invention of Franklin Roosevelt and as a base for spies, saboteurs, and the propagation of communism, the society often called United Nations supporter Eisenhower "a dedicated, conscious agent of the Communist conspiracy."[41] The society was also highly critical of the Warren Court for its decisions on civil rights and civil liberties. Its campaign for the impeachment of Earl Warren was, like most of its other activities, a negative contribution to the political debates of the 1950s.

The censure and subsequent political fall of McCarthy obviously did not end the fear of communism in America. This was well documented in a joint survey conducted in the summer of 1954 by the Gallup Poll and the National Opinion Research Center of the University of Chicago. Written by Samuel Stouffer and published in 1955 under the title, *Communism, Conformity, and Civil Liberties: A Cross Section of the Nation Speaks Its Mind,*[42] this important survey revealed that Americans were still worried about the communist menace and were still distorting its nature and influence. Over half of those surveyed felt that communists should be jailed and that they should be rooted out of American society even if innocent people were hurt in the process. Eighty-nine percent favored firing communists from college teaching posts, 54 percent would not allow socialists to teach in a college or university, and an incredible 84 percent would deny this right to atheists—in these confused times of the fifties, socialists and atheists were often thought to be communists. Over 60 percent favored removing books written by admitted communists from public libraries and firing communists from jobs as radio singers. Sixty-four percent felt that it was right to tap private telephones in order to gather information about communists, and 73 percent felt it was right to report friends and neighbors suspected of communism to the FBI.[43]

Although Americans were against communism, the Stouffer survey indicated that they often did not quite know what it was that they were against. When asked what communists believed in, the most frequently given response was that they were "against religion." Further down the list in their definitions of communists was that they were people who were "immoral, amoral, antifamily," or believed in "political dictatorship," "promoting domination of the world by Russia," "abolition of class distinctions," or "revolution." But only 3 percent said that they had ever known a communist, and only 10 percent said they had known people that they even suspected of being communist. When asked the reasons for their suspicions, they gave answers such as he "would not attend church and talked against God" or "he didn't believe in Christ, heaven, or hell." Others were suspected because of their international views, such as "he was always talking about world peace" and distributed "literature about the United Nations." Then there were those whose suspicions were aroused because "I saw a map of Russia on a wall in his home" or "he wrote his thesis in college on Communism" or "he brought a lot of foreign looking people into his home." A Michigan housewife suspected a relative because he was "a scientist, an atheist, and down on everything," while a Georgia lawyer said that "I suspect it from his conversation and manner. He was well educated and had a high disregard for the mentality of others." One lady in Ohio suspected her brother-in-law because he "drinks and acts common-like," while a farmer expressed the views of many when he said, "I just knew. But I wouldn't know how I knew." In short, the people most likely to be suspected as communists were those who seemed to be different or strange and had ideas disliked or distrusted by the general population.[44]

But the Stouffer survey also revealed something else about Americans in the summer of 1954, for when they were asked what they were most concerned about, over 80 percent listed family, personal, and economic problems—not communism—as their main worries. Although the Cold War was still continuing and the Army–McCarthy hearings were still fresh in people's minds, few were worried about world affairs, war, communism, McCarthy, or any threat to their freedom or civil liberties. Many people thought about these problems, of course, but they just did not place them very high on their lists of concerns. When questioned about the menace of

American communists, only 19 percent felt that they were "a great danger." Apparently many would have agreed with the wife of a Delaware school superintendent who said that "we have to be on the job against Communism" but was willing to leave that job to "Eisenhower and the Army, Navy, and State Department." It was clear, the conductors of the survey concluded, that "the internal communist threat, perhaps like the threat of organized crime, is not directly felt as personal. It is something one reads about and talks about and even sometimes gets angry about. But a picture of the average American as a person with the jitters, trembling lest he find a Red under the bed, is clearly nonsense."[45]

The followers, fears, and ideas that McCarthy exploited and helped inspire lived long after his censure and death. HUAC and the Internal Security Committee were active for the rest of the decade, and the anticommunist crusade was still a burning cause for the DAR, American Legion, J. Edgar Hoover, Buckley, Goldwater, the John Birchers, and other members of the right or radical right. But the worst days of the Great Fear were over by the time of McCarthy's censure in 1954. Stalin was dead, the Rosenbergs were dead, the Korean War was over, and McCarthy was a fading headline. Other problems were coming to the fore, like civil rights, to engage the attention of the nation. Besides, people felt, the good man in the White House would take care of world problems just as he had carried out the defeat of the Nazis and ended the Korean War. Most Americans were ready to put the Red bogey behind them and enjoy the tranquillity and prosperity of the Eisenhower era.

# 11

# *Fighting Jim Crow*

When Eisenhower took office, the nation's 16 million blacks were still at the bottom of the political, social, economic, cultural, and educational ladder. Whether they lived in the North or South or in rural or urban areas, they trailed the white majority in the traditional American criteria of progress and success: income, housing, medical care, education, literacy, and disease and mortality rates. They had little or no political power, held the lowest-paying jobs, lived in segregated residential areas, and were treated as inferiors by the white majority. Like repressed people everywhere, many blacks both resented the way they were treated and often accepted the validity of the stereotyped traits whites ascribed to them—that they were lazy, stupid, slovenly, all the other things whites said they were. And through fear or conviction, blacks everywhere had learned to stay in their place, to act as the white majority expected them to act.

It was in the South, where most of the nation's blacks lived, that they suffered the most from economic deprivation and discrimination. The South was no monolithic region, of course, for in that vast area stretching from Maryland to Texas there were great differences between the upper and the lower South and between urban and rural areas, and southern opinions on blacks and race relations ranged all the way from rabid segregationists to liberals who favored full integration. But overall, the South was still the least urbanized and industrialized part of the country, still trailed the other regions in income and educational levels and most other areas of progress, and was still the region of the country that was most obsessed with Negrophobia and the preservation of white supremacy. It was still the most stable and conservative part of the nation, a land of Bible Belt religious fundamentalism with a strong belief in an orderly and hierarchical society with everything and everybody in its place. And in this conservative hierarchy of things, the superiority of whites, white supremacy, and the separation of the races were considered to be part of God's natural order and therefore should not be disturbed. And finally, nearly a century after the defeats, destruction, and humiliation of the Civil War, Confederate flags still waved over southern state capitols, a proud reminder of a past and a way of life that white southerners were determined to preserve.

As the fifties opened, southern whites and blacks still lived with racial feelings, customs, and laws from deep in the region's past. Ever since the end of the nineteenth century, Jim Crow laws providing for "separate but equal" facilities had forced blacks to live as a subcaste in their own land. The separate-but-equal doctrine still reigned in most private and public facilities—public transportation, theaters, hotels, hospitals, doctors' offices, elevators, churches, libraries, orphanages, prisons, mental institutions, beaches, amusement parks, swimming pools, and golf courses, but chiefly and most disastrously schools. The emphasis was always more on the *separate* than the *equal*, so rarely did the black facilities match those of the white. Segregation extended even into death, for Jim Crow laws also mandated separate morgues, funeral homes, and cemeteries. If it was too expensive to provide two of something, such as a municipal golf course, then the facility eliminated was the black facility. Blacks also had very little political power, having long ago been disfranchised by poll taxes, literacy tests, constitutional interpretation tests, voucher laws requiring a registered voter to "vouch" for the character of a potential voter, "waiting lists" devised by allegedly busy registrars, registration offices that happened to be "closed" when blacks came in to register, and "improperly filled out" registration forms. All of these devices, as well as many others, had been used to keep the voting rolls almost lily white.[1]

To justify his treatment of blacks, the southern white for decades had convinced himself that the treatment was legal, moral, even Christian because of the inferiority of the black race. These rationalizations were often expressed in clichés and shibboleths that varied very little from one part of the South to another. It was an article of faith among whites that blacks were mentally inferior to whites, that they were ignorant buffoons rather than intelligent human beings, that they were lazy, that they were dirty and had offensive body odors, that they could not be trusted with responsibility, that they could perform only the most menial of jobs, that they would steal and loaf whenever they could, that the black male was oversexed and wanted nothing more than to have sexual relations with white women, and that white women were in constant danger of rape from black men. It was an article of faith that segregation was the only way the two different races could live together, that race contact led to race mixing, that race mixing led to intermarriage, that intermarriage and interbreeding had caused the downfall of great civilizations like ancient Egypt, and that to prevent race mixing and the inevitable downfall of civilization southern blacks should be kept in their place by customs, Jim Crow laws, and the antimiscegenation laws that existed in every southern state and in many others as well. It was an article of faith, too, that blacks were happy in the South, did not resent their inferior status and treatment, loved and respected their white superiors, and became upset only when they were agitated by communists, the NAACP, and other outside troublemakers. And added to these myths was one of the greatest myths of all: Southerners, it was believed, had always lived among blacks and understood them far better than northerners did or ever could, and the South could maintain harmonious race relations if outsiders left the question of race relations up to southerners.[2] Some outsiders claimed, as did Richard Long of *The Nation*, that "the Negro they understand exists only in their imagination," but few southerners would have believed it.[3]

Up until the early 1950s, southern whites had the federal government on their side in their attempt to maintain white supremacy and segregation. Ever since the end of Reconstruction the Negro had been virtually forgotten by the federal government that had given him his earlier freedoms. The Supreme Court had overlooked all but the most blatant circumventions of the Fourteenth and Fifteenth Amendments, upholding laws and local practices that effectively disfranchised most blacks in the southern states and ruling in the famous *Plessy* v. *Ferguson* case (1896) and other decisions that the Jim Crow laws were not violations of the Fourteenth Amendment if the segregated facilities were equal. From the Wilson administration on down to Truman's time, the federal government itself had violated the rights of black Americans, maintaining segregation in the armed forces and practicing discrimination in the hiring and promotion of federal workers and in the administration of federal housing programs and other services.

In the first half of the twentieth century, blacks inadvertently took the first step toward gaining full citizenship in white America: They began to leave the rural areas of the South. Seeking better economic opportunities and relief from racial oppression, they began to migrate to the cities, particularly the northern ones, swelling the black populations of New York, Chicago, Detroit, and other industrial cities of the Northeast and Midwest. While in 1900 the great majority of the nation's blacks had lived in the South, this percentage had dropped to 68 percent by 1950 and would decline to 60 percent by the end of the decade.[4] Many blacks found out, as they encountered prejudice and de facto segregation, that the North was not quite the haven they had envisioned, for in the North as in the South racial contact, economic competition, discrimination, fears, and rumors all combined to produce waves of racial violence in urban areas, like the riots that killed forty blacks and eight whites in East St. Louis (Illinois) in 1917, thirty-eight whites and blacks in Chicago in 1919, and nine blacks and twenty-five whites in Detroit in 1943. This racial violence continued on into the fifties, striking in Chicago, New York, Miami, Chattanooga, Birmingham, Atlanta, Kansas City, Cleveland, Indianapolis, Los Angeles, Houston, and several other cities.[5] No part of the country seemed immune from the madness. Long before Eisenhower took office, race relations had ceased to be a southern problem and had become a national problem that would have to be dealt with at the national level.

By 1954 the American Negro stood on the verge of a new era in race relations. Although few Americans—black or white—realized it, the nation was about to undergo a civil rights revolution that would bring more change in race relations than in any period since the Civil War and Reconstruction eras. This new civil rights revolution—the Second Reconstruction, some historians called it[6]—was partly caused by the urbanization of blacks, which led to a new politial and social consciousness, created a new black middle class that would help to lead blacks of all classes in a quest for their rights, and contributed to the formation of the NAACP (1909), the National Urban League (1910), the Congress of Racial Equality (1941), and other organizations dedicated to black progress. It was partly caused by the Second World War and the Korean War, which uprooted millions of black males, broadening their horizons and their contacts with white culture and increasing their resentment of discrimination. The Second Reconstruction was partly fed by television and the consumer culture of the fifties, both of which helped to raise the expectation of the black masses, who now more than ever wanted the material goods and other fruits of the growing prosperity they witnessed on their television screens. It was partly fed by spectator sports and the rest of the entertainment industry, for the exploits of Joe Louis, Jackie Robinson, Willie Mays, and dozens of other black athletes were helping to increase the visibility, respect, and expectations of blacks. And finally, it was promoted by the federal government, which, after decades of neglect, intervened once again to protect the right of black citizens. But unlike the Civil War and Reconstruction periods, when the executive and legislative branches had been the major promoters of civil rights, the major role in the 1950s would be played by the judiciary, with the executive and legislative branches following reluctantly behind.

The Supreme Court had already been quietly chipping away at the walls of segregation before the Brown decision in 1954. By 1950, the Court had outlawed state and local segregated housing laws, segregation on railroads and buses crossing state lines, and the "grandfather clause" and white primaries, two devices used to disfranchise blacks. In a series of decisions handed down from 1939 on, the Court had also attacked the separate-but-equal doctrine in higher education. When the 1953–54 college term began, only five state universities—all in the South—were still segregated. There was still only token integration, but the legal barriers had been broken down. It was obvious to both friends and enemies of the southern black that the separate-but-equal doctrine would soon be under attack at the lower educational levels as well.[7]

The assault would come in the spring of 1954, when segregated schools were required in the nation's capital and in seventeen southern and border states and was a legal option of local governments in four others. It came in a desegregation suit involving a little girl named Linda Brown in Topeka, Kansas. The case had originated back in 1951 when her father, the Reverend Oliver Brown, had tried to enroll her in the fourth grade of Sumner School, an all-white elementary school in Topeka, which was only four blocks from her home and which she had to pass every day on her five-mile trip to the all-black school at Monroe. When the authorities in Topeka refused to admit her to Sumner because she was black, her father took the case to court, and, carried by NAACP lawyers, it finally ended up at the Supreme Court. Several parents from other states had now become parties to the suit, but since Brown's name came first in alphabetical order, he would become the Brown in the famous *Brown* v. *the Board of Education* decision.[8]

The Supreme Court that decided the Brown case was a moderately liberal court headed by a new chief justice, Earl Warren. A moderate Republican, Warren was a Californian who had served as a district attorney, an attorney general, and three-term governor before being appointed by Eisenhower to the Court in September of 1953 to replace Fred Vinson, who had died of a heart attack. He had been a major figure in the Republican party for years, and in 1948 had been Dewey's vice-presidential running mate in the narrow loss to Truman. Ironically, the man who would lead the Warren Court of seventeen different associate justices over sixteen stormy years, who would be identified with civil libertarian causes, and who would be considered the most influential chief justice since John Marshall, had supported as California's attorney general the internment of Japanese-Americans after the attack on Pearl Harbor.[9] Eisenhower would later say that his appointment of Warren was "the biggest damfool mistake I ever made,"[10] but in 1953 it had aroused little opposition from the Republican party, Congress, or the conservative press.

At 12:52 P.M. on Monday, May 17, Warren began reading the decision. In a calm and measured voice, he reviewed the background to the case, the arguments of the parties involved, the history of court opinion on the separate-but-equal doctrine since *Plessy* v. *Ferguson*, and the relevance of the separate-but-equal doctrine in 1954. "We come," he read, "to the question presented: Does segregation of children in the public schools solely on the basis of race, even though the physical facilities and other 'tangible' factors may be equal, deprive the children of equal educational opportunities?" The Court's answer was "that it does. . . . To separate them from others of similar age and qualifications solely because of their race generates a feeling of inferiority as to their status in the community that may affect their hearts and minds in a way unlikely ever to be undone." Warren then read what would become one of the most famous paragraphs in the history of Supreme Court decisions: "We conclude that in the field of public education the doctrine of 'separate but equal' has no place. Separate educational facilities are inherently unequal. Therefore, we hold that the plaintiffs and others similarly situated . . . are, by reason of the segregation complained of, deprived of the equal protection of the laws guaranteed by the Fourteenth Amendment."[11] Warren finished reading at 1:20 P.M. It had taken only twenty-eight minutes to deliver the unanimous decision. It would change history.

News of the Brown decision traveled rapidly across the world, carried by the news media and by Voice of America broadcasts in thirty-four languages. In the American North and most foreign countries, the press lauded it as a long overdue victory over prejudice and discrimination in the world's leading democracy. The American black press and black citizens celebrated it as the biggest victory for black freedoms since Lincoln's Emancipation Proclamation and looked forward to finally becoming first-class citizens in their own land. But in the white South there was little sympathy for the decision, which was widely regarded as an unwarranted judicial intervention in southern affairs and a dangerous attack on the southern way of life. May 17 would be known for years in the South as Black Monday, the day the Court decided to put blacks into the white schools.

Southerners were worried, but in the first few months after the Brown decision there was little hint of open defiance or violence. Uppermost in the minds of most white southerners now was the question an anxious white mother asked a school official in Cleveland, Mississippi, soon after the Brown decision: "Well, are we going to have niggers this fall?"[12] In the spring of 1954, a wide variety of answers to this question were given by school officials and politicians all across the South. Very few of them agreed with the decision, and even those who privately favored it were not foolish enough to say so publicly. Many who would have called themselves liberals or moderates agreed with Senator Estes Kefauver of Tennessee, who said that "while we may not agree with the decision, we must not let this disrupt our school system."[13] In much of the lower South, government officials were less restrained, denouncing the Court in caustic terms and promising to maintain segregated schools forever. But much of this was empty political rhetoric, designed to please the voters while government officials waited for the Court to make its next move. It had provided no specific guidelines for implementing its decision, and many southerners hoped that they might be given years—even decades—to comply.

Between May of 1954 and May of 1955 the Supreme Court heard more arguments on desegregation, and on May 31, 1955, it handed down its second Brown decision. Once again its opinion was unanimous and once again it brought bad news to white southerners, ordering "a prompt and reasonable start toward full compliance with our May 17, 1954, ruling." The Court emphasized that it understood the problems involved and would consider granting "additional time" if necessary, and it left it up to federal district courts to implement the decision and to evaluate whether the states were acting in good faith in carrying out the desegregation decision. But the Court also declared that the district courts were required to move toward the elimination of public school segregation "with all deliberate speed."[14]

"With all deliberate speed"—this vague phrase stunned many southerners. Most did not want integration at all—ever. A Gallup poll of southern opinions on the Brown decision in May of 1955 showed that only 20 percent approved, and this figure would decline as the decade progressed.[15] Now more than at any time since the Civil War and Reconstruction eras, white southerners saw their way of life under attack, and like most groups that suffer from outside attacks, they responded by closing ranks and fighting to defend their region from external enemies. In the face of this perceived threat, southern segregationists tried to force the rest of the South to fall in behind them in defense of the southern way of life. Liberals, moderates, and others who wanted to comply with the Brown decision were quickly reminded by the diehards that "if you're not with us, then you must be against us." All across the South, liberals became afraid to speak out, and many moderates—including moderate politicians who had once been friends of blacks and tried to help them—now joined the ranks of the segregationists. For the rest of the decade, and even longer in the deep South, race relations regressed in a region that felt itself under siege.

In these early days of the civil rights revolution, the American Negro could count on little help from the White House, which was inhabited by a man who was lukewarm on the civil rights issue. In his first state-of-the-union address, Eisenhower had said that the protection of civil rights was "a sacred obligation binding upon every citizen."[16] But action did not follow rhetoric. Eisenhower had had little contact with blacks throughout his life, and he never seemed to understand fully the depth of American racism and the plight of the minority that suffered from it. He was a strong states' righter who genuinely wanted to avoid federal interference in what he regarded as local and state matters, and he believed that segregation was so deeply rooted in American life and the American mind that it could not be eradicated overnight or by force. He felt that people's minds could be changed only through a slow and gradual educational process. Integration in the public schools would come, but it would take a long time, and the place to start was at the college and university level, and then work down. On July 24, 1953, ten months before the Brown decision, he wrote in his diary that "it is my belief that improvement in race relations is one of those things that will be healthy and sound only if it starts locally. I do not believe that prejudices, even palpably unjustified prejudices, will succumb to compulsion."[17]

Eisenhower always refused to comment publicly on the Brown decision, usually on the grounds that his private opinions were not important, that his duty was only to enforce the laws, that his comments would draw the executive branch into a controversy and, as he would later write in his memoirs, "would tend to lower the dignity of government, and would, in the long run, be harmful."[18] When pressed by reporters for a comment, he often stated that Brown was the law of the land and that he would uphold it, and he often reminded them, as he did at a press conference held two days after the first Brown decision, that "the Supreme Court, as I understand it, is not under any administration," and that his administration was not responsible for Brown.[19] But he privately disagreed with the decision. In the 1956 campaign, he told speechwriter Emmet John Hughes that the Brown decision would "*set back* progress in the South *at least fifteen years*. . . . It's all very well to talk about school integration—if you remember that you may also be talking about social disintegration. Feelings are deep on this, especially where children are involved. . . . And the fellow who tries to tell me that you can do these things by *force* is just plain *nuts*."[20]

Feeling as he did, it is not surprising that Eisenhower did very little to further the cause of desegregation until his hand was forced at Little Rock in 1957. When he came into office, he did use his executive authority to complete the desegregation of the armed forces, which had been begun by Truman, and to desegregate naval shipyards at Charleston and Norfolk, all veterans hospitals, and the public schools and other public facilities in Washington, D.C. He also appointed the first black cabinet level official, Assistant Secretary of Labor J. Ernest Wilkins, and the first black presidential aide, E. Frederick Morrow. He was able to do these things without interfering in the rights of the states as he saw them. However, he hurt the civil rights movement and the nation by refusing active support for enforcement of the Brown decision. His talk about states' rights, of the error of trying to force people to accept integration, of gradualism and patience, of changing the hearts and minds of the people—all these statements only encouraged the segregationist diehards, the advocates of massive resistance, and the violence of the Klan and other individuals and groups. If he had only declared publicly that the Brown decision was legally and morally correct and that he intended—as the Constitution required—to enforce it as the law of the land, then the civil rights history of the fifties might have been very different. He was very popular, and if he had used that popularity in the battle for civil rights, the nation's black minority—and the nation itself—might have been spared a great deal of grief.

One of those who felt that Eisenhower failed to provide the moral and political leadership necessary for making the Brown decision work was Earl Warren, and if one of his anecdotes about his relationship with Eisenhower is correct, it is easy to see why he did not provide the leadership. As Warren would later relate in his memoirs, he attended a dinner at the White House while the Brown case was being deliberated by the Court, and as he and Eisenhower left the dinner to go into another room, the president "took me by the arm, and, as we walked along, speaking of the southern states in the segregation cases, he said, 'These are not bad people. All they are concerned about is to see that their sweet little girls are not required to sit in school alongside some big overgrown Negroes!'" Warren often claimed that he and Eisenhower had had cordial relations before the Brown case, but "the Brown case was decided, and with it went our cordial relations." From then on, the president was polite but cool toward Warren.[21]

While Eisenhower was taking a hesitant approach toward the emerging civil rights problem, the South was mounting the greatest resistance to federal power since the Civil War. All across the former Confederacy, segregationists rose up to defy the implementation of the Brown decisions by the judges of the federal district courts. The defiance took many forms, including peaceful but flagrant disobedience of court orders, mass rioting, the bombings of the homes and businesses of black and white desegregation supporters, and regionwide attempts to propagate the "southern point of view" through newspapers, books, magazine articles, letters to friends outside the South, radio programs, literary tracts, pamphlets, and scientific books.[22] At times the defense rose almost to a hysterical level, as some southerners saw their region under attack from a federal government that had become in their eyes a foreign government trying to impose an alien ideology on the South. Northerners were also identified as part of that alien government and were looked upon with fear and hatred.

As the South took the offense against desegregation, all of the old arguments for segregation were rehashed and refined. Once again, as they had so often in past, southerners used as their leading defense the old discredited view that whites were inherently superior to blacks and hence should control society and keep the races separate in order to prevent the mongrelization and subsequent decline of the white race. One of the most widely read and quoted books on the alleged racial superiority of the white race was *The Race Problem from the Standpoint of One Who Is Concerned*

*About the Evils of Miscegenation,*[23] written by Wesley C. George, a prominent research professor at the University of North Carolina Medical School. Although few of their authors seemed to have the credentials of Dr. George, dozens of other books and magazine articles came out, purporting to prove racial differences and the evil results of race mixing. In the January 1956 edition of *Harper's* magazine, for example, southern newspaper editor Thomas R. Waring rehashed these views in "The Southern Case Against Desegregation" and reminded his northern readers that "the Southerner believes that as a practical matter, he is better equipped by experience to cope with race problems than people from other regions, no matter what their intellectual or political attainments."[24] Later that year, in the *Atlantic Monthly,* Charleston writer Herbert Ravenel Sass argued in an article entitled "Mixed Schools and Mixed Blood" that "the mingling or integration of white and Negro children in the South's primary schools would open the door to miscegenation and widespread racial amalgamation," leading to the decline of the white race. White southerners, he said, do not hate the Negro, "nor is there anything that can be called race prejudice. What does exist, strongly and ineradicably, is race preference. In other words, we white Southerners prefer our own race and wish to keep it as it is."[25]

A favorite target of segregationists was the perpetrator of the Brown decision, the United States Supreme Court. Earl Warren received hundreds of letters accusing him and the rest of the Court of upsetting God's will, of aiding and abetting the communist cause, and of furthering the mongrelization of the white race.[26] The American Legion and other patriotic organizations regularly lambasted the Court in their meetings and publications, while politicians like Representative Mendel Rivers of South Carolina went around calling the Court a "greater threat to the Union than the entire confines of Soviet Russia."[27] Some of the most caustic criticism of the Court came from James F. Byrnes of South Carolina, whose long career as a public servant at both the state and national level had included a brief stint as an associate justice on the Court in the early forties. Byrnes accused the Court of making law rather than interpreting it, of usurping the power of Congress and the states, of setting racial progress back fifty years, and of playing into the hands of the communists. He also claimed that "the purpose of those who lead the fight for integration in schools is to break down social barriers in childhood and the period of adolescence, and ultimately bring about intermarriage of the races."[28]

Unfortunately, the resistance to desegregation was often led by prominent southern government officials, who, instead of using their offices and influence to guide the South through difficult times, chose to encourage disobedience and even violent resistance from the rest of the population. The exercise of irresponsible leadership began at the top with southern congressmen, who denounced the Brown decision and used all of their powers to thwart its implementation. The most influential of these men were Senator James Eastland of Mississippi, Senator Herman Talmadge of Georgia, Senator Strom Thurmond of South Carolina, Representative John Bell Williams of Mississippi, and Senator Harry Byrd of Virginia, who called the desegregation problem "the most serious crisis that has occurred since the War Between the States."[29] Between 1954 and 1961, southern congressmen introduced fifty-three bills aimed at retarding or circumventing desegregation. Unable to muster the strength to pass any of these bills or secure a congressional resolution denouncing Brown, southern congressmen, led by Senator Byrd, shocked the rest of Congress and much of the nation in March of 1956 by issuing the Southern Manifesto. Signed by 19 of the 22 southern senators and 82 of the 105 southern representatives, the Southern Manifesto denounced the Brown decision as "a clear abuse of judicial power," praised "the motives of those states which have declared the intention to resist forced integration by any lawful means," and declared that the signatories had pledged "to use all lawful means to bring about a reversal of this decision which is contrary to the Constitution and to prevent the use of force in its implementation."[30] The people back home applauded, and state legislatures began working overtime to come up with ways to resist desegregation. Other problems, even very important and pressing ones, were pushed aside as governors and legislators concentrated on the "crisis in education."

Segregationists controlled many of the governorships in the South, and they used them to attack and block the desegregation decisions. Governor George Timmerman, Jr., of South Carolina went around the state warning that race mixing was "contrary to the divine order of things" and promising that "not in a thousand years will the schools of South Carolina be integrated,"[31] and several other governors adopted similar tactics and rhetoric. But most governors were, like Frank Clements of Tennessee and Leroy Collins of Florida, moderates on the issue of desegregation, which in the context of the times meant that while they made few steps to implement the policy of desegregation and hoped to postpone it for years or maybe forever, they at least did not side with the extreme racists or act or speak in such a manner as to encourage violent resistance or incite riots.

But it was different in the southern legislatures, most of which were dominated by the conservative rural areas because of archaic proportional representation schemes. In the temper of the times, legislators were afraid of being called "nigger lovers" or "integrationists" or even "liberals," and many prosegregation and anti-integration bills were preceded by long discussions in which every legislator seemed compelled to stand up and show that his heart was in the right place. Many of the bills were passed by large majorities, sometimes without even a dissenting vote, and there seemed to be no end to the ingenious devices invented to evade the law of the land. Bill after bill was passed granting state and local police the authority to prevent blacks from entering all-white schools, giving the governors control of the public schools, closing public schools, providing aid to private schools, repealing compulsory school attendance laws, and providing pupil-assignment or pupil-placement schemes designed to prevent integration. Other bills and resolutions were passed condemning the Brown decision, declaring it unconstitutional and hence null and void, tightening up the Jim Crow laws, and outlawing or restricting the activities of the NAACP, which had initiated the Brown decision and most of the other desegregation suits and was widely regarded throughout the South as a communist organization seeking to "stir up" the Negro and create racial conflict.[32]

Southern defiance during Eisenhower's first term also took other forms. One was the formation of White Citizens' Councils, which first sprang up in Mississippi in 1954 and then quickly spread all across the South in 1955 and 1956, enrolling thousands of members. Most councils shunned the violent segregationists who brought so much bad publicity and instead tried to enroll "respectable" white southerners—businessmen, lawyers, doctors, and political officials. Citizen's councils fought desegregation by legal action, by spreading smear literature against desegregation advocates, and by organizing economic boycotts against merchants, newspaper owners, and others who did not support their views. They also used their combined economic power to make it difficult, if not impossible, for blacks or whites who were trying to integrate the schools to get jobs, bank loans, credit at stores, or even to buy food or other products. In some communities they were strong enough to bring about the firing of teachers and ministers who advocated integration. They also tried to develop "right thinking" in the minds of the young by sponsoring school essay contests, giving awards for the best student essays on "Why I Believe in the Social Separation of the Races of Mankind" and "Why the Preservation of States Rights Is Important to Every American."[33] No wonder Thurgood Marshall and other black leaders called the councils Uptown Klans.[34]

Unfortunately, resistance to school desegregation also took all the usual forms of violence that had been standard in racial confrontations for decades: vandalism, arson, bombings of black churches and homes, riots, assaults, and gruesome murders. The violence was worst in the lower South, and particularly in the nation's most impoverished state, Mississippi, where white supremacy was more firmly entrenched than anywhere else in the nation and where authorities from the governor on down routinely ignored the Brown decision and other federal laws they disliked. Three blacks were lynched in that state in 1955, the first examples of that ugly form of vigilante justice in almost five years, and a fourteen-year-old black male, Emmett Till, was kidnapped and murdered after a white woman had claimed that he had whistled at her and asked her for a date. The woman's husband and another man were arrested and tried, but both were acquitted of murder, and a grand jury ruled that there was insufficient evidence to indict them for kidnapping.[35] Till's fate seemed to validate the unwritten rule that had long circulated among black males in the South: Do not ever, ever, become involved with a white woman or even give the appearance of wanting to become involved with one—if you know what is good for you.

In 1956 the level of racially motivated violence increased all across the South and, ominously, began to move from isolated rural areas and city streets into the schools. It began on February 3, when, after a three-year court battle, twenty-six-year-old Autherine Lucy attended her first class as the first black student at the University of Alabama. A mob quickly formed, and for the next few days several hundred university students, nearby high-school students, factory workers, and Ku Klux Klansmen kept the campus in an uproar as they paraded, sang "Dixie," burned crosses, jeered, threw eggs at the automobiles of the authorities escorting Miss Lucy to class, and screamed, "Lynch her, lynch her!" University officials removed her from campus for her own safety, suspended her from class, and then permanently expelled her when in her suit seeking reinstatement she accused them of conspiring with the mob to prevent her from entering the university. University officials had asked Attorney General Brownell for help in dealing with the case, but at this point the Eisenhower administration was still following a nonintervention policy.[36] It would be seven more years before the University of Alabama would be integrated.

In the summer and fall of 1956 racial violence over the schools flared up in the town of Mansfield, Texas, where the Fifth Circuit Court of Appeals had ordered the desegregation of the all-white Mansfield High School that fall. During the summer whites burned crosses in the black section of town and hanged blacks in effigy over city streets and on the flagpole at the school. When registration for the fall term was held during the last of August and the first of September, angry white mobs, sometimes numbering as many as 500 people, came to the school to make sure that no blacks registered. The governor of Texas, Allan Shivers, dealt with the crisis by instructing the school board to refuse registration to anyone whose registration might cause violence and ordering the Texas Rangers to arrest any troublemakers. These orders had the effect of restoring peace in Mansfield and of preventing the desegregation of Mansfield High School, which would not enroll its first black students until well into the 1960s. Again Eisenhower refused to intervene, claiming that the Texas authorities had handled the problem.[37]

But the biggest headlines in 1956 over school violence came in the little Tennessee town of Clinton, whose population (1950 census) of 3,712 included only 220 blacks. A district court in June of 1956 had ordered the desegregation of Clinton High School in the fall of 1956, but when the school term began, the little town was rocked by angry mobs of white youths who attacked blacks and even turned on the police who were vainly trying to restore order as outsiders swelled the mobs to over 2,000 screaming whites. All across the country, Americans were shocked at the news from Clinton and particularly by the pictures of angry youths attacking automobiles containing terrified blacks who feared for their lives as the youths smashed in the windows, slashed the tires, and jumped up and down on the car tops and hoods. Peace was not restored until the Highway Patrol and National Guard moved in with heavy equipment, including seven M-41 tanks and three armored personnel carriers. Later in the fall there would be burnings of Negro homes, cross burnings, Klan marches, and the beating of a white minister who was escorting scared black teenagers to school. Clinton High was functioning as an integrated school by the end of the year, but for the rest of the decade it and the city of Clinton would suffer from racial problems, including a dynamiting that destroyed the high school in 1958.[38]

The record of school desegregation by the end of Eisenhower's first term was not very encouraging for the supporters of the Brown decision. In Washington, Baltimore, and other school districts in the border states, desegregation had proceeded smoothly, with local districts complying in good faith with the Supreme Court's ruling without being pushed by federal district courts. In Washington and the six border states, there had been only minor resistance, few ugly incidents, and no serious unlawful defiance of the federal government. By the end of the 1956–1957 school year, 723 school districts, mostly in the border states, had undergone some desegregation. Desegregation had also begun in two school districts in Tennessee, three in Arkansas, and over a hundred in Texas. But in the eight remaining southern states not a single black student was attending a public school with white children.[39] In these states resistance was hardening, almost to the point of hysteria. Down the road lay the Little Rock crisis and a severe federal-state confrontation that would finally force Eisenhower to take the forceful action he had so hoped to avoid.

One of the greatest civil rights victories won during Eisenhower's first term came not in the schools but in the battle against Jim Crow transportation laws. This victory was won in Montgomery, Alabama, and what was done here in the Cradle of the Confederacy would help to change the whole course of the civil rights movement.

Local black leaders in Montgomery had been looking for the ideal time and person to challenge the city's Jim Crow bus laws, and in December of 1955 they found what they were looking for in Mrs. Rosa Parks, a forty-three-year-old black seamstress and NAACP member who worked at a downtown department store. On the evening of Thursday, December 1, 1955, she was tired as she prepared to catch her usual bus home after a day of working and Christmas shopping. She paid her fare, went to the rear of the bus to board, and sat down near the middle of the bus, since the rear seats were already filled. But at a later stop, the driver picked up several white passengers, and called out, "Niggers move back," which in this case meant that she would have to stand in the rear. But Mrs. Parks refused to budge, not because she was trying to bring a test case, but because, as she said later: "I was just tired from shopping. I had my sacks and all, and my feet hurt."[40] The bus driver then called two policemen, who took her to the police station where she was booked for violating the city's public transportation laws and ordered to appear in court on Monday morning, December 5, for trial.

But between Thursday and Monday, black leaders moved into action to galvanize a massive protest against Mrs. Parks's arrest and the Jim Crow laws that had precipitated it. Meeting in churches over the weekend, they decided to organize a boycott against the city's bus system, which was used primarily by the large number of black citizens who did not own automobiles. During these weekend meetings Martin Luther King, Jr., the twenty-seven-year-old pastor of Dexter Avenue Baptist Church, emerged as the leader of the black community after he was elected president of the Montgomery Improvement Association, formed to conduct the boycott. A native of Atlanta, the young black pastor had graduated from Morehouse College in Atlanta, studied theology and philosophy at Crozer Theological Seminary and the University of Pennsylvania, and completed the requirements for the doctor of philosophy degree in philosophy from Boston University in June of 1955, about nine months after he had taken the pastorate at Dexter Avenue Baptist Church. Little did he know that the Montgomery bus boycott would raise him from obscurity to international fame and make him one of the most loved and hated men in America.

The young and inexperienced King made some mistakes, especially in the early going, but he gradually emerged as a confident, effective, and charismatic leader. From the very beginning, under his leadership, the boycott combined an almost military discipline with old-fashioned revivalistic feelings, and from the beginning he preached and practiced the moral teachings of Christianity—love, patience, tolerance, compassion for one's enemy—and the teachings of Henry David Thoreau and Mohandas Gandhi on nonviolent resistance to unjust laws. Operating within the strong emotionalism of black fundamentalist Christianity, he was able to arouse the black community into action and sacrifice and yet to lead it along peaceful paths and away from the violence and rioting that such high emotionalism could have degenerated into. King constantly urged his followers to eschew violence, to follow Christian principles, and to avoid the retaliations against white oppression that would have destroyed the dignity of the cause and provoked further violence from the opponents. In one of his most famous speeches, delivered at a mass meeting on the night of February 23, 1956, the day after he had been indicted for conspiracy, he told his followers that "this is not a war between the white and the Negro but a conflict between justice and injustice. This is bigger than the Negro race revolting against the white." And then he sounded a familiar theme: "If we are arrested every day, if we are exploited every day, if we are trampled over every day, don't ever let anyone pull you so low as to hate them. We must use the weapon of love. We must have compassion and understanding for those who hate us. We must realize so many people are taught to hate us that they are not totally responsible for their hate."[41]

King and the other Negro leaders told the black community and the city and bus officials that the boycott would not end until the bus company agreed to hire more black drivers, seat passengers on a first-come-first-served basis, and treat black passengers in a courteous fashion. Put into effect on Monday, December 5, 1955, the boycott would last more than a year. It was 90 percent effective by the end of the first week as the black community organized and acted in a disciplined fashion that surpassed the expectations of their leaders and certainly surprised blacks and whites throughout the nation. Throughout the black community a sense of unity in a common, moral cause developed. Many blacks walked or rode bicycles to their destinations to show their determination and loyalty, even when they could have ridden. Black owners of any motor vehicle that would run organized car pools, black taxicab owners carried black passengers for the price of a bus ticket (which was only a fraction of the customary taxi fare), and blacks all over town raised money to buy station wagons to serve as minibuses. It was an extraordinary cooperative effort, one that was sustained through the year by the efforts of the leaders of the black churches, who week after week encouraged their congregations to continue the sacrifices and showed movies of Gandhi's movement in India to illustrate the tactics and results of nonviolence.[42]

The Montgomery boycott attracted nationwide attention, bringing reporters from the television networks and national newspapers and magazines. City and bus officials did not like the publicity, but neither were they disposed to give in to the black demands. There was widespread fear among city authorities and among the white populace that if Montgomery blacks won this battle they would quickly attack other segregation ordinances. The mayor, W. A. "Tacky" Gayle, spoke for many of the city's whites when he said that the black leaders were trying to bring about "the destruction of our social fabric. . . . The white people are firm in their convictions that they do not care whether the Negroes ever ride a city bus again if it means that the social fabric of our community is destroyed."[43] So the city and bus company refused to give in, even though the bus company's ridership fell dramatically and revenues declined by 65 percent.[44]

Although many white citizens of Montgomery cautioned nonviolence and reason, and some even supported integration of the buses, city authorities and many white supremacists retaliated against the boycotters. Mrs. Parks was arrested and jailed for refusing to pay her $10 fine, and King was arrested on a trumped-up drunk-driving charge and then later indicted and jailed, along with about a hundred other black leaders, for conspiring to organize an illegal boycott. The local selective service board canceled the occupational draft deferment of a black lawyer involved in the boycott, insurance companies canceled insurance on some of the black-owned vehicles used in the boycott, and some black participants were fired by their employers. And there was violence. The homes of King and several other black leaders were bombed, the KKK marched through the streets of Montgomery in broad daylight and committed criminal acts of vandalism at night, acid was poured on some of the black automobiles used in the car pooling, and rocks were thrown at private black vehicles. Much of the violence was undoubtedly incited by the White Citizens' Council, which held mass meetings and passed out inflammatory handbills.[45] But the blacks would not give up their struggle. "They can bomb us out and they can kill us," one of their leaders said, "but we are not going to give in."[46]

In 1956, Eisenhower was still refusing to intervene in the racial problems of the South. When asked at a press conference about the boycotters' conspiracy trial, he claimed that he was no lawyer, but as he understood it, "There is a state law about boycotts, and it is under that kind of thing that these people are being brought to trial."[47] Meanwhile, black lawyers had carried the Jim Crow transportation ordinance to the courts, where the case finally wound up in the Supreme Court. On November 13, 1956, the Court ruled that the ordinances were a violation of the Fourteenth Amendment and ordered the end of the discriminatory practices by December 20. At first city officials seemed prepared to defy the federal order, as the city commissioner released a statement saying that the authorities would do all they could "to oppose the integration of the Negro race with the white race in Montgomery, and will forever stand like a rock against social equality, intermarriage, and mixing of the races under God's creation and plan."[48] But finally, city officials agreed to abide by the court order, and in turn King and his followers ended the boycott. King still had to pay an $85 fine for violating the antiboycott laws, but he and the rest of Montgomery's black citizens had won the larger battle over segregated transportation practices.

On the morning of December 21, 1956—381 days after the boycott began—Montgomery's blacks went back to the buses, taking seats in the front and rear, wherever there was an empty seat. King had told his followers that they should not return to the buses with a vengeful or boastful mood but "with an understanding of those who have oppressed us and with an appreciation of the new adjustments that the court order poses for them."[49] Most whites accepted the changed order with resignation and occasionally even with good humor. On one bus a white bank teller said that "they'll find that all they've won in this year of praying and boycotting is the same lousy service I've been getting every day." On another newly desegregated bus, a white man looked at the blacks sitting around him and said, "I see this isn't going to be a white Christmas." A Negro passenger spoke up and said, "Yes, sir, that's right." The bus broke out in laughter.[50] But on another bus, carrying the Rev. Martin Luther King, Jr., on his first ride on a integrated bus, one white man stood near the front rather than take an empty seat at the back, saying that "I would rather die and go to hell than sit behind a nigger."[51] There would be other harsh words, some buses would be fired on by snipers, the home and church of black leader Ralph Abernathy would be bombed, three other black churches would be bombed, and a young black girl would be beaten by a gang of whites while she waited at a bus stop. But after a few weeks the violence died down. The Cradle of the Confederacy had accepted its first loss in the battle to save Jim Crow.

King emerged from the Montgomery bus boycott as an internationally known apostle of nonviolent resistance and as the most famous black leader in America. In the coming months he would found the Southern Christian Leadership Conference and capture the leadership of the nation's civil rights movement. He was admired, almost worshipped by his black followers, but among many southern whites his name was anathema. Many whites felt that he and the "communist-inspired" NAACP were stirring up southern blacks, that he was part of a breed of New Negro who was stepping out of his place and threatening to destroy the proper social order in the South. What most southern whites failed to understand was that all across the South blacks were fed up with racism and with segregation. The so-called New Negro included not just people like King but blacks from all walks of life, even the janitors and the cleaning women and others that whites had prided themselves on understanding but really knew so little about. As one young girl told *New York Times* correspondent George Barret, "The Reverend, he didn't stir us up, we've been stirred up a mighty long time."[52] As for King, the future would bring twelve years of dramatic civil rights battles, numerous demonstrations, nineteen jailings, a Nobel Peace Prize (1964), and—the fate of many charismatic leaders—assassination.

By the end of the Montgomery bus boycott Eisenhower had already been elected for a second term after a campaign that saw both parties trying to shun the civil rights issue in order to avoid alienating the large white southern voting bloc. Both Eisenhower and Stevenson sidestepped serious discussions of the problem and talked in general terms about the need for moderation, patience, and obedience to the laws of the land. The federal courts were still the only branch of the federal government to address the civil rights issues, but in 1957 and the rest of the decade events would move so swiftly and ominously that the executive and the Congress would be drawn into the battle and federal troops would be going into the South to maintain law and order. Jim Crow might be dying, but he was still strong enough to linger for a long, long time.

# 12

# "A Bigger Bang for a Buck"

Along with his undistinguished legislative record and his sidestepping of the McCarthy problem, Eisenhower's failure to provide strong executive leadership during the early days of the emerging civil rights movement contributed to the growing belief among presidential watchers that his claim to presidential greatness would not come from his domestic record but from his achievements in foreign policy. Like his predecessor, Eisenhower's main interest was in foreign affairs, where the main issues were still centered on the problems of the Cold War with the communist world. And perhaps even more than his predecessor, who had plunged the nation into a divisive war over Korea in his pursuit of containment, Eisenhower would be remembered for his accomplishments in preserving the peace while holding the line against communist expansion.

By the time the Republicans took office in 1953, the first era of the Cold War was already drawing to a close. The emergence of Red China was bringing an end to Russia's dominance of international communism and helping to splinter the movement into competing nationalist sects. The European Recovery Program had helped to restore European prosperity and confidence, while the success of the containment policy and the shift of the Cold War to Asia was contributing to the decline in Europe of the fear of communism and the end of automatic adherence to American foreign policy. The age of America's atomic monopoly was also a thing of the past, for after the Soviet Union's first successful atomic bomb test in 1949 that nation had embarked on an atomic weapons program that was bringing it abreast of American atomic power and raising the possibility of mutual destruction. In Asia, the Middle East, and Africa, the anticolonial revolution was in full swing, creating new nations and new battlefields in the Cold War.

These important developments coincided with a change in the leadership of the two superpowers, for Eisenhower's succession of Truman was followed only six weeks later by the death of Joseph Stalin, who had ruled Russia with an iron hand for almost three decades and had consistently followed a hard line in the Cold War. The death of Stalin precipitated a power struggle in the Kremlin among Georgi Malenkov, Nikita Khrushchev, and Nikolai Bulganin, precluding any international adventures for a while. Faced with grave internal political and economic problems, the new leaders would inaugurate a period of "peaceful coexistence" with the West that was in marked contrast to the blunt rhetoric and aggressive actions of Stalin. For the first time since the Cold War began, there was a chance for a real détente between the two superpowers.

In this dangerous age Eisenhower brought to the presidency a broad knowledge of international affairs gained during his long military career. In fact, he had more experience in foreign affairs than any other twentieth-century president, and he used this, along with his acquaintance with many of the world's leaders, to good advantage. He was also a patient, prudent, and practical man who believed in and usually exercised common sense in the conduct of foreign policy, and he always had a serene and confident appearance, even during periods of crisis. This was comforting and attractive to the voters and to the people who worked with him.[1] Part of this was due to his nature, and part to his long experience as a leader. On March 26, 1955, for example, when several members of his own cabinet believed that the United States might soon be fighting in the Formosa Strait over the crisis there, he wrote in his diary that "I believe hostilities are not so imminent as is indicated by the forebodings of a number of my associates. . . . I have so often been through these periods of strain that I have become accustomed to the fact that most of the calamities that we anticipate really never occur."[2]

Like Truman, Eisenhower was an anticommunist hard-liner. Both he and his secretary of state, John Foster Dulles, still viewed communism as a Russian-dominated monolith aimed at world domination, and both felt that the United States had the duty to lead the rest of the world in a crusade against it. In the recent campaign both had attacked the containment policies of the Truman administration for allowing "godless communism" to spread across the globe, and they had made it clear that a Republican victory would bring a radical change in American foreign policy. Instead of fighting a defensive battle against the onrushing communist tide, they said, the United States would go on the offensive, following an aggressive and dynamic foreign policy that would liberate captive peoples behind the Iron Curtain, "unleash" Chiang Kai-shek to reconquer the Chinese mainland, bring a quick end to the seemingly endless Korean War, and take a firm stand against communism wherever it threatened.

But however anticommunist his feelings, Eisenhower was not a rabid Cold War ideologue. Although he believed that the United States could never relax its vigilance against the communist menace, he hoped to obtain more harmonious relations with the communist bloc so as to reduce world tensions and the terrifying dangers of nuclear war. Ironically, the old military hero who now occupied the powerful office at 1600 Pennsylvania Avenue would emerge as the peacemaker in his administration. In spite of all of his Cold War rhetoric, he would show a preference for negotiation over confrontation and conflict, and while building up the nation's military power as a deterrent to war, he would work tirelessly to reduce the tensions of the Cold War through negotiations, summit conferences, and unilateral peace initiatives. His search for peace would reveal that, after a long career devoted to warfare, he had come to understand that in the new nuclear age war had become obsolete, for it would inevitably escalate into a catastrophic nuclear war in which there would be no winners.[3]

Unfortunately, Eisenhower's foreign policy posture often seemed to be at odds with that of his secretary of state. The sixty-five-year-old Dulles had a long background in diplomacy. The nephew of Robert Lansing, Woodrow Wilson's secretary of state, and the grandson of John Foster, secretary of state under Benjamin Harrison, he had attended the Hague Conference in 1907 as a secretary while he was still a Princeton undergraduate, and he later was part of the American delegation to the Paris Peace Conference in 1919. From the 1920s on he practiced law in New York while reading and writing widely in the area of foreign affairs, especially in the history and diplomacy of communist Russia, and he became an expert on communist doctrine, which he could—and often did—quote from memory. He had also worked in the State Department under Roosevelt and Truman, helped to organize the United Nations, served as an adviser to Governor Thomas Dewey, and was the chief negotiator for the peace treaty signed with Japan in 1951. At the Republican convention in 1952 he was the main architect of the platform plank calling for a tough line against communism and the "liberation" of the "captive peoples" behind the Iron Curtain. When Eisenhower appointed him secretary of state, he apparently had the power to carry out his ideas.

Dulles was a twentieth-century Calvinist carved in the mold of a seventeenth-century English Roundhead. He was a staunch Presbyterian, a stern moralist who saw the struggle between the West and communism as a struggle between Christianity and atheism, good and evil, light and darkness. More rigid and dogmatic than the president, he viewed the life-and-death struggle with communism as an irreconcilable and unnegotiable conflict. Hence his bombastic rhetoric about "rollback," "liberation," and "massive retaliation," and his endless trips to foreign capitals (half a million miles in seventy-five months, including four visits to Italy, nineteen to France, eleven to Great Britain, and six to West Germany) trying to persuade America's allies to take a hard line against Russia and China and trying to induce emerging nations to take the American side in the Cold War.[4]

Dulles was highly intellectual, legalistic, methodical, impersonal, confident, pious, and virtually humorless, leading many of his opponents—and some of his colleagues—to circulate a new comparative phrase, "Dull, Duller, Dulles." A workaholic, he usually put in a seven-day work week whether he was in Washington or on one of his many trips abroad, and on weekends he frequently worked in his study at home, drawing upon a pool of three secretaries who alternated the grueling weekend duties. He enjoyed policy-making and personal negotiating but disliked the day-to-day administrative details of running the State Department, which he preferred to turn over to others while he traveled across the globe with his personal diplomacy. It was often said that Dulles "carried the State Department in his hat."[5]

There was another side to the staunch old Calvinist that was not often seen by administration officials or the public. A gregarious man, he loved to attend private parties after working hours and usually gave a New Year's Eve party every year. He had a devoted and tender relationship with his wife of forty years, Janet, who accompanied him on most of his many trips. He loved to swim, was fond of wines, good food, and rye whiskey, and he was a devoted baseball fan who could cite reams of anecdotes and statistics about the sport. He was friendly and almost grandfatherly toward the young secretaries who worked in his office or in his study on weekends, and he was thoughtful and devoted to his friends and closest associates.[6]

What was Dulles's relationship with the president? This would be one of the most widely debated and controversial questions about the making of American foreign policy under Eisenhower. The conventional view of the time was that Eisenhower delegated—some said abdicated—the making of foreign policy to his more knowledgeable and experienced secretary of state, that Dulles dominated the relationship, and that after listening to Dulles's briefings and lists of options and recommendations on some issue, Eisenhower would say, "Do whatever you think is best, Foster," and hurry off to the golf course. But this is far from the truth. It is true that Eisenhower had great confidence in Dulles, that he gave him a great deal of authority and responsibility, perhaps more than any other twentieth-century secretary of state ever enjoyed, and that a very special working relationship developed between the two men in the conduct of foreign policy. "Foster and I worked," Eisenhower once said, "as nearly as can be imagined, as one person."[7] Dulles had more access to the president than anyone except

Sherman Adams and Milton Eisenhower, calling him three or four times a day, striding into his office without a scheduled appointment, and sending cables from overseas each night summarizing the negotiations and actions he had engaged in during the day.

But the Eisenhower–Dulles relationship was a partnership, with the president the senior partner. Eisenhower used Dulles as an instrument of the executive office. Dulles provided him with the facts and options, did the inevitable traveling and negotiating associated with the conduct of personal diplomacy, provided the hard-line rhetoric that so pleased the right wing of the Republican party while Eisenhower appeared as a peacemaker, and served as a lightning rod to draw criticism that would have otherwise been directed at the president. Dulles always came into the office with all the facts, options, problems, and recommendations laid out for the president to see—and Eisenhower was delighted, for it made it easier for him to get to the heart of the problem and make a decision. But he did not accept Dulles's information and advice passively. He had a good knowledge of foreign affairs, asked questions that got to the heart of the issue at hand, made changes in policies or in the working of the documents or speeches that Dulles brought to him, and often overrode Dulles's recommendations in favor of his own. And Dulles never took any important step without first discussing it with the president and getting his approval—hence the frequent phone calls and visits to the Oval Office. He even went over his major speeches with the president, who often penciled in changes, usually to soften the rhetoric from a militant to a more conciliatory tone.[8]

In short, Eisenhower depended heavily upon Dulles and delegated a great deal of authority to him, but he never relinquished control of it. He often referred to Dulles's "encyclopedic knowledge" and praised his acute mind, but very revealingly, he once told speechwriter Emmet John Hughes that "there's only one man I know who has seen *more* of the world and talked with more people and knows more than he does, and that's me."[9] And this provides the key to their relationship: Eisenhower's faith in Dulles was almost unlimited, but he trusted only himself to make the final decisions. He made them, and Dulles went along—sometimes reluctantly—with what the president wanted.

Dulles was not the only controversial member of Eisenhower's circle of foreign policy and defense advisers. Secretary of Defense Charles E. Wilson, chosen by Eisenhower to serve as a watchdog over defense spending, never acquired the influence with Eisenhower that Dulles had, but he often rivaled the secretary of state in his ability to arouse the ire of the public and the press. Aggressive, frank, and opinionated, Wilson left a $600,000 a year job as president of General Motors to take the $22,500 a year position in the cabinet. Even before he took office he became a center of public controversy with a confirmation battle in the Senate over his stockholdings in General Motors and his statement that "what was good for our country was good for General Motors, and vice versa," which was quickly picked up by his opponents and twisted to "what was good for General Motors was good for the country." After the new administration took office, his inability to control his tongue in a sensitive job frequently made him the center of public disputes. Wilson caused a real furor when he attacked government aid to the unemployed by remarking that they should seek out work wherever it existed and that "I've always liked bird dogs better than kennel-fed dogs myself—you know, one who'll get out and hunt for food rather than sit on his fanny and yell."[10] Such intemperate remarks infuriated the president, who often cautioned him to hold his tongue and once blurted out, "Damn it, how in hell did a man as shallow as Charlie Wilson ever get to be head of General Motors?"[11] Wilson's verbal gaffes caused people around Washington to suggest that he suffered from a severe case of foot-in-mouth disease and to circulate reporter James Reston's quip that Wilson had invented the automatic transmission so that he would be free to drive with one foot in his mouth.

Eisenhower's ambitions in foreign relations were tempered by foreign and domestic political and economic realities. Although he was as much of a Cold Warrior as his predecessor, he realized that it was beyond America's military and economic capabilities to police the entire world. He was a staunch advocate of a strong national defense, but he also believed that a strong defense had to be built on the back of a strong economy, that a strong economy was dependent on a balanced budget, and that a balanced budget could only be achieved by holding down defense spending. With limited defense funds and almost unlimited defense needs, the United States had to find a way to reduce the huge sums spent on conventional weapons and to avoid expensive, protracted conventional wars like the Korean conflict, which in addition to being prohibitively expensive also caused great divisions within the United States and the allied camp and produced disappointing military and political results. Eisenhower also believed that future wars would probably be fought almost entirely with nuclear weapons, making large armies and conventional weapons not only wasteful drains on the military budget but virtually obsolete.

Eisenhower's economic and military views led him to unveil during his first year in office plans for a New Look in defense policy. The New Look deemphasized conventional weapons and conventional tactics and concentrated on the development of nuclear weapons and delivery systems that could rain atomic destruction anywhere in the world where communism threatened. From now on, communist expansion would not be met by sending conventional forces to the endangered area but by attacking enemy forces there with small nuclear weapons or even by striking the original source of the aggression—Moscow or Peking. Secretary of Defense Charles E. Wilson, in his usual blunt fashion, said that the new policy would give the United States "a bigger bang for a buck," while Dulles would soon escalate the rhetoric of the New Look by calling it the policy of "massive retaliation," a term destined to send chills down the backs of America's European allies and of others who feared that the new Republican administration was embarking on a dangerous game of nuclear blackmail.

The New Look inevitably meant an even greater reliance on the bomb than before, an increase in the nuclear weapons stockpile, the development of an even larger striking force of B-52s designed to carry atomic weapons long distances, and the construction of more SAC bases in countries allied to the United States. It also entailed the development of nuclear submarines, exotic aircraft and amphibious vehicles, and of small nuclear weapons that could be used in a conventional way. Eisenhower left no doubt that, if necessary, he would use small weapons. "If these things are used on strictly military targets," he said, "I see no reason why they shouldn't be used just exactly as you would use a bullet or anything else."[12] And finally, and very ironically, the New Look meant that a president who had spent most of his adult life in the army had committed himself to a defense policy that inevitably brought a buildup in the air force at the expense of the army and navy. The army suffered the most, subjected to more budget cuts and manpower reductions than any of the military branches during Eisenhower's presidency. In his 1955 budget, for example, Eisenhower called for a $4 billion cut in the army's budget and a $1.5 billion cut in the navy's, while the air force was to receive an $800 million increase.[13] Under his austere defense program, total manpower in the armed forces was cut from 3,555,067 in 1953 to 2,483,771 in 1961, and although all the branches were affected, the army experienced the biggest cutback, from 1,533,815 to 858,622.[14]

Not all policymakers liked the New Look, fearing that it reduced America's military options, dangerously weakened the army, and left the nation too weak to fight small wars in which the stakes were not high enough to risk atomic war. Maxwell Taylor and two other members of the army chiefs of staff chose to resign rather than to support a policy that downgraded the army and eroded the nation's ability to mount a flexible response to any military challenge.[15] Many critics inside and outside the administration complained that the policy made little sense and was indeed dangerous now that Russia also had atomic weapons, and that it meant that any conflict between the superpowers, no matter how small, threatened to escalate into a nuclear war. The "massive retaliation" Dulles boasted of could turn into mutual annihilation.

Much to the chagrin of the American military establishment, Eisenhower refused to engage in a ruinous arms race with the Soviet Union. Such a race, he felt, would bankrupt the nation or at the very least drain off money that could be used for other purposes. As he told the American Society of Newspaper Editors in April of 1953, "Every gun that is made, every warship launched, every rocket fired signifies, in the final sense, a theft from those who hunger and are not fed, those who are cold and are not clothed."[16] Eisenhower also believed that a big buildup would make the country less, rather than more, secure, for it would be matched by the Russians and would escalate the level of destruction each could impose on the other if a war broke out. He was also afraid that a big buildup would make the nation a militaristic state in which too much power would be vested in the hands of the military establishment and the military-industrial complex that fed it. "We don't want to become a garrison state," he said at a press conference in 1953. "We want to remain free."[17]

Eisenhower believed that the country did not have to have overwhelming military superiority to be secure. It was only necessary to have military sufficiency—to have enough power to destroy Russia if she dared to attack the United States or her allies. He held to this idea throughout his two terms, in spite of Russian progress in bombers, missiles, and other sophisticated weapons and in spite of his critics' charges that he was allowing a "bomber gap" and a "missile gap." Eisenhower knew that there was no gap, for from the midfifties on, the missions of the U-2 spy planes revealed that economic and technical problems were preventing the Russians from building up fast enough to catch the United States in nuclear weaponry. So, inheriting a national defense budget of some $50 billion from Truman, he gradually trimmed it to around $40 billion and held it in the $40 to $45 billion range through his two terms while riding out the criticism of his military detractors, who had a hard time arguing with a man of Eisenhower's military experience.[18]

In spite of the inauguration of the New Look and the harsh rhetoric about the rollback of the communist tide, Eisenhower's foreign and defense policies did not radically depart from the containment policies established by Truman—in fact, Eisenhower extended and institutionalized the Cold War policies of his much-maligned predecessor. Like Truman, Eisenhower was a strong supporter of collective security as a means of preserving peace in a war-weary and war-prone world. He was a firm backer of the United Nations and of anticommunist regional alliances like NATO, and after the French had vetoed an American plan for a European Defense Community, he backed a British plan to strengthen Europe and NATO by creating a Western European Union (1955), which ended the Western occupation of West Germany and admitted her to NATO. He also expanded the regional alliance and collective security concept by forming the Southeast Asia Treaty

Organization (SEATO) in 1954 and the Baghdad Pact in 1955, in theory extending the NATO defense line to Southeast Asia and the Middle East but in actuality establishing only weak alliances with weak Third World nations, making these pacts only pale imitations of NATO. He also continued Truman's two-China policy, recognizing Nationalist China and not Red China as the legitimate government of the mainland, using American influence in the United Nations to reject all attempts by Russia and other nations to give Communist China the Nationalist seat in the United Nations, and using the Seventh Fleet and military threats to discourage Mao from launching an invasion of Taiwan.

Eisenhower also continued the economic arm of containment, increasing the foreign aid to underdeveloped countries being swept by anti-imperial revolts and by the revolutions of rising expectations aimed at rapid economic growth and the acquisition of high living standards like those to be found in the Western countries. Misinterpreting these revolutions, as Truman had, as communist revolutions inspired and led by Moscow or Peking, he funneled some $41 billion in foreign aid (with $24 billion of this in military aid) to countries threatened by internal or external revolutionaries and extended the number of American mutual defense pacts to forty-three countries around the world.[19] In the pursuit of defense against communist aggression, America allied with many military dictators and even with fascists, contributing to the growing belief in much of the underdeveloped world that the United States was acting as an imperial or counterrevolutionary force. Meanwhile, in her foreign aid, the Russians were reaping propaganda victories by posing as the supporters of liberation against the imperial Western nations led by the United States.

In the conduct of his foreign policy Eisenhower relied very heavily on the work of the Central Intelligence Agency, headed by Allen Dulles, the brother of the secretary of state. Eisenhower used the CIA to intervene actively in the politics of nations around the world, backing those elements who supported the United States and trying to undermine and overthrow those who did not. Its power undoubtedly augmented by the close working relationship between the Dulles brothers, the CIA engaged in covert actions to try to establish pro-Western governments in Iran, Guatemala, Egypt, Indonesia, Laos, and Cuba, plotted to assassinate Castro and Congolese ruler Patrice Lumumba, and carried out other clandestine activities in countries all across the globe. By 1955 it employed almost 15,000 people, triple what it had in 1950.[20] Operating with few controls from Congress, with only the White House and a few other officials having a knowledge of what it was doing, it justified its Machiavellian tactics on the grounds that communism was an immoral, ruthless, and godless foe that should be fought with any means available. It was widely admired by the public, which saw it as a glamorous cloak-and-dagger organization specializing in espionage and counterespionage, dark secrets, secret and exotic weapons, code words, and incredible feats by agents and double agents.

There were still other signs that Eisenhower's foreign policy brought more of a change in style than in substance and that he was seeking peace rather than conflict. In June of 1953, when discontented workers in Berlin and several other East German cities engaged in strikes, demonstrations, and riots, Russian and East German troops put down the disorders with a firm show of force. The United States did nothing except protest. Eisenhower never even considered intervening, for this would have meant the risk of a third world war. One month later, Eisenhower signed the Korean armistice, settling for a stalemate that vindicated the policy of containment. Neither in Europe nor in Korea had there been any "rollback" of the communist tide or liberation of people enslaved by communism. And in December of 1953, against the wishes of Dulles and many other officials, Eisenhower went before the United Nations with an Atoms for Peace program, proposing that the United States and other atomic powers support the creation of an International Atomic Energy Agency to control the use of atomic energy and find ways to use it for peaceful purposes. The Soviet Union, which trailed the United States in nuclear development, vetoed the plan, giving the United States a propaganda victory.[21]. More and more, Eisenhower was looking like a man of peace, not the anticommunist hardliner the right wing had hoped for.

Eisenhower also acted as a force for peace in the Indochina crisis in the spring of 1954. Ever since the end of the Second World War, a nationalist movement led by communist leader Ho Chi Minh had been fighting the French, who had controlled the country before World War II, evacuated it to the Japanese at the beginning of the war, and then tried to reimpose their rule at the end of the war in spite of the anticolonial spirit sweeping the entire region. Viewing the war as a part of the communist conspiracy to take over all of Asia and the French as America's arm of containment in Southeast Asia, Truman had sent large amounts of aid to the French, and Eisenhower continued it under his "domino theory." At a news conference on April 7, 1954, he told reporters that "you have a row of dominoes set up, you knock over the first one, and what will happen to the last one is the certainty that it will go over very quickly. So you could have a beginning of a disintegration that would have the most profound influences."[22] Not wanting Indochina to become the first of the dominoes to fall, taking the rest of Southeast Asia with it, Eisenhower promised the French $1 billion in 1954. This constituted almost 75 percent of the French effort in Indochina and almost one third of all American foreign aid.[23]

Eisenhower faced a major crisis in Indochina in the spring of 1954, when poor leadership had led thousands of France's best troops to be trapped in the remote jungle fortress at Dien Bien Phu. After a long and exhausting war, the French people back home and the French soldiers in Indochina were losing their will to fight and were on the verge of a military disaster that would result in a communist victory. To avert this calamity, the French appealed to the United States for direct intervention to save Dien Bien Phu. Dulles, Nixon, and several military leaders, including the chairman of the Joint Chiefs of Staff, Admiral Arthur W. Radford, suggested a wide range of options, including the use of American air strikes, ground troops, and even nuclear weapons. However, General Matthew Ridgway and other military leaders warned against getting involved in another land war in Asia that could become another Korea, and so did Senators John F. Kennedy and Lyndon Johnson, two future presidents who would later heavily involve the United States in Vietnam.[24]

Eisenhower was reluctant to involve America in the conflict directly. In spite of this New Look in defense and his campaign rhetoric, he never really considered "massive retaliation" against Communist China, which had supplied the rebel forces, although he did warn the Peking regime that he would use atomic weapons on China if it became directly involved in the war. He did not want to go into the war without allies, and the British, who were liquidating their own empire, firmly indicated that they would not help save France's. More importantly, he realized the problems of fighting a ground war in the jungles of Southeast Asia, thought the French were unreliable allies who had greatly bungled the war, believed that air strikes would not win the war, did not want to get involved in another frustrating and exhausting war like the Korean conflict, and felt the American people would not support the large-scale intervention that would be necessary for saving the French and winning the war.[25] In one of the most important decisions of his presidency, he decided against intervention. On May 7, 1954, the French forces at Dien Bien Phu surrendered.

The defeat at Dien Bien Phu made further French resistance futile and led them to move toward a settlement of the Indochina crisis in an international conference at Geneva called to resolve this problem. On July 21, France signed the Geneva Accords along with Britain, Communist China, and Russia. The Geneva Accords provided for a cease-fire, the granting of independence to Cambodia and Laos, the temporary division of Vietnam along the 17th parallel into a North Vietnam headed by Ho Chi Minh and a South Vietnam headed by French puppet emperor Bao Dai, and elections to be held in 1956 for the unification of Vietnam. The United States, attending the conference only as an observer since it did not recognize the Red Chinese regime, did not sign the accords but verbally agreed to honor them. After eight years of fighting and the deaths of 25,000 Frenchmen and 1 million Vietnamese, the first Indochina war was over.[26] But even as it ended, nearly a million North Vietnamese refugees seeking to avoid communist rule fled to the South, some of them with the help of a large-scale evacuation carried out by the United States Navy.

By rejecting direct American military involvement in Indochina in the spring of 1954, Eisenhower appeared to be the leading dove in his administration. But he was not opposed to indirect involvement in an attempt to prevent all of Vietnam from falling to communism. The ink was barely dry on the Geneva Accords before his administration began to pour money and advisers into South Vietnam. In 1955, General Ngo Dinh Diem ousted Bao Dai and became the sole ruler, announced the cancellation of the unification elections scheduled to be held in the summer of 1956, and staged a rigged presidential election that gave him "98 percent" of the vote. Eisenhower reluctantly approved of these cancellations, saying that if the elections had been held Vietnam would have gone communist.[27] With most of the money to support his regime coming from the United States, Diem followed a repressive policy, arresting, torturing, and executing his enemies, persecuting the Buddhist majority (he was Catholic), and refusing to carry out the land reforms the Eisenhower administration urged on him to win the support of the peasantry.

July 20, 1956, the date set by the Geneva Accords for the unification elections, came and went with little notice back in the United States. But back in Vietnam, communist guerrillas in the South were already in revolt against Diem, while in the North, Ho Chi Minh, feeling that he had been cheated out of his rightful control of all of Vietnam, was preparing for his "war of liberation" against the Diem regime. Few people could see it at the time, but the United States had begun the most protracted, frustrating, and unpopular war in its history. Eisenhower did not go to war in Indochina in 1954, but his decision to back the South Vietnamese government set the United States on the path that would lead to the quagmire of the Kennedy–Johnson–Nixon years.

The fall and winter of 1954 brought Eisenhower another chance to play the role of the peacemaker. In September the Communist Chinese began to shell the offshore islands of Tachens, Quemoy, and Matsu, which were occupied by the Nationalist Chinese, creating a crisis that lasted until the spring of 1955. These shellings were considered by many in Washington to be an attack on America's Chinese ally and a prelude to an actual communist invasion of Taiwan. In the next few months, as the bombings continued, several members of the Joint Chiefs of Staff, National Security Council, and Congress pressured Eisenhower to take a firm stand, even to the point of blockading Red China and attacking her with nuclear weapons.

But Eisenhower resisted the hawks, who included his own secretary of state, and tried to use peaceful methods to defuse the crisis. He signed a mutual defense treaty with Chiang in return for his pledge to stop the provocative guerrilla raids on mainland China, sought and received from

Congress the authority to use force to defend Nationalist China, and persuaded Chiang to agree to evacuate Tachens. In the spring, in messages conveyed through diplomatic channels, he raised the possibility of using atomic weapons against Communist China if it did not stop the bombings. These threats, along with diplomatic pressures put on China by its allies and several neutral Asian nations, apparently had the desired effect. In May of 1955, the bombings tapered off and virtually ceased. Eisenhower's firm stand received a great deal of criticism at home and abroad, for many questioned whether the crisis, or even Chiang's regime itself, was worth going to war over. But it seemed to have worked. And few people outside the administration realized that it was Eisenhower's hand that restrained a flock of hawks who were willing to go to war over China.[28]

To the American public, Eisenhower's handling of the Chinese crisis was yet another example of his skill in preserving the peace while standing firm in the face of aggression. When the crisis ended late in the spring, his popularity rating had risen to 68 percent.[29] The easing of the Chinese crisis coincided with conciliatory overtures from the Russians, who surprisingly agreed in May to sign a peace treaty with Austria, ending another long-standing problem left over from World War II. More and more there was talk of a thaw in the Cold War, and this encouraged the leaders of the major nations to seek an even greater relaxation of tensions by meeting in a summit conference in Geneva in the middle of the summer. Dulles strongly opposed the conference, but Eisenhower was not about to pass up this opportunity to promote world peace.

The first top-level meeting of world leaders since the Potsdam Conference of ten years before, the Geneva Summit Conference (July 18–22) was attended by Eisenhower, Prime Minister Anthony Eden of Great Britain, Premier Edgar Faure of France, and Premier Nikolai Bulganin and Communist Party Secretary Nikita Khrushchev of the Soviet Union. Lower-ranking diplomats and about 1,500 reporters, lobbyists, and interested spectators also attended, along with rising American evangelist Billy Graham, who held a revival attended by about 35,000 people. The conference was characterized by a lot of smiles, amiable conversation, friendly handshakes, exchanges of toasts and gifts, and talk about world peace. But little progress was made on the major items on the agenda, such as German unification, nuclear disarmament, and cultural exchanges. The high point of the conference came when Eisenhower stunned everyone with a speech on nuclear disarmament, proposing that the United States and Russia trade a "complete blueprint of our military establishments, from one end of our countries to the other," and that the two countries open their skies to aerial photography so as to lessen the chances of a surprise attack, thereby leading to a reduction in suspicions and tensions. Britain and France eagerly endorsed the "open skies" proposal, but the Russians opposed it. They feared that it would violate their sovereignty and reveal their developing missile program, and they also suspected that it was nothing more than an American scheme to spy on Russia. So the conference ended without any tangible results, but it did contribute to the thaw in the Cold War and talk about "the spirit of Geneva."[30]

When Eisenhower returned to Washington from Geneva, it was raining in the capital. Vice President Nixon told the officials who were to meet the president at the airport not to provide him with an umbrella, lest it revive memories of Neville Chamberlain's trip back from Munich in September of 1938 at the height of appeasement.[31] But Nixon need not have worried. A Gallup Poll in August showed Eisenhower's popularity rating at an incredible 79 percent, his highest ever.[32] Commenting on this in *The New York Times*, James Reston said that "the popularity of President Eisenhower has got beyond the bounds of reasonable calculation and will have to be put down as national phenomenon, like baseball. The thing is no longer just a remarkable political fact but a kind of national love affair."[33]

The fall of 1955 was one of the warmest periods of the Cold War thaw of the 1950s. The spirit of Geneva was still in the air, the United States was not at war anywhere in the world, and the American people were optimistic about the future of world peace. But then the popular sixty-four-year-old president was stricken with a serious, potentially fatal, illness. On September 23, while vacationing in Denver at the home of Mamie's mother, Mrs. John S. Doud, he played twenty-seven holes of golf and then spent a restful evening at Mrs. Doud's home playing billiards with an old business friend and relaxing with his wife and mother-in-law. He retired around ten o'clock, but at one-thirty the next morning he was awakened by severe chest pains. Twelve hours later, after being treated by his personal physician, he was taken to Fitzsimons Army Hospital, near Denver, where it was determined that he had suffered a moderate heart attack. From then until November 11, Eisenhower would be treated at the army hospital by a team of experts led by Boston cardiologist Paul Dudley White, while press secretary Jim Hagerty released almost daily public reports about the president's condition. During his recovery, he read westerns, worked crossword puzzles with Milton, and listened to recordings of "Stardust," "Clair de Lune," and other musical favorites.[34] On November 11 he walked out of the hospital and flew back to Washington, but he still had to spend several more weeks recuperating at the White House, Camp David, Key West, and Gettysburg.

During his illness his cabinet met under the chairmanship of the vice president, but the other top administrative officials, led by Dulles, drew up plans for an interim government that gave the greatest power to Sherman Adams, not Nixon. Dulles, Adams, and other top officials were suspicious of Nixon's abilities and ambitions, and did not want him and his right-wing followers to acquire power that could be used to capture the Republican party and the nomination in 1956 if Eisenhower were too ill to pursue a second term. So, under an arrangement agreed to by Eisenhower, unable to conduct much official business during the first five weeks of his seven-week stay at the Denver hospital, Sherman Adams went to Denver to serve as the presidential assistant and major decisionmaker during this critical time.[35] On November 26, Eisenhower held a cabinet meeting at Camp David, the first since his heart attack some two months before, and after that gradually resumed his full work schedule. Inevitably, jokes circulated about the ambitious vice president during his crisis in the executive office. One of the more popular ones had Nixon greeting Eisenhower after his return to the capital with a slap on the back and the words, "Welcome back, Mr. President. I'll race you to the top of the steps."[36]

Eisenhower's illness presented a real problem for the Republican party, which desperately needed him to run in 1956. Dr. White pronounced him fit for another campaign and term, but several family members did not want him to seek reelection. Mamie, especially, was opposed. She was worried about his health, was tiring of the public life she had to lead as First Lady, and after decades of living all over the country she wanted the two of them to retire to the farm at Gettysburg and have a home for a change.[37] The president debated the problem for several weeks before deciding that his country, his programs, and his party needed him. He seemed to believe that there was no one else who could continue his policies. On February 29, 1956, in a television address to the nation, he formally announced that he had been given a clean bill of health by his doctors and that he would run again. Then in June he developed ileitis (inflammation of the ileum, a section of the small intestine) and had to undergo abdominal surgery, raising again the question of his medical fitness for the office, but he recovered quickly, reiterated his decision to run again, and was renominated by his party at the convention in August.

The thaw engendered by the spirit of Geneva continued on into 1956, but Secretary Dulles seemed not to have heard of it. In a *Life* magazine interview published on January 16, he boasted that the administration had gone to the brink of war three times—over the ending of the Korean War, the encirclement of the French at Dien Bien Phu, and the crisis over Taiwan—but had managed a peaceful resolution of the conflict at the last possible moment. "You have to take chances for peace," he said, "just as you have to take chances in war. . . . The ability to get to the verge without getting into the war is the necessary art. If you cannot master it, you inevitably get into war. If you try to run away from it, if you are scared to go to the brink, you are lost."[38] Once again, while Eisenhower played the role of peacemaker, the secretary of state was acting as a hard-liner, apparently with the approval of the president. Dulles's rhetoric gave comfort to the right wing of the Republican party, but it also gave some domestic and foreign critics the impression that American foreign policy suffered from a growing case of schizophrenia.

American allies, particularly the British and the French, were outraged at this saber rattling, and so were many domestic critics, who feared that Dulles was playing with fire at a time when advancing nuclear technology was leading the two nuclear superpowers into a "balance of terror" that guaranteed that the next war would be a holocaust. Adlai Stevenson labeled Dulles's policy "the power of positive brinking," and called upon Eisenhower to repudiate Dulles or to fire him.[39] But Dulles continued the moral crusading that had by now made "massive retaliation," "liberation," "roll-back," and "brinkmanship" part of the diplomatic and journalistic jargon of the day. Very few people could have a lukewarm appraisal of such a man. As NBC news analyst and Washington columnist Joseph Harsch wrote in *Harper's* in August of that year, the secretary of state seemed "to arouse either approval bordering on veneration or disapproval ranging close to moral contempt."[40]

Dulles's rhetoric sounded especially bellicose when compared to the statements coming out of the Soviet Union, where Nikita Khrushchev was emerging as Stalin's heir but was contradicting his old boss by preaching "peaceful coexistence" with the West. In February of 1956 he gave a sensational speech at the twentieth Congress of the Communist Party that astonished his fellow communists. In this address, delivered secretly to 1,400 top officials but soon leaked to the Russian people and the West, Khrushchev denounced Stalin as a cruel tyrant who had promoted the "cult of the individual" instead of "collective leadership" and had been led by his paranoia and power mania to practice almost three decades of mass arrests, show trials, tortures, purges, forced labor camps, and executions of millions of fellow Russians. Khrushchev also called for the de-Stalinization of Russia and Eastern Europe and the return of collective leadership, claimed that war between capitalism and communism was not inevitable, and pronounced that there was more than one road to socialism. To the West this speech seemed to portend an even greater thaw in the Cold War, while in Eastern Europe it would encourage attempts to achieve liberalization of Soviet rule.

The thaw continued on into the summer and fall, when the nation was basking in prosperity and preoccupied with the nominating conventions, the election campaign, baseball, vacations, and curiosity about the fall television programs. But then the complacency was broken by the emergence of two crises, one in the Middle East and one in Eastern Europe. The Cold War would temporarily heat up, with the British, French, and Israelis invading Egypt, Russian tanks rolling into Budapest, Khrushchev threatening to use modern weapons on European cities, and East and West tottering on the brink of war.

In the Middle East, the situation that led to the crisis of 1956 was a complex one. By the time Eisenhower took office, the region had become a boiling cauldron. In this oil rich and strategically located bridge to three continents, Arab nationalism was on the rise, former colonial leaders France and Britain were declining as forces of control and stability, Russia was attempting to expand her influence, and border conflicts between Israel (established in 1948) and her hostile Arab neighbors seemed to have become a permanent way of life. To complicate matters more, a military coup d'état in Egypt had deposed King Farouk and brought to power Gamal Abdel Nasser, a strong Arab nationalist with dreams of modernizing Egypt, unifying all Arab states under Egyptian rule, and destroying the state of Israel. In this crucial area the Eisenhower administration attempted to follow the difficult policy of protecting Israel from her hostile neighbors, maintaining Western control of the world's biggest oil reserves, and winning Arab friendship in the Cold War battle against Russia and China.

The Republican administration was heavily involved in Middle Eastern affairs almost from the time Eisenhower took office. In 1953 the CIA initiated a military coup that deposed the anti-Western Iranian premier, Mohammed Mossadegh, who had nationalized the British-owned Anglo-Iranian Oil Company, and replaced him with a friendly and pro-Western government supporting the Shah, Mohammed Riza Pahlavi. In February of 1955 Dulles had helped to construct the Baghdad Pact, an anti-Russian mutual defense treaty signed by Great Britain, Iraq, Iran, Pakistan, and Turkey. Hoping to win Egypt to the American side and use her as a stabilizing and anti-Russian force in that volatile region, the United States also courted Nasser with economic aid, agreeing in December of 1955 to lend him $56 million to help in the construction of the Aswan High Dam on the Upper Nile to provide the hydroelectric and irrigation projects so necessary for feeding Egypt's growing population and launching her on the road to industrialization. These sometimes conflicting American policies were difficult to balance, and were made even more difficult by the Russians, who were busy trying to buy friends and influence of their own in the area.

The dangers of Cold War politics for both big and little powers was illustrated by the Suez crisis that erupted in July of 1956. On July 19, angered by Nasser's recognition of Red China and purchase of arms from Czechoslovakia, Dulles abruptly announced the cancellation of the American loan offer for the Aswan dam project, automatically causing the withdrawal of the British and World Bank loans that were contingent upon the American offer. Nasser retaliated by nationalizing the Suez Canal, the vital waterway between the Mediterranean and the Gulf of Suez, and announcing that he would use the revenues to pay for the Aswan project. The next three months were a tense time of negotiations over control of the canal, operated by the largely French- and British-owned Suez Canal Company, with Eisenhower and Dulles frantically trying to seek a peaceful solution of the problem while the British and French planned a joint military venture to protect their vital oil pipeline if the problem were not soon resolved. On October 29, provoked by eight years of Egyptian border attacks and fear of the Egyptian arms buildup, Israel invaded the Sinai in a drive that would take her to within ten miles of the canal, and two days later the British and French began bombing Egyptian military targets and landing paratroopers to secure the canal.

Preoccupied with the reelection campaign and given no advance warning of the invasion, the Eisenhower administration was caught off guard by the rapidly deteriorating situation in the Middle East. The president publicly condemned the attacks on Egypt, banned the sale of petroleum to Britain and France, and worked through the United Nations for a cease-fire, withdrawal of all outside forces, and the creation of a special United Nations Emergency Force to supervise these. Russia carefully exploited the disarray in the Western camp by joining the United States in condemning the British and French attacks and sponsoring the United Nations resolutions calling for a cease-fire and a withdrawal, providing the rest of the world with the strange spectacle of the United States and the U.S.S.R. voting against the British and French in the United Nations. Khrushchev also threatened to send "volunteers" into Egypt and to fire Russian missiles on French and British cities if their troops were not withdrawn, prompting Eisenhower to counterthreaten to use force to resist Russian intervention in the Middle East.

It was a confusing and dangerous international crisis, threatening to draw not just the Middle East but Russia and America into war. But finally the British, French, and Israelis yielded to pressure from the giants and agreed to a cease-fire and withdrawal. By December all outside forces had withdrawn from the Suez, and the crisis was over. But the British and French had been humiliated, a serious rift had been made in the Western alliance, and the canal had been temporarily closed because of the thirty-two ships Nasser had sunk to block traffic during the crisis. The real winners were Nasser, who had been saved from certain defeat, and the Soviet Union, which had gained by the divisions in the Western camp and the further movement of Egypt into the Russian camp. The whole crisis had demonstrated how hard it was for a great power to impose its will on the "neutrals" in the Cold War and how easy it was for these neutrals to draw the world to the brink of war.

The Suez Crisis gave the Russians a foothold in the Middle East while undermining the power there of Great Britain and France. These and other considerations led Eisenhower to conclude that the United States would have to play a more active role in the area, and on January 5, 1957, he asked Congress to pass a joint resolution authorizing $200 million in military and economic aid to Middle Eastern nations and authorizing the president to dispatch troops to protect any Middle Eastern nation threatened by "overt armed aggression from any country controlled by international communism."[41] Passed by Congress in March, this proposal was inevitably labeled the Eisenhower Doctrine, and like the Truman Doctrine before it, it increased the president's warmaking powers and provided the basis for American intervention in the internal affairs of still more nations around the world.

These Middle Eastern events coincided with a serious crisis in Eastern Europe. In Poland, riots in mid-1956 against Russian rule eventually led Russian leaders to grant concessions leading to de-Stalinization and greater national autonomy under the strong Polish nationalist and communist Wladyslaw Gomulka, by the middle of October. The success of this revolt, coupled with long discontent against Soviet rule and Khrushchev's de-Stalinization speech, sparked another revolt in nearby Hungary, where university students and workers were possibly encouraged by Radio Free Europe messages that seemed to promise American intervention on the side of the rebels. The students and workers attacked government buildings, assaulted the police, destroyed statues and portraits of Russian leaders, and finally toppled the government itself, forcing Khrushchev to agree to relax Russian rule in the country and appoint Hungarian nationalist Imre Nagy as party secretary and head of the government. But the students and new government soon went even further, demanding an end to all Russian rule in Hungary and Hungary's withdrawal from the Warsaw Pact, the communist military alliance forged in 1955 to counter the NATO alliance and Western European Union.

These challenges to Russian rule were unacceptable to Khrushchev. Early in November he sent dozens of tanks and eight divisions of soldiers into Budapest and other centers of revolution, brutally suppressing the revolt and killing perhaps as many as 25,000 Hungarians in the process. Tortures, mass arrests, and executions would continue for three more years, but by the end of November Russia had crushed Hungary and made it clear that de-Stalinization had its limits and would not be allowed to challenge Soviet hegemony in Eastern Europe.

Eisenhower would later write in his memoirs that the dual crisis in Suez and in Hungary were "the start of the most crowded and demanding three weeks of my entire presidency. The drama of those weeks is still so fresh in my memory that I can recite its principal events and our decisions with scarcely a pause."[42] But there was really no agonizing decision on Hungary. In spite of all the talk about liberation, the United States did not intervene, for fear that it would start a land war in Europe that would mushroom to a nuclear confrontation between the two superpowers. So, while the Russians harshly crushed the revolt, the United States looked on helplessly, with Eisenhower unable to do anything beyond praising the brave freedom fighters, announcing that he would provide sanctuary for any of them who sought asylum in the United States, and joining the rest of the noncommunist world in condemning the brutal methods used by Russia to put down the revolt. The Russian leaders responded to American protests and appeals for Hungarian freedom with the blunt assertion that this was a Russian and Hungarian matter that was none of America's business.

The dual crises in the Middle East and Eastern Europe occurred during the campaign and election of 1956. There was no doubt about the Republican nominee—Eisenhower was the best weapon the Republican party had, and at the convention at the Cow Palace in San Francisco in late August he was easily renominated by acclamation on the first ballot. But if the party was sure that it liked Ike, it was not so sure about Richard Nixon. Neither was Eisenhower, who had serious doubts about Nixon's presidential talents and thought that there were other men who might be better qualified, such as Robert Anderson, George Humphrey, Herbert Brownell, and Sherman Adams. In fact, for several months after he announced his candidacy, Eisenhower had refused to endorse Nixon, saying he would leave the decision up to the convention. At one point in the spring he even suggested to Nixon that he might consider accepting a cabinet post, such as defense, rather than the vice-presidency, a humiliating proposal that Nixon refused to entertain. Finally, Eisenhower yielded to Nixon's proven abilities as a campaigner and a political infighter, and on April 26 he informed him that he would openly endorse his candidacy. Although Harold Stassen and others worked to block Nixon's renomination, he was duly chosen by the convention.[43]

There was more suspense in the Democratic camp, where Adlai Stevenson and Estes Kefauver engaged in a spirited battle in the primaries before Kefauver withdrew on July 16 and endorsed Stevenson. Averell Harriman, backed by Harry Truman, then emerged as the only real threat to Stevenson's renomination, but at the convention at the International Amphitheater in Chicago (August 13–17) the Illinois governor won easily on the first ballot, then surprised everyone by throwing the vice-presidential nomination open to the convention, which chose Kefauver after a major battle between his supporters and those of John F. Kennedy of Massachusetts. But the Democrats did not have much of a chance in 1956. Eisenhower was popular, the country was prosperous, and his handling of the Suez crisis appeared to most voters as another sign of his cautious but firm and wise leadership. The Democratic campaign focused on Eisenhower's health, age, "golfing and goofing," weak leadership, agricultural program, and Stevenson's pledge to stop the draft and the testing of nuclear weapons. Little was said about desegregation and the 1954 Brown decision—Stevenson recognized this as a major liability. With Eisenhower so popular, Stevenson concentrated on Nixon, calling him the "heir apparent" and the "heir anointed," a veiled but all-too-obvious reference to the possibility that Eisenhower might not survive a second term. As expected, there were the usual examples of the Stevenson wit, as when he told one audience that "I'm beginning to think that the reason President Eisenhower decided to run again is that he just couldn't afford to retire to his farm in Gettysburg as long as Ezra Taft Benson is Secretary of Agriculture."[44] The Democrats reran some of the buttons and posters of 1952, along with a few new ones: "Adlai Likes Me" and "Adlai and Estes are the Bestes." But none of these could match the most popular Republican button, "We Like Ike."

With Eisenhower's campaign again managed by the prestigious New York advertising firm of Batten, Barton, Durstine, and Osborne, the Republican party refused to be drawn into a real discussion of issues, preferring to emphasize Eisenhower's image, his leadership, peace, and prosperity—"everything's booming but the guns," Republican campaigners happily pointed out. On civil rights, the Republican party asserted that the party accepted the Brown decision and that it would continue to work on the passage of its own civil rights legislation, and in campaigning Eisenhower praised his own administration's work in desegregating the armed forces while rarely mentioning the Brown decision or promising to fight against racial discrimination. The Republican buttons said it all: "America Needs Eisenhower," "The Mighty Tower—Eisenhower," "Let's Back Ike and Dick," "We Still Like Ike," "Peace and Prosperity with Eisenhower," and "Don't Bump a Good Man out of the White House." And Eisenhower looked healthy, defusing all the Democratic references to the possibility that Nixon might have to complete Eisenhower's second term.

Election day was November 6, at the height of the Suez and Hungarian crises, and in spite of the Democrats' claim that the "bankrupt" policies of Dulles and Eisenhower had created the dual crisis, the voters seemed to think that in an uncertain and dangerous world Eisenhower, not Stevenson, was the man of the hour. The president was returned to the White House by a landside, winning 35,590,472 popular votes to Stevenson's 26,022,752. He took 58 percent of the popular vote, while his margin in the electoral college was a whopping 457 to 73. He won all but seven states, again carried several southern states—Virginia, Tennessee, Texas, Florida, and Louisiana—and he drew more black votes (47 percent) than he had in 1952, perhaps because the Brown decision was associated in black voters' minds with the Republican administration. But he could not carry Congress, where the Democrats kept control of the Senate by a vote of 50 to 46 and of the House by 233 to 202.[45] For the first time since 1848, the winning presidential candidate's party had lost both houses of Congress to the opposition party. Once again the voters had shown that they did indeed like Ike, but not necessarily his party.

Still, it was another victory for the general. Republican control of the White House was assured for another four years along with, millions of Americans believed, the continuation of the peace and prosperity Republican rule had brought. The Cold War and the fear of nuclear war were never far out of sight, but most Americans at mid-decade were content to let the man in the White House handle these problems while they enjoyed the greatest period of prosperity and optimism the nation had seen since the Jazz Age of the 1920s.

# 13

# *Good Times*

In the 1950s the United States enjoyed a period of unprecedented prosperity, consumerism, and economic optimism. Signs of the new prosperity were everywhere. At the middle of the decade, the United States, with 6 percent of the world's population and 7 percent of the area, produced almost half of the world's manufactured products and contained within its borders 75 percent of the automobiles, 60 percent of the telephones, and 30 percent of the televisions and radios. Not surprisingly, it also consumed almost half of the world's annual production of energy, 50 percent of the copper, 33 percent of the tin, 60 percent of the aluminum, and 65 percent of the newsprint. During the decade the Gross National Product climbed from $285 billion to $500 billion, per capita income rose by 48 percent, the median family income rose from $3,083 to $5,657, and in spite of the inflation of the Korean War years, real wages rose by almost 30 percent. The number of stockholders jumped from 6.5 million in 1952 to almost 17 million by the early 1960s, and in that same time it was proudly pointed out that the number of millionaires rose from around 27,000 to almost 80,000. Although unemployment was a periodic problem and reached a decade high of 7.5 percent in 1958, the expanding economy continued to create jobs in record numbers: In 1960, when the unemployment rate was 6 percent, the number of working Americans had risen to a record level of 66.5 million.[1]

No wonder many economists were declaring that the nation had become a great worker's paradise in which the old problems of poverty and inequality had been largely solved and superseded by the new, happy problem of what to do with the abundance of consumer goods that were pouring from the factories and farms. No wonder economists rhapsodized about "the affluent society," the "new era of capitalism," and the new "people's capitalism"—in America it was proudly proclaimed, everybody was a capitalist. Never, it seemed, had so many had it so good, and never had so many expected it to get better. To many observers of the American scene, the old adage, "The poor will always be with us," was a thing of the past. When Adlai Stevenson said in the 1952 presidential campaign that "the United States at midcentury stands on the threshold of abundance for all,"[2] he was simply expressing a belief that was already shared by millions of his fellow countrymen.

What were the causes of this prosperity? It was partly due to the consumer spending generated by the savings and deferred demand of the Second World War, when workers saved $150 billion that they would spend in the late 1940s and early 1950s. It was partly caused by the rapid population growth, which greatly expanded the market for homes, furniture, and goods and services for the growing army of young people. It was partly fed by the easy credit policies of banks, other lending institutions, and retail stores, which made it possible, even easy, to buy today and pay tomorrow. It was partly caused by increased productivity due to the introduction of computers, automation, and other labor-saving devices. It was promoted by the federal government, which pumped money into the economy through its welfare programs, subsidies for farmers, foreign-aid programs, and perhaps most of all, through its defense spending, which between 1946 and 1960 totaled over $500 billion and accounted for, on the average, about 10 percent of the annual GNP. By 1960, national defense and veterans' benefits had climbed to $51.3 billion, 55.6 percent of total federal spending, and 10.2 percent of the annual GNP.[3] Peace, real peace, many economists began to understand, would be an economic disaster for the country.

America's economic growth in the 1950s was also aided by an inexpensive, plentiful, and uninterrupted supply of energy. At the beginning of the decade, Eugene Holman, the president of Standard Oil, said that "I don't believe we'll run out of oil in the near or the foreseeable future" and predicted that oil reserves and new processes "will provide our requirements for hundreds of years."[4] This optimistic assessment of energy supplies, made at a time when the nation exported oil and controlled, along with its European allies, most of the world's oil fields, prevailed throughout the decade. The nation went on an energy binge, as Americans filled their homes with new appliances, bought millions of big, gas-guzzling automobiles (averaging 12.7 miles per gallon), and turned away from coal to the more convenient fuel oil and natural gas to heat their homes and run their rapidly expanding industries. Energy use expanded by more than 30 percent during the decade. Gasoline use for passenger cars rose from 25 billion gallons of fuel in 1950 to 42 billion in 1960. In 1955 the country consumed, for the first time in its history, more energy than it produced, and by 1960 was importing 1.8 million barrels of oil a day, 19 percent of all domestic consumption. The roots of future energy crises had been planted.[5]

The prosperity of the decade was also promoted by a phenomenal rise in advertising—in fact, the economic health of the nation in the fifties was more dependent upon advertising than in any previous period in its history. Continuing a trend begun in the 1920s, the economy moved steadily away from a production economy trying to provide the basic needs of society to a consumption economy in which the essentials had already been met and emphasis was placed on consuming more and more luxury items. It was inevitable that the economy would become more and more dependent on advertising. The consumer had to be persuaded to buy not just what he needed, but what he simply wanted or could be convinced that he needed or wanted. As part of this convincing process, the amount of money spent on advertising was more than doubled during the decade, rising from about $6 billion in 1950 to $9 billion in 1955 and to $13 billion in 1963. The biggest spender on advertising was General Motors, which in 1955 alone spent over $162 million attempting to persuade consumers to buy its cars and appliances.[6]

Much of the advertising was based on the assumption that women did most of the buying, not just for themselves but for their children and husbands. Most television commercials, especially during the day, were geared to women, and the typical woman's magazine gave over half its space to advertisements and devoted much of the rest to articles telling the reader how to buy and use the products being poured out by the nation's factories. Advertisers also operated on the assumption that most consumers did not make purchasing decisions on a rational basis—such as real need or intelligent product comparison—but on the basis of deeply rooted, often irrational likes and fantasies. Using the techniques of motivational research, Madison Avenue shrewdly manipulated Americans through advertisements that cast a glamorous aura over a down-to-earth product or service and subtly promised that it would quickly bring youth, health, beauty, sex appeal, friendship, security, power, or status. In addition, advertisers correctly calculated that consumers could be persuaded, through subtle psychological appeals, to give in to buying whims and fantasies, to become dissatisfied with automobiles, appliances, or other products ("psychological obsolescence," the ad men called it) long before they had physically worn out. "If you want it," such ads seemed to say, "don't feel guilty—buy it."

Did consumers know that they were being manipulated? Some did, and tried to make rational choices in spite of the barrage of advertisements they were hit with every day. (Advertisers tried to overcome this rational analysis of needs and products by experimenting with "subliminal advertising," a technique in which a message—such as "Drink Ace Beer"—was flashed on a television or movie screen too fast to be perceived except by the subconscious mind, but a threatened government ban on the ads and their apparent ineffectiveness caused the advertisers to drop the idea.)[7] The techniques of Madison Avenue were often uncovered in magazines and newspaper articles, and in 1957 they were the subject of a widely discussed best-selling book, *The Hidden Persuaders*, by popular sociologist Vance Packard. According to Packard, Americans bought Cadillacs to promote the image of wealth, Fords to promote the image of youth and speed, Gleam toothpaste to reduce their feelings of guilt (it was touted as being for people who "can't brush after every meal"), Maidenform bras because they appealed to fantasies of appearing nude in public ("I dreamed I stopped traffic in my Maidenform bra"), or Marlboro cigarettes because they conveyed masculinity.[8] But the *Hidden Persuaders* or other books (like the same author's work on planned obsolescence and artificial stimulation of consumption, *The Waste Makers*)[9] had little effect on consumers. They might occasionally rebel, as when they rejected the Edsel, but most of the time they bought the products they often did not need for reasons they really did not understand. And Madison Avenue weathered all the criticism that came its way and continued to make millions of dollars by convincing the incredibly gullible consumer of the virtues of almost any product, service, idea, or political candidate it was hired to sell.

By stimulating consumption, Madison Avenue helped promote the rise of a credit society. So did the federal government's Federal Reserve policies and low interest rates for GI housing, retail establishments' convenient charge plans, and the rise of credit card companies. The credit card business began in 1950 with the introduction of the Diner's Club card, which was initially honored only in a few restaurants in New York City but soon spread nationwide, rising to 750,000 card holders in 1958. The Diner's Club card had more holders than any other credit card in the 1950s, though the American Express card, founded in the mid-1950s, trailed not too far behind. Oil companies, motel and hotel chains, and many other companies introduced credit cards in the 1950s as well. Private debt jumped from $73 billion in 1950 to over $196 billion in 1960 as Americans used credit cards and easy installment plans to buy consumer goods, take vacations, and enjoy other pleasures of life offered by the prosperity of the time. By the middle of the decade, 60 percent of all new automobiles were bought on credit, often for as little as $100 down, and by 1960 over 10 million credit customers were shopping at Sears.[10] Many older people, remembering the depression and other hard times of the past, were amazed at how easily and eagerly younger couples incurred thousands of dollars of debt in their search for the good life.

A whole new type of consumer psychology was taking root in prosperous America.

The American economic system was not just growing, it was also undergoing some dramatic transformations. Some older industries—such as mining, iron and steel, lumber, textiles, and leather products—were declining or entering periods of slow growth, primarily because of the boom in synthetic products that had been stimulated by the Second World War. The plastics industry grew by 600 percent in the fifties, as chemical industries turned out a wide variety of plastics to take the place of wood, glass, and metals, and man-made fibers like rayon, Orlon, Dacron, and nylon to take the place of wool, cotton, linen, and silk. The electronics industry, also stimulated by the war, grew to become the nation's fifth largest industry (behind automobiles, steel, aircraft, and chemicals) as it tried to meet the demand for television, radios, hi-fis, tape recorders, home appliances, computers, testing and measuring devices for automation, and sophisticated controls for the complicated weaponry being purchased by the Defense Department. As another mark of the affluent age, it is not surprising that the automotive, home building, and oil and gas industries also grew rapidly in the fifties.[11]

American capitalism was also moving into a new sophisticated era in industrial techniques, research, and information processing. Automation, viewed by more and more industries as a way to boost productivity and cut labor costs, spread rapidly, especially in the chemical, petroleum, automotive, and aircraft industries. Many of these same industries were also turning to the rapidly expanding field of research and development, for the economy was becoming too complex to depend on individual inventors or thinkers or even on small laboratories for new ideas and inventions. Between 1953 and 1964 the amount of money poured into research and development increased by 400 percent, and by the midfifties over 3,000 companies had established research facilities employing a total of almost a half million workers. As might be expected, the largest single funder of research and development was the federal government, which dispensed billions to universities and private think tanks all over the country in an effort to defeat the Russians in the race for development of destructive weapons. The advance of both automation and research and development was aided by the electronic computer, invented during World War II but not commercially marketed until the fifties. As late as 1954 the annual sales of these electronic marvels stood at only 20, but the number jumped to over 1,000 in 1957, over 2,000 in 1960, and over 3,000 in 1961.[12] By the late fifties the computer was already being hailed as a revolutionary breakthrough in the processing and storage of information and as an essential tool for the functioning of complex industrial societies, though its major impact would not come until the 1970s and 1980s.

One of the most significant of all changes occurring in the economy was the rapid growth in the number, size, and power of the large corporations, which, in spite of sporadic governmental attempts at trust busting, had been on the rise ever since the time of their founding in the late nineteenth century. During the fifties the nation's economy became dominated by an economic oligarchy. Some 3,404 smaller companies were absorbed by about 500 larger ones, and by the end of the decade some 600 corporations, representing only one half of 1 percent of all corporations, were responsible for 53 percent of all corporate income, while the 200 largest corporations controlled over 50 percent of all the nation's business assets. The three major automakers produced 95 percent of all new cars, the three major aluminum companies provided 90 percent of all the aluminum, ten aircraft corporations employed 94 percent of all aircraft workers, and similar concentrations of production and workers could be found in the petroleum, steel, tire, office machine, and cigarette industries. Many of the conglomerates were international companies, with plants, investments, and workers all over the world and with annual budgets rivaling or surpassing those of many of the world's smaller countries. All of this was done with the tacit approval of the Department of Justice, which was not in a trust-busting mood in the age of Eisenhower. It was also done with the help of Congress, which promoted corporate profits and growth through generous tax policies on capital gains and depreciation and depletion allowances. In 1957, Humble Oil Company paid only $17 million on a pretax income of $193 million, and in some years some giant corporations paid no taxes at all.[13]

The rise of the giant corporations had a profound effect on American life. A few hundred corporations controlled much of the nation's industrial and commercial assets and enjoyed a near monopoly in some areas. They dominated the seats of economic and political power. They employed millions of workers, a large percentage of whom populated the suburbs that were growing all across America and were helping to transform the country. They promoted a rise in the wage level, helped to make the middle class the largest class in the country, and helped to fight discrimination by adopting hiring practices that were often far ahead of smaller companies. Although their motives were self-serving, their foundations and other forms of charitable activities benefited many communities, organizations, and individuals. And finally, their recruitment and training of the much discussed "organization men" played a major role in the promotion of the conformity that characterized much of American life during the decade.[14]

The changing American economy also experienced dramatic shifts in the composition of the work force. Fewer workers went into traditional fields such as manufacturing, agriculture, and mining, and more went into clerical, managerial, professional, and service fields. In 1956, for the first time in the nation's history, white collar workers outnumbered blue collar ones, and by the end of the decade blue collar workers constituted only 45 percent of the work force. The sexual composition of the work force also changed as more and more women entered the labor market. The influx of women into the work world that had been accelerated by the Second World War continued in the postwar period. By 1950, 16.5 million women were working outside the home, and by the end of 1956 this figure had grown to 22 million, almost a third of the labor force.[15] For both sexes, the dramatic postwar rise in white collar jobs, wages, and college opportunities brought increased possibilities for entering the steadily widening middle class, which was enjoying the prosperity of the fifties and helping to mold the views, values, ideals, and beliefs of that decade. Most surveys showed that some 75 percent of adult Americans considered themselves part of the middle class, lending credence to the growing belief that the nation was becoming one large, prosperous, harmonious middle class.

The shifts in the composition of the work force inevitably affected the fortunes of organized labor. After making tremendous gains in the New Deal and World War II era, organized labor continued to prosper in the fifties, but it seemed to lose much of its vitality and public support. The labor movement was hurt by the changing economy, which was producing fewer jobs in manufacturing, where labor had always been the strongest, and more jobs in the white collar and service sectors, where labor generally made little headway. The labor movement also continued to suffer from antagonistic employers (especially in the South), right-to-work laws and other hostile state enactments, its own antagonism toward female and black workers, the Taft–Hartley Act (which, among other provisions, prohibited the closed shop), and occasional attempts by the government to ferret out supposed communists in unions. Finally, it was hurt by widespread charges of corruption and racketeering involving its leaders, allegations that eventually led in the late fifties to televised hearings of congressional investigating committees, the expulsion of the Teamsters Union from the AFL-CIO (united in 1955), the conviction and imprisonment of Teamster president Dave Beck, the investigation of James Hoffa and other labor leaders, and the passage in Congress of the Landrum–Griffin Act aimed at curbing union activity. No wonder that polls of the time consistently showed that the public held business leaders in high esteem while regarding the unions as unsavory organizations run by "racketeers."[16]

Because of these problems, the number of unionized workers rose only from 14.3 million at the end of the Second World War to 18.5 million in 1957, then declined to around 17 million by the end of the decade.[17] Big labor presented no real threat to big business's control of the economy or to the election or reelection of Eisenhower. In the probusiness atmosphere of the time, labor successfully concentrated on seeking improvements in wages (including a guaranteed annual wage and cost-of-living increases in the automotive industry), pensions, insurance, vacations, sick leave, and other fringe benefits. There were protracted strikes, like the steelworkers' strikes under Truman and again under Eisenhower in 1955 and 1959, but there were no big, pitched battles like those of earlier years. Generally relations were good between labor and management. Most labor leaders were highly paid executives who dressed and lived much like the managers they bargained with and were as conservative as Eisenhower Republicans on most political issues. Unions were strongly anticommunist and antisocialist, still discriminated against blacks and women, and generally opposed the civil rights movement and other emerging social causes of the fifties. In prosperous America, labor, unionized or not, was staunchly lower-middle-class in its attitudes and goals.[18]

Still another economic area undergoing vast changes was agriculture. From 1950 to 1960 agricultural productivity increased by over a third through the use of mechanization, better management, electrification, and the greater use of fertilizers and pesticides produced by the growing biochemical industry. As a result, the United States was in an unprecedented agricultural position, one that made her the envy of much of the rest of the world and would have been undreamed of by people of centuries past. The basic agricultural problem of the United States in the fifties was not how to relieve the scarcity of food, but what to do with all the agricultural surpluses that were piling up and how to arrest the corresponding drop in prices that was hurting so many farmers. Eisenhower dealt with the problems by establishing a flexible government price-support program, inaugurating a soil bank program that paid farmers for not growing food on a certain portion of their land, and shipping surpluses to schools, the military, and to people overseas in the form of charity, disaster relief, and foreign aid. Still, the surpluses accumulated, causing a decline in prices and serious political problems for the president who had entered office with hopes of returning agriculture to the free-market system.[19] Like Roosevelt and Truman before him, Eisenhower never found the key to solving the problems of agricultural abundance.

These agricultural developments were bringing vast changes to the American farm belt. The number of farms declined from 6 million at the end of the Second World War to 3.9 million in 1960, and the number of farmers dropped from over 31 million (25 percent of the population) in 1939 to only 13.7 million (7.1 percent of the population) in the early 1960s. In the 1950s alone, the farm population declined by 17 percent as 1.4 million people left the farms each year seeking better jobs in the city.[20] More and more small farms disappeared, and farming became a big business run by farmers knowledgeable in the ways of modern business and technology. The average acreage of farms grew from 191 in 1945 to 297 in 1960, while the number of people one farmer could feed rose from 14.6 to 25.8.[21] Those who remained on the farm steadily became more like urban dwellers, as the extension of roads, television, and electricity into rural areas ended the historical isolation of farmers and their differences from city dwellers.

What were Americans doing with their newfound prosperity in a land that was producing over half of the world's manufactured products? They bought automobiles, on the order of 5 to 7 million a year. They also bought new houses. By 1960 there were almost 10 million more homeowners than there had been in 1950, 58 percent of all nonfarm families owned their own homes, and 25 percent of all the nation's homes had been built in the previous ten years.[22] Both homeowners and renters filled their homes or apartments with new furniture, and in an age of increasing leisure and backyard barbecues, they bought more and more porch and outdoor furniture—sales of lawn and porch furniture grew from $53.6 million in 1950 to $145.2 million by 1960.[23] Millions more were spent on plastic flamingos, ducks, chickens, deer, and other lawn decorations that supposedly gave a touch of farm and forest to suburban areas. And the swimming pool, which in the past had been affordable only by the rich, now began to appear in the yards of more and more middle-and upper-middle-class homeowners in the suburbs. From 1948 to 1963, the number of residential swimming pools grew from around 3,000 to almost 300,000.[24] And not too far from the swimming pool was the barbecue equipment, a must for every suburban family.

Americans filled the insides of their homes with all the labor-saving appliances and gadgets they could afford to buy with cash or credit. By 1959, 98 percent of electrically wired homes had a refrigerator, 90 percent had a television, 93 percent had an electric washing machine, 37 percent had a vacuum cleaner, 22 percent had a freezer, 18 percent had an electric or gas dryer, and 13 percent had an air-conditioner.[25] Popular magazines of the day were full of articles about the new labor-saving and convenience devices available and predicted even more in the near future. In 1954, in "The Pushbutton Way to Leisure," *House and Garden*[26] used pictures and text to rhapsodize about eighteen new or relatively new devices that were making life more convenient for Americans. "These 18 mechanical servants work part-or-full time," it wrote, and "combine the talents of caretaker, gardener, cook, maid."[27] Among the eighteen servants were electric serving carts to keep food hot, electric dishwashers, automatic incinerators "far more reliable than the local trash collector," food freezers that were the "next best thing to a cook in the kitchen," washers and dryers to "do all the blue jeans, bed linens and beach towels you can toss into them," electric blenders "so easy to operate that children can have a soda fountain at home," automatic coffee percolators, electric lawn trimmers, baby tractors for lawn and garden work, and portable barbecues.

It seemed in the midfifties that convenience products were flooding the market. In 1956, in an article lauding the new products of the previous ten years, *Newsweek* marveled that "hundreds of brand-new goods have become commonplace overnight: TV and hi-fi, frozen, low-calorie, and instant foods, aerosol containers and electronic garbage disposals, power steering and power transmission, the entire field of synthetic chemistry—from plastic squeeze bottles to synthetic textiles."[28] Some consumers had trouble accepting the new products—many were still wary of electric blankets, for example—but for most the biggest problem was not one of acceptance but of keeping the new products in good working order. Americans frequently complained of how often their new gadgets broke down and how difficult and expensive it was to get them repaired. In 1957, there were an estimated 1.8 million repairmen in the country doing $16.6 billion worth of business every year. One appliance that was never allowed to be out of order for long was the television; polls of the decade consistently showed that consumers would pay to have their television repaired even if they had to use rent or house payment money to pay for it. In 1956, television repairs cost some $2 billion, more than the total cost of all new sets sold that year.[29]

Americans also spent more on foods, and as the decade progressed, more and more of it went into convenience foods like TV dinners, instant coffee, frozen orange juice, and frozen and canned foods. The growth of suburbia brought an explosion in outdoor barbecuing, creating a large market for barbecue grills, cooking utensils, beef, pork, poultry, soft drinks, beer, and potato chips. Hot dog production jumped from 750 million pounds in 1950 to 1,050 million pounds in 1960, while potato chip production rose from 320 million pounds to 532 million pounds in that same length of time.[30] As the decade progressed, more and more food and other products were bought in convenient disposable packages. In 1960, for example, the average American family discarded 750 cans.[31] Affluent America was becoming a wasteful, throwaway society.

Americans also began to eat out more, both at traditional restaurants and at the fast-food chains that sprang up across the country in the second half of the decade. Hamburger and hot dog eateries had long been part of the American scene, of course, and even before the fifties began, a few entrepreneurs had built regional chains of fast-food restaurants. But a big change came in 1954 when Ray Kroc, a fifty-two-year-old businessman who had been engaged in several business ventures over the years, paid the McDonald brothers, Maurice and Richard, $2.7 million for the franchise rights to their hamburger diner in San Bernardino, California. Kroc adapted and refined their very successful assembly-line process for making hamburgers, and after opening his own first diner, complete with the soon to be famous golden arches, in Des Plaines, Illinois, in 1955, he established a chain of McDonald restaurants, all offering a highly standardized burger that was 1.6 ounces in weight, 3.9 inches in diameter, and served on a 3.5-inch wide bun with a quarter ounce of onions.

Each McDonald's featured well-dressed employees, clean kitchens and rest rooms, standardized food, and standardized prices. Recognizing that Americans were people on the move, that they wanted a dependable and clean place to eat, and that a fortune could be made from serving whole families, Kroc banned jukeboxes, pinball machines, telephone booths, and other features that would have made his restaurants teen hangouts. In the beginning he even refused to hire young girls, fearing they would attract too many teenage boys. The McDonald's restaurants spread rapidly all across the country, and before the decade was out, in 1959, Kroc opened his one-hundredth restaurant. At that time his famous hamburger still sold for fifteen cents, just as it had under the McDonald brothers and just as it would until 1967, when it went to eighteen cents. In 1959 the average franchise grossed $204,000 a year, and all the restaurants combined had sold a total of 50 million burgers.[32] Kroc's success spawned dozens of imitators, and fast-food chains began to spread across the land.

The affluent nation spent millions on clothing, both for work and school wear and for the faddish, casual clothing that was becoming so popular in an age when large numbers of Americans had so much disposable income and so much leisure time. Over this ten-year period, women's clothes showed a wide range of styles: full skirts worn over crinolines, strapless evening gowns, A-line skirts, tube dresses, sack dresses, short shorts, two-piece bathing suits, bikinis, blue jeans, bobby sox, penny loafers, baggy and tight sweaters—just to mention a few. Some styles had a short life span—the sack dress (also called the chemise, the bag, the loose look, and the Moslem look) lasted less than a year before it was hung in the back of the closet, where, according to some critics, it looked far better on a rack than it ever had on a woman's body. And some fashions caused some women to run into legal problems. Short shorts, which became the rage among teenage girls and even older women in 1956, were widely applauded by males, but in White Plains, New York, and a few other cities women were occasionally fined for violating "indecent exposure" laws. In Southampton, Long Island, several women were fined $10 for violating an ordinance declaring that "no person shall walk or ride in any vehicle upon or along the public streets . . . in any bathing suit, shorts, trunks, or other apparel which does not cover properly the body and limbs from midway between the knees and hips to and including the shoulders."[33]

Clothes for men, who in the past were restricted by convention and designers to drab styles, showed a greater variety than ever before. Conservative types still wore gray flannel suits, blue pinstripes, or tweeds to the office, but more and more men were wearing bolder clothing to work and acquiring a large leisure wardrobe that they often wore to work as well. There was an almost endless range of clothing to fit every age, need, and pocketbook: colorful (even checkered) sports jackets, tuxedos (now in red, yellow, blue, and other colors), white and colored dress shirts, sports and dress shirts with button-down collars, dress shirts with large French cuffs, polo shirts with a crocodile insignia stitched on the breast (given a big sales boost when Eisenhower showed up at the golf course wearing such a shirt), oversize Madras plaid sport shirts, gaudy Hawaiian sports shirts like those sported by President Truman on his vacations, baggy pegged pants, rogue trousers with a white side stripe, slacks with a belt in the back, Bermuda shorts of all colors, canvas shoes, car coats, mohair alpaca sweaters, wing tip shoes, Bass Weejuns, sports caps with a buckle in the back, blue jeans, and leather jackets. In 1955, the male species stunned the world—and perhaps himself—by emerging dressed in pink—pink shirts, Bermuda shorts, slacks, and colonel string ties. Whether he was in the office, in the classroom, or on a motorcycle with the rest of the gang, the male in the fifties came out in all his sartorial splendor.

For both sexes, the trend was toward the casual, convenient, and colorful. In the midfifties, for example, men were buying fewer suits and more separates (different colored slacks and sports coats), 8 million sports jackets (ten times the number they had in the early forties), 62 million pairs of slacks (about five times what they had in the early forties), and 60 percent more sports shirts than dress shirts. Reflecting on these figures, social critic Russell Lynes said that "one would think from this that American men did nothing but hang around country clubs."[34] Looking at the clothing men wore in their backyards, Lynes also observed that the American male wanted "to eat his barbecued spareribs in the backyard dressed like a bird of paradise. For some reason food seems to taste better to him if he has on blue canvas shoes, brick-red or canary-yellow slacks, and a pastel sports shirt which hangs free, like a young matron's maternity smock, outside the pants."[35] As the decade progressed, more and more of the clothing for both sexes was made from the increasing number of synthetic fibers bearing labels promising that they would "drip dry" and required "little or no ironing."

One of the central elements of the prosperity of the fifties was the automobile, which Americans bought in record numbers. Spurred by the growth of the population, suburbs, disposable incomes, easy credit, and advertising, annual sales of passenger cars rose steadily from 6.7 million in 1950 to a record 7.9 million in 1955, then hovered around 5 to 6 million for the rest of the decade. Nearly 58 million automobiles were manufactured during the decade. By 1960, 80 percent of American families owned at least one automobile, and the number of families owning two or more had grown to 15 percent. There were more automobiles in Los Angeles County alone that year than in all of South America or Asia.[36]

The fifties was a time of major innovations and improvements in American automobiles. The decade saw the introduction or widespread adoption of such things as power brakes, power steering, automatic transmissions, high compression V-8 engines that eventually reached over 400 horsepower, ball-joint front suspensions, deep-dish steering wheels, automatic speed controls, torsion-bar suspensions, padded dashboards and seat backs, pop-out windshields, air-cooled engines, rear engines, and fiberglass bodies. These innovations helped make automobiles more comfortable and easier to drive than ever before. Conveniences like air-conditioning, considered a luxury at the beginning of the decade, had become necessities on higher-priced cars by the midfifties. "The only Cadillac buyers here who don't have air-conditioning in their cars are arthritics and old folks who can't stand the chill," claimed one Houston automobile dealer in 1956, when automotive air-conditioning had grown to a $3 billion-a-year industry.[37]

Automobiles also became more expensive than ever before. Although price controls during the Korean War held down price increases in the early fifties, prices rose steadily from 1953 through the rest of the decade, due to increasing costs in materials and labor, major changes in styling and mechanics, and the monopoly of the big three automakers, who steadily squeezed out their smaller competitors and increased their control of the market to 95 percent of domestic production by the end of the decade. By 1959, the average price of a new car was $2,060, up from $1,900 in 1955 and $1,500 in 1946.[38] There was an enormous range, of course, depending on the model and options selected on any particular model. In 1957, for example, a Ford Fairlane could be bought for $2,339, a Chrysler 300-C for $4,929, and a Cadillac Eldorado Brougham for a little over $13,000.[39] What could not be bought in 1957 was a Frazer, Henry J. Kaiser, Clipper, Crosley, or Sears Allstate—the companies that made these cars in the early fifties had gone bankrupt, merged, or discontinued these models. By the end of the decade the Hudson, Packard, De Soto, and other familiar cars had disappeared, too.

The fifties brought a time of rapid changes in styling as automakers vied with one another to persuade the consumer to buy their models and to trade frequently for the newer, more advanced models. As the decade progressed, the automakers dropped, added, and modified their models until the consumer was faced with a bewildering assortment of styles—by 1961, he had to choose from 352 models! Manufacturers lured buyers with longer cars, lower cars, more and more chrome, tail fins, double headlights, multiple taillights, bright colors, two- and even three-tone paint jobs, plush interiors, air-conditioning, a seemingly endless array of gadgets on the dashboard, and new sports cars, like General Motors' Corvette (introduced in 1953) and Ford's Thunderbird (1954). Throughout the decade Detroit practiced "planned obsolescence"—manufacturing and promoting cars in such a way as to induce the consumer to change models frequently before his car had worn out, so that he would not be behind the times. Some critics also claimed that Detroit was also practicing "planned, built-in obsolescence" by deliberately building cars that would wear out quickly so that a new car would have to be bought. As evidence they could point to the 4.4 million cars that were junked in 1955 or the 5 million discarded in 1960, littering the landscape all across the country. Throughout the decade, the average interval between new-car trade-ins was only two years.[40]

One element that automakers made little effort to put into their automobiles was safety. Styling, horsepower, gadgets, and convenience came first, even though 5 million accidents, 40,000 fatalities, and 100,000 permanent disabilities were occurring each year on the nation's highways. The attitude of many automotive executives was summed up by William Mitchell of General Motors, who said in 1956 that only "squares" wanted safe cars and that "there ain't any squares no more,"[41] and by another industry official who said in 1959 that "a square foot of chrome sells ten times more cars than the best safety-door latch."[42] The industry did not want safety devices, the public had little interest in them and certainly did not want to pay for them, politicians were not concerned about an issue that was not an issue for most voters, and the media did not crusade for safety out of fear of losing their lucrative advertising revenues from the automakers. Ammunition for all of these views was provided in 1956, when Ford tried promoting safety with its Lifeguard Design—a package of safety devices made up of safety-door latches, a deep-dish steering wheel, padded seatbacks, seatbelts, and other features—then dropped the idea when sales lagged behind those of General Motors' newly designed Chevrolet that did not offer these devices. Ford's failure gave credence to the slogan around Detroit that "safety doesn't sell." Even when some companies in the late fifties began to offer safety options, they downplayed them in their sales promotions, fearing that the consumer did not want to be reminded that his new machine might maim or kill him and his family.[43]

Throughout the fifties the American automobile, promoted in advertising praising "your Big Pontiac," "the Big M" (Mercury), and increasingly longer Lincolns ("never before a Lincoln . . . so long and so longed for"),[44] continued to get longer, wider, heavier, and gaudier. The peak seemed to be reached in 1957 and 1958 when Chrysler introduced its tail fins and Ford put out a 19-foot 1-inch Lincoln with proud claims of being the longest car on the market. But something happened in 1958—only 4.3 million American automobiles were sold that year, the lowest since 1948, and although the recession undoubtedly played a major role in the sales dip, many analysts claimed that the cars did not sell because they were so ugly. The new styles were widely ridiculed, leading George Romney of American Motors to ask if anyone could "recall a period when a car design was subjected to as much lampooning in newspaper and magazine cartoons?" and industrial designer Carl Sundberg to claim that "panning the American automobile has become a pastime that threatens to replace baseball as a national sport."[45] Cars looked too much like airplanes, spaceships, and tanks and not enough like automobiles, and many consumers decided to pass up the new models.

The automobile that was most often passed up was the Edsel, named after Henry Ford's only son. After years of deliberation, Ford arrived at the decision to produce the car in 1955, during a banner year for the automotive industry, as a medium-priced car to compete with General Motors' cars. Ford executives spared no expense or effort on the new car, spending millions on research, design, production, advertising, and marketing as they tried to make a success of the first new standard-size car introduced by the big three since Ford's own Mercury in 1938. To try to insure that their $250 million investment would pay off, Ford hired the best "motivational research" experts available, created a new division with 800 executives, 15,000 workers, and sixty advertising copywriters, and built a national network of some 1,200 auto dealerships.[46] The car was planned and produced under secrecy and security measures that rivaled the Manhattan Project, as Ford tried to create suspense and to keep photographers and General Motors' spies from learning about Ford's new secret weapon in the battle for the medium-priced car market.

Finally, on September 4, 1957, after a blitz of advertising, the four different models of the new Edsel were unveiled in dealer showrooms with prices ranging from around $2,800 to $4,100. Designed, according to the ads, for the young executive or professional family on its way up, and similar in body style to the Mercury, the new Edsel featured a distinctive oval radiator grill, four front headlights, two large taillights, a powerful engine, and a host of fancy gadgets on the dashboard and steering column designed, according to *Consumer Reports*, to "please anyone who confuses gadgetry with true luxury."[47] The new car was, as Eric Larrabee wrote in *Harper's* in September of 1957, "the logical result of trying to give the consumer what he thinks he wants instead of, as the original Henry gave him, the best car at the cheapest price and no nonsense."[48] An estimated 3 million people visited Edsel showrooms on September 4 to gawk at the new car, and to the delight of Ford executives 6,500 Edsels were sold that first day.

But the car flopped. After the euphoria of the first day, sales never lived up to expectations, and even though Ford introduced design and mechanical changes in subsequent models and continued to bombard consumers with advertising, they refused to buy it. According to one joke making the rounds in this time, thieves even declined to steal it. On November 19, 1959, after selling only 109,446 units in the twenty-six months of the car's existence, far less than 1 percent of all the American automobiles sold during that time, the Edsel was discontinued. According to some estimates, Ford lost close to $350 million on the Edsel, a loss of $3,200 per car. Some analysts suggested that Ford would have come out better if it had decided in 1955 to produce no Edsels at all and to give away 110,000 Mercurys during the next twenty-six months.[49]

Why did the Edsel fail? There were many reasons of course, but perhaps *Time* said it best when it claimed that "the Edsel was a classic case of the wrong car for the wrong market at the wrong time."[50] It debuted right before a major recession, when sales of all cars plummeted to a ten-year low, and it came at a time when many consumers were beginning to rebel against the monstrous gas guzzlers produced by Detroit and to turn to foreign cars. It was also introduced too quickly, before all the mechanical problems had been worked out: Almost half of the owners of the early Edsels complained of serious mechanical defects. It also received poor ratings from automotive magazines and from *Consumer Reports*, which detailed for its 800,000 readers the Edsel's many defects and concluded that it "had no important basic advantage over other brands" and that "too much of the effort apparently went into making a piece of novelty merchandise, too little into creating a superior vehicle."[51] The car's mechanical defects gave it a bad reputation that it was never able to live down, and its famous oval grill, hailed as a major feature of its distinctive styling, became a national joke, with critics debating whether it looked like a horse collar, an egg, a toilet seat, or an Oldsmobile sucking a lemon. Perhaps it failed, too, because all the advance buildup led consumers to expect too much and to reject it when it appeared little different from the ordinary.[52] So, in spite of all the sophisticated motivational research, production and marketing techniques, manpower, and money that went into the production of the Edsel, it failed. In later years, when it became a valuable collector's item, it still remained the standard against which all other automobile lemons would be measured.

At the time of the Edsel fiasco, American automakers were growing increasingly worried about the recession, layoffs, sharp declines in sales, increasing criticism of their cars, and the growing popularity of foreign cars.[53] In 1950, only 16,336 foreign cars were sold in the United States, and even as late as 1955, the big year for American automakers, foreign car sales had climbed only to 51,658 units, less than three quarters of 1 percent of the total market. But then foreign car sales rose dramatically, reaching their highest point of the decade in 1959 with 614,131 units, slightly over 10 percent of all cars sold in the United States, before dropping back to 498,875 and 7.58 percent in 1960.[54] The leading small car was the sturdy, reliable, inexpensive ($1,495 in New York in 1955) Volkswagen, which, with very little advertising, jumped from 330 sales in 1950 to 1,237 in 1953 and nearly 200,000 in 1957.[55] "The Volkswagen people," John Keats noted in *The Insolent Chariots* in 1958, "are so busy trying to fill their orders that they do not need the services of market analysts, researchers, psyche-plumbers, hidden persuaders, and twenty million dollars' worth of advertisers."[56] Clearly, more and more Americans were defecting from Detroit's cars and turning toward cars that were smaller, plainer, more reliable, and cheaper to operate than Detroit's products. For some drivers at least, style, prestige, and fantasy gratification were becoming less important than cheap and reliable transportation.

Detroit reacted to the small-car invasion first by trying to ignore it, then by attacking the cars' quality with phrases like "anyone who wants cheap transportation can always buy a used car," and finally by introducing its own small cars. "If the public wants to lower its standard of living by driving a cheap, crowded car, we'll make it," was the way one Detroit auto executive put it.[57] Ironically, Ford had introduced its first small car, the Falcon, only one month before the Edsel came off the assembly line. As simple and plain as the Edsel was complex and ornate, the Falcon was a success from the very beginning. So was American Motors' compact Rambler, whose sales jumped from 100,000 in 1956 to 500,000 in 1958 and 1959.[58] Finally, in the fall of 1959, General Motors, Ford, and Chrysler introduced their own compact or economy cars, successfully blunting, at least temporarily, the onslaught of European imports.

Meanwhile, a network of good roads was being built throughout the country as the nation went on a road-building binge to handle the growing number of cars that were taking to the highways. Existing dirt roads were paved, new roads were constructed, thousands of miles of toll roads (like the 837-mile series of state turnpikes between New York and Chicago) were built, and the new Interstate system was initiated by the Eisenhower administration. Eisenhower had mounted a strong campaign for federal development and partial financing of a nationwide network of modern four-lane roads to make travel easier and safer, to relieve traffic congestion on the open road and in the cities, to make the cities more accessible while permitting through traffic to bypass them, and to provide for the rapid mobilization of military troops and supplies and the evacuation of urban civilians during an atomic attack. Backed by almost everyone—the politicians, the military, city planners, truckers, oil companies, automakers, road builders, and drivers—the Interstate Highway Act of 1956 provided for the construction of 41,000 miles of freeways to be built over a ten-year period at a cost of $26 billion, to be shared by federal and state governments. It was the largest public works project in American history and the most ambitious road-building plan attempted since the 50,000-mile road system of the Roman Empire. Despite its size, few anticipated that a quarter of a century later the system would still not be completed and that costs would have risen to over $100 billion.[59]

The national Interstate system, along with the toll roads and other road networks, made travel easier, safer, faster, and more convenient and helped to unify the nation as it had never been unified before. It accelerated the growth of the suburbs, contributed to urban flight and the decline of the inner city, accelerated the decline of the railroad and other forms of mass transit, contributed to atmospheric pollution and other environmental problems, and precluded the discussion and development of viable alternatives to the nation's transportation problems. The national Interstate system also committed the nation to a system of transportation based on the private automobile for traveling and on trucks for shipping. The automobile reigned supreme as it never had before, and the nation entered the 1960s with over 3 million miles of roads, almost three fourths of them paved. Total miles traveled by automobile, which had stood at 458 billion miles in 1950, had risen to 800 billion by 1963, when 90 percent of all travel between cities was by private automobile.[60]

It would be difficult to exaggerate the importance of the automobile in the 1950s. It had become an integral part of American life by 1930, when there were some 26 million cars in the country, and the importance of it had steadily increased ever since then. By the early fifties, the automobile was directly or indirectly responsible for one sixth of the GNP, providing jobs for millions in the automotive manufacturing industry, the petroleum industry, all the many companies that made materials that went into the manufacture of new cars, the tourist and travel industry, service stations, drive-in movies and restaurants, advertising, repair shops, and highway construction and maintenance. The automobile was helping to bring rural areas into the mainstream of American life and, along with television and other technological advancements, was helping to make the United States a more homogeneous nation. It was contributing to the growth of suburbia, shopping centers, drive-in movies, drive-in banks, and fast-food chains. It was also promoting the decay of the metropolitan areas, the decline of railway passenger traffic, air pollution (smog was reaching dangerous levels in Los Angeles as early as the 1940s), and traffic jams, traffic accidents, and massive chain-reaction smashups—like the record seventy-four-vehicle collision in Los Angeles in 1955.[61] Ironically, because of the congestion, new highways and powerful automotive engines did not always mean faster travel. Traffic jams in major cities became a way of life.

In spite of the disadvantages of the growth of an automotive society, the average American was convinced that his automobile was a part of his life that he could not live without. It gave him mobility, status, freedom, privacy, and the ability to get to his job and other destinations far easier than ever before. It allowed him to live outside the city while working inside and enjoying all the other amenities of city life without its problems. It made his life easier, more interesting, and more varied, opening up new places to go and new things to do. It was more important even than that other great necessity of the fifties, the television set. Whether it was the teenager with his hot rod or customized '50 or '51 Ford, the sports-car enthusiast with his foreign import or homegrown Corvette or T-Bird, the executive with his Lincoln Continental or Cadillac, the housewife with her boxy station wagon, or the factory worker with his Chevrolet or Ford, the automobile was the key to the good life in Eisenhower's America.

In their celebration of the heavenly benefits of American capitalism, the high priests of the prosperity of the fifties suffered from a severe case of economic myopia. In spite of the widening prosperity, the old inequalities in wealth remained. After all the economic gains of the decade, Americans entered the sixties with the top 1 percent of the population holding 33 percent of the national wealth, the top 5 percent holding 53 percent, and the top 20 percent holding 77 percent. The bottom 20 percent held only 5 percent of the wealth, about the same as at the end of the Second World War. Most Americans were better off than ever before, and the middle class was becoming the largest class, but a small group at the top still got the largest slice of the economic pie.[62] In spite of all the talk about "people's capitalism," over half of Americans throughout the fifties had no savings accounts and over 96 percent held no corporate stock. The Rockefeller family alone owned more stock than all the nation's wage earners combined.[63] There was also a stark contrast in income and life-style between the average American and the corporate rich, like the presidents of General Motors and Du Pont, making close to $500,000 a year in salaries and bonuses in the early fifties, and the board chairmen of the big oil companies with annual salaries between $175,000 and $250,000. The nation's wealthiest citizen, oilman J. Paul Getty, made close to a billion dollars in 1957 alone, yet throughout the decade was known to complain that "a billion dollars isn't what it used to be." Generous tax loopholes allowed wealthy Americans to keep much of what they made, leaving most of the national tax burden to the less fortunate members of the middle and lower classes. In 1959, five Americans with incomes over $5 million paid no taxes at all at a time when private and government studies were beginning to "discover" that millions of Americans lived in poverty.[64]

Little attention was given to the poor in the fifties, but they were there. Poverty was a hard condition to define, but throughout the decade most governmental and private studies of poverty set the poverty-level income at $3,000 annually for a family of four and $4,000 for a family of six. Using these criteria, most studies of poverty showed that from 20 to 25 percent of the population lived in poverty, with perhaps another 10 percent living on the poverty line and struggling desperately to avoid falling below it. If these figures are correct, then in any given year in the fifties something like 40 to 50 million people lived on the edge of poverty or below it.[65]

The existence of such chronic poverty in the midst of plenty was overlooked by most contemporary observers of the economic scene. One reason why it was overlooked was that most Americans believed that it was being eradicated by the prosperity of the times and that soon everybody would become a full member of the affluent society. Another reason was that the poor were largely invisible to those on the economic and social ladder above them and had no influential spokesmen to plead their cause. The poor were the blacks living in the core cities that most Americans were able to avoid as they sped to other destinations on the new expressways being built around the slums. They were the poor whites in the troubled farming and mining industries in the isolated Appalachian areas that stretched from Pennsylvania to Georgia. They were the rural people of both races in the South, left behind by the others who migrated to the North to escape the agricultural and industrial stagnation of these southern regions. They were minorities, like the blacks in urban and rural areas in the North or South, the Puerto Ricans who crowded into New York and other northern cities in the post-World War II period, the Chicanos in rural and urban areas in the Southwest, and the Indians living in squalid conditions on backward reservations or in urban slums. They were the elderly, most of whom had nothing to fall back on after retirement except Social Security checks that almost automatically put them below the poverty line. And they were single, divorced, or widowed mothers with dependent children.

Everyday, when they turned on their television sets, America's poor were reminded they lived in an affluent and consumer-oriented society that had long ago passed the production levels required to meet the basic needs of its citizens and was now pouring out a superabundance of consumer goods that added extras to life. But every day their meager incomes reminded them that they were not full participants in this affluent society—even as their expectations were being raised. It was true, as many analysts said, that America's poor had higher living standards than most of the world's population, an incontrovertible fact that led some defenders in Eisenhower's America to proclaim that the poor should be grateful for what they had and should not complain. But the poor judged their living standards by comparing them with those of middle- and upper-class Americans, not to the peasants of Latin America or China. It was inevitable that they should become envious, frustrated, and resentful. How envious, frustrated, and resentful would not become fully clear until the 1960s, but these feelings existed long before poverty was publicized by Michael Harrington (in *The Other America*) and other social analysts.

But except for the poor, poverty was not an issue in the 1950s, and most Americans felt that the disparities in wealth were more than offset by the low unemployment rate (an average of 4.6 percent throughout the decade), the steady rise in real wages, the low inflation rate (an annual average of 1.5

percent during Eisenhower's two terms), and the plethora of consumer goods that rising wages and easy credit were enabling them to buy.[66] Some economists were disturbed by the periodic recessions of the period and by the slow growth rate. The economy grew rapidly from 1950 to 1952 (spurred by the Korean War), slumped into a recession from 1953 to 1954, entered a period of rapid growth from 1954 through 1957, entered another recession in the middle of 1957 that lasted through the early part of 1958, and then picked up again in late 1958 and performed well until it lapsed into another recession in 1960. After an average annual growth rate of 4.3 percent between 1947 and 1952, the growth rate leveled off for the rest of the fifties and actually ended up with an annual average for the decade of only 2.9 percent, considerably below the 4.5 percent range for most years of the prosperous 1920s.[67]

But poverty, periodic recessions, a slow growth rate, and other economic problems did not detract from the general public belief that the nation had never had it so good. More Americans were working than ever before, and the typical worker was drawing more pay, working fewer hours, and enjoying more of the necessities and luxuries of life than any generation of workers in American history. For white, middle-class males and their white, middle-class families, these were, indeed, good times.

# 14

# The Leisure Society

More consumer goods and creature comforts were not the only elements of the good times of the 1950s. Just as important to many Americans was the fact that this prosperity was accompanied by fewer work hours and more leisure time. By 1953, *Business Week* was able to write that "nothing like it has occurred before in world history. Never have so many people had so much time on their hands—with pay—as today in the United States." The magazine went on to note that "the 40 hour work week, the two-day week-end, three weeks' vacation with pay, 10 minute breaks morning and afternoon for coffee, early retirement on pension—these have created a social upheaval. Leisure has been democratized."[1] Three years later, in an article on automation, *Time* claimed that "once automation hits its full stride, the 30 hour week and the three-day week-end will not be far behind."[2] Equally optimistic was Joseph Prendergast, the executive director of the National Recreation Association, who in that same year predicted that by 1975 the average work week "will not exceed thirty-two hours" and claimed that "the amazing thing is: We haven't seen anything yet." The continuing industrial revolution and automation, he said, would cut the work week even further and add even more leisure time.[3] Clearly, America was entering a new era of leisure.

Rising incomes and increased leisure time were opening up a lucrative leisure market. As early as 1953, *Fortune* magazine reported that Americans were spending over $30 billion for leisure goods and services—double the amount spent on home goods or automobiles and 50 percent more than was spent on shelter or clothing—and as *Fortune* predicted, these figures would steadily increase as the decade progressed.[4] From 1950 to 1960, the amount spent on spectator sports admissions rose from $222 million to $290 million, that spent on radios, televisions, records, and musical instruments from $2.4 billion to $3.4 billion, and that on commercial participant amusements from $448 million to $1.2 billion. Billions more were spent on sports equipment, boats, pleasure aircraft, paint-by-number sets, do-it-yourself books and supplies, books and magazines, eating out, alcoholic beverages, and all kinds of fads and fashions.[5] Americans had never had it so good and had never had so much time to enjoy what they had.

As some critics had predicted, many Americans spent many of their leisure hours lazily slumped in front of the television set. But they also took advantage of their free time to enjoy a host of other activities. One thing they seemed to enjoy most was sports. In the 1950s Americans participated in more sports and watched more sporting events than ever before in the nation's history. In its first issue in August of 1954, *Sports Illustrated*, the new Luce publication, claimed that in sports "the golden age is now," for participant and spectator sports were booming in the United States and indeed in most of the world. The leading participant sports, the magazine reported, were fishing (with 25 million participants), bowling (20 million), hunting (15 million), boating (10 million), and golf (5 million). The leading spectator sport was still baseball: In 1953, the sixteen major league teams drew 14.3 million into their parks, while millions more watched on television and in the ballparks of the minor leagues. Some 2.3 million people also attended professional basketball games while another 7.5 million watched on television; in that same year, 8 million watched college football and countless millions watched basketball games played at lower levels. Football, too, was very popular—the estimated total attendance at football games at all levels was 35 million.[6]

In this golden age television was having a major impact on spectator sports. In the early days of television, some sport observers had worried that television would harm spectator sports by encouraging fans to stay home and watch events in the comfort of their living rooms rather than go out to the parks and arenas. Television did contribute to a slight decline in attendance at high-school athletic events and college football games, and a drastic (from 21 million to 14 million annually) but temporary drop in major-league baseball attendance between 1948 and 1953. It also had a catastrophic effect on minor-league baseball, already suffering from competition from drive-in movies, the outdoor recreation boom, and other forms of leisure and entertainment. Attendance at minor-league games dropped dramatically, and from fifty-nine leagues and 448 teams in 1949, participation shrank to thirty-three leagues and 241 teams in 1955. But with these exceptions, television increased the popularity of all sports by exposing more people to them, making popular figures out of athletic heroes, and pouring money into the treasuries of the sponsors and owners of teams. To cite just one example, the money paid by NBC to major-league owners for televising rights to the World Series jumped from $65,000 in 1947 to $925,000 in 1953 and then, in 1957, to over $16 million for the rights to telecast all World Series and All Star games for the next five years.[7] Thanks to this kind of exposure and financial support, all the major spectator sports boomed in the leisure years of the 1950s, and sports did enter a golden age in both popularity and prosperity.

The most popular spectator sport in the fifties was baseball. It was in one of its golden ages, perhaps even *the* golden age, fielding some of the greatest teams and players in the history of the game. New York took center stage, for the dominance of its teams, quality of its players, and natural media attention helped make that city's teams and players known throughout the country. From the 1950 through the 1960 seasons, the Yankees won nine American League pennants and six World Series, while in the National League the Brooklyn Dodgers won four pennants and one World Series and the New York Giants won two pennants and one World Series. When the Milwaukee Braves won the World Series in 1957, it marked the first time since 1948 that one of the New York teams had not flown the world championship flag in its stadium.

In the 1950s baseball was marked by the parade of one exciting season after another, now followed not only by fans in the ballpark or before radios but by the millions of new and old fans who watched it on television. It was the time when Yankee manager Casey Stengel won ten pennants and seven World Series (including an unprecedented five in a row, 1949–1953), then was released after losing to Pittsburgh in 1960 because, according to Yankee management, he was "too old." It was the decade when the 1951 Dodgers, after being 13½ games ahead of the Willie Mays–led Giants on August 12, ended the season in a dead heat with them; the Dodgers then lost the third and final playoff game to the Giants in the ninth inning, when Bobby Thomson hit a two-out, two-run "home run heard around the world" (off Ralph Branca, wearing uniform number 13). The Dodger fans were thus forced to say, as they had so many times in the past, "Wait till next year." It was the time when the 1954 Giants swept the Cleveland Indians in four straight games, largely through the pinch hitting of Dusty Rhodes and the hitting and fielding of Willie Mays, whose over-the-shoulder catch of Vic Wirtz's 460-foot drive, followed by a rifle-throw back into the infield to hold the runners, is still considered one of the outstanding fielding plays of all time. It was the decade when the 1960 Pittsburgh Pirates, playing in the World Series for the first time since 1927, won the series in the ninth inning of the seventh game on Bill Mazerowski's home run, burying the Yankees

10–9. It was the decade when twenty-year-old Al Kaline of the Detroit Tigers tied Ty Cobb as the youngest man to win the league batting championship, a feat followed two years later in 1957 when thirty-nine-year-old Ted Williams became the oldest man to win the batting title with his .388 average, the highest since his own .406 mark in 1941. It was the time when Pittsburgh Pirates' pitcher Harvey Haddix pitched a perfect no-hitter for twelve innings only to lose the game 1–0 in the thirteenth. It was the time when Stan Musial won three of his six batting titles, and Gil Hodges and Joe Adcock became the fourth and fifth players in history to hit four home runs in one game. It was the decade when Joe DiMaggio ended a thirteen-year career with the Yankees at the end of the 1951 World Series, leaving behind a lifetime batting average of .325, 361 home runs, an unmatched fifty-six-consecutive-game hitting streak, and the reputation as one of the greatest gentlemen ever to play the game. And it was the decade that saw the retirement of such great players as Luke Appling, Bob Feller, Phil Rizzuto, Al Rosen, Jackie Robinson, and Ted Williams.[8]

The decade's end coincided with the retirement of Ted Williams, who in his long career with the Boston Red Sox had acquired numerous hitting records while carrying on a love-hate relationship with the fans and sportswriters. At his last game on a cold September 28, 1960, after being presented with awards and presents from the fans and told that his number 9 was being retired (the first Red Sox number ever retired), the forty-two-year-old Williams walked, flied out twice, and—in his last time at bat in the major leagues—hit a home run over the center field wall off pitcher Jack Fisher. True to form, he refused to tip his cap as he rounded the bases or to come out of the dugout to acknowledge the cheers of the crowd. After the game he packed his gear, announced that he would not go with the team to New York for the last three games of the season, and left the park, ending one of the most successful careers in baseball. In spite of being walked frequently by nervous pitchers and losing several prime baseball years while serving with the marines in World War II and the Korean War, he compiled a lifetime batting average of .344, hit 521 home runs, won the batting title six times and the home run crown three times, and was the last player to hit over .400. In 1960, when his age, ailments, and declining skills had become obvious even to his staunchest fans, Williams still batted .316 and hit twenty-nine home runs, one off pitcher Don Lee, whose father, Thornton Lee, had thrown a home-run ball to him early in the slugger's career.[9] No one could take the Splendid Splinter's place, though a young outfielder playing in the minors at Minneapolis in 1960, Carl Yastrzemski, would try as he opened the season in left field in Fenway Park in the spring of 1961.

Williams was in the twilight of his career in the fifties, playing for a struggling team. Good as he was, the fans outside Boston were far more interested in following the exploits of two young players in New York, Willie

Mays and Mickey Mantle. Throughout the decade, baseball buffs argued over which of the two was the premier centerfielder, in a debate occasionally muddled by those who claimed that the honor really belonged to the Duke of Flatbush, Dodger slugger Duke Snider. Snider was good, good enough to wind up in the hall of fame, but objective observers, when they could be found, conceded that he ran third to his rivals on the Giants and Yankees.

In 1951, as a nineteen-year-old outfielder from Oklahoma, Mickey Mantle broke into the Yankee lineup playing rightfield alongside Joe DiMaggio, whom he was obviously being groomed to replace. In the 1951 World Series against the Giants, he tripped over a drain pipe in center field, damaging the cartilage in his right knee, already weakened from a football injury. Ironically, this injury, which would hamper his career from then on, was suffered while he was backing up Joe DiMaggio's catch of a ball hit by the Giant rookie, Willie Mays, whose baseball idol was DiMaggio. In comparison to Mays, Mantle hit with more power, was a switch-hitter, and was a faster runner when he was healthy. Over the next eighteen seasons he would hit 536 home runs in the regular season and 18 more in the World Series, play on twenty All Star teams, win the Most Valuable Player award three times, play more games (2,401) for the Yankees than anyone else, including Iron Man Lou Gehrig, and win the home-run crown four times and the batting title once. His home runs were legendary—fans still talk about the 565-foot homer he hit off Washington pitcher Chuck Stobb in 1953. In 1956, he became the fourth player in history (behind Rogers Hornsby, Lou Gehrig, and Ted Williams) to win the Triple Crown with a .353 average, fifty-two homers, and 130 runs-batted-in. At the age of thirty-six he would have to retire, and long afterward he and his fans would speculate on what he could have done if he had been a healthier and more durable player.[10]

Mantle's crosstown rival, Willie Mays, a native of Westfield, Alabama, played for the Negro major leagues and two New York Giants farm clubs before being called up to the majors in 1951. When he ended his career in 1973 after twenty years with the Giants and two anticlimatic years with the Mets, he wound up with 660 home runs, 3,283 hits, 1,903 runs batted in, 338 stolen bases, a .302 lifetime batting average, and a sure Place in the Hall of Fame. Impressive as they are, the statistics do not indicate what Willie Mays meant to the game of baseball. His career spanned part of three decades and the administrations of five presidents. He was perhaps the most exciting player ever to play the game, always playing with reckless abandon and always threatening to hit a home run, steal a base, or make his patented "basket catch" or a spectacular over-the-shoulder catch in the outfield. His defensive skills were summed up by Bob Stevens, a reporter at the 1959 All Star Game in Pittsburgh, in which Mays hit a triple in the eighth inning to win it for the National League. "Harvey Kuenn gave it honest pursuit," Stevens wrote, "but the only centerfielder in baseball who could have caught it hit it."[11] Leo Durocher, one of his managers, called him "the greatest outfielder I've ever seen," and Duke Snider gave the ballplayer's ultimate compliment by calling him "a helluva centerfielder."[12] As other admiring players often put it, the Say-Hey Kid always came to play.

After decades of stability, the national pastime underwent several changes in the fifties. One was in the geographical distribution of teams. When the decade opened, there were sixteen major league teams, concentrated in the Northeast, and they were the same sixteen clubs that had made up the National and American leagues since 1903, when Teddy Roosevelt was president. But in the fifties, aging stadiums, traffic congestion, parking problems, declining attendance, and other problems led the Boston Braves to move to Milwaukee, the St. Louis Browns to move to Baltimore, the Philadelphia Athletics to move to Kansas City, and the Brooklyn Dodgers and New York Giants—one of the oldest and hottest rivalries in major league sports—to move all the way to Los Angeles and San Francisco. Many old traditions were destroyed, but baseball became a more national, popular, and prosperous sport.

The fifties also saw further progress in the racial integration of the major league teams. The color barrier had been broken in 1947 by Jackie Robinson, and his success as a player and fan attraction led the Dodgers and other teams to bring in more black players. However, as Branch Rickey of the Dodgers would later admit, many owners followed a quota system in the fifties, gradually bringing in a few black players so as to avoid angering the fans and causing them to stay away from the ballpark. The Yankees would have no black players on their roster until 1955. While several mediocre white players made it to the major leagues, very few mediocre black ones did—to become major leaguers they had to be better than white players. And no matter how good they were, they still were often taunted by the fans, received few offers to endorse commercial products, were paid less than white players of comparable skills, received hate letters from fans, and were the targets of resentment when they threatened to break records held by white players. Nonetheless, by the late fifties there were some fifty black players in the majors, and many were establishing themselves as among the best ever to play the game.[13]

One of the most successful utilizers of black talent was the Brooklyn Dodgers, who had pioneered in the integration of the major-league game. In the 1950s the Dodgers were perennial contenders for the pennant behind the play of Robinson, Roy Campanella, Don Newcombe, Joe Black, Junior Gilliam, and other black stars. Along with such white players as Gil Hodges, Pee Wee Reese, Billy Cox, Carl Furillo, and Duke Snider, these were "the boys of summer," with a fanatical following of fans in Brooklyn and all across the country as they battled the Yankees and Giants for the championship of

New York and the world. When the decade opened, the Dodgers had never won a world championship and had a reputation for losing pennants and World Series on zany plays or errors, and for a while it still appeared that they would never win a world championship. They lost the pennant in 1950 to the Philadelphia Whiz Kids on the last day of the season, lost a 13½ game lead and the playoffs to the Giants in 1951, and lost the World Series to the Yankees in 1952 and again in 1953. But then in 1955, with Robinson, Reese, and other Dodgers slowing with age, the Dodgers finally took the top baseball prize, defeating the Yankees in seven games after losing the first two. The long-awaited title sparked a jubilant celebration all over Brooklyn, with motorists blowing their horns, factories blowing whistles, people standing on front stoops beating on pots and pans, and the *New York Daily News* carrying the headline "THIS IS NEXT YEAR."[14]

But that would be the last Brooklyn celebration. In the 1956 World Series Don Larsen threw a perfect game against the Brooklyn "Bums," and the Yankees took the series in seven games. Then in 1957, in spite of a "Keep the Dodgers in Brooklyn" drive the club was moved to the West Coast for the 1958 season. "Thus ended," *The New York Times* reported, "a colorful and often zany era in Brooklyn," where the Dodgers "had become world famous, first because of their erratic baseball and then because of their winning team."[15] In 1959, when the Dodgers took the World Series from the White Sox, they were the Los Angeles Dodgers, Snider and Furillo were part-time players, Campanella had been crippled in an automobile accident, Reese and Robinson had retired, and Newcombe had been traded to Cincinnati. Brooklyn fans still cheered, but it was not quite the same. The final chapter in the history of the Brooklyn Dodgers was written on February 23, 1960, when Ralph Branca, Carl Erskine, Roy Campanella, catcher Otto Miller (who had played in the first game in Ebbets Field in 1913), and other dignitaries and die-hard fans gathered at Ebbets Field for a short ceremony held in memory of an unforgettable past. Then the wrecking ball began to tear down the historic home of the Bums, to make way for a large apartment complex. The long association between the Dodgers and Brooklyn, dating back to 1890, had come to an end, and so had an era in baseball.[16]

In an age when the Russians were claiming they had been responsible for most modern inventions, it was not surprising that they would claim that they had even invented the great American pastime, baseball. In September of 1952, the Russian magazine *Smena* asserted that long before the United States had even become a nation Russian villagers had played a game called *lapta*, which was later stolen by Americans and made into baseball. What was even worse, according to the article, was that the Americans had taken this Russian game and turned it into a brutal capitalistic sport which often killed or maimed spectators and players and kept the players "in a situation of slaves . . . bought and sold and then thrown out the door when they become unnecessary." The article noted that even the great capitalistic hero, Babe Ruth, was sold at the end of his career against his wishes to another team for $150,000.[17]

Professional football underwent great change and growth in the fifties and by the end of the decade was rivaling professional baseball as the national pastime. As the fifties progressed, the league commissioner, owners, players, and television all combined to change and enrich the game until it became more and more exciting. The decade witnessed the spread of the two-platoon system and elaborate offensive and defensive systems, competition with Canadian football teams, the dismantling or moving of old franchises, and the establishment of new franchises like the Baltimore Colts and the Dallas Cowboys. Profits rolled into club coffers as new attendance records were set each year and contracts were signed with local television stations and with CBS. Attendance around the league rose steadily for eight straight years, going from 1.9 million in 1950 to 2.9 million in 1957, and with each passing year more and more games were sellouts. A 1957 game in Los Angeles between the Rams and San Francisco Forty-niners drew over 102,000 screaming fans. Television, instead of hurting attendance, as some had feared, was giving professional football national exposure and promoting its meteoric rise.[18]

Professional football got a major boost on December 28, 1958, when after one of the most exciting seasons in the history of the game, the Baltimore Colts and New York Giants met in the championship game in New York for what many fans and sports historians still call "the greatest football game ever played." On this warm winter day, over 64,000 fans jammed Yankee Stadium and millions more watched on television as the two teams engaged in an exciting seesaw battle that was sent into overtime in the last seven seconds when Baltimore's Steve Myhra kicked a field goal to tie the score at 17–17. In the sudden-death overtime, the first in the league's history, the Giants failed to score on their possession, and then in twelve plays quarterback Johnny Unitas led the Colts down to the Giant one-yard line, where Alan Ameche plunged over for a touchdown and the 23–17 victory. In Baltimore, a fan listening to the game on his car radio became so excited at the tie-producing field goal that he ran his car into a tree, and when the Colts returned home, 30,000 delirious fans turned out to welcome their conquering heroes.[19]

More than any other football game of the decade, this game captured the attention of the fans and media, created millions of new fans, demonstrated the effectiveness of the growing union between television and pro football, and paved the way for the sport's spectacular increase in popularity in the 1960s. By the end of the 1950s, Johnny Unitas, Jim Brown, Frank Gifford, and Paul Hornung were becoming almost as popular as Mickey Mantle and Willie Mays, and coaches Vince Lombardi of the Green

Bay Packers and Tom Landry of the Dallas Cowboys were building teams that would make them as well-known as Casey Stengel and Leo Durocher. Professional football had come of age, and the day of phenomenal player salaries, Sunday afternoon doubleheaders, and Sunday widows was just around the corner.

After several decades of popularity, college basketball suffered a temporary decline after the fixing scandals of 1951, when players for CCNY, NYU, Kentucky, and several other colleges were involved in taking bribes from professional gamblers to shave points in some forty-nine games in twenty-three different cities. However, the professional game boomed in the sports-minded fifties after the 1949 merger of the National Basketball League and the Basketball Association of America to form the National Basketball Association. The Minneapolis Lakers, with the first real NBA superstar, George Mikan, dominated the game in the first half of the decade, winning four championships. The second half of the decade saw the rise of the phenomenal Boston Celtics, who won the championship in 1957, lost out to St. Louis in 1958, then returned to win in 1959, beginning a string of eight consecutive NBA championships. Although it never attracted as many fans or as much media attention as baseball did, basketball steadily gained in popularity, thanks to the exposure of television, the improving quality of its teams, and the play of Mikan, Bob Cousy, Ed Macauley, Bob Pettit, Adolph Schayes, Paul Arizin, Neil Johnston, Frank Selvy, Elgin Baylor, Wilt Chamberlain, and other stars.[20]

Americans also used some of their leisure time for reading. In spite of all the dire warnings that television would keep people from reading, book sales doubled during the decade. Much of the increase was due to the sale of paperbacks, which had grown rapidly in sales ever since their introduction by Pocket Books in 1939. By 1953 there were 1,061 paperback titles with total sales of 292 million copies. Paperback sales jumped to over 350 million in 1958, and by the early 1960s paperback titles would make up 30 percent of all titles published.[21] Originally concentrating on inexpensive (25 to 75 cents) reprints of hardback originals, and depending on lurid covers to attract readers, paperback companies in the fifties began to print more original titles, to reprint editions of classics, and to produce quality paperbacks in the $1.50 to $2.00 range. The major market continued to be the same outlets magazines had used for decades—drugstores, newsstands, bus stations, supermarkets, army posts, and airports—but paperbacks also began to move into bookstores, college bookstores, and college courses, providing inexpensive reading matter for millions of readers and helping to revolutionize the reading and testing practices of college and universities.

What were Americans reading? Nonfiction was popular, especially books on religion, cooking, do-it-yourself projects, homemaking, popular psychology, health, public personalities, etiquette, and humor. In fiction, several names seemed to appear regularly at or near the top of the best-seller lists: Ernest Hemingway, John Steinbeck, Thomas B. Costain, Taylor Caldwell, J. D. Salinger, John Hersey, James Jones, Herman Wouk, James Michener, John O'Hara, Frances Parkinson Keyes, Allen Drury, Saul Bellow, James Gould Cozzens, and Daphne du Maurier. Americans also read millions of paperback copies of low-brow (some called them "trashy") crime stories, mysteries, westerns, romances, and sexual potboilers like Grace Metalious' *Peyton Place*, one of the all-time best-sellers in America. And in an age of Cold War worries, atomic bomb jitters, and flying saucers, science fiction novels and short stories were popular—almost faddish—especially among the young.[22] Probably the wealthiest and most popular writer of the decade was Mickey Spillane, whose Mike Hammer detective novels were bought by some 27 million readers attracted by his eye-catching titles (*My Gun Is Quick, Vengeance Is Mine*), lurid paperback covers, graphic (for that day) sex, language, and violence, and vigilante justice handed out to murderers, thieves, prostitutes, dope-peddlers, pornographers, sexual deviates, communists, and others who made the streets unsafe for decent, patriotic Americans.[23]

As they had in the past, Americans continued to fill up some of their leisure time reading magazines. Total annual circulation rose during the decade from 147.3 million to 190.4 million and the number of magazines with circulations over a million grew from forty-two to fifty. The most popular magazine was *Reader's Digest*, whose circulation grew from some 9 million in 1950 to 14.5 million in 1963, 5 million more than its nearest competitor, *TV Guide*.[24] Aside from *TV Guide*, the most successful new magazine of the decade was *Sports Illustrated*, which in this sports-minded age drew over 250,000 subscribers even before the first issue appeared in 1954, then grew to a weekly circulation of 575,000 after only six months and to over a million by the end of the decade. One of its biggest fans was Dwight Eisenhower, who was sent a personal copy of the first issue by publisher Henry Luce.[25] The president probably did not read the second most popular new magazine of the time, *Playboy*, whose monthly circulation also reached a million by the end of the decade.

Americans also read comic books. First started as regular publications in 1934 with Eastman Color Printing Company's *Famous Funnies*, comic book titles and sales boomed, reaching a peak in the midfifties with over 600 titles and 90 to 100 million sales each month.[26] They covered a wide range, from the animal stories of Walt Disney to war, crime, humor, the American West, romance, teenagers, horror, science fiction, and illustrated versions of great literary works (Classics Illustrated). Many parents, educators, psychologists, and ministers attacked them, claiming that they were partly responsible for the alarming rise in juvenile crime and delinquency. One of the most dedicated crusaders against comics was Frederic Wertham, who argued his case against comics in a 1954 book, *The Seduction of the Innocents*, and in numerous articles in *Ladies Home Journal* and other magazines. "Mammon is the root of all this," he wrote. "The comic book publishers, racketeers of the spirit, have corrupted children in the past, they are corrupting them right now, and they will continue to corrupt them unless we legally prevent it."[27]

Although many crime authorities, including J. Edgar Hoover, claimed that there was no proof of a link between comic books and antisocial behavior, a few local governments and some states passed laws to regulate the content and sales of comics. The Comic Book Magazine Association of America also tried to deflect criticism by adopting its own code of self-regulation in 1954. Sales did decline in the second half of the decade, dropping to 35 million a month by 1960, primarily because of the competition from television but also because the bad publicity surrounding comics led many parents to limit the types and amount of comics their children could buy.[28] Many teachers and parents might complain about children's comic-book reading habits, but others read and enjoyed them themselves: Studies at mid-decade revealed that comic books were read by 12 percent of the nation's teachers, 16 percent of college graduates, and 25 percent of high school graduates.[29]

Travel was one of the favorite leisure activities of the decade. Aided by cheap gasoline, a growing network of highways, paid vacation time, and more money than ever before, Americans went on a travel binge—to the lakes, mountains, parks, historic homes, battlefields, and dozens of other places. During the decade the number of annual visitors to national parks rose from 13.9 million to 26.6 million, those to national monuments from 5.3 million to 10.7 million, and those using national parkways from 2.8 million to 8.9 million.[30] In July of 1955, tourists had a new type of park to visit when Disneyland opened in California. Attracting visitors from all across the nation and the world, including kings and other heads of state (even Khrushchev wanted to tour it when he came to the country in 1959), Walt Disney's expensive gamble was an instant success, drawing over a million visitors in its first six months and 3 million in 1956, and grossing $195 million in its first ten years.[31] Wherever Americans went, the automobile was the preferred mode of travel. As early as 1953, 83 percent of all vacation trips were by automobile.[32]

The increased vacation travel by automobile was rapidly changing other aspects of American life. Since motoring tourists tried to avoid the congestion of cities, the number and quality of hotels that had served travelers for so long now began to decline, from some 14,000 at the beginning of World War II to 10,000 by the late 1950s. In this same period the number of motels tripled, from 13,500 to over 41,000.[33] These motels were replacing the spartan and often seedy quarters of cabins and motor courts of earlier days and providing more and more conveniences and luxuries to lure the weary traveler: television, air-conditioning, vibrating beds, swimming pools, and other extras. Many of the motels had their own restaurants, and even if they did not, the tourist could usually find a restaurant or fast-food place nearby without having to drive into town. And if he wished to shop or go to a movie, he could usually still avoid the downtown traffic, since the new shopping centers built near the highways provided these and other facilities. Travel was becoming less adventuresome, more predictable, and more standardized. As John Keats observed in *The Insolent Chariots*, "Our new roads, with their ancillaries, the motels, filling stations and restaurants advertising Eats, have made it possible for you to drive from Brooklyn to Los Angeles without a change of diet, scenery, or culture."[34] For the millions of Americans who could remember unhappy adventures on narrow, bumpy roads and in dismal mom-and-pop motor courts and eateries, the new-found predictability and standardization were a welcome change.

Americans were also using their newfound affluence to travel outside the country. In 1950, some 676,000 American tourists traveled abroad, spending around $1 billion. These figures rose to slightly over a million overseas tourists in 1955 spending $1.6 billion, and to 1.6 million tourists in 1960 spending $2.7 billion. Most of the travelers went to Europe and the Mediterranean, the West Indies, and Latin America.[35] Wherever they went, they were conspicuous by their clothing, cameras, language, and, many foreigners complained, by their boastful and arrogant behavior. America was on top of the world in the fifties, and the tourists showed it. Foreigners were grateful for the American dollars, but they were also often resentful of the wealth and manners of the tourists among them.

There was one major recreational activity that actually saw declining attendance and revenues in the fifties. This was the movies, where ticket revenues slipped from $1.4 billion in 1950 to $951 million by the end of the decade. Movie theaters simply could not rival other attractions for people's money and time, and they especially could not compete with television.[36]

Hollywood fought back. In addition to refusing to aid the new industry in any way, it tried to lure the public back to the theaters with contests, door prizes, a heavy advertising campaign declaring that "Movies Are Better Than Ever," and film innovations. First it tried 3-D, which the industry had been experimenting with ever since the early days of filmmaking. Beginning with *Bwana Devil* in 1953 and continuing with *The House of Wax*, *The Charge at Feather River*, and other horror and western movies, viewers wearing special glasses were given the eerie sensation that arrows, knives, monsters, and other human and nonhuman objects were actually coming out into the audience. Commercially successful at first, 3-D movies thrived from

1952 through 1954, but then died as audiences tired of the gimmicks, glasses, and weak plots. Hollywood then tried Cinerama. First introduced in 1952, Cinerama gave viewers the illusion of movement—they actually felt that they were on a roller coaster, train, plane, or speeding car. Cinerama died, too, because the novelty wore off quickly, and most theaters across the country refused to install the costly screens necessary for showing the films.[37]

Finally, with Cinemascope, another old technique from the 1920s resurrected in the hard times of the 1950s, Hollywood hit upon a success. In Cinemascope, the image projected on the screen was two and two thirds as wide as it was high (normal film was shot at a 4 to 3 ratio), giving the illusion of a wide, panoramic picture. The first Cinemascope picture was Twentieth Century Fox's *The Robe*, a spectacular mixture of religion, sex, action, and big stars (Richard Burton, Jean Simmons, Jeff Morrow, and Victor Mature). Released in the spring of 1953, it played to packed houses all across the country, and people talked of waiting in long lines to get in. By the end of the year, it had netted $16 million for the studio. Other studios quickly followed with their imitations and improvements of the process (Todd-AO, Vista-Vision, Vanascope, Vistarama, Glamorama), and by 1954 the industry was producing seventy-five films for the wide screen. Hollywood found that it could lure people back to the theaters with these wide-screen spectaculars, costing unheard of millions to produce because of the large number of stars, extras, animals, and expensive sets. In the midfifties, several expensive spectaculars were made , among them *The Ten Commandments* ($13.5 million), *War and Peace* ($6.5 million). *The King and I* ($6.5 million), *Around the World in Eighty Days* ($6 million), and *Moby Dick* ($5 million). And Hollywood continued to make them through the end of the decade, which ended with the likes of *Ben Hur*, *El Cid*, and *Spartacus*.[38] Then, in 1960, Michael Todd, Jr., and other moviemakers even tried to attract fans by piping odors into the theaters to add realism to what was being shown on the screen, but these "smellies," as Smell-O-Vision and Aroma-Roma were inevitably dubbed, did little to bring the fans back.[39]

Even Cinemascope could not return the good old days, and Hollywood continued to decline. Theaters closed, their number dropping from 14,700 to 12,300 between 1954 and 1958 alone,[40] and weekly attendance still ran less than half of the 85 to 90 million viewers that theaters enjoyed in 1947.[41] Many studios continued to lose money, while others merged or went out of business altogether. The survivors were forced to cut back on the number of actors and other employees, to reduce the number of cartoons, serials, short features, and B films produced, and to shoot more films on location in foreign countries, which was now cheaper than filming on a back-lot set in Hollywood. And finally, as the decade progressed, more and more studios ended their boycott of television and began the lucrative practice of producing *Cheyenne*, *Gunsmoke*, and dozens of other action series for television. Ironically, this new market for Hollywood's products helped many studios to survive the downturn that had been partially caused by the emergence of television. Hollywood had survived, but it would never be the same again.

Fads came and went quickly in the fifties in a nation that had plenty of money to spend on luxury items and that could be led, through the magical power of television, to buy items that other people were buying and to do what others were doing. This was especially true among the impressionable young, who moved quickly from Hopalong Cassidy cowboy paraphernalia at the beginning of the decade to Davy Crockett items in 1955 and then back to cowboy outfits, toy guns, and other items during the heyday of "adult" television westerns in the late fifties. As the decade ended, children were turning to space fads, spending millions of dollars on space suits, ray guns, and other gear for space games.[42]

One of the biggest fads of the fifties was the Davy Crockett craze. The fad was born on December 15, 1954, when the 40 million watchers of the popular *Disneyland* television show saw the first installment of a series on Davy Crockett, played by Fess Parker, a relatively unknown actor. Davy Crockett instantly became a hero among the millions of young children who swallowed Parker's (and Disney's) portrayal of Crockett as a folksy, honest, upright, freshly bathed hero who reigned, as the popular song claimed, as the "king of the wild frontier." Dozens of articles in newspapers and magazines by historians and other writers pointing out that the real Crockett was a dirty, lazy, drunken, cowardly loser who abandoned his wife and children to lead a drifter's life had no impact on the youngsters. Enterprising manufacturers flooded the market with Davy Crockett coonskin caps, knives, bow and arrow sets, guitars, puzzles, moccasins, sheets, towels, rugs, school lunch boxes, pup tents, toothbrushes, toy guns, bicycles, snowsuits, shirts, and other items. The television theme song, "The Ballad of Davy Crockett," sold 4 million copies in just seven months and was recorded in sixteen different versions, including the mambo. But like most fads, the Crockett craze was short-lived. Seven months after it began, it was all over, and as children turned to other interests in the summer of 1955, retailers were caught with large inventories of Davy Crockett items that did not sell even when cut to half price or less. But before it all had ended, over $100 million worth of Davy Crockett paraphernalia had been sold.[43]

Another big fad to hit the country was the Hula Hoop craze of 1958. After being used for years in Australia in gym classes, the Hula Hoop, a slender polyethylene tube manufactured in many colors, was introduced in the United States in 1958 by the small Wham-O Manufacturing Company. It was an instant success. Costing only about 50 cents each to manufacture, the

Hula Hoops sold for $1.98, and demand was so great that the 20,000 produced daily by the company could not meet it. Soon almost forty companies were putting out imitations with such names as Hoop Zing and Hooper Dooper, and by the end of the year total sales of all companies had passed $45 million.

People of all ages and classes were caught up in it—among those photographed with the famous hoop were Jane Russell, Debbie Reynolds, Red Skelton, Steve Allen, and Art Linkletter, who started his own Spin-a-Hoop manufacturing company. The craze quickly spread to England, Germany, France, Holland, Japan, and other countries, and the newspapers noted that Premier Nobusuke Kishi of Japan was given one for his birthday and that Queen Mother Zaine of Jordan brought one back to her country after a trip to Europe. From all across the world came stories of people who were coming to doctors and hospitals with sprained necks and backs and other medical problems caused by twirling the hoops. The British Medical Association warned that "no one with a known heart disease should try it, and anyone who is out of training should not go hard at it right away."[44] Russia and China condemned the hoop as just one more sign of capitalistic degradation and banned it, but Poland, Yugoslavia, and East Germany apparently saw the fad as no threat to the socialist revolution and allowed the people to twirl their hoops. By Christmas of 1958 the fad had peaked, and by the early part of 1959 the Hula Hoop had been relegated to the discount table in retail stores. But for almost a year, it had been one of the hottest fads in American history.[45]

As might be expected, college students were responsible for some of the more bizarre fads of the decade. Whereas previous generations had swallowed goldfish, worn raccoon coats, and engaged in other silly actions, students in the fifties discovered the panty raid. The spring of 1952 was a big year for this activity, which seemed to spread from campus to campus like wildfire. At the University of Missouri, almost 2,000 students stormed the women's dorms before they were driven back by the state militia, a panty raid at the University of Tennessee came to an end only when the Knoxville police arrived to aid the young women in distress, and panty raids at the University of Georgia, University of Pennsylvania, and other colleges and universities also brought the intervention of police or national guardsmen. Most raids seemed to begin when male students had a few drinks too many and decided to raid the women's dorms, and as they marched across campus, they gathered more followers and beer along the way. The women met them with water bombs or inflamed them by waving panties in the air or throwing them down to the mob gathered outside their windows. In some raids, the men broke down locked doors to get into the women's rooms, where they rummaged through bureaus until they found the prize they were seeking, and often the braver among them took panties off women who were wearing them at the time. Sometimes women were roughed up in the melee and men were hurt falling from ledges or windows or in scuffles with the police. Most women seemed to take it in good spirits, even to enjoy it, and at the University of Michigan, Toledo University, and a few other institutions women retaliated by marching on men's dorms in shorts raids. But it all caused a big stir, made headlines in newspapers and feature stories in *Life* and other mass magazines, and prompted the inevitable question, "What is happening to the younger generation?"[46]

University officials were upset by these raids, of course, and tried to determine why they had occurred and how they could be prevented. Some authorities attributed it to simple hell-raising by students who had been cooped up all winter studying. Others said it was a replay of ancient tribal spring ceremonies, with deep symbols of sex and rebirth, or that it was a release for students living in a threatening world of atomic bombs and other problems. Still others said it was an outlet for pent-up sexuality and aggression or that it was just a harmless fad, like the goldfish swallowing of earlier generations. But when the raids happened at the University of Indiana, the institution's resident authority on sex, Dr. Alfred Kinsey, refused to speculate on their cause, claiming that "it is somewhat out of my field."[47] While many deans wanted to implement strict preventive and disciplinarian measures, most seemed to agree with Eric Walter, dean of students at the University of Michigan, who remarked after the panty raids at his school in the spring of 1952 that they were simply "spring madness" that was "bound to happen," and that they could not be prevented. "No human being," he said, "has ever attempted to shift the vernal equinox."[48]

The great panty raids of 1952 were repeated in other years in the fifties. While some occurred in 1953 and 1954, the next big outburst came in 1955, and this time some of the raids got way out of hand. At the University of Nebraska and the University of Connecticut, several coeds were physically harmed in the scuffling, and several students were expelled, while at the University of Massachusetts a panty raid lasting until almost dawn resulted in injuries to several young women when some of the 600 invading males broke into the dorms and yanked underwear off some of the coeds. In 1956 one of the worst panty raids of the decade took place at the University of California at Berkeley, where some 3,000 males attacked twenty-two sororities and a boarding house. In what the student newspaper indignantly called a "night of debauchery," several coeds "were knocked around, assaulted, carried outside in pajamas or nude." The whole ugly affair was not ended until the Berkeley police came to the aid of the campus police, who had not been able to quell the disturbance. Party raids had moved from the level of pranks and mild disorders to that of nearly uncontrollable riots, and authorities began to take strong measures, ranging from expulsion from school to criminal prosecution. Such strong action by the authorities, along with the natural tendency of fads to fade as the novelty wears off and they are replaced by others, contributed to a decline of the panty raid mania in the late fifties. But they occasionally resurfaced, like the one at the Ohio University in 1958 that involved thousands of students and dozens of police, who had to resort to tear gas to force males out of coed dormitories. Few of those involved could know that in just a few short years students and police would again be involved in confrontations, this time over civil rights, the Vietnam War, and other issues that shook the turbulent sixties.[49]

College students got caught up in other fads in the late fifties. In 1959, apparently stimulated by the news of twenty-five South African students who crammed themselves into one telephone booth, college students began to try for cramming records of their own. The cramming fad began in California. At UCLA, only seventeen students were able to get into a booth, while twenty managed to get in at St. Mary's College at Moraga. But at Modesto Junior College, thirty-two students somehow crammed themselves into one booth, and at Fresno State, seven enterprising males stuffed themselves into a phone booth submerged in a swimming pool. Some went on to bigger and better things, such as the forty students in a California college who stuffed themselves into a Volkswagen. From California these and other cramming or stuffing fads spread to other campuses across the country and even to other nations, notably England, though American students proudly pointed out that no college in England had been able to cram more than twenty students into a phone booth. The cramming fad, like most others, lasted only a few months.[50]

Flagpole sitting, a popular fad of the twenties, occasionally resurfaced in the fifties. In 1951, Erma Leach of Eugene, Oregon, spent 152 days in a champagne bubble bath atop a sixty-foot pole in San Francisco as part of an automobile dealer's promotion. For her efforts, she was given a Cadillac, fur coat, and $7,500 in cash. Four years later in Parkland, Washington, a pregnant Kathleen Donham spent 169 days on a sixty-foot pole, passing the time with a telephone and radio while she earned money from commercial sponsors to help pay for the birth of her child. And in 1959, a seventeen-year-old girl, Mauri Rose Kirby, sat atop a flagpole in Indianapolis for twenty-one days. When she came down, she indicated that she would never repeat her performance: "I've missed going places and doing things," she said, "I don't know why in the world I climbed up there."[51]

Another fad of the decade was chlorophyll, introduced by Lever Brothers in a new toothpaste, Chlorodent, in 1951. Its instant commercial success led some forty companies to put it into over a hundred products, including chewing gum, cigarettes, mints, mouthwashes, deodorants, sheets, diapers, mothballs, soaps, shampoos, bubble baths, candles, toilet tissue, inner soles, dog food, and even one brand of vodka. Sales of these products boomed, in spite of medical authorities' warnings that chlorophyll did not fight tooth decay, sweeten the breath, prevent underarm odor, or do most of the other wonders it was supposed to perform. The American Medical Association's journal reminded its readers that goats ate chlorophyll-laden grass all day but smelled no better for it, while the *Wall Street Journal* tried to counter clever advertising jingles with one of its own: "Why reeks the goat on yonder hill, Who seems to dote on chlorophyll?" Gradually, the public realized the uselessness of the products and stopped buying them, and by 1955 the use of chlorophyll was confined primarily to toothpastes, gum, mints, and soaps.[52] The fad had ended, but not before it had made several companies considerably richer.

There seemed to be no end to the fads of the decade. There was canasta, Droodles, and other card and artistic games; paint-by-number kits; fascination with flying saucers and reincarnation (sparked by Morey Bernstein's 1952 book, *The Search for Bridey Murphy*); calypso songs and new dance crazes like rock 'n' roll, the stroll, and the twist; science fiction literature and movies; comic book and baseball card collecting; leotards, pop-it necklaces, and leather motorcycle jackets; poodle and ponytail haircuts for girls and ducktail and Apache haircuts for boys; and the penchant for blaming bad weather, cracked automobile windows, and other problems on hydrogen bomb tests. Most fads lasted only a short while; some, like Frisbee throwing, did not really catch on until the next decade, and others, like rock 'n' roll, turned out not to be fads at all but highly influential, permanent additions to American culture. They were all part of a prosperous, leisure society, with money and time on its hands.

# 15

# *Generation in a Spotlight*

As the 1950s opened, America's adolescents were basically a conservative, unrebellious lot. Although the word *teenager* had come into widespread circulation in the 1940s to describe this distinct age group mired in the limbo between puberty and adulthood, the teenagers of the early fifties had not yet developed a distinct subculture. They had few rights and little money of their own, wore basically the same kind of clothing their parents wore, watched the same television shows, went to the same movies, used the same slang, and listened to the same romantic music sung by Perry Como, Frank Sinatra, and other middle-aged or nearly middle-aged artists. Their idols were Joe DiMaggio, General MacArthur, and other prominent members of the older generation. In spite of what they learned from older kids and from the underground pornography that circulated on school playgrounds, they were amazingly naive about sex, believing well into their high school years that French kissing could cause pregnancy or that the douche, coitus interruptus, and chance could effectively prevent it. Heavy petting was the limit for most couples, and for those who went "all the way" there were often strong guilt feelings and, for the girl at least, the risk of a bad reputation. Rebellion against authority, insofar as it occurred, consisted primarily of harmless pranks against unpopular adult neighbors or teachers, occasional vandalism (especially on Halloween night), smoking cigarettes or drinking beer, and the decades-old practice of mooning. Although most families had the inevitable clashes of opinion between parents and offspring, there were few signs of a "generation gap" or of rebellion against the conventions of the adult world.

But all of this began to change in the early fifties, and by the middle of the decade the appearance of a distinct youth subculture was causing parents and the media to agonize over the scandalous behavior and rebellious nature of the nation's young people. The causes of the emergence of this subculture are not hard to find. One was the demographic revolution of the postwar years that was increasing the influence of the young by producing so many of them in such a short period of time. Another was the affluence of the period, an affluence shared with the young through allowances from their parents or through part-time jobs. As teenagers acquired their own money, they were able to pursue their own life-style, and now American business and advertisers geared up to promote and exploit a gigantic youth consumer market featuring products designed especially for them. Then there were the effects of progressive education and Spockian child-rearing practices, for while neither was quite as permissive or indulgent toward the young as the critics claimed, they did emphasize the treatment of adolescents as unique people who should be given the freedom to develop their own personality and talents.[1] Another factor was television and movies, which had the power to raise up new fads, new heroes, and new values and to spread them to young people from New York to Los Angeles. And finally, there was rock 'n' roll, which grew from several strains in American music and emerged at mid-decade as the theme song of the youth rebellion and as a major molder and reflector of their values.

One of the earliest landmarks in the history of the youth rebellion came in 1951 with the publication of J. D. Salinger's *The Catcher in the Rye*. Infinitely more complex than most of its young readers or older detractors perceived, this novel featured the actions and thoughts of one Holden Caulfield, a sixteen-year-old veteran of several private schools, who roams around New York City in his own private rebellion from home and school. In colloquial language laced with obcenities absent from most novels of the day, Holden tells the reader of his rejection of the phoniness and corruption of the adult world, of how parents, teachers, ministers, actors, nightclub pianists and singers, old grads, and others lie to themselves and to the young about what the world is really like. *The Catcher in the Rye* was popular throughout the fifties with high school and college students, for while young people might not understand all that Salinger was trying to say, they did identify with his cynical rejection of the adult world and adult values. The book was made even more popular by the attempts of school boards, libraries, and state legislatures to ban it. It was one of the first books, if not the first, to perceive the existence of a generation gap in the supposedly happy, family-oriented society of the early 1950s.[2]

Still another sign of the changes occuring in the nation's youth was the rise of juvenile delinquency. Between 1948 and 1953 the number of juveniles brought into court and charged with crimes increased by 45 percent, and it was estimated that for every juvenile criminal brought into court there were at least five who had not been caught.[3] It was especially disturbing that juvenile crimes were committed by organized gangs that roamed—and seemed to control—the streets of many of the larger cities. Street gangs had existed before in American history, but in the fifties they were larger, more violent, and more widespread than ever before. Thanks to modern communications, they tended to dress alike, to use the same jargon, and share the same values all across the country. And they were not just in America—they appeared in England (Teddy Boys), Sweden ("Skinn-Nuttar" or leather jackets), and other industrial countries across the globe. The youth rebellion, including the criminal fringe that made up part of it, was international.

Learning about these gangs in their newspapers and weekly magazines, Americans were horrified by what they read and by how often they read it. It seemed that hardly a week went by without the occurrence of shocking crimes committed by teenagers or even younger children who did not seem to know the difference between good and bad—or worse, deliberately chose the bad over the good. Sporting colorful names like Dragons, Cobras, Rovers, and Jesters, they carried all kinds of weapons—zip guns, pistols, rifles, knives, chains, shotguns, brass knuckles, broken bottles, razors, lead pipes, molotov cocktails, machetes, and lye and other chemicals. They drank alcoholic beverages, smoked reefers, took heroin and other drugs, had their own twisted code of honor, and organized well-planned attacks on other gangs or innocent victims. They also had their own jargon, borrowed from the criminal underworld and spoken by gangs from coast to coast: *dig, duke, gig, jap, jazz, rumble, turf, cool, chick, pusher, reefer,* and hundreds of other slang terms.[4]

To a nation accustomed to believing in the essential goodness of its young people, the behavior of these delinquent gangs was puzzling and frightening. They seemed to pursue violence for the pure joy of violence and to delight in sadistic actions toward other gangs or innocent victims. They engaged in shootings, stabbings, individual and gang rapes, senseless beatings, and unspeakable tortures. They extorted "protection" money from frightened merchants, sprayed crowds in streets or restaurants or subways with rifle fire, doused people with gasoline and set them ablaze, firebombed bars and nightclubs, stole automobiles, vandalized apartments and public buildings, and fought vicious gang wars over girls or invasion of turf or to avenge some real or imagined slight. They often terrorized and vandalized schools and assaulted teachers and students, leading the *New York Daily News* in 1954 to describe "rowdyism, riot, and revolt," as the new three Rs in New York's public schools.[5]

It was particularly disturbing that these young hoodlums often showed no remorse for their actions, recounting with delight to police or social workers the details of a rape, murder, or torture in which they had been involved. One eighteen-year-old who had participated in the torture and murder of an innocent young man in a public park told police that "last night was a supreme adventure for me."[6] Describing his role in the killing of another gang member, one young man told police that "he was laying on the ground looking up at us. I kicked him on the jaw or someplace; then I kicked him in the stomach. That was the least I could do, was kick 'im."[7] In another incident a gang member described his part in a stabbing by saying: "I stabbed him with a bread knife. You know, I was drunk, so I just stabbed him. [Laughs] He was screaming like a dog."[8]

The rise of juvenile delinquency, and especially its organized forms in the street gangs of the major cities, caused agonizing soul-searching among anxious parents, school authorities, psychologists, and other experts on adolescent and criminal behavior. Parents of delinquents anxiously asked, "What did we do wrong?" and many admitted to school, police, and court authorities that they could not control their children. The experts came up with a whole range of explanations of juvenile criminality, blaming it on poverty, slum conditions, permissive parents, lack of religious and moral training, television, movies, comic books, racism, parents who were too busy working or pursuing their own pleasures to rear their children properly, the high divorce rate with the resulting broken homes, anxiety over the draft, and decline of parental discipline and control. Early in the decade most authorities tended to blame it on the problems of poverty and slum living, but as the decade wore on, it became very clear that many of the delinquents were from middle- and upper-class families that provided a good environment for their children. So then it was blamed on society or on simple "thrill seeking" by bored, pampered, and jaded youths. As the problem worsened, many were inclined to agree with Baltimore psychologist Robert Linder, who claimed that the young people of the day were suffering from a form of collective mental illness. "The youth of the world today," he told a Los Angeles audience in 1954, "is touched with madness, literally sick with an aberrant condition of mind formerly confined to a few distressed souls but now epidemic over the earth."[9]

Whatever the causes of juvenile delinquency, and they were certainly multiple and complex, it was obvious that delinquent and criminal acts by individual adolescents and organized gangs were increasing every year and were making the streets of many large cities dangerous for law-abiding citizens. And while many people thought of the problem as one that plagued primarily the slums of the big cities of the Northeast or California, it soon became clear that it was spreading to large cities all across the country, to the new suburbs, to the rural areas which were so accessible now to middle-class teenagers with automobiles, and to the South, which had often prided itself on not having the problems of the big northern cities. In 1954 *New York Times* education editor Benjamin Fine wrote a much-discussed book on the problem, *1,000,000 Delinquents,* which correctly predicted that during the next year 1 million adolescents would get into serious trouble that would bring them into the courtroom.[10] In that same year *Newsweek* published an article entitled "Our Vicious Young Hoodlums: Is There Any Hope?"[11] By now, many people thought that there was none and found themselves in the unusual position of being afraid of their own children.

By the midfifties Americans had become so saturated with stories of juvenile delinquency that there was a tendency among many to stereotype all teenagers as bad, especially if they adopted the clothing, ducktail haircuts, or language of gangs. But the truth was that few teenagers were juvenile delinquents or gang members, very few used drugs (except for alcohol), and very few ever got into trouble with the police. And many teenagers resented the stereotyped image the adult world had of them. As one seventeen-year-old high school girl said in 1955, "I've never set a fire, robbed a gas station, or beaten a defenseless old man. In fact, I don't even know anyone who has. . . . I wish someone would think of the 95% of us who *aren't* delinquents. Because we're here, too."[12] The young woman was correct, of course, for most teenagers were not delinquents. But they were changing in ways that were disturbing even the parents of "good" teens, and one of the major causes of these changes was the rise of a new musical form, rock 'n' roll.

Rock 'n' roll was a musical amalgam that comprised many strains of American music—country and western, rockabilly, rhythm and blues, gospel, jazz, folk, popular, and swing. These strains had come from many parts of the country—from the rural South, New Orleans, Chicago, St. Louis, Detroit, Harlem, and dozens of small and large towns across the land. By the late forties and early fifties, much of this music had been fused into what was called race music or rhythm and blues, and because of its association with blacks and its strong sexual overtones, it had been recorded only by small black record companies and played on black radio stations. While the majority of whites were still listening to show tunes and the idealistic popular music of white crooners, a musical revolution was building in the background.

The early 1950s had provided a portent of the musical future with the records and singing style of Johnny Ray, a white singer who was dubbed the Million Dollar Teardrop and the Nabob of Sob when he released in 1952 a 4-million-seller record with a hit on each side, "Cry" and "The Little White Cloud That Cried." The lyrics of his songs were traditional romantic ones, but his delivery was not: He cried, squirmed, twisted, fell on his knees, almost collapsed on stage. His emotionally charged singing sometimes caused miniriots as excited fans rushed the stage to tear off his clothes as souvenirs, and he often had to be rescued by the police. No singer had caused such fan reaction since Frank Sinatra back in the early 1940s. In his popularity with teenagers and his emotional singing style, Ray helped pave the way for the rock 'n' roll idols of the second half of the decade, though his own popularity was short-lived.[13]

A key man in the history of rock 'n' roll was Alan Freed, a trained engineer who had also studied music theory and the classical trombone before beginning his radio career on a classical music show in Pennsylvania. His career gradually moved toward popular music, and in Cleveland in the early fifties he began to play and promote the race music of Fats Domino, Chuck Berry, and other black artists. In 1951, he began to refer to their music as rock 'n' roll, a phrase which had appeared in many race songs and which in the black community had long stood for dancing and sexual intercourse. It was on his Cleveland radio show that many white audiences first began to hear race music, and they liked it. In the midfifties he moved to radio station WINS in New York, where he became the widely acknowledged spokesman for rock 'n' roll, publicizing the new music, appearing in rock 'n' roll movies, sponsoring live concerts in which black groups played to mixed audiences, and gaining even greater notoriety when some of his live shows ended in riots or near-riots. More than any other single individual, he introduced rock 'n' roll to white audiences and promoted its rapid rise.[14]

Except for Alan Freed and a few other disc jockeys, most white radio shows in the early fifties refused to play rock 'n' roll performed by black artists because it was widely regarded by white station owners and white audiences as "nigger music." So in these crucial years of rock 'n' roll's history, the major record companies put out white versions (called covers) of songs originally recorded by black singers. Thus most white audiences in these years heard Georgia Gibbs's version of "Tweedle Dee" and "Dance with Me Henry" rather than LaVerne Baker's original versions, and June Valli's very popular cover of "Crying in the Chapel," rather than Sonny Till and the Orioles' earlier recording. However, by 1954 rhythm and blues was becoming so popular that white audiences began to buy the original black versions of the songs they were hearing, and in the spring of that year *Billboard Magazine* was noting that rhythm and blues "is no longer identified as the music of a specific group, but can now enjoy a healthy following among all people, regardless of race or color."[15] And in that same year the record "Sh-Boom" appeared, and in its black version by the Chords and its white version by the Crew Cuts it became the fifth best-selling song of 1954. It was, according to most musical historians, the first rock 'n' roll hit.[16]

The year 1955 was a crucial year in the history of rock 'n' roll. The year began with traditional popular songs like "Let Me Go, Lover" and "Pledging My Love" heading the best-selling list, and for the entire year the number one song was "Unchained Melody," followed by "The Ballad of Davy Crockett," "Cherry Pink and Apple Blossom White," "The Yellow Rose of Texas," and "Melody of Love." But in April *Life* magazine carried an article about the new rock 'n' roll music-and-dance craze that was sweeping the country and causing so much controversy. Accompanied by a picture of two teenagers dancing in a supermarket parking lot in Los Angeles with a large crowd of onlookers watching and clapping their hands, the article claimed that "some American parents, without quite knowing what it is that their kids are up to, are worried that it's something they shouldn't be."[17] Twelve of the year's top fifty songs that year were rock 'n' roll songs, and there was an increase in the number of black songs covered by white artists. And most importantly, 1955 saw the appearance in the spring of the movie, *The Blackboard Jungle*, with its revolutionary theme song, "Rock Around the Clock."

*Blackboard Jungle* appeared at a critical time in the history of American education and American teenagers. The schools were already under attack from many quarters, and the concern that Americans had for their troubled schools was matched by the concern they were acquiring for their troubled youth. *Blackboard Jungle* focused on both in a volatile way. The main plot of the movie was centered around the problems a young teacher (Glenn Ford) was experiencing in trying to teach a group of unruly, hostile teenagers in a run-down vocational high school in the Bronx. But the movie's plot was secondary to its music, particularly its theme song, "Rock Around the Clock," written in 1953 by two white middle-aged Philadelphia song writers and recorded the next year by Bill Haley and the Comets, an all-white group of conservative young men who mixed country and western with rhythm and blues and electric guitars and drums.

"Rock Around the Clock" had an electrifying effect on the young. In many theaters they spontaneously jumped from their seats and danced in the aisles when it was played, and in several American and European cities excited teenagers rioted inside and outside the theaters, sometimes damaging property on streets for blocks around. All across the nation, public school principals and teachers held special meetings with town officials to try to determine how to handle the young when the movie came to their town, and some cities dealt with the problem by banning the movie. Clare Boothe Luce, the American ambassador to Italy, joined with other political figures in an attempt (unsuccessful) to prevent the movie from being shown in foreign countries, claiming that it presented a bad image of the United States at a time when it was trying to exercise world leadership.[18] Troubled adults everywhere began to identify rock 'n' roll with rioting, rebellion, and juvenile delinquency. Many agreed with Bosley Crowther, music critic for

*The New York Times*, who called the movie "a vivid and hair-raising film" that "treats of a contemporary subject that is social dynamite," and questioned whether it was "a desirable stimulant to spread before the young."[19]

"Rock Around the Clock" quickly went to the top of the record charts in the summer of 1955, sold some 15 million copies by the late 1960s, and became one of the best-selling single records of all times. Many consider it to be the real birth of rock 'n' roll, not just because of its sales but because through the movie it introduced rock 'n' roll to many young people who had heard little of it before on white radio stations. It was the first rock 'n' roll record to gain national and world popularity among teenagers, who now felt that they had a music of their own, a unifying force that gave them a common consciousness and set them off from their elders. As Bill Haley often claimed, Alan Freed might have coined the phrase *rock 'n' roll*, and he might be its greatest promoter, but Haley and his Comets were the true founding fathers of the music through the international sensation created by "Rock Around the Clock" and through their blend of country and western with rhythm and blues, and their driving electric guitars, loud drums, and dynamic repetitions of chords and phrases.[20] Haley was an unlikely teen idol—he was overweight, nearing middle age, and had a wife and five children—but for months he was met with wild excitement from fans everywhere. He was the first teenage idol of the fifties, but he would soon be pushed aside by two more suitable candidates, James Dean and Elvis Presley.

Born in the small town of Fairmount, Indiana, on February 8, 1931, James Dean led a life much like that of the troubled youth he later came to portray in his movies. His mother died when he was nine, and he was reared on the farm of his aunt and uncle with only brief glimpses of his father. A confused adolescent, he went to California after his graduation from high school, attended Santa Monica City College and UCLA, and played some small parts in movies before going back to New York to study acting in 1951. In 1954 he came back to Hollywood as an admirer of Marlon Brando, motorcycles, and fast cars. He quickly earned a reputation as a lazy, undisciplined, ill-mannered star who often stayed out all night long and then showed up on the set too tired to do good work.[21] His first major film, *East of Eden* (1955), brought him instant fame through his portrayal of the sensitive son suffering from the fear that his father does not love him, but his rise as a teenage idol came later in the year through his performance as a misunderstood and rebellious teenager in *Rebel Without a Cause*. Costarring Natalie Wood and Sal Mineo, the film was released to the theaters in the fall of 1955, only two weeks after Dean's tragic death in a high-speed wreck between his Porsche and a Ford on a lonely California highway. By the time the just-completed *Giant* was released, in November of 1956, an astonishing cult had sprung up around the young star and his death, so senseless, at the age of twenty-four.

The legends that grew up around James Dean were the greatest since the death of Rudolph Valentino. Young people saw Dean as the embodiment of their restlessness, confusion, and rejections, as a rebel fighting, like them, against the rules and conformity the adult world was trying to impose upon them. But while Valentino and most other movie legends had appealed as sex symbols, Dean appealed to an age group—to young males and females between fourteen and twenty-four. Young males saw him as a symbol of their own rebellious and troubled nature, while young girls saw him as an attractive, sensual male who needed mothering as much as sexual love.[22] Although Dean was a good actor with great promise, his acting reputation was exaggerated beyond all reality by the myths and legends that shrouded his life and acting career after his premature death.

Within a few weeks after Dean's death, Warner Brothers was swamped with hundreds of letters. Their number rose to 3,000 a month by January of 1956 and to 7,000 a month by July, some with money enclosed for a picture of the dead star. The fan magazines played the Dean legend for all it was worth, publishing thousands of pictures and stories. In these magazines and across the national teenage grapevine, the rumors flew: that he was not really dead, that he had been so disfigured from the wreck that he had gone into hiding or been sent to a sanatorium, that he was just a vegetable in a secret hospital room known only to his close friends, that he had talked to some of his fans from beyond his grave, and that his tomb in Fairmount, Indiana, had been emptied by grave robbers or by Dean's own miraculous resurrection. Several records appeared—"Tribute to James Dean," "The Ballad of James Dean," "His Name Was Dean," "The Story of James Dean," "Jimmy Jimmy," and "We'll Never Forget You." Dozens of biographies and other literary tributes were rushed to the market, along with the inevitable movie, *The James Dean Story*. When the wreckage of his car was put on display in Los Angeles, over 800,000 people paid to view it. The adulation swept teens all across America and even in Europe. In England, a young man legally changed his name to James Dean, copied his clothing and mannerisms, went to America twice to visit the real Dean's family and grave, and claimed to have seen *Rebel Without a Cause* over 400 times.[23] As *Look* magazine observed, the subject of this almost psychopathic adulation was "a 24-year old who did not live long enough to find out what he had done and was in too much of a hurry to find out who he was."[24]

Along with *The Wild One*, a 1954 film starring Marlon Brando as the leader of a motorcycle gang, *The Blackboard Jungle* and the films of James Dean helped to spawn a series of films aimed specifically at young people. In addition to the films of Elvis Presley and other teen idols, the second half of the fifties saw a spate of second-rate rock movies—*Rock Around the Clock*, *Don't Knock the Rock*, *Rock Pretty Baby*, *Rock Around the World*, and *Let's*

*Rock*—and a series of shallow, trashy movies about young people and delinquency, such as *Girls in Prison*, *Eighteen and Anxious*, *Reform School Girl*, *Hot Rod Rumble*, and *High School Confidential*. For better or worse—mostly worse—teenagers were getting their own movies as well as their own music.[25]

In 1955 teenagers had their music, their movies, their idols—dead and alive—but as yet they had no one who combined all three of these and served as a focal point for their growing consciousness as a subculture. But he was waiting in the wings, for in that year a young performer with a regional reputation was making records and gaining a wide following among teenagers, especially young girls, with live performances in southern cities that were often punctuated by desperate attempts by the police to prevent these screaming fans from rushing the stage to tear off his clothes. He was a James Dean fan, who had seen *Rebel Without a Cause* several times, could recite the script by heart, and had been wearing tight pants, leather jackets, and a ducktail haircut with long sideburns for several years. In 1956 he would burst on the national entertainment stage and proceed to become one of the most popular and influential musical performers of all time, rivaling Rudy Vallee, Bing Crosby, Frank Sinatra, and other singers before him. His name was Elvis Presley, and he was destined to claim the title of King of Rock 'n' Roll.

Elvis Aaron Presley and his twin, Jesse Garon Presley (who died at birth), were born in Tupelo, Mississippi, on January 8, 1935. Young Elvis grew up in poverty and in the religious atmosphere of Pentecostal and Assembly of God churches, and from an early age he sang gospel music in church and revival meetings and listened to gospel and country music on the radio. When he was eleven years old, his mother bought him a $13 guitar, and after he taught himself a few simple chords, he learned to play and sing by imitating the music he heard on the radio. When he was fourteen, his parents moved to Memphis, Tennessee, where his father worked in a factory and Elvis worked at odd jobs after school—mowing lawns, ushering at a movie theater, and driving a truck. In high school he wore a ducktail haircut and long sideburns, long before they became popular nationally, and was known for wearing outlandish clothes. But few people at Humes High School, from which he graduated in 1953, paid much attention to him. One of his classmates would later recall that "he had no personality, if you know what I mean. Just acted kind of goofy, sitting in the back of class, playing his guitar. No one knew that he was ever going to be *anything*."[26]

But in 1953 Elvis went into a small Memphis company associated with Sun Records and paid $4 to record "My Happiness" and "That's Where Your Heartaches Begin" for his doting mother. Company executives were impressed enough to back his first commercial release in August of 1954: "That's All Right, Mama" on one side and "Blue Moon of Kentucky" on the other. Local radio stations received many requests to play the record, and it sold several thousand copies in a few weeks. Presley then began to record other songs and to make personal appearances at country music shows and on the Grand Ole Opry. During one of his country music shows he began to make undulating, suggestive movements with his body—a technique he had picked up from revivalistic preachers—and the audience went into a frenzy. A surprised Presley began to incorporate these movements permanently into his act, and as he rose as a regional performer in small towns across the rural South, he was met by swooning and squealing teenage girls, frowning police, and criticism from local ministers.[27] By the end of 1955 his contract with Sun Records had been purchased by RCA Victor for $40,000, he had acquired a manager (Colonel Parker), and he was only weeks away from emerging as the first superstar of rock 'n' roll.

The year 1956 saw Presley's meteoric rise to fame. He began the year with a new movie contract from Twentieth Century–Fox, a hit record in "Heartbreak Hotel," and a series of public appearances on the television shows of Jimmy Dorsey, Milton Berle, and Steve Allen. Each appearance brought him more fame, more record sales, more complaints from viewers about his suggestive gyrations, and high ratings that clobbered the opposition on rival networks. At first Ed Sullivan had sniffed that "Presley is not my cup of tea" and that he would not have him on his "family-type show at any price,"[28] but when Presley's appearance on Allen's show edged Sullivan's show into second place in the ratings, Sullivan hired him for three fall appearances at $50,000 per appearance, more than three times what he had paid any previous performer. On the first appearance, Sullivan instructed the cameramen to keep the cameras focused above the waist so as not to reveal Presley's wriggles. An estimated 54 million people saw this show, setting a record for the Sullivan show that would not be surpassed until the Beatles appeared on the show in February of 1964 before 67.5 million viewers.[29]

The year 1956 was a phenomenal one for Presley. In addition to his television appearances, the release of the first (*Love Me Tender*) of his nearly thirty movies, and dozens of personal appearances commanding $25,000 per night, he made history with his record sales. At a time when a record was considered a hit when sales reached the 100,000 mark, each Presley record easily sold over a million copies, and for the year his "Don't be Cruel," "Love Me Tender," "I Want You, I Need You," and other hits sold over a total of 10 million copies, the most in any one year by any entertainer before that time. From January of 1956 until he was drafted into the army in March of 1958, he had fourteen consecutive million-seller records. Within five years he had an unprecedented thirty-eight gold records, and within ten years he had sold over 115 million records grossing some $150 million.[30] In 1956 and subsequent years he also made millions more from the sale of Elvis Presley embroidered jeans, perfumes, belts, bracelets, books, sneakers, bobby sox, T-shirts, hats, caps, plaster of Paris busts, color photographs, guitars, bookends, pillows, diaries, stuffed hound dogs, and cosmetics, including lipstick that came in three colors: Hound Dog Orange, Heartbreak Hotel Pink, and Tutti-Frutti Red. Sales of these items in 1956 alone amounted to over $20 million. Presley became the first rock star to have a successful singing career, movie career, and souvenir business all running simultaneously. Nothing like this had ever been seen before in the entertainment industry.[31]

How can such a remarkable success be explained? Certainly not just on singing talent, for although Presley could sing all kinds of songs from rock 'n' roll to ballads and gospel, his voice was not at all that unusual, his guitar playing was mediocre, and he could not even read music. But as Presley knew, it was not his music but the combination of his music and his body movements that attracted the fans. "Without my left leg, Ah'd be dead,"[32] he drawled in 1956, and he later said: "I'm not kidding myself. My voice alone is just an ordinary voice. What people come to see is how I use it. If I stand still while I'm singing, I'm dead, man. I might as well go back to driving a truck."[33] Colonel Parker and Presley's other managers understood this, too, and they carefully promoted the image of Elvis the Pelvis, the rebellious, sexy, rock 'n' roll singer joining with the kids in rebellion against the sexual and social conventions of the time, yet a young man who was, conversely, an all-American boy who did not smoke or drink, did not hang around in nightclubs, was religious and patriotic, polite to his elders, and loved his parents, even buying them a $40,000 house to live in after a lifetime of poverty. Very importantly, Presley took rhythm and blues, rockabilly, country and western, and gospel and synthesized them into his own unique style and sound, and because he was white, he could get away with singing black music before white audiences (many people who heard Presley before they ever saw him thought that he was black), and singing them in a sexually suggestive manner. Presley came along at the right time—the rise of rock 'n' roll, *The Blackboard Jungle*, and the life and death of James Dean had all paved the way for him—and he and his managers exploited the opportunity to the fullest.[34]

Parents and music critics reacted to Presley with horror, especially in the beginning. In August of 1956, in an article entitled "He Can't Be—But He Is," *Look* called him "a wild troubadour who wails rock 'n' roll tunes, flails erratically at a guitar and wriggles like a peep-show dancer." While conceding that the twenty-one-year-old former truck driver had some good points, *Look* declared that "Elvis is mostly nightmare. On stage, his gyrations, his nose wiping, his leers are vulgar."[35] In that same month, in "Elvis—a Different Kind of Idol," *Life* claimed that Presley was different from Frank Sinatra and other previous idols and that he was worrying a lot of parents, clergymen, and civic leaders. "He does not just bounce to accent his heavy beat," *Life* declared. "He uses a bump and grind routine usually seen only in burlesque. His young audiences, unexposed to such goings-on, do not just shout their approval. They get set off by shock waves of hysteria, going into frenzies of screeching and wailing, winding up in tears."[36] Some of the most severe criticism of Presley came from Jack Gould of *The New York Times*, who wrote that "on the Sullivan program he injected movements of the tongue and indulged in wordless singing that were singularly distasteful" and that "when Presley executes his bumps and grinds, it must be remembered by the Columbia Broadcasting System that even the 12-year-old's curiosity may be overstimulated."[37] Jack Crosby of the *New York Herald-Tribune* called Presley "an unspeakably untalented and vulgar entertainer," and asked, "Where do you go from Elvis Presley, short of obscenity—which is against the law?"[38]

But the teenagers adored him. Young girls bought all of his records, as much of his monogrammed merchandise as their parents or allowances could afford, and stood in long lines to see his forgettable movies. Young males were at first a little resentful of all the attention directed toward him by girls of their age group, but they also came to like his music, to copy his style of dress and hair, to imitate his sullen facial expressions and swaggering walk, and to see him as a focal point of their rebellion against social convention. Among both girls and boys Presley was popular because he dealt with sex more directly than any previous singer had, and he was the first singing idol that they did not have to share with their elders. After Presley, music and teenagers would never be the same again.

After Presley's incredible success opened the flood gates to rock 'n' roll, the nation was inundated with the new music. Although Pat Boone and other artists still put out covers of black originals, the years from 1956 to 1960 would see Chuck Berry, Ray Charles, Little Willie John, Fats Domino, the Platters, Little Richard, Sam Cooke, and dozens of other black artists rise to fame and fortune through their recordings, television and movie appearances, and personal appearances before white, black, and even mixed audiences. At the same time, Presley, Buddy Holly, Pat Boone, Jerry Lee Lewis, and other white singers provided a steady stream of white rock 'n' roll. Many of the new singers were teenagers who rose to fame partly because of their musical talents and partly because they looked like—and often were—high-school-age performers with whom young record buyers could identify. Fabian was only fifteen, Rick Nelson and Frankie Avalon were only seventeen, and Bobby Rydell only nineteen when they had their first hits and became teen idols, and many other popular singers of the day were in their teens or, like Bobby Darin, their early twenties when they made it big.

Record sales soared with the coming of rock 'n' roll. Aided by the affluence of the time, the invention of the 45 rpm and 33⅓ rpm records, and the introduction of high fidelity, record sales had steadily climbed from 109 million in 1945 to 189 million in 1950 and to 219 million in 1953, then with the arrival of rock 'n' roll rose to 277 million in 1955 and to 600 million in 1960. In 1956 alone, RCA Victor sold over 13.5 million Elvis Presley singles and 3.75 million Presley albums.[39] By 1957, the new 45s and 33⅓s had driven the 78s out of production. Teenagers bought most of the inexpensive and convenient 45s and most of the long-playing rock 'n' roll albums, whereas adults bought most of the long-playing albums of traditional popular music, jazz, and classical music. While in 1950 the average record buyer was likely to be in his early twenties, by 1958, 70 percent of all the records sold in the United States were purchased by teenagers. Most of the popular singles were purchased by girls between the ages of thirteen and nineteen, the group most receptive, as one critic said, to "little wide-eyed wishes for ideal love and perfect lovers, little songs of frustration at not finding them."[40] Thanks to these revolutions in the musical world, record sales, which had stood at only $7.5 million in 1940, had risen to a healthy $521 million in 1960.[41]

Why was rock 'n' roll so popular? One of the reasons, of course, was that it was written and performed by young people and was centered upon what was important to them: love, going steady, jealousy, high school, sex, dancing, clothing, automobiles, and all the other joys and problems of being young. The lyrics were just as silly, sentimental, and idealistic as the music of the crooners of the first half of the decade, but it was written just for the young and the singing styles, beat, electrical amplification, and volume of the music was much more dynamic than that of the earlier period. Teens were attracted to its celebration of sexuality, expressed in the more explicit lyrics, driving tempo, movements of the rock 'n' roll performers, and in new dances at high school hops and private parties. Perhaps Jeff Greenfield, a member of this first generation of rock 'n' roll fans, expressed it best in his *No Peace, No Place*: "Each night, sprawled on my bed on Manhattan's Upper West Side, I would listen to the world that Alan Freed created. To a twelve- or thirteen-year-old, it was a world of unbearable sexuality and celebration: a world of citizens under sixteen, in a constant state of joy or sweet sorrow. . . . New to sexual sensations, driven by the impulses that every new adolescent generation knows, we were the first to have a music rooted in uncoated sexuality."[42] And very importantly, rock 'n' roll gave young people a sense of cohesion, of unity, all across the nation. It was *their* music, written for them and for them only, about their world, a world that adults could not share and did not understand. As such, it was one of the major harbingers of the generation gap.[43]

It was not long after teenagers acquired their own music and movies that they also acquired their own television show. *American Bandstand* began as a local television show in Philadelphia in 1952, and in August of

1957 it premiered as a network show on ABC over sixty-seven stations across the country, from 3:00 to 4:30 in the afternoon, with twenty-six-year-old Dick Clark as the host. The first network show featured songs by Jerry Lee Lewis, the Coasters, and other top rock 'n' roll artists, and guest star Billy Williams singing "I'm Gonna Sit Right Down and Write Myself a Letter." Some of the early reviews of the show were not complimentary. According to *Billboard*, "The bulk of the ninety minutes was devoted to colorless juveniles trudging through early American dances like the Lindy and the Box Step to recorded tunes of the day. If this is the wholesome answer to the 'detractors' of rock 'n' roll, bring on the rotating pelvises."[44] But by the end of 1958 the show was reaching over 20 million viewers over 105 stations, and had spawned dozens of imitations on local stations. This was a show about teens, and its consistent high rating and longevity proved that they liked it, regardless of what adults said about it.

*American Bandstand* had a great influence on popular music and on America's teenagers. Clark's good looks, neat clothing, and civilized manner helped reassure American parents that rock 'n' roll was not a barbarian invasion that was turning the young into juvenile delinquents. All the dancers on the show in the fifties were white, adhered to a strict dress code (coats and ties for boys, dresses and skirts and blouses for girls, and no jeans, T-shirts, or tight sweaters), and followed a strict language code that even prohibited the use of the term "going steady." One of Clark's most embarrassing moments on the show came when a young girl told him that the pin she was wearing was a "virgin pin."[45] Stars with unsavory reputations were not allowed on the show, so when the news of Jerry Lee Lewis's marriage to his thirteen-year-old cousin broke, Clark joined other disc jockeys and promotors across the country in canceling all future appearances of the pioneer rock 'n' roll star. The show also featured the biggest stars of the day and helped launch the careers of Connie Francis, Fabian, Frankie Avalon, and several other singers. The new dances performed on the show—such as "the stroll," "the shake," and "the walk"—were soon copied all across the country. Teenagers everywhere also imitated the slang and the dress of this very influential show and bought the records its regulars danced to. The success of this dance show brought popularity and wealth to its host, who freely admitted that "I dance very poorly," yet became a millionaire by the age of thirty.[46]

The rise of rock 'n' roll, teen movies, teen television shows, and teen magazines helped create the teen idol. Many of the idols were singers, like Elvis Presley, Rick Nelson, Frankie Avalon, Bobby Darin, Fabian, Pat Boone, Connie Francis, and Annette Funicello. Others were movie or television actors, like James Dean and Marlon Brando, though of course many of the singers also went on to movie careers which might be called, at best, undistinguished. Most of the idols were teenagers themselves or in their twenties, and it is important to note here that while earlier generations had tended to create idols much older than themselves—like Bing Crosby, Perry Como, and Clark Gable—the teenagers of the late fifties made idols of people from their own generation. And although clean-cut stars like Ricky Nelson or Frankie Avalon were chosen as idols, many young people also idolized Brando and Dean, who seemed so much like them in their agonizing over the problems of life. This inclination of the young to idolize those who portrayed problem youth was puzzling and disturbing to parents who wanted their children to grow up to be clean-cut, middle-class kids who went to church, obeyed their parents and other authorities, drank nothing harder than a soft drink, had no sexual experience before marriage, saved and studied for college, hung around soda shops rather than pool rooms, and after college went into a respectable career with a good income and a secure future. In short, they wanted their children to be like Pat Boone.

Born in Jacksonville, Florida, in 1934, Boone rose to fame while still a college student by winning first place on Ted Mack's *Original Amateur Hour* and *Arthur Godfrey's Talent Scouts* in 1954. He became a regular on Godfrey's morning show, and then began a career as a singer, movie star (*Bernadine* and *April Love*, both in 1957), and television star with his own show (*Pat Boone Chevy Showroom*). Many of his recordings were covers of original black songs like "Tutti-Frutti" and "Ain't That a Shame," and traditional romantic tunes such as "Friendly Persuasion," "April Love," and "Love Letters in the Sand." Boone was an all-American boy, a dedicated Christian and family man who had not been spoiled by his success, although at the age of twenty-four he was already popular and wealthy, earning $750,000 annually. He had an attractive wife, four pretty daughters, a baccalaureate degree from Columbia University, a love of milk and ice cream, and a severe distaste for strong drink, tobacco, and anything else immoral.[47] He attracted wide publicity in 1958 when he refused to kiss Shirley Jones in the movie *April Love*, saying that "I've always been taught that when you get married, you forget about kissing other women." However, after talking it over with his wife, he agreed to do the kissing scene, although "she would prefer to keep that part of our lives solely to ourselves."[48] This old-fashioned wholesomeness enabled him to hit the best-seller list in 1958 with *'Twixt Twelve and Twenty*,[49] a moral and social guide for teenagers that reflected Boone's conservative view of sex and his deeply religious outlook on life. Some teenagers found Boone hopelessly "square," but many others admired his moral rectitude. He was immensely popular in the fifties, perhaps second only to Elvis.

In spite of the existence of clean-cut white performers like Pat Boone, much of the adult world was against the new rock 'n' roll. Many musicians and music critics condemned it on musical grounds, disliking its primitive beat, electrical amplification, witless and repetitive lyrics, loudness, and screams. But most adults opposed it for other reasons. Many objected to its suggestive lyrics and claimed that it fomented rebellion against parents and other authorities, bred immorality, inflamed teenagers to riot, and was un-Christian and unpatriotic. They agreed with Frank Sinatra, who called it "the martial music of every sideburned delinquent on the face of the earth."[50] Others objected to its racial background and content, even claiming, as many southerners did, that rock 'n' roll was a plot jointly sponsored by the Kremlin and the NAACP, and that rock musicians and disc jockeys were dope addicts, communists, integrationists, atheists, and sex fiends. To many whites, North and South, it was "nigger music," and as such was designed to tear down the barriers of segregation and bring about sexual promiscuity, intermarriage, and a decline in the morals of young whites.[51]

The fears of parents and other adults were fed by the isolated incidents of rioting that accompanied rock 'n' roll concerts in Boston, Washington, D.C., and several other cities. As a result of these headline-getting events, rock 'n' roll concerts were banned in many cities or else accompanied by heavy police security and strict regulations as to what the performers could do or say on stage. In many cities, city councils and other local groups also tried to ban rock 'n' roll from record stores or jukeboxes. In San Antonio, Texas, the city council even went so far as to ban the music from the jukeboxes of public swimming pools, claiming that it "attracted undesirable elements given to practicing their gyrations in abbreviated bathing suits."[52] A disc jockey in Buffalo was fired when he played an Elvis Presley record, and across the country disc jockeys were similarly punished for playing the new music or were pressured into boycotting it. Some disc jockeys broke rock 'n' roll records on the air, while radio station WLEV in Erie, Pennsylvania, loaded over 7,000 rock 'n' roll records into a rented hearse and led a funeral procession to Erie Harbor, where the records were "buried at sea." Ministers preached against it, claiming, like the Rev. John Carroll in Boston, that the music corrupted young people and that "rock and roll inflames and excites youth like jungle tom-toms readying warriors for battle,"[53] and many churches held public burnings of rock 'n' roll records. Some were even willing to resort to the ugliest kinds of violence to try to stem the advance of rock music. On April 23, 1956, in Birmingham, Alabama, where the White Citizens' Council had succeeded in removing all rock 'n' roll records from jukeboxes, five men connected with the council rushed the stage of the city auditorium and assaulted black ballad singer Nat King Cole, who was badly bruised before the police stopped the attack.[54]

The debate over rock 'n' roll continued through the end of the decade, carried on in the press, over radio and television, in teachers' meetings, pulpits, and city council meeting rooms. By 1960 the debate had begun to die down, with parents coming to see that the music was not going to fade away, that it had not made delinquents of their children, and that all the other dire predictions had not come to pass, either. Some even began to admit grudgingly that they liked some of it, though they wished that it were not played so loudly. Some of the older professional musicians had also come to defend it—Benny Goodman, Sammy Kaye, Paul Whiteman, and Duke Ellington had kind words for the new music from the very beginning, and Whiteman and Kaye publicly recalled that most new musical forms, including their own swing music, had been condemned when it first appeared.[55] And in the May 1959 issue of *Harper's*, critic Arnold Shaw noted that "perhaps it should be added (although it should be self-evident) that just as hot jazz of the twenties (then anathema to our grandparents) did not destroy our parents, and swing (anathema to our parents) did not destroy us, it is quite unlikely that rock 'n' roll will destroy our children."[56]

The spectacular rise of rock 'n' roll should not obscure the fact that the older music continued to thrive. In 1957, when rock 'n' roll claimed seven of the top ten records of the year, the number one song was "Tammy," recorded by both Debbie Reynolds and the Ames Brothers, and Perry Como remained a favorite of young and old throughout the decade. In a 1956 poll by *Woman's Home Companion*, teenage boys and girls chose Como as the best male vocalist, with Presley, Boone, and Sinatra trailing behind.[57] Johnny Mathis, Paul Anka, Pat Boone, Bobby Darin, the Everly Brothers, and many other teen idols also continued to sing fairly traditional love songs, and in the late fifties, building on a tradition established early in the decade by the Weavers, the Kingston Trio brought a revival of folk music to college students with a touch of rock and protest in songs like "Tom Dooley," "Tijuana Jail," and "A Worried Man," paving the way for the folk music explosion in the early 1960s. Rock music dominated from 1956 to 1960, but it did not completely push the older music aside.

In addition to obtaining their own music, movies, television shows, and idols, teenagers of the fifties also acquired their own fashions, and here they followed the trend toward casual dress that was characterizing the rest of society. The favorite dress of high school boys was denim jeans with rolled-up cuffs, sport shirts, baggy pegged pants, pleated rogue trousers with a white side stripe, slacks with buckles in the back, V-neck sweaters, button-down striped shirts, blazers, white bucks, and loafers. In 1955 they also joined older males on college campuses and executive offices in the pink revolution, donning pink shirts, pink striped or polka dot ties, and colonel string ties. Hair styles ranged from the popular flat top or crew cut to the Apache or ducktail (banned at some high schools). "Greasers" of course shunned the Ivy League and pink attire as too effeminate, sticking to their T-shirts (often with sleeves rolled up to hold a cigarette pack), jeans, leather jackets, and ducktails. For girls, the fashions ranged from rolled-up jeans to casual blouses or men's shirts, full dresses with crinolines, skirts and sweaters, blazers, occasional experiments with the tube dress and sack dress and other disasters foisted upon older women by fashion designers, short shorts (with rolled-up cuffs) that got progressively shorter as the decade wore on, two-piece bathing suits (few were bold enough to wear the bikini, imported from France in the late forties), brown and white saddle shoes and loafers, and hair styles from the poodle to the ponytail. Couples who were going steady wore one another's class rings, identification tags, and necklaces or bracelets, and often adopted a unisex look by wearing matching sweaters, blazers, and shirts.[58]

Like the generations before them, the teenagers of the fifties also had their slang. Much of it was concerned, of course, with the great passion of teens, cars. Cars were *wheels*, tires were *skins*, racing from a standing start was called a *drag*, the bumper was *nerf-bar*, a special kind of exhaust system was called *duals*, and a car specially modified for more engine power was a *hot rod* or *souped up car* or *bomb*. A drive-in movie was a *passion pit*, anything or anyone considered dull was a *drag*, and a really dull person was a *square* or a *nose-bleed*. An admirable or poised individual or anything worthy of admiration or approval was *cool* or *neat* or *smooth*, someone who panicked or lost his *cool* was accused of *clutching*, and people admonished not to worry were told to *hang loose*. Teenagers also borrowed lingo from the jazz and beatnik world, such as *dig*, *hip*, *cat*, *bread*, and *chick*. A cutting, sarcastic laugh at someone's bad joke was expressed by *a hardeeharhar*. And teenagers also shared the jargon of the rest of society—*big deal*, *the royal screw* or *royal shaft*, *up the creek without a paddle*, *forty lashes with a wet noodle*, *wild*, *wicked*, *crazy*, *classy*, *horny*, *BMOC*, *looking for action*, *bad news*, *out to lunch*, *gross*, *fink*, *loser*, *creep*, *dumb cluck*, *doing the deed*, *going all the way*, or *coming across*. Many of these colloquialisms were borrowed from earlier generations, sometimes with modifications in meaning, while some had been regionalisms that now became national through the great homogenizing power of television.[59]

By the mid-1950s there were 16.5 million teenagers in the United States. About half of them were crowding the nation's secondary schools, while the rest had entered college or the work world. Wherever they were, they had become, as Gereon Zimmerman would write in *Look* magazine, a "Generation in a Searchlight," a constant subject of media attention and a constant source of anxiety for their parents and the rest of the adult world. As Zimmerman observed, "No other generation has had so much attention, so much admonition, so many statistics."[60]

Zimmerman might also have added that no other young generation had had so much money. One of the most revolutionary aspects of the teenage generation was its effects on the American economy, for by the midfifties teenagers made up a very lucrative consumer market for American manufacturers. By mid-decade teenagers of this affluent era were viewing as necessities goods that their parents, reared during the depression, still saw as luxuries, such as automobiles, televisions, record players, cameras, and the like. By the midfifties, teenagers were buying 43 percent of all records, 44 percent of all cameras, 39 percent of all new radios, 9 percent of all new cars, and 53 percent of movie tickets.[61] By 1959, the amount of money spent on teenagers by themselves and by their parents had reached the staggering total of $10 billion a year. Teenagers were spending around $75 million annually on single popular records, $40 million on lipstick, $25 million on deodorant, $9 million on home permanents, and over $837 million on school clothes for teenage girls.[62] Many teenagers had their own charge accounts at local stores and charge cards issued especially for them, such as Starlet Charge Account, Campus Deb Account, and the 14 to 21 Club. Like their parents, teenagers were being led by the affluence and advertising of the age to desire an ever-increasing diet of consumer goods and services and to buy them even if they had to charge them against future earnings.

Many adults had a distorted image of this affluent young generation, focusing too much on its delinquency, rock 'n' roll, unconventional hair styles and clothing, and dating and sexual practices. Only a very small percentage were delinquents or problem-ridden adolescents. Most were reasonably well-groomed, well-behaved, and active in school and extracurricular functions. Most were interested in sports, automobiles, movies, rock 'n' roll, dating, dancing, hobbies, radio, and television. Their major worries were the typical problems of youth in an affluent age: problems with their parents, their popularity with other teens, their looks and complexions, proper dating behavior, sex, first dates, first kisses, love, bad breath, body odors, posture, body build, friends, schoolwork, college, future careers, money, religion, and the draft.[63]

These teenagers that parents worried so much about were remarkably conservative. Survey after survey of young people in the fifties found that over half of them—and sometimes even larger percentages—believed that censorship of printed materials and movies was justified, that politics was beyond their understanding and was just a dirty game, that most people did not have the ability to make important decisions about what was good for them, that masturbation was shameful and perhaps harmful, that women should not hold public office, and that the theory of evolution was suspect and even dangerous. Like their parents, they were also very religious as a group, tending to believe in the divine inspiration of the Bible, heaven and hell, and a God who answered the prayers of the faithful. They were suspicious of radical groups and were willing to deny them the right to assemble in meetings and to disseminate their ideas, and they saw nothing wrong with denying accused criminals basic constitutional rights, such as the right to know their accuser, to be free from unreasonable search or seizure of their property, or to refuse to testify against themselves. Teenagers were also very conformist: They were very concerned about what their friends thought of their dress, behavior, and ideas, and they tried very hard to be part of the group and not be labeled an oddball or individualist. In short, in this age of corporation man, the country also had corporation teen.[64]

Most teens were also conservative in their approach to dating, sex, and marriage. Religious views, social and peer pressure, and fear of pregnancy all combined to create this conservatism and to ensure that most teens kept their virginity until marriage or at least until the early college years, though heavy petting was certainly prevalent among couples who were engaged or "going steady," a practice reflecting society's emphasis on monogamy. These conservative attitudes toward sexual behavior were reinforced by the authorities teenagers looked to for guidance—parents, teachers, ministers, advice to the lovelorn columnists like Dear Abby and Ann Landers (both of whom began their columns in the midfifties), and books on teenage etiquette by Allen Ludden, Pat Boone, and *Seventeen* magazine. In his book for young men, *Plain Talk for Men Under 21*,[65] Ludden devoted an entire chapter to such things as "That Good Night Kiss"—discussing whether to, how to, and the significance of it if you did. And in the very popular *The Seventeen Book of Young Living* (1957), Enid Haupt, the editor and publisher of *Seventeen* magazine, advised young girls to "keep your first and all your romances on a beyond reproach level" and to save themselves for the one right man in their lives. Acknowledging that "it isn't easy to say no to a persuasive and charming boy," she offered one answer for all potentially compromising situations: "'No, please take me home. Now.'"[66]

The conservatism of the young would continue over into the college-age population, where it would remain entrenched for the rest of the fifties. The decade witnessed a boom in higher education, as rising prosperity, G.I. benefits, increasing governmental and private financial aid, fear of the draft, and a growing cultural emphasis on higher education all contributed to a great increase in the number of college students, faculty, programs, and buildings. The boom occurred at all levels—undergraduate, graduate, professional, and in the burgeoning junior- and community-college movement. The number of students, which had stood at 1.5 million in 1940 and 2.3 million in 1950, steadily rose in the decade and reached 3.6 million in 1960, and while the population of the country grew by 8 percent in the decade, the college population grew by 40 percent. By the end of the decade, almost 40 percent of the eighteen-to-twenty-one-year-old age group was attending some institution of higher education.[67]

The conservatism of the college students of the 1950s led them to be called the Silent Generation. Why was it so silent? One of the most important reasons was that it mirrored the conservatism of the society at large, a society caught up in the materialistic and Cold War mentality of the decade. Like their elders, students were seeking the good life rather than the examined one, and as the Great Fear spread to the campuses, many were afraid of acquiring a radical reputation that might jeopardize their scholarships and their future careers in private industry, government service, or the military. Many were veterans, and their military experience, especially for those who had served in Korea, had tended to confirm their conservatism. Many others were in college in order to evade or at least defer the draft, and did not want to do or say anything that might endanger their deferred status. And finally, most students were white and drawn from the middle and upper-middle classes of society. The doors of higher education were still closed to most minority groups and to the economically and socially disadvantaged—groups who might have brought questioning or even radical attitudes into the field of higher education had they been part of it. It is not surprising then that most college students were hardworking, conservative, and career-oriented, truly deserving of their Silent Generation label.

The conservatism of the college generation prevailed throughout the decade. In a study of the college generation in 1951, *Time* magazine noted that "the most startling thing about the younger generation is its silence. . . . It does not issue manifestoes, make speeches, or carry posters." Most students, *Time* found, were worried about the Korean War and its effects on their plans for careers and marriage, but they pushed these fears into the background and concentrated on earning good grades and landing a good job. They were serious and hardworking, in rebellion against nothing, and had no real heroes or villains. Born during the depression years, they were primarily interested in a good job and security, and they did not want to do or say anything that would jeopardize these goals. "Today's generation," *Time* concluded, "either through fear, passivity, or conviction, is ready to conform."[68]

Soon after the end of the Korean War, *Newsweek* studied college students in seven institutions, and its findings were little different from those of *Time* two years before. In "U.S. Campus Kids of 1953: Unkiddable and Unbeatable," *Newsweek* reported that students were hardworking, ambitious conformists who looked forward to secure jobs and a happy married life. Going steady was more popular then ever before, a sign of the period's emphasis on marriage and of young people's desire for the security that a going-steady relationship brought. Most students, *Newsweek* found, were not very interested in politics or international affairs, and they avoided being linked with unpopular causes. One Vassar girl told the magazine, "We're a cautious generation. We aren't buying any ideas we're not sure of." Another said that "you want to be popular, so naturally you don't express any screwy ideas. To be popular you have to conform." And a Princeton senior said that "the world doesn't owe me a living—but it owes me a job." *Newsweek* also saw a renewed interest in religion, as reflected in increasing enrollments in religion courses and frequent "religious emphasis weeks." The magazine found much to admire in the hardworking materialistic class of 1953, although it did concede that "they might seem dull in comparison with less troubled eras."[69]

Similar collegiate characteristics were reported in a 1955 study by David Riesman, who found that students were ambitious, very sure of what they wanted to do, but also very unadventurous—they wanted secure positions in big companies and were already concerned about retirement plans. As one Princeton senior saw it, "Why struggle on my own, when I can enjoy the big psychological income of being a member of a big outfit?" Most males had already decided that they wanted middle-management jobs—they did not want to rise to the presidential or vice-presidential level because that would require too much drive, take time away from their family life and leisure time, and force them to live in a big city. Most had already decided upon the kind of girl they would marry, how many kids they would have, and which civic clubs and other organizations they would join—and they would be joiners, for they liked the gregarious life and knew it would help their careers. They wanted educated wives who would be intellectually stimulating, yet they wanted them to be dutiful and obedient and to stay at home and raise the kids. Many said they wanted as many as four or five kids, because they felt that a large family would bring happiness, security, contentment. One Harvard senior said that "I'd like six kids. I don't know why I say that—it seems like a minimum production goal."[70] They did not know or care much about politics, but they did like Ike and said that they would probably be Republicans because corporation life dictated that they should be.

These attitudes still seemed to prevail in 1957, when *The Nation* surveyed college and university professors about what their students were reading and thinking. Most reported that their students still read the standard authors—Hemingway, Wolfe, Lawrence, Orwell, Huxley, Faulkner, and Steinbeck—but shied away from fiction or nonfiction that dealt with economic, social, or political protest. One professor lamented that "the only young novelist I have heard praised vociferously is J. D. Salinger, for his discovery of childhood," and complained that "when a liberal and speculative voice is heard in the classroom, it is more likely than not to be the professor's, despite whatever caution the years may have taught him." The director of the Writing Program at Stanford University claimed that students were "hard to smoke out. Sometimes a professor is baited into protest by the rows and circles of their closed, watchful, apparently apathetic faces, and says in effect, 'My God, *feel* something! Get enthusiastic about something, plunge, go boom, look alive!'" A Yale English professor complained that "the present campus indifference to either politics or reform or rebellion is monumental." And most agreed with a University of Michigan professor's claim that to the student of 1957, "college has ceased to be a brightly lighted stage where he discovers who he is. It is rather a processing-chamber where, with touching submissiveness, he accepts the remarks of lecturers and the hard sentences of textbooks as directives that will lead him to a job."[71]

What did the members of the Silent Generation do when they were not studying, planning what company they intended to find a safe niche in, deciding what kind of mate they would marry or how many kids they would have, or planning for retirement? They played sports, drank beer, ate pizzas and hamburgers, went to football games and movies, participated in panty raids, dated, dreamed of the opposite sex, read novels and magazines, watched television, and listened to recordings of jazz, classical music, or the popular crooners of the day. For most, the hottest issues on campus were what to do about a losing football coach or who should be elected homecoming queen or student body president. Both sexes wore conservative preppy clothes, and at many coeducational institutions women were forbidden to wear jeans or shorts to class. Those who could afford to joined one of the fast-growing number of fraternities or sororities in order to party, find identity and security, and form friendships that might later be useful in the business world they hoped to enter after graduation. College students were, indeed, an unrebellious lot.

By the late fifties America's teenagers had acquired a distinct subculture of their own. They had their own money, music, movies, television shows, idols, clothing, and slang. In contrast to previous generations, they were more affluent, better educated, talked more openly about sex, had greater mobility through the widespread ownership of automobiles by their parents or themselves, demanded and received more personal freedom, had more conflicts with their parents, and were the subject of more media and parental concern. But they were not yet in rebellion, for although their life-style had departed from the conventions of their elders, their basic ideas and attitudes were still the conservative ones that mirrored the conservatism of the affluent age in which they grew up.

Still, their parents were worried. As *Look* magazine reported in 1958 in an article entitled "What Parents Say About Teenagers," "many parents are in a state of confusion or despair about their teenagers. And they don't exactly know what to do about it. They would like to sit down with their children and talk over their mutual problems, but often this desire is thwarted by the teenagers themselves."[72] The much-heralded generation gap was coming into view. In the next decade, when the junior high and senior high school students of the fifties crowded the colleges, marched in civil rights demonstrations, protested the Vietnam War, and engaged in unconventional sexual and drug practices, it would take on the temper of a revolution.

# 16

# Women, Love, and Sex in Eisenhower's America

Teenagers were not the only group of Americans in the national spotlight during the prosperous years of Eisenhower's America. In the midfifties, the nation seemed to be caught up in a great love affair with the American woman. In countless books, newspaper and magazine articles, and radio and television shows, Americans were being reminded again and again of the importance of women in American life. They were told that for the first time women now outnumbered men (there were 100 women for every 98.6 men), that women were marrying earlier and earlier (the median age of marriage for women in 1956 was 20.2), that women were having over 4 million babies each year, that the 22 million working women made up a third of the work force, and that half of all married women were working outside the home. Women, it seemed, were having an increasingly heavy impact on almost every facet of American life.[1]

Perhaps nowhere was the celebration of the American woman more lavishly done than in October 16, 1956, issue of *Look* magazine. In a long article entitled "A New Look at the American Woman," American women were lauded as a new breed greatly different from their mothers and grandmothers. They were healthier, had more home conveniences, were crowding American colleges, had more freedom than ever before, and were achieving success in many different fields, although they "gracefully conceded the top rungs to men." Furthermore, the magazine continued, "this marvelous creature . . . looks and acts far more feminine than the 'emancipated' girl of the 1920's or even 1930's."[2] Not to be outdone by its competitor, *Life* magazine devoted a special issue at the end of the year to "The American Woman: Her Achievements and Troubles," [3] featuring articles on working women, the beauty business, pregnancy, clubwork, politics, divorce, widows, and other interests and problems of the nation's 83 million women. Perhaps never in American history had the American woman been the subject of so much analysis and adoration, and perhaps never before had the real truth about American women been more obscured.

The truth was that in the 1950s the United States was still a sexist nation. In spite of all the progress of the previous half-century, American women still lived in a society in which the men controlled the wealth and power, made the rules under which both sexes lived, and stacked them in favor of men. Politics, government, religion, economics, education, the media—all were controlled by men and used by them to maintain their power and perpetuate the myth of female inferiority. Women were placed, as in the past, on pedestals, but what they were being exalted for was as wives and babymakers and skilled practitioners of traditional female occupations—teachers, nurses, librarians, secretaries, office and store clerks. For most women of the fifties, the women's movement that would bring so much upheaval and so many benefits in the sixties and seventies was hardly even a dream.

To justify the sexism that they consciously and unconsciously practiced, men resorted to the same tactic that had long been used by racists to perpetuate racial discrimination: the invention and dissemination of the big lie. In race relations, the big lie was the myth of black inferiority, which maintained that since blacks were an inferior race they should be controlled and kept in their place by the superior white race. In sex relations, the big lie was, as one woman writer has put it, "the idea of women's inferiority, a lie so deeply ingrained in our cultural behavior that merely to recognize it is to risk unraveling the entire fabric of civilization."[4]

Although women were in the majority, they were treated, like blacks, as an inferior minority group. They were stereotyped, singled out as different, discriminated against on the basis of alleged differences, and treated almost as a separate caste. Like blacks, women were alleged to be mentally and physically inferior to the dominant group—less intelligent and talented, emotionally unstable, irresponsible, weak, and submissive. They were deprived of supervisory positions, subjected to sexual harassment, paid less than men, feared as competitors in the job world, and subjected to ridicule, hostility, and even retaliation if they stepped outside their traditional place. Like blacks, who had learned to behave in the stereotyped manner whites ascribed to them and expected of them, women learned to survive and even thrive in a world that treated them as inferiors by using smiles, flattery, teasing looks, affectations of ignorance and helplessness, and other feminine wiles to outwit the dominant group. Like blacks, they were considered to be satisfied with their traditional role and therefore content to "stay in their place"—the place assigned to them by men. And like blacks, many women accepted the dominant group's teachings and fully believed that they were inferior beings and hence deserving of the discrimination they suffered.[5] As feminist leaders would discover in the 1960s, much to their dismay, a major obstacle to the destruction of sexism was the belief of many women that they were inferior and should be kept in their place—a testament to the effectiveness of the brainwashing of the male-dominated society.

The conscious and unconscious sexism that permeated American society was continuously taught and reinforced by all the major institutions and communication systems. Sexist teachings began in the home, where parents taught their children the myth of male superiority along with narrow conceptions of male and female sex roles. It continued in the public schools, where teachers, the curriculum, textbooks, extracurricular activities, and peers all served to reinforce narrow ideas of what boys and girls are like and what they should grow up to be: Boys should grow up to be lawyers, doctors, firemen, and other leaders and protectors of society, while girls should grow up to be their assistants: wives and mothers or—if they worked at all—teachers, nurses, librarians, or secretaries. It was taught in colleges and in the universities, too, where young men trained for business, law, and medicine—and young women, if they aspired to these professions, and if they were admitted as students, were urged to learn typing and stenography along with their other studies, because that was how you got "in." And all along the way, from childhood, adolescence, adulthood, and into old age, sexism was perpetuated by newspapers, magazines, radio, television, the movies, the churches, professional organizations, the world of work, and other formal and informal organizations and communication systems. And what was so insidious about it all was that few people of the time recognized sexism for what it was—a pervasive prejudice that relegated one half of the population to inferior status, and prevented both men and women from realizing their full potential as human beings.

A strong promoter of sexism in America in the 1950s was the widespread popularity of Freudian views on the nature and function of males and females. These views were disseminated through the works of hundreds of Freudian writers, but the most popular and most influential work was undoubtedly *Modern Woman: The Lost Sex*,[6] by Marynia Farnham, a psychiatrist, and Ferdinand Lundberg, a journalist. Published in 1947, *Modern Woman: The Lost Sex* is based on the popular Freudian idea that "anatomy is destiny": There are natural differences between men and women that determine their basic nature and program them for the basic function each sex is to fulfill in life. In this stereotyped concept of the sexes, men are naturally strong, aggressive, independent, rational, and competitive, so they are the natural breadwinners, protectors, and leaders of society. Women, by contrast, are naturally soft, passive, emotional, obedient, gentle, and maternal, so they are the natural wives, mothers, and homemakers. Society functions best if each sex follows the role nature predetermined for it. If individuals try to deny their natural instincts and perform functions relegated to the opposite sex, they will become unhappy, perhaps even neurotic, their marriages will suffer, and society will suffer. The normal woman can reach full contentment and happiness only by being a passive, dependent mother and wife.

Farnham and Lundberg's theories inevitably led them to the conclusion that marriage was the only normal state for adults and that single people, male or female, were abnormal—so abnormal, in fact, that they should seek psychotherapy. They recommended that bachelors over the age of thirty be required to see a psychiatrist, while spinsters should be prevented from teaching because they were obviously so emotionally warped that they would harm the children placed in their care. Furthermore, they proposed that the government should encourage domesticity through a special tax on bachelors over the age of thirty, the payment of bonuses for having children, and propaganda aimed at promoting marriage, domesticity, and childbearing.[7]

Farnham and Lundberg's views on bachelor taxes and spinster teachers were considered extreme even in the fifties, but their other views were accepted with little or no questioning by the majority of the population, whether male or female, educated or not. Selling widely in hard cover and paperback, the book was liberally quoted and paraphrased by hundreds of academic and popular authors of books and articles on the sexes, and its ideas were widely accepted among psychiatrists and other professionals who treated women for various mental and physical problems. These ideas also pervaded the pages of *McCalls*, *Good Housekeeping*, *Ladies Home Journal*, and the dozens of other women's magazines read by millions of American women.[8]

The sexism of the fifties was perpetuated by the colleges and universities. It was widely believed that even women who were fortunate enough to attend college should prepare themselves for marriage and motherhood. In 1950 Lynn White, a prominent educator and president of Mills College in California, wrote in *Educating Our Daughters* that women are not as gifted as men in areas of abstract thinking, such as in natural science and mathematics, and that attempts to compete in these areas would only lead to frustration, failure, and an abandonment of their true roles as wives and mothers. Women should be educated as women, in courses in home economics, ceramics, flower arranging, and other crafts that suited their aptitudes as women and prepared them for their life as homemakers.[9]

Women were often taught by their mothers, high school teachers, and college curricula and professors that they should not become too intellectual and should not enter academic fields and careers that would put them in competition with men. Betty Friedan would later claim that "the one lesson a girl could hardly avoid learning, if she went to college between 1945 and 1960, was not to get interested, seriously interested, in anything besides getting married and having children, if she wanted to be normal, happy, adjusted, feminine, have a successful husband, successful children, and a normal, feminine, adjusted, successful sex life."[10] This was a great exaggeration, of course. Many young college women did avoid that lesson, or ignored it. They took serious courses, majored in liberal arts rather than home economics, excelled academically, and went on after college to balance marriage and motherhood with a career outside the home. But for many others, Friedan's remark was all too true.

Sexism also reared its ugly head in higher education in other ways. The number of female college students almost doubled in the 1950s, from 721,000 to 1.3 million, while the number of male students jumped only from 1.6 million to 2.3 million. But male students still greatly outnumbered female ones, and while over 55 percent of male college students graduated, only 37 percent of female students did.[11] Over half the female students who dropped out did so because, as people joked at the time, they had gained their MRS. degree and were now working on their Ph.T.—"Putting Hubbie Through." Of the women who did graduate, only a small number went to graduate or professional school. In 1960, in spite of all the real educational gains of the decade, women obtained only 25,727 master's degrees, about half as many as men (51,965), and only 1,028 doctorates, about one eighth as many as men (8,801).[12] Most graduate and professional schools admitted only a small percentage of female applicants, usually under a quota system that favored men, who, it was presumed, were the more intelligent species, the real breadwinners and leaders of society, and would not have to waste their time by retiring to the home after marriage and children.

Television was also a prime purveyor of sexism. From the very beginning of telecasting, men and women were portrayed in stereotyped roles, with the men doing the important work in life (working at the office, chasing down criminals in Manhattan or the Old West, saving lives in hospital operating rooms, or winning big battles in court) while women stayed at home as wives and mothers or worked in traditional female occupations. Women appeared as zany housewives (Lucy), perfect wives and mothers (Harriet Nelson), addled wives of entertainers (Gracie Allen), battling wives (Alice Kramden), giggly and excited game show contestants, singers and dancers on musicals and variety shows, or as wronged wives, adulterers, shrews, and jezebels on daytime soap operas. Rarely were women shown working outside the home, and when they did venture out into the work world, it was not as doctors and lawyers but as schoolteachers (*Our Miss Brooks*), secretaries (Ann Sothern as Susie McNamara on *Private Secretary*), or as nurses and salesclerks. And in thousands of commercials, women were depicted as contented housewives who spent most of the day trying to decide which detergent got their clothes the whitest, which toothpaste was best for their children, and what to cook for their man for dinner when he came home from the real world. Day after day and night after night, television perpetuated the sexism of the day.

One of the most prominent teachers of sexism in the fifties was the movie industry, which was desperately trying to find the right formula for reversing the dramatic declines at the box office. In addition to experimenting with 3-D, Cinerama, and Cinemascope, the industry tried to feature movies with the right kind of female starlet to lure people back to the theater. In contrast to the forties, when women had often been portrayed as strong, individualistic, career-oriented or patriotic women doing their best for the war effort, the movies of the fifties paraded before audiences a variety of stereotyped women in stereotyped sex roles. A favorite theme of the decade was "woman chasing after her man," as in *Seven Brides for Seven Brothers*, *Gentlemen Prefer Blondes*, *How to Marry a Millionaire*, and *Three Coins in the Fountain*. In most of these, the woman chased her man until she finally got him, but in order to win him over, she had to prove that she was not the strong independent type and would let her man control her. Other prominent themes were "woman preparing for marriage" (*Father of the Bride*, *High Society*, *The Catered Affair*), "discontented wives" (*Written on the Wind*, *From Here to Eternity*, *The Country Girl*), "romancing widows" (*Not as a Stranger*, *The Magnificent Obsession*, *Love Is a Many Splendored Thing*,), and "the woman alone" (*Streetcar Named Desire*, *The Fugitive Kind*, *Picnic*, *Suddenly Last Summer*). In these and other films, women were portrayed as inferior beings, as emotional weaklings, as lonely, incomplete singles, wives, or widows who experienced true happiness only when they found the right man who swept them off their feet and made them feel the way a woman ought to feel.[13]

To play romantic leads, Hollywood seemed to choose three types of women: the girl next door, the sexy mammary bombshell, and the temptress. Sweet, funny, innocent yet mischievous, the wholesome girl-next-door type fought off the advances of her man until he finally agreed to marry her. The most popular girl next door was Doris Day, whose engaging smile, blond hair, freckles, and wholesome image carried her through picture after picture and prompted Oscar Levant, who had appeared in her first movie, to quip that he had known her "before she became a virgin."[14] Not nearly as strong or lucky a woman was June Allyson, an unselfish martyr who spent most of her time in movies waiting, crying, and suffering for the men she so desperately loved in performances that led her to be looked upon by her approving public as the ideal doting wife.[15]

To attract people away from their television sets, Hollywood in the fifties also tried to appeal to the prurient interest of Americans by giving them a constant parade of sex bombs on the screen. In this age of mammary mania, the most popular girl with the big bust was Marilyn Monroe, the preeminent sex goddess of the decade and perhaps of the entire post-World War II period of American history. An illegitimate child whose real name was Norma Jean Baker, Marilyn Monroe lived in twelve different foster homes and an orphanage before marrying (at age sixteen) a twenty-year-old aircraft worker, James Dougherty, in order to escape her rootless life. Discovered by Hollywood from some pictures of her accompanying a *Yank* article on women engaged in war work, she first appeared in small roles in movies in 1950 but quickly rose to become the biggest female star in the business. Between 1950 and 1961 she made twenty-three films—including *The Asphalt Jungle*, *Some Like It Hot*, *The Seven Year Itch*, and *Gentlemen Prefer Blondes*—which grossed over $200 million and brought her great fame and wealth. Although she had considerable acting talent, Hollywood never developed it, preferring instead to exploit her most obvious assets: a 37½–23–36 figure, blond hair, a soft, sexy voice, blue eyes, sexy walk, moist lips, and a beautiful face. Her role rarely varied, for she almost always played the dumb blond who walked around in skintight clothing, sang sexy songs, made innocent but suggestive comments, and naively ignored the verbal and physical advances of the men who panted after her. As the press invariably wrote at that time, she radiated sex, on screen and off. She enjoyed shocking reporters, like the female reporter who, upon learning of a nude calendar photo Marilyn had posed for earlier, gasped, "You mean you didn't have anything on?" and was told by Marilyn, "Oh, yes, I had the radio on,"[16] or the male reporter who asked her what she wore to bed and was told, "I only wear Chanel No. 5."[17]

Many Americans viewed her as the ideal woman, but her real life was far from ideal. She married three times, but her marriage to the aircraft worker lasted only two years, her marriage to Joe DiMaggio only nine months, and her union with Arthur Miller only four years, and she had other men before, during, and after her marriages to these three very different individuals. She took acting lessons under the Strasbergs, hoping to make it as a serious actress like Jean Harlow, Greta Garbo, and others she was often compared to, but the studios still cast her in dumb-blond roles. In the late fifties, the depressed star turned more and more to alcohol and pills and was chronically late for work or absent for days or weeks at a time. Her declining dependability finally caused her to be fired from the cast of *Something's Got to Give* in 1962. Later that year, after a life of tragedy and success, poverty and wealth, obscurity and fame, a life spent in trying to find love and acceptance, she died from an overdose of sleeping pills while a stack of Frank Sinatra records played on her record player. America's favorite sex symbol, the epitome of woman as sex symbol and object, the child woman who was never allowed to grow up, the lusty woman who shocked so many by giving the impression that she liked sex and would have it anytime she wished, had lived only to the age of thirty-six. She had many imitators—Jayne Mansfield (who had her bust, variously reported to measure somewhere between 40 and 44 inches, insured for $1 million), Diana Dors, Mamie Van Doren, Anita Eckberg, and Kim Novak, just to mention a few—but none of her busty contemporaries could match her fame and influence.[18]

Another female type popular in movies in the 1950s was the wily, seductive temptress, the modern-day Eve constantly in wait to snare the modern-day Adam. The most popular native-born actress to play this type was Elizabeth Taylor, a child star who grew up to be a voluptuous beauty and major sex symbol in the fifties. Beautiful, sultry, scandalous in films, she was equally beautiful, sultry, and scandalous in real life. Her love affairs, marriages, and divorces were eagerly followed by her public. She first married Nicky Hilton, hotel-chain heir, divorced him and married Michael Wilding, then divorced Wilding and married Mike Todd, who was tragically killed in a plane crash. She then became involved with the breakup of the Eddie Fisher-Debbie Reynolds marriage, and wound up married to Fisher before the end of the decade. Marriages to Richard Burton and others would follow in the 1960s and 1970s. Her love life on and off the screen scandalized many people and led many, during this decade that venerated marriage, motherhood, and fidelity, to regard her as little more than a vamp and to overlook her very real talents as an actress in such films as *Father of the Bride* (1950), *A Place in the Sun* (1951), *Giant* (1956), and *Suddenly Last Summer* (1959). She usually played strong women, greatly different from the virginal Doris Day and spineless June Allyson, so she did not fit the image of what an ideal woman in America should be.[19]

Although the 1950s was seen as a golden age of marriage and domesticity, the truth of the matter is that the decade saw an acceleration of women, married and single, into the work force, seeking economic survival, a higher standard of living for their families, or personal enrichment and fulfillment. As late as 1940, the number of female workers stood at 13.8 million, representing 25 percent of all workers and 28 percent of all women. The number of female workers rose to 18 million by 1950, 20 million by 1955, and 23.2 million in 1960, when women made up 33 percent of the labor force and when 36 percent of all women were employed. The percentage of married women working outside the home by 1960 had reached 32 percent, representing 54 percent of all working women. Of all the industrial countries of the world, only Russia had a higher proportion of women—married or single—working outside the home.[20] Tradition might have it that a woman's place was in the home, but the statistics indicated otherwise.

Women who entered the job market soon discovered that there was a strong sexual division in labor and pay. The jobs traditionally regarded as female occupations—clerical workers, telephone operators, teachers, nurses, social workers, and assembly-line workers in textile and clothing industries—were low in pay and prestige (though not necessarily in skill). In 1956, an estimated 60 percent of female high-school graduates who entered the labor force went into clerical work, and 60 percent of female college graduates who went to work became teachers. In 1960, women constituted 85 percent of all librarians, 97 percent of all nurses, and 57 percent of all social workers. Few of them went into high-prestige or high-pay occupations. Women in 1960 made up only 3.5 percent of all lawyers, 19 percent of all college presidents and professors, and 6.8 percent of all physicians. In whatever field they worked, women were rarely given jobs in supervisory positions, especially over men, or jobs that required travel, the spending of huge sums of money, or the exercise of great power. And naturally they were paid less; in 1956, among all occupations, the median income of women was only two thirds that of men, and among female factory workers, the pay was 70 percent that of male factory workers, even though they often performed the same job as the men they worked along side of.[21]

The discrimination suffered by women in the economic world was more than matched on the political stage. Although women had had the vote for over three decades, it was still widely believed that they did not know enough about politics to participate deeply in the political process. At political conventions, fashion shows were always arranged to keep the wives of preoccupied politicians entertained while their husbands caucused and conferred. Most married women, though certainly not all, voted as their husbands did, and most women believed, as did the men, that a woman's place was in the home and not in the mayor's office, the governor's mansion, White House, or halls of the state legislatures or U.S. Congress. A woman president was simply out of the question. Women were thought to be too emotional and too ignorant to hold important offices and make daily decisions affecting the lives of millions. In the U.S. Congress, there was only one female senator and nine female representatives in the 1949–1950 session, two senators and eleven representatives in the 1953–1954 session, and one senator and sixteen representatives in the 1959–1960 session.[22] In politics as in other areas of life, men made the rules and kept women in their place.

Women of the fifties were also victimized by the prevailing romantic views on love and sex. Romantic love had long been a part of American culture, but in the 1950s it seemed to reach new heights. Americans were in love with love, and the love they were so obsessed with was an idealistic, sentimental, fictionalized concept that treated courtship as a game and men and women as players, as objects to be pursued and won. It was widely believed that people "fell in love" quickly, with a glance, a stare, a brief conversation, a dance, in an instant of mutual attraction and understanding. Love was regarded as a jealous, exclusive, demanding, and possessive thing, and it was centered upon the physical characteristics of the loved one—his or her physique, clothing, eyes, voice, and touch. Love was also something that no one could live without—for without the desired person, life was empty, meaningless. Love was something that came along just once—there was one right person for everyone, and if you could not capture him or her you were doomed to a lifetime of loneliness and unhappiness. And finally, love was something that should result in marriage and eternal happiness.[23]

The concept of romantic love was shot through with inconsistencies and with an idealistic perception of human beings and their relationships, but it was a vital part of American culture in the fifties. The fact that love and marriage rarely approached the ideal did not seem to undermine most Americans' belief in this concept. Romantic love was the theme of the great majority of American songs, movies, novels, and television shows and even of religious movies like *The Ten Commandments*. Madison Avenue used love as the theme of thousands of ads produced for magazines, newspapers, radio and television, all emphasizing that love could be won by buying certain brands of toothpaste, mouthwash, soap, automobiles, clothing, or a host of other products. Many Americans believed all this, and were not deterred by the warnings of psychologists like Erich Fromm, who suggested that Americans' "obsession with love symbols" was a sign of the absence of real love in people's lives ("when people are hungry," he wrote, "they never tire of the promise of food") and an indication of a widespread incapacity to form true loving relationships.[24]

It was appropriate in this age of romantic love that a young woman from Philadelphia would be swept up in a fairy-tale romance that would culminate in one of the most publicized weddings of the fifties or of any other decade. The princess in the fairy tale was Grace Kelly, daughter of a Philadelphia millionaire, who made eleven motion pictures in a short career from 1951 to 1956, ranging from the western *High Noon* (with Gary Cooper), to the Hitchcock films that made her famous (*Dial M for Murder*, *Rear Window*, and *To Catch a Thief*), and to her last, *High Society* (with Bing Crosby and Frank Sinatra). She also appeared in live television drama on *Kraft Television Theatre*, *Philco Playhouse*, and *Studio One*. Like Audrey Hepburn, she did not fit the usual Hollywood molds represented by Doris Day, Marilyn Monroe, or Elizabeth Taylor, for she had a rare beauty and presence that led her many admirers to describe her as classy, aristocratic, regal, and elegant. At the Cannes Film Festival in 1954 she met the prince of the story, Prince Rainier III of Monaco, perhaps the most eligible bachelor in all of

Europe, and thus began the storybook romance that made her the envy of every schoolgirl in America as she was courted and finally won by the wealthy prince of the tiny Mediterranean principality. In April of 1956, at the age of twenty-six, she was married to Rainier in civil and religious ceremonies in Monaco attended by dignitaries from all over the world and by some 1,800 reporters and photographers, who came to dispatch reports and pictures of the wedding to the interested millions who could not attend. Grace Kelly of Philadelphia now became Her Serene Highness, Princess Grace of Monaco, leaving America and Hollywood behind and entering into a new life as dutiful wife and mother (her first pregnancy was joyfully announced in August) in a splendid European castle. In the romantic, monogamous fifties, it was the stuff that dreams were made of.[25]

The emphasis on romantic love in the fifties naturally meant that there was a great emphasis placed upon youth and beauty—the ideal man and ideal woman were supposed to be good-looking and young. But important as this was for men, it was even more important for women, for men were valued for their intelligence and economic skills while women were idealized for their looks and figures. The cultural obsession with beauty led American women to spend billions of dollars on products and services designed to make them more beautiful and attractive to the male species, and entire industries and advertising agencies grew up to promote and satisfy the need to be beautiful. As Philip Wylie wrote, the real message of most the ads aimed at the American woman was, "Madam, are you a good lay?"[26] Wylie was only half right, for the ads were also asking, "Madam, are you a good watch fob?"—a thing of beauty to be envied by your man's friends. In 1956, American women spent $1.3 billion on toiletries and cosmetics, $660 million at beauty parlors, $400 million on soaps and electric hair dryers and other electric beauty aids, and millions of dollars on lingerie and other clothing chosen not for comfort but for the effect it had on males. Women also spent $65 million in 1956 trying to reduce, with over $25 million of this going to the Slenderella parlors across the United States.[27]

Most women could not live up to the standards of beauty set for them, standards they saw constantly paraded in magazines, advertisements, movies, television, and songs. Just as most men did not look like Clark Gable or Rock Hudson, most women could not measure up to the physical standards of Marilyn Monroe, Debbie Reynolds, or Doris Day, and even young women who came close to these ideals moved away from them as the natural effects of aging and the demands of marriage, childbirth, child rearing, housekeeping, and working outside the home took their toll. For those who were not blessed by nature with voluptuous figures to start with, personal happiness was often hampered by feelings of inadequacy caused by their inability to live up to the standards of beauty popularized in American culture. Men suffered too, of course, but it was upon women that society placed the greatest burden of looking pretty and inviting to the opposite sex. In addition to suffering from sexism, then, women also were discriminated against because of their looks and their age.[28]

Confused as they were about romantic love, Americans were even more confused in their attitudes and practices regarding sex. Nationwide, lip service was given to an unofficial Puritanical code that restricted sexual relations to married heterosexuals, treated homosexuality as either a dangerous abnormality or an affectation to make fun of, and frowned on premarital and extramarital sex relations, heavy petting, masturbation, public nudity, talk about sex (especially in mixed company or before the children), incest and other perversions, and abortion. This code existed in the midst of a society permeated with sexual hypocrisy and titillation. Female clothing was designed to tease, to suggest the great treasures underneath, yet to promise more than the woman was supposed to give. The movies paraded before their audiences a series of voluptuous women who seemed to have sex whenever they wanted to, and magazine and television commercials used sexual titillation to sell a wide range of products. Although nude pictures of white women did not appear in respectable magazines until the arrival of *Playboy* in 1953, several generations of males had grown up looking at pictures of nude dark-skinned natives in the pages of *National Geographic* and ogling naked white women in such nudist magazines as *Sunshine and Health* and *Modern Sunbathing*. There was also an irrepressible network of producers and distributors of pornographic books, magazines, comic books, calendars, playing cards, and hundreds of other erotic items.

All this existed in a nation that advocated celibacy among unmarried people, banned birth control devices in several states, and had a self-imposed movie code that sanctioned much on-screen violence but prohibited the use of the words "pregnant," "virgin," "seduction," and "birth control." The lesson was clear: Nudity and sex are dirty, to be avoided by all except the married, and women are desirable but dirty human beings. No wonder many young people were bewildered about sex or that many women did not know whether to choose Doris Day or Eve as a role model.

The widespread violation of the Puritan code indicated that premarital sexual abstinence was no longer the code of urban, industrial America. Actually, in the fifties several codes seemed to coexist. The most popular was the old Victorian double standard, which allowed men to sow a few wild oats while requiring "good" women to remain pure until the wedding night. But the Victorian code had been under attack since before the outbreak of the First World War, and by the fifties it was crumbling rapidly. Large numbers of unmarried people, particularly young dating couples, had loosened the code enough to allow for quite a bit of heavy petting, and many a young woman prided herself on being a "good girl" long after her virginity had become little more than a technicality. As the fifties proceeded and sexual attitudes became more liberal, even premarital intercourse was held by some to be permissible between two people who loved each other and planned to marry—after all, the reasoning went, it's *so* hard to wait, and we *do* plan to get married. Still others, but certainly a minority, claimed that premarital intercourse was permissible even when it was based on a simple physical attraction without love and with no plans for marriage.[29] This was a radical, almost scandalous view, and it was fraught with great danger, because the existing birth-control methods were often unreliable or even unavailable (New York and Connecticut banned the sale of contraceptives) to many dating couples, and abortion was illegal. The birth control pill was still in the research stage and would not be marketed until 1960.

Ever since colonial times, Americans had tried to write their sexual codes into law. As the fifties opened, almost every state in the union had laws prohibiting homosexual acts, oral sex, anal sex, and sex with animals, and a few states even outlawed sexual intercourse between unmarried heterosexual couples. Typical was the law of Kansas, which imposed severe penalties for "every person who shall be convicted of the detestable and abominable crime against nature, committed with mankind or with beast." Some states went as far as Indiana, which provided stiff sentences for "whoever entices, allures, instigates or aids any person under the age of twenty-one (21) years to commit masturbation or self-pollution," with the crime being punishable by as much as a $1,000 fine and fourteen years in prison.[30] The problems of apprehending or convicting people involved in these sexual acts made enforcement difficult if not impossible, and as the decade wore on and sexual attitudes slowly changed, even occasional attempts to enforce these laws ended, and some laws were rewritten in more permissive language or eliminated altogether.

As the decade progressed, there were growing indications that America's sexual attitudes and practices were changing. One of the earliest signs of these changes came with the publication of Dr. Alfred C. Kinsey's reports on American sexuality. A professor of zoology at the University of Indiana, Kinsey had spent twenty years studying the gall wasp before he turned his attention to the investigation of human sexuality, a topic he pursued with such obsession that Mrs. Kinsey is supposed to have remarked that "I hardly see him at night since he took up sex."[31] His studies resulted in the publication in 1948 of *Sexual Behavior in the Human Male*,[32] a very comprehensive statistical study based on some 18,000 case histories. Although it was 804 pages long and cost $6.50, it sold over a quarter of a million copies within a year's time. In 1953 he published his 842-page study of *Sexual Behavior in the Human Female*,[33] based on some 6,000 case histories. He was so obsessed with the collection of sexual case histories that he invited to his Institute for Sex Research the controversial Christine

Jorgenson, who as George Jorgenson had undergone a sex-change operation in Copenhagen in 1952 that made headlines across the world. He also once traveled 1,500 miles to interview a man who claimed sexual experiences with hundreds of adults, children, and animals.[34] Never had so much sexual data been collected, analyzed, and disseminated. Although the Kinsey reports contained many inaccuracies in the handling of samples and statistics, they did provide important insights into the sexual behavior of the American people.

When Americans read the Kinsey reports, or the many summaries of them in newspapers and magazines, they were shocked, for Kinsey's researches suggested that Americans, male and female, married and unmarried, were much more sexually active than most people had thought. If Kinsey were to be believed, from 68 to 90 percent of American males and some 50 percent of American females had engaged in premarital intercourse, 92 percent of the males and 62 percent of the females had engaged in masturbation at least once, 37 percent of males and 13 percent of females had engaged in at least one homosexual experience, 50 percent of males and 26 percent of females committed adultery before they reached the age of forty, some 8 percent of the males and 4 percent of the females had engaged in some form of sexual contact with animals, and 83 percent of males and 37 percent of females had experienced nocturnal orgastic dreams. The reports also confirmed what most people knew and what the double standard sanctioned: Males were much more promiscuous than females, having earlier sexual experiences, more partners, and more frequent orgasms. But what was not expected, and what was so shocking, was the revelation that women were much more promiscuous than people had thought, that each generation of women was getting more promiscuous than the previous one, and that more and more women were sleeping in the nude and engaging in sexual practices that previous generations—and the American sexual code of the fifties—had deemed unnatural, abhorrent, immoral, and even illegal.[35]

The Kinsey reports shocked the nation. Many bookstores refused to stock the books, while others kept them behind the counter, away from the curious eyes of juveniles or casual browsers who wanted to look, not to buy. Some communities banned the sale of the books, and some librarians refused to buy them for their collection or decided to put them in their noncirculating collection, forcing red-faced patrons to come to the desk and ask the librarian for them. Even many college libraries refused to put the books in open circulation. Kinsey was often attacked in the press, and so much controversy arose over the book that the Rockefeller Foundation, which had financed his Institute for Sex Research, dropped its support in the mid-1950s after the uproar over the 1953 study on female sexuality.[36] But in spite of the controversy surrounding the Kinsey studies, they were read, and they had an enormous influence. Many people read the reports to see if they were "normal" or not, and the widespread discussions of his studies helped to liberalize ideas about sex, to bring more understanding and toleration of homosexuality, more understanding of female sexuality, and a greater inclination to study sex with the same attitudes employed in investigating other human functions. The Kinsey reports, like the writings of Freud and Havelock Ellis earlier and Masters and Johnson later, helped to demystify sex, to liberalize American attitudes about it, and to have it looked upon as a commonplace human activity rather than some secret, dirty, prohibited perversion.[37]

Kinsey's 1953 study of female sexuality was joined in that same year by the publication of an English translation of Simone de Beauvoir's *The Second Sex*,[38] a 732-page encyclopedic study of women. A famous French novelist, essayist, existentialist, and mistress of Jean-Paul Sartre, de Beauvoir drew on several disciplines to present a pioneer study of the nature of women and their long history of oppression by men. Her major argument was that throughout human history, from ancient times to the present, the physically stronger male species had used its power to control society and to dominate women, who were regarded as objects rather than equal persons. In short, women had been treated as second-class citizens, just like Jews, blacks, and other minority groups. This had deprived them of their equal rights and power in society and stymied their search for fulfillment as human beings. One of the major weapons used by men to dominate was the perpetuation of the myth that women's primary function in life was as wives and mothers. De Beauvoir denied that motherhood was woman's sole reason for existing, claimed that a woman could be a truly good mother only if she was a whole, fulfilled woman, called for equal work opportunities for women, and urged men and women to work together to end the centuries-long oppression of women.[39]

Perhaps the most revealing thing about the reaction to the appearance of *The Second Sex* in the United States was that there was so little reaction. It was not widely discussed in the press, on television, or in academic circles, probably because the author was a foreigner and a woman and because the work was a difficult and controversial study of a problem that most Americans refused to recognize as a problem. Reviewers tended to treat it in a hostile, condescending manner. In the *Atlantic Monthly*, Charles J. Rolo claimed that there was a "chip in Mademoiselle de Beauvoir's shoulder" and contended that "so extreme is her picture of woman's enslavement that one doubts that" such conditions exist "even in the harem of the most unspeakable merchant of Baghdad."[40] In the *Saturday Review*, which did consider the book important enough to be reviewed by a panel of experts from various fields, noted psychiatrist Karl A. Menninger called the book "a scholarly and at the same time a pretentious and inflated tract on feminism" and predicted that some readers "will be disquieted by the plaintive, mildly paranoid wails that dot almost every page." Other panel members disagreed, however. Author Philip Wylie asserted that "what this great woman sets forth is the Truth," and noted anthropologist Margaret Mead wrote that although the book was encumbered by factual errors and bias, "the main argument . . . is a sound one."[41] But most publications gave little attention to the book, as did most women, though future leaders of the feminist movement would later credit the book with being one of the catalysts of the modern woman's movement.

Another landmark in the history of sex attitudes also came in 1953 with the publication of the first issue of *Playboy* magazine, started by Hugh Hefner, a young graduate of the University of Illinois who had formerly worked for *Esquire* magazine. In December of 1953 he launched his new publication with $600 borrowed from a bank and finance company (with his furniture and 1950 Studebaker used as collateral) and about $7,000 raised by selling stock to his friends. Priced at fifty cents per copy, the first issue sold around 53,000 copies, largely because it contained a nude photograph of Marilyn Monroe, which Hefner had bought from a calendar printer for $200. The first *Playboy* was primarily a girlie magazine, though Hefner intended the magazine to be much more than that. In an editorial in the first issue, he claimed that "we believe we are filling a publishing need only slightly less important than the one just taken care of by the *Kinsey Report*."[42] The surprising profits from the first issue enabled Hefner to put out a second and third, all edited on a card table in his Chicago apartment, and from then on sales of the magazine soared. Within a year, each issue was selling over 175,000 copies, and the circulation rose rapidly after that, climbing to over a million by 1960. Hefner's wealth rose with his success, and in 1959 he branched out and began to organize Playboy Clubs in Chicago and other large cities across the country, charging from $25 to $100 for membership keys and the opportunity to be served drinks and food by scantily-clad waitresses sporting bunny-ears headgear. By 1961, *Playboy*'s profits before taxes had reached nearly $1.8 million, and profits from his Playboy Clubs had climbed to almost $1.5 million.[43]

Hefner had obviously found the right formula for success, and he was apparently meeting the needs, as he anticipated, of a large audience. The magazine was aimed at urban males between the ages of eighteen and thirty-four who liked a sophisticated magazine dealing with the good (male) life. Although the nudes, bawdy cartoons, off-color jokes, and articles and stories with sexual themes were always a prominent part of the magazine, *Playboy* also featured short stories and nonfiction by some of the decade's best writers (including Carl Sandburg, Alberto Moravia, Evelyn Waugh, and Nelson Algren) and sophisticated features on food, drink, entertainment, sports, sports cars, men's fashions, and music. The centerfold and other nudes were always antiseptic, airbrushed photographs exposing the breasts but deftly concealing the other private parts of the female body by clothing, a book, a fan, the lighting, or the angle of the camera. The centerfold was the most talked about part of the magazine, and jokes abounded all across the country about the thousands of young males who were growing up thinking that women had a staple where the navel was supposed to be. The magazine spawned a host of imitators, like *Escape*, *Nugget*, *Rogue*, and *Gent*, but they were essentially girlie magazines with few if any of the other sophisticated features of Hefner's original.

In the beginning, the magazine was widely attacked by conservative ministers and concerned citizens, newsstands kept copies behind the counter so they would not be read by juveniles or nonbuyers, subscribers received their copies in the mails in plain brown envelopes, and men who purchased the magazine at newsstands and drug stores often looked furtively around as they paid for the magazine and requested that it be put in a paper bag. Some small towns attempted to ban it from stores and libraries, and in 1955 Hefner had to go to court to force the U.S. Post Office to grant his application for second-class mailing privileges normally accorded other magazines.[44] But by the end of the decade *Playboy* was openly displayed on many newsstands and even so-called respectable men openly admitted that they read it, though they often hastened to explain that they bought it for the articles and not for the pictures.

*Playboy* had a great influence. Like the Kinsey report, the magazine helped to demystify sex, though instead of statistical analysis it used portraits of nude women in full color and treated sex like any other aspect of human existence. It also celebrated the idea that sex is fun and that it is a normal activity, not something to be ashamed of. It did, unfortunately, often treat sex in juvenile, almost locker-room style, and it contributed to the sexism of the time by portraying women as objects put on earth as man's plaything. But in the long run it helped promote more open attitudes and discussions about sex.

Another milestone in the history of sex attitudes came in September of 1956 with the publication of the controversial novel *Peyton Place*,[45] written by Grace Metalious, a thirty-two-year-old housewife and wife of a school principal in the small town of Gilmanton, New Hampshire. A first novel by an unpolished writer, *Peyton Place* lacked sophistication and literary merit, but as the book jacket promised, it was an "extraordinary new novel that lifts the lid off a small New England town." The novel offered a scorching tale of lust, rape, incest, adultery, murder, alcoholism, and hypocrisy in what had been a respectable little town. The subjects, language, and sexual content of *Peyton Place* all seem tame by today's standards, but in 1956 people were shocked—and apparently curious and entertained, since the novel sold 6 million copies by March of 1958 and soon at 10 million became the best-selling novel up to that time, bypassing Erskine Caldwell's *God's Little Acre*.

*Peyton Place* was a sensation. Most reviewers dismissed it as trash, while some agreed with Princeton professor Carlos Baker, who in *The New York Times* referred to the novel as a "small town peep show," called Metalious "a pretty fair writer for a first novelist," but offered his hope that "Mrs. Metalious can turn her emancipated talents to less lurid purposes."[46] Some small towns banned the book, teachers confiscated it from their students, and librarians refused to put it in their circulating collection, but millions of readers bought the hardcover or paperback edition or borrowed it from friends. Housewives read it, talked about it, and lent it to their friends, while junior high and high school students kept it in their lockers and pocketbooks or put false covers on it so that their scandalized teachers would not confiscate it. It was widely condemned as an obscene book, but millions read (and often reread) "the dirty parts," reviewing again and again the passage where Thomas Makris orders Constance to "untie the top of your bathing suit . . . I want to feel your breasts against me when I kiss you," or the part where she begs Makris, "Again, darling. Again," or the part where Allison loses her virginity in a very explicit scene and tells her older, married lover that "I thought I was dying . . . and it was the loveliest feeling in the world."[47] These people enjoyed sex—even the women enjoyed it, and they were not ashamed to enjoy it! And to naive teenagers of the day, and so many of them were, the book seemed to offer, through its explicit sex scenes, instructions on how to make love. Like the *Kinsey Report*, *Playboy*, and other publishing events of the decade, *Peyton Place* helped to demystify sex. Its influence was magnified by the 1957 movie, a tame version of the novel, which was nominated for nine Academy Awards but won none.

*Peyton Place* was soon followed by other literary challenges to the conservative moral code. In 1958 Vladimir Nabokov's novel *Lolita*, featuring the famous nymphet, was number three on the fiction best-seller list, selling 153,000 hardback and over 3 million paperback copies and later being made into a movie. In that same year, after numerous court battles and after being smuggled in from Europe and read by countless thousands of American readers for three decades, D. H. Lawrence's *Lady Chatterley's Lover* was published in an unexpurgated Grove Press edition, and in 1959 it rose to number five on the best-seller list. It, too, was made into a movie, albeit in a rather prim, old-fashioned interpretation. And in 1960, Irving Wallace's *The Chapman Report* reached the number four spot.[48] All of these novels were roundly condemned by town councils, libraries, and ministerial groups. But millions of curious citizens read them anyway.

The movie industry was also undergoing rapid changes as it attempted to draw people away from television by satisfying their apparently growing prurient interests. The Production Code, which had governed Hollywood since the 1920s, broke down as the industry tried to deal more directly with sensitive subjects. Beginning with *From Here to Eternity* (1953), with its lusty beach scene and portrayal of adultery, Hollywood moved to deal with drugs in *The Man with the Golden Arm* (1955), with miscegenation in *Island in the Sun* (1957), with homosexuality in *Compulsion* (1959), and with abortion in *Blue Denim* (1959). Hollywood also turned out several movies of Tennessee Williams's plays with sensitive themes and sultry performances by Elizabeth Taylor, Carroll Baker, and other actresses of the day: *A Streetcar Named Desire* (1951), *The Rose Tattoo* (1955), *Baby Doll* (1956), *Cat on a Hot Tin Roof* (1958), *Suddenly Last Summer* (1959), and *The Fugitive Kind* (1959). The most controversial of these movies was *Baby Doll*, appearing a few months after the novel *Peyton Place* in the winter of 1956. *Time* magazine called *Baby Doll* "just possibly the dirtiest American-made motion picture that has ever been legally permitted" and asserted that "the moviegoer can hardly help wondering if the sociological study has not degenerated into the prurient peep."[49] Apparently others agreed, for some cities banned the movie, others forced the theaters to cut some of the offensive scenes, the U.S. Army refused to show it to GIs in its armed forces theaters, the Catholic League of Decency banned it, and New York's Francis Cardinal Spellman called it "revolting" and "morally repellant."[50] But long lines formed to see it, and it was a smash at the box office.

There were still other signs of change. In 1957, Elizabeth Taylor's reign as the supreme celluloid temptress was challenged by French import Brigitte Bardot, who was only twenty-two years old when *And God Created Woman* shocked and titillated American audiences. One cause of her appeal was her nationality—the French were supposed to know more about sex and deal with it more openly than Americans, and actually to brag about enjoying it. She also had a rare combination of youth, beauty, sexuality, seductiveness, and animalism—a little girl, sex kitten, and whore all combined in one beautiful body. And she was willing, she almost begged, to disrobe before the camera. She was not the ideal American woman—she was too carnal, too independent, too strong.[51] She was also widely condemned. The Rev. James T. Lyng of Lake Placid, New York, for example, called the film "an assault on each and every woman of our community and nation, living or dead—our mothers, sisters, wives, and daughters."[52] All across the country the film was boycotted and banned, and children were forbidden by their parents to see it. And all across the country people flocked to the theater to stand in long ticket lines to see it (the film grossed over $4 million in the United States) and her other films. Bardot's films helped to get Americans interested in other foreign films, such as *La Strada* and *The Seventh Seal*, which were often shown in small theaters and referred to as art flicks.[53] In the long run her films also helped liberalize the film codes of Hollywood studios, which realized that in spite of all the uproar surrounding films like *And God Created Woman*, Americans wanted more flesh in their movies and would pay to see it.

At the same time that Bardot was raising temperatures inside the theaters, Sandra Dee was helping to redefinc thc character of the girl next door. Miss Dee possessed many of the little-girl traits of Debbie Reynolds and the girl-next-door traits of Doris Day, but exhibited more sexuality. In *The Reluctant Debutante* (1958), *Imitation of Life* (1959), *A Summer Place* (1959), and *Gidget* (1959), she established herself as one of the top-ten box office attractions in the country. In *A Summer Place*, in which she costarred with Troy Donahue, unmarried Sandra was even gotten pregnant by her boyfriend—a calamity that would never have happened to Debbie or Doris. Within four months of its opening in December of 1959, *A Summer Place* had grossed almost $2 million. The popularity of this movie was more evidence that teenagers, women, and the times were changing, that the conservative moral codes of the fifties were about to give way to the sexual revolution of the sixties.[54]

By 1960, more and more women were coming to examine their sexual, marital, maternal, and career roles as more of them went to college, entered the job market, read the more sexually explicit novels and viewed the more open movies of the time, and considered what they had read about sex and women in *The Second Sex*, the *Kinsey Reports*, and *Playboy*. But few women were ready to rebel in 1960. Most had simply been too conditioned to accept their roles as inferior beings, and rebellion against their oppressors would mean rebellion against the people they loved: their fathers, brothers, boyfriends, husbands, and other close relatives and friends. This intimate relationship with their opressors, and the latter's continuing economic and emotional control, made rebellion too difficult for most women in 1960. But it would come, and when it did, it would radically change the face of America.

# 17

# *God's Country*

In 1955 Morris L. Ernst, a lawyer, civil liberties activist, and author, published a remarkable book, *Utopia 1976*, predicting that in just a little over twenty years, on the two-hundreth anniversary of the founding of the nation, the United States would be an industrial paradise. The work week would be reduced to thirty hours or less, travel to foreign countries would be commonplace, spectator sports would decline as people became participants rather than spectators, people would use their leisure time more creatively, cheap nuclear power and heretofore untapped sources of power (solar, wind, and ocean) would be available for homes and factories, food production would be revolutionized through climate control and the use of new techniques and chemicals, and homes would be changed so much by better construction and new appliances and gadgets that they would be "unrecognizable, in 1976, by the people of today."[1] Prosperity, along with new forms of contraception (including a pill), would bring earlier marriages, better child planning and rearing, better family relations, and more women entering the work force because they wanted to work rather than because they had to work.

And that was not all. There would be more and better schools and teachers and a boom in education at all levels, including the fledgling field of adult education. Americans would also be much healthier, for "all the present important diseases will be detectable, preventable, and curable by 1976," including the common cold. Travel would be revolutionized. Nuclear energy would be used to power airplanes, rockets would be used to transport mail from city to city, vertical lift airplanes would become commonplace, and automobiles would become smaller, more comfortable, and more functional, with less emphasis on chrome and other frills. And there would be, he predicted, no nuclear war, for the very destructiveness of the nuclear bomb "reduces its potential for employment." The list of anticipated wonders goes on and on: more material goods, less racism and sexism, more open and natural sexual attitudes and practices, less alcohol and drug abuse. Truly, in Eisenhower's America, the present and the future looked very bright.[2]

Ernst's book was only the latest in a growing body of literature praising the performance of American capitalism and predicting even better things for the future. The first half of the decade had seen an outpouring of paeans to American capitalism, including Peter Drucker's *The New Society* (1950), the editors of *Fortune's U.S.A.: The Permanent Revolution* (1951), Frederick Lewis Allen's *The Big Change: America Transforms Itself, 1900–1950* (1952), John Kenneth Galbraith's *American Capitalism* (1952), and David M. Potter's *People of Plenty: Economic Abundance and the American Character* (1954). A common theme of these and dozens of lesser-known works was that American capitalism was revolutionizing American society, producing a plethora of consumer goods, narrowing the gap between rich and poor, and producing an unprecedented worker's paradise. Ernst's *Utopia 1976* simply carried the optimism of these more earth-bound works to its logical conclusion, and in doing so he was not standing out on a literary limb. In the midfifties, many other rosy predictions appeared, most notably the editors of *Fortune's The Fabulous Future: America in 1980*,[3] an anthology of several articles attempting to foretell what America would be like twenty-five years in the future. Containing articles by eleven distinguished Americans—among them Adlai E. Stevenson, David Sarnoff, George Meany, Earl Warren, and Henry R. Luce—*The Fabulous Future* predicted that the expansion of the American economy and technology under the free enterprise system would create a utopian life-style within the next twenty-five years. Similar views were expressed in dozens of magazine articles celebrating the progress of the previous ten or twenty years and projecting even more wonders in the years ahead. As these literary effusions made clear, the peace and prosperity of the mid-1950s was leading many Americans to believe that it was a good time to be alive, and that Eisenhower's America was a good place to live.

The Eisenhower years were, indeed, a time of confidence and optimism for many Americans. Almost everywhere they looked, they saw reason to be content with the present and optimistic about the future. The great compromiser and soother, Dwight Eisenhower, was leading the nation away from the dangerous international strife and debilitating domestic political quarrels of the Truman years. Stalin had been in his grave since early 1953, and his successors were following the policy of peaceful coexistence, toning down Russia's traditional anti-Western rhetoric, meeting with Western leaders at Geneva, signing a peace treaty with Austria, and taking other steps to continue the thaw in the Cold War. The Korean War was a fading memory, and so was McCarthy and the hysterical period of anticommunism in America. And the economic system, though still plagued with occasional downturns and inequities, was providing most Americans with unprecedented prosperity and leisure time.

Medical advances were also giving Americans cause for optimism, for the decade was seeing dramatic breakthroughs in the prevention and treatment of many of man's oldest maladies. Penicillin was already in widespread use, and beginning with Terramycin, developed in 1950, the march of antibiotics continued, until by the middle of the decade over a dozen varieties were in common use, along with hundreds of other drugs used for the treatment of arthritis, diabetes, cancer, heart disease, allergies, diseased organs, and many other medical problems which only a few years before would have brought debilitation or death. In 1956, 80 percent of the prescription drugs in use had been unknown as recently as 1941. In addition, surgeons were making significant advancements in open-heart surgery, the repair and artificial replacement of heart valves, the installation of pacemakers, and other forms of heart surgery, along with revolutionary developments in kidney surgery, kidney transplants, and surgical treatment of other organ disorders. Tranquilizers, developed by the French in the late 1940s, were not mass-marketed in the United States until the midfifties, when Miltown appeared, but by the end of the decade middle- and upper-class Americans, particularly suburban women, were paying almost $5 million a year for the 1.2 million pounds of tranquilizers ("don't give a damn pills," *Time* called them) they were using to cope with the problems of modern society.[4] And in 1953, at Cambridge University, an English physicist, Francis Crick, and an American chemist, James D. Watson, uncovered the secret of life, DNA (deoxyribonucleic acid), opening the door to revolutionary developments in genetics and medical research.

But undoubtedly the most dramatic medical wonder of the decade was the discovery of a preventive for polio. After years of research and testing, Dr. Jonas Salk of the Pittsburgh Medical School developed his killed-virus polio vaccine, and in 1955 the federal government helped sponsor a nationwide inoculation program that encouraged millions of children to stand in line to receive immunity from the dread disease. After epidemics afflicting over 58,000 in 1952 and 38,000 in 1954 and again in 1955, the inoculation program would produce a dramatic decline in the number of new cases, down to 5,700 in 1958 and to 3,277 in 1960. Quite understandably, Dr. Salk was hailed as a medical giant and national hero. Further improvements would come with Dr. Albert Sabin's live-virus vaccine, developed at the end of the decade but not licensed for use until the early 1960s. Sabin's vaccine would soon replace Salk's, and by 1971 the number of new cases would drop to only twenty-one. One of the oldest and most-feared of all diseases, polio would at last be conquered, at least in the United States and other developed countries.[5]

The decade was also seeing a parade of scientific and technological discoveries. Older wonders, like television, transistors, and computers, were being steadily improved upon, while new ones appeared with amazing regularity. Among other advances, the decade saw the discovery of einsteinium and several other new elements, the discovery of antiprotons and antineutrons, the unveiling of Einstein's General Field Theory, the synthetic manufacture of amino acids, the first artificial earth satellites, moon rockets, solar batteries, atomic-powered submarines, atomic power plants, the first jet transports, rocket planes traveling over 2,000 miles an hour, and weather satellites—just to mention a few. There was another side to the coin of course, for science and technology were also being harnessed to build thermonuclear bombs, supersonic bombers, nuclear missiles, and other weapons of death. But most Americans were able to put these horrors in the backs of their minds while they enjoyed the positive benefits of science and technology and contemplated the wonders still to come.

For most Americans in the midfifties, the United States was a very good place to live. This was not true for many blacks and other minority groups, or for the poor of all races. And it did not seem true to a small group of critics who condemned Eisenhower's affluent America for its materialism, its worship of success, its complacency, its mediocrity, its consumerism, its racism, its hypocrisy, and its mass culture, which was reducing the arts to the lowest common denominator. But most Americans were satisfied with themselves and with their country. Not since the 1920s had so many worshipped at the altar of prosperity and felt that they lived in God's Country. In spite of the tensions of the Cold War and the growing threat of nuclear annihilation, the prevailing climate of Eisenhower's America was one of confidence, optimism, and complacency.

With this atmosphere, it was perhaps inevitable that the midfifties would be a time of consensus. Not for many decades had so many Americans agreed upon so many fundamental issues. America, it was widely believed, was the greatest country on earth, superior to all contemporary, and even to most past, civilizations. As such, it was morally obligated to lead the free world in the battle against the greatest evil in the history of the world—international communism, led by the Soviet Union. It was widely believed, too, that the American economic system—democratic capitalism or people's capitalism, it was often called—was working exceptionally well, and that while inequalities of wealth and other problems might exist, they would eventually be solved by the continuing economic growth that was providing full employment and abundance for all and moving most Americans into the broad, prosperous middle class. Most felt that the New Deal could not and should not be dismantled, and that the main issue was over how far and how fast it should be extended. Most, even if they had never heard of John Maynard Keynes, believed in Keynesian economics—that the government should manipulate the fiscal and monetary system to promote full employment and prosperity. Most were also coming to believe that social problems, insofar as they existed, could be solved through rational study and the intervention of governmental and private agencies. And most believed that the United States was not, and never really had been, troubled with class divisions and class struggles like those that had plagued Europe for so many decades.[6]

Signs of this conservative consensus—the Eisenhower Consensus, it was sometimes called—were easy to find. Most of the electorate moved toward the political center and so did the political parties, causing Adlai Stevenson to remark during the 1952 campaign that "the strange alchemy of our time has somehow converted the Democrats into the truly conservative party of this country,"[7] and ADA chairman Joseph Rauh to complain in 1956 that "the Congressional Democrats have become practically indistinguishable from the party they allegedly oppose."[8] As most people drifted toward the broad political center, the socialist and the communist parties dwindled to insignificant factions. Although there was racial conflict, there was less class conflict than there had been in the thirties and forties, and organized labor had lost what little radicalism it had ever had and was striving for wage increases and fringe benefits that would give blue collar workers the same life-style and security enjoyed by the white collar and professional classes. High school students, in spite of their fondness for rock music and leather-jacket-clad idols, were as conservative on most issues as their parents were, and college students were earning the Silent Generation label as they buried their heads in their books and prepared for secure jobs in the corporation womb. There was a return to family life and to the home. And increasingly, in an age of mass production and mass consumption, Americans were buying the same consumer goods, living in the same types of houses, moving to standardized suburbs that varied little from New York to Los Angeles, eating the same foods, wearing the same dress, watching the same television shows and commercials, and thinking the same thoughts. America was becoming homogenized.

Why had this occurred? Basically, the conservative consensus developed out of the upheavals and anxieties of the depression, Second World War, and Cold War years. Americans wanted a breathing spell from personal sacrifices, social and economic experimentation, and change. They wanted to go forward, but not too far and not too fast. The wealth seemed more evenly distributed than ever before, and capitalism seemed to be working so well that there was no reason to make radical changes in it. Communism and fascism, the philosophies that did advocate radical changes, had both been discredited—fascism by the horrors perpetrated by the Nazis and the Japanese during World War II and communism by the aggressive actions of Russia in postwar Europe and China in postwar Asia. The discrediting of these extremes seemed to make the moderate middle of the political spectrum the only respectable place to be. In addition, the threat of international and internal communism naturally caused most Americans to rally around Old Glory and to equate Americanism with anticommunism and even with antisocialism and anti all ideologies of the left. And the tensions of the Cold War along with the rootlessness of an age of rapid economic, social, and geographical mobility, combined to encourage people to find what security, stability, and meaning they could in a renewed emphasis on religion, family life, and other traditional values. And other broad homogenizing forces were at work too, including the decline in immigration and the corresponding drop in the number of foreign-born in the population, mass production and mass consumption, the growth of television and the rest of the mass media, and the spread of common values by the nationwide growth of suburbs and corporations.[9]

The conservatism of the period was not confined to the masses. It was also characteristic of the intellectuals, the class that historically had often been alienated from bourgeois values and had served as the conscience of a complacent society. But like the rest of the population, the intellectual classes had moved toward conservative, middle-class respectability. The intelligentsia were sharing the prosperity of the time, for many had comfortable jobs in universities, foundations, the government, industry, and mass communications. It is not surprising that they adopted materialism, success, family life, and other middle-class values and became more interested in financial security than in political and social causes.[10] They also felt, like the rest of the population, that capitalism was working well and that America was becoming a land of plenty and a place where poverty was being abolished. Quite naturally, they also saw the conflict between the free world and totalitarian communism as the major issue of the day and tended to rally around the flag like everyone else.

There were still other reasons for the intellectual conservatism of the time. Intellectuals had been one of the major targets of McCarthy and the other anticommunist witchhunters. In a time of anticommunism, they were remembered for their alleged sins of the past, when many had embraced or flirted with communism and other ideologies of the left as a way of curing the depression or fighting the rise of fascism. In a time of anti-intellectualism, they were widely branded as eggheads, bleeding-heart liberals, pinkos, fellow travelers, and dupes. Under this pressure, they became less outspoken and tried to show that they were good Americans and anticommunists like everybody else. Hence the rash of confessions, repentances, and conversions in the late forties and early fifties, the parade of informers in Hollywood and elsewhere, and the flight from noble causes, even from pacifism or civil rights or civil liberties. Most intellectuals took refuge in moderate liberalism or even neoconservatism and avoided the ideals and causes of the left.[11]

The left, as Daniel Bell and others pointed out, virtually disappeared in the fifties. Most intellectuals were democratic liberals who supported the anticommunist and counterrevolutionary policy of containment in foreign affairs, distrusted all mass movements and radical ideologies, believed that capitalism was an essentially sound system that was creating a workers' paradise, supported only modest extension of New Deal social welfare programs, and maintained that America was a pluralistic society in which business, labor, farmers, and other groups competed with each other as equals to secure the blessings of a successful capitalistic system. A sizable number of intellectuals, including Russell Kirk, Clinton Rossiter, and Peter Viereck, made up a new camp of scholarly conservatives who espoused what was called the new conservatism. Although many shades of opinion could be found within this group, most of the new conservatives had high praise for free enterprise, private property, leadership by the political and cultural elite, and traditional institutions and values, while showing contempt for big government, social welfare programs, leftist ideologies, mass politics, mass society, mass movements, mass anything.[12]

No wonder many people of the time had trouble telling intellectual conservatives and intellectual liberals apart. No wonder that *Time* magazine would write, in a 1956 cover story on intellectuals, that most of them were not alienated from America as many intellectuals had been in the past, and in fact were happy with their country. Citing Jacques Barzun as an example of "a growing host of men of ideas who not only have the respect of their nation, but who return the compliment," *Time* declared that American intellectuals had not fled the nation to live a self-imposed exile in Europe, as they had in the 1920s. In the 1950s, in spite of McCarthy, "the American intellectual stayed at home and even found himself feeling at home."[13] No wonder that sociologist Daniel Bell, himself an intellectual of the consensus school, would declare in *The End of Ideology*, published at the end of the decade, that the fifties had seen the exhaustion of the old intellectual ideologies, causes, and utopian visions.

The intellectual conservatism of the time showed up in many areas. Besides appearing in the hymns to capitalism published by economic and social thinkers, it was revealed in the writings of a large number of influential academic historians who made up a new school of "consensus" or "neoconservative" historians. Louis Hartz, Clinton Rossiter, Daniel J. Boorstin, Richard Hofstadter, and others wrote new interpretations of the American past that downplayed class, sectional, and ideological conflicts while emphasizing that the movement of American history had been characterized by consensus and continuity in basic American values and purposes. According to Henry Steele Commager, for example, the New Deal "was no revolution, but rather the culmination of half a century of historical development," and Franklin Roosevelt was "the greatest conservative since Alexander Hamilton."[14] Other consensus historians claimed that the American Revolution was not a radical revolution but a conservative one that preserved the freedoms that Americans were already enjoying, that there were few differences between the Hamiltonians and the Jeffersonians, and that the antebellum North and South were really not as distinct as they had been made out to be. Many other historians of the fifties, such as Arthur Schlesinger, Jr., still reminded their readers of the great conflicts in America's past, but the consensus and continuity school dominated American historiography for most of the decade.[15]

This conservative view of America's past was also taught in the public schools, where historians collaborated with educators to produce textbooks emphasizing traditional American values and portraying the United States as the greatest nation in the world. The United States was pictured as a land that had never had many internal conflicts, had always served as the melting pot of the world's people and cultures, had always been in the forefront of democracy, freedom, and technology, and was made up of common-sense people who were almost uniformly practical, hardworking, tolerant, patriotic, and civic minded. Unlike textbooks of the past, which had usually given little attention to foreign affairs, the texts of the fifties devoted considerable space to America's rise to global power and to her leadership in the life-and-death struggle between Western democracy and totalitarian communism.[16] Because of the McCarthy hysteria and the desire to acquire large markets for their books all across the country, publishers were very concerned not to offend anyone, an understandable goal at a time when southern states would not adopt textbooks showing white and black children playing together, when some states required textbook authors to sign loyalty oaths before their books could be adopted, and when the legislature of Texas passed a resolution requiring that "the American history courses in the public schools emphasize in the textbooks our glowing and throbbing history of hearts and souls inspired by wonderful American principles and traditions."[17] This bland, patriotic, false interpretation of the past would be taught in public schools all across the nation until the events of the 1960s forced educators to provide a more realistic picture of the American past.

The decline of ideology and other aspects of the conservatism of the age also showed up in literature. Much of the fiction of the day was concerned with individual alienation that led to despair, suicide, murder, rape, and other desperate acts of lonely individuals in mass society. Except for Ralph Ellison's *The Invisible Man* (1952) and a few other novels, there were few novels of social protest or social criticism like those that had often characterized American fiction in the past. This was, after all, the age of Salinger, not of Sinclair Lewis and H. L. Mencken. Even Jack Kerouac and the other Beatniks, who felt so out of place in Eisenhower's middle America, retreated into individual preoccupations with their music, poetry, Zen Buddhism, and sex and drugs, instead of serving as a literary vanguard for social and economic change.[18]

This is not to say that there were no serious critics of America in the fifties, for there were. The growing trend toward conformity was dissected by many writers, notably David Riesman in *The Lonely Crowd* (1950) and William H. Whyte in *The Organization Man* (1957). Will Herberg complained of the secularization and homogenization of religion in *Protestant–Catholic–Jew* (1955). In *The Power Elite* (1956) and other works, sociologist C. Wright Mills protested that America was ruled by an elite group of business, political, and military rulers and that the great majority of the population was essentially powerless. Philosopher Herbert Marcuse used Freudian psychology and Marxism in his *Eros and Civilization* (1955) to criticize the whole range of political, social, and economic values and institutions in a society he viewed as a quasi-totalitarian technocracy ruled by a small but powerful group of experts in business, government, and the other seats of power. In 1959, popular sociologist Vance Packard depicted the American people's obsession with class and status in *The Status Seekers*. And at the end of the decade, in *Growing Up Absurd* (1960), Paul Goodman emerged as a major critic of the schools and other institutions that were stifling the growth and creativity of the nation's people—especially the young. Many of these writers would become the heroes of the New Left and counterculture of the 1960s, but in the 1950s they were minority voices in a complacent land.[19]

It is not surprising that the conservative fifties saw a major revival of religion. Year after year the statistics pointed to unprecedented increases in church membership, which grew from 86.8 million in 1950 to over 114 million in 1960.[20] Each year saw record contributions to churches and other religious organizations, construction of new churches and synagogues and related religious buildings, record enrollments in college religion courses, overcrowding in religious seminaries, and growth in the prestige of clergymen. Poll after poll showed that each year more and more Americans affirmed a belief in God, an afterlife, the Bible as the literal word of God, the power of prayer, and the divinity of Jesus. The radio airwaves were full of religious songs like "I Believe," "It is No Secret What God Can Do," "The Man Upstairs," "Vaya Con Dios," and "Big Fellow in the Sky," while

Hollywood churned out *The Robe, The Ten Commandments, A Man Called Peter*, *Ben Hur*, and other movies with religious themes. The sales of Bibles reached an all-time high, aided by the publication in 1952 of the new—and somewhat controversial—Revised Standard Version, which sold 2 million copies in its first year and continued to sell well throughout the decade. Year after year, nearly half the books on the nonfiction best-seller list were religious books. Americans rushed to the bookstores not only to buy Norman Vincent Peale's *The Power of Positive Thinking* and Catherine Marshall's *A Man Called Peter*, but also books with such titles as *Pray Your Weight Away* and *The Power of Prayer on Plants*.[21] Newspapers and magazines published frequent articles on religious issues and religious leaders, newspapers carried Bible stories in their feature and comics sections, and the influential publisher, Henry R. Luce, a close friend of Billy Graham, Bishop Sheen, and Norman Vincent Peale, saw to it that these and other religious figures got a steady stream of favorable publicity in his *Time* and *Life* magazines.[22]

The return to religion was manifested in many other ways as well. College and high schools regularly held "religious emphasis" weeks, and athletic contests were often preceded by a brief prayer or moment of silent meditation, as were many public and private meetings. Radio and television shows often provided a moment of meditation, and in Dallas officials at a bathing beauty contest decreed that the opening festivities would begin with a prayer.[23] In 1954, the Ideal Toy Company marketed a doll with flexible knees that could be made to "kneel in a praying position," the company's response, it said, to "the resurgence of religious feeling and practice in America today."[24] And in 1956, the Rev. John Sutherland Bonnell of the Fifth Avenue Presbyterian Church in New York introduced Dial-A-Prayer, taking out an ad in *The New York Times* promising that "for a spiritual life in a busy day, Dial-A-Prayer. Circle 6-4200. One Minute of Inspiration in Prayer."[25]

If there was piety throughout the country in the fifties, there was also piety along the Potomac. It began at the top with a president who had attended church only sporadically throughout his life, did not belong to any church until after his election, knew little about the profundities or subtleties of religious faith, yet felt it was important to believe in something. Eisenhower, according to the Republican National Committee, was "not only the political leader, but the spiritual leader of our times."[26] The president exhibited this leadership by beginning his inaugural address with a prayer, by opening each cabinet meeting with a prayer, by attending church with Mamie almost every Sunday, and by making frequent statements about the importance of faith and the close ties between Christianity and Americanism in a country battling against godless communism. The lead float in his 1953 inaugural was "God's Float," exhibiting pictures of churches and other religious places and the slogans "In God We Trust" and "Freedom of Worship" written in Gothic script. He was also close friends with many religious leaders, especially Billy Graham, who often gave the president advice and visited with him at the White House.

The Supreme Court and Congress followed the executive branch's lead in promoting the religious revival. In 1952, shortly before Eisenhower took office, the Court overturned a 1948 decision by proclaiming that it was constitutional for public schools to provide released time for religious instruction. In the midfifties, Congress passed legislation changing the pledge of allegiance to include "under God," making "In God We Trust" an official slogan to be placed on all currency, and appropriating money for a new congressional prayer room. Several senators also supported Senator Flanders's unsuccessful attempt to procure a Constitutional Amendment proclaiming that "this nation devoutly recognizes the authority and law of Jesus Christ, Saviour and Ruler of Nations, through whom are bestowed the blessings of Almighty God."[27] The postal service did its part to promote religion by issuing a red, white, and blue 8-cent stamp bearing the "In God We Trust" slogan. And all across Washington, government officials attended frequent prayer breakfasts, just as pious executives and businessmen were doing all across the country.

In the 1950s, after decades of declining prestige and power, men of the cloth reclaimed some of the popularity and influence they had once enjoyed. The most popular evangelist of the 1950s was undoubtedly Billy Graham, who entered full-time evangelism with the Youth for Christ organization in 1945 but became a national figure only after his successful revival in Los Angeles in 1949. In 1950, he incorporated his organization as the Billy Graham Evangelist Association and began his rise to national and world fame. His success was made possible by his good looks, dynamic speaking style, simple message, carefully planned and promoted crusades, and his skillful use of mass communications to reach millions of people. It was also partly due to the promotion of Graham by the Luce publications, *Readers Digest*, and other popular magazines of the day. By 1954 a *Time* magazine cover story on Graham was describing him as "the best known, most-talked about Christian leader in the world today, barring the Pope,"[28] and succeeding years brought even larger audiences and successes. By the midfifties he was conducting crusades in America and abroad, had a regular television and radio show, a daily newspaper column, two best-selling books, *Peace With God* (1953) and *The Secret of Happiness* (1955), the friendship of President Eisenhower, and the adoration of millions in America and all across the world.

Graham's message, with its literal interpretation of the Bible, warnings of the imminent end of the world, and concentration on individual conversion, had a wide appeal to fundamentalist Christians in an anxious age. His message rarely changed. "Time is running out," he warned in *Peace with God* and many of his sermons. "The seconds are ticking away toward midnight. The human race is about to make the fatal plunge. Which way shall we turn?"[29] Like many other evangelists of the day, he also often equated Christianity with Americanism and with anticommunism, claiming that "a great sinister anti-Christian movement masterminded by Satan has declared war upon the Christian God."[30] He rarely discussed social issues, but he did preach a color-blind faith to his integrated audiences at a time when it was unpopular to do so. As for his critics who claimed that his techniques belonged more to show business and to Madison Avenue than to the church, he usually replied, as he did in 1954, that "I am selling the greatest product in the world; why shouldn't it be promoted as well as soap?"[31]

There were other evangelists with regional crusades, television and radio programs, and regional success who preached essentially the same gospel as Graham, but none of them achieved his fame and influence. Then there were right-wingers like Billy James Hargis, who was obsessed with the dangers of the internal communist conspiracy and used his daily radio program and *Christian Crusade* magazine to rail out against communism, the United Nations, the civil rights movement, liberals, and the National Council of Churches. And there were faith healers, of whom the best known was Oral Roberts, an Oklahoma Pentecostal Holiness preacher who rose rapidly in the fifties after a 1951 article in *Life* magazine brought him national attention. He was soon drawing large crowds and building up a large empire based on his traveling healing ministry, his books, his television show, and his carefully promoted reputation as a faith healer. By the midfifties he had a 280-acre ranch near Texas, a twelve-passenger plane, a runway for his plane on his farm, an overseas ministry, a television and radio show airing on 400 stations, and $53 million in annual revenues. Always criticized by mainline Protestants, the American Medical Association, and other organizations for his healing claims, he and his empire began to run into trouble in the late fifties when a Detroit woman he had supposedly cured of diabetes stopped taking her insulin, went into a diabetic coma, and died, and a California woman who had supposedly been cured of cancer on his television show died from her tragic illness. But devoted followers still maintained their faith in his miraculous healing powers and sought guides to success in his popular autobiography and guidebook, *God's Formula for Success and Prosperity* (1955), which contained chapters with such titles as "God's Poultry and Real Estate Man" and "God's Plumbing Supply Man."[32]

The first clergymen to become a television star was the Most Reverend Fulton J. Sheen, auxiliary bishop of New York, whose weekly *Life Is Worth Living* show was on national television from 1952 through 1957. For much of that time he was on opposite the popular Milton (Uncle Miltie) Berle, whose show was sponsored by Texaco; Berle called his competition Uncle Fultie and claimed that "we both work for the same boss—Sky Chief." Bishop

Sheen took the kidding in good stride.[33] His thirty-minute show was made up largely of anecdotes and moral lessons ranging over a broad range of topics—God, science, teenagers, death, democracy, and war—but the subject he turned to again and again was communism and its dangers to America and the rest of the Christian world. Frequently telling his viewers that communism was infiltrating America's public schools, colleges, government, and other institutions, he warned that no peace was possible with Russia, the leader of international, godless communism. "Fellow citizens, be not deceived," he said on one broadcast. "Remember, when Russia talks peace, it is a tactic, and a preparation for war. . . . A peace overture of Russia will be the beginning of another Pearl Harbor." He warned over and over again that America must save the world from the hammer and sickle, just as she had once saved it from the swastika. Early in 1953, he became the talk of the nation when he said that "Stalin must one day meet his judgment."[34] A few days later, the Russian dictator died, leading many viewers, newspapers, and magazines to ponder whether the good bishop was also a clairvoyant. It was a sign of the times that a program like Sheen's could have such popularity and longevity. He was watched not only by Catholics but also by Jews and by Protestants of all denominations. At the height of his popularity, he had an audience of 10 million people, received over 8,000 letters a week from viewers, and sold thousands of copies of his most popular books, *Life Is Worth Living* and *Peace of Soul.*[35]

Probably the most popular—and wealthiest—religious figure of the 1950s was Norman Vincent Peale. An ordained Methodist minister, he began his career as a minister and writer in the 1930s, but his greatest success came after World War II and peaked in the fifties, when he was at the height of his influence as the best-known promotor of what he called positive thinking. His *Guideposts* magazine had reached a circulation of 800,000 by the end of the decade, he had his own television and radio show, which aired several times each week, and he had a regular column in *Look* magazine and also wrote frequently for the other magazines and newspapers of his day. He also sold millions of copies of his book, records and printings of his sermons, and his greeting and Christmas cards. In the lounge of his church in New York City was a salesroom offering long-playing records of his sermons ($4.50 each), subscriptions to *Guideposts* ($2.00), a maroon-colored binder to hold a year's worth of his sermons ($3.00), and other paraphernalia.[36] When his most popular book, *The Power of Positive Thinking*, was published at $2.95 in 1952, it quickly went to the top of the nonfiction best-seller list and stayed there for 112 consecutive weeks. In 1954 it sold more copies than any other book except the Bible, and in that same year Peale was named one of the Twelve Best U.S. Salesmen.[37]

What was he selling, what was the appeal of Peale? In an age of anxiety, he sold the gospel of reassurance and self-assurance, merging religion, psychology, and the old American ideal of success, practicing mass counseling on an unprecedented scalc through the means of modern communication. In all of his books, sermons, records, and radio and television shows, he gave the same simple message over and over again: You can overcome any obstacle, have anything you want, obtain health, peace of mind, success, and popularity simply by believing in yourself, thinking positive thoughts, avoiding negative thoughts, convincing yourself that problems do not exist, using simple formulas, and taking God as a partner in life. In the preface to *The Power of Positive Thinking*, he tells the reader that "the powerful principles contained herein are not my invention but are given to us by the greatest Teacher who ever lived and who still lives. This book teaches applied Christianity; a simple yet scientific system of practical techniques of successful living that works."[38]

Record church attendance, best-selling religious books and records, the airwaves filled with popular religious songs and television and radio shows, piety in the White House and on Capitol Hill, the popularity of Graham, Sheen, Peale—all these pointed to a religious revival of the fifties. Or did they? Many critics and cynics of the time felt that they did not, that the supposedly religious revival was not a true religious renaissance at all but a reflection of the anxiety, materialism, and conformity of the time. The revival of religion was a part, according to Reinhold Niebuhr, "of a rather frantic effort of the naturally optimistic American soul to preserve its optimism in an age of anxiety."[39] Billy Graham offered salvation and eternal life in a world whose very existence was threatened by atomic war. Fulton Sheen appealed to the millions of Americans who equated Christianity and Americanism and saw the world locked in a life-and-death struggle between godless communism and Christian democracy, and everyone knew whose side God was on, thus reducing God, as one critic of popular religion said, "to the level of the fierce tribal diety of the early Old Testament."[40] So pervasive was this nationalization of Christianity in the fifties that atheists were automatically considered to be unpatriotic, un-American, and perhaps even treasonous. In 1958, a Gallup Poll showed that 80 percent of Americans would never vote for an atheist for president. Christianity had become a civic religion, and as one critic of the merging of Christianity and patriotism complained in *The Christian Century* in 1954, it had become "un-American to be unreligious."[41]

In an age of conformity, religion also offered a sense of belonging, of finding identity in a secular, troubled, impersonal, and increasingly homogenized world. As Will Herberg pointed out in 1955 in his classic study of religion, *Protestant–Catholic–Jew*, "the religious revival under way in this country today . . . is a reflection of the social necessity of 'belonging,' and today the context of 'belonging' is increasingly the religious community."[42] Religion itself was homogenized—there was more toleration, differences among the faithful were downplayed, and most people accepted others as long as they believed in something. According to the polls of the day, 95 percent of Americans claimed to be religious. Sixty-eight percent identified themselves as Protestant, 23 percent as Catholic, and 4 percent as Jewish. At a time when religion had become an important badge of identity, only 5 percent had "no preference."[43]

As for Peale and the other positive thinkers, they were attractive to materialistic and individualistic people seeking reassurance and simple steps to the success they craved so much. "The high priest of this cult of reassurance," as one critic[44] called Peale, offered simple solutions to the complex problems of life, and as many of his critics pointed out, his books, sermons, and records belonged in the same category as the popular books of the day on how to lose weight without dieting and how to learn a foreign language without studying. Peale turned God into a friend and business partner, and he transformed religion into a practical faith, into a tool for solving life's problems and for achieving happiness, prosperity, peace of mind, and success that was often measured in monetary rewards. One of the best examples of his shallow approach to life's problems occurred on his television show when, after talking to a child suffering from anxiety and insomnia because of what he had heard about atomic bombs, Peale patted the boy on the head and told him not to worry any longer, for God was looking out for him and no atomic bombs would ever fall on New York. Such incidents caused many physicians, psychiatrists, and counselors to complain that people with serious physical or psychological problems might not seek the professional help they needed because of Peale's teaching that life's problems will go away if you stop worrying about them and think positively.[45]

In this age of religious revival, many Americans were shockingly ignorant of the history and tenets of the faith they claimed to hold so strongly. Polls and other studies of religious knowledge regularly revealed that most Americans were hard pressed to explain what their basic beliefs were, to distinguish between Protestantism and Catholicism, to explain or even identify the Christian trinity, to distinguish the Old Testament from the New, or even to name the first four books of the New Testament. In fact, a 1951 Gallup poll showed that 53 percent of Americans could not even name *one* of the gospels. The faithful also flocked to the theaters, often at the urgings of ministers and Sunday school teachers, to see "biblical movies" like *The Ten Commandments*, a romantic spectacular that bore little resemblance to the epic portrayed in the Old Testament. At a time when the Legion of Decency was condemning *Baby Doll* for its shameful sexuality, *The Ten Commandments*, masquerading as a religious film, was playing to packed houses, where on the screen, as critic Murray Kempton said, Cecil De Mille "was serving up flesh in pots," while in the lobbies of some theaters children were lining up to buy souvenir coloring pencils in Protestant, Catholic, or

Jewish versions bearing such messages as "Thou Shalt Not Commit Adultery."[46] This film was a triumph of Hollywood and American capitalism, but many viewers came away calling it a moving religious experience.

These distortions of the biblical message caused many to complain that the Bible was frequently bought but rarely read, that Americans had a childlike "faith in faith" itself, that they believed in "the magic of believing,"[47] and that these misconceptions of the real tenets of Christianity and Judaism led to the further error of equating Christianity with belief in patriotism, the American way of life, and success. Such misconceptions also led to the irreverent humanizing of God, to regarding him as a chum, the man upstairs, even, in Jane Russell's words, as "a living doll." They led to the view of God as some kind of a cosmic bellhop who ran to cater to man's latest wish for comfort, peace of mind, happiness, and success. They led to a secular, man-centered faith, and to the denial of the social message of religion—most Americans wanted comfort and practical guides from their faith, not exhortations to tackle racism, poverty, and the other problems of the time. Billy Graham preached individual conversion, not the social gospel, and popular counselor Peale was an archconservative who had attacked Franklin Roosevelt as a dictator, was devoted to the nineteenth-century philosophy of laissez-faire capitalism, and was opposed to unions, taxes, Social Security, and minimum wage and hour laws. He had endorsed General MacArthur for president in 1948, and although he stayed out of politics in the fifties, afraid that it would hurt his various enterprises, he reentered the political arena in 1960 to oppose John F. Kennedy because of the candidate's Catholicism.[48]

Yet, in spite of the critics, religion boomed in the fifties, and nowhere was it more evident than in the suburbs, where new churches were going up rapidly to serve a materialistic, transient population seeking not only God and salvation but identity, companionship, and reassurance. The peace-of-mind religion was especially popular here, for materialistic suburbanites moved to the suburbs to get away from the problems of the city and did not want to be reminded of these problems—or any other—here in their pleasant suburban environment. They wanted comforting and inspiring sermons, not appeals to shun materialism for spiritualism or to go out and solve the social problems of their time. As Stanley Rowland put it in *The Nation*, "the homogenized suburbanite likes his religion, unlike his martinis, diluted," and he looked at his church as a "comfort station." It is not surprising that drive-in church services, usually held in the parking lots of drive-in theaters, enjoyed the geatest popularity in the suburbs, or that a New York clergyman who conducted these services said that he did it to make it "more convenient and comfortable" to worship.[49]

The religious revival seemed to affect all classes, races, educational levels, and regions of the country. Although the popular revivalists, right-wing anticommunists, and peace-of-mind groups seemed to set the tone for the rest of the society, important religious thinking was going on in many colleges and seminaries across the country. While intellectuals were appalled by the Peales and Grahams, they were attracted to the writings of serious theologians who grappled with serious religious problems in a secular age that had recently experienced Nazism and the Holocaust and was now trying to find meaning in a world facing the prospect of atomic annihilation. The writings of Karl Barth, Paul Tillich, Jacques Maritain, Martin Buber, Reinhold Niebuhr, and other theologians had a wide following, and intellectual journals and popular liberal newsmagazines like *The Nation*, *The New Republic*, and the *Saturday Review* carried important reflections by serious thinkers on the precarious predicament of modern man.[50]

The great religious revival of the fifties reached its peak in the midfifties and seemed to wane in the latter half of the decade as the country moved farther and farther away from the dark days of the Korean War and McCarthyism, learned to live with the bomb, and submerged itself in the materialism of the age. Rock 'n' roll helped to drive popular religious music from the airwaves, sales of religious books leveled off, books and articles critical of popular religion began to appear in greater numbers, and the percentage of Americans attending church each Sunday declined from a high of 51 percent in 1957 to 47 percent in 1960.[51] At the end of the decade, the movie *Elmer Gantry* played to packed houses, won several awards, and made the hypocritical, silver-tongued, boozing, skirt-chasing evangelist almost as well known as Billy Graham. As these and other events of Eisenhower's second term would make clear, the nationwide conservative consensus of the midfifties would begin to break down in the last years of the decade as the nation moved toward a more questioning and more turbulent time.

# PART THREE

# Trouble in God's Country, 1957–1961

# 18

# *Rocky Road*

On January 20, 1957, Dwight David Eisenhower began his second term as president of the United States. Since the twentieth fell on Sunday, he and Vice President Nixon were sworn in in a private ceremony that day in the White House, with the public inauguration to come the following day. It was cold and overcast in Washington on inauguration day, but a respectable crowd braved the weather to attend the ceremonies, while 75 million others watched them on the television sets that by now were in most homes in the country. Looking healthy in spite of his two recent illnesses, the president was sworn in by Chief Justice Earl Warren. After delivering a thirteen-minute address, the president ate a lunch containing more salt than his doctors would have liked, then went to the reviewing stand for a three and a half hour parade that included not only the obligatory floats, military and boy scout units, and pretty marching baton twirlers, but also some of the new guided missiles the country was developing as part of its defense program. When the parade was over, *Life* reported, "the Eisenhowers and thousands of other Republicans changed into dinner clothes for the liveliest and happiest round of parties . . . in capital memory."[1]

Eisenhower began his second term with the country basking in unparalleled prosperity and the president himself enjoying great popularity among his countrymen—polls at the time of his inauguration showed that 79 percent of the population approved of the way he was handling his job. Most domestic and foreign problems seemed under control, and fears of atomic war were fading, even as the weapons of atomic destruction were multiplying in number and intensity. Americans had learned to live with the unthinkable by not thinking about it or by believing that America's superiority in atomic weaponry precluded any real threat of a Russian attack. Besides, there were more important things to think about: getting that second car or perhaps even a second home, raising the kids, saving for their college educations, and acquiring more and more of the consumer goods that kept flowing out of the American horn of plenty. Americans were satisfied with themselves and with their president, and they looked forward to four years of peace, prosperity, and tranquillity presided over by a good man who would not let anything bad happen to the country.

But it was not to be. Eisenhower's second term would be much more troublesome for him and for his countrymen than his first term had been. There would be, it seemed, one problem after another, domestic and foreign. In contrast to the first term, Eisenhower would fall under heavy criticism from the press, the public, his own party, and, of course, the Democrats. There would be more talk about the "lack of leadership in Washington," of Eisenhower's "golfing and goofing," of "crises of confidence" inside the administration and throughout the country, of "the decline of the Eisenhower consensus," and of "the search for a national purpose." The decade would end with the emergence of new domestic and foreign problems and with the rejection of the Republican party in the elections of 1960.

Eisenhower found his second term much less satisfying than the first. He continued to have health problems, suffering a mild stroke in November of 1957. The Twenty-second Amendment, limiting presidential terms to two, made him a lame duck, shorn of the power that a potential reelection gives to a first termer. He was still under attack from the right wing of his own party, and with the Democrats controlling both houses of Congress throughout his second term he was forced to continue to turn to Lyndon Johnson, Sam Rayburn, and other Democrats to get his programs through. And to make matters even worse, Eisenhower would lose several key officials: Attorney General Herbert Brownell, Secretary of Defense Charles Wilson, and Secretary of Treasury George Humphrey left in 1957, presidential assistant Sherman Adams resigned in the midst of a scandal in 1958, and then the worst blow of all came in the spring of 1959 when Secretary of state Dulles's terminal cancer forced him to step down in favor of Christian A. Herter. Eisenhower, who had never liked politics in the first place, seemed to enjoy it even less as his problems mounted and his former key officials were not around to help him in his battles with Congress and the Russians.

Eisenhower's relations with the Eighty-fifth Congress (1957–1959) were stormy, with frequent battles over the budget, social programs, and other matters and with Eisenhower resorting to the veto more often than he had in his first term. However, there were some positive legislative accomplishments. In domestic areas, the Congress passed—and Eisenhower signed—bills to protect blacks' right to vote, admitting Alaska to statehood, establishing the National Defense Education Act to aid education, founding the National Aeronautics and Space Administration, creating a weak joint federal-state civil defense program, and providing aid to farmers and to the ailing railroad industry. In foreign policy, Congress approved the Eisenhower Doctrine, the International Atomic Energy Treaty, more financial and technical assistance to the European Atomic Energy Community, the extension of presidential authority to negotiate reciprocal tariff agreements, and a military reorganization bill. The mood on Capitol Hill and in the Oval Office was still basically conservative, with both branches refusing to broaden the New Deal significantly or to deal with civil rights, poverty, and other festering problems.

The president's political troubles were aggravated by the recession that hit the country in the fall of 1957. Fed by decreases in defense spending, in exports, and in investments in factories and factory equipment, the recession quickly became the worst economic downturn since World War II. As unemployment climbed to over 5 million, equal to almost 7 percent of the labor force, criticism of Eisenhower (Eisen-Hoover, some critics called him) mounted in Congress, the press, and the public. Eisenhower dealt with the recession by increasing federal spending and unemployment compensation and urging the Federal Reserve System to ease monetary restrictions. But he would not cut taxes or approve heavy spending for public works projects, public housing, or welfare. The policies seemed to work, for by the summer of 1958 the worst of the recession was over, though unemployment continued to be a problem for the rest of the decade. For Republicans, who prided themselves on knowing more about business than the Democrats, the recession was a major embarrassment, and to many people, it brought back haunting memories of the depression of the 1930s and Herbert Hoover's failure to act in that crisis—on which Democrats had been harping for over twenty years.

Eisenhower's second term would also be plagued by continuing civil rights problems. As the year began, Eisenhower still showed no signs of using his popularity or the powers of his office to lead the nation toward compliance with the Brown decisions. In his state of the union message in January of 1957, for example, he called for more federal aid to education "uncomplicated by provisions dealing with the complex problems of integration."[2] But the "complex problems of integration" were becoming more and more complex in 1957. In the 1956–1957 school year, some two hundred school districts were desegregated for the first time, bringing to 712 the total number of districts desegregated since the Brown decision of 1954. But most of these had come in the border states, where little resistance was met. In the other southern states the desegregation orders had been met with legal defiance and even with violence. Southern resistance was hardening in 1957, and from then on the pace of desegregation slowed down; only thirty-eight districts desegregated in 1957–1958, thirteen in 1958–1959, nineteen in 1959–1960, and seventeen in 1960–1961. And in Georgia, South Carolina, Alabama, and Mississippi, black children would not attend school with whites until the Kennedy administration.[3]

The beginning of Eisenhower's second term coincided with a period of hardening resistance to desegregation. All across the South, there was an increase in the power and activities of White Citizens' Councils, the KKK, and other vigilante groups. Some governors were threatening to do everything in their power, including closing the schools, to prevent desegregation, while southern legislators were rushing to introduce resolutions and bills circumventing the Brown decision and providing for more—not less—segregation. In Montgomery, Alabama, for example, a law passed in 1957 made it "unlawful for white and Negro people to play together in any game: baseball, football, golf, track, dice, cards, dominoes, checkers, pool, billiards, or at swimming pools, beaches, lakes or ponds."[4] In some towns and cities, teachers, professors, and preachers who dared to speak out for desegregation were harassed and sometimes fired. Books supporting school desegregation or anything else contrary to the southern way of life were banned from the bookstores and libraries, leading in some communities to the removal from the shelves of such offending magazines as *Life*, *Look*, and the *National Geographic*. In Florida in 1958 segregationists even tried to force a librarian to take a new edition of "The Three Little Pigs" off the shelves because it allegedly showed that black pigs were stronger than white ones.[5]

The KKK was experiencing a revival in the mid- and late 1950s. After reaching its height in the early 1920s, the Klan had declined in the late twenties and depression years, but it was rejuvenated by the Brown decision in 1954. The Klan of the fifties was weaker than its earlier versions, primarily because it splintered into at least fifteen competing Klans, was discredited by its violence, and because respectable whites—even those who opposed desegregation—wanted nothing to do with the Klan and regarded it as a blight on the southern lanscape. The Klan found its strongest support in Alabama, Mississippi, central Georgia (particularly the Atlanta area), Florida, South Carolina, and parts of North Carolina. But most southerners rejected it, preferring the middle-class White Citizens' Councils, which seemed to be more respectable.[6]

The Klan of the late fifties attracted the losers of society—those at the bottom of the social and educational ladder who had no one to look down upon except blacks and who would lose what little status this gave them if blacks were allowed to rise. Many Klansmen were unemployed, some had criminal records, some were mentally unstable, and some were outcasts even from the white race that they were claiming to protect—a pathetic group, who might have been pitied had their potential for cruelty and harm not been so extreme. They joined the Klan for any number of reasons: to gain a sense of belonging (of Klannishness); to find an outlet for violence or sadomasochism, which they could practice with the anonymity bestowed on them by sheets and hoods and the clandestine nature of their actions; to make money by selling memberships and robes and other paraphernalia to other Klansmen; and to overcome their own sense of inferiority. Some even joined because they really believed, as the Klan initiations and literature claimed, that they were protecting womanhood, motherhood, Americanism, Christianity, morality, and the white race.

The concern for protecting his race reveals the typical Klansman's Negrophobia and obsession with the white supremacy that often gave him his only source of identity and satisfaction. At a rally in South Carolina in October of 1955, for example, a Klan speaker had boasted that "our kind of whites were elected to rule the world and everything in it." And at a rally in Lakeland, Florida, in July of 1956, the same theme was elaborated by the Klan speaker who boasted that "the Ku Klux Klan is the only white Christian Protestant 100 per cent American organization in America today. . . . Klansman are the cleanest and most perfect people on earth." And at other rallies Klansmen pledged that "we are gonna stay white, we are going to keep the nigger black, with the help of our Lord and Saviour, Jesus Christ," and "I've been a white man all my life and I always will be."[7] The Klan gave its members status, power, significance, a cause or a mission—they believed that they could save the country that was being swept by social and economic changes that they did not understand.

The Klan's image was often damaged by the silly and disgraceful actions of some of its individuals and local groups and by the frequency with which its leaders made the headlines for involvement in sex scandals and criminal activity. It made a hero, for example, out of traveling racial agitator John Kasper, who then later testified in a Florida trial that he had once had an affair with a black girl when he ran a book store in New York.[8] But perhaps the greatest humiliation came in 1958 at a rally held in Robeson County, North Carolina, by Rev. James W. "Catfish" Cole. Assembled for the purpose of teaching the Lumbee Indians proper respect for superior white people like the Klansmen, the rally broke up when it was attacked by a large group of Lumbees; the startled Klan members, and a small group of whites who came to watch, panicked and beat a hasty retreat. The whole country laughed when pictures of Klansmen running for their lives from attacking Indians appeared in newspapers and popular magazines all across the country, causing great embarrassment for Klansmen and their sympathizers everywhere. Readers were particularly amused to read that the sheriff of

Robeson County, Malcolm McLeod, was able to disperse the Indians by telling them that they had better hurry home or they would miss *Gunsmoke* on television.[9]

But to its victims the Klan was no laughing matter. Some of its activities were indeed chilling and repulsive, and signs of sick and twisted minds at work. One of the most grisly episodes came in Birmingham, Alabama, in the fall of 1957, when six members of the local "Ku Klux Klan of the Confederacy" kidnapped a black man from a Birmingham street to use in an initiation rite for a new member. The victim, a thirty-three-year-old handyman named Judge Aaron, was stripped of his clothing, beaten, tortured, and forced to crawl around on his hands and knees before his taunting captors. He was then castrated with a razor blade, and after turpentine had been poured on his groin area to magnify the pain, he was dumped by the side of the road and left to die. But he survived, and during a sensational trial two of the six Klansmen involved turned state's evidence against the other four, who were convicted and given twenty-year prison sentences.[10] The convictions were unusual, for in most of the lower South in the midfifties, whites were rarely punished for committing violent acts against blacks.

The Klan was not the only perpetrator of violence, for many individuals and groups or mobs not associated with the Klan also joined in the lawlessness that swept many southern communities in the second half of the 1950s. Between January 1, 1955, and January 1, 1959, a total of 225 acts of racially inspired violence were committed in the eleven southern states. These acts included six murders, twenty-nine shootings, forty-four beatings, five stabbings, thirty bombings and eight burnings of homes, four bombings and two burnings of schools, seven bombings of churches and two of Jewish temples, and the bombing of a YWCA. While most of the victims of these cowardly acts were blacks, some were Jews and some were whites who had committed such crimes against the white race as having black friends, advocating desegregation, urging moderation or compliance with the Brown decisions, or advocating "race-mixing."[11]

Racially inspired violence was not limited to the South, for the northern states also had their share of bombings, shootings, arson, and mob action, though here the precipitator was not school desegregation but residential desegregation—"blockbusting." One of the most publicized incidents occurred in Levittown, Pennsylvania, which was founded in 1952 and had no black citizens among its 55,000 residents until August of 1957, when William and Daisy Myers, a college-educated couple with three children, purchased a $12,000 house and moved into town. Antiblack mobs quickly formed, and for eight days ruled the neighborhood, burning crosses, yelling "nigger" and a host of obscenities, and making threatening telephone calls to the black couple and to the whites who befriended them. They even rented a vacant house behind the Myerses' house to use as the headquarters for their activities, flying a Confederate flag from its roof and playing "Old Man River" over a loudspeaker day and night. The harassment was finally ended when the local police and state troopers were called in to quell the violence and the state attorney general, Thomas D. McBride, issued a court order charging eight neighbors with "evil conspiracy" and directing the community to stop harassing the Myerses. Gradually, the uproar died down, and the Myerses were accepted into the neighborhood. Their opponents then turned their energies toward fighting the fluoridation of the water supply and preventing the new high school from being named after J. Robert Oppenheimer.[12]

But as white resistance to desegregation in the South grew, so did the courage and determination of southern blacks. In 1957, a Gallup Poll showed that 69 percent of the South's 10 million blacks supported enforcement of the Brown decision, while 13 percent opposed it. In that same year, Martin Luther King, Jr., and several other black leaders formed the Southern Christian Leadership Conference, with King as president, to fight for black rights, and they led a march on Washington to dramatize the need for civil rights legislation. The march and protest attracted around 15,000 participants, helping to demonstrate the growing dissatisfaction of blacks at the inaction of the federal government in the racial problems facing the nation. But although the majority of blacks supported desegregation, many were still reluctant to speak out for it, especially in front of whites.[13]

In the late summer of 1957 the federal government did take one small step to promote civil rights with the enactment of the Civil Rights Act of 1957, the first significant piece of civil rights legislation since 1875. The Civil Rights Act was a watered-down version of legislation first introduced by the administration in 1956 and finally passed after a sixty-three-day debate in Congress and a marathon one-month filibuster by Senator Strom Thurmond, who set a new record for an individual by talking for twenty-four hours and eighteen minutes before finally giving in. Eisenhower had lobbied with congressmen behind the scenes to get this bill passed, but as was characteristic of him, he did little to pressure Congress openly or try to drum up public support, adding to the public impression that he was lukewarm on the issue of civil rights. Consequently, Lyndon Johnson would get most of the credit for the weak bill that was passed.[14]

Signed by the president on September 9, 1957, the bill gave the attorney general the power to obtain court injunctions against attempts to obstruct or deprive anyone of his voting rights, created a six-man executive Commission on Civil Rights to study the civil rights question, created a Civil Rights Division in the Department of Justice headed by a new assistant attorney general, and provided for trials without jury for individuals charged with violating the voting rights of others. But even this weak bill was not strongly enforced by the executive department, creating the need for a stronger bill with more enforcement powers, which would be passed in 1960.

At the time he signed the Civil Rights Act on September 9, 1957, Eisenhower was also facing the most serious domestic crisis of his presidency, and it too involved civil rights. It occurred in Little Rock, Arkansas, a progressive southern city with a good past history of race relations. The crisis was precipitated by Governor Orval Faubus, who had been regarded as a moderate when he was elected in 1954 but had apparently decided in the summer of 1957 that his future political career could be better promoted by the rabid segregationists than by the moderates he had courted in the past. In late August he began to circulate the rumor that he had knowledge of impending violence if the city school board's court-approved gradual desegregation plan was put into effect and nine blacks were enrolled in the all-white Little Rock Central High School in September. On the evening of September 2, the day before classes were scheduled to begin at the 2,000-student high school, Faubus ordered a 270-man contingent of the Arkansas National Guard to surround the school. About an hour later he appeared on television to explain that the troops had been sent to "maintain or restore the peace and good order of the community" and that they "will not act as segregationists or integrationists, but as soldiers called to active duty to carry out their assigned tasks."[15] Their assigned task, of course, was to prevent the black students from entering the high school. There was little sign of any violence until Faubus stirred things up, and although he claimed that he was acting to prevent disorder, he had actually caused the trouble and was now using the authority of the state to prevent the carrying out of federal law.

On Tuesday, September 3, the nine black students assigned to Central High School followed the advice of the school board and stayed home to avoid trouble. But the next day, accompanied by two white and two black ministers, the nine students tried to enter the high school, only to be turned away by the leaders of the National Guard. The black students left, as calm and as dignified as they had come, ignoring the curses, jeers, and threats of the large white mob of students and townspeople who had gathered that morning. Pictures and stories of the day's events were circulated all over the world. One of the most dramatic scenes was that of the actions of Elizabeth Eckford, a courageous fifteen-year-old Negro girl who walked calmly for about a hundred yards through a throng of cursing whites. Most Americans were outraged and shamed, as were the friends of America all over the world. But communist countries gloated over the stories coming out of Little Rock and gleefully suggested that Americans concerned with human freedoms should stop condemning the Russian actions in Hungary and instead investigate what was going on in Little Rock. And in Africa, Asia, and other countries peopled by nonwhites—the countries America was trying to woo to its side in the Cold War—leaders wondered about the sincerity of American claims to be the friend of freedom-loving people everywhere.

Governor Faubus's irresponsible actions presented Eisenhower with a crisis that he had hoped would never occur. For the next eighteen days, the Arkansas governor defied federal law and used troops to keep blacks from entering the school while Eisenhower worked behind the scenes to try to defuse the crisis. The president sent FBI agents to Little Rock to investigate the situation, conferred with the mayor of Little Rock, and met with Faubus at the president's vacation retreat at Newport, Rhode Island. Finally, on Friday, September 20, in obedience to a federal district court order, Faubus ordered the National Guard to evacuate Central High, leaving only the city police to handle any problems that might arise on Monday morning. Faubus then left to attend a governors' conference in Georgia. On Saturday, when he was introduced at a college football game at Grant Field in Atlanta, he received a standing ovation.[16]

After a tense weekend, school reopened on Monday, September 23, with 150 local policemen present to keep order. A large white crowd had gathered long before the opening bells and grew to over a thousand by late in the morning. When the black students arrived around 8:45 and were escorted by police into the school through the delivery entrance, the crowd became an angry mob, crying, "The niggers are in our school," and trying to rush the school, but were held back by the police. The hysterical mob attacked any blacks they found on the streets, taunted, kicked, and beat "Yankee" reporters and photographers, yelled "nigger" and "nigger-lover" and accused the police of being traitors.[17] One policeman took off his badge and walked away. Around 9:00, Mayor Woodrow Mann telegraphed the president that "the immediate need for federal troops is urgent. . . . Mob is armed and engaging in fisticuffs and other acts of violence. Situation is out of control and police cannot disperse the mob."[18] At 11:30 the authorities removed the black students from the school for their own safety. When the crowd still refused to believe the Negro students had left, authorities allowed Mrs. Allen Thevenet of the Mother's League to enter and search the school. When she came out, she triumphantly reported that "we went through every room in the school and there were no Negroes there."[19]

Eisenhower's hand had been forced. Later that day he released a statement denouncing the "disgraceful occurrences" at Little Rock and issued a proclamation ordering "all persons engaged in such obstruction of justice to cease and desist therefrom, and to disperse forthwith."[20] The next day, Tuesday, September 24, the black students did not return to school but some 200 whites showed up to demonstrate. Eisenhower now did what he had to do, carrying out, according to Sherman Adams, "a constitutional duty which was the most repugnant to him of all his acts in his eight years at the White House."[21] He ordered 1,100 army paratroopers from the 101st Airborne Division into Little Rock and federalized the Arkansas National Guard, taking them out from under Govenor Faubus and putting them under the control of the president of the United States and under the command of Major General Edwin A. Walker. For the first time since Reconstruction days, federal troops had been sent into the South to protect the civil rights of blacks. Eisenhower took this strong action because of the disorders and Faubus's defiance of federal court action—not because he felt he should further the cause of desegregation. To Eisenhower it was a presidential duty required by the Constitution—not a moral duty.[22]

On Wednesday, September 25, the soldiers accompanied the nine blacks to class as cursing whites looked on. Although the paratroopers would leave by the end of November, the National Guard would stay on until the end of the school term in May of 1958. Faubus continued to rant and rave about illegal federal intervention, complained that the president's usurpation of his authority was comparable to Truman's firing of General MacArthur, and often referred to his "crucifixion" at the hands of federal authorities. He also circulated stories that the federal government had tapped his telephone, that federal authorities had planned to arrest him, and that soldiers accompanied teenage girls into bathrooms and dressing rooms.[23] Faubus had gotten what he wanted: a classic federal-state confrontation that allowed him to pose as the protector of states rights and the southern way of life, a pose that would be worth thousands of votes in the 1958 gubernatorial election.

So, with the help of federal troops, Central High was integrated. Although feelings at the school soon calmed down, the use and continued presence of federal troops had certainly brought serious disruptions to the educational process. Although most of the white students either ignored the blacks or accepted them grudgingly, a small group of whites continued to harass their black classmates through most of the school year. The black students were threatened, cursed, spat upon, kicked, and pushed, and there were several attempts to burn or dynamite the school. The school superintendent, principal, and several teachers were subjected to threatening phone calls and other forms of harassment, and the school superintendent, Virgil Blossom, was the target of an unsuccessful assassination attempt. But eight of the blacks stayed the entire year, and one, Ernest Green, graduated in the spring with the rest of the senior class and received a scholarship to Michigan State University. His yearbook, signed by fourteen of his classmates, contained pictures of soldiers but no other references to the troubles that had made for such a memorable school year.[24]

Eisenhower's actions in the Little Rock crisis were consistent with his moderate views on civil rights. But as expected, he was both praised and damned for his actions. Adlai Stevenson and ex-presidents Hoover and Truman publicly applauded his use of federal troops in Little Rock, and Gallup polls showed that 64 percent of the American people, including 36 percent of southerners, also approved.[25] But many liberals felt that he dragged his feet in the Little Rock crisis. By waiting so long to exercise his leadership, his critics claimed, Eisenhower allowed the Little Rock situation to develop into a major crisis and gave Faubus and the rabid segregationists almost three weeks to bask in the headlines, encouraging segregationists everywhere in the South and bringing the United States into disrepute all over the world. Some even claimed that Eisenhower had encouraged Faubus and his supporters by his past inactions and by his press conference statements about the need for moderation and patience in race relations and of the dangers of using force to change old prejudices. As late as September 3, the day after Faubus had precipitated the crisis by sending the National Guard to Central High School, Eisenhower had told reporters that "you cannot change people's hearts simply by laws" and that southerners "see a picture of mongrelization of the races, they call it."[26]

But many thought that Eisenhower had gone too far. Senator Richard Russell of Georgia wired the president his disapproval of the action and compared the federal soldiers at Little Rock to "Hitler's storm troopers."[27] Faubus became a hero in his own state and throughout the South, and the emotions generated by the Little Rock crisis contributed to the hardening of race relations and of resistance to federal law for the next two to three years. In August of 1958 Faubus would win reelection for a third term by a landslide, and would win three more terms after that. In the 1958–1959 school year, Faubus closed all the schools in Little Rock, while in Virginia Governor Almond, elected in the fall of 1957 during the Little Rock turmoil, became the leader of massive resistance in that state. As more and more southerners attacked Eisenhower and the federal government for "ramming race-mixing down the throat of the South," liberals and moderates became even more afraid to speak out, and those who did speak out and run for office were buried under avalanches of votes for their segregationist opponents. Perhaps the chief victim of this black backlash was Congressman Brooks Hays of Arkansas, who had tried to act as a mediator in the Eisenhower–Faubus confrontation. In the 1958 elections he was defeated by a write-in campaign for Dr. T. Dale Alford, a rabid segregationist. School segregation, white supremacy, and other elements of Jim Crow might be dying, but fear, hatred, prejudice, ignorance, and demogoguery were making a strong last stand in the last years of the decade.

# 19

# *Sputnik*

The events at Little Rock had barely disappeared from the headlines when America was faced with still another crisis, one that dealt a serious blow to America's belief in its scientific and technological superiority and seemed to threaten its very existence as a nation. On Friday, October 4, 1957, the Russians launched man's first artificial satellite, Sputnik ("fellow traveler" [of the earth]). This feat would be widely viewed as a "technological Pearl Harbor" which laid bare the nation's defenses and opened the way for military conquest by an alien power and ideology. After nearly fifteen years of superiority in atomic bombs, long-range bombers, and other weapons, the United States appeared, on that dark day in October, to have fallen behind the Russians in the deadly game of weapons development.

The first word of the launching reached the United States Friday evening, and within minutes radio and television broadcasters were sending the news all across the country. Americans huddled around their radio and television sets all evening, and the next morning eagerly devoured the front-page stories about it in the newspapers. They quickly became familiar with the figures: The satellite was 22 inches in diameter, weighed 184.3 pounds, had a maximum height of 560 miles, traveled at 18,000 miles per hour, and circled the earth once every ninety-five minutes or fifteen times a day. It also had two radio transmitters sending back a *beep-beep-beep* signal so that Soviet scientists could track it. In an attempt to get maximum exposure and propaganda mileage, and to show just how well the satellite had been launched and controlled, Soviet scientists had placed it in an orbit circling the most populated parts of the earth so that it could be tracked by scientific observatories and even at times be seen with a small telescope or binoculars. The Russians had clearly scored a great scientific and propaganda victory. *Tass* proudly claimed that Sputnik demonstrated the superiority of Russia's "socialist society," and Khrushchev could not help gloating that "fighter bomber planes can now be put into museums" and that his country would soon be "turning out long-range missiles like sausages."[1]

There had already been signs that Russia was catching up with the United States in weapons technology, for after acquiring the atomic bomb in 1949, she had matched each American atomic breakthrough within a few months. Unable to rival American bomber technology or to ring America with air bases, the Russian leaders in the early 1950s began to concentrate on the development of missiles that they hoped would make long-range bombers obsolete. By 1955 Russia had acquired a clear lead in missile research, and in August of 1957 she successfully tested an intercontinental ballistic missile, fifteen months before America had tested her first ICBM. Leading Democrats had stepped up their attacks on the Eisenhower administration for being so shortsighted and parsimonious as to allow the United States to fall behind the Russians in missile development. Actually, the "missile gap" was more apparent than real, for although the Russians were developing rockets with more thrust, capable of carrying large warheads long distances, the United States had already achieved the "thermonuclear breakthrough" of reducing the size and weight of the warhead in relation to the megaton yield. In other words, the United States could send more destructive nuclear weapons aloft on smaller missiles requiring less thrust.[2] But these crucial distinctions had been lost in the summer of 1957, when most Americans could understand only that the Russians were developing missiles that could travel over three times farther than America's and that someday missiles fired from Russia would be able to reach American cities. In October, these fears were greatly magnified when the Russians sent Sputnik into orbit.

Sputnik destroyed the ingrained American belief that Russian science and technology was vastly inferior to that of the United States and that America would always hold a decisive military edge over its implacable enemy. The nation was stunned, perhaps more than at any other time in the fifties, even more than at the beginning of the Korean War or the firing of General MacArthur. The nation was also humiliated, and scared. Rumors flew. Some said it was just a hoax, just more Russian propaganda, but this idea had to be dropped as American scientific instruments picked up the telltale *beep-beep-beep* and citizens all across the country saw it with the unaided eye. Some said that it contained spy cameras or that it carried a nuclear bomb or some other weapon. These allegations were false, but the military implications were obvious: If the Russians could use that much thrust to get that large an object off the ground and into orbit, then they could not be very far away from being able to send large nuclear warheads almost anywhere in the world. After all, had they not just a few weeks earlier successfully tested an ICBM? Up until this time, nuclear warheads delivered by bombers had not seemed like the harbingers of doomsday—bombers could be shot down, and so far Americans had far more and far better bombers than the Russians had. But large missiles were something else. They would be much harder to defend against, and were much faster and much more destructive, than bombers. And now the possibility of invisible missiles raining nuclear death down on Americans began to seem very real indeed.

Americans had to blame someone for the Russian feat, and as they so often do in times of trouble, they placed the blame squarely on the administration in power. The Democrats, who had already been complaining about the "missile gap," now began to talk about a "space gap" and to blame the Eisenhower administration for failing to spend enough money for missile and space defense and for allowing inefficient and overlapping programs to delay America's missile and space program. Even some Republicans joined the chorus of criticism, especially those who had always liked Ike but who had also always felt that for a former general he sure did not want to spend enough for defense. The press also joined the criticism, providing analyses of Russian and American military strength, research programs, and scientific education that usually concluded that the United States was losing the military and space race. And many scientists agreed with Edward Teller, who claimed that the United States had lost "a battle more important than Pearl Harbor."[3] So on and on it went, as the American people sought explanations and scapegoats for the Russian victory and politicians sought explanations and political gain.

The criticism accelerated on November 3 when Russia launched Sputnik II. Americans were astonished that the Russians had launched a second satellite less than a month after the breathtaking first one, and they were even more amazed when they learned that at 1,120 pounds Sputnik II was six times as large as Sputnik I, that its orbit reached a height of 1,056 miles, that it contained important scientific instruments for studying the earth's atmosphere, weather, and outer space, and that it carried a passenger, a little dog named Laika, with medical instruments strapped to its body to monitor and transmit back to earth important information about the ability of living things to survive in outer space. The implication was inescapable: The Russians were even further ahead in rocket technology than Sputnik I had revealed, and they were planning to send men into space, undoubtedly to the moon, which could one day become a dangerous extraterrestrial military base.

At about the same time that the nation was jolted by the two Sputniks, some other distressing news began to pour in about the country's military readiness. In the spring of 1957, Eisenhower had appointed a civilian commission to study the status of America's defense. Chaired by H. Rowan Gaither, a lawyer and chairman of the Ford Foundation and the Rand Corporation, the committee presented its report to the president in October, shortly after Sputnik. The forty-page Gaither report concluded that the U.S.S.R. was spending far more on defense than the United States was, that she was better prepared to fight a conventional war, that America's main line of defense—the SAC—was very vulnerable and probably would not survive a nuclear attack, and that by as early as 1959 the U.S.S.R. could deliver a massive knockout blow against the United States. The Gaither report was considered classified information, but most of its conclusions and recommendations leaked to the press, causing still more criticisms of the president.[4]

At about the same time as the Gaither report appeared, a Rockefeller Brothers Fund study of the nation's defense and military policies was also released. Largely written by Henry Kissinger, who at thirty-four had already served as a consultant on defense to Truman and Eisenhower and had written *Nuclear Weapons and Foreign Policy*, the Rockefeller report also painted a dismal picture of the nation's defense. Both the Gaither and Rockefeller reports called for dramatic increases in spending for defense and for weapons research and development.[5] In the fall and winter of 1957–1958 defense analyses from dozens of other sources appeared in the newsmagazines, newspapers, *Foreign Affairs*, and other publications, and they generally all pointed to the same conclusion: The United States had fallen dangerously behind the U.S.S.R. and had better spend billions to catch up.

Government officials and scientists were not totally surprised by the Sputnik launchings. Ever since 1955 both the United States and the Soviet Union had been working on artificial satellites. Eisenhower had deliberately given the project low priority while concentrating on the long-range development of IRBMs and ICBMs carrying nuclear warheads, while the Russians, hoping to reap military and propaganda rewards by beating the United States in the development of huge rockets capable of launching satellites into outer space, had given priority to their satellite project. From early 1957 on, the CIA and the air force had confirmed Russian governmental announcements and press reports that a Russian satellite would be launched in the fall of the year, while scientific officials working on the American Vanguard project had informed the president that an American satellite could not be launched before the late spring of 1958. But although American government and scientists were not surprised by the Russian achievement, they were stunned at the magnitude of it. The satellites were heavier, went higher, and required more rocket thrust to propel them into orbit than they had thought the Russians could develop. The enemy had achieved a major breakthrough in research and development of rockets, missiles, and satellites.[6]

Eisenhower and the leading members of his administration were concerned about the Russian achievements, for they exceeded anything that had been expected. And the president was certainly worried over the political implications of the Sputnik success. The Russian feat could not have come at a worse time, for it trumpeted Russia's technological success all around the globe at a time when America was in a recession and when the eyes of the nation and the world were focused on the embarrassing problems at Little Rock. The polls showed that his popularity was slipping, dropping from a Gallup poll approval rating of 79 percent in January of 1957 to 57 percent in the early part of November.[7]

But while Eisenhower was alarmed at Sputnik, he refused to panic or to embark on a crash space program to beat the Russians to the moon, as many of his critics and advisers were clamoring for. His first priority was still missile development, not the launching of satellites and ships to the moon. He preferred, he said, to have "one good Redstone nuclear-armed missile than a rocket that could hit the moon. We have no enemies on the moon."[8] Besides, as he often pointed out to nervous members of the cabinet, Russia would not dare strike first, even if it could, because America had her surrounded with bases and SAC bombers and could retaliate with unacceptable punishment. He also knew that America was not really very far behind Russia in space technology but had simply emphasized missile development over the satellite project, and he knew from military intelligence, partly gathered from high-flying reconnaissance planes taking astonishingly clear pictures of Russian military installations, that the Gaither report and similar studies had greatly overestimated Russia's military strength.[9]

Eisenhower wisely refused to be stampeded, but he did not stand pat either. On November 7 he went before the nation on radio and television to try to calm his countrymen's fears by telling them that while Sputnik was "an achievement of first importance," the nation was in no real danger, for it and the rest of the free world were still far ahead of the communist world in scientific and military technology. He also announced that he was appointing a special assistant for science and technology, James R. Killian (president of MIT), and that the federal government was going to give more aid and encouragement to scientific study and research.[10]

In the weeks and months after Sputnik, Eisenhower ordered an acceleration of America's missile and space program, secured from a willing Congress $1.37 billion for missile development and production, and submitted a 1958 budget with defense increases that bloated the budget to a record peacetime figure of $73.9 billion. In September of 1958 he supported congressional passage of a National Defense Education Act to upgrade

American education from kindergarten through graduate school. And in July of 1958, he secured from Congress legislation providing for the establishment of the National Aeronautics and Space Administration, to coordinate the nation's various missile and space programs. NASA would begin operation in October of 1958, and one of its first acts was to begin Project Mercury, aimed at manned spaceflight. The United States had entered the space race.

But first, it had to get a satellite rocket off the ground. After Sputnik's success in October, the American effort was accelerated. On December 6, 1957, in a nationally televised test of the Vanguard missile, the rocket rose about two feet off the launch pad at Cape Canaveral and crashed. As the foreign press wrote about "Flopnik" and "Stay-putnik," there was more national humiliation and more criticism of the administration's missile and defense program. Finally, on January 31, 1958, the first American satellite, carried by a Jupiter C rocket, was successfully launched from Cape Canaveral. Americans felt a little better, though Explorer I weighed only 31 pounds, in comparison to Sputnik I's 184 pounds and Sputnik II's 1,160 pounds. From then until the end of Eisenhower's second term, the United States would launch a total of thirty-one scientific satellites. But the Russians would maintain their lead for several more years, becoming the first nation to send a space probe past the moon and into orbit around the sun (January 1959), to land a probe on the moon and transmit pictures of the dark side of the lunar surface back to earth (October 1959), and to send a man into orbit (Yuri Alexseyevich Gagarin, April of 1961). It was not until February 20, 1962, that an American, Lt. Col. John Glenn, finally orbited the earth.

Actually, the space gap was never much of a gap. Although hampered by her emphasis on missile rather than satellite development and by rivalry among the military branches for control of the missile and satellite programs, the United States still trailed by only a few months the Russian feats that received so much worldwide attention. After their early victories, the Russians ran into technical difficulties, and with increased spending by the Eisenhower administration and an all-out effort by the Kennedy administration, the United States would be able to surge ahead of the Soviet Union in space exploration in the 1960s. On July 20, 1969, Americans Neil Armstrong and Edwin Aldrin would become the first earthmen to walk on the moon, fulfilling President Kennedy's 1961 promise to beat the Russians to the moon and to get there by the end of the decade.

It was perhaps inevitable that the national soul-searching and scapegoating that followed the Sputnik launching would soon come to center on the public schools that trained America's scientists and technicians. Even before Sputnik, many Americans had come to believe, as Senator William

Benton had said after a tour of Russian schools, that the nation was engaged in a "new 'cold war' of the classrooms."[11] Sputnik brought a rapid heating of this Cold War, and accelerated a national debate over the nation's schools that had been growing in the United States since the beginning of the decade.

Most of the attacks on the schools in the first half of the fifties had come from two groups, from those who thought the schools were centers of subversion and from those who attacked the schools for practicing the methods of progressive education that produced poorly trained and poorly educated students. The first group, made up of local and national right-wingers, was caught up in the hysteria of the McCarthy era. As McCarthyism declined after 1954, the number and influence of these right-wing critics of education also waned, though they never died out completely. More influential than the right-wing critics of education were those who criticized the schools not for harboring subversives but for harboring progressive educators. Progressive education had always had its dedicated defenders and equally dedicated critics, and while both often misunderstood what it was, they and most of the public had become familiar with its language: "educating the whole child," "recognizing individual differences," "creative self-expression," "teaching children, not subjects," "personality development," "life adjustment," and a whole host of other words and phrases that allowed people who knew a great deal about education or indeed very little at all to discuss educational matters for hours on end.

By the end of World War II, progressive education had come to dominate American educational thought and practice, but even as it won its victory, its critics began to be more numerous and vocal. In the late forties, books and articles critical of progressive education began to appear, but the greatest and most influential criticism would come in the early fifties, and it came from professional educators, professors of the academic disciplines in the colleges and universities, politicians, and other public figures and journalists. The attack intensified in the fall of 1953, when four very important books critical of American education were published in a month's time: Albert Lynd's *Quackery in the Public Schools*, Paul Woodring's *Let's Talk Sense About Our Schools*, Arthur Bestor's *Educational Wastelands*, and Robert Hutchins's *The Conflict in Education*. Reviewing the first three of the books in the *Saturday Review* in December of 1953, Fred M. Hechinger, education editor of the *New York Herald Tribune*, wrote that "never has so much been written about education by so many within so brief a period as this fall."[12] Others would quickly follow, like Rudolf Flesch's *Why Johnny Can't Read and What You Can Do About It*, and dozens of other books with catchy titles. Newspapers and magazines also published article after article on the "crisis" in education.

Although the background and expertise of the critics varied greatly, the message in all of these books and articles was essentially the same: Progressive education had failed to educate America's young people in the way they should be educated. It had failed because it was too permissive and had wasted time on trying to train children how to adjust to life, play in groups, or fulfill themselves, rather than on teaching them academic subject matter. The proposed remedies were usually the same, too: Schools must return to the three Rs, to a rigid and serious curriculum, to discipline, to more work and less play—to academic training rather than life adjustment.

After Sputnik, everybody seemed to get into the debate over the nation's schools, from the president on down. Many Americans seemed to believe, as Paul Woodring wrote in *A Fourth of a Nation* in 1957, that "just as war is too important to be left to the generals, education is too important to be left to the educators. It must concern us all."[13] Newspapers and magazines were again full of articles about the new "crisis" in education, and a new flood of books hit the market analyzing the problems in American education and proposing remedies for them. Education became the center of conversation and of radio and television news reports. Americans talked almost in crisis tones of the "Cold War of the classrooms" that had become part of the battle for survival against international communism. Over and over again American schools were compared with Russian schools and American students with Russian students, with American schools and students almost always coming off second best to their Russian counterparts. The media often concentrated on the worst aspects of American education, describing how American students took courses in cooking, music, and other frills while Russian youngsters were studying math and science and all the other hard subjects that had enabled them to beat America into space, would allow them to beat her to the moon, and maybe defeat her in a nuclear showdown.

Were the Russian schools better than America's? This was a very difficult question to answer, as are all questions involving comparisons of educational systems in different countries. It does seem, however, that the curriculum in the Russian schools was at every level more rigorous and demanding than America's. Russian students began the study of natural science, math, and foreign languages much earlier than American students did, and studied them more intensively. The classes and school days were longer, there were fewer electives, stricter grading standards, little time for play, and virtually no frills courses or life-adjustment courses. The Russian high school graduate had as much education as the American student did at the end of two years of college. These hard facts led Alvin C. Eurich, vice president of the Ford Foundation for the Fund for the Advancement of Education, to say, after a tour of Russian schools in the spring of 1958, that "Soviet education today combines the rigorous European system with the mass education of the United States—a phenomenal attempt."[14]

But there were others who were not quite so sure that Russian schools were really better. As evidence they pointed to the fact that while John Dewey's progressive educational theories had not penetrated the Russian schools, Karl Marx's teachings had, and that the daily indoctrination in Marxism–Leninism took time away from academic studies and constituted a form of life adjustment of its own—adjustment to an authoritarian state. Some skeptics also pointed out that Russian students received little education in the social sciences and the humanities, were allowed little freedom to develop the creative aspects of their nature, and were not taught to think or to question accepted doctrines. This one-sided education, critics pointed out, made Ivan a good technocrat but a dull boy with a rigid authoritarian mind. Besides, mass education in Russia stopped at the secondary level—only the truly gifted were sent on to college, where they had to study subjects and pursue careers that were useful to the state.

But few Americans listened to those who claimed that Russian schools were inferior to theirs—had not Sputnik shown otherwise? Was not that technological feat a sure sign that America was losing the educational cold war, and that if it did not reverse things, disaster awaited in the future? This was certainly the view of Admiral H. G. Rickover, the much respected father of the atomic submarine, who expressed his ideas in speeches and articles and in his highly influential book, *Education and Freedom*, published in 1959. Throughout his book he emphasized the Russian danger, warned Americans not to "underestimate an opponent because we reject his political means and goals," and urged them to spare no effort or expense in the attempt to upgrade the schools and win the educational Cold War.[15] Similar views were expressed in the writings and speeches of Arthur Bestor, a historian and longtime critic of progressive education who wrote in 1958 that "we have wasted an appalling part of the time of our young people on trivialities. The Russians have had sense enough not to do so. That's why the first satellite bears the label, 'Made in Russia.'"[16] Dozens of other books and articles echoed these same alarms.

One of the most influential journalistic studies of American education appeared in a five-part *Life* magazine series entitled "The Crisis in Education," published in the spring of 1958. "The schools are in terrible shape"[17] *Life* wrote in the introduction, and proceeded in the rest of the series to explain why. Frequent references were made to the educational Cold War, such as Sloan Wilson's assertion, in an article entitled "It's Time to Close Our Carnival," that "it goes without saying that the outcome of the arms race will depend eventually on our schools and those of the Russians."[18] Well-illustrated and well-written for the layman, the *Life* series caused widespread discussion and controversy, for as a mass magazine it reached far more people than did the more scholarly books and articles of the day on the education crisis. Many educators were upset by the series, particularly the National Association of Secondary School Principals, which sent a form letter to its 20,000 members urging them to cancel their *Time* and *Life* subscriptions "as long as they have an attitude and policy inimical to education."[19]

Perhaps the most widely discussed of the *Life* articles was the first one in the series, "Schoolboys Point Up a U.S. Weakness," portraying in photographs and words the school life of a typical American high school student, Stephen Lapekas of Chicago, and a typical Russian high school student, Alexei Kutzkov of Moscow. Both were sixteen-year-old boys, but there the resemblance seemed to end. Stephen was described as "an average student, likable, considerate, good-humored—the kind of well-adjusted youngster U.S. public schools are proud of producing." Stephen was not a very serious student, and his school day seemed to revolve around his girlfriend and his other extracurricular activities, "which leave him little time for hard study." Although the school curriculum demanded very little of Stephen, he was lagging in mathematics and making mediocre grades in his other courses. But he was a popular member of the student body and a star swimmer. Alexei, by contrast, was described as "hardworking, aggressive, above average in his grades—the kind of student the Russian system ruthlessly sets out to produce." Good grades were the most important thing in his life, and the rigors of the Russian curriculum and his own desire to excel left little time for dating or other extracurricular activities. He also had good teachers, good equipment, strong discipline, and few electives. *Life* conceded that the American system developed "flexibility" while the Soviet one developed "rigidity and subservience to an undemocratic state. But there is no blinking at the educational results. Academically, Alexei is two years ahead of Stephen."[20]

A great deal of the educational criticism was directed at the teachers and at the institutions that trained them. Teachers colleges and educational departments at other colleges and universities fell into disrepute as study after study ridiculed them for concentrating on methods rather than subject matter, for offering courses on how to run film projectors and provide proper room ventilation, and for awarding masters and doctorates to students who had a marginal command of the English language and used it to write dissertations on such weighty matters as the planning of bathroom locations and schedules and the use, care, and location of pencil sharpeners. More and more, teachers colleges and educational departments were portrayed as inferior schools with inferior professors teaching inferior students how to go out and become inferior teachers. A popular joke on many college campuses in the late fifties was that "a teachers college is a place where false pearls are cast before real swine."[21]

The furor over education aroused by Sputnik helped to promote a growing belief in the need for federal aid to education, which had always had strong opposition from the Roman Catholic Church, business and patriotic organizations who thought it was socialistic, and southern legislators who thought it would provide the federal government with another tool for advancing integration. On January 27, 1958, Eisenhower sent a message to a very receptive Congress calling for a broad program of federal aid to education. After months of deliberation, including testimony from Dr. Wernher von Braun, director of the Development Operation Division of the Army Ballistic Missile Agency and the nation's foremost expert on rocketry, Congress finally responded in September of 1958 with the National Defense Education Act, the most significant federal educational legislation since the land grant acts of the Civil War era. The act provided for a broad spectrum of educational aid, including $295 million in low-interest loans to college students (especially those interested in becoming teachers), $280 million in matching funds for laboratories and other facilities and materials for teaching science, math, and foreign languages in the public schools, $82 million to provide over 5,000 fellowships annually for graduate students preparing to become college teachers, and additional money for improving foreign language instruction in the colleges and for promoting the use of television and other audiovisual techniques. As the title of the bill indicated, this was all to be done in the interest of national defense and security, and individuals receiving money under these various programs had to sign a clause affirming loyalty to the United States and swearing that they were not, and never had been, involved in any subversive activities. The relics of McCarthyism were still around.[22]

In the closing years of the fifties Americans rushed to close the educational gap that had been opened up by Sputnik. Between 1957 and 1964, federal, state, and local appropriations for public education doubled.[23] Educators were busy at all levels revising the curricula, raising standards, putting more emphasis on languages, science, and mathematics, purging the worst of the life-adjustment courses, experimenting with new ways of teaching, introducing more programs for gifted students, and putting more emphasis on I.Q. and college board scores. At the college level, federal money poured in to train public school and college teachers, to pay for the educations of veterans and foreign exchange students, to experiment with new teacher training programs with more emphasis on academic preparation than on educational courses, and to provide more money for research, especially in the sciences and in the areas related to weapons development and other areas of national defense. More and more universities became dependent on federal funds for research, becoming, in the words of Clark Kerr, president of UCLA, "federal grant" universities.[24]

Did all of the money and experiments pay off? It was too early to tell in 1960, of course, but most observers felt that it had. Certainly, the schools and the students *seemed* more serious, the curricula were more rigorous and the standards more demanding, more small rural high schools were being consolidated into comprehensive high schools structured along the lines suggested in James B. Conant's *The American High School Today* (1959), the colleges were training more teachers, and university research labs were developing more ways to destroy the enemy. But urban and suburban schools still provided better educations than rural ones and northern schools better education than southern ones. Most southern school systems were still segregated, and all across the country the schools were still suffering from a surfeit of students and a shortage of teachers. At the collegiate level, a disproportionate amount of the federal aid went to a few of the nation's largest and best universities, leaving the others to scramble for what was left. And in spite of all the money and effort that went into the educational system, many students would rebel against them in the sixties, while in the seventies and eighties Americans would again go through a period of soul-searching about the quality of the schools.

Ironically, while Americans were idolizing and imitating Soviet schools, the Russians were going through an educational debate of their own. Faced with continued industrial and agricultural shortages, rising consumer unrest over the lack of consumer goods, labor shortages, and signs of Western-style student restlessness, the Russian leaders at the very time of the Sputnik success were reexamining their educational system. On April 19, 1958, Khrushchev said that "it is high time, I think, to repattern decisively the system of schooling for our growing generation."[25] By the fall of that year he was announcing that the Russian educational system had been modified to decrease the amount of time spent on math and science, to teach a larger number of practical and technical subjects, and to require all students—from the elementary grades on—to devote part of their day to work in factories or farms in an attempt to help remedy the severe labor shortage. Reporting on these changes in *Newsweek* magazine, Leon Volkov gave his opinion that the Russian educational changes "might well give the West a strategic advantage in the desperate race for scientific and technological dominance."[26]

Three months after it stunned the world, Sputnik fell out of orbit and disintegrated in a fiery death. Its impact had been tremendous. It had served the purpose of its builders, giving Russia a tremendous propaganda victory in the Cold War. It inaugurated the space age—after it, would come dozens of other satellites, over 180 American astronauts and Russian cosmonauts, twelve Americans who walked on the moon, space stations, and probes to other planets. It paved the way for rapid advances in missile research and for communication satellites that would help to revolutionize communications, military surveillance, and weather forecasting. And it brought something its builders probably had not anticipated—it woke America up, much as Pearl Harbor had some sixteen years before, spurring the nation to reexamine and reform some of its basic institutions, to recast some of its priorities and goals, and to plunge full force into the space age.

# 20

# *Living with the Bomb*

If Sputnik signaled that man had entered the space age, opening up the exciting possibility of exploring other worlds and learning more about the mysterious universe, it also signified something else: Man had taken one more step in the dangerous atomic arms race that threatened to destroy life on this planet long before he would have the opportunity to explore outer space. In the years since Hiroshima, atomic weapons and guidance and delivery systems had made incredible progress and had locked the Soviet Union and the United States into a nightmarish arms race that was threatening to spiral out of control. After twelve years of learning to live with the bomb, the introduction of guided missiles and space satellites increased the chance that man would die with it.

From the beginning of the atomic age, the bomb had been viewed as the cheapest and most effective weapon—in fact, as the ultimate weapon which would never have to be used since the very threat of its use would deter aggression. And from the very beginning the research and development of atomic and nuclear weapons had been conducted in a crisis and competitive atmosphere, as part of a deadly race. The United States won the race against the Axis powers during World War II, held a monopoly until Russia tested her bomb in 1949, and tested the first hydrogen bomb on November 1, 1953, nine months before the first successful Russian test. After Truman and Stalin were removed from the world stage early in 1953, Eisenhower and the new Russian rulers continued the race, firmly believing that the other side would launch an attack if it were provoked or developed a clear military superiority. The best defense, both sides believed, was a good offense.

The race continued, and the stakes got higher and higher. In 1955 Russia became the first to drop a hydrogen bomb from an airplane, a feat duplicated by the United States in May of 1956. The United States continued to build its superior fleet of B-47 bombers and to surround Russia and China with air bases and in 1956 began to phase in its new B-52 superbombers, which were far superior to anything the Russians had, as the mainstay of the SAC fleet. At mid-decade the United States had an overwhelming superiority over Russia in bombers by a margin of 9 to 1, but the U.S.S.R., realizing it could never win the bomber race, had concentrated on missile research and development and surged ahead in that field. In the last part of the decade, however, Russia lost this lead as she ran into technical and economic problems and as the United States put more money and effort into closing the "missile gap."[1] Meanwhile, nuclear submarines and other sophisticated war machines were being developed by both sides, the bombs got bigger and bigger, and Britain and France joined the atomic and nuclear weapons club.

In spite of Russia's advantage in military manpower and all the talk about "missile gaps," and "space gaps," and other gaps, the United States and its Western allies retained a large military edge over the U.S.S.R. throughout the fifties. The Gaither report and other defense analyses of the late fifties overestimated the number and destructive power of Soviet weapons and underestimated the strength of the United States, which during Eisenhower's two terms was never vulnerable to a Russian first-strike victory. In the second half of the decade, the U.S.S.R. was capable of inflicting serious, unacceptable damage on Western Europe and perhaps even the United States, but at the same time the United States and her Western allies had attained a state of "maximum deterrence" through their ability to destroy the military and industrial power of the Soviet Union.[2] By 1961, the United States had over 100 intermediate and intercontinental missiles, 1,700 intercontinental bombers, 300 carrier-based planes with nuclear weapons, 80 Polaris missiles, and around 1,000 supersonic land-based fighter planes armed with nuclear warheads. The Russians, by contrast, had only 50 ICBMs, 150 intercontinental bombers, and 400 intermediate missiles.[3] No wonder Eisenhower always bristled at the mention of missile and space "gaps" or "lags" and responded indignantly to all charges that he had gambled with America's defense and security in his attempts to hold down defense spending.

Besides having a weapons edge on the Soviet Union, the United States was also protected by an elaborate defense warning system. In addition to its SAC bases and planes encircling the Soviet Union, the United States had a

Distant Early Warning system, which became operational in July of 1957. Running all across the North American continent from Alaska to Baffin Island, the DEW Line was a sophisticated detection system made up of about fifty radar stations and a network of planes and ships with advanced detection devices. The headquarters of the entire operation was in Colorado Springs. Since the Dew Line was about 1,200 miles north of the border between the United States and Canada, and since the manned bombers of 1957 flew about 600 miles an hour, the DEW Line would detect incoming Russian planes about two hours before they reached the United States. This gave a warning period of about two hours in which planes or missiles could be launched to shoot down the incoming bombers and initiate a counterattack against the Soviet Union.

No one knew for sure how well the system worked, but it was widely believed at the time that very few Russian planes would be able to slip through the detection network and reach their targets in New York, Washington, and other prime sites. General Earle E. Partridge, appointed commander-in-chief of the North American Air Defense Command in the fall of 1957, said that America could shoot down most of the Russian planes but "it wouldn't be 100 per cent. It's like shooting down all the birds in a flock of ducks. If the conditions are good, we would get most of them. If they're bad, or the ducks are exceptionally adept, we might miss a good many."[4] The possibility that some Russian planes might get through always worried some Americans, but many were just as worried about the possibilities of an accidental nuclear war. What if the blips on the radar were really just birds or friendly planes, and the military responded by sending SAC planes to bomb Russian cities? What if some madman got control of the buttons and dispatched atomic bombs toward the Kremlin? The military dismissed these fears as impossible scenarios because of all the safety checks built into the system, but many civilians were still not convinced.

Eisenhower was never comfortable with the reliance on such horrible weapons, and he often worried about the dangers of atomic war and the nightmarish predicament weapons technology had led man into. At a press conference in 1955 he told reporters that the threat of atomic destruction was "so serious that we just cannot pretend to be intelligent human beings unless we pursue with all our might, with all our souls . . . some way of solving this problem."[5] So he worried, refused to engage in budget-busting crash programs to develop and stockpile new weapons, and resisted the pressure of advisers who urged him to rattle the atomic swords in public statements or even use the weapons in some of the crises his administration was faced with. Yet he allowed Dulles to go around talking about "brinkmanship" and "massive retaliation," and he threatened (through discreet diplomatic channels) to use the bomb to resolve the Korean conflict in 1953 and the Formosan crisis in 1954 and 1955. And he made only a few halting steps toward meaningful arms control.

Throughout the fifties both Russian and American leaders gave lip service to the need for arms control through occasional unilateral disarmament proposals, such as Eisenhower's Open Skies suggestion at the Geneva Conference in 1955. Disarmament was also discussed at other forums, particularly the United Nations Subcommittee on Disarmament, which held dozens of sessions. But in spite of all the talks, little was done to control either conventional or nuclear weapons in these tension-filled Cold War years. America and her allies steadfastly insisted that all disarmament and test-ban agreements include provisions for international aerial or on-site inspections, which the Russians usually rejected on the grounds that these inspections would be nothing more than a stratagem for espionage and would be a violation of national sovereignty. Actually, neither side seemed to want a meaningful disarmament agreement. As Bertrand Russell said, "Each is only concerned to find ways of advocating it without getting it."[6] The United States was ahead in the arms race and wanted to stay ahead, and Russia was behind and wanted to catch up. But finally in the latter part of 1958 the United States, Britain, and Russia began an informal "voluntary moratorium" on nuclear testing while the diplomats labored at Geneva to achieve some kind of agreement prohibiting or limiting atomic tests. These moratoriums lasted until the summer of 1961, during the early months of the new Kennedy administration, when Khrushchev ordered a series of tests of superbombs, including one of fifty-eight megatons. The United States resumed testing the next year.[7]

Living with the bomb had never been easy, but it had been done. From Hiroshima onward, most Americans had accepted the bomb as a terrible but necessary weapon. From 1945 through 1948, both the American government and the American people had basked in the knowledge that the nation had a monopoly on the weapon and hence would never suffer its terrible consequences, but this security disappeared with the Russian test in 1949 and the subsequent frantic race to build superbombs. Now, Americans, too, were threatened by the kinds of death and suffering they had seen in the magazine photographs and newsreels of the Hiroshima victims. But faced with these realities, most seemed to react to the threat by denying that it could ever happen to them—God, the American government, and the nation's incredible good luck would prevent it. This denial was partly a natural coping mechanism of the human mind, but it was also partly due to the fact that no major war had been fought on American soil since the Civil War. Unlike Europeans, who had suffered the carnage of two world wars within a generation's time, Americans had fought their modern wars in someone else's territory and had not experienced infantry attacks, occupations, shellings, and terrifying air raids. These were things that always happened to someone else, not to a nation that had led a charmed life.

As the atomic age proceeded, atomic and nuclear bombs, along with the ever-present threat of a war fought with them, became such a commonplace part of American life that most people pushed them into the back of their minds as they went about the routine tasks of life. Most became accustomed to the bomb tests, to the civil defense messages and drills, to the maps of the United States showing prime target areas Russia would be expected to hit, and to the maps of New York and other large cities showing the various levels of destruction radiating out from the center of the blast. Jokes about atomic energy and atomic war also became commonplace, and even people who lived near atomic test zones out in the desert were getting used to the bomb. Early in 1951 a test blast startled Robert Orr, a sixty-five-year-old resident of the mining town of Pioche in the Nevada hills, but his reaction was that "I reckoned there wasn't much I could do about it. So I just sat down and ate my breakfast." The same blast was heard by all-night gamblers at the Golden Nugget in Las Vegas. One of them looked up from the table, commented that it "must be an A-bomb," and continued to roll the dice.[8] And in 1952 a couple who lived near the testing grounds in Nevada was awakened in the middle of the night by a lightning flash and a sound wave that rocked the house. The husband woke up with a start, but was told by his wife, "Oh, go back to sleep. It's only an atomic bomb." The husband replied, "All right. I was afraid one of the kids had fallen out of bed."[9]

In the search to build a better bomb, the United States conducted 122 atomic bomb tests during the fifties, the Russians at least 50, and the British 21. Little was known at the time about the dangers of the radioactive fallout produced by these tests. However, as countries rushed to test bigger and better hydrogen bombs, concern arose about their dangers. More and more evidence was collected to indicate that radioactive fallout could endanger life thousands of miles from the test site, carrying strontium-90 and other radioactive isotopes that caused leukemia and other cancers, birth defects, genetic defects for an undetermined number of generations, perhaps even horrible mutations in human and animal species and irreversible damage to the genetic pool of the entire human race, and countless other unknown dangers if the tests continued long enough. As the decade progressed, other radioactive substances were found in the soil, water, milk, rice, wheat, and other foods all over the world. The public was confused about all of these claims, for it was a new and complex field, little was known, and scientists seemed divided on the real effects of fallout.

The American government and its scientists took the position that although little was known about radioactive fallout, it did not seem to be very dangerous, and that even if it were, the United States had to take the risks because Russia was testing and building the terrible weapons. It was, it was often said, in the "national interest" that America continue the tests. One of the major advocates of this view was the father of the H-bomb, Dr.

Edward Teller. "Sober consideration of the facts make it perfectly clear that we must continue testing nuclear weapons," he wrote in a *Life* article in 1958. "Such tests do not seriously endanger either present or future generations." He also claimed that "American tests *are* leading to the development of a clean bomb" with less radiation and consequently reduced damage to civilians.[10] And America had to build them, clean or not, because they were needed as a deterrent to Russian attack. Like so many other supporters of atomic tests, Teller seemed to believe that the Russian danger was so great that America's superiority in weapons must be preserved, regardless of the effect it had on the government budget or the health of the population.

Most of the popular press seemed to agree with Teller and the government. Newspapers and magazines often ran stories on the results of the tests, but generally downplayed the dangerous effects and insisted that America had to continue them for security reasons. Some conservative publications tried to convince the public that the risks were small and that opponents of the tests were poorly informed alarmists, communist dupes, or communists and fellow travelers. In "What It's Like to Live on Earth's Most A-Bombed Area," *U.S. News and World Report* reported in 1957 on the effects of the atomic bomb tests in an area around Las Vegas, where forty-nine tests had taken place. According to the magazine, it had talked to residents of the area and found that "most people in this desert region seem to agree that living here appears to be just as safe as living anywhere else." One citizen was quoted as saying that "the tests don't worry me. I think the guys who are doing it are competent. If they weren't, they wouldn't be doing it." Another reasoned that "it might be dangerous—this fall-out and all—but I'd rather have us first find out about all this atomic business so the Russians won't be the only ones."[11] And in another 1957 article, the magazine claimed that the protests came only against American and British bomb tests, but "when the Soviet Union explodes a nuclear weapon, the protestors are strangely silent," leading American and British officials to see "a pattern which suggests that much of the agitation against British and American bomb tests is Communist inspired." The article also asserted, as the American government frequently had, that the protestors were badly misinformed, for the ordinary citizen received far more radiation from the natural environment and from dental and medical X rays than he ever got from the fallout from nuclear tests.[12]

In addition to minimizing the dangers of the atom, both government officials and the media glamorized the peaceful uses of atomic energy resulting from the research into how to make better bombs. Over and over again Americans were told that atomic energy would light entire cities, revolutionize the diagnosis and treatment of disease, and make possible all kinds of wonderful gadgets and conveniences that would make life in the dawning atomic age better than man had ever dreamed of. Early in the decade, these views were perhaps best expressed in an editorial, "Our Atomic Tomorrow," in a 1953 issue of *Holiday* magazine. Writing about an atomic bomb test that had been carried out in Nevada on April 22, the editor declared that the successful test "implied clearly that use of the atom's forces for beneficent purposes is closer than ever, that the day when such energy will power cars, ships, planes, and industry is near, that civilization will be better for the work in the desert." The editor then went on to proclaim that "the good living which is *Holiday*'s theme is closer than the eternal desert where the experiments took place. Perhaps not tomorrow, but maybe the day after, the ships will sail, the craft will fly and there will be a fusion-powered society of less work, more leisure."[13]

The decade saw an outpouring of articles and books on the marvelous power of the atom. Typical in its treatment of this topic was David O. Woodbury's *Atoms for Peace* (1956), which declared that the atomic age had arrived and that "there is a fabulous future in it for American talent in general, at all levels and in hundreds of different trades and professions. Never have our young people looked ahead with so much new territory to explore." Woodbury painted a rosy picture of atomic advances and the jobs to be had in the atomic field, and proclaimed that "America is awake to the atomic age. Atoms are for everybody. Whether they are to be destroyers or builders of life, is for the people themselves to decide—by training, by thought, by the substitution of knowledge for ignorance."[14] Still, many Americans worried about nuclear tests and other problems of the atomic age. Many were troubled by the possibilities of nuclear accidents involving workers at atomic power plants and research facilities and bombers carrying nuclear payloads. Back in 1945 and 1946, ten people had been accidentally exposed to radiation at the Los Alamos Scientific Laboratory, and while eight recovered, the other two died within a month's time. In early 1954, a shift in wind currents after an American H-bomb test caused radioactive debris to fall on some of the ships involved in the test, on residents of the Marshall Islands, and on the crew of the *Lucky Dragon*, a Japanese tuna trawler. Although the trawler was sixty-five miles away from the test site, several crew members came down with radiation sickness and the ship's radio operator died from it six months later. Ironically, the first victims of the hydrogen bomb were Japanese, like those of the first atomic bombs in 1945. In 1958, a serious accident involving a reactor killed a workman at Los Alamos, and an accident at a chemical plant at Oak Ridge exposed eight men to radiation; although they suffered from short-term weakness, nausea, vomiting, hair loss, and blood damage, there were no apparent lasting effects. In that same year a B-47 accidentally lost one of its atomic bombs while flying over South Carolina, but luckily the trigger device was not activated so only the TNT in the bomb exploded when it fell, damaging a nearby house.[15] These and other incidents caused a growing number of Americans to question whether the new atomic age was as marvelous as its promoters claimed it was.

In 1956 a new concern was added when private utility companies began to build nuclear power plants. The companies, the Atomic Energy Commission, and the press generally downplayed the danger of these plants while emphasizing that they would provide a cheap, clean, and almost unlimited source of power for industries and homes in the future. Both the power companies and the AEC knew that there were many gaps in their knowledge about radiation and radioactive wastes and that there were significant risks of malfunctionings and accidents, but they suppressed this information so as to encourage public acceptance of the new plants. Luckily, there were no serious accidents involving these plants in the pioneer days of the late fifties, and except for successful efforts by citizens' groups opposing the dumping of radioactive wastes into the ocean near Boston and Cape God, there were few individuals or organizations who complained about the construction of public or private nuclear power plants.[16]

The public seemed to accept what the government and the press said about the beneficial effects of atomic energy, but it still worried about it. The press was full of stories about atomic tests and fallout, and movie after movie appeared dealing with animal and human monsters created by nuclear war or radiation accidents. Millions went to the theaters to see such cinematic travesties as *The Beast from 20,000 Fathoms*, *The Creature from the Black Lagoon*, *The Creature Walks Among Us*, *The Blob*, *Godzilla*, and *Them*. In most cases, the radiation-created monsters terrorized entire communities or even the entire world before they were finally destroyed by the American military authorities. A symbol of the age, the movies revealed that Americans were beginning to fear what man had created in the atomic bomb and other heralded technological breakthroughs.[17]

Monster movies were not the only examples of the effects of the nuclear age on the entertainment industry, for the fifties also brought the boom of science fiction literature and movies. The technology of World War II and the late forties had brought about rapid developments in weapons and space technology, creating the possibilities of space travel, invasions from outer space, interplanetary and intergalactic wars, and the destruction of the human race—themes science fiction had been dealing with for decades. The Cold War, with its international rivalries, anxieties, and harnessing of scientists to build doomsday weapons also contributed to the rise of science fiction, as did the flying saucer scare of the late forties and fifties.[18]

The basic themes of science fiction movies appeared quite early in the decade. In the 1950 film *Destination Moon*, taken from a Robert A. Heinlein novel, a wealthy industrialist, wanting the United States to beat the Russians to the moon, finances a rocket trip to the moon after the United States government had turned down the idea. In *The Day the Earth Stood Still* (1951), the earth is invaded by aliens of superior intellect who come to earth to warn human beings of the danger of the atomic bomb and threaten to destroy the planet if earthlings do not abolish all atomic weapons and all wars (a common theme in science fiction during the 1950s). In *The Thing from Another World* (1951), from a 1938 story by John W. Campbell in *Astounding Science Fiction*, an alien invader found in the Arctic ice terrifies an isolated Arctic base before it is destroyed by the army. There were many other science fiction films, ranging from reasonably intelligent films like *The Invasion of the Body Snatchers*, *Forbidden Planet*, and *The Incredible Shrinking Man* to mindless space battle and monster films. In the late fifties, there was a blessed decline in monster movies and other silly exploitation films, and then in 1959 came the most intelligent and chilling science fiction film of the decade, *On the Beach*.

Published as a novel by Nevil Shute in 1957 and serialized in many newspapers, *On the Beach* was a literary and cinematic success. Starring Gregory Peck, Fred Astaire, and Ava Gardner, the Stanley Kramer film gave a chilling portrait of the last days of the human race as they are played out in Australia after a nuclear war in 1964 had destroyed the Northern Hemisphere but temporarily spared South America and Australia, which faced eventual doom as radioactive clouds headed their way with certain death. One of its most dramatic moments came when an American nuclear submarine that had been stranded in Melbourne made a trip to California to find the source of a mysterious radio signal that seemed to indicate that there had indeed been survivors. But the signal turned out to be caused by a window shade blowing against a Morse code key. The end of the film showed a tattered Salvation Army poster proclaiming that "THERE IS STILL TIME BROTHER." *The New York Times* called it "a deeply moving picture" conveying the theme that "life is a beautiful treasure and man should do all he can to save it from annihilation, while there is still time." The *Times* also felt that "the great merit of this picture, aside from its entertaining qualities, is the fact that it carries a passionate conviction that man is worth saving, after all."[19]

Science fiction novels and short stories also flourished in the new Cold War and atomic age. As early as 1950, *The New York Times* was reporting that "more science fiction novels and anthologies will be published this fall alone than in any previous year." The *Times* correctly predicted that "the future of science fiction seems assured" because "new readers are being lured daily to the new medium, and once attracted they became devotees."[20] Science fiction had been around for a long time, of course, but it now gained an unprecedented popularity. There was an almost endless variation of basic themes revolving around space travel, space adventures, time travel, fear of science, monsters and other mutations caused by atomic radiation, atomic wars, and speculations about man's future in an age when there might be no future. Throughout the decade Ray Bradbury, Isaac Asimov, Arthur C. Clarke, Robert A. Heinlein, and other literary masters helped to raise science fiction to new heights of imagination and popularity. Dozens of book publishers, especially the paperback ones, flooded the market with science fiction works, and at one time nearly a hundred science fiction magazines were being published.[21]

The atomic anxieties of the fifties were also reflected in the rash of reports of "flying saucers" or Unidentified Flying Objects (UFOs) that appeared in that decade. Actually, such sightings were not new, for back in 1896 and 1897 citizens in several states had reported seeing strange "airships" traveling from five to two hundred miles per hour accompanied by strange noises, blue, red, and green lights, and people looking out the windows at the earthlings below. These were the first reported sightings in the United States, but they ended as quickly as they came, not to appear again until the 1940s. Many American pilots reported strange UFOs on bombing missions over Germany and Japan, and from 1946 through 1948 there was an outbreak of UFO reports in Western European and Scandinavian countries.[22]

Undoubtedly related to the dawn of the atomic age and the tensions of the Cold War, the modern era of American UFO sightings began in 1947 when a pilot reported that while flying over the state of Washington he had seen nine aircraft resembling flying saucers moving across the sky at approximately 1,200 miles an hour. In these anxious days of the Cold War, his story was widely circulated by the press and widely discussed throughout the nation, with most people speculating that the saucers had come from outer space or were the latest weapons of the Russians in their drive to defeat the United States and dominate the world. All told, there were seventy-nine reported sightings in 1947, and from then until the end of the 1950s hundreds of UFO sightings were reported each year. These reports were investigated by the U.S. Air Force, which was entrusted with this task because of the military implications of the sightings. According to the air force, which spent close to $500,000 investigating these reports between 1947 and 1960, there were 169 sightings in 1950, but these jumped to a decade high of 1,501 in 1952, then dropped off to around 500 each year until 1956, when they jumped to 778. They rose again to 1,178 in 1957 (the year of Sputnik), before dropping off to 573 in 1958, 364 in 1959, and 462 in 1960.[23]

Most of these sightings, the air force concluded, were of weather balloons, planets, lightning, artificial satellites (after 1957), regular aircraft, and other natural and man-made happenings, along with the inevitable hoaxes and optical illusions. It also admitted that some of the sightings simply could not be explained. But throughout the fifties, many people claimed that the air force and civilian government officials were dragging their feet or were covering up the real dangers of UFOs so as to prevent public hysteria or to avoid revealing the government's own inability to investigate or intercept the strange aircraft.

The UFO scare produced many bizarre stories. Hundreds of people reported sightings of all types of spaceships carrying all kinds of alien beings. There were strange meetings with aliens, tours of spacecraft, rides on spacecraft at the invitation or command of their pilots, and warnings from aliens that man was heading for destruction unless he stopped the atomic race and learned to live in peace on earth. Some even claimed that aliens had explained some or all of the mysteries of the universe that had puzzled man since the dawn of human civilization. Across the United States a network of people arose who claimed these experiences, wrote books and pamphlets about them, gave interviews to reporters, appeared on television and radio, gave lectures, and attended conventions where they exchanged stories and tried to sell one another souvenirs of their experiences or books they had written about them. Many Americans believed their tales, while others attributed them to the tensions of the Cold War, the desire for fame and profit, or the manifestations of hysteria and other mental aberrations. Some cynics suggested that these stories were probably inspired by *The Day the Earth Stood Still* and other science fiction films, books, and short stories of the day.[24]

While the claims made by the UFO witnesses might be suspect, many of the stories were certainly quite imaginative. In *Inside the Space Ships* (1955), George Adamski narrated his account of being taken on board spaceships from Mars, Venus, Saturn, and Jupiter, and of meeting beautiful women and superintelligent men from civilizations far superior to any that could be found on earth. These aliens had first contacted him in bars and cafés in Los Angeles and for some reason had chosen him as the medium for warning man to stop the wars and atomic weapons race that were endangering the entire solar system. Then there was David Fry, who related in his *White Sands Incident* how he had been picked up by a flying saucer at the White Sands Proving Ground in New Mexico and flown to New York City and back. His hosts seemed to be quite fluent in English, for they said such things as "Better not touch the hull, pal, it's still hot!" and "Take it easy, pal, you're among friends." Orfeo Angelluci also seemed to have extraterrestrial pals, for he related in *Secret of the Saucers* in 1955 of meetings he had had with aliens in out-of-the-way places like the Greyhound bus terminal in Los Angeles. On one of these strange encounters he met none other than Jesus Christ. And finally there was Buck Nelson, who claimed that he had been taken on flying saucers to the moon, Mars, and Venus. As proof of his latter trip, he sold packets of hair which he claimed were from a 385-pound Venusian St. Bernard dog.[25]

Most Americans were less concerned about UFOs and friendly or unfriendly alien visitors than they were about the down-to-earth dangers of nuclear war. Although Americans learned to live with the fear, it was always there: newspapers, television programs, magazines, and government reports provided a steady stream of information about what would happen to America's cities if the bombs fell. No one really knew, of course, how great the destruction would be. The only real-life examples of atomic attack had been at Hiroshima and Nagasaki, and the destruction of those little bombs would be dwarfed by the huge weapons expected to be used in the next war. The extent of the destruction would depend upon many factors, such as how many Russian planes got through America's defenses, how close they came to the targets, how long the war lasted, weather conditions, and other variables.

In 1958 and 1959, a special Radiation Subcommittee of the Joint Committee on Atomic Energy did a study of the hypothetical impact of a Russian atomic attack on the United States. The study focused on the probable effects if Russia had dropped a series of hydrogen bombs totalling 1,500 megatons (a moderate, not heavy, bomb attack) on American cities and military installations at noon on October 17, 1958. Released in June of 1959, the study contained some very disturbing conclusions. Twenty million Americans would be killed on the first day and 22 million more would die in the following sixty days from radiation sickness, making a grand total of 42 million, 28 percent of the population. The East Coast would be destroyed by the explosion of the bombs and resulting fire storms, and the percentage of the population killed here would be especially high—65 percent in metropolitan New York, 91 in Boston, 80 in Philadelphia, 92 in Baltimore, and 81 in the capital. Destruction and death in the rest of the country would be severe but not as great as on the East Coast.[26]

The study also revealed that a 20-megaton blast would cause fatal burns to anyone out in the open for as far away as 20 miles from the center of the explosion, blisters on anyone up to 25 miles away, lung damage up to 6 miles away, eardrum ruptures up to 10 miles away, and the destruction of steel and concrete skyscrapers 2.5 miles away. The attack would bring burned forests and cropland, urban rubble, erosion, floods, fires, food shortages, medical service shortages, a panicky and perhaps disorderly population, the breakdown of transportation and communication, and the interruption of almost all governmental, industrial, and medical services. There would also be long-term environmental and climatic changes: "The sun will shine through a dust-laden atmosphere; the landscape in mid-January would be snow-covered or blackened by fire; at higher latitudes, blizzards and subzero temperatures would add death and discomfort."[27] For decades to come, there would be diseases and death from radioactive fallout. The country could survive and rebuild, and ecological balance would be gradually restored, but it would take a long time, the report concluded.

At the same time as the subcommittee report appeared, a whole new type of literature on the strategy of thermonuclear warfare was coming out. Henry Kissinger (*Nuclear Weapons and Foreign Policy*) and other academicans were carving out names for themselves in the field, but the best known of the new theorists was Herman Kahn, a Rand scientist, civil-defense strategist, and futurologist at the Princeton Institute for Advanced Study. In the summer of 1959 he gave a series of lectures at the institute that were published in 1960 as *On Thermonuclear War*.[28] The book sold 30,000 copies, an unusually high figure for a university press book, and it was widely read in governmental, educational, and military circles.

In a cold, analytical fashion, Kahn reasoned that there would never be worldwide disarmament, that war would never be outlawed, and that future wars would probably be nuclear ones whether policymakers wanted them to be or not. Therefore, America must be prepared to fight and win a nuclear war, not just to survive it. With these assumptions, he went on to analyze how to win such a war, how many people would be killed and how many would survive, what was an "acceptable" level of civilian deaths and property damage and what was not. He also advocated heavy spending for nationwide fallout shelter construction. Kahn's work helped to popularize such phrases as "thinking about the unthinkable," "doomsday machine," and "escalation," and it had a great influence in military and governmental circles. But his emphasis on a "rational" approach to thermonuclear war also earned him the reputation of being a cold-blooded, half-mad, amoral theorist who was willing to sacrifice millions of lives for a military victory over the enemy.[29]

At the time of Kahn's work, America's civil defense policies had changed very little from the vastly inadequate ones of the Truman years, when Congress had decided that the federal government would serve primarily as a public information service and leave most of the responsibility for civil defense up to the states. From 1950 to 1958, the federal government had spent $490 million on civil defense for various programs, but had very little to show for it. In 1958 the Civil Defense Act of 1950 was amended by Congress to make civil defense a "joint" responsibility of the states and the federal government, but still little was done. Throughout the fifties, Congress refused to appropriate money for public bomb shelters, an important first step in any civil defense program, for most government officials believed that it was up to individuals to provide their own shelters.[30]

The federal government seemed to think it was doing enough by publishing such pamphlets as *Education for National Survival: A Handbook on Civil Defense for Schools* (1956) and *The Family Fallout Shelter* (1959). In addition to providing information on preparing for and surviving a nuclear war, these and similar publications minimized the destructive effects of nuclear war and used Cold War rhetoric to rally the population behind the nation's defense and atomic testing policies. In *What You Should Know About the National Plan for Civil Defense and Defense Mobilization,* for example, the reader was told that "studies of possible attack patterns and their probable effects indicate that a large majority of the total population can survive," and was reminded that "national survival requires that we not only survive the immediate effects of an attack but go on to recover and win."[31] *Education for National Survival* claimed that "the forces of totalitarianism are adamant in their determination that their form of government shall prevail not only in their own lands but throughout the world," and warned that the "aggressor nations are making tremendous strides in the development of intercontinental bombers, nuclear weapons, and guided missiles."[32]

Under the Eisenhower administration, fallout shelters steadily increased in popularity and became a major emphasis of the federal government's civil defense program. Government officials and scientists warned that all Americans who could should build some kind of a fallout shelter. An increasing number of them did, but they still constituted a minute portion of the population—only 5 percent by the end of the decade. To most it was still something of a fad promoted by the federal government, bomb shelter contractors, and the popular press. In August of 1959, for example, *Life* magazine ran an article entitled "Their Sheltered Honeymoon," a story of a Mr. and Mrs. Melvin Mininson of Miami, who spent their honeymoon in an 8-by-14-foot steel and concrete shelter twelve feet undergound. The feat was sponsored by a bomb shelter contractor who gave the couple a two-week vacation in Mexico for spending fourteen days—the most critical period of fallout danger—in the shelter. The Mininsons' shelter had a telephone and radio but no television, but they survived the ordeal, according to *Life*, with very little discomfort. Bomb shelter life, the article seemed to say, was not all that bad.[33]

But government civil defense pamphlets and stunts like the Mininson sheltered honeymoon could not hide the fact that the United States really had no viable civil defense program in the fifties. There was no effective coordinated program to give adequate advance warning of an attack, to supervise the evacuation of target areas, to provide for food, water, shelter, basic government services, and long-range recuperation after an attack. Bomb shelters would have provided significant protection, but very few individuals could afford private shelters, and the government would not help finance private shelters or large public ones. As a Gallup Poll in October of 1961 revealed, over 90 percent of the population had made no effort to acquire fallout shelters or even to stockpile food. In almost all areas of civil defense planning, the United States trailed far behind the U.S.S.R., Great

Britain, the Netherlands, and the Scandinavian countries.[34] If the United States had fought a nuclear war anytime in the fifties, and if significant Russian striking forces had gotten through to their targets, the United States would have experienced a civilian disaster of nightmare porportions, one from which the nation might not have recovered.

But the development of large hydrogen bombs and the rapid progress in guided missile research convinced many people that no civil defense program could be very effective in the event of war. The evacuation routes and procedures so carefully worked out by civil defense officials would only result in hopelessly clogged highways and prevent the movement of emergency vehicles. If by chance some did escape the cities, where would they go, where would they find food and other essentials? Hiding under desks or tables, lying in a fetal position in the fortified corner of the basement, or burrowing underground in a shelter also seemed to offer little protection against the superbombs. Shelters might survive the initial blast, but the inhabitants might still be killed by asphyxiation or incineration. And even if some did survive the immediate blast or the first few days of fallout, what would be the point of coming out of the shelters to a world of burned forests, flattened cities, contaminated water and food and air, lingering radiation sickness, and anarchy, where the human race would act like animals in the jungle? Television and radio were already carrying stories of people hoarding supplies in their own little bomb shelters and promising to shoot anyone who approached their sanctuary in a postatomic world.

In 1960 one Queens, New York, accountant told a reporter that "survival with fallout . . . would be miserable," and a Manhattan bank teller said that in a nuclear attack he would probably "run under the bomb and get it over with quickly."[35] Many felt that the end would come quickly, and there were many who experienced fleeting moments of fear when they thought the end had come. One observer of the decade has written that for him the moment came "on an evening in the autumn of 1956, during the Suez crisis." He remembered "walking along Fifth Avenue in New York as a low-flying jet roared suddenly overhead and thinking immediately, This Is It."[36]

As the decade progressed a growing number of Americans began to argue that the key to a national survival was not a civilian defense program or a deterrent nuclear force but a worldwide ban on nuclear tests, the manufacture of nuclear weapons, and ultimately of war itself. These people were small in number in the first half of the decade and were usually dismissed by the government and the press as communists, socialists, dupes, or wild-eyed kooks. But in the midfifties, as the bombs grew bigger and the hazards of nuclear tests became clearer, the peace movement began to attract more supporters and attention, especially when its leaders came to include some of the country's—and the world's—greatest scientists and thinkers in other fields. One of the most prominent of these was Nobel Prize–winning chemist Linus Pauling, whose *No More War!* (1958) graphically detailed the dangers of strontium-90 and other effects of fallout, warned of the terrible probable effects of nuclear war, and proclaimed his belief that "the way to avert nuclear war is to begin making safe, just, and effective international aggreements; and . . . the first of these should include the stopping of the tests of all nuclear weapons."[37] In England, the indefatigable philosopher Bertrand Russell pursued similar objectives through his publications and public peace demonstrations. In his *Common Sense and Nuclear Warfare* (1959), Russell said his book was aimed at all countries, communist or not, with no bias to either side: "the appeal is to human beings, as such, and is made equally to all who hope for human survival."[38] Nobel Prize–winner Albert Schweitzer also added his influential voice to the protest, as in his April of 1957 radio appeal to fifty nations asking for the termination of all nuclear tests.

By the time of Schweitzer's plea in the spring of 1957 the peace movement was picking up steam. In June of 1957, Linus Pauling led some 11,000 scientists from all across the world, including some 3,000 from the United States, in signing a petition calling for "immediate action . . . to effect an international agreement to stop the testing of all nuclear weapons," an action which led the Senate Internal Security Subcommittee to investigate his patriotism.[39] Then in the summer of 1957, peace activists finally formed a national organization, the National Committee for a Sane Nuclear Policy (SANE), which on November 15, 1957, took out a full page ad in *The New York Times* calling for an end to nuclear testing. From this modest beginning, SANE would grow rapidly, having 130 chapters and 25,000 members by the summer of 1958 and counting among its members such notables as Norman Cousins, Norman Thomas, Oscar Hammerstein II, Walter Reuther, John Hersey, and Erich Fromm. It also included many well-known and obscure figures from the old left and the emerging new left, Quakers, and other groups that had been active in the peace movement since early in the decade. SANE would eventually be joined in its efforts by other groups. One was the Student Peace Union, made up of student pacifists and socialists, which was organized in 1959 and claimed 5,000 members by the end of the decade. Another was the Committee for Non-Violent Action (CNVA), formed in the fall of 1958, which engaged in peaceful acts of civil disobedience, like trespassing on AEC property or in areas where testing projects were being carried out.[40]

Members of these and other peace groups often made the headlines in the late fifties. On the twelfth anniversary of the Hiroshima bombing on August 6, 1957, Albert Bigelow and several other pacifists were arrested when they illegally entered an AEC testing ground in Nevada as a protest against nuclear tests. In the spring of 1958, Bigelow and four Quaker pacifists, members of CNVA, were taken into custody when they tried to sail the ship *Golden Rule* into a Bikini test zone in the Pacific where tests were scheduled to be held. They were jailed until the tests were over. And in July of 1958, pacifists on the *Phoenix* who were trying to enter a nuclear test zone in the Pacific were arrested and given prison sentences.[41]

The peace movement reached its height in 1960. In May a large crowd jammed Madison Square Garden for a SANE rally and nearly 3,000 pacifists demonstrated in San Francisco. In July a Walk for Disarmament demonstration was held in Los Angeles, and in August several thousand demonstrators calling for nuclear disarmament marched on the U.N. in New York. In that same year, pacifists in some of New York City's public schools and in each of its public colleges refused to join in civil defense drills on the grounds that they were really part of the preparations for war. And at Harvard, Berkeley, and other college campuses, students formed peace societies, circulated peace petitions, and demonstrated.[42]

In spite of all their efforts, the peace protesters of the late fifties failed to alter the policies of the government or to change public opinion on nuclear tests and weapons or on protesters themselves. The government and most of the public still viewed pacifists and opponents of nuclear tests to be communists or well-meaning but naive and ill-informed dupes of the communists. However, the peace movement of the late fifties did bring an important public debate on nuclear tests, the nuclear arms race, and the perils of thinking about the unthinkable—even if the majority of the public was not listening. And it also revealed the existence of a significant body of dissent from the prevailing ideology of the Cold War and showed that not all intellectuals and college students of the fifties were part of the Silent Generation. The seeds of nonviolent and violent protests against war had been planted, to be nurtured later by a war in Southeast Asia that would bring nationwide peace demonstrations, drive one president from office, and force another to pull American forces out of an unpopular and unwinnable war.

# 21

# *Troubled Times*

By the late fall of 1957 it had become increasingly clear that Eisenhower's second term would not be as satisfying for him as the first had been. There had already been unpleasant battles with the Democratic Congress, the economic recession, the Little Rock crisis, the shock of Sputnik, more criticism from the press and Congress, and, as he wrote in his diary during the Little Rock crisis, growing demands from many quarters that he "'do something.'"[1] Then to make matters worse, he had another serious illness. On November 16, at the height of the national handwringing over Sputnik, Eisenhower suffered the third illness of his presidential career, a mild cerebral stroke that left him with a slight speech hesitation but did not damage his reading, writing, and reasoning abilities. Following doctors' orders, the president reduced his workload and tried to get more rest, but he did not enter the hospital, and he continued to carry out his presidential duties, including traveling to Paris in December for an important NATO meeting and delivering his state-of-the-union message to Congress in January.

Eisenhower's third illness caused more concern throughout the nation about his health and his ability to perform the complex and stressful duties of the presidency—after all, the stroke came on the heels of a heart attack in 1955 and ileitis surgery in 1956. Some Democrats and even a few Republicans joined newspaper and magazine editorialists in suggesting that the sixty-seven-year-old president was too old and sick to run the nation and that he should step down for the good of himself and the country. Eisenhower was hurt and angered by these calls for his resignation. He did realize the dangers the stroke posed for him and the country, but he felt that his abilities to do the job had not been impaired, and he had taken the precaution of privately working out with Nixon plans for a vice-presidential takeover if he became incapacitated. His ingrained sense of duty also prevented him from seriously considering resignation—the presidency, he told reporters in December, is a "job you may die from but it's not a job you resign from."[2] He continued to perform his job well, amazing his close colleagues by his stamina and healthy appearance. On March 1, 1958, his doctors pronounced him completely recovered from the stroke.

If 1957 had been a bad year for Eisenhower, 1958 would be no better. In fact, he would call it "the worst of his life."[3] At home, he and Congress were embroiled in arguments over how to cure the recession and how to close the alleged space, missile, and educational gaps opened up by Sputnik. And in foreign affairs, little crises seemed to pop up everywhere as the Cold War spread into the non-Western world. The Middle East continued to be a center of Arab–Israeli conflicts, Russian–American competition, Arab nationalism, and Nasser-inspired revolts against pro-Western Middle Eastern regimes. Drawing on that convenient excuse for intervention, the Eisenhower Doctrine, Eisenhower had sent the Sixth Fleet to the eastern Mediterranean in the spring of 1957 to protect Jordon's King Hussein against rebel forces. In July of 1958, at the request of Lebanon's president, Camille Chamoun, he dispatched 1,700 marines, later followed by almost 14,000 reinforcements, to defend Beirut and its airport from rebel attack while Chamoun restored order in the rest of the country and Britain intervened to stabilize Hussein's shaky regime in Jordan. In August, there was another crisis in Asia, where, after nearly three years of relative peace between Taiwan and Communist China, the latter began to shell Quemoy and Matsu and Mao and Chiang exchanged threats of war. In this crisis, Eisenhower used diplomacy and a naval show of force in the waters between the two nations to prevent a potentially dangerous conflict. The Chinese Communists stopped the shelling, though shortly afterward they began a new policy of lobbing a few shells toward Quemoy on odd-numbered days of the month.

Eisenhower's troubles with Latin America also garnered dramatic foreign policy headlines in 1958. Throughout most of the fifties, the United States had neglected Latin America as it concentrated on the Cold War in other parts of the world. The United States sent little foreign aid to Latin America, and what little she did send went to right-wing dictators who used it to prop up their regimes rather than to make land reforms and other fundamental changes that might lead to stable and democratic governments. This policy was deeply resented in Latin America, as was the United States' claim—often called the Dulles Doctrine—that she had the right to intervene in Latin American affairs whenever her interests were threatened, even to the point of overthrowing a government hostile to American interests. Latin America was certainly ripe for communist subversion—most of its nations were characterized by poverty, illiteracy, poor transportation systems, little industrialization and little capital to initiate it, exploitation of poor peasants by large landowners and the government, frequent riots and demonstrations against governments, and frequent changes in government as one dictator succeeded another.

To help improve relations with the United States' southern neighbors, Eisenhower sent Vice President Nixon on an eighteen-day goodwill tour of eight Latin American nations in the spring of 1958. What had been expected to be an uneventful trip turned out to be a nightmare for the vice president as he and his party received a hostile reception at almost every stop. His speeches were interrupted by hecklers, he was spat upon and pelted with eggs and fruit, and greeted with cries of "Yankee Imperialist," "Yankee Go Home," and "Death to Nixon." In Caracas, Venezuela, he and his party were met by well-organized mobs. Again he was spat upon and pelted with various objects and his motorcade was attacked by angry demonstrators with eggs, rocks, steel pipes, axes, and poles. The mob smashed the windows of several automobiles, injuring some of those inside, and then, in a horrifying experience, part of the mob surrounded the vice president's car and rocked it up and down, trying to turn it over. Nixon barely escaped with his life. Eisenhower sent an armada of six destroyers and an aircraft carrier loaded with helicopters and marines, and alerted American forces in Puerto Rico and Guantánamo Bay.[4] The forces were not needed, however, and Nixon came back to the United States as a hero. In Latin America, of course, the armada was deeply resented as another example of Yankee imperialism and intervention.

Not long after the vice president's ordeal in Latin America, the Eisenhower administration was shaken by a major scandal involving Sherman Adams, the assistant to the president. The Adams controversy began in June of 1958, when the House Committee on Legislative Oversight reported that some rather unsavory transactions had taken place between Adams and wealthy New England industrialist Bernard Goldfine. It seemed that Goldfine, a friend of Adams for eighteen years, had been a very good friend indeed, having given the assistant to the president many gifts—including a $2,400 Oriental rug and a $700 vicuña coat—and having paid a $3,000 hotel tab that Adams had run up in Boston, New York, and Plymouth, Massachusetts. Adams had returned these favors, it was alleged, by interceding on Goldfine's behalf with the Federal Trade Commission and the Securities and Exchange Commission, which were investigating Goldfine's violation of federal laws. Adams told Eisenhower that "I made a mistake, but I'm no crook,"[5] and he made the same claim in testimony before the House committee, where he admitted accepting the gifts but denied using his influence to help Goldfine. The committee cleared Adams of all charges but cited Goldfine for contempt. Goldfine would later be sent to jail for income tax evasion.

Eisenhower was stunned at the charges leveled at the good friend who had been so valuable in running the White House staff. On June 18, the day after Adams had appeared before the House committee, the president held a press conference and announced that Adams had been imprudent but not dishonest, and went on to say that "I personally like Governor Adams. I admire his abilities. I respect him because of his personal and official integrity. I need him."[6] The last phrase was quickly picked up by the press and circulated as just more proof that Adams was really the assistant president and that Eisenhower could not govern without him. Many other Republicans did not like or need Adams, whose gruff ways had made many enemies over the years, and they began to clamor for his resignation, claiming that he would be an enormous liability in the upcoming fall elections, which already promised dim prospects for the party.

Eisenhower felt that Adams was being hounded by Democrats and Old Guard Republicans and resisted all attempts to dump him. But as the days passed, the pressure to get rid of him mounted and became irresistible in September when, in the traditionally Republican state of Maine, Senator Frederick Payne, who had received gifts and a loan from Goldfine, was trounced by Democratic challenger Edmund Muskie. Eisenhower now decided that for the sake of the party, Adams would have to go, and he sent Nixon and the GOP national chairman, Meade Alcorn, to persuade him to do the right thing. On September 22, Adams handed in his resignation. Eisenhower accepted it with deep regret for losing such a close and valuable aide but with relief that he had not been forced to fire Adams or ask for his resignation in person.[7] Adams's forced departure was a bitter defeat for Eisenhower, who for years afterward would maintain that Adams was innocent of the charges and was the victim of his own bad judgment and the political atmosphere of the time that forced his resignation.

The problems of 1957 and 1958 were taking their toll on the president and his party, and the Republicans went into the 1958 elections with fears of a major setback. They were right, for the party suffered a stunning defeat. The Democrats gained 47 seats in the House and 13 in the Senate, giving them a majority of 282–154 in the House and 64–34 in the Senate. The Democrats had their biggest victory since 1936, and for the first time since 1867 the opposing party had the power to override the vetoes of the president. Eisenhower now had the dubious distinction of being the first president ever to have three consecutive Congresses in the hands of the opposition party. Out in the states, the Democrats had won twenty-six gubernatorial races, so they now controlled the governorships in thirty-four states.[8] It was truly a disaster, and a personal blow to the president. Although he himself was still very popular, the voters seemed to have rejected his policies and his party. The lame duck seemed to have become lamer.

Eisenhower's last two years in office were plagued by problems with the heavily Democratic Eighty-sixth Congress. In public speeches and press conferences he attacked the "lavish spending" of the Democrats, and he used his veto power and the help of Southern Democrats and conservative Republicans to block proposals for federal aid for school construction and teachers' salaries, large increases in the minimum wage, and health care for the aged and poor. He did approve the Kerr-Mills bill, a weak measure that provided federal matching funds for states that established health insurance programs for the elderly poor over the age of sixty-five. In turn, Congress rejected administration bills to create thirty-five new federal judgeships, raise postal rates, and increase gasoline taxes. It cut funds from Eisenhower's mutual foreign aid programs, passed over his veto a $750 million pay raise for federal employees, and after passing his 1959 budget with few changes, added $600 million to the 1960 budget. It also rejected, after a long and bitter debate, Eisenhower's appointment of Lewis L. Strauss as secretary of commerce to succeed Sinclair Weeks, the first time since 1925 that the Senate had turned down a cabinet appointee. Angry and depressed, Eisenhower told his secretary that "this was the most shameful thing that had happened in the U.S. Senate since the attempt to impeach a President many, many years ago."[9]

The civil rights issue continued to be front page news in the last two years of Eisenhower's presidency. He was still reluctant to use his powers to advance the civil rights cause, in spite of the fact that the nation was becoming more receptive to civil rights reforms and black organizations were becoming more militant. On May 19, 1958, near the end of the turbulent school year in Little Rock, he spoke before an all-black audience in Washington's Presidential Arms Hotel at a luncheon sponsored by the National Newspaper Publishers Association. At the end of his speech before the overflow crowd, he said that "no one is more anxious than I am to see Negroes receive first-class citizenship in this country, but you must be patient." His listeners were shocked. One of them, Jackie Robinson, would later say that he felt like jumping to his feet and saying, "Oh, no! Not again." The speech received a great deal of publicity, resulted in a flood of indignant phone calls and letters, and strengthened the view in the black community that the president, in spite of his (belated) use of force in Little Rock, was basically unsympathetic to their cause and would not provide the national leadership necessary for faster civil rights progress.[10]

The despair of American blacks over the president's leadership was heightened a month later when Martin Luther King, Jr., and several other black leaders met with Eisenhower at the White House in a vain attempt to persuade him to endorse the Brown decision publicly and to use his influence to get meaningful civil rights legislation passed through Congress. At this June 23 meeting, Eisenhower listened politely but refused to commit himself to any of the proposals presented to him. As the black leaders left the room, Eisenhower told King, "Reverend, there are so many problems . . . Lebanon, Algeria. . . ." Depressed and disgusted, King departed with the impression that Eisenhower had good intentions but did not know how to deal with the civil rights issue and "could not be committed to anything which involved a structural change in the architecture of American society. His conservatism was fixed and rigid, and any evil facing the nation had to be extracted bit by bit with a tweezer because the surgeon's knife was an instrument too radical to touch this best of all possible societies."[11]

The schools continued to be the focus of most of the civil rights battles of the late fifties. By the fall of 1958, most of the southern states had adopted legislation authorizing the governor to close the schools to prevent desegregation. But outside of Little Rock, Arkansas, only Virginia, the leader of "massive resistance" ever since the Brown decision in 1954, chose this reactionary course. Ironically, the state had experienced little of the racial violence that had plagued some of her sister states to the south. Yet, in September of 1958, invoking powers granted to him by the legislature, Governor Almond closed the schools in Warren County, Charlottesville, and Norfolk, affecting some 12,700 students. Although federal court orders and public pressure served to reopen most of the closed schools in Virginia midway through the 1958–1959 school year, the crisis would continue in Prince Edward County, which closed all its public schools in the fall of 1959.

The school closings of 1958 were only one sign of the extremism sweeping parts of the South. The reactionaries were still in control, and many moderates were still afraid to speak out. Nearly thirty faculty members left the university of Alabama after the Autherine Lucy incident. Black state colleges that showed any signs of agitating for civil rights saw their funds curtailed by state legislatures. In Mississippi in 1958, a black professor at Alcorn College who tried to enter the summer session at the University of Mississippi was arrested and put in an insane asylum, and for months whites in the state joked that "any nigger who tries to enter Old Miss *must* be crazy."[12] In 1959 when a black army veteran, Clyde Kennard, tried to register at Mississippi Southern College, he was harassed by the local authorities—the police stopped him for "reckless driving," claimed to discover illegal whiskey in his car, and later arrested him for allegedly stealing a bag of chicken feed. After fighting these trumped-up charges, he was given a seven-year prison sentence by the judge.[13] Moderate politicians were voted out of office in favor of their rabid segregationist opponents. Books were banned in school and municipal libraries, textbooks were banned or censored, and in Mississippi, after the DAR in 1959 had circulated a list of "satisfactory" and "unsatisfactory" textbooks, the state legislature in 1960 was moved to pass a law giving its apparently omniscient governor, Ross Barnett, the final authority over the selection of textbooks in the public schools. Barnett eagerly accepted the new duty, exhorting the state to "clean up our textbooks. Our children must be properly informed of the Southern and true American way of life."[14]

And the violence continued. In 1959 Mississippi made national headlines again in the case of Mack Charles Parker, a black accused of raping a pregnant white woman. Even though the victim could not positively identify her assailant in a lineup of twenty black men, Parker was jailed. His trial was scheduled for April 27, 1959, but some could not wait for justice to be done. On the night of April 25, nine masked men broke into the Poplarville jail, took Parker from his cell, and dragged him down the metal stairway with his head hitting each stair as he clawed at the steps. He was taken to the Pearl River, the boundary between Mississippi and Louisiana, shot twice through the chest, and thrown into the rain-swollen waters. His body was found on May 4, and although many people in the community knew who the killers were, none would come forward to implicate them, and they were never brought to trial. When the grand jury was impaneled on November 2, 1959, circuit judge Seba Dale told the eighteen jurors that the Supreme Court's decisions probably caused the death of Parker and referred to the court as a "board of sociology, sitting in Washington, garbed in Judicial robes." On January 14, 1960, the grand jury refused to issue an indictment, claiming that there was no "basis for prosecution in the case."[15]

There were southerners who spoke up against this madness, and few were more vocal than Harry Golden, a transplanted New York Jew who lived in Charlotte, North Carolina, where he published a bimonthly newspaper, the *Carolina Israelite*. The paper had a small circulation, perhaps 15,000 before his book, *Only in America*,[16] rose to the top of the best-seller list in 1958, bringing national fame to Golden and thousands of new subscribers to the newspaper. Even before that, its subscribers had numbered some of the most influential people in America, including Harry Truman, Adlai Stevenson, Earl Warren, and William Randolph Hearst. Golden took on many important causes, with integration being one of his favorite ones and logic, wit, sarcasm, and satire being his standard literary tools.

One of his most widely circulated and quoted articles was "The Vertical Negro Plan," written after the North Carolina legislature had passed in 1956 its latest laws to circumvent the Brown decision. Noting that the South had always been willing to take the money of its 12 million black citizens, and that whites and blacks had always been allowed to *stand* together in lines at drugstore counters, bank teller windows, grocery stores, and dime and department stores, Golden observed that "it is only when the negro 'sets' that the fur begins to fly." Therefore, he proposed that at the next session the legislature adopt his Golden Vertical Negro Plan for the public schools, which would entail taking all the seats out of the public schools and replacing them with desks. "The desks should be those standing-up jobs, like the old-fashioned bookkeeping desk. Since no one in the South pays the slightest attention to a VERTICAL NEGRO, this will completely solve our problem. . . . In whatever direction you look with the GOLDEN VERTICAL NEGRO PLAN, you save millions of dollars, to say nothing of eliminating forever any danger to our public education system upon which rest the destiny, hopes, and happiness of this society."[17]

In other columns he described his Golden Out-of-Order Plan, which advocated that out-of-order signs be placed over all the "white only" water fountains. This would lead, he predicted, to whites drinking from the "colored" fountains and eventually to the need for only one fountain, for "it is possible that the whites may accept desegregation if they are assured that the facilities are still 'separate,' albeit 'Out-of-Order.'" And in his Carry-the-Books Plan, he proposed to remedy the objections to school desegregation by having black children carry the books of their white classmates and by having black girls wear aprons to school—since whites were used to having black domestics around, they would be willing to go to school with blacks if they appeared in their domestic guise.[18] Golden's brilliant satire was widely appreciated but not universally so, for he received many obscene complaints and threats in the same mail that brought accolades and orders for new subscriptions.

In 1959 the South seemed to turn the corner on race relations. Desegregation was initiated that year in a few districts in Texas and Florida, in two high schools in Little Rock, and in two cities (High Point and Durham) and two counties in North Carolina. Even Governor Almond of Virginia seemed to see the futility of further defiance; in the first part of 1959, he reopened the schools. In many places in the South, it seemed, change was coming as people tired of the violence and interruption of the educational process caused by defiance, came to prefer integration to the closing of the schools, and began to look at the situation more realistically. The president had shown that he would use force if necessary to prevent mobs from closing the schools, and the federal courts, NAACP, and other groups pushing for desegregation had shown that they were not going to back down. Moderates were becoming more numerous, courageous, and outspoken, and more organizations were being formed to work for peaceful integration. More and more businessmen, fearing that the violence and school closings were scaring off potential industries looking to relocate in the

South, began to urge compliance so that industries and people would be attracted to their communities. Progress was slow and setbacks were numerous, but desegregation was advancing.

Still, at the end of 1960, as Eisenhower prepared to give way to Kennedy, southern education was still segregated in most school districts. When Kennedy took office, only 765 of the South's 7,000 school districts were desegregated, and only 7 percent of black pupils in the South attended integrated schools. No schools had been integrated in South Carolina, Alabama, Georgia, and Mississippi, and the schools in Prince Edward County in Virginia, closed in 1959, would remain closed until 1963.[19] Few blacks voted, either. The Civil Rights Act of 1957 had weak provisions and weak enforcement—the Justice Department brought only ten suits against voting rights violators between 1957 and the enactment of a new act in 1960. The number of black voters in the South, which had stood at around 1 million in 1952, had increased to only 1.4 million in 1960, and they still made up only 28 percent of southern blacks of voting age. And in Mississippi, where few blacks had the vote, only 5 percent of black adults went to the polls.[20]

In the spring of 1960 civil rights won a minor victory when Congress overcame a long southern filibuster and eight-week debate to pass a new civil rights bill aimed at strengthening the 1957 act. Pushed through Congress by Lyndon Johnson, who was trying to stake out a claim as a national leader and presidential candidate, the Civil Rights Act of 1960 authorized federal judges to appoint "referees" to supervise registration and voting in areas where patterns and practices of discrimination existed, made it a federal crime to attempt to obstruct a federal court order, and provided for criminal penalties for bombings or threatened bombings of buildings.[21] Calling it "an historic step forward in the field of civil rights,"[22] Eisenhower signed the bill into law on May 6. But A. Philip Randolph, Martin Luther King, Jr., and other black leaders criticized both parties for failing to support a stronger bill that would have provided better enforcement of voting rights and attacked discrimination in employment, public accommodations, and other areas.

However, blacks were making progress in some areas in the late 1950s. They almost dominated the lucrative rock 'n' roll record business. Fifteen of the sixteen major league baseball clubs had black players on their rosters, and in the 1958 World Series Elston Howard of the Yankees was one of the stars. Blacks were also starring in the professional basketball and football leagues, were dominating boxing (with the likes of Floyd Patterson and Sugar Ray Robinson), and Althea Gibson was even breaking into the lily-white world of international championship tennis. Blacks were moving into politics, too: Marian Anderson was a delegate to the United Nations, Ralph Bunche was under secretary of the United Nations, and Clifton R. Wharton was the United States minister to Romania. Blacks were also serving in the

U.S. Congress (four), in the legislatures of fifteen states, and on the city councils of fifteen southern cities. They also made up 10 percent of the government employees of federal, state, and local governments. Many blacks had higher living standards than most people in other parts of the world. Negro college enrollment in the United States was larger than the total college enrollment of West Germany, and the number of black owners of automobiles in the United States exceeded the total number of automobile owners in the Soviet Union. And the black middle class was growing in the United States.[23] These and similar facts and figures were often broadcast abroad by the Voice of America and other government organs trying to combat the negative criticism directed at the United States from other countries during the civil rights battles of the fifties. They were often cited, too, by conservative groups who wanted to show that blacks were better off than people thought and that civil rights and minority job opportunities should not be pushed any harder.

But these facts still ignored the main points: While blacks were becoming better off, most were actually losing ground to the white population, for the economic boom of the fifties was raising the living standards of whites faster than that of blacks and widening the gap between them. While a few blacks were excelling in the sports and entertainment business and were becoming visible in government and business circles, the doors to most careers and vocations were still closed or virtually inaccessible, especially in the South, where most blacks in government and private industry worked as janitors and in similar menial jobs. In 1957, for example, the Ford Motor Company employed only 21 blacks among its 1,588 workers in Atlanta, 9 among its 2,991 in Dallas, 35 among its 1,458 in Memphis, and 9 among its 1,628 in Norfolk–Portsmouth, Virginia. In that same year, the general manager of a Ford plant in Atlanta undoubtedly spoke for many companies when he said that "when we moved into the South we agreed to abide by local custom and not hire Negroes for production work. This is no time for social reforming in that area, and we're not about to try."[24] While the nation's 19 million black citizens might be better off than the inhabitants of non-Western and even some Western nations, this was small consolation to a minority that was at the bottom of the economic heap in America and was still denied many of the rights and privileges that the majority obtained just by being born white. And while Americans might cheer at the individual exploits of Willie Mays, the baseball star would have trouble buying a house in a white section of San Francisco when the Giants moved out to the West Coast.[25] There was progress for many blacks and real prosperity for some, but the fifties would end with this tenth of the American population still at the bottom of the ladder to the American dream.

Just how far blacks still had to go before they became accepted into American society was dramatically illustrated in a 1960 book about a very unusual experience of a very unusual man. The book was *Black Like Me*, the author was John Howard Griffin, and the experience he related was the tragic story of how the skin color of American blacks determined white people's perception and treatment of them. Griffin was a thirty-nine-year-old writer and white Texan who had been blinded for ten years by diabetes and World War II injuries and then miraculously regained his sight in 1957. In 1959, as part of a writing assignment for *Sepia* magazine, a black publication with a circulation of around 61,000, Griffin shaved his straight brown hair and used the help of a dermatologist to darken his skin by oral medication, vegetable dye, and ultraviolet light treatment. He then enbarked upon a tour of the Deep South, to learn what it was like to be black in the geographical heart of white racism and segregation. For six weeks he traveled through Dixie, passing for black among blacks and whites and keeping a journal of his experiences that was published in *Sepia* and as a separate book.

In a manner that no sociological study could ever approach, *Black Like Me* graphically portrayed what it was like to have black skin in the Deep South. Just because his skin was black and for no other reason, Griffin was denied service in restaurants, hotels, and other public and private facilities and subjected to one subtle and not-so-subtle racial slur after another. White strangers, for example, came up to him and asked if his wife had ever slept with a white man or told him that they were trying to get rid of "his kind" in the community. Describing these experiences, he wrote that "the real story is the universal one of men who destroy the souls and bodies of other men (and in the process themselves) for reasons neither really understands. It is the story of the persecuted, the defrauded, the feared and detested. I could have been a Jew in Germany, a Mexican in a number of states, or a member of any 'inferior group.' Only the details would have differed. The story would have been the same."[26]

The *Sepia* articles and the book were widely read and discussed in 1960, bringing fame and success to the author and racial understanding to his white readers. Griffin gave several interviews to reporters and even appeared on the Mike Wallace and Dave Garroway television shows. But many seemed to miss the central message. Griffin received many threatening phone calls and letters accusing him of betraying his own race and threatening to "get" him. He was hanged in effigy in Forth Worth; the dummy was half white, half black, with a yellow streak down its back. He had to request police surveillance of his home and that of his parents, who received so many threats that they decided to move to Mexico. The experiences related in the book, and the reaction of some who read or heard about them, revealed how deep and irrational southern racism was, and indicated that the battle against it would not be easily won. Griffin was so shaken by his experiences that he began to lose faith in the integrity of the white race. As he told reporters in March of 1960, "I like to see good in the white man . . . but after this experience, it's hard to find it in the southern white."[27]

In spite of festering domestic problems, Eisenhower continued in the last half of his second term to give more attention to foreign affairs, where his expertise and interest lay and where he suffered fewer shackles on his freedom of action from the Democratic Congress. The Cold War was continuing to spread into new areas and to take on new dimensions. Strains in the Western alliance were beginning to appear, as evidenced by the actions in the Suez Crisis, while the growing power of China and the problems Russia was having with its Eastern European satellites indicated that the communist world was no longer—if it ever had been—a monolith led by Russia. In Russia itself, the struggle for power that began at the moment of Stalin's death had come to an end in March of 1958 when Nikita Khrushchev became premier and secretary of the Communist Party and the undisputed ruler of Russia. Even before he assumed that mantle of power, Khrushchev had forged a new type of leadership in Russia to challenge the West for global domination. Unlike Stalin, who had been reluctant to travel outside Russia and meet with Western leaders, Khrushchev and his colleagues embarked on trips to Western countries seeking "peaceful coexistence" and new victories in the propaganda theater of the Cold War. While continuing to probe and exploit any weaknesses that appeared in the Western alliance, Khrushchev talked frequently of "peaceful coexistence" and of the dangers of nuclear war while boasting that the Soviet Union would outstrip and eventually bury capitalism by the sheer force of Soviet technological and industrial superiority. Like Eisenhower, Khrushchev was plagued by pressures from both hawks and doves in his government, perhaps explaining why he seemed to alternate between bellicosity and peaceful coexistence. The new Soviet rulers were masters of propaganda, and their propaganda victories, along with real successes in science and technology, like the launching of Sputnik, convinced many Americans during Eisenhower's second term that the general had let the United States fall behind the Russians and that America was now losing the worldwide war against communism.

New tensions emerged between the two superpowers in the last part of 1958. There had been hopeful signs of better relations between them when Eisenhower announced on August 22 that the United States was suspending nuclear testing and the Russians, after hurrying to complete a last series of tests, announced their own suspension of tests in November. But in the fall Khrushchev created a new international crisis over Berlin, a frequent hot spot in the Cold War. Located deep inside East Germany, it gave the Western powers a foothold inside the communist bloc, acted as a center for espionage activities, and served as a haven for East Germans fleeing the workers' paradise in East Germany. In November, Khrushchev announced that the intolerable West Berlin problem must be solved and threatened to turn the Soviet zone over to East Germany if the Allies did not negotiate an end to the problem. This would force the Allies to negotiate with a country they had steadfastly refused to recognize since its creation in 1949. The United States, France, and Britain firmly refused to give in to these demands, reiterating that they would deal only with Russia on the Berlin question and would discuss it only in the context of the wider question of the reunification of Germany. Tension over Berlin continued into the early months of 1959, but Khrushchev gradually softened his stance and made overtures for better East–West relations.

These offers were well-received by President Eisenhower. As his presidency neared its final two years, he seemed more and more to see himself as a man of peace who could use his personal influence and the power of the United States to bring peace to the world. This was especially true after May of 1959, when Secretary of State Dulles died after a long bout with cancer. Dulles had been a consistent hard-liner against Russia and had opposed the 1955 summit conference and other presidential attempts to thaw the Cold War. Following Dulles's recommendation, Eisenhower named Christian A. Herter, a former Massachusetts governor and congressman, as his new secretary of state. But Herter was himself troubled by health problems, suffering so badly from arthritis that he had to use crutches when he walked. Herter was a competent man, but Eisenhower, who had formerly relied heavily on Dulles, now exercised even greater control over foreign policy. As he had been planning since late 1958, he now began to make more peace overtures and to try to make arrangements for personal meetings between Russian and American rulers in order to reduce tensions and work out some of the problems dividing the two superpowers.

Efforts in this direction had already been made even before Dulles's resignation. Khrushchev quietly dropped his ultimatum over Berlin in the spring of 1959, and the establishment of a cultural exchange program opened the way for exchange visits at very high levels. In late June Deputy Premier Frol R. Koslov came to New York to be the official opener of a Soviet exhibition of science, technology, and culture at the New York Coliseum. Less than a month later, on July 22, Koslov's counterpart, Vice President Nixon, left for a thirteen-day tour of the Soviet Union. Nixon received a warm welcome from Russian officials and from the Russian crowds that followed him wherever he went. There were frequent public discussions and exchanges between Nixon and his host, Khrushchev, with the most famous one coming after the two had drunk Pepsi Colas together in the kitchen of a model American home that was part of the American exhibit at Sokolniki Park in Moscow. Clearly embarrassed by the American exhibit, which showed Russian visitors and television viewers a range of American consumer products that Russian citizens could only dream about, Khrushchev engaged Nixon in an extemporaneous debate on the merits of Soviet communism and American capitalism. Before the curious crowd and millions of television viewers, Khrushchev boasted that the Russian economic system would catch up with America's in seven years. As Khrushchev jammed his thumb into Nixon's chest, Nixon waved a menacing finger in the premier's face as he argued the superiority of the American system. The "kitchen debate," or the Sokolniki Summit as some reporters called it, showed the combative nature of the two leaders, won both of them points with the home viewers, and pointed up the competitiveness of the two countries. And although the debate ended with a friendly toast, it helped improve Nixon's status at home as a man who could talk with the Russians while still maintaining a tough stance. At the tour's end, Khrushchev promised to accept Eisenhower's invitation to visit the United States later in the year.[28]

On August 3, Eisenhower announced that he and Khrushchev would exchange visits in the fall, and on August 26 he left for Europe on the first of four goodwill tours he would make in the closing months of his administration. Lasting until September 7, the European tour was a diplomatic and popular success. Everywhere he went in West Germany, England, and France the obviously healthy and energetic president was welcomed by large and enthusiastic crowds. The general had been a hero to Europeans during the Second World War, and now, some fifteen years after D-Day, they showed that they still liked Ike. He returned home on September 7, having achieved something of a propaganda coup by his triumphant tour of Europe just days before the expected arrival of the Soviet premier.

Khrushchev arrived in the United States on September 15 on a trip that the Soviets had obviously orchestrated to achieve the maximum propaganda effect. Not wishing to relive the embarrassment he had suffered in 1955 when he came to the Geneva summit in a two-engine plane, he landed at Andrews Air Force Base in Maryland in a TU-114, the most advanced jet of the age. Before he left home, Russian scientists had fired a rocket at the moon, and a few hours before he arrived in the United States his government announced that the 858-pound rocket had landed on the moon with pennants inscribed with the hammer and sickle. As soon as Khrushchev, his wife, two daughters, son, and sixty-three Russian bureaucrats got off the plane, the Russian ruler announced the successful moon probe, and a few hours later he presented a small model of it to Eisenhower. Angered at his guest's poor political manners and still smarting over the critical fallout from Sputnik, Eisenhower received it coolly.[29] That evening he entertained Khrushchev in White House ceremonies that included a concert by Fred Waring and the Pennsylvanians, and the next day the rotund Russian ruler embarked on a tour of the United States with

Ambassador Henry Cabot Lodge as his escort and guide. During the trip, Khrushchev told Lodge that "the plain people of America like me. It's those bastards around Eisenhower that don't."[30]

Khrushchev's whirlwind tour was eagerly followed by the American people, who were astonished at the spectacle of a Russian ruler traveling across their country. This would have been unimaginable in Truman's day—could anyone have envisioned Stalin dining with Truman in the White House and being escorted around the country by Truman or Dean Acheson? That Khrushchev's tour was possible in 1959 was a testament to the thawing of the Cold War and the enormous faith the American people had in their president. If Eisenhower approved (actually he had grave reservations about the trip), then it must be all right. Some disagreed, of course. William F. Buckley, Jr., wanted to dump red dye into the Hudson River so that the Russian dictator would be welcomed to New York by a "river of blood."[31]

Khrushchev's journey was a headline-gathering event. Some 375 reporters and photographers followed his every step during the two-week stay. He was on the television newscasts at night, and was the subject of several specials, such as NBC's "Khrushchev in America," CBS's "Eyewitness to History," and ABC's "Mr. Khrushchev Abroad." He made good copy—often smiling and friendly, then coy, then combative, then boastful, then bellicose, and often crude and boorish. He toured Washington, New York, Los Angeles, San Francisco, Pittsburgh, and farms in the Midwest, visiting industrial plants, supermarkets, farms, and Hollywood studios. In New York he addressed the United Nations and managed to insult Eleanor Roosevelt at Hyde Park, in Washington he flashed an angry temper at reporters at a press conference, and in Iowa he talked with farmers and marveled at American agriculture. Everywhere he talked of American–Soviet friendship, yet boasted that "we will bury you" in the long run economically. In San Francisco, he got into an altercation with Mayor Norris Poulson over his "we will bury you" remark, and in a private meeting with a seven-member labor delegation led by Walter Reuther he became embroiled in an argument and lashed out at labor leaders as tools of American capitalists, bringing a smile to the lips of Walter Reuther. In Los Angeles, where he was allowed to view the filming of *Can-Can*, he complained that the dancing was immoral and that "a person's face is more beautiful than his backside." When the mayor refused to let him visit Disneyland, which would have presented a security nightmare, Khrushchev became angry and asked, "Have gangsters taken hold of the place?"[32]

Khrushchev capped his trip with a three-day meeting with Eisenhower at Camp David. At this presidential retreat in the Maryland mountains, the rulers of the two most powerful states in the world shared meals, talked, looked at western movies, and made a brief journey to the president's Gettysburg farm to look at his prize cattle. The two leaders were unable to resolve any of the major problems dividing their two countries, but Khrushchev did withdraw all deadlines for solving the Berlin question and agreed to meet with Eisenhower and the British and French leaders in a new Geneva summit meeting to discuss Berlin and other problems. Eisenhower's trip to Russia was rescheduled for the spring of 1960.

Before he left to return to the Soviet Union, Khrushchev also appeared on American television, where in a friendly and gracious manner he reiterated his desire for better relations with the United States and assured his audience that "everybody in the Soviet Unions wants all countries to live in peace, everybody wants peaceful coexistence." But he also managed to boast of Russian advances under communism and to predict that Russia would catch up with the United States in the economic sphere. He ended his speech by thanking Eisenhower and the American people for their hospitality, and expressing the wish that his trip and Eisenhower's forthcoming visit to the Soviet Union would promote friendliness between the two countries. He closed with "Good-bye and good luck, friends."[33]

Khrushchev's visit to the United States had resulted in no solutions to the problems dividing the two countries. But it did lessen tensions between the superpowers and gave rise to a new "spirit of Camp David" to replace the dying "spirit of Geneva." More and more, governments and journalists talked of the real possibility of "peaceful coexistence," a topic that Khrushchev had mentioned often and to which he devoted an eighteen-page article that appeared in the October of 1959 issue of *Foreign Affairs*. In this article he reiterated his view that the rise of destructive nuclear weapons made it imperative that the United States and Russia learn to live side by side and repudiate war as a means of settling disputes. "In our day there are only two ways: peaceful coexistence or the most destructive war in history," he wrote. "There is no third choice." However, he still felt compelled to assert that communism was superior to capitalism and that "the idea of communism will ultimately be victorious throughout the world, just as it had been victorious in our country, in China and in many other states."[34]

In the fall of 1959, Eisenhower's search for peace seemed to be bearing fruit at home and abroad. A genuine thaw in the Cold War seemed to be underway. On December 3, he went globetrotting again, embarking on a three-week goodwill tour that would take him 22,000 miles in nineteen days and to eleven countries in Europe, Asia, and Africa. Whether he was in New Delhi, Casablanca, Rome, or Paris, the result was the same as large crowds turned out to welcome a genuine American hero and searcher for world peace. Near the end of his tour he met in Paris with Charles de Gaulle and Prime Minister Harold Macmillan, and they agreed to hold a four-power summit with Khrushchev in Paris in May to discuss Berlin and other problems. Eisenhower flew home buoyed by the success of his tour and the progress of the East–West thaw.

In February of 1960 he flew off again, this time to Latin America, where less than two years earlier Vice President Nixon had been the target of riots and demonstrations. But Eisenhower received warm welcomes as he toured Puerto Rico, Brazil, Uruguay, Argentina, and Chile. He returned to the United States convinced once again that his personal diplomacy was bringing positive benefits. His critics, however, felt otherwise, as they saw his trips as little more than attempts to escape the growing problems at home and to divert attention from the failures of his administration. In May of 1960, for example, Richard Rovere wrote in *Harper's* that Eisenhower "has provided the spectacle, novel in the history of the presidency, of a man strenuously in motion yet doing essentially nothing—traveling all the time yet going nowhere."[35] But the American people did not agree with the journalistic critics: Gallup polls at the first of 1960 showed that confidence in Eisenhower's leadership had risen five points since November to a three-year high of 71 percent.

The globetrotting in late 1959 and early 1960 proved to be the high mark of Eisenhower's peacemaking, for the last year of his presidency would be plagued by foreign policy crises all across the globe in the countries of Cuba, South Vietnam, Laos, Cambodia, and the Belgian Congo. But the most dramatic crisis of all occurred in May of 1960, for it involved the two superpowers, a spy plane, a personal confrontation between Eisenhower and Khrushchev, and an end to the seven-year thaw in the Cold War that began with the death of Stalin in 1953.

The crisis centered around another product of the Cold War, an American U-2 spy plane. The U-2 was a high altitude Lockheed reconnaissance plane, which had been making regular flights over Russian territory since 1956 in order to gather information on the state of Russian ICBM development. The flights were carried out in great secrecy and carefully kept from the American people. The Russians knew about the flights but had not been able to stop them. Although the high-flying planes took good pictures from a height of fourteen miles and were hard to track by radar, the chance of detection and interception was great, so great than when Khrushchev visited the United States Eisenhower had ordered a temporary halt in the flights so that no embarrassing incidents could occur. But in the spring of 1960, with so much talk about a "missile gap" and so little information on just how many operational missiles the Russians had, Eisenhower seemed willing to risk the flights even though the summit conference was only two weeks away.

On May 1, 1960, Francis Gary Powers was flying a U-2 over Russia to take pictures of a suspicious site that photographs from previous U-2 flights suggested might be an operational ICBM base. About 1,300 miles inside the Soviet Union, near Sverdlovsk, his plane was hit by a Russian rocket, causing it to spin toward the earth and forcing the pilot to bail out. Powers had been given training on how to evade capture, how to escape if captured, and how to kill himself with a needle tipped with curare, a deadly poison that could kill a man in minutes. But he never had a chance to escape or to commit suicide—which he never considered—for he was quickly captured. He was then questioned by the KGB for sixty-one days, given a showcase trial in the Hall of Columns in Moscow, where Stalin's purge trials of the thirties had been held, and then sentenced on August 19, 1960, to ten years in prison for espionage. (He would be released in exchange for Russian spy Rudolph Abel in 1962.)[36] However, his own personal fate was pushed into the background, as the thirty-year-old pilot from Virginia and his sophisticated plane became a new focal point in the Cold War.

The U-2 incident provided Khrushchev with great propaganda opportunities and with awkward problems. He wanted better relations with the West, but he was both puzzled and angered at Eisenhower's betrayal of trust and by the problems this caused him at home, for he had had about as much trouble selling "peaceful coexistence" to the Russian leadership as Eisenhower had in selling it to his own government and to the American people. He was also having troubles with Communist China, which was gradually emerging as a rival for control of the communist movement and had long accused him of appeasing the West. In the summer of 1959 Khrushchev had refused to share the secrets of atomic and nuclear weaponry with the Chinese, and in the winter of that same year relations had deteriorated so badly that he had withdrawn all Russian technical aides from China. Although no one knows for sure why Khrushchev acted as he did in the U-2 affair, it seems that he used it to score a propaganda victory against the West and to assure his colleagues, the Chinese, and communist leaders everywhere that he was not an appeaser and that he was just as anti-imperialist and as communist as they were.[37]

For whatever reason, Khrushchev cleverly exploited the propaganda plum that had fallen from the sky into his lap. He gradually released the information he had in such a way as to draw the United States into a trap. On May 3, NASA announced that one of its weather planes was missing somewhere in Turkey. In a speech on May 5, Khrushchev claimed that an American plane had been shot down over Russian territory and reminded his listeners at home and abroad that if a Soviet plane had appeared over New York or other American cities SAC bombers would have headed toward Russia and "that would mean the outbreak of war." American officials, still thinking that the Russians had only detected the plane on radar, announced that it was a weather plane and that it had not deliberately violated Soviet air space. Then on May 7, speaking before the Supreme Soviet, Khrushchev sprang his surprises: He had the pilot, Francis Gary Powers, "alive and kicking," and he had the pilot's confession, the plane, and the photographic equipment that proved that Powers was on a spy mission.[38]

Caught in its own web of evasions and lies, the State Department said that an American intelligence plane had "probably" flown over Russian territory, and that such flights were necessary for American security since the Russians had not accepted Eisenhower's Open Skies proposals at Geneva in 1955. Up until this point, the State Department had handled this case and had deliberately given the impression that the president had not been involved. But finally, on May 11, always sensitive to his critics' assertion that he often did not know what was going on in his own administration, Eisenhower read a statement at his morning press conference confirming that he had approved of the flights because "no one wants another Pearl Harbor" and he had "to protect the United States and the free world against surprise attack and to enable them to make effective preparations for defense." Such espionage activities were "a distasteful but vital necessity."[39]

In spite of the uproar over the U-2 incident, Eisenhower made plans to attend the Paris Summit conference. So did Khrushchev, who continued to attack the "aggressive acts" of the United States and threaten retaliation against Turkey and other countries that had allowed U-2 flights to originate from bases on their soil. On May 16, the first day of the summit, Khrushchev stood up and angrily denounced the United States, accusing Eisenhower of "treachery" and demanding that he apologize for past flights, promise to discontinue them, and punish those responsible for them. He also canceled Eisenhower's invitation to visit Russia and demanded that the Summit Conference be postponed until another president took office. Angry but controlled, Eisenhower defended the U-2 flights on the grounds that they were necessary to prevent a sneak Russian attack, but announced that they had been discontinued and would not be resumed. But he refused to accede to Khrushchev's other demands and accused the Russian leader of traveling thousands of miles to sabotage the conference. The Paris summit meeting broke up before it really got started, and the leaders went back to their countries, but not before Khrushchev held a lengthy news conference before about 3,000 newsmen from all over the world in order to get in a few last-minute denunciations of Eisenhower and the United States. Khrushchev had put on quite a show, one that was intended as much or more for communist leaders at home and across the world as for the Paris audience.[40]

The U-2 incident brought a temporary end to "peaceful coexistence" and opened up a new era of acrimony in Soviet–American relations that would bring new crises for Eisenhower and his successor and would climax with the Cuban missile crisis in 1962. The U-2 affair hurt American prestige abroad and gave Russia a propaganda victory in the Cold War, for it was a humiliation and embarrassment for the president and for the United States, which had been cleverly drawn into a trap and forced to admit that it had committed espionage and had lied about it to its own people and to the international community. Although most Americans saw Khrushchev and not Eisenhower as the villain, especially after the Russian leader's rude performance at Paris, it did cause some Americans to question the president's handling of foreign policy and gave the Democratic party ammunition for attacking the Republican administration. It also gave Khrushchev the opportunity to mend political fences at home and among the world's communist leaders, though it did not heal the rift in the Soviet–Chinese alliance or halt the splintering of the world communist movement. Finally, it ended all hopes for a summit during the rest of Eisenhower's term, and retarded progress in East–West discussions on disarmament, nuclear test bans, Berlin, and other pressing problems.

The U-2 debacle coincided with another foreign crisis, a gathering storm centered on the Caribbean island of Cuba. Since the turn of the century the United States had regarded the island off the Florida coast as a special American protectorate to be dominated by the American government and by American investors. In the 1950s American investors gained an even larger control of the Cuban economy, while the American government supported the Cuban dictator, Fulgencio Batista, one of the worst tyrants in Latin America, providing him with most of his military equipment and training most of his army officers. The Cuban people, meanwhile, suffered from poverty, ignorance, illiteracy, disease, exploitation by the small group of wealthy landowners who controlled almost half of the land, and ruthless governmental oppression.[41]

The winds of change in Cuba began to blow in the mid-1950s. In 1956 Fidel Castro, a graduate of Havana Law School who had once lived in exile in New York City and had already spent two years in jail for opposing Batista's regime, began a guerrilla campaign against Batista from his headquarters in the Sierra Maestra Mountains. Castro and his 26th of July Movement quickly picked up support from the Cuban people, while in the United States romantic newspaper stories of the bearded revolutionary leader led some Americans to smuggle money and weapons to his rebel band. By the end of 1958 Batista's unpopular regime had collapsed, and as his army deserted or defected to Castro's camp, he went into exile in the Dominican Republic. On January 1, 1959, Castro rode into Havana on top of a tank and proclaimed his takeover of the Cuban government. When he heard of Castro's takeover, John Foster Dulles, still trying to work while suffering from the cancer that would soon take his life, could only say that "I don't know whether this is good for us or bad for us."[42]

Castro's victory was very popular in the United States at first. The press portrayed him as a liberator of his people, the government extended diplomatic recognition, and in April of 1959 Castro even made a trip to the country, where he was welcomed by enthusiastic crowds in New York and Washington and spent three hours in consultation with Vice President Nixon. But relations between the United States and the new Cuban regime deteriorated quickly. Castro began to carry out speedy trials and executions of Batista's supporters and Castro's opponents, to break up large landholdings, and to confiscate foreign investments—including around $1 billion held by Americans—in Cuban industries and farms. As the United States protested and indicated that there would be no more American economic aid unless Castro stopped these revolutionary changes, Castro began to step up his anti-American statements and confiscation of foreign assets in Cuba. Relations continued to deteriorate in 1959 and early 1960 as Castro moved leftward and increased his attacks on "Yankee imperialists," signed long-term trade agreements with the U.S.S.R., and gave diplomatic recognition to Red China. Meanwhile, Cuban refugees were pouring into the United States, bringing stories of Castro's atrocities and of growing communist influence in their country, and the CIA was compiling more and more information on growing communist influence in Cuba.

In 1960 Eisenhower gradually moved toward a complete break with Cuba. He stopped all economic aid, cut Cuban sugar imports to 700,000 tons and then ended them all together, and embargoed all exports to Cuba. He also increased naval patrols in the Central American waters and approved a CIA plan to train Cuban refugees in Guatemala for an invasion of Cuba. Meanwhile, Castro signed trade agreements with several Eastern European communist states, made threats against the American naval base at Guantánamo, confiscated more American and British-owned companies, and received a Russian pledge to defend Cuba against an attack from the United States. Finally, on January 3, 1961, during his last days in office, Eisenhower broke diplomatic relations with the Cubans. By the time he left office, the Cold War had already come to Latin America, with Russia supporting a Cuban revolutionary regime that was popular throughout Latin America for the heroic stand of a heroic leader against the Yankee colossus to the north. A Russian satellite, it appeared, had been established just ninety miles from Florida.[43]

The deteriorating situation in Latin America was matched by a deteriorating situation in Southeast Asia, where ever since 1954 the United States had been supporting the authoritarian and anticommunist regime of General Diem as the bulwark against communist expansion in that region. The United States had funneled millions of dollars in military and economic aid to prop up Diem's unpopular regime, including nearly three quarters of a billion dollars between 1958 and 1960 alone. Most of this aid had been used by Diem to beef up his army and internal security forces, while very little had gone to education, health, agriculture, industrial development, and other areas that would have improved the living conditions of the people. Diem had made few reforms, ruthlessly suppressed all opponents to his regime, and convinced the Eisenhower administration that all of his opponents were communists and that the Hanoi regime in North Vietnam was the source of the communist subversion of his country.[44]

In 1959 and 1960 both communist and noncommunist opposition to the corrupt and tyrannical Diem regime grew, as did the frequency of terroristic attacks against the government. On November 11, 1960, Diem's own paratrooper battalions, considered among the most loyal supporters of the government, attempted to assassinate him. The coup was put down only after a bloodbath that left some 400 dead. In December of 1960, after six years of unofficial existence, the National Liberation Front, dominated by communists but also made up of noncommunist opponents of Diem, was officially established as the political arm of the rebellion against the Diem regime. By now the United States had over 1,000 military advisers in South Vietnam.[45] Most of them saw that the Diem regime did not have the support necessary to stay in power much longer and that the entire populace was turning against the repressive dictator. On January 17, three days before Kennedy was to inherit Eisenhower's problems in Vietnam and other parts of the world, Brigadier General Edward Lansdale prophetically warned that "the free Vietnamese, and their government, probably will be able to do no more than postpone eventual defeat—unless they find a Vietnamese way of mobilizing their total resources and then utilizing them with spirit."[46] Eisenhower went out of office with Diem's regime on the verge of collapse, while in neighboring Laos and Cambodia, supposedly made neutral by the Geneva agreements of 1954, communism was making great inroads and challenging the fragile governments of these two countries.

The last months of Eisenhower's administration were played out against a background of a steadily deteriorating situation in world affairs. These were probably the most unsatisfying months of his entire presidency. Russia and America were moving further apart, Cuba was drifting into the communist orbit, and South Vietnam was moving to the verge of collapse and anarchy. In June, when the president was on a new goodwill tour in the Far East, widespread rioting by Japanese student leftists over the new ten-year security pact between the United States and Japan led the Japanese prime minister to cancel the president's proposed trip to Japan for his own safety. This limited his Far East journey to Taiwan, the Philippines, and South Korea and marked the second time in two months that a head of state had withdrawn an invitation to the president. On July 1 an American RB-47 reconnaissance plane was shot down by Russia over the Barents Sea; its two surviving airmen were imprisoned by the U.S.S.R. and not released until the first year of the Kennedy administration. In July, shortly after the Belgians had left the newly created independent Republic of the Congo, a complex civil war broke out that would involve the massacre of innocent civilians, army rebellions, secessions of component states, the intervention of the Belgian army to restore order, and the intervention of the United States, Russia, and the United Nations in an attempt to solve the problem.

In the fall, Cuban–American relations moved toward the breaking point they would reach early in the next year, and as the Congo crisis raged Khrushchev came to the United Nations in September to use that international forum to attack the United States. He called the United States a "disgrace to civilization," accused her of causing the Congo crisis, and hammered on the desk with his fist as he boasted of Russia's military strength and leveled more attacks at the United States. He also rudely interrupted a speech by Harold Macmillan and took off his shoe and pounded it on the desk during an address by a member of the Filipino delegation. At this same U.N. session, Khrushchev's new friend Castro delivered a four-hour diatribe against Yankee imperialism.[47] This time Eisenhower refused to meet with the powerful dictator he had entertained at Camp David for three days only a year before, and for security reasons would not allow him to venture outside New York City during his three-week visit. The president was infuriated by the Russian's leader's boorish behavior, and his own famous temper showed itself when he commented privately that if he were a dictator he would "launch an attack on Russia while Khrushchev is in New York."[48] Summitry, and the world peace it was supposed to promote, was postponed until another day and another president.

# 22

# *The Winds of Change*

It was obvious by the late fifties that the conservative consensus that had numbered so many adherents during Eisenhower's first term was beginning to break down during his troubled second one. The president was still popular, of course, but more and more critics were rising to attack his administration's unwillingness or inability to deal with pressing domestic issues or to reverse the decline in America's prestige and influence that had begun with Sputnik in 1957 and continued down through the U-2 incident and other problems of 1960. More critics were rising, too, to challenge some of America's basic institutions, values, and beliefs. Although few people realized it at the time, the growing criticism was a sign that the nation was undergoing great change and that an ostensibly placid decade was about to give way to the turbulent sixties.

Some of the changes affecting the nation were demographic in nature. The population was still growing rapidly, reaching over 179 million in 1960, up some 30 million over the 1950 figure. It was still moving to the suburbs and into the western states, particularly California, and at decade's end the nation gained population by adding new states to the union for the first time since 1912. Both Alaska and Hawaii had applied for statehood before, but the long distances involved, the lack of contiguity with the other forty-eight states, and partisan politics (Alaska was traditionally a Democratic stronghold and Hawaii a Republican one) had always kept them out. But by 1959 the jet airplane had helped to solve the distance problem, and the need for air bases and other military installations helped to overcome most other objections. Democrats and Republicans moved to compromise. Alaska, with more than twice the land area of Texas but with the smallest population of any of the other states, was admitted on January 3, 1959; Hawaii, which Mark Twain had once called "the loveliest fleet of islands that lies anchored in any ocean," became the fiftieth state on August 21 of that year.[1]

Important changes were also occurring in transportation as passenger trains and ocean liners gave way to the airliner. The automobile had already undermined the American romance with the railroads, which had carried over a billion passengers a year in the early 1920s and still transported 916 million as late as 1944. After the war the railroads had spent millions of dollars on diesel engines and new passenger cars, including air-conditioned slumber coaches and Vista-Dome cars. They also used advertising to lure passengers to the railroads, like a 1950 full-page advertisement in *Time* telling businessmen that "it's good business to Go Pullman" because it is "COMFORTABLE, DEPENDABLE, AND—ABOVE ALL—SAFE."[2] But ridership continued to drop, to 488 million passengers in 1950 and to 327 million in 1960, partly due to poorly maintained equipment and mismanagement but more to the growing attraction of the automobile for short trips and the airplane for longer ones. As the railroads lost money, they cut back on the number of coaches, number of markets served, and the number of daily runs between markets—all causing, of course, a further decline in passengers. At the end of the 1950s Americans still had a romantic, emotional attachment to the railroads, but when they wanted to travel or ship goods, they turned to the automobiles, buses, and tractor trailers that were clogging the highways and to the commercial airlines that were beginning to crowd the skies.[3]

The private airline industry boomed in the late fifties. The government helped with funds to construct airports and other forms of aid, airplane manufacturers provided faster, safer, and more comfortable planes, and automobile traffic jams and declining railroad service encouraged more and more people to turn from trains, buses, and private automobiles to planes. Air travel saved time, making it possible for business people and vacationers to spend more hours at work or play and less time trying to get there. In 1950, airlines carried only 24 percent of all combined airline-railroad traffic, but by the end of the decade they were carrying 61 percent.[4] A big boost came to the airlines in 1958 with the introduction of jet passenger service for both domestic and international air travel, cutting air travel time in half. The British inaugurated the first transatlantic jet service in October of 1958 with the De Havilland Comet and were quickly followed by the Pan American Boeing 707s, while in December National Airlines began regularly scheduled jet service between New York and Miami. In that year for the first time in history, the number of passengers crossing the Atlantic by plane outnumbered those going by ship. More and more, people preferred a ten-hour jet flight over the Atlantic to a four- or five-day trip on the fastest ocean liners. By the end of the decade the great days of the luxury ocean liner, like those of the railroads, were becoming a thing of the past.

The last years of the decade also saw a genuine rebellion against the beliefs and values of Eisenhower's America carried out by a small group of nonconformists, the Beatniks. Descendents of the Lost Generation of the twenties and the "bohemians" of the thirties and forties, the Beats first appeared on the West Coast in the early fifties in coffeehouses, bars, and other hangouts in Los Angeles and San Francisco, then across the continent in New York's Greenwich Village, then in other large cities and college campuses. The first Beat novel, John Clellon Holmes's *Go*, was published in 1952, and in that same year *The New York Times Magazine* published the same author's "This Is the Beat Generation." However, the Beats did not get national attention until 1956 when an obscenity trial involving *Howl and Other Poems* (1956), written by Allen Ginsberg and published by Lawrence Ferlinghetti's City Lights publishing company, made headlines all across the country. The book was seized by the San Francisco police in a raid on Ferlinghetti's City Lights Bookshop. During a sensational, nationally publicized trial, in which the ACLU successfully defended Ginsberg and Ferlinghetti, the nation first learned of the existence of a Beat Generation with unusual members like Ginsberg, Ferlinghetti, Jack Kerouac, Gary Snyder, Gregory Corso, Lawrence Lipton, and William S. Burroughs. Soon, the media began to publicize them and to convince Americans that there was a Beat Generation and a Beat Movement.

There was no general agreement even among the Beats as to what the word meant. Some said it was a shortening of "beatitude" or "beatific" and carried a meaning of inner spiritual peace, while others claimed that it came from being "beaten down" by society. Perhaps it came from the world of jazz, for ever since the early 1940s jazz musicians had used the phrase, "I'm beat right down to my socks."[5] Generally the press and public called them Beatniks, a term despised by most of these nonconformists, who rarely referred to one another as Beatniks and preferred to be called Beats, or, in the case of males, cats, after the animal that resists being sexually domesticated.[6] But whatever they were called, it was clear to most Americans that they were different from everyone else and therefore somewhat suspicious or even dangerous.

Who were the Beats? They were not really a movement, for they were too few in number and too individualistic, disorganized, and nonpolitical to be called that. As a group they are difficult to characterize, though certain traits did stand out. They definitely were not youthful protestors like the hippies and yippies of the 1960s, for many of them had served in World War II or in the Korean War and were in their twenties, thirties, or even older.

Most of them were white males, and many came from the middle class and had had some college training. Although many of them kept their middle-class dress or wore working-class clothing common to blue-collar workers, an unofficial dress code seemed to have evolved by the mid- and late fifties. Beat males wore khaki pants or jeans, sweaters, sandals or well-worn sneakers, beards, and hair as short as any Ivy Leaguer of the time. Beat women wore black leotards, no lipstick, and so much eyeshadow that they came to be called "raccoons." As part of their rejection of society, they consorted with, and romanticized, society's outcasts and misfits—blacks, drug addicts, prostitutes, bums, migrant farm workers, and petty criminals.

The life-style of the Beats was decidedly unconventional by the standards of the fifties. Many of them lived in cheap apartments or rooms they called pads and tried to have as few furnishings, belongings, and responsibilities as possible. Sexually promiscuous in an age that extolled premarital chastity, monogamy, and the happy home, male and female Beats often lived together without benefit of clergy and without shame. They proudly celebrated their sexual freedoms, including homosexuality, bisexuality, and interracial sex. They smoked marijuana (called reefers or pot) in an age that knew little about it and considered it scandalous. The drug had been around for a long time in the criminal and musical world, and was part of the culture of the young street gangs of the nation's large cities. The Beats liked the drug for its mild hallucinogenic effect and for its role, when smoked in a group, as a social ritual that made the group feel and think as one.[7] To heighten their sensory awareness, some used stronger drugs, like peyote or heroin. Many also took benzedrine pills or tore open benzedrine inhalers and sniffed the drug, a practice that led Jack Kerouac and several other Beatniks to develop thrombophlebitis in the legs. Alcohol was also a part of the Beat culture, usually as beer or cheap wine.

The Beats tried to spend their time doing what they wanted to do. Most tried to avoid work (indeed, in the Beat lexicon "work" meant sexual intercourse), though some did try to pick up part-time jobs long enough to buy the few necessities of life or to be able to travel abroad. Some Beat women, though certainly a minority, practiced the world's oldest profession when they needed money. Most Beats did not own a television and rarely watched one, and most did not read newspapers or popular magazines, which to them simply reported on the superficial happenings of a society they had rejected.[8] Most Beats liked jazz, the blues, or folk music, and many of them played the guitar and other instruments. Some also wrote novels or poetry, often with themes and language considered vulgar by the rest of society. They delighted in shocking straight people with the use of four letter words in their writings or in public encounters with the square world. The Beats also had their own slang—*like*, *cool*, *pad*, *hip*, *hep*, *square*, *chick*, *bread*, *spade*, *bug*—which was mostly borrowed from black jazz musicians and from young street gangs. Their religion was borrowed from the East—many Beats studied Zen Buddhism and other Eastern religions and philosophies that emphasized the "inner peace" they were seeking. This Eastern influence also showed up in other ways, as in the Oriental furniture, floor pillows, short Japanese tea tables, oriental prints and tapestries, and other fixtures found in many of their apartments.

The Beats denounced the middle-class ethic of consumer America—the dedication to hard work, success, materialism, patriotism, suburbanism, consumerism, conformity, and organized religion. To them American society was hopelessly corrupt and hypocritical, far beyond peaceful reform or even revolutionary change. Most were nonpolitical, believing that government and politics, like the rest of America, were corrupt at all levels, that all elections were rigged, and that big business and advertising controlled the country and made all important decisions. Most did not vote, feeling that under these circumstances voting was useless.[9] The Beats were not rebels or revolutionaries. They had no program or cause, did not engage in demonstrations or violence, and were not active agents of social change. They dropped out of society and treated it with disdain, boredom, and detachment. They were not trying to reform the world but to live apart from it. They were nonconformists, but not revolutionaries. They rejected society and simply wished to be left alone.

The most popular and influential of the Beats was Jack Kerouac, a French Canadian Roman Catholic who played football at Columbia University during World War II, served in the navy, taught at the New School for Social Research in the late forties, and made several cross-country trips by bus and car, bumming around and writing, in the late forties and early fifties. In 1950 this wanderer published *The Town and the City*, but it was the publication in 1957 of *On the Road*[10] that made him and his Beat friends famous. An undisciplined, rambling, often dull account of the camaraderie and cross-country wanderings of a group of free spirits, *On the Road* sold 500,000 copies and created something of a sensation, coming as it did not long after the Ginsberg trial. Gilbert Millstein of *The New York Times* called it "a major novel" and claimed that its "publication is a historic occasion."[11] *Time* magazine said that "with his barbaric yawp of a book, Kerouac commands attention as a kind of literary James Dean."[12] The book had a great impact on the Beats, giving them national fame and serving as kind of a Bible for their movement, and it had a major effect on many young people who were not Beats but were looking for something that expressed their yearning for freedom and meaning in the last years of the Eisenhower era.

The book's effect was heightened, of course, by all the media attention Kerouac and the other Beats were now receiving. It was also increased by the myth, spread by Kerouac himself, that it was written in "spontaneous prose," a concept borrowed from jazz musicians who improvised their music instead of following formulas. Kerouac claimed that it was written in just three weeks, that the ideas came to him so spontaneously that he tried to write as fast as possible, and that he wrote the book on a 120-foot roll of United Press teletype paper, which allowed him to write for days without putting in new paper. It was not revised or rewritten, he claimed, except for the last few pages, which had to be redone when a dog chewed up the last few feet of the roll.[13] Actually, this was not true. The book was written and then revised several times over a nine-year period. But the legend persisted. Novelist Norman Mailer, who publicized the Beats, counted himself among their number, and claimed that his essay "The White Negro" was part of their literature, related Kerouac's version to Truman Capote on the David Susskind show. This prompted Truman Capote's famous remark, "That's not writing, it's just . . . typing."[14]

Kerouac was an unlikely hero for the young nonconformists of the late fifties. He was thirty-five years old when *On the Road* was published, and in spite of all his rhetoric about alienation and freedom from the social conventions of the day, he never escaped his conservative French Canadian Catholic background. He was anti-Semitic, once accused Ferlinghetti and Lawrence Lipton of being communists, and told his friends that if he had voted in 1956 he would have voted for Eisenhower.[15] He also promoted his books by giving interviews to reporters and by appearing on radio and television shows, including *Mike Wallace Interviews*, and he was very much interested in the size of the royalties he received from his books. But to the people who read and worshipped him, he was the symbol of their alienation and yearnings for freedom and the open road.

Jack Kerouac was the best-known of the Beat figures, but nearly as famous was Lawrence Ferlinghetti, a native of Paris, who had served in the navy, worked in the mail room at *Time* magazine, and acquired degrees from Columbia and the Sorbonne. In 1953 he and a friend established the City Lights Bookshop in San Francisco, the first all-paperback book store in the United States and a hangout for many of the major Beat writers. He soon began his own publishing company, City Lights Books, and began publishing his own poetry and that of other Beats. Among Ferlinghetti's best-known works were "Coney Island of the Mind" and "Tentative Description of a Dinner to Promote the Impeachment of President Eisenhower." The latter was published, read in public poetry sessions, and recorded with drums in 1957.[16]

One of the most controversial of the Beats was Allen Ginsberg, who had first met Kerouac when the two were students at Columbia. Ginsberg had worked as a book reviewer and market research consultant before undergoing psychotherapy, which, he often said, had changed his life. His famous apocalyptic poem, "Howl," written in one weekend under the influence of peyote, amphetamines, and Dexedrine, seemed to attack all the values and beliefs of Eisenhower's America, and it made the thirty-year-old rebel the poet and prophet of the Beat movement all across the country.[17] Even the literary establishment praised his poetry, though it frowned at his homosexuality and other traits, which were regarded as unconventional even for a poet. To the establishment he was still, however, more acceptable than fellow poet Gregory Corso, who had spent much of his early life in foster homes and prisons, was self-educated (largely through reading at Harvard University's library), never combed his hair, and had a wit that was often overshadowed by his irreverent and crude public remarks. At public readings he was prone to utter obscenities just for the shock value and to shout such nonsense as "all life is a rotary club" and "Fried shoes. Like it means nothing. Don't shoot the warthog."[18]

The Beats were a small group, numbering around 400 to 500 legitimate rebels at best,[19] but they received media attention far out of proportion to their numbers or influence. They were the subject of television documentaries and talk shows, books, and articles in popular magazines and in small literary magazines and journals. Hollywood made a movie of Kerouac's *The Subterraneans* and also turned out a second-rate feature with the obligatory title, *The Beat Generation*. The Beats made good copy, and the public was fascinated with them, regarding them as quaint deviants or lazy bums rather than serious rebels. Most of the publicity was negative—over and over again they were portrayed as immature, superficial, even neurotic people with beards and strange clothing, an aversion to work and bathing, and a disposition for writing bad poetry and following an Eastern philosophy that they distorted to justify their dislike of work and responsibility. They were also denounced for using drugs, for practicing sexual promiscuity, and for including so many of society's losers and outcasts in their ranks. And over and over again they were attacked for being anti-intellectual and conformist. Critic Harold Rosenberg called them "a herd of independent minds," while Norman Podhoretz labeled them "the know-nothing bohemians" and claimed that they were anti-intellectuals who extolled emotions and ignorance over reason and intelligence and who bore no resemblance to the serious bohemians who had criticized life and values in earlier times.[20]

In August of 1958 *Look* magazine called the Beats "fugitives from the great American middle class—people who have chosen to retire for a while from the rat race of everyday living." According to *Look*, "There's nothing really new about the Beat philosophy. It consists merely of the average American's value scale—turned inside out. The goals of the Beat are *not* watching TV, *not* wearing gray flannel, *not* owning a home in the suburbs, and especially—*not* working."[21] Not to be outdone by its competitor, *Life* magazine featured many critical articles on the Beats, the most notable of which was "The Only Rebellion Around," written by staff writer Paul O'Neil. According to O'Neil, "the wide public belief that the Beats are simply dirty people in sandals is only a small if repellent part of the truth." O'Neil claimed that "Beat philosophy seems calculated to offend the whole population, civil, military, and ecclesiastic," and that its followers "are against work and they are often ill-fed, ill-clothed, and ill-housed by preference." O'Neil then went on to ask, "Whoever heard of rebels so pitiful, so passive, so full of childish rages and nasty, masochistic cries?" and to complain that "a hundred million squares must ask themselves: 'What have we done to deserve this?' "[22] Throughout all the criticism in the popular press, and in the serious literary magazine, was a refusal to take the Beats seriously and a penchant for concentrating on their life-style rather than on their ideas and writings.

All the publicity about the Beats was bound to spawn followers and silly imitators. On college campuses and in cities across the country, coffeehouses and other hangouts sprang up where Beats or pseudo-Beats got together to talk, listen to music, strum the guitar, and read poetry. As time passed the number of people affecting the Beat life-style undoubtedly came to outnumber the few genuine Beats. Beat culture quickly lost its freshness and became a stylized, ritualized culture. Suburbanites and college students trying to be "with it" held Beat parties, where guests dressed like Beat men and women, tried to copy the Beat lingo, and discussed Zen Buddhism and other elements of Oriental culture. In San Francisco and other cities it was possible to buy a Beatnik "kit"—complete with sandals, pants, shirts, and a book of terminology. In the consumer culture of the fifties, it was perhaps inevitable that "the only rebellion around," as *Life* had called it, would degenerate into a commercial fad. Beatniks had also become objects of derision. Standup television comedians began to incorporate a mandatory joke about Beats into their routine, and television and radio shows began to feature Beatnik characters as guest characters or cast regulars.

The Beatnik movement—if it ever was that—began to decline by the end of the decade. It had attracted a great deal of attention, given birth to a host of followers and imitators, and precipitated a great deal of amused and sometimes angry criticism from a middle-class society that refused to take it seriously but still regarded it as a danger to "the American way of life." It also left behind a body of writing, notably *On the Road* and the poetry of Ginsberg, Ferlinghetti, and other poets, often published in little magazines like the *Black Mountain Review* and the *Evergreen Review*, and hundreds of underground mimeographed literary outlets. Few real converts to the Beat philosophy appeared in the fifties, but the Beats did raise a valuable voice of protest against America's consumer culture that was heard and even heeded by a few. They were the progenitors of the hippies, yippies, and other youthful members of the counterculture of the sixties, who would embrace the Beat's love of freedom and drugs and disdain for middle-class values but would go beyond the apolitical Beats to be very active agents of social change. A few Beats, like Allen Ginsberg, would carry their protests into the sixties and seventies, often showing up at peace rallies, the Chicago Seven trial, and other counterrevolutionary events, and ironically, participating in university seminars and other activities of the establishment.

On a hot Saturday afternoon in August of 1960, a thirty-nine-year-old respected Harvard psychologist sat down with five friends in Cuernavaca, Mexico, and ate from a bowl of sacred mushrooms that Indians had been using in religious rites for hundreds of years to produce heightened consciousness and visions. Dr. Timothy Leary had heard of the marijuana being smoked by the Beats and other members of the urban underworld, but he had never before taken any mind-altering drugs and had apparently never heard of the experiments being conducted with peyote, mescaline, lysergic acid diethylamide, and other mind-altering drugs by people like Alan Watts, Dr. Albert Hoffman, and Aldous Huxley (who had described his experiences in *The Doors of Perception*). But Leary's four-hour high on the magic mushrooms produced a dramatic conversion to visionary drugs as the key to understanding and inner peace. Before the year was out, he and Richard Alpert, a Harvard colleague who had been with him at the experiment in Mexico, had founded the Center for Research in Personality and embarked on a crusade to study and legalize powerful mind-altering drugs. Partly through their efforts, the drug culture was about to emerge from the underground and enter the mainstream of American life as the "psychedelic revolution" of the turbulent 1960s.[23] Leary often claimed that he was a follower of Ginsberg and some of the other Beats. Quite naturally, one of the first participants in Leary's own Harvard experiments in drugs would be Allen Ginsberg.[24]

The Silent Generation of students was showing signs of restlessness in 1960. Only one year before, the new president of the University of California, Clark Kerr, had said that "the employers will love this generation. . . . They are going to be easy to handle. There aren't going to be any riots." But events were already moving past the distinguished university leader. Even before he made his optimistic remarks, thousands of students across the country had been drawn to demonstrations against segregation, war, nuclear tests, and ROTC programs on college campuses. In the same year as his remarks, students at the University of Chicago formed the Student Peace Union, and students at Wisconsin began publishing *Studies on the Left*, and in 1960 youthful protesters became even more numerous, vocal, and influential. They formed new organizations like the Students for a Democratic Society and the Student Nonviolent Coordinating Committee, attended SANE rallies and other pacifist demonstrations, participated in sit-ins all across the South, and showed up outside San Quentin to protest the execution of convicted killer Caryl Chessman.[25]

In the spring of 1960 the entire country seemed to be caught up in the Chessman case. The thirty-eight-year-old resident of San Quentin's death row had been arrested in 1948 as the famous Red Light Bandit, who had terrorized couples in lovers' lanes in Los Angeles County with robberies and rapes. Convicted of kidnapping and sexual assault upon two young women, he had been sentenced under California's Little Lindbergh Law, which carried the mandatory death penalty. But for the next twelve years, Chessman, who had a grade-school education and an I.Q. of 136, worked in his small prison cell to obtain his freedom, reading hundreds of law books, filing his own legal briefs, making fifteen appeals to the United States Supreme Court, holding press conferences, and publishing four books, including *Cell 2455 Death Row* (1954), which sold half a million copies and was translated into over a dozen foreign languages. His literary and legal talents kept him alive for twelve years, securing eight stays of execution and creating a public debate over capital punishment that eventually forced Governor Pat Brown to call a special session of the California state legislature to consider the issue. In the spring of 1960, Brown received from all across the world thousands of letters and telegrams requesting clemency, including a petition from Brazil with 2 million signatures. At the same time a Sacramento schoolteacher went on a hunger strike in support of Chessman, and a popular song, "The Ballad of Caryl Chessman," was playing on radio stations and jukeboxes.[26] But time had run out for Chessman. On May 2, with thousands of college students and other protesters from the San Francisco area gathered outside San Quentin in protest, he was executed. Nineteen other men still remained on death row in California along with 140 others across the country, but Chessman's case had helped to inspire an anticapital-punishment movement that would continue to grow and produce results in state after state in the 1960s.

On May 13, less than two weeks after Chessman's execution, students from several local colleges came to City Hall in San Francisco to protest the House Un-American Activities Committee's hearings on communist activities in the region. Denied admission to the hearings, they began to sing civil rights songs on the steps outside the building. Suddenly, without warning or provocation, the police moved in with high-pressure water hoses and kicked, clubbed, pushed, and dragged the passive students down the steps. Twelve people were injured and fifty-two were arrested before the melee was over, but the next day close to 5,000 students from nearby campuses came back to demonstrate in front of City Hall protesting the previous day's actions by the police. The radical student activities of the sixties were near at hand.[27]

Early in 1960 the civil rights movement took an important new turn with the emergence of the sit-in movement. It began at 4:30 in the afternoon on February 1, 1960, when Ezell Blair, Jr., Joseph McNeil, David Richmond, and Franklin McLain—black freshmen from North Carolina Agricultural and Technical State College in Greensboro, North Carolina—sat down at the all-white lunch counter at the F. W. Woolworth store in downtown Greensboro and ordered coffee. "The waitress looked at me as if I were from outer space," Blair later said.[28] After being told that "we do not serve Negroes," the young men sat at the counter for another hour until the counter was closed.[29] But the next day, they returned with five other students to continue the sit-in, and as they came back each day, they were joined by still others. The blacks were courteous, well-behaved, and dignified, presenting quite a contrast to some of the young whites who harassed them on the streets by waving Confederate flags, yelling insults, and hurling cigarette butts at them.

The sit-ins quickly spread to the lunch counters of Woolworth's and other chain stores in other North Carolina towns—Durham, Winston-Salem, Fayetteville, Charlotte, and High Point—and by March 1, one month after they had begun, to stores in cities in seven other states in the South, in spite of efforts by managers to end the protests by raising prices or removing the seats. In many cities, especially in Mississippi and other states in the Deep South, the passive and stoic demonstrators were met with resistance: They were knocked off lunch-counter stools, kicked, beaten, shot, stabbed, tear-gassed by police, bitten by police dogs, and hauled off to jail. And at several colleges, including some black ones, students who joined in the sit-ins were expelled and faculty members who participated were fired.[30]

The sit-ins electrified the black community throughout the South, causing a massive awakening of blacks and also attracting thousands of white sympathizers, many of them young students, from all across the nation. Yale divinity students marched in support in New Haven, students from Harvard and other universities in the Boston area petitioned Woolworth stores, and expressions of support surfaced at other colleges and universities. In the South, white students began to sit at the lunch counters with Negro protesters. The sit-ins quickly spread to other civil rights battlefields: swimming pools, public libraries, movie theaters, hotels and motels, public parks, beaches, and other segregated public and private facilities. These sit-ins, stand-ins, and wade-ins often provoked violence from rabid white segregationists and arrests from unsympathetic local police. But gradually the white establishment gave in, for the sit-ins were bringing bad publicity to their communities and the economic boycotts were disrupting business and causing great economic losses. In Greensboro, for example, the Woolworth's store where it all began saw a 20 percent decline in sales and a 50 percent decline in profits in 1960. In June, the store manager came to the mayor and said, "For God's sake, do something, my business is going to pot."[31] By the early summer of 1960, lunch counters had been desegregated in Greensboro and several other southern cities. By the end of the year, over 50,000 people, most of them young, had participated in sit-ins and some 3,600 of them had gone to jail for their efforts.[32] But lunch counters and other public facilities had been integrated in 126 cities across the South. As one participant in the Greensboro sit-ins said, "That dime store . . . was the birthplace of a whirlwind."[33]

The sit-ins were more than just a protest against segregation. They were also a rebellion against the Uncle Tomism that had been so prevalent among southern blacks in the past. The participants in the sit-ins were not the respectable middle-class older black leaders, nor were they "agitators" from outside the South who were stirring up formerly happy and contented blacks, as many white southerners had always believed. They were young black southerners taking charge of the movement from older and more conservative black leaders who had often preached patience and accommodation. They were part of the New Negroes, who were not willing to adapt themselves to white racism or wait patiently for years while liberal whites and middle-class blacks fought the battle for them in the courts. Their mood was aptly expressed by Bob Moses, a former Harvard graduate student who was living in a Harlem apartment at the time he saw pictures of the Greensboro sit-inners. "The students in that picture had a certain look on their faces," he later said, "sort of sullen, angry, determined. Before, the Negro in the South had always looked on the defensive, cringing. This time they were taking the initiative. They were kids my age, and I knew this had something to do with my own life."[34]

In April of 1960 some 200 students met at Shaw University in Raleigh, North Carolina, to discuss ways of coordinating the sit-ins and other protests against desegregation. Out of this meeting and another one held at Atlanta later in the spring came the Student Nonviolent Coordinating Committee (SNCC). Members of this organization dedicated themselves to Martin Luther King's philosophy of nonviolence, but they also proclaimed that "arrest will not deter us" and that "this is no fad. . . . We're trying to eradicate the whole system of being inferior."[35] And although they cooperated with CORE, SCLC, and other civil rights organizations run by older black leaders, they declined to be officially affiliated with any of them. In the months and years to come, young members of SNCC and other groups would move across the South with "We Shall Overcome" as their theme song and the destruction of the walls of segregation as their goal. Ahead lay the Freedom Rides and the terrible, violent, civil rights battles of the turbulent 1960s.

The Negro was becoming more vocal and important now and could not be ignored or turned back. In the election of 1960, both parties pledged support for civil rights in their platforms, and Democratic candidate John F. Kennedy intervened to secure the release of King after his arrest during a demonstration in Atlanta. With the election of Kennedy, the civil rights movement was poised to move rapidly to the forefront of the nation's attention and bring rapid progress to the 19 million blacks who were residents of the United States but were not yet full citizens under the law.

There were signs, too, as the decade ended, that the American woman was growing unhappy with home and hearth and was beginning to yearn for more fulfillment in life. More and more women were entering the work world and going to college, and a few were joining the Beatnik underworld and participating in civil rights sit-ins and in peace demonstrations. A rash of articles and books were appearing on the dissatisfactions of American women. As *Newsweek* said in a March 1960 article on "Young Wives," the educated, middle- and upper-middle-class woman "should be pleased with herself, and yet, she is not. . . . By her own admission, this thrice-blessed woman feels herself troubled in these good times. She is dissatisfied with a lot that women of other lands can only dream of. Her discontent is deep, pervasive, and impervious to the superficial remedies which are offered at every hand." What was she discontented with? With a society that still treated her as an inferior being and measured her worth according to how she rated as wife and mother. The article quoted Margaret Mead as saying that "family life is not an end in itself. A woman's career should last longer than a boxer's or a ballet dancer's. Her goal should be development of herself as an individual, not because she is a wife or mother, but because she is a human being."[36]

This same theme was echoed in an article by Betty Friedan in the September 1960 issue of *Good Housekeeping*. In "Women Are People Too," this housewife, writer for women's magazines, and future feminist leader wrote that "there is a strange stirring, a dissatisfied groping, a yearning, a search that is going on in the minds of women. This is not easy to put into words because those women who struggle with it struggle alone, afraid to admit that they are asking themselves the silent question 'Is this all?' as they make the beds, shop for groceries and new curtains, eat peanut-butter sandwiches with the children, chauffeur Cub Scouts and Brownies to and from meetings, or lie beside their husbands at night." In this pioneer article on the frustrations of women in a sexist society and on the need for greater female self-fulfillment, Friedan asks, "Who knows what women can be when they finally are free to become themselves?"[37] In the same month as Friedan's article, *Redbook* magazine ran a contest offering a $500 prize for the best account of "Why Young Mothers Feel Trapped." Much to their surprise, the editors received 24,000 entries.[38] American women were still marrying as young (age 20.3 on the average) as they had in the early fifties and were still having babies in record numbers, but the winds of change were blowing.

The changes were helped along in May of 1960 when the United States Food and Drug Administration announced the approval of the sale by prescription of Enovid, the first oral contraceptive for women. For around $10 a month and the effort required to take twenty pills according to a rigidly prescribed monthly schedule, the pill brought a safe, convenient, and nearly 100 percent effective method of contraception, according to G. D. Searle and Company, its manufacturer. Millions of women rushed to their physicians to get prescriptions for the new pill that would free them from the unwanted pregnancies that had always inhibited female sexual activity, provided a rationale for the double standard in sexual relations, and hampered the spontaneity and enjoyment of sex relations for both partners. Few people seemed to realize it at the time—*The New York Times* buried the story of the Food and Drug Administration's action on page 75—but the sexual revolution of the sixties was about to begin.[39]

Unknown to most Americans, several writers were at work in the late fifties on books that would help to revolutionize the sixties and seventies. Betty Friedan was ignoring the advice of her editors—one of whom told her literary agent that "Betty has gone off her rocker"—and was researching her pioneer study of female repression that would appear in 1963 as *The Feminine Mystique*.[40] Rachel Carson, a prominent marine biologist who had already written two best-selling books about the mysteries and beauties of the sea, was laboring over a study of the effects of chemical pesticides on the environment and human body that would appear in 1962 as *Silent Spring*, helping to spark the modern ecological movement. A young socialist and political activist, Michael Harrington, was investigating poverty, something that was not supposed to exist in Eisenhower's America, and the publication of his *The Other America* in 1962, with its revelations that close to 20 to 25 percent of the population lived in poverty, would help to inspire the Kennedy–Johnson War on Poverty. And Ralph Nader, a young graduate of Harvard Law School whose quest for a long and healthy life had led him to give up alcohol, tobacco, women, and driving automobiles, was already writing articles on auto safety that would bring *Unsafe at Any Speed: The Designed-In Dangers of the American Automobile* (1965), raising nationwide concern and congressional legislation on automobile safety.[41]

The end of the decade coincided with a growing belief that American morality was in decline. Some critics claimed that the movies seemed to have lost all sense of decency and public responsibility as they loosened their code to deal with provocative sexual themes or exhibit lascivious bodily poses in such films as *Baby Doll* and *And God Created Woman*. In literature, many pointed to declining artistic and moral standards exemplified by the publication of *Peyton Place* and the appearance in 1958 of Vladimir Nabokov's *Lolita*, the story of a middle-aged man's obsession with adolescent girls and his seduction by a wily twelve-year-old nymphet, a story so outrageous that even *The New Republic*, which rarely got upset about such matters, was moved to label it an "obscene chronicle of murder and a child's destruction."[42] And in 1959 came the publication by Grove Press of an unexpurgated version of *Lady Chatterley's Lover*, opening the way for an influx of previously banned novels that for decades had been smuggled into the country by determined entrepreneurs. As one social observer wrote in 1960, "Books are now available at the counter newsstand . . . . which would have raised a storm of indignation as recently as five years ago."[43]

Some of those who claimed to perceive a decline in morality in movies and literature also seemed to find evidence for it in other areas of American life. They pointed to such things as the scandals that brought down Sherman Adams, to the indictment for income tax evasion of the Reverend Adam Clayton Powell, popular black leader and Democratic congressman from Harlem, to a congressional investigating committee's unearthing of fraud and racketeering in labor unions, to books and magazine articles about widespread cheating on examinations and term papers by college students at the nation's finest institutions, to involvement by police in New York and other large cities in burglary rings, and to an all-night sexual orgy with a fourteen-year-old girl in a Yale dormitory that resulted in the expulsion of eleven Yale students. They also pointed to the signs that Americans were losing their belief in absolute right and wrong and coming to believe that it was all right to do anything you wanted to do as long as it was legal and did not hurt anyone else. And they pointed to the surveys that revealed that few Americans were upset at the kind of cheating that went on when citizens filled out their income tax returns or when contestants won big money on television quiz shows.[44]

There were many observers of the American scene who felt that the quiz show scandals were still more evidence of declining morality. The quiz shows had been popular ever since the appearance in 1955 of *The $64,000 Question*, which had spawned *The $64,000 Challenge*, *Twenty-One*, and other imitators. The shows had a very dramatic setting: Two individuals, isolated in separate glass-enclosed booths, were pitted against one another in a contest of brains for high monetary rewards; the questions were kept in a bank vault and then brought to the studio at air time by a bank executive and two armed guards, and the contestants returned week after week until one finally emerged as the champion and entered another round with a new challenger. The contestants on these shows acquired a large national audience, which followed and rooted for their favorites every week. A spellbound public watched as Dr. Joyce Brothers won $134,000 as a boxing expert, as seventy-one-year-old Myrt Power from Georgia won $32,000 on one show and $16,000 on another as a baseball expert, as child star Patty

Duke became one of the country's richest eleven-year-olds by winning $32,000 as an expert on singing groups, as an army depot clerk with an eighth-grade education named Teddy Nadler won $252,000, and as other famous or heretofore obscure contestants took home large monetary prizes.

The most popular of all the contestants was Charles Van Doren, a thirty-three-year-old assistant professor of English at Columbia University and member of one of the nation's most famous literary families. In 1956, Van Doren, who was making $4,400 a year teaching at Columbia, won $129,000 in fourteen weeks on *Twenty-One*. He received a great deal of fan mail from parents and teachers praising him for being such an inspiration for young people, and was given $50,000 a year by NBC to serve as a consultant and as a commentator on Dave Garroway's *Today Show*. Overnight, through the magic power of television, an obscure English professor had become an academic and show-business star.

The quiz show brought fame and wealth to the contestants and big profits to the networks and the sponsors. *The $64,000 Question*, which started it all, soon attracted 85 percent of the audience in its time slot, and its sponsor, Revlon, which was trying to overcome the success of rival Hazel Bishop, saw its sales rise so rapidly that for weeks it could not meet the demand for its products as they sold out in retail stores all across the country.[45] Since high audience ratings meant increased profits for sponsors and the network, and since the program executives had always regarded the shows not as legitimate educational programs but as entertainment, it was perhaps inevitable that the shows would be rigged so as to provide maximum audience appeal. Contestants were taught how to smile, frown, bite their lips, clench their fists, hesitate in giving answers, and do all the other little things that enhanced their show business appeal and built up the suspense that kept the viewers sitting on the edge of their chairs and tuning in each week. The contestants who were most popular with the studio and home audiences were given extra coaching, which included being fed the correct answers. As soon as a contestant's popularity began to wane, or when a more attractive challenger was found, the producers would arrange for the reigning champion to lose at a most dramatic moment by instructing him to miss a question deliberately or by giving the correct answer to his opponent in advance. It was all good show business, but it was also gross deception.[46]

It was inevitable that in time some of the losing candidates, resentful at being arbitrarily eliminated from competition, would turn public informer. In 1958 Herb Stempel, a CCNY student who had won $49,000 on *Twenty-One* before being dethroned by Van Doren, took his story to the New York newspapers and to the Manhattan district attorney, and the facts began to come out. A New York grand jury opened an investigation into the charges, and in 1959 a congressional Subcommittee on Legislative Oversight, which watched over the FCC, started its own probe. Gradually the sordid details of the fixed programs were unraveled. Van Doren handled himself very badly, at first protesting his innocence to NBC officials, to his own lawyer, to the audience of *The Today Show*, to the grand jury, and to the Senate investigating committee. But finally in the fall of 1959 he admitted the truth of the charges and revealed before 120 reporters and seventeen photographers in the investigating committee room how as a young college professor he had been lured by the promise of wealth and fame into accepting extensive coaching on his acting and on his answers. "I was involved, deeply involved, in a deception," he admitted, explaining that "I was almost able to convince myself that it did not matter what I was doing because it was having such a good effect on the national attitude toward teachers, education, and the intellectual life."[47] Van Doren was not alone in this public embarrassment. Teddy Nadler, Patty Duke, Myrt Power, and several of the other popular contestants also admitted to accepting correct answers or to being coached in ways that allowed them to defeat their opponents at the proper time for maximum dramatic benefit and audience appeal.

At first the nation was stunned. It felt betrayed by the networks and the contestants, and was outraged that such dishonesty could be allowed. The quiz shows were so discredited that most were taken off the air, and the contestants suffered acute embarrassment, severely damaged reputations, and legal problems. As Judge Edward F. Breslin told Van Doren, "How deep and acute your humiliation has been is quite evident. I have seen it on your face and the faces of the others in this case."[48] Van Doren was fired from the Dave Garroway show despite an avalanche of mail urging the network to retain him. He was also dismissed from his Columbia position, in spite of protests from Columbia students. Teddy Nadler later took a written test for a $13-a-day job as a census taker in St. Louis, but this time the man with the encyclopedic memory failed to come up with enough correct answers and did not qualify for the job. Thirteen of the contestants on the shows were indicted for perjury, and several, including Van Doren, received suspended sentences.[49]

But some of the others were not hurt too badly. Dr. Joyce Brothers was cleared of all charges by a House investigating committee and went on to a successful career as a television talk show host and author of a syndicated column on psychological problems, and Patty Duke, whose participation in the rigged shows had been revealed in *The New York Post* under the headline, "They Even Fixed the Kid," appeared with Anne Bancroft in the 1959 Broadway Show, *The Miracle Worker*, and went on to a successful acting career. But for many contestants, even those who had not received any coaching, the embarrassment lingered for years. The television networks shied away from quiz shows with large cash prizes and were forced by the FCC to draw up strict regulations for all future quiz programs. But after the initial shock many came to believe that the contestants had not really done anything wrong, and polls revealed that three fourths of the American people felt that most people in Van Doren's situation would have done what he did.[50] This toleration of deception, pundits pointed out, was just one more sign of declining morality in a nation that was moving away from good old-fashioned moral absolutes and toward moral relativisim.

At the time of the quiz show problems the entertainment industry was struck by still another seamy revelation. Called the payola scandal, this public disgrace involved the music industry and would not have come to light without the glare of publicity surrounding the quiz show investigations or the widespread prejudice in conservative adult circles against rock 'n' roll. Investigations conducted by the Federal Communications Commission and the House Committee on Interstate Commerce revealed that thousands of disc jockeys across the country had been accepting money and presents from record companies in return for playing their music on the air. The investigations also showed that some disc jockeys, promoters, and managers also held stock in record companies or music publishing companies, a clear case of conflict of interest.

The hearings into these changes were conducted in a highly emotional atmosphere, which revealed not just the outrage over the alleged wrong-doing but a widespread belief that rock 'n' roll was a decadent form of popular music and would not have become so popular if disc jockeys had not been paid to play it. Dick Clark, who had sold out some of his investments in record companies, music publishing firms, and distributors before he was called to testify, was even accused by one investigating committee of deliberately slighting some of the older singers like Bing Crosby and Perry Como. Clark was not convicted of actually accepting payola, but his spotless reputation was tarnished by the revelations of his record company holdings and other conflicts of interest. The more controversial Alan Freed, long considered by many of the detractors of rock 'n' roll to be one of the sinister figures behind the rise of that music, was convicted of accepting payola and given a $300 fine and a six-month suspended jail sentence. His career, already on the decline, was ruined. All across the country other disc jockeys were fired by their stations as local owners and the national broadcasters moved to root out payola and other unsavory practices. The scandal even brought down the chairman of the FCC, John Doerfer, who was forced to resign after it was revealed that he had accepted favors from one of the major broadcasters he was supposedly policing.[51]

The foreign and domestic problems troubling the nation at the end of the decade contributed to a debate over national prestige and national purpose that had been growing ever since the early months of Eisenhower's second term. America had entered the fifties in a confident mood as the strong and prosperous leader of the free world in the battle against communism. In military power, prosperity, and prestige the nation was number one in the world. But that confidence had gradually eroded in the fifties as Russia caught up in atomic and nuclear weaponry, as America fought the Korean War to a frustrating stalemate, as in spite of all its efforts communism made rapid progress in Asia, the Middle East, and Latin America. For a brief time America had basked in the peace and prosperity of Eisenhower's first term, but then in 1957 the decline in national prestige and confidence began: Little Rock, Sputnik, the recessions, the rise of anti-American feeling in Latin America and other parts of the world, the government scandals that brought down the president's close friend and assistant, the quiz show scandals, the payola scandals, cheating in the schools, the appearance of a communist state on America's own back doorstep, and the U-2 affair. These problems resulted in the rise of criticism of American basic values, institutions, and, as they always do when things seem to be going wrong, the government. They inaugurated a period of self-examination.

Books, magazine and newspaper articles, and politicians—especially Democratic ones—began to spread the message that American prestige and power were declining in the world and that the United States had lost the energy, the spirit, the drive, the sense of mission and purpose that had helped it to become a great nation. The nation was criticized for its conformity, materialism, complacency, apathy, dull homogeneity, and confusion about its national purpose and goals. It was criticized for the existence of poverty in the midst of plenty, for urban slums, crime, the hedonistic pursuit of pleasure, slow economic growth, missile gaps, space gaps, educational gaps, and gaps in other areas. The United States, it was said, was in serious danger of losing its leadership and becoming number two in the world behind the Soviet Union. A Rockefeller study released in separate reports between 1958 and 1960 and published in a single volume in 1961 as *Prospect for America* claimed that "the number and the depth of the problems we face suggests that the very life of our free society may be at stake" and that most of the problems were related to "the mortal struggle in which we are engaged" with the Soviet Union. The report concluded that if the nation drew upon its human and material resources and responded to "challenges" and "opportunities" as it had in the past, "there is every reason to face the future with all confidence."[52]

The debate over the national purpose quickened in 1960. *The New York Times* and *Life* ran special series on the national purpose, with the five-part *Life* series gaining a wide audience in the spring and early summer because it coincided with the furor over the U-2 affair and because of the stature of its contributors, which included Adlai Stevenson, Archibald MacLeish, Billy Graham, David Sarnoff, John Gardner, Clinton Rossiter, and Walter

Lippman. Covering a wide range of issues, it added little that was new to the national soul-searching but did help, through the magazine's mass circulation, to disseminate existing ideas to wide audiences. The president himself had entered the debate in February of 1960 when he set up a ten-member President's Commission on National Goals, headed by Henry M. Wriston, the president of Brown University. The commission's report, entitled *Goals for Americans*, was clearly written under the shadow of the Cold War. "The nation is in grave danger," the introduction warned, "threatened by the rulers of one third of mankind." The report contained several direct and indirect references to the Eisenhower administration's failure to respond properly to the Soviet threat and to domestic problems, and called for massive federal spending to remedy the deficiencies in both areas.[53]

Deeply disappointed with the report, Eisenhower delayed its release until after the November elections. But he need not have bothered, for the report's main proposals had already been debated in a campaign that saw the electorate decide, by a narrow margin, that the goals of the nation could best be met by the Democrats and their new young leader, John F. Kennedy.

# 23

# *The Torch Is Passed*

The agonizing over the national purpose and declining national prestige would be an integral part of the campaign of 1960. Jockeying for the party nominations began after Eisenhower's reelection in 1956, for the Twenty-second Amendment that prevented the ever-popular general from seeking a third term left the race wide open for both parties in 1960. The Democrats had several strong contenders, but by the opening of the convention in Los Angeles in July Senators Hubert Humphrey, Stuart Symington, Lyndon Johnson, and all the other aspirants for the office had been crushed by the strong organization, popularity, and campaigning of Senator John F. Kennedy of Massachusetts. Nominated on the first ballot, Kennedy balanced the ticket by choosing Senate Majority Leader Lyndon Johnson as his running mate. On the Republican side, Vice President Richard Nixon was again troubled by Eisenhower's reluctance to give him a strong endorsement, but he was able to thwart several "stop Nixon" movements in his own party and defeat his two main rivals from the opposing wings, Governor Nelson Rockefeller of New York and Senator Barry Goldwater of Arizona. In July he was duly nominated by his party on the first ballot at the convention in Chicago, and as his running mate he chose the experienced and popular ambassador to the United Nations, Henry Cabot Lodge, whom Kennedy had defeated for the Senate in 1952.

Kennedy and Nixon had much in common. Both had been elected to Congress in 1946, and both were now running for the highest office in the land against great odds: Nixon was trying to become the first vice president since Martin Van Buren to succeed to the presidency through the electoral process rather than the death of the incumbent, while Kennedy, the first Catholic nominee since Al Smith in 1928, was attempting to become the first Catholic ever elected president. Both men were young, though at forty-three Kennedy seemed much younger than the forty-six-year-old Nixon. Both men believed in a strong presidency, the continuation of the New Deal, a strong defense, and the need for the United States to lead the Western world in the worldwide battle against international communism. While Kennedy was considered the more liberal of the two, the opposing candidates were not far apart in their basic political philosophies, leading some to characterize Kennedy as "the Democratic Nixon." Both men were consummate politicians who understood how the game of politics worked and how to play it.

The differences between the two men were not differences of substance but of style. Early in the 1960 campaign, even before the two men received the nominations for their party, reporter Richard Rovere wrote in *Harper's* that along with all the other presidential contenders, Kennedy and Nixon "tend more and more to borrow from one another's platforms and to assume one another's commitments; by election eve, they are practically united in their schemes for the future and divided principally by their views of the past."[1] Eric Sevareid also noted that there was little to choose from between the two candidates and that "the 'managerial revolution' has come to politics, and Nixon and Kennedy are its first completely packaged products. The Processed Politician has finally arrived."[2] Ironically, both men, as Rovere observed, were competing to succeed one of the most popular presidents in history by trying in their emphasis on strong leadership to imply that they would not be like him.[3]

Kennedy had many assets. He came from a very wealthy and influential Massachusetts family with business and personal contacts spanning the nation and going all the way back to the Roosevelt administration, when Joe Kennedy was the ambassador to the United Kingdom. John Kennedy was young, good looking, athletic, urbane, witty, intellectual, and articulate. He was a Harvard graduate, a genuine World War II hero who rescued several of his men when his PT boat was sunk in the Pacific by the Japanese, and the author of a million-copy best-seller (*Profiles in Courage*) on senators who at crucial times in American history had chosen duty and honor over political expediency. He had money, an attractive wife, and one of the most efficient political organizations ever assembled in the drive for the presidency, as Humphrey and others had discovered when the Kennedy bandwagon rolled over them in the primaries. He also had some serious liabilities—his religion, his reputation as a brash and immature playboy, and the cynical suspicion in some Democratic party circles that he was a superficial and immature young man with questionable liberal credentials who could not win the presidency or govern if he were lucky enough to capture it. Harry Truman, whose eight-year absence from Washington had done little to diminish his sharp tongue, expressed the views of many of the party faithful by frequently referring to him as a "boy" with a rich father who would try to buy the election and influence him once he had been elected. "It's not the Pope who worries me," he said. "It's the pop." But like most Democrats, Truman campaigned for Kennedy once he was nominated, and in traditional style he told an audience in San Antonio that Texans who voted for Nixon ought "to go to hell."[4]

In his campaign Kennedy rarely attacked Eisenhower personally—the president was too popular for that. Instead, he concentrated on assaulting the eight years of Republican rule that had caused the United States to decline in prestige and power at home and abroad, to lose her sense of mission and direction, to stagnate economically and fall behind the growth rate of the Russian economy, to trail in the missile and space races, and to allow communism to expand and even to gain a foothold just ninety miles off the coast of Florida. It was time, he reiterated, to reverse this decline, to look ahead rather than behind, to move America forward. And although he had not established strong liberal credentials during his Senate years, he now called for vigorous federal action to stimulate economic growth, end racial discrimination in all areas of life, establish medical care for the aged, provide federal aid to education and the troubled cities, increase the minimum wage, establish a peace corps, and reverse the recession and unemployment troubling the nation. As much of a Cold Warrior as Nixon, he called for the buildup of American armed forces and courageous resistance to the spread of communism wherever it might threaten. And throughout his campaign he emphasized, as he had in his acceptance speech at the Democratic convention, that "it is time for a new generation of leadership" as America moved into "a New Frontier—the frontier of the 1960s—the frontier of unknown opportunities and perils."[5]

Kennedy faced the religious issue straightforwardly, proclaiming that he believed in the separation of church and state, was against federal aid to parochial schools, and would not let the pope or any other outside authority influence his presidency in any way. "Contrary to common newspaper usage," he said, "I am not the Catholic candidate for President; I am the Democratic Party's candidate for President, who happens also to be a Catholic. I do not speak for my church on public matters—and the church does not speak for me."[6] While he dealt with many questions directly, he nimbly sidestepped others or deflected them with his humor, as when he told a campaign audience that he had received a telegram from his wealthy father saying, "Dear Jack: Don't buy a single vote more than is necessary—I'll be damned if I'm going to pay for a landslide."[7] And when Nixon continued to use his Kitchen Debate with Khrushchev as an example of his experience in diplomacy, Kennedy quipped that "Mr. Nixon may be very experienced in kitchen debates," but "so are a great many other married men I know."[8] Many people, especially the young and particularly the college-educated young, were attracted to Kennedy's youthful idealism, intellectualism, and confidence that the nation could be turned around and placed on a proper course. He had charisma, as sympathetic reporters and followers never tired of saying, and he and his young, attractive, pregnant wife drew large crowds and enthusiastic responses wherever they went. He was popular with the press and received a steady stream of favorable publicity.

Richard Nixon did not have charisma, but he did have eight years' experience as vice president and a loyal following in his party and throughout the nation. He tried to take the high road in the campaign, leading to a lot of talk about the New Nixon and a lot of Democratic jabs about how there had been so many Nixons that no one could ever be sure which one was the real one. Democrats still referred to him as Tricky Dick and asked, "Would you buy a used car from this man?" Nixon attacked Kennedy for his immaturity, impulsiveness, pie-in-the-sky proposals, and big spending ideas, but he did not raise the religious issue. He concentrated on emphasizing his own experience, moderation, and maturity, while pledging to continue the peace and prosperity that eight years of Republican rule had brought the nation. He also talked of the need to have strong leadership, to move ahead, to build on the good record and performance of Dwight Eisenhower. He portrayed himself as a vigorous and experienced leader, a man who had courageously faced rioters in Latin America and stood up to Khrushchev in the Kitchen Debate in Moscow. He constantly emphasized that he would not be a caretaker president or a mere conciliator, but a man of action, a leader of Congress and the nation. He seemed to be promising—though he did not explicitly say so—that he would not be a weak president like Eisenhower but would be a strong and vigorous chief executive. Eisenhower strongly resented this implication, and there were many close to the outgoing president who felt that Eisenhower's campaigning was aimed not so much at electing Nixon, about whom he had always had reservations, but at defeating the brash senator from Massachusetts.[9]

The relationship between Eisenhower and Nixon was still a strained, enigmatic one. At the time of the 1952 campaign, the two men had barely known one another. They had met only a few times, and they had never sat down to have a drink or meal together or socialized in any other way.[10] There was a great age difference—twenty-three years between their dates of birth—and while Eisenhower had been a world-famous figure before he came to the presidency, Nixon was a relative newcomer on the national political stage. A graduate of Whittier College and Duke University Law

School, the navy veteran successfully ran for Congress in 1946 and 1948, and built a national reputation as a member of HUAC and central figure in the Hiss investigation. In 1950 he won election to the Senate by defeating Congressman Helen Gahagan Douglas, a former stage star and wife of movie star Melvyn Douglas, in a no-holds-barred campaign in which he called her the "pink lady" and accused her of communist sympathies. He continued to attract national attention as a senator by his aggressive support of the domestic and international battle against communism, earning a reputation that helped him gain the vice-presidential nomination in 1952. Coming from two very different backgrounds, the slick politician and the seemingly nonpolitical military hero found themselves on the same ballot in 1952 and 1956, providing additional proof of the old saying about politics making strange bedfellows.

Eisenhower had an enormous influence on the young Californian's career in both positive and negative ways. He chose him for the vice-presidency in 1952, almost dumped him from the ticket in the controversy over the "slush fund," accepted him back into the fold after the Checkers speech, considered dropping him from the ticket in 1956, and seemed lukewarm in his support of his bid for the presidency in 1960. Although he could describe Nixon in his diary as "not only bright, quick, and energetic—but loyal and cooperative,"[11] Eisenhower rarely sought Nixon's advice on difficult decisions, did not consider him a creative thinker, did not think that he was good presidential material or that he would ever be a great statesman. Eisenhower always seemed to think that Nixon was "too political," but he was not above using him to do the dirty work of politics that Eisenhower did not want to do—attacking Stevenson and others during the campaigns of 1952 and 1956, mending fences with disgruntled elements in the Republican party, and dealing with McCarthy and other troublesome members of the right wing. For his part, Nixon looked upon the president as a father figure who could make or break his career, and as he revealed privately and in his *Six Crises* and *Memoirs*, he was often embarrassed, hurt, and angered by Eisenhower's treatment of him. In spite of eight years as political allies and colleagues, and the courtship and 1968 marriage of Nixon's daughter, Julie, to Eisenhower's grandson, David, the president and vice president never became close friends and always seemed to have an awkward relationship.[12]

Eisenhower played a dubious role in the 1960 election. He endorsed Nixon only because he felt that he was better than all the alternatives. His personal choice was Robert Anderson, his old friend and treasury secretary, but Anderson refused to run. As for Nixon's main rival, Nelson Rockefeller, Eisenhower believed that he did not have the intelligence or character for the job and was too liberal and too much of a big spender.[13] So, he was left with Nixon. But here he dragged his feet, withholding a strong public endorsement until the party nominated Nixon in July. He also played a passive role up until the final week, partly because of his own disinclination to become embroiled in partisan politics and partly because he and Nixon both felt that he should stay in the background while the vice president staked out his own position as an independent candidate and party leader, showing that he was not a mere puppet of the president.

Although Eisenhower was less than enthusiastic about the Nixon-Lodge ticket, he felt it was far better that what the opposition had to offer. He was infuriated at Kennedy's claims that he had allowed the nation to fall behind the Soviet Union in arms development and endangered the nation's security. He also disliked the whole Kennedy family. Early in the campaign he told one of his friends that if Kennedy were elected "we will never get them out—that there will be a machine bigger than Tammy Hall ever was." And he told another that "I will do anything to avoid turning my chair and the country over to Kennedy." He also disliked Kennedy's running mate, Lyndon Johnson, whom he called "the most tricky and unreliable politician in Congress."[14]

Eisenhower's campaign posture certainly hurt Nixon, who had hoped for enthusiastic support from one of the most popular presidents in history. While Nixon wanted to run as his own man, he desperately wanted the president to use his "nonpartisan" public appearances to praise his abilities and to tout his contributions to the Eisenhower team over an eight-year period. But given his reservations about Nixon, Eisenhower found this difficult to do. Besides, he too often saw the campaign not as a battle between Nixon and Kennedy but as a defense of his own administration. On August 24, Eisenhower further damaged Nixon's chances with a hasty remark he made at the end of a long press conference that he was hurrying to bring to a close. When asked by a reporter if he could name one important idea that Nixon had contributed to a White House decision in his eight years as vice president, Eisenhower replied, "If you give me a week, I might think of one. I can't remember."[15] This ill-considered remark caused wide comment and cast further doubt on Nixon's ability and the president's conception of him as the heir apparent. Eisenhower later called Nixon and apologized for the remark, but the damage had been done.[16] And during the rest of the campaign Eisenhower did little to rectify it, for in his press conferences and other public appearances he still declined to characterize Nixon as a major decision-maker within his administration.

Finally in the last week of October, as Eisenhower became eager to campaign against the young upstart who was accusing him of lax leadership and as Nixon began to feel that the president's help was needed in what was obviously going to be a close election, Eisenhower emerged as a direct participant in the campaign. He appeared in rallies in Philadelphia, New York, Cleveland, Pittsburgh, Washington, and other cities, defending his administration, endorsing Nixon, and attacking the inexperience and immaturity of Kennedy. However, he often seemed to spend more time defending his own administration against Kennedy than in endorsing Nixon. Meanwhile, the Democrats got considerable political mileage out of claiming that Nixon was trying to ride "piggyback" into the White House.[17]

The campaign was long, arduous, and expensive. More than in any previous campaign in American history, both men relied heavily on large complex organizations composed of advisers, speech writers, advance men, pollsters, researchers, crowd organizers and controllers, and thousands of volunteers at all levels all across the country. Kennedy traveled an estimated 75,000 miles and visited forty-six states, while Nixon traveled some 60,000 miles as he fulfilled his campaign pledge to visit all fifty states. Both men spent huge sums of money, much of it on television commercials. The Republicans spent $7.6 million for television, and the Democrats $6.2 million—a record up to that time. This indicated the growing power and importance of television, as did the intense preparations both men put into the four televised debates—the first in American history—that were held in September and October and attracted audiences ranging from 61 million to 75 million.[18] Many people felt that these debates aided Kennedy more than they did Nixon, since they helped Kennedy become better known and since Nixon, suffering from a knee infection incurred when he bumped his knee on a car door while campaigning in North Carolina, looked pale and ill during the first debate.

In the last month of the election everyone knew it was going to be close. In the middle of October George Gallup even refused to forecast the winner, and comedian Mort Sahl joked that "neither candidate is going to win."[19] But in the last few days before the election most pollsters predicted a narrow win for Kennedy. On November 8 almost 69 million voters—close to two thirds of those eligible—went to the polls and gave a very narrow verdict in favor of Kennedy. The electoral margin was 303 to 219, while in the popular vote the margin was only 118,000, or about one fourth of 1 percent of the vote, the closest popular vote margin since 1884. If only 12,000 voters in five states had voted differently, Nixon would have won. In the congressional races the Republicans gained seats in both houses but the Democrats still maintained a 65–35 margin in the Senate and a 262–174 majority in the House.[20]

The closeness of the vote made it difficult for analysts to explain why Kennedy won. Most agreed that his victory could be explained partly by the strength of his organization, by his performance in the television debates, and by his appeal to the large industrial states of the Midwest, the large cities, the South (thanks partly to Lyndon Johnson), and to Catholics, Jews, blacks, and women. Some believed that he won in spite of his religion, since his Catholicism may have cost him as many votes as it attracted. Many agreed that his appeal to blacks was heightened in the last days of the campaign when his brother Robert put in a call to the local authorities in Georgia to secure the release on bail of Martin Luther King, Jr., who had been arrested and sentenced to four months' imprisonment for his role in a sit-in at a restaurant in Rich's Department Store in Atlanta. John also called Mrs. King to express his concern for the civil rights leader.[21]

The closeness of the election and charges of voting irregularities in several states, particularly Texas and Illinois, could have led Nixon to call for a recount that could have thrown the election into the House of Representatives. However, Nixon conceded the victory to Kennedy rather than tie up the nation in a divisive and paralyzing constitutional crisis. But he was bitter. He felt that he had been defeated by a slanted press, fraudulent voting, and dirty tricks of the Kennedy organization. Years later, he would write in his memoirs that "we were faced by an organization that had equal dedication and unlimited money that was led by the most ruthless group of political operators ever mobilized for a presidential campaign." "From this point on," he wrote, "I had the wisdom and wariness of someone who had been burned by the power of the Kennedys and their money and by the license they were given by the media. I vowed that I would never again enter an election at a disadvantage by being vulnerable to them—or anyone—on the level of political tactics."[22] Kennedy, of course, could afford to take a more generous view of the outcome, saying that "the margin is narrow, but the responsibility is clear."[23]

Eisenhower was bitterly disappointed at the results of the election of 1960, regarding it as a "repudiation of everything I've done for eight years."[24] In spite of his reservations about Nixon, Eisenhower was deeply disturbed by what he considered to be a rejection of his policies and a victory for the brash, young, free-spending Democrat. He also had second thoughts about his own role in the election, and he often pondered what the outcome might have been if he had played an earlier and more active part in the campaign. Years later, in his memoirs, he wrote that during his eight years in office "my principal political disappointment was the defeat of Dick Nixon in 1960. . . . I shall never cease to wonder whether a more extensive program of political speaking on my part might have had a favorable effect on the outcome."[25] Many contemporary and later observers of the elections wondered along the same lines. Some of Eisenhower's biographers, including Stephen Ambrose, who has written very favorably of the man and his presidency, have concluded that Eisenhower's words and actions (or inactions) in the 1960 campaign may have cost Nixon the victory both men wanted so badly.[26]

After the November election, Eisenhower still had two and a half months in office before power was transferred to the young Kennedy. There was little opportunity for him to rest and reflect on his presidency, for the problems kept coming into the Oval Office from the Congo, Vietnam, Laos, Guatemala, Cuba, and other hot spots in the world. At home, the recession continued to defy quick solutions and unemployment reached 7 percent. But the president remained popular right to the end. Just before the end of his term, a Gallup poll showed that 59 percent of Americans still approved of his handling of his job. If he could have run again in 1960, he would most certainly have won a third term.[27]

In these last weeks Eisenhower did all he could to bring about an orderly transfer of power. On December 6, 1960, and Janauary 19, 1961, the president-elect visited the White House and met with Eisenhower in a friendly atmosphere very unlike the tense and awkward climate surrounding Eisenhower's own visits with Truman eight years before. Although he had earlier harbored grave reservations about Kennedy's maturity and abilities, the president was very impressed by "the young man who was to be my successor," particularly by "his pleasing personality, his concentrated interest and his receptiveness." At both meetings Kennedy was given detailed information on the organization and running of the government and on the major issues in foreign policy, and on several other occasions Kennedy and his top advisers were briefed by officials from the CIA and other agencies. It was at one of these meetings that he first heard from Allen Dulles of plans for using refugees for the invasion of Cuba. At the second meeting in the White House Kennedy was also informed, Eisenhower later wrote, of "the significance of the satchel filled with orders applicable to an emergency and carried by an unobtrusive man who would shadow the President for all his days in office." Eisenhower also wrote that he had impressed the young Kennedy by pushing a button and saying, "Send a chopper," which landed on the White House lawn just outside the Oval Office only six minutes later.[28]

At 8:30 P.M. on January 17, three days before he left office, Eisenhower appeared on radio and television to give his farewell address to the nation. He had labored over it for several days, for he considered it to be one of his most important speeches ever as he brought to a close nearly fifty years of public service that had begun before the airplane had become an important military weapon and was ending with both Russia and the United States pointing deadly ICBMs at one another. His fifteen-minute speech touched on several points, mostly warnings about the dangers that the nation faced at home and abroad. But the most prophetic part of his speech came when he cautioned that "in the councils of government, we must guard against the acquisition of unwarranted influence, whether sought or unsought, by the military industrial complex. The potential for the disastrous rise of misplaced power exists and will persist." While the growth of the military and the arms industry had been an inevitable necessity, he said, the nation's economy had become too dependent on military and defense spending, and the military establishment and arms industry had too much influence in government and society. It was possible, he suggested, that the continued growth of the military industrial complex could "endanger our liberties or our democratic processes."[29] These were strong words, coming as they did from a man who had spent nearly two thirds of his life in uniform.

Thursday, January 19, was Eisenhower's last full day in office. He was already packed, ready and eager to go to his retirement at his Gettysburg farm. Still, in spite of all the burdens of the job, and especially those of the past year, it was hard for a man who had held power for so long to give it up. A few days before, as he watched workmen erect a reviewing stand for Kennedy's inaugural, he told a friend that "it's like being in the death cell and watching them put up the scaffold."[30] He spent his last day attending to last-minute correspondence, signing the hundreds of documents that presidents have to sign every day, meeting with president-elect Kennedy and his staff, and attending to last-minute details. That afternoon a courier arrived from the Treasury Department with his last presidential paychecks—a salary check of $5,416.69 and an expense check for $2,708.31.[31] Before he left his office around five o'clock that afternoon, Washington had been blanketed by a swirling snowstorm that eventually dumped eight inches on the capital, snarling traffic and forcing fourteen White House secretaries to spend the evening in the bomb shelter in the basement of the White House. That night, while President and Mrs. Eisenhower spent a quiet evening in the White House and John Kennedy attended preinaugural ceremonies until nearly 4 A.M., city workers and some 3,000 servicemen from nearby army bases manned shovels, snowplows, and trucks to clear the streets so that the festivities surrounding the transfer of power could proceed as scheduled.

Inauguration day was beautifully clear but cold and windy, with the temperature still hovering around 20 degrees at the noon inauguration. John and Jacqueline Kennedy had coffee in the Red Room at the White House with the Eisenhowers and Nixons, then at around 11:30 the president-elect and the president walked down the front steps of the White House to the waiting limousines for the ride along Pennsylvania Avenue to the inaugural stand at the Capitol Plaza. As they rode together the two men talked easily and casually, mostly about Eisenhower's two previous inaugurations and about the Second World War. Then, along with the rest of the large crowd, Eisenhower braved the cold through the prayers of Richard Cardinal Cushing, the dedicatory poem of Robert Frost, and the swearing in of the thirty-fifth president by Chief Justice Earl Warren. He then listened attentively to the eloquent and idealistic address of the new president as he promised national renewal, sacrifice, hope, and greatness and proclaimed that "the torch has been passed to a new generation of Americans, born in this country, tempered by war, disciplined by a hard and bitter peace, proud of our ancient heritage, and unwilling to witness or permit the slow undoing of those human rights to which this nation has always been committed, and to which we are committed today at home and around the world." He listened, too, as Kennedy exhorted America to "ask not what your country can do for you—ask what you can do for your country."[32]

After the inaugural, the Eisenhowers went to a luncheon at the F Street Club hosted by Mr. and Mrs. Lewis Strauss and attended by the key officials of his administration. Then the seventy-year-old Eisenhower, the oldest man to serve as president up to that time, left Washington and the fate of the country to John Kennedy, at forty-three the youngest man ever elected president. Eisenhower would live quietly at Gettysburg until his death in March of 1969, relaxing, golfing, playing bridge, painting, reading, enjoying his grandchildren, writing his memoirs, and occasionally offering private advice to his successors but rarely giving public criticism of them or their policies. He would outlive by over five years his young successor, who would be struck down by an assassin's bullets on November 22, 1963.

On the night of the inaugural ceremonies, Richard Nixon dined with his family, while in happier circumstances John Kennedy continued to enjoy the festivities of his inaugural. The past few months had been difficult ones for the ex-vice president. He had lost the election by an incredibly narrow margin, and then later, following the stipulations of the Constitution, he had to exercise his duties as president of the Senate and count the electoral ballots in front of the senators and representatives and certify that John F. Kennedy had defeated Richard M. Nixon for the presidency. Then on January 26 he had had coffee with the president-elect and attended his inauguration. That night he had his official chauffeur of eight years, John Wardlaw, drive him around the icy, hazardous streets of the city that had been his political home for the past fourteen years. In the course of the drive he went to Capitol Hill, and there he went out on a balcony of the Capitol and looked out over the mall at the Washington and Lincoln monuments, which seemed more beautiful than ever in the snow-covered ground and even more difficult to leave. But as Nixon would later write, "As I turned to go inside, I suddenly stopped short, struck by the thought that this was not the end—that someday I would be back here. I walked as fast as I could back to the car."[33]

Angry and bitter, Richard Nixon went back home to California to rebuild a political career that would, indeed, bring him back to Washington and the national limelight.

# 24

# In Search of the Fifties

With the election and inauguration of John F. Kennedy, the decade of the fifties came to a close. But even before it ended, historians were beginning to write its epitaph. At the beginning of 1960, in a *Harper's* article entitled "Good-By to the Fifties—and Good Riddance," Eric Goldman expressed the opinion of most historians of the time when he wrote that "we've grown unbelievably prosperous and we maunder along in a stupor of fat. . . . We live in a heavy, humorless, sanctimonious, stultifying atmosphere, singularly lacking in the self-mockery that is self-criticism. Probably the climate of the late fifties was the dullest and dreariest in all our history." As for the president who reigned over it all, Goldman saw him as "an overwhelmingly public hero, who persists in talking platitudes straight out of the old days of the Rutherford B. Hayes Marching Societies."[1] And later that year, as Eisenhower's troubled second term drew to a close, historian and journalist William V. Shannon wrote that the fifties "have been years of flabbiness and self-satisfaction and gross materialism. . . . [The] loudest sound in the land has been the oink and grunt of private hoggishness. . . . It has been the age of the slob."[2]

Long before the decade ended, liberal intellectuals were already writing off the Eisenhower presidency. In a 1958 article in *Commentary*, Shannon claimed that "although Eisenhower has two years still to serve, his place in history and the significance of his presidency are already becoming clear. Eisenhower is a transitional figure. He has not shaped the future nor tried to repeal the past. . . . When he leaves office in January of 1961, the foreign policies and the domestic policies of the past generation will be about where he found them in 1953. No national problem . . . will have been advanced importantly toward solution nor its dimensions significantly altered. The Eisenhower era is the time of the great postponement."[3] Eisenhower's troubled last year in office only confirmed the earlier liberal assessments of his presidency. In October of 1960, historian Norman A. Graebner of the University of Illinois wrote that "never has a popular leader who dominated so completely the national political scene affected so negligibly the essential historic process of his time."[4] Overall, Graebner viewed Eisenhower's presidency as one that failed to solve the basic domestic and foreign problems of the day.

At the end of the fifties, then, historians had come to an agreement on the major characteristics of the era and of the popular president who reigned over it. It was, they said, a dull, placid, and sterile age, a time of materialism, selfishness, conformity, apathy, conservatism, consensus, and security. Presiding over it all was a popular military hero, a grandfatherly figure loved and respected for who he was rather than for what he did, a naive man who stood aloof from the partisan politics he detested so much, a man who turned the running of the country over to Dulles and Adams and other subordinates while he read westerns, played bridge with his millionaire friends, or headed off to the nearest golf course. Under this good but naive and incompetent president, the nation drifted along with a calm surface but with problems boiling underneath that would later surface to plague future presidents. Strongly Democratic in their political affiliation, most historians were ready to get Eisenhower behind them, and they looked forward to the presidency of a young liberal intellectual who would get the country moving again.

The traditional views of the fifties and of President Eisenhower were little challenged over the next decade. Meanwhile, the nation entered one of the most turbulent and terrible times in its history, probably the worst since the divisive 1850s and the Civil War era. The decade of the sixties brought the assassinations of President Kennedy, Martin Luther King, Jr., and Robert Kennedy. It brought a full-scale revolt against the establishment's rulers and values by students, blacks, women, American Indians, and other dissatisfied and radicalized groups. It brought the murder of freedom riders in the South, massive civil rights demonstrations, violent riots in Watts and other black ghettoes in cities all across the country, peaceful and violent protests against the Vietnam War, student riots at Berkeley and other campuses, the rise of the New Left and of a counterculture of young people—hippies, yippies, and others—protesting against the values of bourgeois society. It brought the widespread use of drugs, public nudity, and public sexual intercourse among "flower children" and other members of the counterculture, the rise of a feminist movement, and other radical changes. Near the end of the sixties came the riots outside the Democratic convention in Chicago and the election of Richard Nixon, back from the political dead. Ahead lay Kent State, Watergate, and other troubles of the early seventies.

As Americans entered the 1970s, they began to look back on the 1950s through nostalgic eyes. By then, the Eisenhower era appeared not as a bland and sterile age, but as a simple, happy time before the deluge of the sixties. This longing for the golden age of the fifties first became widespread in 1972. In June of that year *Life* magazine observed in "The Nifty Fifties" that "it's been barely a dozen years since the '50s ended and yet here we go again, awash in the trappings of that sunnier time, paying new attention to the old artifacts and demigods." *Life* noted that Elvis Presley's concerts were very popular, *Grease* was packing them in on Broadway, the airways were full of the music of Chuck Berry, Billy Haley, Little Richard, and other relics of the fifties, the group Sha Na Na was doing 200 concerts a year and making over $1 million a year parodying and recalling the age, and ponytails and ducktail haircuts were popular again. "Kids barely old enough to remember what a fall-out shelter was are digging the hand jive and the bunny hop, circle skirts and cinch belts, penny loafers, saddle shoes, white bucks, shirts with cigarette packs tucked into their sleeves."[5]

Many dismissed this nostalgia as a temporary phenomenon, but as 1972 continued, the fad spread and intensified. In the fall of that year *Newsweek* wrote in "Back to the '50s" that "in the grand sweep of American history, the 1950s were one of the blandest decades ever. But now a revival of those very same quiet years is sweeping across the nation like a runaway Hula Hoop."[6] Some observers decried this epidemic of nostalgia for the fifties. In "Must We Be Nostalgic for the Fifties?" in the October 1972 issue of *Horizon*, Thomas Meehan reminded his readers that the happy days of the fifties was also the time of the Korean War, McCarthyism, atomic war scares, and other unhappy events. He also dismissed the period as "a Golden Age of Kitsch. Formica in the kitchen, barbecue grills in the backyard, Hula Hoops, *Confidential*, Davy Crockett hats, ankle bracelets, Barbie dolls, Metrecal soups, and a plastic pink flamingo in postage-stamp-sized suburban front lawns. The memory of it all, to lapse once again into the slang of the fifties, is enough to make one want to toss one's cookies, upchuck, and barf."[7]

Apparently millions of Americans disagreed with Meehan, for the fad that swept the country in 1972 continued on into the midseventies before it entered a slow decline at the end of the decade. Many compared the decade to the jazz age of the 1920s, another happy era of prosperity, popular Republican presidents, and zany fads like the Charleston, raccoon coats, and goldfish swallowing. There was a major revival of fifties clothing, records, dances, movies, Hula Hoops, and other "artifacts," as *Life* called them, along with Presley, Berry, Rick Nelson, and other "demigods." *Grease* would turn out to be the longest-running show in Broadway history, up till that time. Movies about the fifties, such as *The Last Picture Show* and *The Way We Were*, were a big success, as was *American Graffiti*, which was ostensibly about the year 1962 but captured the atmosphere of the late fifties with its portrayal of the automobiles, clothing, "cruising," haircuts, and other customs and styles of the preceding decade. A host of television shows about the decade appeared, led by *M*A*S*H*, *Laverne and Shirley*, and *Happy Days*. And the midseventies would see the publication of popular and academic books attempting to recapture, describe, and explain the decade and the American people's continuing fascination with it.

The causes of the fascination were not difficult to find. As *Life* pointed out in June of 1972, "Pop psychologists—and many of the kids—see the flight to the '50s as a search for a happier time, before drugs, Vietnam and assassination."[8] And in October of that year, *Newsweek* claimed that "the appeal of the '50s today represents nothing so much as the exhaustion of the hope and energy that fired the '60s."[9] The nostalgia was, indeed, a natural yearning after the troubled sixties to return to a happier, simpler time, especially for the young, who had grown up in an age that robbed them of a carefree, optimistic youth. The nostalgia was also a part of some older Americans' desire to relive their youth, to remember a time before their lives became complicated with jobs, marriages, children, and the turbulent events of the sixties. As so often happens after periods of change and strife, people sought escape from the present by turning back to a golden age, yearning for a time they never had or, for the older generation, for a time they once had had, but now had lost.[10]

The events of the sixties and early seventies that caused Americans to yearn for the good old days also contributed to other revivals, this time of the personal popularity of President Truman and the historical reputation of President Eisenhower. Although most historians had always given Truman's presidency high marks, the public had not. During the darkest days of the Korean War and the "Truman scandals," public opinion polls revealed that the number of Americans approving of the way he handled his job dropped to 26 percent and finally to a low of 23 percent, which was below the rating of any of his predecessors or successors, including Richard Nixon at the time of his resignation from the presidency in 1974.[11] By the time he left office in January of 1953 Truman's approval rating had risen only slightly, to 30 percent, and his personal popularity would remain low for the rest of the decade.

However, as the passage of time created a better perspective on Truman's presidency and blurred the controversial events of the Korean War era, Truman's personal popularity began to rise to the level of his historical reputation. The events of the 1960s and 1970s dramatically elevated his popularity among older Americans and among younger ones who had no personal memory of his era, for Lyndon Johnson's abuses of presidential power in the conduct of the Vietnam War and Richard Nixon's resignation in the wake of the Watergate scandal made the plain-speaking, hard-hitting, but honest and open man from Missouri more attractive than ever before. By the middle of the 1970s he was the subject of several favorable television documentaries, James Whitmore's one-man performances of the stage play *Give 'em Hell, Harry*! were attracting rave reviews and overflow audiences, the song "Harry Truman" by the rock group "Chicago" had climbed near the top of the charts, students were wearing Harry Truman T-shirts, automobiles were displaying bumper stickers reading "America needs you, Harry Truman," popular magazines were running articles on "Trumania" and "Truman nostalgia," and Senator Barry Goldwater, President Gerald Ford, and presidential aspirant Jimmy Carter and other politicians from both parties were claiming that Truman was one of their favorite presidents. Meanwhile, polls of historians and political scientists continued to rank him as the eighth or ninth best president in American history. In his own right, and certainly in contrast to most of his successors, Truman was looking better all the time.[12]

So was Eisenhower. Unlike Truman, he had never fallen out of favor with the majority of the American public, which always liked him better than did the historians, reporters, and other presidential watchers. Eisenhower had left office more popular than when he came in, and he continued to hold the public's love and respect during his retirement years. In 1968, after the rapidly failing general had suffered his sixth heart attack, twenty healthy adults called Walter Reed Army Hospital offering to save his life by donating their own hearts to be used as a transplant. And three months before his death in March of 1969, a poll revealed that Eisenhower led the list of the top ten most admired men in the country.[13] Still, the historians did not think much of his presidency, continuing to regard him as a good and well-meaning man who let the country drift toward the disasters of the 1960s. Arthur Schlesinger's 1962 poll ranked Eisenhower near the bottom of the list of "average" presidents, tied for twenty-first with Chester A. Arthur and just ahead of Andrew Johnson. In a poll of the Organization of American Historians published in 1970, Eisenhower ranked number nineteen in "general prestige" and twentieth in accomplishments.[14]

There had always been some respected political observers who disagreed with their colleagues' low opinions of Eisenhower. In 1956, Samuel Lubell had written that Eisenhower was not a "five-star babe in the political woods" but was instead "as complete a political angler as ever fished the White House."[15] In that same year Arthur Krock of *The New York Times* wrote that Eisenhower was a hardworking, intelligent president who loved his job and was "remarkably well informed in a vast field of government operations."[16] In 1960 George E. Allen, a writer and close friend of the president, wrote in *The Saturday Evening Post* that "the man who took office mistrusting politics and politicians will leave office having proved himself one of the most successful politicians ever to occupy the Presidency." Allen also claimed that Eisenhower, not Adams or Dulles or anyone else, ran the presidency, and that he ran it very well.[17]

A few other critics spoke well of Eisenhower in the 1960s, but the first major reevaluation of him came in *Esquire* in 1967, when one of his old detractors, columnist Murray Kempton, wrote in "The Underestimation of Dwight Eisenhower" that Eisenhower had pulled the wool over the eyes of his liberal critics. Eisenhower, Kempton claimed, was much more intelligent, complex, and devious than most people had thought. "He was the great tortoise upon whose back the world sat for eight years. We laughed at him; we talked wistfully about moving; and all the while we never knew the cunning beneath the shell." Kempton admitted that he was not impressed when he first met Eisenhower during the 1952 campaign, but "I was too dumb to understand him then. It would be ten years before I looked at his picture and realized that the smile was always a grin."[18]

Eisenhower died less than two years after Kempton's article. By then the nation had lost two of the Kennedy brothers and Martin Luther King, Jr., to assassins, the ghettoes of the cities had been set ablaze, and the colleges and streets were being taken over by antiwar demonstrators. Eisenhower and the decade he presided over began to look better and better, and Garry Wills and other political analysts were describing him as a "political genius" and "a brilliant man."[19] The seventies saw the Kent State and Watergate tragedies, the resignation of Richard Nixon, and the weak presidencies of Gerald Ford and Jimmy Carter. Meanwhile, Eisenhower's own cabinet members and other advisers close to the president and the events of the 1950s began to write their memoirs and assessments of his presidency, and scholars were sifting through, editing, and publishing Eisenhower's private papers. Herbert S. Parmet, Charles C. Alexander, Robert H. Ferrell, Stephen Ambrose, and other revisionist historians published new studies of Eisenhower portraying him as one of the best presidents of the twentieth century. In 1982, when a new poll of historians was taken, he was ranked ninth among the Ten Best, sandwiched between Harry Truman and James K. Polk.[20]

Obviously, Eisenhower's elevated reputation was partly due to the perspective offered by the passage of time, new historical materials, and new bases of comparison. In the fifties and sixties, he had been compared—generally unfavorably—to Harry S. Truman and Franklin D. Roosevelt, strong activist presidents who were greatly admired by the Democratic historians who wrote the histories and who outnumbered the fewer Republicans when historians were polled to provide the presidental rankings that appeared in scholarly publications and the popular press. But in the 1970s, he could be viewed against the turbulent 1960s and compared—usually favorably—with Kennedy, Johnson, Nixon, Ford, and Carter. And the publication of his private papers, many of which were not declassified until the 1970s, provided new insight into the mind and actions of the man with the big grin who seemed to play golf so much.

It is still too early for a definitive evaluation of Eisenhower—indeed, a final verdict on Eisenhower or any other major historical figure or event will never be possible. But with the perspective offered by the passage of a quarter century and by the abundance of new materials on the man and his administration, it seems clear that the elevation of his historical reputation was long overdue. Although some of the revisionists have gone overboard and praised him too much, he does deserve to be labeled a "near great" president and to be ranked among the top ten presidents in American history. He was not a political genius or a brilliant man, but he was much smarter than most of his contemporary critics gave him credit for. Eisenhower, not Adams or Dulles or any of his other advisers, ran the presidency. He made the decisions, and he was a skillful politician who worked behind the scenes to move men, policies, and events in the direction he wanted them to go. He was an intelligent, good, and decent man who maintained the dignity of his office, exercised common sense, avoided the sharp political divisions that had polarized the nation and paralyzed the presidency under Truman, and acted as a healer and unifier of a nation that wanted a breathing spell after the crises and conflicts of the Truman years. He inspired trust, and for good reason.

In domestic affairs, his accomplishments were considerable. Under his leadership the nation had nearly eight years of prosperity, low inflation, low taxes, recessions but no depression, and high employment. Although he did little to expand it, he kept the New Deal and convinced most of his party that it should be accepted. He extended the Social Security program to an additional 10 million Americans and established the Department of Health, Education, and Welfare. He supported and signed legislation establishing the Interstate Highway System, providing federal aid to education, establishing NASA, authorizing the construction of the St. Lawrence Seaway, and bringing Alaska and Hawaii into the union. He appointed five new justices to the Supreme Court, including one of the best chief justices in the history of the court, Earl Warren (although Eisenhower himself later came to regard that as a mistake). And while he kept the nation's defenses strong, he held down defense spending and refused to give in to those who wanted enormous defense budgets and an even greater arms race.

But it was in foreign affairs that he achieved the most. He retained the internationalist foreign policy of his Democratic predecessors, and his prestige forced his party to go along with this. Once the Korean War ended, six months after he came into office, he spent the rest of his presidency trying to bring peace to the world. After Korea, not a single American soldier died in combat for the rest of his administration. It was a dangerous time, a time of crises that could have plunged America and the world into war, but as Max Lerner wrote in 1971, Eisenhower "vetoed the apocalypse whenever it was proposed."[21] He refused to go to war over Indochina, the Formosan Strait, Berlin, East Germany and Hungary, the Suez, and Cuba. "The United States never lost a soldier or a foot of ground in my administration," he boasted after he left office. "We kept the peace. People asked how it happened—by God, it didn't just happen, I'll tell you that."[22] Eisenhower also strengthened NATO, maintained good relations with old allies like the British and the French and new ones like Japan and West Germany, signed a peace treaty with Austria that ended ten years of allied occupation, and cultivated good relations with Latin America until the Cuban problem took center stage. And he genuinely sought to improve relations with the Soviet Union and reduce the tensions that could lead to nuclear war.

There were marks on the negative side, of course. He failed to provide moral leadership in dealing with McCarthy and the civil rights issues, and he did little for education, medical care, urban decline, air and water pollution, or the poor and the elderly. He failed to modernize and unite the Republican party, to bring good leadership into it, or to groom his own successor—Nixon lost his bid for the presidency in 1960, and after that the right wing gained control of the party and brought on the Goldwater disaster of 1964. In spite of all his efforts to promote world peace and a lessening of tensions between the United States and the U.S.S.R., when he left office in 1961 the U-2 debacle and other problems had caused American–Soviet relations to decline to their lowest point in almost a decade. He liberated no country from communist control; in fact, the Korean truce left communism in control in North Korea, and communism also spread into North Vietnam and Cuba. While he had avoided war in Vietnam in 1954, his domino theory and his support of South Vietnam embroiled America deeper in Vietnam and perhaps made inevitable the escalation policies of Kennedy and Johnson. His excessive fear of communism caused him to misread the problems of the Third World, to intervene in the internal affairs of Iran and other underdeveloped nations, to support right-wing dictators, and to overcommit the United States with defense pacts with little countries across the globe. And finally, in spite of his Atoms for Peace and Open Skies proposals, his treaty with Russia outlawing nuclear tests in Antarctica, and the two-year moratorium on nuclear tests declared in the last two years of his second term, his distrust of the Russians prevented him from seeking and obtaining a truly significant agreement on arms control and nuclear testing.

Eisenhower's record was mixed, like that of all American presidents, and it was achieved against great odds. He came into office with little knowledge of domestic events and politics, he presided during dangerous times when many domestic and foreign events were beyond his control, he inherited great problems (such as Korea and McCarthy) from his predecessor, and his freedom of action was hindered by opposition from the right wing of his own party and from the Democratic party that controlled Congress during three quarters of his presidency. But in spite of these problems, Eisenhower, like Truman, always tried to do his best as he saw it, he was right more often than he was wrong, and the good things that he did far outweighed the bad. There is "no wonder," as Stephen Ambrose has written, that "millions of Americans felt that the country was damned lucky to have him."[23] There is no wonder that he is the only twentieth-century president besides Franklin Roosevelt to leave office more popular than when he came into it or that he is the only president since Roosevelt to serve two full terms. And there is no wonder, either, that a growing number of American historians are joining the I Like Ike club that has numbered so many adherents during the past generation of American history.

Was the decade of the fifties the golden age it has often been portrayed to be? The answer given now, twenty-five years after the end of the decade, would have to be a qualified yes. The period that most of the nostalgic feelings have centered upon is the time sandwiched between the end of the Korean War in the summer of 1953 and the launching of Sputnik in October of 1957, a space of a little over four years. These were the best years of the decade, the prosperous and peaceful interlude between the strife of the McCarthy and Korean War era and the decline of American confidence and prestige after the Russians seemed to win the space race.[24] Like the nostalgia for most periods, the nostalgia for the fifties was highly selective, emphasizing the best times and overlooking the bad ones. And for some Americans, primarily the blacks and other minorities, the poor, and many of the elderly, no part of the decade seemed to be a golden age.

But for most white, middle-class Americans, and particularly white, middle-class males, the fifties was perhaps the best decade in the history of the republic. It certainly was the most prosperous decade in the nation's history, and unlike the twenties, with which it has sometimes been compared, it was not followed by a great economic crash and paralyzing depression. It was a time of prosperity and of peace at home and abroad (after Korea), a plethora of consumer goods, and a popular president who inspired trust and confidence, helped heal the wounds of earlier times, and could not be hated even by the most partisan Democrats. It was a time when America still reigned as the strongest nation in the world and was still respected by her friends and allies and feared by her enemies. It was a time when the Cold War was still seen as an unambiguous battle between good and evil. It was a time when people were proud to be Americans, trusted their leaders, and shared a consensus on basic beliefs and values. It was a time when, in spite of all the critics of American materialism and popular culture, Americans were happy with their homes, their automobiles, their televisions and other consumer goods, and the popular culture they consumed daily. It was a time when Americans had the highest standard of living in the world and did not know or care that the critics of materialism and mass culture condemned their values and tastes and told them that they should be unhappy.

The fifties was also a time of puzzling paradoxes. It was an age of American military dominance yet declining world influence, of peace sought through constant preparation for war, of widespread faith in progress along with the constant fear of nuclear Armageddon, and of a new Red Scare in the face of a minor internal communist threat. It was also a time of unprecedented prosperity and great poverty, of the glorification of marriage and motherhood and the veneration of the carefree single life, and of widespread lip service to democracy and equality along with the practice of rampant racial and sexual prejudice and discrimination. And it was a time when the major peacemaker in Washington was not one of the civilian bureaucrats but Dwight D. Eisenhower, the old general who had devoted his career to war.

The fifties was not a placid and sterile decade—how could it have been when it experienced the continuing paranoiac fear of being blown up by the Russians, the Korean War, the McCarthy hysteria, the Montgomery bus boycott, riots over integration at Little Rock and Clinton and other southern cities, the birth of the hydrogen bomb, ban-the-bomb movements, the birth of the space age, the appearance of a teenage subculture, the rise of the Beatniks, the suburban and baby booms, the spread of television to 90 percent of the nation's population, the birth of the pill, and other developments? The decade would later appear to be serene and dull only because it was seen through the events of the terrible decade that followed. To those who lived through the sixties and seventies, the fifties seemed calm and static by contrast.

The fifties was a good time for the majority of Americans, though it was never the golden age it was made out to be. It was an exciting, paradoxical, and seminal age, a time when the seeds of future dramatic changes were sown. And because of the continuing nostalgia for the period and because the events of the time helped to mold the years that followed, the decade now seems almost contemporary, as if it ended only the day before yesterday, rather than a quarter century ago.

# NOTES

## *PREFACE*

1. "Back to the '50s." *Newsweek* 80 (16 October 1972): 82.

### *Chapter 1: Entering the Fifties*

1. Gordon Wright, *The Ordeal of Total War, 1939–1945* (New York: Harper & Row, 1968), p. 234.
2. Ibid., p. 263.
3. "The American Task," *Life* 28 (2 January 1950): 28.
4. George H. Gallup, *The Gallup Poll: Public Opinion, 1935–1971*, 3 vols. (New York: Random House, 1972), 2: 881, 899, 916, 919.
5. "To a Brave New Year," *The Nation* 172 (6 January 1951): 1.
6. John O'Sullivan and Edward F. Keuchel, *American Economic History: From Abundance to Constraint* (New York: Franklin Watts, 1981), pp. 197, 213.
7. Frederick Lewis Allen, *The Big Change: America Transforms Itself, 1900–1950* (New York: Harper & Row, 1952), pp. 231–32; editors of *Fortune*, *The Changing American Market* (Garden City, N. Y.: Hanover House, 1955), p. 178.
8. United States Department of Commerce. Bureau of the Census. *Historical Statistics of the United States: Colonial Times to 1970*, bicentennial ed. (Washington: U.S. Government Printing Office, 1975), p. 716.
9. Editors of *Consumer Guide*, *Cars of the 50s* (New York: Beekman

House, 1978), pp. 16, 20, 24, 42; John B. Rae, *The American Automobile: A Brief History* (Chicago: University of Chicago Press, 1965), p. 176.

10. Lawrence J. White, *The Automobile Industry Since 1945* (Cambridge: Harvard University Press, 1971), pp. 290–92.

11. "Housing," *Time* 56 (7 August 1950): 17.

12. Harold G. Vatter, *The U. S. Economy in the 1950s* (New York: W. W. Norton & Co., 1963), p. 175; *Fortune, Changing American Market*, pp. 117–18.

13. John Brooks, *The Great Leap: The Past Twenty-five Years in America* (New York: Harper & Row, 1966), pp. 161–62; Douglas T. Miller and Marion Nowak, *The Fifties: The Way We Really Were* (Garden City, N. Y.: Doubleday & Co., 1977), p. 344; *Historical Statistics*, p. 796.

14. Norman Cousins, "The Time Trap," *Saturday Review* 32 (24 December 1949): 20.

15. Edwin Emery and Michael Emery, *The Press and America: An Interpretative History of the Mass Media*, 4th ed. (Englewood Cliffs, N. J.: Prentice-Hall, 1978), p. 404.

16. Russel B. Nye, *The Unembarrassed Muse: The Popular Arts in America* (New York: Dial Press, 1970), p. 406.

17. Arnold Shaw, *The Rockin' '50s* (New York: Hawthorn Books, 1974), pp. 32–34.

18. Jim Miller, ed., *The Rolling Stone History of Rock and Roll* (New York: Rolling Stone Press, 1976), p. 24; Jeff Greenfield, *No Peace, No Place: Excavations Along the Generational Fault* (Garden City, N. Y.: Doubleday & Co., 1973), pp. 44–46.

19. Bill C. Malone, *Country Music U.S.A.: A Fifty Year History* (Austin: University of Texas Press, 1968), p. 231.

20. Ibid., pp. 236–38.

21. Martin Quigley, Jr., and Richard Gertner, *Films in America, 1929–1961* (New York: Golden Press, 1970), p. 187; Erik Barnouw, *A History of Broadcasting in the United States*, 3 vols. (New York: Oxford University Press, 1966–1970), vol. 2, *The Golden Web* (1968), pp. 290–91.

22. Brooks, *Great Leap*, p. 21; Thomas W. Bohn and Richard L. Stromgren, *Light and Shadows: A History of Motion Pictures*, 2d ed. (Sherman Oaks, Calif.: Alfred Publishing Co., 1978), pp. 318–19.

23. Leo Bogart, *The Age of Television: A Study of Viewing Habits and the Impact of Television on American Life*, 3d ed. (New York: Frederick Unger, 1972), p. 163.

24. Al Hine, "The Drive-Ins," *Holiday* 12 (July 1952): 7.

25. "Miscellany," *Time* 56 (18 September 1950): 124.

26. *New York Times*, 1 October 1950.

27. *Historical Statistics*, p. 810.

28. James Playsted Wood, *Magazines in the United States*, 3d ed.

(New York: Ronald Press, 1971), p. 431; Theodore Peterson, *Magazines in the Twentieth Century* (Urbana: University of Illinois Press, 1964), pp. 60–62.

29. Nye, *Unembarrassed Muse*, p. 239.

30. Jerry Robinson, *The Comics: An Illustrated History of Comic Strip Art* (New York: G. P. Putnam's Sons, 1974), pp. 186–92.

31. Alice Payne Hackett and James Henry Burke, *80 Years of Bestsellers, 1895–1975* (New York: R. R. Bowker, 1977), pp. 152–53.

32. Allen, *Big Change*, p. 273.

33. Arthur J. Snider, "Medicine's Golden Era: 1937–1957," *Science Digest* 41 (January 1957): 34; *Historical Statistics*, p. 56.

34. "Runner-Up," *Time* 56 (25 December 1950): 41.

35. Paul Sann, *Fads, Follies, and Delusions of the American People* (New York: Crown Publishers, 1967), pp. 127–32.

### *Chapter 2: The Man from Independence*

1. Robert J. Donovan, *Conflict and Crisis: The Presidency of Harry Truman, 1945–1948*. (New York: W. W. Norton & Co., 1977), p. xv.

2. Margaret Truman, *Harry S. Truman* (New York: William Morrow & Co. 1973), p. 209.

3. "U.S. Closes Ranks Under Truman," *Newsweek* 25 (23 April 1945): 27.

4. Ken Hechler, *Working With Truman: A Personal Memoir of the White House Years* (New York: G. P. Putnam's Sons, 1982), p. 22.

5. John Hersey, *Aspects of the Presidency: Truman and Ford in Office* (New York: Ticknor and Fields, 1980), p. 7.

6. Hechler, *Working With Truman*, p. 223.

7. Robert Underhill, *The Truman Persuasions* (Ames: Iowa University Press, 1981), pp. 337–38.

8. Merle Miller, *Plain Speaking: An Oral Biography of Harry S. Truman* (New York: G. P. Putnam's Sons, 1973), p. 378.

9. Harry S. Truman, *Mr. Citizen* (New York: Random House, 1960), p. 164.

10. Miller, *Plain Speaking*, pp. 5, 26.

11. Robert H. Ferrell, ed., *Off the Record: The Private Papers of Harry S. Truman* (New York: Harper & Row, 1980), pp. 1–3.

12. H. S. Truman, *Mr. Citizen*, p. 224.

13. Alfred Steinberg, *The Man from Missouri: The Life and Times of Harry S. Truman* (New York: G. P. Putnam's Sons, 1962), p. 345.

14. Ferrell, *Off the Record*, p. 226; Steinberg, *Man From Missouri*, pp. 345–46.

15. Hechler, *Working With Truman*, p. 17; Hersey, *Aspects of the Presidency*, pp. 11–12.

16. Steinberg, *Man from Missouri*, pp. 346–47: Ferrell, *Off the Record*, p. 226.
17. Underhill, *Truman Persuasions*, p. 239.
18. Ferrell, *Off the Record*, pp. 233–34.
19. Hechler, *Working With Truman*, pp. 219–20.
20. Dean Acheson, *Present at the Creation: My Years in the State Department* (New York: W. W. Norton & Co., 1969), p. 730.
21. Donovan, *Conflict and Crisis*, p. 148.
22. Underhill, *Truman Persuasions*, p. 37.
23. Donovan, *Conflict and Crisis*, p. 146; Robert H. Ferrell, *Harry S. Truman and the Modern American Presidency* (Boston: Little, Brown & Co., 1983), pp. 183–84.
24. Margaret Truman, *Letters from Father: The Truman Family's Personal Correspondence* (New York: Arbor House, 1981), p. 15.
25. Marianne Means, *The Woman in the White House: The Lives, Times, and Influence of Twelve Notable First Ladies* (New York: Random House, 1963), p. 219.
26. Underhill, *Truman Persuasions*, pp. 238–39.
27. J. B. West, *Upstairs at the White House* (New York: Warner, 1974), p. 75.
28. Means, *Woman in the White House*, p. 231.
29. Ferrell, *Harry S. Truman*, p. 189.
30. Donovan, *Conflict and Crisis*, p. xvi.
31. "The Letter," *Time* 56 (18 December 1950): 17.
32. Ibid.
33. Ibid.
34. Ferrell, *Off the Record*, p. 204.
35. Monte Poen, ed., *Strictly Personal and Confidential: The Letters Harry Truman Never Mailed* (Boston: Little, Brown & Co., 1982), pp. 25, 121, 126.
36. Underhill, *Truman Persuasions*, p. 44.
37. Means, *Woman in the White House*, p. 235.
38. Cabell Phillips, *The Truman Presidency: The History of a Triumphant Succession* (New York: Macmillan Co., 1966), pp. 142–43; Steinberg, *Man from Missouri*, pp. 356–57.
39. M. Truman, *Harry S. Truman*, pp. 487–88; Steinberg, *Man from Missouri*, pp. 390–91.
40. Ferrell, *Off the Record*, p. 198.

### *Chapter 3: "A Hell of a Job"*

1. Victor Albjerg, "Truman and Eisenhower: Their Administrations and Campaigns," *Current History* 47 (October 1964): 221.
2. Phillips, *Truman Presidency*, p. 245.

3. Ibid., p. 21.

4. Albjerg, "Truman and Eisenhower," pp. 223–24.

5. Eric F. Goldman, *The Crucial Decade—And After: America, 1945–1960* (New York: Vintage Books, 1960), p. 90.

6. Alonzo Hamby, *Beyond the New Deal: Harry S. Truman and American Liberalism* (New York: Columbia University Press, 1973), p. 293.

7. Thomas A. Bailey, *Presidential Greatness: The Image and the Man from George Washington to the Present* (New York: Appleton-Century, 1966), p. 323; Albjerg, "Truman and Eisenhower," p. 222.

8. Donovan, *Conflict and Crisis*, p. 284.

9. Stephen E. Ambrose, *Rise to Globalism: American Foreign Policy, 1938–1980*, 2d rev. ed. (New York: Penguin Books, 1980), p. 147.

10. Sidney Lens, *The Day Before Doomsday: An Anatomy of the Nuclear Arms Race* (Garden City, N. Y.: Doubleday & Co., 1977), p. 3.

11. Goldman, *Crucial Decade*, p. 136.

12. Chalmers Roberts, *The Nuclear Years: The Arms Race and Arms Control, 1945–1970* (New York: Frederick A. Praeger, 1970), p. 8.

13. William Manchester, *The Glory and the Dream: A Narrative History of America, 1932–1972* (Boston: Little Brown, 1974), pp. 573–74; editors of Time-Life Books, *This Fabulous Century*, 7 vols. (New York: Time-Life Books, 1970), vol. 6, *1950–1960*, p. 30.

14. Time-Life Books, *Fabulous Century*, 6: 31.

15. Fred J. Cook, *The Warfare State* (New York: Macmillan Co., 1962), p. 332.

16. Miller and Nowak, *Fifties*, p. 50.

17. John M. Fowler, ed., *Fallout: A Study of Superbombs, Strontium 90 and Survival* (New York: Basic Books, 1960), p. 125.

18. Miller and Nowak, *Fifties*, p. 50.

19. New York: New York World-Telegram, 1951, p. 2.

20. Vol. 14, pp. 33–35.

21. Time-Life Books, *Fabulous Century*, 6: 25; Miller and Nowak, *Fifties*, p. 51.

22. New York: Farrar, Straus, & Young, 1952, p. 275.

23. Lawrence S. Wittner, *Cold War America: From Hiroshima to Watergate.* (New York: Praeger, 1974), pp. 86–87.

24. Phillips, *Truman Presidency*, pp. 365–72.

25. Acheson, *Present at the Creation*, p. 360.

26. Goldman, *Crucial Decade*, p. 125.

### *Chapter 4: The Great Fear*

1. Richard Rovere, *Senator Joe McCarthy* (New York: Harcourt, Brace & Co., 1959), pp. 122–23.

2. Thomas C. Reeves, *The Life and Times of Joe McCarthy: A Biography* (New York: Stein & Day, 1982), p. 224.

3. Rovere, *McCarthy*, p. 13.

4. Phillips, *The Truman Presidency*, p. 388.

5. Robert Griffith, *The Politics of Fear: Joseph R. McCarthy and the Senate* (Lexington: University Press of Kentucky, 1970), p. 101.

6. Ibid.

7. David M. Oshinsky, *A Conspiracy So Immense: The World of Joe McCarthy* (New York: Free Press, 1983), pp. 158–62.

8. Gallup, *The Gallup Poll*, 2: 912.

9. Rovere, *McCarthy*, pp. 48–52.

10. Oshinsky, *Conspiracy So Immense*, pp. 31–33; Rovere, *McCarthy*, p. 95.

11. Peter Lewis, *The Fifties* (New York: J. B. Lippincott, 1978), pp. 74–75.

12. Griffith, *Politics of Fear*, pp. 75, 87.

13. Robert P. Ingalls, *Point of Order: A Profile of Senator Joe McCarthy* (New York: G. P. Putnam's Sons, 1981), p. 68.

14. Griffith, *Politics of Fear*, p. 182.

15. Jack Anderson and Ronald May, *McCarthy: The Man, the Senator, the "Ism"* (Boston: Beacon Press, 1952), p. 206.

16. Rovere, *McCarthy*, p. 52.

17. Hamby, *Beyond the New Deal*, p. 396.

18. Rovere, *McCarthy*, pp. 37–38: Griffith, *Politics of Fear*, 181–82.

19. New York: Alfred A. Knopf, 1965, p. 72.

20. Rovere, *McCarthy*, pp. 8, 70–72.

21. Oshinsky, *Conspiracy So Immense*, p. 183.

22. Richard Nixon, *The Memoirs of Richard Nixon* (New York: Grosset & Dunlap, 1978), pp. 138–39; Oshinsky, *Conspiracy So Immense*, p. 180.

23. Robert J. Donovan, *Tumultuous Years: The Presidency of Harry S. Truman, 1949–1953* (New York: W. W. Norton & Co., 1982), p. 166.

24. Rovere, *McCarthy*, p. 65.

25. Ibid., pp. 13–14.

26. David Caute, *The Great Fear: The Anti-Communist Purge Under Truman and Eisenhower* (New York: Simon & Schuster, 1978), p. 113.

27. Ingalls, *Point of Order*, p. 66; Donovan, *Tumultuous Years*, p. 165.

28. Rovere, *McCarthy*, p. 269.

29. Phillips, *Truman Presidency*, pp. 387–88.

30. Ferrell, *Off the Record*, pp. 176–77.

31. Hersey, *Aspects of the Presidency*, p. 138.

32. "Loyalty Needs Better Friends," vol. 124 (4 February 1952): 11.

33. Merle Curti, *The Growth of American Thought*, 3d ed. (New York: Harper & Row, 1964), pp. 757–58.

34. Caute, *Great Fear*, pp. 229, 274–75.

35. Phillips, *Truman Presidency*, pp. 374–77; Hamby, *Beyond the New Deal*, pp. 411–13.

36. Herbert S. Parmet, *Eisenhower and the American Crusades* (New York: Macmillan Co., 1972), p. 227; Caute, *Great Fear*, pp. 70–74.

37. Walter Schneir and Miriam Schneir, *Invitation to an Inquest* (Garden City, N. Y.: Doubleday & Co., 1965), pp. 1–2; Caute, *Great Fear*, pp. 62–66.

38. Schneir and Schneir, *Invitation to an Inquest*, pp. 170–71..

39. Ibid., pp. 2–3.

40. Caute, *Great Fear*, p. 487; Miller and Nowak, *Fifties*, p. 316.

41. Miller and Nowak, *Fifties*, p. 316.

42. John Cogley, *Report on Blacklisting*, 2 vols. (n.p.: Fund for the Republic, 1956), vol. 1, *The Movies*, pp. 219–20.

43. Stefan Kanfer. *A Journal of the Plague Years* (New York: Atheneum, 1973), pp. 189–92.

44. Lewis, *Fifties*, p. 65.

45. Barnouw, *History of Broadcasting*, 2: 265–67.

46. Ibid., 269–71.

47. Marty Jezer, *The Dark Ages: Life in the United States, 1945–1960* (Boston: South End Press, 1982), p. 101.

48. Caute, *Great Fear*, p. 421.

49. Lewis, *Fifties*, p. 81.

50. Vol. 30, pp. 23–28.

51. Caute, *Great Fear*, p. 454; Goldman, *Crucial Decade*, p. 258.

52. Geoffrey Perrett, *A Dream of Greatness: The American People, 1945–1963* (New York: Coward, McCann & Geoghegan, 1979), p. 258; Caute, *Great Fear*, p. 22.

53. Charles Einstein, *Willie's Time: A Memoir* (New York: J. B. Lippincott, 1979), pp. 14–15.

54. Fred J. Cook, *The Nightmare Decade: The Life and Times of Senator Joe McCarthy* (New York: Random House, 1971), p. 20.

55. "The Perils of Conformity," vol. 35 (12 January 1952), p. 7.

56. Victor S. Navasky, *Naming Names* (New York: Viking Press, 1980), p. 26.

57. Caute, *Great Fear*, pp. 185–86; Navasky, *Naming Names*, p. 26.

58. David A. Shannon, *The Decline of American Communism: A History of the Communist Party of the United States Since 1945* (New York: Harcourt, Brace & Co., 1959), p. 364.

59. Donovan, *Tumultuous Years*, p. 170.

### *Chapter 5: Mr. Truman's War*

1. David Rees, *Korea: The Limited War* (New York: St. Martin's Press, 1964), p. 4.

2. John G. Stoessinger, *Why Nations Go to War*, 2d ed. (New York: St. Martin's Press, 1978), p. 77.

3. Donovan, *Tumultuous Years*, pp. 196–97, 201–203; Acheson, *Present at the Creation*, pp. 405–406.

4. Harry Truman, *Memoirs*, 2 vols. (Garden City, N. Y.: Doubleday & Co., 1956–1958), vol. 2, *Years of Trial and Hope*, pp. 332–33.

5. Stoessinger, *Why Nations Go to War*, pp. 80–81.

6. H. S. Truman, *Memoirs*, 2: 463.

7. Richard F. Haynes, *The Awesome Power: Harry S. Truman As Commander in Chief* (Baton Rouge: Louisiana State Press, 1973), p. 172.

8. 29 June 1950.

9. Stoessinger, *Why Nations Go to War*, p. 85.

10. Haynes, *Awesome Power*, p. 172.

11. Hamby, *Beyond the New Deal*, pp. 403–404.

12. Goldman, *The Crucial Decade*, pp. 158–59.

13. Donovan, *Tumultuous Years*, p. 283.

14. Ferrell, *Off the Record*, p. 200.

15. Robert Smith, *MacArthur in Korea: The Naked Emperor* (New York: Simon & Schuster, 1982), p. 95.

16. Rees, *Korea*, pp. 117–20; Haynes, *Awesome Power*, p. 201.

17. John W. Spanier, *The Truman-MacArthur Controversy and the Korean War* (Cambridge: Harvard University Press, 1959), p. 112; Phillips, *The Truman Presidency*, p. 322.

18. Rees, *Korea*, p. 155.

19. Haynes, *Awesome Power*, p. 212; Donovan, *Tumultuous Years*, p. 305.

20. Donovan, *Tumultuous Years*, p. 319.

21. Phillips, *Truman Presidency*, p. 331.

22. Rees, *Korea*, pp. 173–74.

23. Ferrell, *Off the Record*, p. 2.

24. Miller, *Plain Speaking*, p. 294.

25. Phillips, *Truman Presidency*, pp. 328–29; Donovan, *Tumultuous Years*, p. 345.

26. Spanier, *Truman-MacArthur Controversy*, p. 67.

27. Matthew B. Ridgway, *The Korean War* (Garden City, N. Y.: Doubleday & Co., 1967), pp. 152–53.

28. Phillips, *Truman Presidency*, p. 327.

29. Spanier, *Truman-MacArthur Controversy*, pp. 200–201.

30. James David Barber, *The Presidential Character: Predicting Performance in the White House*, 2d ed. (Englewood Cliffs, N. J.: Prentice-Hall, 1977), p. 287.

31. Richard Rovere and Arthur Schlesinger, Jr., *The General and the President* (New York: Farrar, Straus, and Young, 1951), p. 170.

32. Ferrell, *Off the Record*, pp. 210–11.
33. Truman, *Memoirs*, 2: 445.
34. Haynes, *Awesome Power*, p. 263.
35. Miller, *Plain Speaking*, p. 287.
36. Ferrell, *Harry S. Truman*, pp. 128–29.
37. Rees, *Korea*, pp. 218–19.
38. Rovere and Schlesinger, *General and President*, p. 267.
39. Rees, *Korea*, pp. 8–9; Haynes, *Awesome Power*, p. 256.
40. Rees, *Korea*, p. 222.
41. Spanier, *Truman-MacArthur Controversy*, p. 212; Rees, *Korea*, pp. 221–22.
42. William Manchester, *American Caesar: Douglas MacArthur, 1880–1964* (Boston: Little, Brown & Co., 1978) , p. 651.
43. Time-Life Books, *Fabulous Century*, 6: 38.
44. Phillips, *Truman Presidency*, p. 345.
45. Rovere and Schlesinger, *General and President*, p. 12; Spanier, *Truman-MacArthur Controversy*, p. 211; Donovan, *Tumultuous Years*, p. 360.
46. Douglas MacArthur, *Reminiscences* (New York: McGraw-Hill, 1964), pp. 400–404.
47. Rees, *Korea*, p. 227.
48. Rovere and Schlesinger, *General and President*, p. 16.
49. Manchester, *American Caesar*, p. 662.
50. Rovere and Schlesinger, *General and President*, p. 285.

### *Chapter 6: The Magic Box*

1. Brooks, *Great Leap*, pp. 30–31.
2. Jeff Greenfield, *Television: The First Fifty Years* (New York: Henry N. Abrams, 1977), p. 32; Barnouw, *History of Broadcasting*, 2: 126–28; Tim Brooks and Earle Marsh, *The Complete Directory to Prime Time Network TV Shows: 1946–Present* (New York; Ballantine Books, 1979), pp. viii–ix.
3. Greenfield, *No Peace, No Place*, p. 108.
4. Landon Y. Jones, *Great Expectations: America and the Baby Boom Generation* (New York: Coward, McCann, and Geoghegan, 1980), p. 42.
5. Nye, *The Unembarrassed Muse*, p. 406.
6. *Historical Statistics*, p. 796; Brooks, *Great Leap*, p. 162.
7. Brooks and Marsh, *Complete Directory*, p. 555.
8. Bogart, *The Age of Television*, p. 70.
9. Erik Barnouw, *A History of Broadcasting in the United States*, 3 vols. (New York: Oxford University Press, 1966–1970), vol. 3, *The Image Empire (1970), pp. 6–7;* Time-Life Books, *Fabulous Century*, 6: 253; Greenfield, *Television*, p. 106.

10. Arthur Shulman and Roger Youman, *How Sweet It Was* (New York: Bonanza Books, 1966), p. 52.

11. Ibid., p. 111.

12. Time-Life Books, *Fabulous Century*, 6: 274.

13. Greenfield, *Television*, pp. 132–41; Time-Life Books, *Fabulous Century*, 6: 274–76.

14. Harold Mehling, *The Great Time-Killer* (Cleveland: World Publishing Co., 1962) p. 257; Miller and Nowak, *Fifties*, p. 348.

15. Mehling, *Great Time-Killer*, p. 241.

16. Ibid., pp. 62–63.

17. Barnouw, *History of Broadcasting*, 3: 22–23; Mehling, *Great Time-Killer*, pp. 58–60.

18. Vol. 39, pp. 36–50.

19. Shulman and Youman, *How Sweet It Was*, p. 8.

20. Bogart, *Age of Television*, p. 209.

21. Louis Kronenberger, *Company Manners: A Cultural Inquiry Into American Life* (New York: Bobbs-Merrill, 1954), p . 84.

22. Bogart, *Age of Television*, pp. 273, 280.

23. Ann Usher, "TV . . . Good or Bad for Your Children?" *Better Homes and Gardens* 33 (October 1955), pp. 208–209.

24. Bogart, *Age of Television*, pp. 124–25.

25. Greenfield, *No Peace, No Place*, pp. 116–19.

26. Barnouw, *History of Broadcasting*, 3: 149–52.

27. Mehling, *Great Time-Killer*, pp. 323–24.

### *Chapter 7: Home, Sweet Home*

1. Walter T. K. Nugent, *Modern America* (Boston: Houghton Mifflin Co., 1973), p. 419; Jones, *Great Expectations*, p. 38; Miller and Nowak, *Fifties*, p. 134; Jezer, *Dark Ages*, p. 188.

2. Perrett, *Dream of Greatness*, pp. 549–51.

3. Miller and Nowak, *Fifties*, p. 133.

4. *Historical Statistics*, p. 639; Jones, *Great Expectations*, p. 39.

5. John Keats, *The Crack in the Picture Window* (Boston: Houghton Mifflin Co., 1956), p. 25.

6. Ibid., p. xi.

7. Harry Henderson, "The Mass Produced Suburbs," two parts, *Harper's* 207 (November and December 1953), part 1 (November), p. 31.

8. *Big Change*, p. 288.

9. Henderson, "Mass Produced Suburbs," part 2 (December), p. 81.

10. Ibid.

11. "The Roots of Home," *Time* 75 (20 June 1960): 14–18.

12. Congressional Quarterly. Editorial Research Reports. *The Women's Movement* (Washington: Congressional Quarterly, 1973), p. 36; Jones, *Great*

*Expectations*, p. 24; James Gilbert, *Another Chance: Postwar America, 1945–1968* (New York: Alfred A. Knopf, 1981), pp. 56–58.

13. Marjorie Rosen, *Popcorn Venus: Women, Movies, and the American Dream* (New York: Coward, McCann, and Geoghegan, 1973), p. 246; Lois W. Banner, *Women in Modern America: A Brief History* (New York: Harcourt Brace Jovanovich, 1974), pp. 218–19.

14. 30 January 1955.

15. James Joslyn and John Pendleton, "The Adventures of Ozzie and Harriet," *Journal of Popular Culture* 7 (Summer 1973): 23–41.

16. Betty Friedan, *The Feminine Mystique*, 10th anniversary ed. (New York: W. W. Norton & Co., 1974), p. 48.

17. Ruth N. Sedam, "Who Wants to Go Back to the Good Old Days?" *Parents Magazine* 31 (October 1956): 38.

18. *New York Times*, 7 March 1954.

19. Henderson, "Mass Produced Suburbs," part 1, p. 28.

20. Nugent, *Modern America*, p. 288; Jones, *Great Expectations*, p. 336.

21. Jones, *Great Expectations*, p. 21.

22. William Peterson, "The New American Family: Causes and Consequences of the Baby Boom," *Commentary* 21 (January 1956): 1–4; Jones, *Great Expectations*, pp. 24–35.

23. "The First Baby," *Life* 41 (24 December 1956): 57–63.

24. "Rocketing Births: Business Bonanza," *Life* 44 (16 June 1958): 83.

25. Charles C. Alexander, *Holding the Line: The Eisenhower Era, 1952–1961* (Bloomington: Indiana University Press, 1975), p. 129.

26. Jones, *Great Expectations*, pp. 50–51.

27. Time-Life Books, *Fabulous Century*, 6: 167; Jones, *Great Expectations*, pp. 56–57.

28. Miller and Nowak, *Fifties*, p. 271.

29. Jones, *Great Expectations*, p. 48.

30. June Sochen, *Herstory: A Woman's View of American History* (Port Washington, N. Y.: Alfred Publishing Co., 1974), pp. 369–70.

31. "The Inheritors," *Time* 89 (6 January 1967), pp. 18–23.

32. "The Baby Boomers Come of Age," *Newsweek* 97 (30 March 1981), pp. 34–37.

33. Jones, *Great Expectations*, p. 2.

34. Miller and Nowak, *Fifties*, pp. 138–39.

35. Time-Life Books, *Fabulous Century*, 6: 158.

36. John B. Rae, *The Road and the Car in American Life*, (Cambridge: MIT Press, 1971), p. 230.

37. Garden City, N. Y.: Hanover House, 1955, pp. 184–96.

38. Jezer, *Dark Ages*, p. 172.

39. Vatter, *U. S. Economy in the 1950s*, p. 255.

40. *Fortune, Changing American Market*, pp. 142–43.
41. Ibid., p. 144.
42. Jezer, *Dark Ages*, p. 171.
43. *Fortune, Changing American Market*, p. 147.
44. "Roots of Home," p. 18.

### Chapter 8: Time for a Change

1. Harry Truman, *Memoirs*, 2: 488–89.
2. Ferrell, *Off the Record*, p. 177.
3. Steinberg, *The Man From Missouri*, p. 409.
4. Arthur M. Schlesinger, Jr., Fred L. Israel, and William P. Hansen, eds., *The Coming to Power: Critical Presidential Elections in American History* (New York: Chelsea House, 1971), p. 403.
5. Goldman, *Crucial Decade*, p. 221.
6. Emery and Emery, *Press and America*, p. 483; Bill Adler, comp. and ed., *The Stevenson Wit* (Garden City, N. Y.: Doubleday & Co., 1966), p. 29.
7. Donovan, *Tumultuous Years*, p. 394.
8. Martin Mayer, *Madison Avenue, U.S.A.* (New York: Harper & Row, 1958), pp. 296–97.
9. Hamby, *Beyond the New Deal*, p. 497.
10. Wittner, *Cold War America*, p. 106.
11. Richard M. Fried, *Men Against McCarthy* (New York: Columbia University Press, 1976), p. 235.
12. Hamby, *Beyond the New Deal*, p. 497.
13. Ibid., p. 500.
14. Phillips, *The Truman Presidency*, p. 403.
15. Ibid., pp. 402–14.
16. Alexander, *Holding the Line*, p. 15.
17. Barnouw, *History of Broadcasting*, 2: 299.
18. Adler, *Stevenson Wit*, p. 29.
19. Ibid., p. 30.
20. Schlesinger et al., *Coming to Power*, p. 422.
21. Richard Hofstadter, *Anti-intellectualism in American Life* (New York: Alfred A. Knopf, 1966), pp. 221–22.
22. John Mason Brown, *Through These Men: Some Apects of Our Passing History* (New York: Harper & Brothers, 1956), pp. 25–27.
23. Stephen E. Ambrose, *Eisenhower*, 2 vols. (New York: Simon & Schuster, 1983–1984), vol. 1, *Soldier, General of the Army, President-Elect, 1890–1952*, p. 55.
24. Schlesinger et al., *Coming to Power*, p. 428.
25. Thomas A. Bailey, *Voices of America: The National Story in Slogans, Sayings, and Songs* (New York: Free Press, 1976), p. 444–47; Cook, *Nightmare Decade;* p. 6.

26. Schlesinger et al., *Coming to Power*, p. 414.
27. Fried, *Men Against McCarthy*, p. 233.
28. Ambrose, *Eisenhower*, 1: 557.
29. Richard Nixon, *Six Crises* (Garden City: Doubleday & Co., 1962), p. 93.
30. *New York Times*, 24 September 1952.
31. Ambrose, *Eisenhower*, 1: 561.
32. Ibid., p. 569.
33. Hamby, *Beyond the New Deal*, p. 502.
34. Fried, *Men Against McCarthy*, p. 237.
35. Donovan, *Tumultuous Years*, p. 399.
36. Schlesinger et al., *Coming to Power*, pp. 428–29.
37. Ibid, p. 37.
38. Kenneth S. Davis, *The Politics of Honor: A Biography of Adlai E. Stevenson* (New York: G. P. Putnam's Sons, 1967), p. 291.
39. Parmet, *Eisenhower*, p. 144.
40. Ferrell, *Off the Record*, p. 263.
41. Steinberg, *Man from Missouri*, p. 415.
42. Ferrell, *Off the Record*, pp. 274–75.
43. Steinberg, *Man from Missouri*, p. 417.
44. Brown, *Through These Men*, p. 39.
45. Steinberg, *Man from Missouri*, pp. 418–19.
46. Brown, *Through These Men*, p. 45.
47. Merle Miller, *Plain Speaking*, p. 337.
48. Donovan, *Tumultuous Years*, p. 409.
49. Alexander, *Holding the Line*, p. 228.
50. Acheson, *Present at the Creation*, p. 730.
51. Phillips, *Truman Presidency*, p. 402.
52. William E. Leuchtenburg, "Give 'em Harry," *New Republic* 190 (21 May 1984): 22.
53. Ibid., p. 23.
54. Phillips, *Truman Presidency*, p. 402.
55. Bailey, *Presidential Greatness*, p. 24.
56. Steve Neal, "Our Best and Worst Presidents," *Chicago Tribune*, 10 January 1982, section 9 (*Chicago Tribune Magazine*), p. 9.

### *Chapter 9: Ike*

1. Robert L. Branyan and Lawrence H. Larsen, eds., *The Eisenhower Administration, 1953–1961: A Documentary History*, 2 vols. (New York: Random House, 1971), 1: 26–31.
2. Dwight D. Eisenhower, *The White House Years: A Personal Account*, 2 vols. (Garden City, New York: Doubleday & Co., 1963–1965), vol. 1. *Mandate for Change, 1953–56*, p. 102.

3. Ambrose, *Eisenhower*, 1: 528.

4. Robert H. Ferrell, ed., *The Eisenhower Diaries* (New York: W. W. Norton & Co., 1981), p. xiv.

5. Ibid., p. 225.

6. Ambrose, *Eisenhower*, 1: 555.

7. Sherman Adams, *First-Hand Report: The Story of the Eisenhower Administration* (New York: Harper & Brothers, 1961), p. 86.

8. Stephen E. Ambrose, *Eisenhower*, 2 vols. (New York: Simon & Schuster, 1983–1984), vol. 2, *The President*, p. 27; Robert Keith Gray, *Eighteen Acres Under Glass* (Garden City, N.Y.: Doubleday & Co., 1962), pp. 166–69.

9. Gray, *Eighteen Acres Under Glass*, p. 143.

10. A. Merriman Smith, *Meet Mr. Eisenhower* (New York: Harper & Row, 1955), p. 162.

11. Ibid., p. 165.

12. Paul F. Boller, Jr., *Presidential Anecdotes* (New York: Oxford University Press, 1981), p. 297.

13. Gray, *Eighteen Acres Under Glass*, p. 205.

14. A.M. Smith, *Meet Mr. Eisenhower*, pp. 151–52.

15. Adams, *First-Hand Report*, pp. 428–29; Eisenhower, *White House Years*, 1: 265.

16. Virgil Pinkley with James F. Scheer, *Eisenhower Declassified* (Old Tappan, N. J.: Fleming H. Revell Co., 1979), p. 281; Barber, *Presidential Character*, p. 166; Robert J. Donovan, *Eisenhower: The Inside Story*. (New York: Harper & Brothers, 1956), pp. 206–207.

17. Ferrell, *Eisenhower Diaries*, pp. 270–71.

18. Paul Hutchinson, "The President's Religious Faith," *Life* 36 (22 March 1954): 151–70, passim.

19. Peter Lyon, *Eisenhower: Portrait of the Hero* (Boston: Little, Brown & Co., 1974), p. 477.

20. Wittner, *Cold War America*, p. 123.

21. Lyon, *Eisenhower*, p. 477.

22. Parmet, *Eisenhower*, p. 176.

23. A.M. Smith, *Meet Mr. Eisenhower*, p. 214.

24. Goldman, *The Crucial Decade*, p. 291.

25. William Bragg Ewald, Jr., *Eisenhower the President: Crucial Days, 1951–1960* (Englewood Cliffs, N.J.: Prentice Hall, 1981), p. 170.

26. Brown, *Through These Men*, p. 61.

27. Emmet John Hughes, *The Ordeal of Power: A Political Memoir of the Eisenhower Years* (New York: Atheneum, 1963), pp. 24–25.

28. Ambrose, *Eisenhower*, 2: 53.

29. Kay Summersby Morgan, *Past Forgetting: My Love Affair with Dwight D. Eisenhower* (New York: Simon & Schuster, 1976).

30. Pinkley with Scheer, *Eisenhower Declassified*, pp. 361–68; Ferrell, *Eisenhower Diaries*, p. xv; Steve Neal, *The Eisenhowers: Reluctant Dynasty* (Garden City, N.Y.: Doubleday & Co., 1978), pp. 175–79.

31. Neal, *Eisenhowers*, p. 461.

32. Ibid.

33. Means, *Woman in the White House*, p. 250.

34. Lester David and Irene David, *Ike and Mamie: The Story of the General and His Lady* (New York: G. P. Putnam's Sons, 1981), pp. 194–99.

35. Ibid., pp. 219–21.

36. Barber, *Presidential Character*, p. 159.

37. Fred I. Greenstein, *The Hidden-Hand Presidency: Eisenhower as Leader* (New York: Basic Books, 1982), p. 50.

38. Stephen E. Ambrose, "The Ike Age," *The New Republic* 184 (9 May 1984): 34.

39. Boller, *Presidential Anecdotes*, p. 298.

40. Ferrell, *Eisenhower Diaries*, p. xiii.

41. Greenstein, *Hidden-Hand Presidency*, p. 57.

42. Norman L. Rosenberg and Emily S. Rosenberg, *In Our Times*, 2d ed. (Englewood Cliffs, N. J.: Prentice-Hall, 1982), p. 55.

43. Greenstein, *Hidden-Hand Presidency*, pp. 4–5.

44. "Dreaming of the Eisenhower Years," *Time* 116 (28 July 1980): 32.

45. Garry Wills, *Nixon Agonistes: The Crisis of the Self-Made Man* (Boston: Houghton Mifflin Co., 1970), p. 122; Norman A Graebner, "Eisenhower's Popular Leadership," *Current History* 39 (October 1960): 234.

46. Ambrose, *Eisenhower*, 2: 27, 53, 346.

47. Ibid., p. 114.

48. Alexander, *Holding the Line*, pp. 34–35.

49. Gray, *Eighteen Acres Under Glass*, pp. 32–33: Eisenhower, *White House Years*, 2: 311.

50. Rosenberg and Rosenberg, *In Our Times*, p. 57.

51. Greenstein, *Hidden-Hand Presidency*, pp. 146–47; Lyon, *Eisenhower*, p. 502.

52. Goldman, *Crucial Decade*, p. 240.

53. Ewald, *Eisenhower the President*, p. 189; Ferrell, *Eisenhower Diaries*, p. 238.

54. Ewald, *Eisenhower the President*, pp. 71–72; Parmet, *Eisenhower*, p. 176; Greenstein, *Hidden-Hand Presidency*, p. 113.

55. Ambrose, *Eisenhower*, 2: 80, 623.

56. Ewald, *Eisenhower the President*, p. 65.

57. Greenstein, *Hidden-Hand Presidency*, pp. 91–92.

58. Barber, *Presidential Character*, p. 163.

59. Adams, *First Hand Report*, p. 73.

60. Ewald, *Eisenhower the President*, pp. 88–89, 104.
61. Ambrose, *Eisenhower*, 2: 203.
62. Greenstein, *Hidden-Hand Presidency*, p. 4.
63. "Dossier: Dwight David Eisenhower," *Esquire* 100 (December 1983): 567.

### *Chapter 10: Charting a New Course*

1. I. F. Stone, *The Haunted Fifties* (New York: Random House, 1963), p. 6.
2. *Historical Statistics*, pp. 1116, 1123–24.
3. Schneir and Schneir, *Invitation to an Inquest*, pp. 248–49.
4. Ibid., pp. 249–50.
5. *New York Times*, 20 June 1953.
6. Rees, *Korea*, pp. 323–26. Admiral Turner Joy, *How Communists Negotiate* (New York: Macmillan Co., 1955), pp. 4–5, 18.
7. Eisenhower, *White House Years*, 1: 95.
8. Robert A. Divine, *Eisenhower and the Cold War* (New York: Oxford University Press, 1981), pp. 30–31; Alexander, *Holding the Line*, pp. 34–35.
9. Rees, *Korea*, pp. 331–32.
10. Branyan and Larsen, *Eisenhower Administration*, 1: 172.
11. Rovere, *McCarthy* pp. 199–205.
12. Parmet, *Eisenhower*, p. 261.
13. Greenstein, *Hidden-Hand Presidency*, p. 175.
14. Ibid., pp. 177–78.
15. Ferrell, *Eisenhower Diaries*, pp. 233–34.
16. Griffith, *Politics of Fear*, p. 199; Ambrose, *Eisenhower*, 2: 57.
17. Fried, *Men Against McCarthy*, pp. 254–55.
18. Ambrose, *Eisenhower*, 2: 59.
19. Greenstein, *Hidden-Hand Presidency*, pp. 165–66; Ambrose, *Eisenhower*, 2: 59–61.
20. Eisenhower, *White House Years*, 1: 275.
21. Branyan and Larsen, *Eisenhower Administration*, 1: 365.
22. Perrett, *Dream of Greatness*, pp. 268–69.
23. Griffith, *Politics of Fear*, p. 249.
24. Oshinsky, *Conspiracy So Immense*, p. 377
25. Griffith, *Politics of Fear*, p. 253.
26. Barnouw, *History of Broadcasting*, 3: 52.
27. Ibid.
28. Ambrose, *Eisenhower*, 2: 186–89.
29. Michael Straight, *Trial by Television* (Boston: Beacon Press, 1954), pp. 251–53; Ingalls, *Point of Order*, pp. 128–29.
30. Alexander, *Holding the Line*, pp. 60–61.
31. Ingalls, *Point of Order*, p. 145.

32. Oshinsky, *Conspiracy So Immense*, p. 498.
33. Stone, *Haunted Fifties*, p. 115.
34. Thomas C. Reeves, *The Life and Times of Joe McCarthy: A Biography* (New York: Stein & Day, 1982), pp. 673–74.
35. Bailey, *Voices of America*, p. 448.
36. Rovere, *McCarthy*, p. 250.
37. Vol. 42 (7 June 1957): 143–44.
38. Chicago: Henry Regnery Co., p. 335.
39. Ronald Lora, *Conservative Minds in America* (Chicago: Rand McNally & Co., 1971), p. 207.
40. Michael W. Miles, *The Odyssey of the American Right* (New York: Oxford University Press, 1980), pp. 244–46; Lora, *Conservative Minds in America*, pp. 208–209; "All the President's Magazines," *Time* 116 (15 December 1980): 78.
41. Miles, *Odyssey of the American Right*, p. 249.
42. Garden City, N. Y.: Doubleday & Co.
43. Ibid., pp. 22–43.
44. Ibid., pp. 166–78.
45. Ibid., pp. 59–87.

## *Chapter 11: Fighting Jim Crow*

1. Anthony Lewis and *The New York Times*, *Portrait of a Decade: The Second American Revolution* (New York: Random House, 1964), pp. 130–31.
2. William Peters, *The Southern Temper* (Garden City, N. Y.: Doubleday & Co., 1959), pp. 193, 206–209.
3. Richard A. Long, "Those Magnolia Myths," *The Nation* 183 (7 July 1956): 17.
4. Nugent, *Modern America*, p. 300.
5. Charles Abrams, *Forbidden Neighbors: A Study of Prejudice in Housing* (New York: Harper & Brothers, 1955), pp. 86–89.
6. C. Vann Woodward, *The Strange Career of Jim Crow*, 3d rev. ed. (New York: Oxford University Press, 1974), pp. 8–9.
7. Ibid., p. 145.
8. James D. Weaver, *Warren: The Man, the Court, the Era* (Boston: Little, Brown & Co., 1967), pp. 212–13.
9. Alexander, *Holding the Line*, p. 122.
10. Peter Lyon, *Eisenhower: Portrait of the Hero* (Boston: Little, Brown & Co., 1974), p. 563.
11. Benjamin Muse, *Ten Years of Prelude: The Story of Integration Since the Supreme Court's 1954 Decision.* (New York: Viking Press, 1964), pp. 283–86.
12. Walter Lord, *The Past That Would Not Die* (New York: Harper & Row, 1965), p. 60.

13. Muse, *Ten Years*, p. 20.

14. Ibid., p. 26; Woodward, *Strange Career*, p. 153.

15. Numan V. Bartley, *The Rise of Massive Resistance: Race and Politics in the South During the 1950s* (Baton Rouge: Louisiana State University Press, 1969), p. 277.

16. Lyon, *Eisenhower*, p. 555.

17. Ferrell, *Eisenhower Diaries*, p. 246.

18. Dwight D. Eisenhower, *The White House Years: A Personal Account*, 2 vols. (Garden City, New York: Doubleday & Co., 1963–1965), vol. 2, *Waging Peace, 1956–1961*, p. 150.

19. James C. Duram, *A Moderate Among Extremists: Dwight D. Eisenhower and the School Desegregation Crisis* (Chicago: Nelson Hall, 1981), p. 110.

20. Hughes, *Ordeal of Power*, p. 201.

21. Earl Warren, *The Memoirs of Earl Warren* (Garden City, N. Y.: Doubleday & Co., 1977), pp. 291–92.

22. Muse, *Ten Years*, pp. 160–61; Bartley, *Rise of Massive Resistance*, pp. 170–89.

23. Birmingham, Ala.: n. pub., 1955.

24. Vol. 222 (January 1956): 40.

25. Vol. 198 (November 1956): 47.

26. Warren, *Memoirs*, pp. 302–303.

27. Clifford Lytle, *The Warren Court and Its Critics* (Tucson: University of Arizona Press, 1968), p. 16.

28. James F. Byrnes, "The Supreme Court Must Be Curbed," *U.S. News and World Report* 40 (18 May 1956): 56.

29. Bartley, *Rise of Massive Resistance*, p. 110.

30. Muse, *Ten Years*, pp. 64–65.

31. Ibid., p. 59.

32. Bartley, *Rise of Massive Resistance*, pp. 185–187.

33. Ibid., p. 225.

34. I. A. Newby, *Challenge to the Court: Social Scientists and the Defense of Segregation, 1954–1966*, rev. ed. (Baton Rouge: Louisiana State University Press, 1969), p. 16.

35. Peters, *Southern Temper*, p. 202.

36. Lewis, *Portrait of Decade*, pp. 107–108; Muse, *Ten Years*, 53–54.

37. Muse, *Ten Years*, 89–92.

38. Ibid., pp. 92–94.

39. Woodward, *Strange Career*, pp. 160–61; Muse, *Ten Years*, pp. 36–37.

40. Henry F. Bedford, *Trouble Downtown: The Local Context of Twentieth-Century America* (New York: Harcourt Brace Jovanovich, 1978), p. 141.

41. Lewis, *Portrait of Decade*, p. 74.
42. George R. Metcalf, *Black Profiles*, expanded ed. (New York: McGraw-Hill, 1970), pp. 270–71; Lewis, *Portrait of Decade*, p. 82.
43. Metcalf, *Black Profiles*, p. 273.
44. Lewis, *Portrait of Decade*, p. 72.
45. Parmet, *Eisenhower*,, p. 442.
46. Stephen B. Oates, *Let the Trumpet Sound: The Life of Martin Luther King, Jr.* (New York: Harper & Row, 1982), p. 92.
47. Lewis, *Portrait of Decade*, p. 106.
48. Bedford, *Trouble Downtown*, p. 164.
49. Martin Luther King, Jr., *Stride Toward Freedom: The Montgomery Story* (New York: Harper & Row, 1958), p. 172.
50. "A Great Ride," *Time* 68 (31 December 1956): 10.
51. King, *Stride Toward Freedom*, p. 173.
52. Lewis, *Portrait of Decade*, p. 81.

### *Chapter 12: "A Bigger Bang for a Buck"*

1. Devine, *Eisenhower and the Cold War*, pp. vii, 11.
2. Ferrell, *Eisenhower Diaries*, p. 296.
3. Greenstein, *Hidden-Hand Presidency*, pp. 47–48.
4. Alexander, *Holding the Line*, pp. 65–66.
5. Townsend Hoopes, *The Devil and John Foster Dulles* (Boston: Little, Brown & Co., 1973), pp. 141, 396–400.
6. Roscoe Drummond and Gaston Coblentz, *Duel at the Brink: John Foster Dulles' Command of American Power* (Garden City, N. Y.: Doubleday & Co., 1960), pp. 229–39; Parmet, *Eisenhower*, pp. 187–88.
7. Drummond and Coblentz, *Duel at the Brink*, p. 23.
8. Drummond and Coblentz, *Duel at the Brink*, pp. 21–25; Divine, *Eisenhower and the Cold War*, pp. 21–23; Greenstein, *Hidden-Hand Presidency*, pp. 87–91; Douglas Kinnard, *President Eisenhower and Strategy Management: A Study in Defense Politics* (Lexington: University Press of Kentucky, 1977), pp. 128–29.
9. Hughes, *Ordeal of Power*, pp. 251.
10. Time-Life Books, *Fabulous Century*, 6: 43.
11. Ewald, *Eisenhower the President*, p. 192.
12. Ambrose, *Rise to Globalism:* p. 193.
13. Alexander, *Holding the Line*, pp. 69–70.
14. *Historical Statistics*, p. 1141.
15. Ambrose, *Rise to Globalism*, pp. 191–92.
16. Ibid., p. 192.
17. Gilbert, *Another Chance*, p. 140.
18. O'Sullivan and Keuchel, *American Economic History*, p. 203.
19. Vatter, *U. S. Economy in the 1950s*, p. 271.
20. Wittner, *Cold War America*, pp. 151–57.

21. Parmet, *Eisenhower,* p. 389.
22. Branyan and Larsen, *Eisenhower Administration,* 1: 330.
23. George McTurnan Kahin and John W. Lewis, *The United States in Vietnam,* rev. ed. (New York: Dial Press, 1967), p. 32.
24. Stanley Karnow, *Vietnam: A History* (New York: Viking Press, 1983), p. 197; Parmet, *Eisenhower,* p. 367.
25. Ewald, *Eisenhower the President,* pp. 105–120; Divine, *Eisenhower and the Cold War,* pp. 48–51.
26. Kahin and Lewis, *United States in Vietnam,* pp. 48–55; Wittner, *Cold War America,* p. 163.
27. Karnow, *Vietnam,* pp. 223–24.
28. Divine, *Eisenhower and the Cold War,* pp. 61–65.
29. Parmet, *Eisenhower,* p. 399.
30. Alexander, *Holding the Line,* pp. 95–98; Parmet, *Eisenhower,* pp. 405–407.
31. Goldman, *Crucial Decade,* p. 289.
32. Lyon, *Eisenhower,* p. 664.
33. Parmet, *Eisenhower,* p. 407.
34. Neal, *Eisenhowers,* pp. 368–69.
35. Parmet, *Eisenhower,* pp. 416–18.
36. Lyon, *Eisenhower,* p. 671.
37. Parmet, *Eisenhower,* p. 427.
38. James Shepley, "How Dulles Averted War," *Life* 40 (16 January 1956): 70–80.
39. W. A. Swanberg, *Luce and His Empire* (New York: Charles Scribner's Sons, 1972), p. 373.
40. "John Foster Dulles: A Very Complicated Man," vol. 213 (September 1956) :27.
41. Branyan and Larsen, *Eisenhower Administration,* 2: 710–11.
42. Eisenhower, *White House Years,* 2: 58.
43. Ewald, *Eisenhower the President,* pp. 177–84.
44. Adler, *Stevenson Wit,* p. 14.
45. Alexander, *Holding the Line,* pp. 181–82.

### *Chapter 13: Good Times*

1. G. T. Seaborg, "The Future Through Science," *Science* 124 (28 December 1956): 1275; John Brooks, *Great Leap,* pp. 80, 132–35; Alexander, *Holding the Line,* pp. 102, 107.
2. Miller and Nowak, *Fifties,* p. 109.
3. O'Sullivan and Keuchel, *American Economic History,* p. 203.
4. North Bigbee, "Why We Aren't Running Short of Oil," *Reader's Digest* 56 (January 1950): 126.
5. O'Sullivan and Keuchel, *American Economic History,* pp. 210, 213.

6. Vance Packard, *The Hidden Persuaders* (New York: David McKay, 1957), p. 121; Mayer, *Madison Avenue U.S.A.*, pp. 26–27.

7. Brooks, *Great Leap*, p. 90.

8. Pages 53, 68, 85, 86, 95–97.

9. New York: David McKay, 1960.

10. Miller and Nowak, *Fifties*, p. 119: Brooks, *Great Leap*, p. 139.

11. Vatter, *U. S. Economy in the 1950s*, pp. 12, 179–80.

12. Thomas C. Cochran, *American Business in the Twentieth Century* (Cambridge: Harvard University Press, 1972), p. 160; *Vatter, U. S. Economy in 1950s*, p. 165: Brooks, *Great Leap*, pp. 267–68.

13. Wittner, *Cold War America*, pp. 115–16; Alexander, *Holding the Line*, p. 108.

14. Brooks, *Great Leap*, pp. 45–47.

15. "Women Hold Third of Jobs," *Life* 41 (24 December 1956): 31.

16. Alexander, *Holding the Line*, pp. 114–15; Vatter, *U.S. Economy in 1950s*, pp. 238–44.

17. O'Sullivan and Keuchel, *American Economic History*, p. 207.

18. Alexander, *Holding the Line*, p. 112; Wittner, *Cold War America*, pp. 132–33; Perrett, *Dream of Greatness*, pp. 530–31.

19. Alexander, *Holding the Line*, pp. 39, 163–64.

20. Helen Hill Miller, "Farming Isn't What It Was," *The New Republic* 140 (2 March 1959): 9–12; Brooks, *Great Leap*, p. 104.

21. O'Sullivan and Keuchel, *American Economic History*, pp. 211–13.

22. Time-Life Books, *Fabulous Century*, 7 vols. (New York: Time-Life Books, 1970), 6: 160; Vatter, *U. S. Economy in 1950s*, p. 225.

23. Time-Life Books, *Fabulous Century*, 6: 161.

24. William E. Leuchtenberg and the editors of *Life*, *The Great Age of Change* (New York: Time-Life Books, 1964), pp. 153–54.

25. Vatter, *U. S. Economy in 1950s*, p. 175.

26. Vol. 105 (March 1954): 135–37.

27. Ibid., p. 135.

28. "Buying New," *Newsweek* 48 (17 December 1956): 83.

29. "Out of Order," *Time* 70 (14 October 1957): 102.

30. Time-Life Books, *Fabulous Century*, 6: 123.

31. Peter Lewis, *Fifties*, p. 40.

32. Max Boas and Steve Chain, *Big Mac: The Unauthorized Story of McDonald's* (New York: E. P. Dutton & Co., 1976), pp. 19–28.

33. "Short Shorts Become Permanent in U.S. Scene," *Life* 41 (10 September 1956): 52.

34. Russell Lynes, *A Surfeit of Honey* (New York: Harper & Brothers, 1957), p. 67.

35. Ibid., p. 69.

36. Rae, *American Automobile*, p. 192; Lewis, *Fifties*, p. 18; Edith Horsley, *The 1950s* (London: Bison Books, 1978), p. 231.

37. "Buying New," p. 84.
38. Rae, *American Automobile*, pp. 199–200.
39. Editors of *Consumer Guide*, *Cars of the 50s*, pp. 15, 23, 41.
40. Brooks, *Great Leap*, p. 120; Lewis, *Fifties*, p. 23.
41. Miller and Nowak, *Fifties*, p. 141.
42. Ralph Nader, "The Safe Car You Can't Buy," *The Nation* 188 (11 April 1959): 311.
43. White, *Automobile Industry Since 1945*, pp. 239–40.
44. Jezer, *Dark Ages*, pp. 144.
45. Paul C. Wilson, *Chrome Dreams: Automobile Styling Since 1893* (Radnor, Penn: Chilton Book Co., 1976), p. 238.
46. Manchester, *Glory and the Dream*, p. 815.
47. "The New Edsel," vol. 23 (January 1958): 32.
48. "The Edsel and How It Got That Way," vol. 215 (September 1957): 68.
49. John Brooks, *The Fate of the Edsel and Other Business Adventures* (New York: Harper & Row, 1963), pp. 66–68.
50. "The $250 Million Flop," vol. 74 (30 November 1959): 87.
51. "The New Edsel," pp. 30–33.
52. Brooks, *Fate of the Edsel*, p. 60.
53. Eric Larrabee, "Detroit's Great Debate: Where Did We Go Wrong?" *The Reporter* 18 (17 April 1958): 16–21.
54. White, *Automobile Industry Since 1945*, pp. 290–95.
55. Edgar Snow, "Herr Tin Lizzie: Saga of the Volkswagen," *The Nation* 181 (3 December 1955): 474–76.
56. Philadelphia: J. B. Lippincott, 1958, p. 113.
57. Ibid., p. 230.
58. Vatter, *U. S. Economy in 1950s*, p. 162.
59. Richard O. Davies, *The Age of Asphalt: The Automobile, the Freeway, and the Condition of Metropolitan America* (New York: J. B. Lippincott, 1975), p. 6; O'Sullivan and Keuchel, *American Economic History*, p. 211.
60. Brooks, *Great Leap*, p. 121.
61. Miller and Nowak, *Fifties*, p. 143.
62. Wittner, *Cold War America*, p. 112.
63. Miller and Nowak, *Fifties*, p. 113.
64. Alexander, *Holding the Line*, p. 110.
65. Brooks, *Great Leap*, p. 136.
66. Vatter, *U.S. Economy in 1950s*, pp. 4–5.
67. Ibid., p. 7.

### *Chapter 14: The Leisure Society*

1. "The Leisured Masses," (12 September 1953): 142.

2. "Automation," Vol. 67 (19 March 1956): 106.

3. Joseph Prendergast, "Non-Working Time Continues to Expand," *Recreation* 49 (March 1956): 107.

4. *Fortune, Changing American Market*, p. 197.

5. *Historical Statistics*, p. 401.

6. "The Golden Age Is Now," vol. 1 (6 August 1954): 51.

7. Bogart, *Age of Television*, pp. 181–83.

8. Lawrence Ritter and Donald Honig, *The Image of Their Greatness: An Illustrated History of Baseball from 1900 to the Present*. (New York: Crown Publishers, 1979), pp. 223–71, passim.

9. Herbert Warren Wind, ed., *The Realm of Sport* (New York: Simon & Schuster, 1966), pp. 63–71.

10. Charles Einstein, ed., *The Third Fireside Book of Baseball*. (New York: Simon & Schuster, 1968), pp. 238–44.

11. Einstein, *Willie's Time*, p. 114.

12. Wind, *Realm of Sport*, p. 72.

13. David Q. Voight, *America Through Baseball* (Chicago: Nelson-Hall, 1976), pp. 121–23.

14. Damon Rice, *Seasons Past* (New York: Praeger, 1976), pp. 414–15.

15. *New York Times*, 9 October 1957.

16. Rice, *Seasons Past*, p. 434.

17. *New York Times*, 16 September 1953.

18. David S. Neft, Roland T. Johnson, Richard M. Cohen, and Jordan A. Deutsch, *The Sports Encyclopedia: Pro Football* (New York: Grosset & Dunlap, 1974), p. 105.

19. Wind, *Realm of Sport*, pp. 336–38; for a full account, see Dave Klein, *The Game of Their Lives* (New York: Random House, 1976).

20. Frank G. Menke, *The Encyclopedia of Sports*, 6th rev. ed. (Garden City, N.Y.: Doubleday & Co., 1979), pp. 172, 180–81.

21. Thomas E. Cooney, "The Booming Bust of the Paperbacks," *Saturday Review* 37 (6 November 1954): 13–16, 64–65; Peterson, *Magazines in the Twentieth Century*, pp. 50–51.

22. Hackett and Burke, *80 Years of Bestsellers*, pp. 152–82.

23. Christopher La Farge, "Mickey Spillane and His Bloody Hammer," *Saturday Review* 37 (6 November 1954): 11–12, 54–59; Nye, *Unembarrassed Muse*, pp. 263–64.

24. Peterson, *Magazines in the Twentieth Century*, pp. 60–62, 232–43; Wood, *Magazines in the United States*, p. 431.

25. Robert T. Elson, *The World of Time, Inc.: The Intimate History of A Publishing Enterprise*, 2 vols. (New York: Atheneum, 1968, 1973), 2: 353.

26. Nye, *Unembarrassed Muse*, p. 240.

27. Frederic Wertham, "It's Still Murder," *Saturday Review* 38 (9 April 1955): 48.

28. Peterson, *Magazines in the Twentieth Century*, pp. 357–60.
29. "Comic Strips Down," *Time* 65 (14 March 1955): 86.
30. *Historical Statistics*, p. 396.
31. Richard Schickel, *The Disney Version: The Life, Times, Art, and Commerce of Walt Disney* (New York: Simon & Schuster, 1968), pp. 310–17.
32. Rae, *Road and the Car*, pp. 142–43.
33. John Brooks, *Great Leap*, p. 99.
34. Philadelphia: J.B. Lippincott, 1958, pp. 14–15.
35. *Historical Statistics*, p. 403.
36. Ibid., p. 401.
37. Charles Higham, *Hollywood at Sunset* (New York: Saturday Review Press, 1972), pp. 92–95.
38. Bohn and Stromgren, *Light and Shadows*, pp. 320–21, 335; Higham, *Hollywood at Sunset*, pp. 99–100.
39. Paul A. Carter, *Another Part of the Fifties* (New York: Columbia University Press, 1983), pp. 204–205.
40. Brooks, *Great Leap*, p. 168.
41. Nye, *Unembarrassed Muse*, p. 384.
42. "Fads of the Fifties," *Look* 24 (2 February 1960): 88.
43. Paul Sann, *Fads, Follies, and Delusions*, pp. 27–30; Time-Life Books, *Fabulous Century*, 6:58–59.
44. Manchester, *Glory and the Dream*, p. 821.
45. Sann, *Fads, Follies, and Delusions*, pp. 145–49; Manchester, *Glory and the Dream*, pp. 820–21.
46. "Spring Madness," *Life* 32 (7 April 1952): 59–60.
47. Sann, *Fads, Follies, and Delusions*, pp. 293–97.
48. "Spring Madness," p. 59.
49. Sann, *Fads, Follies, and Delusions*, pp. 294–96.
50. Ibid., p. 297; Time-Life Books, *Fabulous Century*, 6: 60–61.
51. Sann, *Fads, Follies, and Delusions*, p. 46.
52. Time-Life Books, *Fabulous Century*, pp. 66–67; Sann, *Fads, Follies, and Delusions*, pp. 133–35.

### Chapter 15: Generation in a Spotlight

1. Miller and Nowak, *Fifties*, p. 270.
2. Warren French, ed., *The Fifties: Fiction, Poetry, Drama* (Deland, Fla.: Everett Edwards, 1970), pp. 23–29.
3. Benjamin Fine, *1,000,000 Delinquents* (Cleveland: World Publishing Co., 1955), p. 27.
4. Harrison E. Salisbury, *The Shook-Up Generation* (New York: Harper & Row, 1958), pp. ix–x; Dale Kramer and Madeline Karr, *Teen-Age Gangs* (New York: Henry Holt & Co., 1953), pp. 241–44.
5. "The New Three Rs," *Time* 63 (15 March 1954): 68–69.
6. Fine, *1,000,000 Delinquents*, p. 19.

7. Lewis Yablonsky, *The Violent Gang* (New York: Macmillan Co., 1962), p. 5.

8. Ibid.

9. "Rebels or Psychopaths?" *Time* 64 (6 December 1954): 64–65.

10. Miller and Nowak, *Fifties*, p. 280.

11. Vol. 44 (6 September, 1954): 43–44.

12. Elizabeth Evans, "In Defense of My Generation," *NEA Journal* 44 (March 1955): 139–40.

13. Nik Cohn, *Rock: From the Beginning* (New York: Stein & Day, 1969), pp. 11–12; Miller and Nowak, *Fifties*, pp. 294–95.

14. Arnold Shaw, *The Rockin' '50s* (New York: Hawthorn Books, 1974), pp. 104–11; Greenfield, *No Peace, No Place*, pp. 46–47; Sann, *Fads, Follies, and Delusions*, pp. 277–80.

15. Greenfield, *No Peace, No Place*, p. 50.

16. Shaw, *Rockin' '50s*, pp. 76–77.

17. "Rock 'n' Roll," *Life* 38 (18 April 1955): 166–68.

18. Quigley, and Gertner, *Films in America*, p. 234.

19. *New York Times*, 21 March 1955.

20. David Ewen, *All the Years of American Popular Music* (Englewood Cliffs, N.J.: Prentice-Hall, 1977), pp. 554–55; Cohn, *Rock*, p. 16.

21. George Scullin, "James Dean: The Legend and the Facts," *Look* 20 (16 October 1956): 123–24.

22. Rosen, *Popcorn Venus*, p. 287; Peter Lewis, *Fifties*, p. 125.

23. Shaw, *Rockin' '50s*, p. 170; John Montgomery, *The Fifties* (London: George Allen and Unwin, 1965), p. 213.

24. Scullin, "James Dean", p. 122.

25. Jim Miller, *Rolling Stone History*, pp. 350–52; Miller and Nowak, *Fifties*, p. 334.

26. Miller, *Rolling Stone History*, p. 33.

27. Ewen, *All the Years*, pp. 557–58.

28. Shaw, *Rockin' '50s*, p. 151.

29. Sann, *Fads, Follies, and Delusions*, p. 361; Ewen, *All the Years*, p. 558.

30. Ewen, *All the Years*, p. 559; Miller, *Rolling Stone History*, p. 36.

31. "The Great Elvis Presley Industry," *Look* 20 (13 November 1956): 98–104.

32. "He Can't Be—But He Is," *Look* 20 (7 August 1956): 84.

33. Henry Pleasants, *The Great American Popular Singers* (New York: Simon & Schuster, 1974), p. 272.

34. Miller and Nowak, *Fifties*, pp. 300–302.

35. Vol. 20 (7 August 1956): 84.

36. Vol. 41 (27 August 1956): 101.

37. *New York Times*, 16 September 1956.

38. Shaw, *Rockin' '50s*, p. 151.

39. Charlie Gillett, *The Sound of the City: The Rise of Rock and Roll* (New York: Outerbridge and Dienstfrey, 1970), p. 360.

40. Bernard Asbell, "Disc Jockeys and Baby Sitters," *Harper's* 215 (July 1957): 77.

41. Richard Schickel, "The Big Revolution in Records," *Look* 22 (15 April 1958): 27; Jones, *Great Expectations*, p. 64.

42. Page 53.

43. Miller and Nowak, *Fifties*, p. 303; Greenfield, *No Peace, No Place*, p. 54.

44. Ewen, *All the Years*, p. 567.

45. Dick Clark and Richard Robinson, *Rock, Roll, and Remember* (New York: Thomas Y. Crowell Co., 1976), p. 81.

46. Ibid., 108.

47. "Pat Boone: All American Boy," *Look* 22 (5 August 1958): 81–85.

48. Rosen, *Popcorn Venus*, p. 291.

49. Englewood Cliffs, N. J.: Prentice-Hall, 1958.

50. Sann, *Fads, Follies, and Delusions*, p. 278.

51. Gillett, *Sound of the City*, p. 21; Greenfield, *No Peace, No Place*, p. 61.

52. Ewen, *All the Years*, p. 568.

53. Shaw, *Rockin' '50s*, p. 154.

54. Wilma Dykeman and James Stokely, *Neither Black Nor White* (New York: Rinehart & Co., 1957), p. 260.

55. Shaw, *Rockin' '50s*, p. 155.

56. "Mr. Harper's After Hours: Upheaval in Popular Music," *Harper's* 218 (May 1959): 82.

57. "Cool Facts About Teen-age Fads," *Woman's Home Companion* 83 (July 1956): 53.

58. Ibid., p. 53; Time-Life Books, *Fabulous Century*, 6:74–79.

59. Howard Junker, "As They Used Say in the 1950s," *Esquire* 72 (August 1969): 70–71, 141.; Time-Life Books, *Fabulous Century*, 6: 80.

60. "Generation in a Searchlight," Vol. 20 (24 January 1956): 32.

61. Manchester, *Glory and the Dream*, p. 724.

62. "A New $10 Billion Power: The U.S. Teen-age Consumer," *Life* 47 (31 August 1959): 78, 83.

63. James S. Coleman, *The Adolescent Society: The Social Life of the Teenager and Its Impact on Education* (New York: Free Press, 1961), p. 13. H. H. Remmers and D. H. Radler, *The American Teenager* (Indianapolis: Bobbs-Merrill Co., 1957) pp. 53–119, passim.

64. Remmers and Radler, *American Teenager*, pp. 7, 15–17, 52–53, 156, 225–26.

65. New York: Dodd, Mead, 1954.

66. New York: David McKay, 1957, pp. 155–56.

67. John S. Brubacher and Willis Rudy, *Higher Education in Transition: A History of American Colleges and Universities, 1636–1976*, 3d ed., rev. and enl. (New York: Harper & Row, 1976), p. 257.

68. "The Younger Generation," vol. 58 (5 November 1951): 46–52.

69. Vol. 42 (2 November 1953): 52–53.

70. "The Found Generation," *American Scholar* 25 (Autumn, 1956): 427, 434.

71. "The Careful Young Men," *The Nation* 184 (9 March 1957): 200, 202–203, 206.

72. "What Parents Say About Teen-agers," *Look* 22 (2 September 1958): 65.

***Chapter 16: Women, Love, and Sex in Eisenhower's America***

1. Margaret Mead, "She Has Strengths Based on a Pioneer Past," *Life* 41 (24 December 1956): 26–27.

2. Vol. 20, p. 35.

3. Vol. 41 (24 December 1956).

4. Molly Haskell, *From Reverence to Rape: The Treatment of Women in the Movies* (New York: Holt, Rinehart & Winston, 1974), p. 1.

5. Betty Roszak and Theodore Roszak, eds., *Masculine/Feminine: Readings in Sexual Mythology and the Liberation of Women* (New York: Harper & Row, 1969), pp. 130–40.

6. New York: Harper & Bros., 1947.

7. William H. Chafe, *The American Woman: Her Changing Social, Economic, and Political Roles, 1920–1970* (New York: Oxford University Press, 1972), pp. 202–06; William L. O'Neill, *Everyone Was Brave: The Rise and Fall of Feminism in America* (Chicago: Quadrangle Books, 1969), pp. 336–37; June Sochen, *Movers and Shakers: American Women Thinkers and Activists, 1900–1970* (New York: Quadrangle Books, 1973), pp. 198–207.

8. Friedan, *Feminine Mystique*, pp. 42–44; O'Neill, *Everyone Was Brave*, p. 336.

9. Chafe, *American Woman*, pp. 207–208.

10. Friedan, *Feminine Mystique*, p. 156.

11. *Historical Statistics*, p. 383; Friedan, *Feminine Mystique*, p. 163.

12. *Historical Statistics*, p. 385.

13. Rosen, *Popcorn Venus*, pp. 246–50, 257–58.

14. Sochen, *Herstory*, p. 367.

15. Rosen, *Popcorn Venus*, p. 250.

16. *New York Times*, 6 August 1962.

17. "Hollywood Topic A-Plus," *Life* 32 (7 April 1952): 104.

18. Rosen, *Popcorn Venus*, p. 271; Manchester, *Glory and the Dream*, pp. 688–91.

19. Sochen, *Herstory*, pp. 364–65.

20. Robert Jay Lifton, ed., *The Woman in America* (Boston: Houghton Mifflin Co., 1965), pp. 145, 205.

21. Robert Smuts, *Women and Work in America* (New York: Columbia University Press, 1959), pp. 65, 104; Carol Hymowitz and Michaele Weissman, *A History of Women in America* (New York: Bantam Books, 1978), p. 315.

22. Congressional Quarterly, *Women's Movement*, p. 36.

23. Albert Ellis, *The American Sexual Tragedy* (New York: Lyle Stuart, 1954), p. 109.

24. Huston Smith, ed., *The Search for America* (Englewood Cliffs, N. J.: Prentice-Hall, 1959), pp. 124–25.

25. "Portrait of a Lady," *Newsweek* 100 (27 September 1982): 36–47; Edith Horsley, *1950s*, p. 172.

26. Manchester, *Glory and the Dream*, p. 776.

27. "Billions of Dollars for Prettiness," *Life* 41 (24 December 1956): 121, 124.

28. Ellis, *American Sexual Tragedy*, p. 34.

29. Ira Reiss, *Premarital Sexual Standards in America* (New York: Free Press of Glencoe, 1960), pp. 83–84.

30. Donald Webster Cory, *The Homosexual in America: A Subjective Approach* (New York: Greenberg, 1951), pp. 284–85.

31. Manchester, *Glory and the Dream*, p. 478.

32. Philadelphia: W. B. Saunders Co.

33. Philadelphia: W. B. Saunders Co.

34. Perrett, *A Dream of Greatness*, pp. 313–17.

35. Ellis, *American Sexual Tragedy*, pp. 256–59; Manchester, *Glory and the Dream*, pp. 478–80.

36. Perrett, *Dream of Greatness*, p. 317.

37. Paul Robinson, *The Modernization of Sex* (New York: Harper & Row, 1976), p. 118.

38. New York: Alfred A. Knopf.

39. Sochen, *Movers and Shakers*, pp. 200–203.

40. "Readers Choice," *Atlantic Monthly* 191 (April 1953): 86.

41. "A SR Panel Takes Aim at 'The Second Sex,'" *Saturday Review* 36 (21 February 1953): 27–28, 31.

42. Peter Lewis, *Fifties*, p. 61.

43. Peterson, *Magazines in the Twentieth Century*, p. 319.

44. Ibid., p. 318.

45. New York: Julian Messner, 1956.

46. September 23, 1956.

47. Pp. 149, 277, 365.

48. Hackett and Burke, *80 Years of Bestsellers*, pp. 174–81.

49. "New Picture," *Time* 68 (24 December 1956): 61.

50. "The Trouble With Baby Doll," *Time* 69 (4 January 1957): 100.
51. Rosen, *Popcorn Venus*, p. 280.
52. Time-Life Books, *Fabulous Century*, 6: 222.
53. Rosen, *Popcorn Venus*, p. 281.
54. Ibid., p. 294.

### *Chapter 17: God's Country*

1. New York: Random House, 1955.
2. Ibid., pp. 276, 288–305, passim.
3. New York: E. P. Dutton & Co., 1955.
4. Snider, "Medicine's Golden Era," pp. 34–36; John Brooks, *Great Leap*, p. 141.
5. Jones, *Great Expectations*, p. 58.
6. Godfrey Hodgson, *America in Our Time* (Garden City, N. Y.: Doubleday & Co., 1976), pp. 72–76.
7. J. Rogers Hollingsworth, "Consensus and Continuity in Recent American Historical Writing," *South Atlantic Quarterly* 61 (Winter 1962): 41.
8. Wittner, *Cold War America*, p. 183.
9. Hollingsworth, "Consensus and Continuity," pp. 40–41.
10. Hodgson, *America in Our Time*, p. 96; Wittner, *Cold War America*, pp. 127–28.
11. Miller and Nowak, *Fifties*, pp. 231–37; Hollingsworth, "Consensus and Continuity," pp. 40–41.
12. Miller and Nowak, *Fifties*, pp. 223–27.
13. "Parnassus, Coast to Coast," vol. 67 (11 June 1956): 65–66.
14. Hollingsworth, "Consensus and Continuity," pp. 46–47.
15. Ibid., pp. 44–49.
16. Frances Fitzgerald, *America Revised: History Schoolbooks in the Twentieth Century* (Boston: Little, Brown & Co., 1979), pp. 56–57, 128.
17. Ibid., p. 38.
18. Wittner, *Cold War America*, pp. 129–30; Alexander, *Holding the Line*, pp. 156–57.
19. Alexander, *Holding the Line*, pp. 157–58; Hodgson, *America in Our Time*, pp. 154–56.
20. Leo Rosten, ed., *Religions in America*, rev. ed. (New York: Simon & Schuster, 1963), p. 232.
21. Miller and Nowak, *Fifties*, pp. 86–87.
22. Swanberg, *Luce and His Empire*, p. 341.
23. Paul Hutchinson, "Have We a 'New' Religion?" *Life* 38 (11 April 1955): 138.
24. "Words and Works," *Time* 64 (20 September 1954): 65.
25. Eric Goldman, "Good-by to the Fifties—and Good Riddance," *Harper's* 220 (January 1960): 28.

26. Miller and Nowak, *Fifties*, p. 90.

27. William Lee Miller, "Piety Along the Potomac," *The Reporter* (11 August 1954): 25.

28. "The New Evangelist," *Time* 64 (25 October 1954): 54.

29. Billy Graham, *Peace With God* (New York: Doubleday & Co., 1953), p. 23.

30. Peter Lewis, *Fifties*, pp. 73–74.

31. "The New Evangelist," p. 55.

32. James Morris, *The Preachers* (New York: St. Martin's Press, 1973), pp. 57–126, passim.

33. Shulman and Youman, *How Sweet It Was*, p. 406.

34. Fulton J. Sheen, *Life Is Worth Living* (New York: McGraw-Hill, 1953), pp. 154, 251.

35. Edward L. R. Elson, *America's Spiritual Recovery* (n.p.: Fleming H. Revell, 1954), pp. 41–42.

36. William Lee Miller, "Some Negative Thinking About Norman Vincent Peale," *The Reporter* 12 (13 January 1955): 19.

37. Donald Meyer, *The Positive Thinkers: A Study of the American Quest for Health, Wealth, and Personal Power from Mary Baker Eddy to Norman Vincent Peale* (Garden City, N. Y.: Doubleday & Co., 1965), p. 262.

38. New York: Prentice-Hall, 1952, p. xi.

39. Reinhold Niebuhr, "Varieties of Religious Revival," *New Republic* 132 (6 June 1955): 13.

40. Harry C. Meserve, "The New Piety," *The Atlantic Monthly* 195 (June 1955): 35.

41. A. Roy Eckardt, "The New Look in American Piety," *The Christian Century* 71 (17 November 1954): 1396.

42. Garden City, N. Y.: Doubleday & Co., 1956, p. 54.

43. Ibid., p. 59.

44. Hutchinson, "Have We a 'New' Religion?" p. 148.

45. W. L. Miller, "Some Negative Thinking About Norman Vincent Peale," p. 23; Hutchinson, "Have We A 'New' Religion?" p. 23.

46. Murry Kempton, *America Comes of Middle Age: Columns, 1950–1962* (Boston: Little, Brown & Co., 1963), p. 73.

47. Herberg, *Protestant-Catholic-Jew*, p. 103.

48. Meyer, *Positive Thinkers*, pp. 282–87.

49. Stanley Rowland, Jr., "Suburbia Buys Religion," *The Nation* 183 (28 July 1956): 79–80.

50. Alexander, *Holding the Line*, p. 136; Miller and Nowak, *Fifties*, p. 88.

51. J. Paul Williams, *What Americans Believe and How They Worship*, rev. ed. (New York: Harper & Row, 1962), p. 474.

### *Chapter 18: Rocky Road*

1. "A Solemn Inaugural and a Gay Celebration," *Life* 42 (4 February 1957): 25.
2. Stone, *Haunted Fifties*, p. 183.
3. Lewis and *The New York Times*, *Portrait of a Decade*, p. 119.
4. Dykeman and Stokely, *Neither Black Nor White*, p. 253.
5. Bartley, *The Rise of Massive Resistance*, p. 234.
6. James W. Vander Zanden, "The Klan Revival," *American Journal of Sociology* 65 (March 1960): 457.
7. Ibid., p. 460.
8. Bartley, *Rise of Massive Resistance*, p. 206.
9. David M. Chalmers, *Hooded Americanism: The History of the Ku Klux Klan*, 2d ed. (New York: New Viewpoints, 1981), p. 348.
10. Peters, *Southern Temper*, p. 203; Perrett, *Dream of Greatness*, p. 382.
11. Muse, *Ten Years of Prelude*, p. 50.
12. "When a Negro Family Moved into a White Community," *U.S. News and World Report* 43 (30 August 1957): 29–32; David B. Bittan, "Ordeal in Levittown," *Look* 22 (19 August 1958): 84–86.
13. Muse, *Ten Years of Prelude*, p. 203.
14. Alexander, *Holding the Line*, p. 197.
15. Muse, *Ten Years of Prelude*, pp. 126–27.
16. Ibid., p. 137.
17. Virgil T. Blossom, *It Has Happened Here* (New York: Harper & Brothers, 1959), pp. 104–107.
18. Duram, *A Moderate Among Extremists*, p. 155.
19. Perrett, *Dream of Greatness*, p. 430.
20. Branyan and Larsen, *Eisenhower Administration*, 2: 1129–30.
21. Adams, *First Hand Report*, p. 355.
22. Duram, *Moderate Among Extremists*, p. 144.
23. Muse, *Ten Years of Prelude*, p. 142.
24. Peters, *Southern Temper*, p. 86.
25. Parmet, *Eisenhower*, p. 512.
26. Lyon, *Eisenhower*, p. 747.
27. Lewis, *Portrait of Decade*, p. 55.

### *Chapter 19: Sputnik*

1. Norman Moss, *Men Who Play God: The Story of the H-Bomb and How the World Came to Live with It* (New York: Harper & Row, 1968), pp. 193–94.
2. Alexander, *Holding the Line*, p. 212.
3. Neal, *Eisenhowers*, p. 390.
4. Morton H. Halperin, "The Gaither Committee and the Policy Process," *World Politics* 13 (April 1961): 364–69.

5. Alexander, *Holding the Line*, pp. 223–30.

6. Willy Ley, *Rockets, Missiles, and Men in Space* (New York: Viking Press, 1968), p. 314; Ewald, *Eisenhower the President*, pp. 283–86.

7. Lyon, *Eisenhower*, p. 758.

8. Manchester, *Glory and the Dream*, p. 796.

9. Parmet, *Eisenhower*, pp. 536–37; Alexander, *Holding the Line*, p. 226.

10. Alexander, *Holding the Line*, p. 215.

11. Andrew R. MacAndrew, "Are Soviet Schools Better Than Ours?" *The Reporter* 18 (20 February 1958): 11.

12. Fred M. Hechinger, "The Fate of Pedagoguese," *Saturday Review* 36 (12 December 1953): 18.

13. New York: McGraw-Hill, 1957, p. 1.

14. Alvin C. Eurich, "Russia's New Schooling," *Atlantic Monthly* 201 (April 1958): 55.

15. New York: E. P. Dutton & Co., 1959, p. 249.

16. Arthur Bestor, "What Went Wrong with U. S. Schools?" *U.S. News and World Report* 44 (24 January 1958): 69.

17. "Crisis in Education," *Life* 44 (24 March 1958): 25.

18. Vol. 44 (24 March 1958): p. 37.

19. "Reaction to a Letter," *Life* 44 (28 April 1958): 16.

20. Vol. 44 (24 March 1958): 27, 33.

21. John Keats, *Schools Without Scholars* (Boston: Houghton Mifflin Co., 1958).

22. R. Alton Lee, *Dwight D. Eisenhower: Soldier and Statesman* (Chicago: Nelson-Hall, 1981), pp. 285–86.

23. Brooks, *Great Leap*, p. 223.

24. Perrett, *Dream of Greatness*, p. 477.

25. Fred M. Hechinger, *The Big Red Schoolhouse* (Gloucester, Mass.: Peter Smith, 1968), p. 138.

26. "Behind K's 'Hard Work' Revolution . . . In Education," *Newsweek* 6 (6 October 1958): 87.

### *Chapter 20: Living with the Bomb*

1. Alexander, *Holding the Line*, p. 203; Roy E. Licklider, "The Missile Gap Controversy," *Political Science Quarterly* 85 (December 1950): 600–15, passim.

2. Alexander, *Holding the Line*, pp. 203–204.

3. Wittner, *Cold War America*, p. 145.

4. "Two-hour Warning Against Sneak Attack," *U.S. News and World Report*, 43 (6 September 1957): 76.

5. Merlo J. Pusey, *Eisenhower the President* (New York: Macmillan Co., 1956), p. 114.

6. Peter Lewis, *Fifties*, p. 88.

7. Alexander, *Holding the Line*, p. 210.

8. "The Atom," *Time* 57 (5 February 1951): 11.

9. "Life in These United States," *Reader's Digest*, 61 (October 1952): 52.

10. Edward Teller and Albert Latter, "The Compelling Need for Nuclear Tests," *Life*, 44 (10 February 1958): 64.

11. Vol. 42 (28 June 1957): 79, 81–82.

12. "What's Back of the 'Fall-Out' Scare," *U.S. News and World Report* 42 (7 June 1957): 25.

13. Vol. 12 (August 1952): 5.

14. New York: Dodd, Mead & Co., 1956, pp. 245, 250.

15. Fowler, *Fallout*, p. 455; Peter Lewis, *Fifties*, pp. 96–97.

16. Miller and Nowak, *Fifties*, pp. 68–73.

17. Brian Murphy, "Monster Movies: They Came from Beneath the Fifties," *Journal of Popular Film*, 1 (Winter, 1972): 38.

18. John Brosnan, *Future Tense: The Cinema of Science Fiction* (New York: St. Martin's Press, 1978), pp. 72–73.

19. *New York Times*, 18 December 1959.

20. *New York Times*, 24 September 1950.

21. Douglas Menville and R. Reginald, *Things to Come: An Intellectual History of the Science Fiction Film* (New York: The New York Times Book Co., 1977), p. 80.

22. David Michael Jacobs, *The UFO Controversy in America* (Bloomington: Indiana University Press, 1975), pp. 5–36, passim.

23. Ibid., p. 304.

24. Ibid., pp. 120–21.

25. Ibid., pp. 110–114, 120.

26. Fowler, *Fallout*, p. 176.

27. Ibid., p. 179.

28. Herman Kahn, *On Thermonuclear War* (Princeton, N. J.: Princeton University Press, 1960).

29. For summary of Kahn's ideas, see Moss, *Men Who Play God*, pp. 243–64.

30. Fowler, *Fallout*, p. 133.

31. Office of Civil and Defense Mobilization. *What You Should Know About The National Plan for Civil Defense and Defense Mobilization* (Washington: U.S. Government Printing Office, 1958), pp. 8, 25.

32. U.S. Department of Health, Education, and Welfare. Office of Education. *Education for National Survival: A Handbook on Civil Defense for Schools* (Washington: U.S. Government Printing Office, 1956), pp. 1, 13.

33. Vol. 47 (10 August 1959): 51–52.

34. Lens, *The Day Before Doomsday*, p. 135; Fowler, *Fallout*, pp. 133–35.

35. Lawrence C. Wittner, *Rebels Against War: The American Peace Movement, 1941–1960* (New York: Columbia University Press, 1969), p. 266.

36. Thomas Meehan, "Must We Be Nostalgic About the Fifties?" *Horizon* 14 (Winter 1972): 8.

37. New York: Dodd, Mead & Co., 1958, p. 111.

38. New York: Simon & Schuster, 1959, p. 7.

39. Wittner, *Cold War America*, p. 199.

40. Wittner, *Rebels Against War*, pp. 243–47; Wittner, *Cold War America*, p. 199.

41. Wittner, *Rebels Against War*, pp. 248–49.

42. Wittner, *Cold War America*, pp. 198–200; Wittner, *Rebels Against War*, pp. 266–77.

## *Chapter 21: Troubled Times*

1. Ferrell, *Eisenhower Diaries*, p. 347.
2. *New York Times*, 23 December 1957.
3. Ambrose, *Eisenhower*, 2: 486.
4. Lyon, *Eisenhower*, pp. 768–69.
5. Ambrose, *Eisenhower*, 2: 468.
6. Branyan and Larsen, *Eisenhower Administration*, 2: 921–22.
7. Eisenhower, *White House Years*, 2: 315–17; Ambrose, *Eisenhower*, 2: 480–82.
8. Parmet, *Eisenhower*, p. 523; Alexander, *Holding the Line*, p. 243.
9. Ambrose, *Eisenhower*, 2: 530.
10. Parmet, *Eisenhower*, p. 553.
11. Oates, *Let the Trumpet Sound*, p. 134.
12. Lord, *Past That Would Not Die*, p. 76.
13. Ibid.
14. Ann Lyon Haight, *Banned Books: Informal Notes on Some Books Banned for Various Reasons at Various Times and in Various Places*, 3d ed. (New York: R. R. Bowker, 1970), p. 119.
15. Lewis and *The New York Times, Portrait of a Decade*, pp. 213–14.
16. New York: World Publishing Co., 1958.
17. Ibid., p. 122.
18. Ibid., pp. 123–24.
19. Lewis and *The New York Times, Portrait of a Decade*, p. 119.
20. Bartley, *Rise of Massive Resistance*, pp. 7–8; Alexander, *Holding the Line*, p. 200.
21. Paul L. Murphy, *The Constitution in Crisis Times, 1918–1969* (New York: Harper & Row, 1972), pp. 554–55.
22. Parmet, *Eisenhower*, p. 555.

23. "How Negroes Are Gaining in U.S.," *U.S. News and World Report* 42 (28 June 1957): 105–106; "Negroes: Big Advances in Jobs, Wealth, Status," *U.S. News and World Report* 45 (28 November 1958): 90–92.

24. Peters, *Southern Temper*, p. 261.

25. Wittner, *Cold War America*, p. 139.

26. Boston: Houghton Mifflin Co., 1960, p. 121.

27. "Black Like Me," *Time* 75 (28 March 1960): 90.

28. Nixon, *Six Crises*, pp. 255–58; Goldman, *Crucial Decade*, pp. 329–30.

29. Goldman, *Crucial Decade*, p. 331.

30. Neal, *Eisenhowers*, pp. 407–08.

31. Ambrose, *Eisenhower*, 2: 536.

32. Parmet, *Eisenhower*, pp. 549–51; Goldman, *Crucial Decade*, pp. 331–32.

33. *New York Times*, 28 September 1959.

34. Vol. 38 (October 1959): 5, 7.

35. "Eisenhower and the New President," vol. 220 (May 1960): 32.

36. David Wise and Thomas B. Ross, *The U-2 Affair* (New York: Random House, 1962), pp. 196–97, 211–12.

37. Edward Crankshaw, *Khrushchev: A Career* (New York: Viking Press, 1966), pp. 274–75.

38. Parmet, *Eisenhower*, pp. 556–58; Alexander, *Holding the Line*, pp. 264–65.

39. Branyan and Larsen, *Eisenhower Administration*, 2: 1238–39.

40. Parmet, *Eisenhower*, p. 558; Alexander, *Holding the Line*, p. 266; Goldman, *Crucial Decade*, pp. 337–38.

41. Alexander, *Holding the Line*, pp. 256–57.

42. Parmet, *Eisenhower*, p. 540.

43. Ibid., pp. 561–62; Alexander, *Holding the Line*, pp. 257–62.

44. Peter A. Poole, *The United States and Indochina, from FDR to Nixon* (Hinsdale, Ill.: Dryden Press, 1973), pp. 44–45.

45. Stoessinger, *Why Nations Go to War*, p. 117.

46. Parmet, *Eisenhower*, p. 563.

47. Lee, *Eisenhower*, p. 316.

48. Ambrose, *Eisenhower*, 2: 590.

### *Chapter 22: The Winds of Change*

1. Lee, *Eisenhower*, pp. 290–91; Leuchtenberg, *Great Age of Change*, p. 132.

2. January 9, 1950, p. 29.

3. John F. Stover, *The Life and Decline of the American Railroad* (New York: Oxford University Press, 1970), p. 214; *Historical Statistics*, p. 729; Peter Lyon, *To Hell in a Day Coach: An Exasperated Look at American Railroads* (Philadelphia: J. B. Lippincott, 1968), pp. 195–97.

4. Stover, *Life and Decline of American Railroad,* p. 218.

5. Bruce Cook, *The Beat Generation* (New York: Charles Scribner's Sons, 1971), p. 6.

6. Lawrence Lipton, *The Holy Barbarians* (New York: Julian Messner, 1959), p. 157.

7. Ibid., p. 171.

8. Ibid., p. 296.

9. Ibid., p. 307.

10. New York: Viking Press.

11. *New York Times*, 5 September 1957.

12. "The Ganser Syndrome," *Time* 70 (16 September, 1957): 120.

13. Cook, *Beat Generation*, pp. 72–74.

14. Ibid., p. 96.

15. Ibid., p. 84.

16. Manchester, *Glory and the Dream,* p. 726.

17. Cook, *Beat Generation*, p. 64.

18. Ibid., p. 7; Time-Life Books, *Fabulous Century*, 6: 93.

19. William O'Neill, ed., *American Society Since 1945* (Chicago: Quadrangle Books, 1969), p. 79.

20. Cook, *Beat Generation*, p. 9; Norman Podhoretz, "The Know-Nothing Bohemians," *Partisan Review* 25 (Spring 1958): 305–18, passim.

21. "The Bored, the Bearded, and the Beat," *Look* 22 (19 August 1958): 65.

22. Vol. 47 (30 November 1959): 115, 130.

23. Cook, *Beat Generation*, pp. 187–89.

24. Hodgson, *America in Our Time*, p. 325.

25. Miller and Nowack, *Fifties*, pp. 395–96.

26. "The Quality of Mercy" *Time* 75 (29 February 1960): 21–22; "The Chessman Affair," *Time*, 64 (21 March 1960): 16–20.

27. Wittner, *Cold War America,* pp. 199–201; Miller and Nowak, *Fifties*, pp. 395–96.

28. Hodgson, *America in Our Time*, p. 184.

29. William H. Chafe, *Civilities and Civil Rights: Greensboro, North Carolina, and the Black Struggle for Freedom* (New York: Oxford University Press, 1980), p. 99.

30. Howard Zinn, *SNCC: The New Abolitionists*, 2d ed. (Boston: Beacon Press, 1965), pp. 16, 20, 30.

31. Chafe, *Civilities and Civil Rights*, p. 136.

32. Zinn, *New Abolitionists*, p. 16; Alexander, *Holding the Line*, p. 121.

33. Chafe, *Civilities and Civil Rights*, p. 137.

34. Zinn, *New Abolitionists*, p. 17.

35. Oates, *Let the Trumpet Sound*, p. 154.
36. "Young Wives," *Newsweek* 55 (7 March 1960): 57, 60.
37. Vol. 151 (September 1960): 59, 162.
38. Jezer, *The Dark Ages*, p. 233.
39. Manchester, *Glory and the Dream*, pp. 849–50.
40. Friedan, *Feminine Mystique*, p. 3.
41. Manchester, *Glory and the Dream*, pp. 1255–56.
42. Perrett, *Dream of Greatness*, p. 498.
43. Eric Larrabee, *The Self Conscious Society* (Garden City, N. Y.: Doubleday & Co., 1960), p. 102.
44. Goldman, *The Crucial Decade*, pp. 324–25.
45. Barnouw, *History of Broadcasting*, 3: 57–58.
46. Ibid., p. 125.
47. Manchester, *Glory and the Dream*, p. 851.
48. Sann, *Fads, Follies, and Delusions*, p. 339.
49. Ibid., p. 336.
50. Goldman, *Crucial Decade*, p. 324.
51. Shaw, *Rockin' '50s*, pp. 269–70; Manchester, *Glory and the Dream*, p. 852.
52. Hodgson, *America in Our Time*, p. 70.
53. Ibid., p. 71.

### *Chapter 23: The Torch Is Passed*

1. Richard Rovere, "Measuring the Presidential Candidates," *Harper's* 220 (June 1960): 86.
2. Herbert S. Parmet, *The Democrats: The Years After FDR* (New York: Oxford University Press, 1977), p. 167.
3. Rovere, "Measuring the Presidential Candidates," p. 83.
4. Steinberg, *Man From Missouri*, p. 428.
5. Alexander, *Holding the Line*, p. 274.
6. Bailey, *Voices of America*, p. 456.
7. Theodore C. Sorenson, *Kennedy* (New York: Harper & Row, 1965), p. 119.
8. Paul F. Boller, *Presidential Campaigns* (New York: Oxford University Press, 1984), p. 303.
9. Ewald, *Eisenhower the President*, p. 310.
10. Ambrose, *Eisenhower*, 1: 555.
11. Ferrell, *Eisenhower Diaries*, p. 242.
12. Bruce Mazlish, *In Search of Nixon: A Psychohistorical Inquiry* (New York: Basic Books, 1972), p. 98; Wills, *Nixon Agonistes*, pp. 123–28; Ambrose, "The Ike Age," p. 28.
13. Ambrose, *Eisenhower*, 2: 546, 559–60, 593.
14. Ibid., p. 597.

15. Lyon, *Eisenhower,* p. 823.
16. Ambrose, *Eisenhower*, 2: 600–601.
17. Boller, *Presidential Campaigns*, p. 300.
18. Barnouw, *History of Broadcasting*, 3: 164–65.
19. Boller, *Presidential Campaigns*, p. 300.
20. Alexander, *Holding the Line*, p. 279; Arthur M. Schlesinger et al., *Coming to Power,* pp. 456–57.
21. Manchester, *Glory and the Dream*, pp. 882–83.
22. Nixon, *Memoirs*, pp. 225–26.
23. Schlesinger et al., *Coming to Power*, p. 457.
24. Ewald, *Eisenhower the President*, p. 314.
25. Eisenhower, *White House Years*, 2: 652–53.
26. Ambrose, *Eisenhower*, 2: 594.
27. Alexander, *Holding the Line*, p. 288.
28. Eisenhower, *White House Years*, 2: 603, 617.
29. Branyan and Larsen, *Eisenhower Administration*, 2: 1373–77; Fred J. Cook, *Warfare State* pp. 2–3.
30. Lyon, *Eisenhower*, p. 825.
31. Gray, *Eighteen Acres Under Glass*, p. 351.
32. Sorenson, *Kennedy*, pp. 245–48.
33. Nixon, *Memoirs*, p. 228.

### *Chapter 24: In Search of the Fifties*

1. Vol. 220 (January 1960); 27.
2. Cited by Richard Rovere, "Eisenhower Over the Shoulder," *The American Scholar* 31 (Spring 1962): 176.
3. "Eisenhower as President: A Critical Appraisal of the Record," vol. 26 (November 1958): 390.
4. Graebner, "Eisenhower's Popular Leadership," p. 230.
5. Vol. 72 (16 June 1972): 39.
6. Vol. 80 (16 October 1972): 78.
7. Meehan, "Must We Be Nostalgic About the Fifties?" p. 13.
8. "The Nifty Fifties," p. 39.
9. Ibid., p. 79.
10. Miller and Nowak, *Fifties*, p. 5.
11. Leuchtenburg, "Give 'em Harry," p. 20.
12. "Trumania in the '70s," *Time* 105 (9 June 1975): 45; Ferrell, *Harry S. Truman*, p. 191.
13. Lyon, *Eisenhower,* p. 857; Parmet, *Eisenhower,* p. 4.
14. Lee, *Eisenhower,* p. 333; Vincent De Santis, "Eisenhower Revisionism," *The Review of Politics*, 38 (April 1976): 196; Bailey, *Presidential Greatness*, p. 24.
15. De Santis, "Eisenhower Revisionism," p. 192.

16. Ibid., p. 193.

17. "My Friend the President," vol. 232 (9 April 1960); 54.

18. *Esquire*, 68 (September 1967), 108–109, 156.

19. Lee, *Eisenhower*, pp. 333–34; De Santis, "Eisenhower Revisionism," pp. 198–99.

20. Neal, "Our Best and Worst Presidents," section 9, p. 9.

21. Paul S. Holbo and Robert W. Sellen, *The Eisenhower Era: The Age of Consensus*, (Hinsdale, Illinois: Dryden Press, 1974), p. 10.

22. Lee, *Eisenhower*, p. 323.

23. Ambrose, *Eisenhower*, 2: 627.

24. Ibid., p. 425.

# WORKS CITED

A comprehensive bibliography of all the materials consulted in the preparation of this book would take up far too much space. What follows is a list of all the works cited in the text.

### *I. Government Publications*

Office of Civil and Defense Mobilization. *The Family Fallout Shelter*. Washington: U.S. Government Printing Office, 1959.

———. *What You Should Know About the National Plan for Civil Defense and Defense Mobilization*. U.S. Government Printing Office, 1958.

U.S. Department of Commerce. Bureau of the Census. *Historical Statistics of the United States: Colonial Times to 1970*. Bicentennial ed. Two parts. Washington: U.S. Government Printing Office, 1975.

U.S. Department of Health, Education, and Welfare. Office of Education. *Education for National Survival: A Handbook on Civil Defense for Schools*. Washington: U.S. Government Printing Office, 1956.

### *II. Documentary Collection*

Branyan, Robert L., and Lawrence H. Larsen, eds. *The Eisenhower Administration, 1953–1961: A Documentary History*. 2 vols. New York: Random House, 1971.

### *III. Articles*

Albjerg, Victor. "Truman and Eisenhower: Their Administrations and Campaigns." *Current History* 47 (October 1964): 221–28.
"All the President's Magazines." *Time* 116 (15 December 1980): 78.
Allen, George E. "My Friend the President." *Saturday Evening Post* 232 (9 April 1960): 23–25, 50–54.
Ambrose, Stephen E. "The Ike Age." *The New Republic* 184 (9 May 1981): 26–34.
"The American Task." *Life* (2 January 1950): 28.
Asbell, Bernard. "Disc Jockeys and Baby Sitters." *Harper's* 215 (July 1957): 77–80.
"The Atom." *Time* (5 February 1951): 11.
"Automation." *Time* 67 (19 March 1956): 98–106.
"The Baby Boomers Come of Age." *Newsweek* 97 (30 March 1981): 34–37.
"Back to the '50s." *Newsweek* 80 (16 October 1972): 78–82.
Bestor, Arthur. "What Went Wrong with U.S. Schools." *U.S. News and World Report* 44 (24 January 1958): 68–77.
Bigbee, North. "Why We Aren't Running Short of Oil." *Reader's Digest* 56 (January 1950): 123–26.
"Billions of Dollars for Prettiness." *Life* 41 (24 December 1956): 121–26.
Bittan, David. "Ordeal in Levittown." *Look* 22 (19 August 1958): 84–86.
"Black Like Me." *Time* 75 (28 March 1960): 90.
"The Bored, the Bearded, and the Beat." *Look* 22 (19 August 1958): 65–68.
"Buying New." *Newsweek* 48 (17 December 1956): 83–84.
Byrnes, James F. "The Supreme Court Must Be Curbed." *U.S. News and World Report* 40 (18 May 1956): 50–58.
"The Careful Young Men." *The Nation* 184 (9 March 1957): 199–214.
"The Chessman Affair." *Time* 64 (21 March 1960): 16–20.
"Comic Strips Down." *Time* 65 (14 March 1955): 86.
"'Cool' Facts About Teen-Age Fads." *Woman's Home Companion* 83 (July 1956): 53.
Cooney, Thomas E. "The Booming Bust of the Paperbacks." *Saturday Review* 37 (6 November 1954): 13–16, 64–65.
Cousins, Norman. "The Time Trap." *Saturday Review* 32 (24 December 1949): 20.
"Crisis in Education." *Life* 44 (24 March 1958): 25.
Davies, A. Powell. "Loyalty Needs Better Friends." *The New Republic* 124 (4 February 1952): 11–13.
De Santis, Vincent. "Eisenhower Revisionism." *The Review of Politics* 38 (April 1976): 190–207.
"Dossier: Dwight David Eisenhower." *Esquire* 100 (December 1983): 567.
"Dreaming of the Eisenhower Years." *Time* 116 (28 July 1980): 32.
Eckardt, A. Roy. "The New Look in American Piety." *The Christian Century* 71 (17 November 1954): 1395–97.

"Elvis—a Different Kind of Idol." *Life* 41 (27 August 1956): 101–109.

Eurich, Alvin C. "Russia's New Schooling." *Atlantic Monthly* 21 (April 1958): 55–58.

Evans, Elizabeth. "In Defense of My Generation." *NEA Journal* 44 (March 1955): 139–40.

"Fads of the Fifties." *Look* 24 (2 February 1960): 83–88.

"The First Baby." *Life* 41 (24 December 1956): 57–63.

Flynn, John T. "Who Owns Your Child's Mind?" *Reader's Digest* 30 (October 1951): 23–28.

Friedan, Betty. "Women Are People Too." *Good Housekeeping* 151 (September 1960): 59–61, 161–162.

Fuess, Claude M. "The Perils of Conformity." *Saturday Review* 35 (12 January 1952): 7–8, 30.

"The Ganser Syndrome." *Time* 70 (16 September 1957): 120.

Goldman, Eric. "Good-by to the Fifties—and Good Riddance." *Harper's* 220 (January 1960): 27–29.

Graebner, Norman A. "Eisenhower's Popular Leadership." *Current History* 39 (October 1960): 230–36.

"The Great Elvis Presley Industry." *Look* 20 (13 November 1956): 98–104.

"A Great Ride." *Time* 68 (31 December 1956): 10.

Halperin, Morton H. "The Gaither Committee and the Policy Process." *World Politics* 13 (April 1961): 360–84.

Harsch, Joseph C. "John Foster Dulles: A Very Complicated Man." *Harper's* 213 (September 1956): 27–34.

"He Can't Be—but He Is." *Look* 20 (7 August 1956): 82–85.

Hechinger, Fred M. "The Fate of Pedagoguese." *Saturday Review* 36 (12 December 1953): 18–20.

Henderson, Harry. "The Mass Produced Suburbs." Two parts. *Harper's* 207 (November and December 1953): 25–32, 80–86.

Hine, Al. "The Drive-Ins." *Holiday* 12 (July 1952): 6–11.

Holland, Gerald. "The Golden Age Is Now." *Sports Illustrated* 1 (6 August 1954): 46–52, 83–94.

Hollingsworth, J. Rodgers. "Consensus and Continuity in Recent American Historical Writing." *South Atlantic Quarterly* 61 (Winter 1962): 40–50.

"Hollywood Topic A-Plus." *Life* 32 (7 April 1952): 101–104.

"Housing." *Time* 56 (7 August 1950): 17.

"How Negroes Are Gaining in the U.S." *U.S. News and World Report* 42 (28 June 1957): 105–106.

Hutchinson, Paul. "Have We a 'New' Religion?" *Life* 38 (11 April 1955): 138–58.

———. "The President's Religious Faith." *Life* 36 (22 March 1954): 151–70.

"The Inheritors." *Time* 89 (6 January 1967): 18–23.

Joslyn, James, and John Pendleton. "The Adventures of Ozzie and Harriet." *Journal of Popular Culture* 7 (Summer 1973): 23–41.

Junker, Howard. "As They Used to Say in the 1950's." *Esquire* 72 (August 1969): 70–71, 141.

Kempton, Murray. "The Underestimation of Dwight D. Eisenhower." *Esquire* 68 (September 1967): 108–109, 156.

Khrushchev, Nikita. "On Peaceful Coexistence." *Foreign Affairs* 38 (October 1959): 1–18.

La Farge, Christopher. "Mickey Spillane and His Bloody Hammer." *Saturday Review* 37 (6 November 1954): 11–12, 54–59.

Larrabee, Eric. "Detroit's Great Debate: Where Did We Go Wrong?" *The Reporter* 18 (17 April 1958): 16–21.

———. "The Edsel and How It Got That Way." *Harper's* 215 (September 1957): 67–73.

Lawrence, David. "Justice to the Memory of Senator McCarthy." *U.S. News and World Report* 42 (7 June 1957): 144, 139–43.

"The Leisured Masses." *Business Week* (12 September 1953): 142.

"The Letter." *Time* 56 (18 December 1950): 16–17.

Leuchtenburg, William E. "Give 'em Harry." *New Republic* 190 (21 May 1984): 19–23.

Licklider, Roy E. "The Missile Gap Controversy." *Political Science Quarterly* 85 (December 1970): 600–15.

"Life in These United States." *Reader's Digest* 61 (October 1952): 52.

Long, Richard, A. "Those Magnolia Myths." *The Nation* 183 (7 July 1956): 16–17.

MacAndrew, Andrew R. "Are Soviet Schools Better than Ours?" *The Reporter* 18 (20 February 1958): 10–14.

Mead, Margaret. "She Has Strengths Based on a Pioneer Past." *Life* 41 (24 December 1956): 26–27.

Meehan, Thomas. "Must We Be Nostalgic About the Fifties?" *Horizon* 14 (Winter 1972): 4–17.

Meserve, Harry C. "The New Piety." *The Atlantic Monthly* 195 (June 1955): 34–37.

Miller, Helen Hill. "Farming Isn't What It Was." *The New Republic* 140 (2 March 1959): 9–12.

Miller, William Lee. "Piety Along the Potomac." *The Reporter* 11 (17 August 1954): 25–28.

———. "Some Negative Thinking About Norman Vincent Peale." *The Reporter* 12 (13 January 1955): 19–24.

"Miscellany." *Time* 56 (18 September 1950): 124.

Murphy, Brian. "Monster Movies: They Came from Beneath the Fifties." *Journal of Popular Film* 1 (Winter 1972): 31–38.

Nader, Ralph. "The Safe Car You Can't Buy." *The Nation* 188 (11 April 1959): 310–13.

Neal, Steve. "Our Best and Worst Presidents." *Chicago Tribune*, 10 January 1982, section 9 (*Chicago Tribune Magazine*), pp. 8–16.
"Negroes: Big Advances in Jobs, Wealth, Status." *U.S. News and World Report* 45 (28 November 1958): 90–92.
"The New Edsel." *Consumer Reports* 23 (January 1958): 30–33.
"The New Evangelist." *Time* 64 (25 October 1954): 54–60.
"A New Look at the American Woman." *Look* 20 (16 October 1956): 35–54.
"New Picture." *Time* 68 (24 December 1956): 61.
"A New $10 Billion Power: The U.S. Teen-age Consumer." *Life* 47 (31 August 1959): 78–85.
"The New Three R's." *Time* 63 (15 March 1954): 68–70.
*New York Times*, 1950–1961.
Niebuhr, Reinhold. "Varieties of Religious Revival." *The New Republic* 132 (6 June 1955): 13–16.
"The Nifty Fifties." *Life* 72 (16 June 1972): 38–46.
O'Neil, Paul. "The Only Rebellion Around." *Life* 47 (30 November 1959): 114–30.
"Our Atomic Tomorrow." *Holiday* 12 (August 1952): 5.
"Our Vicious Young Hoodlums: Is There Any Hope?" *Newsweek* 44 (6 September 1954): 43–44.
"Out of Order." *Time* 70 (14 October 1957): 102.
"Parnassus, Coast to Coast." *Time* 67 (11 June 1956): 65–70.
"Pat Boone: All American Boy." *Look* 22 (5 August 1958): 81–85.
Peterson, William. "The New American Family: Causes and Consequences of the Baby Room." *Commentary* 21 (January 1956): 1–6.
Podhoretz, Norman. "The Know-Nothing Bohemians." *Partisan Review* 25 (Spring 1958): 305–18.
"Portrait of A Lady." *Newsweek* 100 (27 September 1982): 36–47.
Prendergast, Joseph. "Non-Working Time Continues to Expand." *Recreation* 49 (March 1956): 107.
"The Pushbutton Way to Leisure." *House and Garden* 105 (March 1954): 135–37.
"The Quality of Mercy." *Time* 75 (29 February 1960): 21–22.
"Reaction to a Letter." *Life* 44 (28 April 1958): 16.
"Rebels or Psychopaths?" *Time* 64 (6 December 1954): 65–65.
Riesman, David. "The Found Generation." *American Scholar* 25 (Autumn 1956): 421–36.
"Rock 'n Roll," *Life* 38 (18 April 1955): 166–68.
"Rocketing Births: Business Bonanza." *Life* 44 (16 June 1958): 83–89.
Rolo, Charles J. "Reader's Choice." *Atlantic Monthly* 191 (April 1953): 82–86.
"The Roots of Home." *Time* 75 (20 June 1960): 14–18.
Rovere, Richard. "Eisenhower and the New President." *Harper's* 220 (May 1960): 31–35.

———. "Eisenhower Over the Shoulder." *The American Scholar* 31 (Spring 1962): 176–79.
———. "Measuring the Presidential Candidates." *Harper's* 220 (June 1960): 82–86.
Rowland, Stanley, Jr., "Suburbia Buys Religion." *The Nation* 80 (28 July 1956): 78–80.
"Runner-Up." *Time* 56 (25 December 1950): 41.
Sass, Herbert Ravenel. "Mixed Schools and Mixed Blood." *Atlantic Monthly* 198 (November 1956): 45–49.
"A Saturday Review Panel Takes Aim at 'The Second Sex.'" *Saturday Review* 36 (21 February 1953): 26–31, 41.
Schickel, Richard. "The Big Revolution in Records." *Look* 22 (15 April 1958): 26–39.
"Schoolboys Point Up a U.S. Weakness." *Life* 44 (24 March 1958): 26–34.
Scullin, George. "James Dean: The Legend and the Facts." *Look* 20 (16 October 1956): 120–28.
Seaborg, G. T. "The Future Through Science." *Science* 124 (28 December 1956): 1275–78.
Sedam, Ruth N. "Who Wants to Go Back to the Good Old Days?" *Parents Magazine* 31 (October 1956): 38–39.
Shannon, William V. "Eisenhower as President: A Critical Appraisal of the Record." *Commentary* 26 (November 1958): 390–98.
Shaw, Arnold. "Mr. Harper's After Hours: Upheaval in Popular Music." *Harper's* 218 (May 1959): 80–83.
Shepley, James. "How Dulles Averted War." *Life* 40 (16 January 1956): 70–80.
"Short Shorts Become Permanent in U.S. Scene." *Life* (10 September 1956): 49–54.
Snider, Arthur J. "Medicine's Golden Era: 1937–1957." *Science Digest* 41 (January 1957): 32–38.
Snow, Edgar. "Herr Tin Lizzie: Saga of the Volkswagen." *The Nation* 181 (3 December 1955): 474–76.
"A Solemn Inaugural and a Gay Celebration." *Life* 42 (4 February 1957): 24–33.
"Spring Madness." *Life* 32 (7 April 1952): 59–60.
Teller, Edward, and Albert Latter. "The Compelling Need for Nuclear Tests." *Life* 44 (10 February 1958): 64–72.
"Their Sheltered Honeymoon." *Life* 47 (10 August 1959): 51–52.
"To a Brave New Year." *The Nation* 172 (6 January 1951): 1.
"The Trouble with Baby Doll." *Time* 69 (15 January 1957): 100.
"Trumania in the '70s." *Time* 105 (9 June 1975): 45.
"Two-Hour Warning Against Sneak Attack." *U.S. News and World Report* 43 (6 September 1957): 72–85.

"The $250 Million Flop." *Time* 74 (30 November 1959): 87–88.

"U.S. Campus Kids of 1953: Unkiddable and Unbeatable." *Newsweek* 42 (2 November 1953): 52–55.

"U.S. Closes Ranks Under Truman." *Newsweek* 25 (23 April 1945): 27.

Usher, Ann. "TV. . . . Good or Bad for Your Children?" *Better Homes & Gardens* 33 (October 1955): 145, 176, 202–209.

Vander Zanden, James W. "The Klan Revival." *American Journal of Sociology* 65 (March 1960): 456–62.

Volkov, Leon. "Behind K's 'Hard Work' Revolution . . . in Education." *Newsweek* 52 (6 October 1958): 86–87.

Waring, Thomas R. "The Southern Case Against Desegregation." *Harper's* 212 (January 1956): 39–45.

Wertham, Frederic. "It's Still Murder." *Saturday Review* 38 (9 April 1955): 11–12, 46–48.

"What It's Like to Live in Earth's Most A-Bombed Area." *U.S. News and World Report* 42 (28 June 1957): 79–82.

"What Parents Say About Teen-agers." *Look* 22 (2 September 1958): 65.

"What to Do in Case of an Atomic Bomb Attack." *World Almanac*, 1951. New York: New York World-Telegram, 1951.

"What TV Is Doing to America." *U.S. News and World Report* 39 (2 September 1955): 36–50.

"What's Back of the 'Fall-Out' Scare." *U.S. News and World Report*. 42 (7 June 1957): 25–28.

"When a Negro Family Moved Into a White Community." *U.S. News and World Report* 43 (30 August 1957): 29–32.

Wilson, Richard. "Atomic Weapons Will Save Money—They May Stop War." *Look* 14 (10 October 1950): 33–55.

Wilson, Sloan. "It's Time to Close Our Carnival." *Life* 44 (24 March 1958): 36–37.

"Women Hold Third of Jobs." *Life* 41 (24 September 1956): 30–35.

"Words and Works." *Time* 64 (20 September 1954): 65.

"Young Wives." *Newsweek* 55 (7 March 1960): 57–60.

"The Younger Generation." *Time* 58 (5 November 1951): 46–52.

Zimmerman, Gereon. "Generation in A Searchlight." *Look* 20 (24 January 1956): 30–32.

### *IV. Memoirs, Diaries, and Letters*

Acheson, Dean. *Present at the Creation: My Years in the State Department*. New York: W. W. Norton & Co., 1969.

Adams, Sherman. *First-Hand Report: The Story of the Eisenhower Administration*. New York: Harper & Brothers, 1961.

Clark, Dick, and Richard Robinson. *Rock, Roll, and Remember*. New York: Thomas Y. Crowell, 1976.

Eisenhower, Dwight D. *The White House Years: A Personal Account*. 2 vols. Garden City, N. Y.: Doubleday & Co., 1963–1965. Vol. 1: *Mandate for Change, 1953–1956* (1963); Vol. 2: *Waging Peace, 1956–1961* (1965).

Ewald, William Bragg, Jr. *Eisenhower the President: Crucial Days, 1951–1960*. Englewood Cliffs, N. J.: Prentice-Hall, 1981.

Ferrell, Robert H., ed. *The Eisenhower Diaries*. New York: W. W. Norton and Co., 1981.

———. *Off the Record: The Private Papers of Harry S. Truman*. New York: Harper & Row, 1980.

Hechler, Ken. *Working With Truman: A Personal Memoir of the White House Years*. New York: G. P. Putnam's Sons, 1982.

Hughes, Emmet John. *The Ordeal of Power: A Political Memoir of the Eisenhower Years*. New York: Atheneum, 1963.

MacArthur, Douglas. *Reminiscences*. New York: McGraw-Hill, 1964.

Morgan, Kay Summersby. *Past Forgetting: My Love Affair with Dwight D. Eisenhower*. New York: Simon & Schuster, 1976.

Nixon, Richard. *The Memoirs of Richard Nixon*. New York: Grosset & Dunlap, 1978.

———. *Six Crises*. Garden City, N. Y.: Doubleday & Co., 1962.

Poen, Monte, ed. *Strictly Personal and Confidential: The Letters Harry Truman Never Mailed*. Boston: Little, Brown & Co., 1982.

Truman, Harry. *Memoirs*. 2 vols. Garden City, N. Y.: Doubleday & Co., 1956–1958. Vol. 1: *Year of Decision* (1956); Vol. 2: *Years of Trial and Hope* (1958).

———. *Mr. Citizen*. New York: Random House, 1960.

Truman, Margaret. *Letters from Father: The Truman Family's Personal Correspondence*. New York: Arbor House, 1981.

Warren, Earl. *The Memoirs of Earl Warren*. Garden City, N. Y.: Doubleday & Co., 1977.

### V. *Biographies*

Ambrose, Stephen E. *Eisenhower*. 2 vols. New York: Simon & Schuster, 1983—1984. Vol. 1: *Soldier, General of the Army, President-Elect, 1890–1952* (1983); Vol. 2; *The President* (1984).

Anderson, Jack, and Ronald May. *McCarthy: The Man, the Senator, the "Ism."* Boston: Beacon Press, 1952.

Crankshaw, Edward. *Khrushchev: A Career*. New York: Viking Press, 1966.

David, Lester, and Irene David. *Ike and Mamie: The Story of the General and His Lady*. New York: G. P. Putnam's Sons, 1981.

Davis, Kenneth S. *The Politics of Honor: A Biography of Adlai E. Stevenson*. New York: G. P. Putnam's Sons, 1967.

Donovan, Robert J. *Conflict and Crisis: The Presidency of Harry Truman, 1945–1948*. New York: W. W. Norton & Co., 1977.

———. *Eisenhower: The Inside Story*. New York: Harper & Brothers, 1956.

———. *Tumultuous Years: The Presidency of Harry S. Truman, 1949–1953*. New York: W. W. Norton & Co., 1982.

Einstein, Charles. *Willie's Time: A Memoir*. New York: J. B. Lippincott, 1979.

Ferrell, Robert H. *Harry S. Truman and the Modern American Presidency*. Boston: Little, Brown & Co., 1983.

Ingalls, Robert P. *Point of Order: A Profile of Senator Joe McCarthy*. New York: G. P. Putnam's Sons, 1981.

Lee, R. Alton. *Dwight D. Eisenhower: Soldier and Statesman*. Chicago: Nelson Hall, 1981.

Lyon, Peter. *Eisenhower: Portrait of the Hero*. Boston: Little, Brown & Co., 1974.

Manchester, William. *American Caesar: Douglas MacArthur, 1880–1964*. Boston: Little, Brown & Co., 1978.

Mazlish, Bruce. *In Search of Nixon: A Psychohistorical Inquiry*. New York: Basic Books, 1972.

Means, Marianne. *The Woman in the White House: The Lives, Times, and Influence of Twelve Notable First Ladies*. New York: Random House, 1963.

Metcalf, George R. *Black Profiles*. Expanded ed. New York: McGraw-Hill, 1970.

Miller, Merle. *Plain Speaking: An Oral Biography of Harry S. Truman*. New York: G. P. Putnam's Sons, 1973.

Morris, James. *The Preachers*. New York: St. Martin's Press, 1973.

Neal, Steve. *The Eisenhowers: Reluctant Dynasty*. Garden City, N. Y.: Doubleday & Co., 1978.

Oates, Stephen B. *Let the Trumpet Sound: The Life of Martin Luther King, Jr.* New York: Harper & Row, 1982.

Oshinsky, David M. *A Conspiracy So Immense: The World of Joe McCarthy*. New York: Free Press, 1983.

Parmet, Herbert S. *Eisenhower and the American Crusades*. New York: Macmillan Co., 1972.

Phillips, Cabell. *The Truman Presidency: The History of a Triumphant Succession*. New York: Macmillan Co., 1966.

Pinkley, Virgil, with James F. Scheer. *Eisenhower Declassified*. Old Tappan, N. J.: Fleming H. Revell, Co., 1979.

Pusey, Merlo J. *Eisenhower the President*. New York: Macmillan Co., 1956.

Reeves, Thomas C. *The Life and Times of Joe McCarthy: A Biography*. New York: Stein & Day, 1982.

Rovere, Richard. *Senator Joe McCarthy*. New York: Harcourt, Brace & Co., 1959.

Schickel, Richard. *The Disney Version: The Life, Times, Art, and Commerce of Walt Disney*. New York: Simon & Schuster, 1968.

Smith, A. Merriman. *Meet Mr. Eisenhower*. New York: Harper & Row, 1955.

Smith, Robert. *MacArthur in Korea: The Naked Emperor*. New York: Simon & Schuster, 1982.

Sorenson, Theodore E. *Kennedy*. New York: Harper & Row, 1965.

Steinberg, Alfred. *The Man from Missouri: The Life and Times of Harry S. Truman*. New York: G. P. Putnam's Sons, 1962.

Swanberg, W. A. *Luce and His Empire*. New York: Charles Scribner's Sons, 1972.

Truman, Margaret. *Harry S. Truman*. New York: William Morrow & Co., 1973.

Weaver, James D. *Warren: The Man, the Court, the Era*. Boston: Little, Brown & Co., 1967.

Wills, Garry. *Nixon Agonistes: The Crisis of the Self-Made Man*. Boston: Houghton Mifflin Co., 1970.

### *VI. Special and General Studies*

Abrams, Charles. *Forbidden Neighbors: A Study of Prejudice in Housing*. New York: Harper & Brothers, 1955.

Adler, Bill, comp. and ed. *The Stevenson Wit*. Garden City, N. Y.: Doubleday & Co., 1966.

Alexander, Charles C. *Holding the Line: The Eisenhower Era, 1952–1961*. Bloomington: Indiana University Press, 1975.

Allen, Frederick Lewis. *The Big Change: America Transforms Itself, 1900–1950*. New York: Harper & Row, 1952.

Ambrose, Stephen E. *Rise to Globalism: American Foreign Policy, 1938–1980*. 2d rev. ed. New York: Penguin Books, 1980.

Bailey, Thomas A. *Presidential Greatness: The Image and the Man from George Washington to the Present*. New York: Appleton-Century, 1966.

———. *Voices of America: The National Story in Slogans, Sayings, and Songs*. New York: Free Press, 1976.

Banner, Lois W. *Women in Modern America: A Brief History*. New York: Harcourt Brace Jovanovich, 1974.

Barber, James David. *The Presidential Character: Predicting Performance in the White House*. 2d ed. Englewood Cliffs, N. J.: Prentice-Hall, 1977.

Barnouw, Erik. *A History of Broadcasting in the United States*. 3 vols. New York: Oxford University Press, 1966–1970. Vol. 2: *The Golden Web* (1968); Vol. 3: *The Image Empire* (1970).

Bartley, Numan V. *The Rise of Massive Resistance: Race and Politics in the South During the 1950's*. Baton Rouge: Louisiana State University Press, 1969.

Bedford, Henry F. *Trouble Downtown: The Local Context of Twentieth-Century America.* New York: Harcourt Brace Jovanovich, 1978.

Blossom, Virgil T. *It Has Happened Here.* New York: Harper & Brothers, 1959.

Boas, Max, and Steve Chain. *Big Mac: The Unauthorized Story of McDonald's.* New York: E. P. Dutton & Co., 1976.

Bogart, Leo. *The Age of Television: A Study of Viewing Habits and the Impact of Television on American Life.* 3d ed. New York: Frederick Unger Publishing Co., 1972.

Bohn, Thomas W., and Richard L. Stromgren. *Light and Shadows: A History of Motion Pictures.* 2d ed. Sherman Oaks, Calif.: Alfred Publishing Co., 1978.

Boller, Paul F., Jr. *Presidential Anecdotes.* New York: Oxford University Press, 1981.

———. *Presidential Campaigns.* New York: Oxford University Press, 1984.

Boone, Pat. *'Twixt Twelve and Twenty.* Englewood Cliffs, N. J.: Prentice-Hall, 1958.

Brooks, John. *The Fate of the Edsel and Other Business Adventures.* New York: Harper & Row, 1963.

———. *The Great Leap: The Past Twenty-five Years in America.* New York: Harper & Row, 1966.

Brooks, Tim, and Earle Marsh. *The Complete Directory to Prime Time Network TV Shows: 1946–Present.* New York: Ballantine Books, 1979.

Brosnan, John. *Future Tense: The Cinema of Science Fiction.* New York: St. Martin's Press, 1978.

Brown, John Mason. *Through These Men: Some Aspects of Our Passing History.* New York: Harper & Brothers, 1956.

Brubacher, John S., and Willis Rudy. *Higher Education in Transition: A History of American Colleges and Universities, 1636–1976.* 3d ed., rev. and enlarged. New York: Harper & Row, 1976.

Buckley, William F., and L. Brent Bozell. *McCarthy and His Enemies.* Chicago: Henry Regnery Co., 1954.

Carter, Paul. *Another Part of the Fifties.* New York: Columbia University Press, 1983.

Caute, David. *The Great Fear: The Anti-Communist Purge Under Truman and Eisenhower.* New York: Simon & Schuster, 1978.

Chafe, William H. *The American Woman: Her Changing Social, Economic, and Political Roles, 1920–1970.* New York: Oxford University Press, 1972.

———. *Civilities and Civil Rights: Greensboro, North Carolina, and the Black Struggle for Freedom.* New York: Oxford University Press, 1980.

Chalmers, David M. *Hooded Americanism: The History of the Ku Klux Klan.* 2d ed. New York: New Viewpoints, 1981.

Cochran, Thomas C. *American Business in the Twentieth Century*. Cambridge, Mass.: Harvard University Press, 1972.

Cogley, John. *Report on Blacklisting*. 2 vols. N. p.: Fund for the Republic, 1956.

Cohn, Nik. *Rock: From the Beginning*. New York: Stein & Day, 1969.

Coleman, James S. *The Adolescent Society: The Social Life of the Teenager and Its Impact on Education*. New York: Free Press, 1961.

Congressional Quarterly. Editorial Research Reports. *The Women's Movement*. Washington: Congressional Quarterly, 1973.

*Consumer Guide*, Editors of. *Cars of the 50s*. New York: Beekman House, 1978.

Cook, Bruce. *The Beat Generation*. New York: Charles Scribner's Sons, 1971.

Cook, Fred J. *The Nightmare Decade: The Life and Times of Senator Joe McCarthy*. New York: Random House, 1971.

———. *The Warfare State*. New York: Macmillan Co., 1962.

Cory, Donald Webster. *The Homosexual in America: A Subjective Approach*. New York: Greenberg, 1951.

Curti, Merle. *The Growth of American Thought*. 3d ed. New York: Harper & Row, 1964.

Davies, Richard O. *The Age of Asphalt: The Automobile, the Freeway, and the Condition of Metropolitan America*. New York: J. B. Lippincott, 1975.

De Beauvoir, Simone. *The Second Sex*. New York: Alfred A. Knopf, 1953.

Divine, Robert A. *Eisenhower and the Cold War*. New York: Oxford University Press, 1981.

Drummond, Roscoe, and Gaston Coblentz. *Duel at the Brink: John Foster Dulles' Command of American Power*. Garden City: Doubleday & Co., 1960.

Duram, James C. *A Moderate Among Extremists: Dwight D. Eisenhower and the School Desegregation Crisis*. Chicago: Nelson Hall, 1981.

Dykeman, Wilma, and James Stokely. *Neither Black Nor White*. New York: Rinehart & Co., 1957.

Einstein, Charles (ed.). *The Third Fireside Book of Baseball*. New York: Simon & Schuster, 1968.

Ellis, Albert. *The American Sexual Tragedy*. New York: Twayne Publishers, 1954.

Elson, Edward L. R. *America's Spiritual Recovery*. N. p.: Fleming H. Revell, 1954.

Elson, Robert T. *The World of Time, Inc.: The Intimate History of a Publishing Enterprise*. 2 vols. New York: Atheneum, 1968, 1973.

Emery, Edwin, and Michael Emery. *The Press and America: An Interpretative History of the Mass Media*. 4th ed. Englewood Cliffs, N. J.: Prentice-Hall, 1978.

Ernst, Morris L. *Utopia 1976*. New York: Rinehart & Co., 1955.

Ewen, David. *All the Years of American Popular Music*. Englewood Cliffs, N.J.: Prentice-Hall, 1977.

Farnham, Marynia, and Ferdinand Lundberg. *Modern Woman: The Lost Sex:* New York: Harper & Brothers, 1947.

Fine, Benjamin. *1,000,000 Delinquents*. Cleveland: World Publishing Co., 1955.

Fitzgerald, Frances. *America Revised: History Schoolbooks in the Twentieth Century*. Boston: Little, Brown & Co., 1979.

*Fortune*, Editors of. *The Changing American Market*. Garden City, N. Y. Hanover House, 1955.

———. *The Fabulous Future: America in 1980*. New York: E. P. Dutton & Co., 1955.

Fowler, John M., ed. *Fallout: A Study of Superbombs, Strontium 90 and Survival*. New York: Basic Books, 1960.

French, Warren, ed. *The Fifties: Fiction, Poetry, Drama*. Deland, Fla.: Everett Edwards, 1970.

Fried, Richard M. *Men Against McCarthy*. New York: Columbia University Press, 1976.

Friedan, Betty. *The Feminine Mystique*. 10th anniversary ed. New York: W. W. Norton & Co., 1974.

Gallup, George H. *The Gallup Poll: Public Opinion, 1935–1971*. 3 vols. New York: Random House, 1972.

George, Wesley C. *The Race Problem from the Standpoint of One Who is Concerned About the Evils of Miscegenation*. Birmingham, Ala.: n. pub., 1955.

Gilbert, James. *Another Chance: Postwar America, 1945–1968*. New York: Alfred A. Knopf, 1981.

Gillett, Charlie. *The Sound of the City: The Rise of Rock and Roll*. New York: Outerbridge and Dienstfrey, 1970.

Golden, Harry. *Only in America*. New York: World Publishing Co., 1958.

Goldman, Eric F. *The Crucial Decade—And After: America, 1945–1960*. New York: Vintage Books, 1960.

Graham, Billy. *Peace With God*. Garden City, N. Y.: Doubleday & Co., 1953.

Gray, Robert Keith. *Eighteen Acres Under Glass*. Garden City, N. Y.: Doubleday & Co., 1962.

Greenfield, Jeff. *No Peace, No Place: Excavations Along the Generational Fault*. Garden City, N. Y.: Doubleday & Co., 1973.

———. *Television: The First Fifty Years*. New York: Harry N. Abrams, 1977.

Greenstein, Fred I. *The Hidden-Hand Presidency: Eisenhower as Leader*. New York: Basic Books, 1982.

Griffin, John Howard. *Black Like Me*. Boston: Houghton Mifflin Co., 1960.

Griffith, Robert. *The Politics of Fear: Joseph R. McCarthy and the Senate*. Lexington: University Press of Kentucky, 1970.

Hackett, Alice Payne, and James Henry Burke. *80 Years of Bestsellers, 1895–1975*. New York: R. R. Bowker, 1977.

Haight, Ann Lyon. *Banned Books: Informal Notes on Some Books Banned for Various Reasons at Various Times and in Various Places*. 3d ed. New York: R. R. Bowker, 1970.

Hamby, Alonzo. *Beyond the New Deal: Harry S. Truman and American Liberalism*. New York: Columbia University Press, 1973.

Haskell, Molly. *From Reverence to Rape: The Treatment of Women in the Movies*. New York: Holt, Rinehart & Winston, 1974.

Haupt, Enid A. *The Seventeen Book of Young Living* New York: David McKay, 1957.

Haynes, Richard F. *The Awesome Power: Harry S. Truman As Commander in Chief*. Baton Rouge: Louisiana State Press, 1973.

Hechinger, Fred M. *The Big Red Schoolhouse*. Gloucester, Mass.: Peter Smith, 1968.

Herberg, Will. *Protestant–Catholic–Jew: An Essay in American Religious Sociology*. Garden City, N. Y.: Doubleday & Co., 1956.

Hersey, John. *Aspects of the Presidency: Truman and Ford in Office*. New York: Ticknor and Fields, 1980.

Higham, Charles. *Hollywood at Sunset*. New York: Saturday Review Press, 1972.

Hodgson, Godfrey. *America in Our Time*. Garden City, N. Y.: Doubleday & Co., 1976.

Hofstadter, Richard. *Anti-intellectualism in American Life*. New York: Alfred A. Knopf, 1966.

———. *The Paranoid Style in American Politics*. New York: Alfred A. Knopf, 1965.

Holbo, Paul S., and Robert W. Sellen. *The Eisenhower Era: The Age of Consensus*. Hinsdale, Ill.: Dryden Press, 1974.

Hoopes, Townsend. *The Devil and John Foster Dulles*. Boston: Little, Brown & Co., 1973.

Horsley, Edith. *The 1950s*. London: Bison Books, 1978.

Hymowitz, Carol, and Michaele Weissman. *A History of Women in America*. New York: Bantam Books, 1978.

Jacobs, David Michael. *The UFO Controversy in America*. Bloomington: Indiana University Press, 1975.

Jezer, Marty. *The Dark Ages: Life in the United States, 1945–1960*. Boston: South End Press, 1982.

Jones, Landon Y. *Great Expectations: America and the Baby Boom Generation*. New York: Coward, McCann, and Geoghegan, 1980.

Joy, Admiral Turner. *How Communists Negotiate*. New York: Macmillan Co., 1955.

Kahin, George M., and John W. Lewis. *The United States in Vietnam*, rev. ed. New York: Dial Press, 1969.

Kahn, Herman. *On Thermonuclear War*. Princeton, N. J.: Princeton University Press, 1960.

Kanfer, Stefan. *A Journal of the Plague Years*. New York: Atheneum, 1973.

Karnow, Stanley. *Vietnam: A History*. New York: Viking Press, 1983.

Keats, John. *The Crack in the Picture Window*. Boston: Houghton Mifflin Co., 1956.

———. *The Insolent Chariots*. Philadephia: J. B. Lippincott, 1958.

———. *Schools Without Scholars*. Boston: Houghton Mifflin Co., 1958.

Kempton, Murray. *America Comes of Middle Age: Columns, 1950–1962*. Boston: Little, Brown & Co., 1963.

King, Martin Luther, Jr., *Stride Toward Freedom: The Montgomery Story*. New York: Harper & Row, 1958.

Kinnard, Douglas. *President Eisenhower and Strategy Management: A Study in Defense Politics*. Lexington: University Press of Kentucky, 1977.

Kinsey, Alfred C., Wardell B. Pomeroy, Clyde E. Martin, and Paul H. Gebhard. *Sexual Behavior in the Human Female*. Philadelphia: W. B. Saunders, 1953.

———. *Sexual Behavior in the Human Male*. Philadelphia: W. B. Saunders, 1948.

Klein, Dave. *The Game of Their Lives*. New York: Random House, 1976.

Kramer, Dale, and Madeline Karr. *Teen-Age Gangs*. New York: Henry Holt & Co., 1953.

Kronenberger, Louis. *Company Manners: A Cultural Inquiry into American Life*. New York: Bobbs-Merrill, 1954.

Larrabee, Eric. *The Self-Conscious Society*. Garden City, N. Y.: Doubleday & Co., 1960.

Lens, Sidney. *The Day Before Doomsday: An Anatomy of the Nuclear Arms Race*. Garden City, N. Y.: Doubleday & Co., 1977.

Leuchtenberg, William E., and the editors of *Life*. *The Great Age of Change*. Vol. 12 of the *Life History of the United States*. New York: Time-Life Books, 1964.

Lewis, Anthony, and *The New York Times*. *Portrait of a Decade: The Second American Revolution*. New York: Random House, 1964.

Lewis, Peter. *The Fifties*. New York: J. B. Lippincott, 1978.

Ley, Willy. *Rockets, Missiles, and Men in Space*. New York: Viking Press, 1968.

Lifton, Robert J., ed. *The Woman in America*. Boston: Houghton Mifflin Co., 1965.

Lipton, Lawrence. *The Holy Barbarians*. New York: Julian Messner, 1959.

Lora, Ronald. *Conservative Minds in America*. Chicago: Rand McNally & Co.,. 1971.

Lord, Walter. *The Past That Would Not Die*. New York: Harper & Row, 1965.

Ludden, Allen. *Plain Talk for Men Under 21!* New York: Dodd, Mead, & Co., 1954.

Lynes, Russell. *A Surfeit of Honey*. New York: Harper & Brothers, 1957.

Lyon, Peter. *To Hell in a Day Coach: An Exasperated Look at American Railroads*. Philadelphia: J. B. Lippincott, 1968.

Lytle, Clifford. *The Warren Court and Its Critics*. Tucson: University of Arizona Press, 1968.

Malone, Bill C. *Country Music U.S.A.: A Fifty Year History*. Austin: University of Texas Press, 1968.

Manchester, William. *The Glory and the Dream: A Narrative History of America, 1932–1972*. Boston: Little, Brown & Co., 1974.

Mayer, Martin. *Madison Avenue, U.S.A*. New York: Harper & Row, 1958.

Mehling, Harold. *The Great Time-Killer*. Cleveland: World Publishing Co., 1962.

Menke, Frank G. *The Encyclopedia of Sports*. 6th rev. ed. Garden City, N. Y.: Doubleday & Co., 1977.

Menville, Douglas, and R. Reginald. *Things to Come: An Illustrated History of the Science Fiction Film*. New York: The New York Times Book Co., 1977.

Meyer, Donald. *The Positive Thinkers: A Study of the American Quest for Health, Wealth, and Personal Power from Mary Baker Eddy to Norman Vincent Peale*. Garden City, N. Y.: Doubleday & Co., 1965.

Miles, Michael W. *The Odyssey of the American Right*. New York: Oxford University Press, 1980.

Miller, Douglas T., and Marion Nowak. *The Fifties: The Way We Really Were*. Garden City, N. Y.: Doubleday & Co., 1977.

Miller, Jim, ed. *The Rolling Stone Illustrated History of Rock and Roll*. New York: Rolling Stone Press, 1976.

Montgomery, John. *The Fifties*. London: George Allen & Unwin, 1965.

Moss, Norman. *Men Who Play God: The Story of the H-Bomb and How the World Came to Live with It*. New York: Harper & Row, 1968.

Mowry, George E. *The Urban Nation, 1920–1960*. New York: Hill & Wang, 1965.

Murphy, Paul L. *The Constitution in Crisis Times, 1918–1969*. New York: Harper & Row, 1972.

Muse, Benjamin. *Ten Years of Prelude: The Story of Integration Since the Supreme Court's 1954 Decision*. New York: Viking Press, 1964.

Navasky, Victor S. *Naming Names.* New York: Viking Press, 1980.

Neft, David, Roland T. Johnson, Richard M. Cohen, and Jordan A. Deutsch. *The Sports Encyclopedia: Pro Football.* New York: Grosset & Dunlap, 1974.

Newby, I. A. *Challenge to the Court: Social Scientists and the Defense of Segregation, 1954–1966.* Baton Rouge: Louisiana State University Press, 1967.

Nugent, Walter T. K. *Modern America.* Boston: Houghton Mifflin Co., 1973.

Nye, Russel B. *The Unembarrassed Muse: The Popular Arts in America.* New York: Dial Press, 1970.

O'Neill, William L. *Everyone Was Brave: The Rise and Fall of Feminism in America.* Chicago: Quadrangle Books, 1969.

O'Neill, William L., ed. *American Society Since 1945.* Chicago: Quadrangle Books, 1969.

O'Sullivan, John, and Edward F. Keuchel. *American Economic History: From Abundance to Constraint.* New York: Franklin Watts, 1981.

Packard, Vance. *The Hidden Persuaders.* New York: David McKay, 1957.

———. *The Waste Makers.* New York: David McKay, 1960.

Parmet, Herbert S. *The Democrats: The Years After FDR.* New York: Oxford University Press, 1977.

Pauling, Linus. *No More War!* New York: Dodd, Mead, & Co., 1958.

Peale, Norman Vincent. *The Power of Positive Thinking.* New York: Prentice-Hall, 1952.

Perrett, Geoffrey. *A Dream of Greatness: The American People, 1945–1963.* New York: Coward, McCann & Geoghegan, 1979.

Peters, William. *The Southern Temper.* Garden City, New York: Doubleday & Co., 1959.

Peterson, Theodore. *Magazines in the Twentieth Century.* Urbana: University of Illinois Press, 1964.

Pleasants, Henry. *The Great American Popular Singers.* New York: Simon & Schuster, 1974.

Poole, Peter A. *The United States and Indochina, from FDR to Nixon.* Hinsdale, Ill.: Dryden Press, 1973.

Quigley, Martin, Jr., and Richard Gertner. *Films in America, 1929–1969.* New York: Golden Press, 1970.

Rae, John B. *The American Automobile: A Brief History.* Chicago: University of Chicago Press, 1965.

———. *The Road and the Car In American Life.* Cambridge: MIT Press, 1971.

Rees, David. *Korea: The Limited War.* New York: St. Martin's Press, 1964.

Reiss, Ira. *Premarital Sexual Standards in America.* Glencoe, Ill.: Free Press, 1960.

Remmers, H. H., and D. H. Radler. *The American Teenager*. Indianapolis: Bobbs-Merrill Co., 1957.

Rice, Damon. *Seasons Past*. New York: Praeger, 1976.

Rickover, H. G. *Education and Freedom*. New York: E. P. Dutton & Co., 1959.

Ridgway, Matthew B. *The Korean War*. Garden City, N. Y.: Doubleday & Co., 1967.

Ritter, Lawrence, and Donald Honig. *The Image of Their Greatness: An Illustrated History of Baseball from 1900 to the Present*. New York: Crown Publishers, 1979.

Roberts, Chalmers. *The Nuclear Years: The Arms Race and Arms Control, 1945–1970*. New York: Frederick A. Praeger, 1970.

Robinson, Jerry. *The Comics: An Illustrated History of Comic Strip Art*. New York: G. P. Putnam's Sons, 1974.

Robinson, Paul. *The Modernization of Sex*. New York: Harper & Row, 1976.

Rosen, Marjorie. *Popcorn Venus: Women, Movies, and the American Dream*. New York: Coward, McCann, and Geoghegan, 1973.

Rosenberg, Norman L., and Emily S. Rosenberg. *In Our Times*. 2d ed. Englewood Cliffs, N. J.: Prentice-Hall, 1982.

Rosten, Leo, ed. *Religions in America*. Rev. ed. New York: Simon & Schuster, 1963.

Roszak, Betty, and Theodore Roszak, eds. *Masculine/Feminine: Readings in Sexual Mythology and the Liberation of Women*. New York: Harper and Row, 1969.

Rovere, Richard, and Arthur Schlesinger, Jr. *The General and the President*. New York: Farrar, Strauss, and Young, 1951.

Russell, Bertrand. *Common Sense and Nuclear Warfare*. New York: Simon & Schuster, 1959.

Salisbury, Harrison E. *The Shook-Up Generation*. New York: Harper & Row, 1958.

Sann, Paul. *Fads, Follies, and Delusions of the American People*. New York: Crown Publishers, 1967.

Schlesinger, Arthur M, Jr., Fred L. Israel, and William P. Hansen, eds. *The Coming to Power: Critical Presidential Elections in American History*. New York: Chelsea House, 1971.

Schneir, Walter, and Miriam Schneir. *Invitation to an Inquest*. Garden City, N. Y.: Doubleday & Co., 1965.

Shannon, David A. *The Decline of American Communism: A History of the Communist Party of the United States Since 1945*. New York: Harcourt, Brace & Co., 1959.

Shaw, Arnold. *The Rockin' '50s*. New York: Hawthorn Books, 1974.

Sheen, Fulton J. *Life Is Worth Living*. New York: McGraw-Hill, 1953.

Shirer, William L. *Midcentury Journey*. New York: Farrar, Straus & Young, 1952.

Shulman, Arthur, and Roger Youman. *How Sweet It Was*. New York: Bonanza Books, 1966.

Smith, Huston, ed. *The Search for America*. Englewood Cliffs, N. J.: Prentice-Hall, 1959.

Smuts, Robert. *Women and Work in America*. New York: Columbia University Press, 1959.

Sochen, June. *Herstory: A Woman's View of American History*. Port Washington, N. Y.: Alfred Publishing Co., 1974.

———. *Movers and Shakers: American Women Thinkers and Activists, 1900–1970*. New York: Quadrangle Books, 1973.

Spanier, John W. *The Truman-MacArthur Controversy and the Korean War*. Cambridge: Harvard University Press, 1959.

Stoessinger, John G. *Why Nations Go to War*. 2d ed. New York: St. Martin's Press, 1978.

Stone, I. F. *The Haunted Fifties*. New York: Random House, 1963.

Stouffer, Samuel A. *Communism, Conformity, and Civil Liberties: A Cross-section of the Nation Speaks Its Mind*. Garden City: Doubleday & Co., 1955.

Stover, John F. *The Life and Decline of the American Railroad*. New York: Oxford University Press, 1970.

Straight, Michael. *Trial By Television*. Boston: Beacon Press, 1954.

Time-Life Books, Editors of. *This Fabulous Century*, 7 vols. New York: Time-Life Books, 1970. Vol. 6: *1950–1960*.

Underhill, Robert. *The Truman Persuasions*. Ames: Iowa University Press, 1981.

Vatter, Harold G. *The U.S. Economy in the 1950s*. New York: W. W. Norton & Co., 1963.

Voigt, David Q. *America Through Baseball*. Chicago: Nelson Hall, 1976.

West, J. B. *Upstairs at the White House*. New York: Warner, 1974.

White, Lawrence J. *The Automobile Industry Since 1945*. Cambridge: Harvard University Press, 1971.

Williams, J. Paul. *What Americans Believe and How They Worship*. Rev. ed. New York: Harper & Row, 1962.

Wilson, Paul C. *Chrome Dreams: Automobile Styling Since 1893*. Radnor, Penn.: Chilton Book Co., 1976.

Wind, Herbert Warren, ed. *The Realm of Sport*. New York: Simon & Schuster, 1966.

Wise, David, and Thomas B. Ross. *The U-2 Affair*. New York: Random House, 1962.

Wittner, Lawrence S. *Cold War America: From Hiroshima to Watergate*. New York: Praeger, 1974.

———. *Rebels Against War: The American Peace Movement, 1941–1960*. New York: Columbia University Press, 1969.

Wood, James Playsted. *Magazines In the United States*. 3d ed. New York: Ronald Press Co., 1971.

Woodbury, David O. *Atoms for Peace*. New York: Dodd, Mead & Co., 1956.

Woodring, Paul. *A Fourth of a Nation*. New York: McGraw-Hill, 1957.

Woodward, C. Vann. *The Strange Career of Jim Crow*. 3d rev. ed. New York: Oxford University Press, 1974.

Wright, Gordon. *The Ordeal of Total War, 1939–1945*. New York: Harper & Row, 1968.

Yablonsky, Lewis. *The Violent Gang*. New York: Macmillan & Co., 1962.

Zinn, Howard. *SNCC: The New Abolitionists*. 2d ed. Boston: Beacon Press, 1965.

## *VII. Novels*

Kerouac, Jack. *On the Road*. New York: Viking Press, 1957.

Metalious, Grace. *Peyton Place*. New York: Julian Messner, 1956.

# Index